CHARLATANS, SPIRITS AND REBEL

'Stephen Ellis was—in my view at least—the greatest Africanist of his generation, and his death from leukaemia at the tragically early age of sixty-two remains a source of lasting regret. This volume provides a guide to the study of Africa that is far more than the sum of its parts, and will be of central importance to any understanding of the continent and its peoples.

Ellis pioneered a way of looking at Africa that starts from the ways in which Africans look at themselves, their societies, and the worlds in which they live. He was by training and inclination a historian, but (unlike all too many historians of Africa) sought to advance the understanding of what are, after all, the oldest human societies on earth by looking at the origins of these societies, and at the ways in which Africans continue to think and therefore behave in the modern world. This search for a genuinely decolonised study of Africa underlies almost everything he wrote, and especially his emphasis on the epistemologies and spiritualities that remain of central importance.'

—Professor Christopher Clapham, Centre of African Studies, University of Cambridge, and former editor of *The Journal of Modern African Studies.*

'This judicious collection of Stephen Ellis's writings on Africa exemplifies why he is considered to be the most important Africanist of his generation. In all of these his sterling qualities are evident: an ability to make confident judgments that derived from thorough research, an interest in reaching a wide audience, and, partly through his extensive travel in Africa and his deep intelligence and sympathy, his anxiety to give events their true historical setting. He was my friend and prime mentor, always generous and helpful, never condescending. This collection is a fitting tribute.'

—Lansana Gberie (PhD), Ambassador of Sierra Leone to Switzerland, author of *A Dirty War in West Africa*

'This wide-ranging collection of twenty essays by Stephen Ellis—examining method, rebellion, repression, religion, crime, and public engagement—is a must-read for everyone with an interest in Africa. The Reader displays Ellis's incisive and analytical mind and his ability to make accessible to a broad audience the complex politics of Africa. A trained modern historian, Stephen Ellis was astute in his recognition of how Africa's history, religion and culture shaped its contemporary politics, or the reality of Africa's "dual registers". The result were nuanced studies of the culture of power, the religious dimension to contemporary conflicts, the exercise of power and its experience by ordinary people, and the perversion of power. A scholar-activist and a commentator on contemporary African politics, Ellis was a keen student of organisations, the formal and informal, the political and criminal. His knowledge was encyclopaedic, and he wrote with

deep familiarity about countries as geographically distant as Madagascar, South Africa, and Liberia. The Reader is a serving of Ellis's remarkable erudition.'
—Emmanuel Akyeampong, Ellen Gurney Professor of History, and also Professor of African and African American Studies, Harvard University

'Stephen Ellis, one of the most prominent and prolific Africanist scholars of his generation. He died in 2015, leaving behind a substantial intellectual legacy. Ellis's work was extraordinary in terms of both depth and range, and the collection presented here, under the editorship of Tim Kelsall, will be of interest to a diverse group of readers within the broad field of 'African Studies': historians, anthropologists, geographers, political scientists, journalists and policy-makers.'
—Richard Reid, Professor of African History, University of Oxford

'This powerful book amply illustrates the scope, originality and boldness of Stephen Ellis's influential work. From Madagascar to the politics of religion, from the inner life of revolutionary parties to Liberia, from civil violence to the international politics of crime: few scholars of Africa have made defining contributions to such a wide set of debates. That Ellis did so in elegant, precise and captivating prose is testament to the clarity of his thought as well as its enduring relevance for a wide readership.
—Ricardo Soares de Oliveira, Professor of the International Politics of Africa, University of Oxford

'Stephen Ellis never stopped focusing on what he thought was important, and he did so with honesty, moral integrity and academic excellence, making his work highly sophisticated and impossible to pigeonhole. This approach often put him in difficult situations and earned him both enemies and misunderstandings, even a lawsuit brought against him by a head of state. Towards the end of his life, when he knew he was sick, he revealed Nelson Mandela's membership in the South African Communist Party, which had been denied for various reasons for years.
Despite his brilliant academic career, Stephen was discreet about his professional achievements, which many of us only discovered when he passed away. He was a true gentleman historian'
—Solofo Randrianja, Professor of History, University of Toamasina

'Stephen Ellis was the centre of a scholarly enterprise that prioritised the cultural and social aspects of politics in Africa. His writings collected here bring into focus the different ways political authority has been exercised, including through the spiritual realm, and how it shaped the continent's development. Anyone who seeks to understand how Africa works and the real challenges of creating just and durable political orders should read this book.'
—Will Reno, Professor of Political Science, Northwestern University, author of *Warfare in Independent Africa*

STEPHEN ELLIS

Charlatans, Spirits and Rebels in Africa

The Stephen Ellis Reader

Edited by
TIM KELSALL

Foreword by
SOLOFO RANDRIANJA

Afterword by
JEAN-FRANÇOIS BAYART

HURST & COMPANY, LONDON

First published in the United Kingdom in 2022 by
C. Hurst & Co. (Publishers) Ltd.,
New Wing, Somerset House, Strand, London, WC2R 1LA

Printed in Great Britain by Bell and Bain Ltd, Glasgow

A Cataloguing-in-Publication data record for this book
is available from the British Library.

ISBN: 9781787383302

www.hurstpublishers.com

CONTENTS

Preface (Solofo Randrianja):   vii
Stephen Ellis: The Gentleman Historian

Introduction by Tim Kelsall   1

SECTION ONE
METHOD

1.   Writing Histories of Contemporary Africa   29

2.   Africa's Wars of Liberation: Some Historiographical   61
Reflections

3.   Tuning in to Pavement Radio   93

4.   Rumour and Power in Togo   105

5.   Violence and History: A Response to Thandika Mkandawire 127

SECTION TWO
REBELLION AND REPRESSION

6.   The Political Elite of Imerina and the Revolt of   153
the *Menalamba*. The Creation of a Colonial Myth
in Madagascar, 1895–1898

7.   Mbokodo: Security in ANC Camps, 1961–1990   171

8.   The Historical Significance of South Africa's Third Force   193

9.   Liberia 1989–1994: A Study of Ethnic and Spiritual Violence 253

Section Three
RELIGION

10. Religion and Politics: Taking African Epistemologies   291
    Seriously (co-authored by Gerrie ter Haar)

11. Religion and Politics in Sub-Saharan Africa   311
    (co-authored by Gerrie ter Haar)

12. The Occult Does Not Exist: A Response to Terence   337
    Ranger (co-authored by Gerrie ter Haar)

13. Witch-Hunting in Central Madagascar 1828–1861   355

Section Four
CRIME

14. The New Frontiers of Crime in South Africa   387

15. Africa and International Corruption: The Strange Case   411
    of South Africa and the Seychelles

16. This Present Darkness: A History of Nigerian   445
    Organised Crime

17. West Africa's International Drug Trade   467

Section Five
PUBLIC ENGAGEMENT

18. How to Rebuild Africa   495

19. The Roots of African Corruption   509

20. South Africa and the Decolonization of the Mind   523

Afterword (Jean-François Bayart): State and Religion in Africa,   539
or Two or Three Things that Stephen Ellis Taught Me

Notes   563

Stephen Ellis Bibliography compiled by Jos Damen   627

Copyright Permissions and Publisher's Acknowledgement   649

PREFACE

STEPHEN ELLIS (13 JUNE 1953–29 JULY 2015)
THE GENTLEMAN HISTORIAN

Solofo Randrianja
(University of Toamasina, Madagascar)

Nothing I could write would ever match the honour of my friendship with this gentleman—a friendship that he referenced towards the end of his life in the preface to his last book.[1]

I first met and listened to Stephen Ellis speak at one of Professor Françoise Raison's seminars, which would often be held at the Paris Diderot University–Paris VII, in the Third World Africa Centre. It was then a rare if not the only site in France for research on Madagascar, and Dr Raison was on the lookout for all those researching the island nation. If I remember correctly, this was the first time that an Anglophone historian had participated in the seminar—in the late 1970s, French university circles were still predominantly French-speaking, except for a few pioneers like Jean François Bayart. Stephen gave his presentation in the language of Molière, which he commanded perfectly and with masterful ease, thanks to the time he had spent in Africa and Madagascar.

Stephen had come to talk about the Menalamba uprising, a topic that he was then researching for a thesis at Oxford.[2] Paris VII, the site of this research centre, was known for its post-1968, Third-Worldist positions. It was expected that Stephen, in his presentation, would join these ranks, that he would rely on Marxist or at the very least anticolonial analyses. Instead, the seminar did not conform to the expected leftist bent, which was then known colloquially as the general 'esprit de Jussieu', after the name of the university campus. Ours was the student generation that saw the end of grand paradigms, and we were in quest of both academic excellence and values to which we might cling.

While the official record of Malagasy and Francophone nationalist literature stated that the Menalamba uprising was part of a long list of anticolonial movements, Stephen presented it in his talk as proto-nationalist, basing his argument on texts in Malagasy written by the movement's leaders. The approach was slightly iconoclastic to say the least, and Stephen would double down on it several years later.[3] When it was published, his thesis would begin by describing on the very first page the brutal murder of a British missionary and his whole family, obliterating any shred of nationalist sympathy.

The discussions that followed Stephen's presentation were heated and disconcerted some of the audience, who failed to classify him into familiar categories. At the time, speakers had to be chosen according to their obedience to prevailing thought and orthodoxy. Stephen's presentation earned him respect because of his commitment to the truth, that of the archives.

After his speech, Stephen showed an interest in my own work on the anticolonial movement in Madagascar in the inter-war years, which mainly militated for the mass naturalisation of the island's inhabitants.[4] I too dissented from the nationalist mainstream opinion, which viewed any anticolonial movement as militating for independence. At the time of Stephen's presentation, Madagascar had begun a slow economic decline marked by societal violence, political instability and serious economic difficulties, the product of this extreme type of nationalism that valued indigenousness. With so much in common, Stephen and I hit it off very quickly.

On his initiative, the Royal African Society hosted my first public lecture in English in London some time later. Stephen introduced me to the British way of writing history. I discovered writers like Moses Finley (who was a member of his thesis jury) and Benedict Anderson, among many others. During my stay at the University of Natal in Durban, South Africa, just as Nelson Mandela was taking office as president, Stephen invited me to take part in a collective project[5] that took us to Dakar in Senegal. There I met colleagues from the Council for the Development of Social Science Research in Africa (CODESRIA), a pan-African research organisation founded by Samir Amin. Stephen had started to associate with them and never missed any of the organisation's meetings. He was not without scepticism, but still hoped that something would come out of this unique institution. He was sceptical because, despite the Marxist and Afro-centric convictions of many within the organisation, CODESRIA survived on grants from European countries, undermining the anti-Western diatribes of many of its members. He remained hopeful because, in spite of everything, CODESRIA had enabled important researchers to make themselves known in the global academic community.

Stephen Ellis attended these meetings, often on behalf of *African Affairs*, the journal of the esteemed Royal African Society, seeking out these emerging and promising African scholars, many of whom he published. Some stayed at the African Studies Centre in Leiden, where he was based. Many became his friends, inspiring him and rooting him in the African world. Despite his brilliant academic career, Stephen was discreet about his professional achievements, which many of us only discovered when he passed away. He was always very humble and respectful and considered his colleagues as equals. He was willing to discuss all subjects and did not mind translating articles by French-speaking authors into English to increase their visibility.

Just as much as his time with Amnesty International, his closeness to these colleagues, some of whom lived modestly if not precariously, accentuated his mistrust of trends and ways of thinking that were fashionable, and therefore impermanent.

Thus, in the majority of his writings on Africa, Stephen never stopped focusing on what he thought was important, and he did so with honesty, moral integrity and academic excellence, making his work highly sophisticated and impossible to pigeonhole. This approach often put him in difficult situations and earned him both enemies and misunderstandings,[6] even a lawsuit brought against him by a head of state. Towards the end of his life, when he knew he was sick, he revealed Nelson Mandela's membership in the South African Communist Party, which had been denied for various reasons for years.

His approach towards nineteenth-century Madagascar fits with this perspective. While the period is often presented as an unfinished model of 'development' defeated by conquest and colonisation by the French, Stephen highlighted that it had been shaped by extreme violence. What I remember from our discussions is that the prevailing vision of the past reflects the Westernisation of contemporary elites, who have capitalised on a certain representation of history for their own benefit. It excludes from history slaves, their descendants and all subalterns. Stephen's approach led to other studies that we intended to develop further. Violent contacts—with Europeans—did indeed set Madagascar into a kind of decline that prefigured the postcolonial twentieth and twenty-first centuries. At the same time, this phenomenon was first set in motion, as is logical, at least as far back as the seventeenth century[7] with the coastal kingdoms, which were the first to enter into sustained trade with Europeans. Viewed in this way, the history of Madagascar is a shared history, due to the circulation of political models over the course of several centuries in spite of persistent ethnicity.

Grounded in these values and positions, our friendship would be consolidated by the culmination of years of research—fifty cumulative years of experience as professional historians, he used to say—in the work *Madagascar: A Short History*, which was hailed as an important contribution, in English, to our common discipline.

In his own words, Stephen Ellis revealed something of the general spirit of his work, as well as his spirit of friendship, in something he said during a discussion with our host and mutual friend Ralph Austen at the University of Chicago:

'I can accept that someday, a certain scientific discipline or another might prove me to be of inferior intelligence, but no discipline would ever convince me that I were morally inferior.'

I interpret this statement, with sadness and hope, as a grand declaration of love for the whole continent[8] from a true gentleman historian.

INTRODUCTION

When Stephen Ellis died on 29 July 2015, tributes flooded in from around the world. African studies had lost 'one of the greatest Africanists of his generation',[1] 'an invaluable colleague and an inspiring mentor',[2] 'a giant baobab', and 'somebody to be trusted and respected absolutely'.[3] Stephen Ellis was a prolific author. Although only sixty-two when he died, his bibliography included some twenty books and more than 130 published articles.[4] A recognized expert on the history and politics of Madagascar, South Africa, Liberia and Nigeria, he also had an active role outside academia, spending periods working for Amnesty International, South Africa's Truth and Reconciliation Commission and the International Crisis Group, as well as contributing to publications for various judicial inquiries, governmental and intergovernmental commissions and acting as a frequent advisor to the Government of the Netherlands. In my own tribute, I recalled what a pleasure and a privilege it was for me to work with him on the journal *African Affairs*, the present success of which he did much to shape.[5]

Stephen Ellis's first engagement with Africa came at age eighteen, when he took up a teaching position with VSO in a Catholic missionary school in Cameroon. He went on to read history at Oxford, and subsequently, under Anthony Kirk-Greene, to complete a doctorate in the history of Madagascar. Unable initially to find a job as a professional historian, he worked as a researcher for Amnesty International and then as editor of the newsletter *Africa Confidential*. In the 1980s he met his life partner, the Dutch scholar of religion Gerrie ter Haar, and subsequently took up a position as Director of the African Studies

1

Centre in Leiden, an institution to which he remained affiliated for the rest of his career.

These early experiences were to shape his future interests, which revolved around violence—in particular the abuses that surrounded rebellions and their repression—crime, religion, and various forms of political struggle. I sometimes wondered what drove Stephen to investigate the topics he did, which were often disturbing and sometimes provocative. In an address written for his funeral, he invoked Sir Isaac Newton: 'I do not know what I may appear to the world; but to myself I seem to have been only like a boy playing on the seashore, and diverting myself in now and then finding a smoother pebble or a prettier shell than ordinary, whilst the great ocean of truth lay all undiscovered before me'. Be that as it may, he was also drawn to some of the bigger stones, overturning them to expose what crawled beneath. Such was certainly the case with his research into the ANC in exile, which earned him many enemies in South Africa, and his work on Nigerian organized crime, which also risked offending sensibilities. As more than one obituary has noted, however, Stephen Ellis was a scholar of great courage (Trewhela 2015): 'Stephen consistently chose to tell the truth against established opinion, out of a profound sense of intellectual honesty and moral duty' (ter Haar 2017, 22). One of the best illustrations was his long libel case with Liberian President Charles Taylor, accused by Ellis of eating human body parts; Ellis was later to face Taylor in the Special Court for Sierra Leone.

Although one will find references to Karl Marx, Max Weber, Clifford Geertz, Michel Foucault, Achille Mbembe and others in his work, Stephen Ellis's writing was not theory-driven; the empirical facts—for he did believe in such things—always propelled the analysis. Nor was it obviously ideologically flavoured, being neither socialist, conservative, liberal nor post-modern. In fact, Stephen Ellis was a scholar of considerable sophistication and subtlety, with the consequence that his work escapes easy categorization. It is partly for this reason, and for what it tells us about early twenty-first century Africa, that it deserves a sustained attention.

To that end, this collection aims to provide an introduction, covering some of his work's main themes, pieces that describe or illustrate his method, as well as some examples of writing penned for a more popular or policy-oriented audience. The collection encompasses his main geographical interests, historical and contemporary subjects, well- and lesser-known articles. I hope that readers will consider his arguments and their implications seriously, and be inspired to delve deeper into his broader corpus of work. In the remainder of this introduction I provide a summary of the articles, grouped under the sections, 'Method', 'Rebellion and Repression', 'Religion', 'Crime', and 'Public Engagement'. It concludes by touching on some of the unanswered questions and perplexing features of his oeuvre.

Method

Although Stephen Ellis's interests ranged over contemporary politics, religion and public affairs, he was first and foremost a historian. His PhD was on the topic of a colonial revolt in Madagascar, and although, as we shall see, some of the themes of that study were to reappear in his later work, its method was entirely conventional. The thesis was published as a book by Cambridge University Press and in French by Karthala, yet Ellis was unable immediately to find a job as a historian. Instead he went to work for Amnesty International and from there to the newsletter *Africa Confidential*. Arguably these early professional experiences were to shape his subsequent, distinctive, historiographical style—which focused, to a greater extent than that any other historian I know, on contemporary events, and which employed not only the traditional techniques of the historian, in particular archival research and interviews, but also novel sources such as rumour, or 'pavement radio'.

Stephen Ellis's approach is laid out in detail in Chapter 1 of this Reader, 'Writing Histories of Contemporary Africa' (S. Ellis 2002a). This article has three main themes. The first is that histories of contemporary Africa are relatively rare, with accounts of recent events on the continent dominated by journalists, political scientists and other commentators. While some of these accounts may be excellent, the historian's rigour, thinks Ellis, can potentially shed new light on contemporary problems and change the way people think about Africa, 'by picking out strands from its past that are sometimes unnoticed, or by combining these threads in new ways' (S. Ellis 2002a, p. 33 of this book).

To do so, however, he calls for a new periodization of African history. Ellis argues against the conventional chronological division of Africa's past into pre-colonial, colonial and independent periods, with the rather brief colonial period 'the fulcrum around which African history turned' (S. Ellis 2002a, p. 34 in this book). The 1970s, a decade of global economic crisis which comprehensively changed the prospects for African states and societies, might be a more obvious point from which to trace Africa's twenty-first century problems. An additional disadvantage of conventional periodizations is that, by viewing contemporary Africa through the prism of the post-independence moment, when the ideals of liberation and modernization were in high fashion, the present inevitably appears as a failure (p. 36). But Africa's current problems are neither the result of the imposition of colonial institutions on an 'authentic Africa', nor a 'botched decolonization'. By extending our gaze further back in time, post-colonial Africa might be portrayed, less pessimistically, perhaps, as 'groping to reconnect with deeper currents of its own history' (42).

This is a theme that Ellis had also discussed in the second article in this collection, 'Africa's Wars of Liberation: Some Historiographical Reflections' (S. Ellis 2000). Here he discusses a tendency on the part of historians, in thrall to the idea that the colonial era 'marked a watershed of some sort' (S. Ellis 2000, p. 69 of this book), to interpret violent resistance struggles in Africa as episodes in some ultimately teleological process, liberating Africans progressively from colonial, neo-colonial or national oppression. Yet given the disappointing results of each of these successive 'liberations', there are reasons to be sceptical. A more fruitful approach, he argues, would be to attempt to re-read 'the late colonial and postcolonial period of African history [without] any ideological prism' (p. 85). The call is to view Africa's wars of liberation 'in a wide context of social, economic and political history' (p. 86), with some of the recent scholarship on culture, subjectivities and identities, war and religion, war as an economic activity, and the 'politics of extraversion' conceivably representing steps in the right direction. The idea has crumbled that nationalism was a heroic project whose armed struggles were inevitable—but we have yet to fully escape the 'now-classic division of African history into three periods defined by their relationship to colonial rule' (p. 88).

Returning to the previous article, 'Writing Histories', Ellis argues that the scarcity of contemporary histories of Africa may also be related to sources. With the demise of the bureaucratic states established by colonialism, the compilation and maintenance of archives, the traditional domain of the historian, has deteriorated. That does not mean, however, that the historian's task is futile. Indeed, an abundance of alternative sources exists, including accounts of events authored contemporaneously or near-contemporaneously, in memoirs or autobiographies, eye-witness accounts in newspapers, periodicals and pamphlets, novels, and information broadcast via television, radio, film or the internet. None of these sources are without problems, and 'historians are well-advised to follow their basic precepts concerning evidence, asking themselves who has produced a particular document and why' (p. 47). Interviews are another, sometimes neglected source: as Thucydides, one of the greatest ever historians maintained, 'history' was 'that which he could elicit through skillful questioning from people who could still remember the events he wanted to describe' (p. 54).

The article also includes a discussion of the importance of *radio trottoir*, sometimes pejoratively dismissed as 'rumour' or 'gossip' in English. This forms the subject of the third piece in this collection, 'Tuning in to Pavement Radio' (S. Ellis 1989). Pavement radio is the modern successor of what used to be called the 'bush telegraph', and may be defined as, 'the popular and unofficial discussion of current affairs in Africa, particularly in towns' (S. Ellis 1989, p. 89 of this book). The article argues that it is 'a phenomenon worthy of study by scholars' (p. 89) for two main reasons. To begin with, *radio trottoir* has effects. In a continent where the news media is often unreliable and elections of dubious quality, pavement radio provides a space for government critique, and may serve to support or undermine incumbent governments, a kind of 'populist restraint on government' (p. 98). Indeed, so influential is it that national leaders sometimes engage with it directly, denying, like Paul Biya of Cameroon, the veracity of unfavourable stories, or, like Omar Bongo of Gabon, indirectly mimicking or infiltrating it, sowing the seeds of rumours that reflect more favourably on themselves. Second, pavement radio provides an important insight into popular opinion and concerns. As such, it should be thought of as a window on modern African society, a form of contemporary oral history (p. 99).

'[I]t is fair to say', writes Ellis in 'Rumour and Power in Togo', the fourth article in this collection, 'that analysts have tended to steer clear of *radio trottoir*, for the good reason that most of the information it conveys is impossible to check and its sources are generally impossible to verify'. Despite these difficulties, its rumours are worthy of study, 'for the light they shed on the nature of political legitimacy and authority [...] and the means by which they are contested' (p. 103 of this book). The article tells the story of how *radio trottoir* provided a crucial medium of support for President Eyadéma at a pivotal moment in the country's history when he was being challenged by oppositional elements in a National Conference: 'In the end, despite his legal destitution, President Eyadéma still had the appearance of power and Prime Minister Koffigoh had not' (p. 114). *Radio trottoir* was a 'crucial element in the interplay of forces between state and civil society' (p. 118), paving the way for Eyadéma's re-ascendency, post 1991. The article is typical of Stephen Ellis's method, in the sense of recounting in forensic detail the events surrounding a political crisis, before delving beneath the surface to consider the symbolic and cultural forces that gave meaning to the struggle.

This was also the approach taken in his research on the Liberian civil war. We will discuss one of his most famous articles about Liberia later. In this section on method, however, I have included his article, 'Violence and History: a response to Thandika Mkandawire', not because of what it says about the specifics of that case, but because of what it reveals about Stephen Ellis's view of history and historiography. Briefly, Mkandawire took issue, in an earlier article, with Ellis's extended analysis of cannibalism in the Liberian conflict, critiquing it as a 'poorly veiled racist' attack on 'African culture' (S. Ellis 2003, p. 123 of this book). In his response, Ellis rejects these claims, pointing out that nowhere in his work is there an appeal to race or genetics, or even to 'African' or 'Liberian' culture. Nevertheless, in attempting to explain some of the distinctive forms taken by violence in the Liberian civil war, he admits to treating violence, in the words of Anton Blok, as an 'historically developed cultural form of meaningful action' (p. 132), referring to, 'a range of symbols concerning power that are widely understood and historically rooted' (p. 136) and transmitted through institutions, in this case religious and political, that transcend the lifespan of individual generations (p. 124). This leads on to a broader discussion of how to reinvigorate social science in an era where confidence in some of its most influential models and paradigms is on the wane: 'What appears most desirable' he argues, 'is a two-step approach that consists, first, in understanding local ideas in their own context, and only then considering the light such ideas may throw on established modes of behaviour known to the social sciences' (p. 138). At the same time social science should be premised on the assumption that, 'all human beings have fundamental qualities, tendencies and abilities in common, and on the assumption that it is possible to reach a sophisticated and informed understanding of what these qualities are, exactly' (p. 140).

Rebellion and repression

A major theme in Stephen Ellis's work is the study of rebellions, resistance movements, and, in some cases, their repression. To this, he brought his characteristic concern to present the facts and place them in context. Never in service of grand historical narrative or ideological conviction did he manipulate, ignore or finesse the facts, and he never shrank from presenting truths that might be inconvenient or upsetting. Both in his published work and his public service engagements, Ellis implied that individuals, whoever they were, should be held responsible for their actions; at the same time those actions needed to be viewed on a wide canvas. Often his writing, especially when recounting details of atrocious and shocking events, took on a rather detached and dispassionate tone; yet when interpreting the causes of violence, it could become more empathetic, even compassionate. Certainly, he rarely set out to vilify individuals, but had instead a keen appreciation for the tragedy, and occasional tragicomedy, inherent in human affairs.

The seventh chapter in this collection, 'The Political Elite of Imerina and the Revolt of the Menalamba', his first published article in English (S. Ellis 1980), helped establish his reputation as an expert on the history of Madagascar. Using previously unopened archival sources, it provides a painstaking reconstruction of the revolt of the *Menalamba* in the two years following the French invasion of Madagascar in 1895, which Ellis describes as 'One of the most puzzling and fascinating of all resistance movements' (S. Ellis 1980, p. 149 of this book). It tells the story of the French suppression of the uprising and prosecution of its alleged organisers, a miscarriage of justice that portended a shift in French colonial policy. Here, in embryo, can be found several of the themes—rebellion and resistance, elite politics, rumour and conspiracy, spirit mediums and religion, and nationalist myth-busting—that would come to dominate Ellis's later work.

Stephen Ellis was also an expert on South Africa, studying the country for more than twenty-five years. In 'Mbokodo: security in ANC camps, 1961–1990', he discusses evidence surrounding two episodes of serious repression in the ANC's military camps in exile, one in 1967–9, and one in 1981–4, in which rank and file members of the ANC's armed wing were subjected to harsh discipline, torture, and were in some cases killed. The first episode led, via the Morogoro Conference, to the South African Communist Party exerting an increased influence not just over the ANC's armed wing, but over the entire organisation. This included the creation of an intelligence and security department run along East European lines, which promoted a single, ideologically-correct line, and which stifled debate and dissent. One of the officials in the intelligence and security department, named in passing as one of the individuals responsible for abuses in ANC camps, was Jacob Zuma. In what now seems a prescient passage, Ellis writes: 'ANC headquarters in Johannesburg continued to employ many of the officials of the Security Department who were found to have participated in abuses in Angola and who presumably would be well-placed to hold political or other high office in a future government' (p. 187). The implications for South Africa are explored further in his controversial book, *External Mission: The ANC in Exile 1960–1990* (S. Ellis 2014).

Addressing abuses on the other side of the political divide, 'The Historical Significance of South Africa's Third Force', narrates the crucial role that the South African state's violent and clandestine security networks played in the transition from apartheid, and their lasting influence on South African politics and society. The Third Force, according to Ellis, 'was not responsible for all the political violence which occurred in this period, but there is reason to believe that they were in some way its most important sponsors' (S. Ellis 1998, p. 193 of this book). 'Murder, torture, smuggling, forgery, propaganda and subversion were instruments used by both sides in this struggle, but it was the state which brought the greatest resources to bear in these domains' (S. Ellis 1998, p. 194 in this book). The article details how a contingent of South African policemen who honed their counterinsurgency skills in Rhodesia, emerged at the heart of the underground war, or 'organised network of illegal repression' (p. 209) against the ANC, SACP, and PAC. In the late 1970s, at the same time as other structures in the South African state were being centralized with a view to defending apartheid against insurgency, Special Forces were being granted an increased degree of autonomy, especially with respect to revenue generation. Covert military operatives, 'ran ivory, hardwood, diamonds and other products out of Angola through a front company on a large scale from the late 1970s' (p. 212). The extent of covert criminal operations expanded greatly in the 1980s. For the rank and file of the special units, 'total war meant simply war without rules' (p. 215). 'The culture of cynicism and illegality' Ellis argues, 'penetrated very deep' (p. 215). This carried on into the transition period, when the Vlakpaas, one of the most notorious special units, sold guns to Inkatha.

The Third Force, Ellis argues, was empowered by a group of senior politicians and security officers whose aim was not to sabotage or stop the negotiations, but to prolong them until such point at which a political settlement more favourable to white South Africa might be found. Unfortunately for them, the strategy backfired, since the covert units and the course of historical events they unleashed were never sufficiently under their control. As South Africa stared into a violent abyss, 'The ANC helped De Klerk to rein in the Third Force by having the wisdom to offer the National Party constitutional terms which were broadly acceptable to the SADF generals' (p. 240). Although the Third Force's sponsorship of political violence was brought to heel, many of its operatives escaped prosecution and, post-transition, may remain influential in criminal networks that continue to exert a pernicious effect on politics and society in South Africa and beyond.

'Liberia 1989–1994: A study of ethnic and spiritual violence' (S. Ellis 1995) is the extraordinary article that first drew my attention, as a young PhD student, to Stephen Ellis. Here, Ellis is at the height of his powers, combining chronology, political economy, and interpretive imagination to explain how the Liberian civil war, with its cannibalism, random violence and torture, sometimes perpetrated by young fighters wearing women's clothing or other bizarre accoutrements, took such a 'peculiarly horrible' form (S. Ellis 1995, p. 249 in this book).

The article begins by tracing the roots of the civil war first to Samuel Doe's 1980 coup and thence to the 1989 invasion of Liberia from Côte d'Ivoire, by Charles Taylor's National Patriotic Front of Liberia (NPFL). It then details the intervention of a Nigerian-led peace-keeping force, the capture and murder of Doe by an NPFL splinter group, the emergence of new armed groups, the Cotonou Ceasefire, the ineffective 1994 Transitional Government, and the subsequent multiplication of armed militias, accompanied by escalating levels of violence and atrocity. It then proceeds to an analysis of the causes of collapse, describing the system of political patronage erected by Americo-Liberian presidents Tubman and Tolbert over the hinterland, and the stresses placed on this by the need to incorporate a greater number of 'country people' during a period in which the Liberian economy was shrinking. A combination of social change and institutional sclerosis within the army, meanwhile, set the stage for Samuel Doe's 1980 coup. Doe subsequently instituted a system of marauding ethnic violence, galvanizing the NPFL—initially a vehicle for Mano and Gio interests—that was soon to be commandeered by the relentlessly ambitious Charles Taylor, who secured backing from 'the unlikely trio' of Côte d'Ivoire, Burkina Faso and Libya (p. 267). Taylor was then joined by other warlords, the majority of whom combined ethnicity with violence as a means of building political constituencies. At the same time, the violence was becoming increasingly divorced from any overarching ideological aims and was becoming more of an economic activity: 'A veritable mode of production had evolved in which the main aim was enrichment through looting, and wealth was sucked upwards within the militias' rudimentary hierarchies, from fighters to their officers' (p. 272).

It is in a section on 'Liberian concepts of power', however, that the article is most astonishing. Here, Ellis discusses secret societies and other cultic organisations, common throughout most parts of Liberia, in which ritual sacrifice and murder were symbolized and sometimes practised as a means of representing and ordering power. At the heart of the Poro initiation, Ellis claims, is a terrifying and morally ambiguous ritual of death and rebirth, represented as the act of being eaten by a wild spirit. The bush spirits are represented by masked officers of the society, who educate boys in the duties of manhood, while demonstrating 'that the power of the wild and dangerous spirits of the bush has been tamed and made socially productive by the Poro' (p. 274). Although analogues of Poro ritual have been appropriated by modern politicians and military leaders alike, the ability of the cults actually to impose social control has long been eroded, and in parts of the country all but destroyed during the recent conflict:

> In the civil war, in a world grown anarchic, acts of violence are daily performed in the familiar language of the secret society rituals, but now out of control. Ritual murders are no longer carried out by officers of established cults, but by unqualified adolescents. Whereas cultic violence is properly performed by society elders wearing masks, in Liberia today young fighters improvise masks with any objects they have to hand: dark glasses, women's wigs, shower caps, and so on. (p. 280)

And while the object of militia warfare is to gain wealth and power through violence, the cultic aspects are 'a means of spreading terror and also psychologically strengthening fighters, using a lexicon of symbols which is widely understood' (p. 279).

While not diminishing the awfulness of these violent acts, Ellis's interpretation at least bespeaks their rationality in the currency of a local material and symbolic economy. With spiritual and political life disordered, and, at the time, little prospect of an American intervention in Liberia, Ellis proffers that religion might be the most likely means of rebuilding Liberian society: 'Healing, in these circumstances, lies in the spiritual field at least as much as in the political one, and at the local level rather than the national one. The spirit world is the only domain in which constructive action is still detectable, and in this a leading role may fall to the churches' (p. 284).

Religion

Running through all the works discussed above, in addition to the themes of rebellion and resistance, is the importance of religious belief to understanding African thought and society. An apprehension of this is evident even in Ellis's earliest work; but it undoubtedly acquired greater shape through conversations with his life partner Gerrie ter Haar, a scholar of religion in Africa, whom he met in the 1980s. In this section, I showcase three articles he co-wrote with her.

The first is, 'Religion and Politics: Taking African Epistemologies Seriously', which, partly by responding to critiques of their earlier work, arguably sets out the authors' position in the most emphatic terms. In it, Ellis and ter Haar propose a two-step process for understanding religion in Africa: first by listening to what ordinary Africans say about religion, or, in other words, grasping its *emic* terms, before translating these into the more detached and universal, *etic*, categories of social science. On the basis of this method, they argue that a common feature of African epistemologies is a holistic view of the world in which, 'material and immaterial aspects of life cannot be separated, although they can be distinguished from each other, much as the two sides of a coin can be discerned but not parted' and that religion in sub-Saharan Africa is thus best understood as, 'a belief in the existence of an invisible world, distinct but not separate from the visible one, that is home to spiritual beings with effective powers over the material world' (S. Ellis and G. ter Haar 2007). This, they argue, is a radical departure from traditional social scientific approaches, which typically operate on the basis of a structural separation between the religious and material domains, encouraging them either to ignore religion, as with most political science and economics, or to focus on explaining it as the product of sociological phenomena, as with much of anthropology. Taking African epistemologies seriously, by contrast, opens new vistas in the understanding of politics, economics and development, by providing greater purchase on what people in Africa believe and desire. What is more, the model may have wider application and might be profitably deployed to understand other societies which presume a close relation between the visible and invisible worlds, and in which religion constitutes an increasingly powerful political currency.

More detail is provided in their earlier article 'Religion and Politics in Sub-Saharan Africa' (S. Ellis and G. ter Haar 1998). It begins by drawing attention to the proliferation of popular religious tracts in Africa that purport to describe mystical voyages, experiences of witchcraft, and journeys into the underworld. Such texts, although literally believed by their authors, can also be seen, argue Ellis and ter Haar, as 'a commentary on a world in which power is seen as being too often an instrument of evil people who use it to destroy peace and harmony. To that extent, they are also an oblique criticism of government or misgovernment' (p. 308). They proceed to the claim that, 'Religious belief', often derived from traditional cosmologies, 'operates at every level of society in Africa' (p. 309), before sketching a theory of the relationship between religion and politics quite different to that found in conventional political science or even anthropology:

> Religion and politics are both systems of ordering the power inherent in human society, in the process of which elements of authority and hierarchy tend to emerge. As such, religion and politics are closely related. In the modern Western tradition these two systems of harnessing or manipulating power have been subject to sharp organizational and intellectual distinctions which conform to the separation of politics and religion or church and state [...] However, it is clear that a large number of the world's people continue to regard these two spheres of power as impinging upon one another or even, in some circumstances, of being virtually indistinct. (p. 326)

Following a brief exegesis of a couple of remarkable, yet typical, popular religious tracts, they provide various examples of the importance Africa's national political leaders have attached to religion. It is not unusual, say the authors, for politicians all over the world to try to court popular support via public expressions of religious piety; what perhaps separates Africa from the West is that in many cases political elites consult religious experts, use protective objects, divination, and even sacrifice, since they believe that 'access to the spiritual world is a vital resource in the constant struggle to secure advantage over their rivals in political in-fighting' (p. 320). Meanwhile many of the new religious revival movements in Africa, 'can be seen as attempts to revive a known source of power' (p. 325).

13

Fundamentalist movements, in particular, can be seen as attempts to reorder society by imposing simplified, dualistic categories on current political and moral confusion. Indeed, in parts of Africa where the state has more or less collapsed, religious movements may offer a new basis not just for legitimizing power, but for creating an apparatus that can fulfil some of the functions of government. The challenge for Africans will be to develop a new language of politics which, while incorporating a notion of politicians as upholders of a cosmic order, is capable of being 'comprehensible internationally' (p. 331). For academics, it is, 'to understand this language of public affairs not as a symptom of a new form of exoticism, but as a debate on the proper function of power in Africa' (p. 332).

In the third co-written article in this section, 'The Occult Does Not Exist' (S. Ellis and G. ter Haar 2009), Ellis and ter Haar respond to a review article by Terence Ranger which opens with a discussion of the investigation in London of the presumed ritual murder of a young boy, of probable West African origin, dubbed by the British police as 'Adam'. In the article, Ranger 'admonishes the British police for making use of a crude stereotype of Africa', before presenting his own views via a review of recent works on religion and 'the occult' in Africa (p. 333). In their response, Ellis and ter Haar take issue with terms such as 'magic', 'witchcraft', and 'the occult', which come attached, they think, with a heavy ideological load. They trace this to earlier ideas about 'good' and 'bad' religion, originating in early European history, taken up by the early Christian Church, and zealously imposed on Africa during colonialism. The effect was to relegate much existing African religion to a residual and stigmatized category, a segregation that is echoed in much modern social science, with unfortunate consequences. One is to make almost impossible any balanced discussion of practices, which evidence suggests are quite common and widespread in Africa, that emanate from the search for spiritual power, and which have important consequences for human life and human rights. In remedy, Ellis and ter Haar propose that these activities ought first to be incorporated under their 'morally neutral and value-free' (p. 334) concept of religion, which I earlier introduced: 'Socially positive and socially harmful practices both exist within the field of religion. Referring to a specific act or practice as "religious" does not imply any definite moral value since, academically speaking, religion itself is neither good nor bad, but morally ambiguous. Placing so-called "occult" practices within a broader religious field helps us to understand the full range of their moral, social and political meanings' (p. 344). The article is interesting as an illustration of how to incorporate local meanings within a value-neutral social science terminology, while still having an opinion about the desirability or morality of the phenomena described.

The final article in this section, 'Witch-Hunting in Central Madagascar 1828–1861', tells the fascinating story of a poison-ordeal administered *en masse* by the Imerina state in the nineteenth century (S. Ellis 2002b). A faithful operationalisation of Ellis and ter Haar's advice on method, it proceeds in two stages: first by describing 'witchcraft' or *mosavy* in local, contextual terms, and then by analysing its relation to and role in larger social processes, which included political centralisation, massive population movements, war, disease and its decay. Ellis then explores the possibilities of a cautious comparative analysis of witchcraft, best approached, he thinks, as a 'comparative sociology of scapegoating' (p. 375). In conclusion, argues Ellis,

> the great witch-hunts were intrinsic to the articulation of a religious and political power that proved unable to endure, not least because of the vast inequities and ambiguities with which it was associated. For power does not reside in persons or things, but 'in the interstices between persons and between things, that is to say *in relations*'. This, too, is precisely where the artefact we call witchcraft is perceived to exist (p. 379).

Crime

In Chapter 14, 'The New Frontiers of Crime in South Africa', Ellis explains the roots of contemporary South Africa's chronic crime wave in apartheid and the resistance to it. Briefly, apartheid created a political and economic system in which the proper place of blacks was intended to be rural homelands, so despite the apartheid economy's demand for black industrial labour, black townships were never treated as permanent residences. One by-product was that the state made little attempt to police ordinary crime in black urban communities, as opposed to political activities; townships consequently saw the growth of fearsome criminal gangs. Initially marginal to the struggle around

15

apartheid, both the ANC and the National Party recognised by the late 1970s that these gangs could be their allies, and in some cases deliberately trained, armed, and encouraged them to foment disorder or attack their opponents. When the ANC and National Party finally settled their differences, these groups' violent activities returned to being more overtly criminal, but in enhanced form, confronted by a police force with little support among the black population and in some cases a history of collusion with the very elements it was supposed to be policing: 'Thus many of the social groups which participated in the struggle for South Africa continue to pursue their factional interests by violence. Today, this is generally labelled as criminal rather than political violence, but the change of vocabulary should not blind us to the fact that the actors remain largely the same' (p. 395). In addition, during the years of apartheid, the South African security forces were overwhelmingly focused on countering what they saw as the Soviet-backed threat of the ANC and SACP. This left them ill-prepared to cope with the massive growth in international cross-border criminality that accompanied the end of the Cold War and the decline in the formal economies of many states on their doorstep. Ironically, some of its own security agents, who had been given carte blanche to engage in smuggling and money laundering operations in the fight against the ANC, have found common cause with former enemies and are now key players in complex networks of politically connected licit and illicit business activity. Private security guards and fortified suburbs seem to be a permanent feature of the South African landscape, and the real question is whether South Africa's present levels of criminality can be contained, or whether they will ultimately overwhelm the core of a functioning state.

In 'Africa and International Corruption', Ellis broadens his gaze from South Africa itself to consider some of crime and corruption's transnational aspects (S. Ellis 1996). In a dizzying tale of money laundering, intelligence agencies, mafia-style organizations and shell-companies, that ties political events in the Seychelles to national and geopolitical processes involving the US, Soviet Union, South Africa, Italy and France, among others, Ellis explains how grand corruption, 'sometimes masquerading as *raison d'état*, shapes the environment in which individual politicians, diplomats and business people are obliged to operate' (p. 408). Secret or covert networks, created with the aim of advancing geopolitical interests, he argues, attract the attention of professional criminals and tempt otherwise honest people to steal— since the funds involved are publicly unaccountable.

In Chapter 17, 'West Africa's International Drug Trade' (S. Ellis 2009b), Ellis delves deeper into one dimension of this. The article traces West Africa's insertion into global narcotics markets to the colonial period, explaining how the trade nevertheless expanded greatly in the 1980s, in a period during which African formal economies were under severe stress, while financial and other forms of globalization were gathering pace. Focusing on Nigeria, with additional insights from elsewhere in West Africa, the article details certain features of the Nigerian drugs industry. Characterized by flexible, ad hoc relations among 'drugs barons', 'strikers' and 'couriers', and described by a US anti-drugs official as 'some of the most sophisticated and finely-tuned transshipment, money-moving and document-forging organizations in the world', its structure is difficult for law enforcement officers to pin down (p. 477). The article goes on to discuss some of the more localised features that may serve to give Nigerians a comparative advantage in this field, including a state in which law enforcement is generally weak, economic aspirations are high, and solidarity and secrecy can be cemented by means such as oathing. 'The emergence of shadow states with networks that have become globalized through commerce and migration opens up an important debate in historical sociology concerning the degree to which predation in the last quarter of the twentieth century was the consequence of a specific context in the 1980s, and the extent to which its historical roots go much deeper' (p. 487).

In his last book, Stephen Ellis again picks up this theme, setting out to answer the sensitive questions of how it is that the Nigerian state has achieved such a reputation for corruption, and why Nigerians appear to be disproportionately represented in such fields as international drug trafficking, prostitution, and internet fraud. Responding to former US Secretary of State Colin Powell's view that, 'Nigerians as a group, frankly, are marvelous scammers. I mean, it is in their natural culture' (S. Ellis 2016, p. 443 in this book),[6] Ellis asks whether culture can be an explanation for such behaviour. His answer takes the form of a complex historical narrative, explaining how elements of precolonial religion and society combined with the forces of colonialism and indirect rule to produce an entrepreneurial culture subject to weakened legal and moral restraints, channeled into politics in the run up to Independence, then amplified with the oil boom and exported among the Nigerian diaspora, concluding that 'Nigerian organized crime is not created by culture, but it does arise from a particular history. Where else could it possibly come from?' In this collection, we reproduce the Introduction and first chapter, which discusses how precolonial culture and indigenous religion shaped 'the psychology of Nigerian organised crime' (p. 445), while the theory and practice of early colonialism, especially in Southern Nigeria, provided an early contribution to 'a culture of corruption' (p. 461).

Public engagement

This collection also includes three pieces written for a more popular, or policy audience. The first, 'How to Rebuild Africa', focuses on the problem of Africa's 'failed' or 'fragile states' at the turn of the twenty-first century. Failed states, argues Ellis, are typically viewed by policymakers as being like machines, which, with some well-known technical inputs, can be fixed. A better metaphor is that they are sick patients, each with their own peculiarities, which require careful diagnosis before being nursed back to health. In addition to this basic error, the conventional wisdom on rebuilding African states suffers from three major defects: it is short-termist; it overestimates, in some cases, the degree of capacity that these states ever had; and it is overly focused on individual nations as its unit of analysis. What are needed are longer-term, international or regional solutions, that in some cases re-imagine what it is a state can realistically achieve, and which other actors and institutions might fulfil typical state functions instead. In a few cases, thinks Ellis, a new form of international trusteeship can be advocated: 'multilateral joint ventures in which certain countries and institutions share control over key operations'. The partial surrender of sovereignty this entails will doubtless be a bitter pill to African nationalists (p. 501). Nevertheless, 'These arrangements would avoid the evils of colonialism and the errors of more recent peacekeeping and state-building efforts. The outcome—a healthier, more stable, and more secure Africa—would benefit everyone, on the continent and around the world' (p. 504).

The second, 'The Roots of African Corruption', picks up what for us by now is a familiar theme: the use of the 'hollowed out' institutions of the postcolonial state by 'secret services, money launderers, offshore bankers, corporate lawyers, sanctions busters, drug traffickers, arms smugglers, and others', not to mention political elites, for personal gain. Underlying this, of course, is the imposition of legal-rational institutions by colonial powers on indigenous societies, the economic decline that has beset the continent since the 1970s, and a perception on the part of African leaders that the international system is rigged against them. 'As long as this mood prevails' argues Ellis, 'corruption in Africa will continue' (p. 517).

This leads us to the final piece in our collection, the inaugural lecture Ellis gave on accepting the Desmond Tutu Chair at Vrije Universiteit Amsterdam (S. D. K. Ellis 2009a). As well as being a meditation on the contemporary situation in South Africa, which has failed, sadly, to realize Tutu's 'Rainbow Nation' vision, it is perhaps the clearest statement we have of Ellis's view of the way forward for Africa, a task which requires, echoing Ngugi wa Thiongo, a 'decolonization of the minds' of both Africans and Europeans. Africans must, as have some other non-European peoples, take responsibility for their own history, including that of colonialism, neither seeking to revive a mythical African 'authenticity', nor playing the role of perennial victims of Western machinations. At the same time, Europeans must rid themselves of the delusion that their continent has some special place in history, that development consists in shepherding other countries past already-achieved Western milestones, or that Africa has nothing from which Europeans themselves can learn: 'We should cease believing almost instinctively that ideas from Africa must be wrong, since our underlying assumption is that they are destined to be replaced with ideas made in Europe [...] We Europeans, too, have to decolonize our minds' (p. 532).

Closing thoughts

In the words of his editor, Michael Dwyer, 'Stephen Ellis's rigour as a researcher and writer was matched by an unflinching search to understand Africa and its historical vicissitudes and to explain these to the reader'. I hope that this Introduction and the collection's articles provide a sense of the tremendous contribution Stephen Ellis made to African studies. However, Ellis's approach was often controversial and in this section I try, briefly, to clear up some of the confusion by discussing issues of ontology, epistemology, ethics and style.

From an ontological point of view, Ellis worked with a conception of a world in which social, political, economic—and conceivably, spiritual—forces shaped but did not fully determine the actions of individuals, while historically-transmitted cultural institutions provided a kind of language or grammar through which those actions could be understood. This approach, and especially the emphasis on culture, put him on a collision course with African nationalists and Marxists. As a reaction to colonialism's culture-based claims to superiority and authority, many African nationalists have downplayed culture as a significant explanatory variable or object of study. Marxists, meanwhile, have eschewed culture in favour of a materialist ontology, which, in its cruder versions, envisages fundamental economic laws producing inevitable historical outcomes. As expressions of the Enlightenment, nationalists and Marxists tend also to cleave to a 'Whiggish' version of history, in which individuals can be on either the right or wrong side. By taking culture seriously, however, Ellis inadvertently identified himself as a reactionary, and thus invited accusations of 'Afro-pessimism' and even 'racism'. In reality, Ellis merely had a richer, more holistic view of the world: history has no inevitability and there are no objective grounds by which one epoch can be assumed superior to another. Far from being racist, he was at pains to stress that Europe had much to learn from Africa. His allegedly 'negative' portrayal of the continent was more a consequence of his subject matter: war, crime, corruption, violence and their cultural aspects, than a manifestation of bias or malicious intent.

Epistemologically and methodologically, Ellis believed that it was necessary to rid the mind of normative preconceptions in order to fully understand a phenomenon. As with various approaches to theological hermeneutics, interpretive sociology and anthropology, the aim in the first instance is to approach the issue in cultural context and from the actor's point of view. In this spirit, he goes to considerable lengths to avoid ideologically loaded terms such as 'magic' and the 'occult' and even, at least in his later work, 'cannibalism'. Because of this, one sometimes gets the impression that one is reading the work of a moral or cultural relativist, especially when combined with his rejection of teleological or Whiggish views of history, development and progress. This might be unsettling, at times, to readers from a human rights or development background. Ellis, however, was keen to distance himself from a 'crude moral relativism' (see *Season of Rains*, 167), and a sort of moral judgement infuses many of his conclusions and much of his policy advice. What, then, was Ellis's normative standpoint?

To my knowledge, Stephen Ellis was never explicit in his writings about his ethical worldview. Raised a Catholic and always deeply interested in religion, he returned to his spiritual roots at the end of his life; the association of the Chair he held at Amsterdam with Bishop Tutu was for him a source of pride. In addition, and as we have seen, Ellis spent his early career working for Amnesty International, while in some of his work he refers to the UN's Human Development Index as a potential yardstick against which to measure social progress (e.g., *Season of Rains* 154; *European Journal of Development Research*). Perhaps the most we can say, then, is that Ellis's worldview was influenced by Christianity and humanism and these informed his attitude to the topics he studied and the solutions he proposed. It was another reason why he was distrustful of nationalism and historicism, both ideologies which tended to abrogate the rights of the individual in favour of an objectively-determined collective good. Whether an attachment to humanistic values can be squared with an epistemology that begins by understanding cultures from the inside, I leave it to readers to decide. What is not in doubt, however, is that Ellis's genuine interest in African cultures, combined with a worldly hard-headedness about power and politics, places his work on a different level to that of most authors writing from a human rights background. Indeed, Ellis's policy advice tended to urge pragmatic solutions that, in contrast to ideologically driven ones, should take the realities of African societies into account (see *Season of Rains*, esp. 147–170).

Another consistent feature of Ellis's worldview was his abhorrence of secrecy. Much of his work is concerned with the baleful effects of secret societies, cliques, shadowy networks and censorship. It was in these closed spaces that power was likely to assume its most damaging forms. Stephen saw it as his vocation as a journalist and a historian to shine a light on these areas and expose the truth, even if that involved confronting long-held beliefs and cherished myths. Nowhere was this more evident than in his book about the ANC in exile, in which his distrust of nationalism, Marxism and secrecy combine in a powerful expose of dishonesty, factionalism, human rights abuse, crime and corruption. Even Nelson Mandela does not escape criticism. 'Why not choose a more uplifting subject?' Ellis asks in an appendix to the book. The answer, he says, is that the ANC's mythology is no longer serving South African society well, and that as new historical information has come to light, it is useful to show how the myth is inconsistent with the facts. In the view of some commentators, the present author included, Ellis's claim that the ANC in exile was basically a front organization for the South African Communist Party, strays a little close to violating his own injunction that historians should 'resist to the best of their ability the temptation to extend contemporary ideas or concerns back into the past in a single-minded manner' (2000, page 85 in this book). Nevertheless, most readers will appreciate that *External Mission* is a powerful story and important contribution to debates on South Africa's past and present.

Another feature of Ellis's writing that will likely make it challenging for some is its style. Stephen did not let political correctness or what are now called 'snowflake sensibilities' get in the way of the truth; he did not write to spare other people's feelings. His book on crime in Nigeria, for example, while apparently well-received in that country, may make uncomfortable reading for law-abiding Nigerians in the diaspora, anxious about negative stereotypes of their country and its offspring. While Ellis does at various points qualify his findings, one wonders, in a world where some are keen, for reasons of prejudice or political gain, to stigmatize particular African nations or Africans in general, whether he could or should have done so more vigorously. In any case, I urge readers to come to Ellis's work with an open mind: to set aside what they think they know about Africa or how they would like Africa to be, and to concentrate on what he is really telling them.

The final difficulty concerns the role of causation in his work. Stephen Ellis was a historian who presented us with enthralling, meticulously researched narratives of historical and contemporary events. His work has many insights to offer political science. But he was not a political scientist and these were not *causal narratives* in a scientific sense. To give one example, in *This Present Darkness,* Ellis is persuasive in arguing that the growth of Nigerian organized crime is associated with a constellation of factors, one of which is the history of secret societies. But that is not the same, and nor does he explicitly claim, that the remarkable growth and resilience of Nigerian crime is *caused*, even partly, by a historical tradition of having secret societies. To get a better handle on this, it would be necessary to engage at greater length in counterfactual thought experiments, to compare Nigeria to other countries sharing similar characteristics, but differing in this one respect, or to assess the prevalence of crime in other countries that have a secret society tradition but lack some of Nigeria's other features. Only via the logic of comparison can we know whether secret societies are an essential causal ingredient in the story of Nigerian organized crime, or, by contrast, whether they merely provide local colour. Although Stephen Ellis's work did include a comparative dimension, it did not take this approach. That was not his style, and the application of a systematic comparative framework may have denuded his writing of some of what makes it rich and interesting, not to mention its élan. Yet this type of knowledge would be useful, in theory, to policymakers wishing to know to what extent secret societies should be a focus for anti-crime policy.

Puzzles and possible oversights notwithstanding, I hope to have demonstrated in this chapter that by empirically describing and historically illuminating the blurring of crime, conflict, politics and violence that affected much of Africa at the turn of the twenty-first century, and by suggesting routes out of the impasse, Stephen Ellis's work should be an inspiration to social scientists and policymakers for years to come.

References

Ellis, prof. dr. S.D.K. (2009), 'South Africa and the Decolonization of the Mind'. Inaugural lecture, Desmond Tutu chair in the Faculty of Social Sciences, VU University, Amsterdam, 2009. No ISBN Online version: http://hdl.handle.net/1871/15351.

Ellis, Stephen (1980), 'The political elite of Imerina and the revolt of the Menalamba. The creation of a colonial myth in Madagascar, 1895–1898', *Journal of African History,* 21, 219-34.

———— (1989), 'Tuning in to pavement radio', *African Affairs,* 88 (352), 321-30.

———— (1994), 'Mbokodo: security in ANC camps, 1961–1990', *African Affairs,* 93 (371), 279-98.

———— (1995), 'Liberia 1989–1994: a study of ethnic and spiritual violence.', *African Affairs,* 94 (375), 165-98.

———— (1996), 'Africa and international corruption: the strange case of South Africa and the Seychelles', *African Affairs,* 95 (165-196).

———— (1998), 'The historical significance of South Africa's Third Force', *Journal of Southern African Studies,* 24 (2), 261-99.

———— (2000), 'Africa's wars of liberation: some historiographical reflections', in P. Konings, W. van Binsbergen, and G. Hesseling (eds.), *Trajectoires de libération en Afrique contemporaine* (Paris: Karthala), 69-91.

———— (2002a), 'Writing histories of contemporary Africa', *Journal of African History,* 43, 1-26.

———— (2002b), 'Witch-hunting in central Madagascar 1828–1861', *Past and Present,* (175), 90-123.

———— (2003), 'Violence and history: a response to Thandika Mkandawire', *Journal of Modern African Studies,* 41 (3), 457-75.

———— (2009b), 'West Africa's international drug trade', *African Affairs,* 108 (431), 171-96.

———— (2011) *Season of Rains. Africa in the World.* Forew. by Archbishop Desmond Tutu. Auckland Park, Jacana & London, Hurst & Co.

———— (2014), *External Mission: The ANC in Exile. 1960–1990* (London: Hurst and Company).

———— (2016), *This Present Darkness: A history of Nigerian organised crime* (London: Hurst and Company).

Ellis, Stephen and ter Haar, Gerrie (1998), 'Religion and Politics in Sub-Saharan Africa', *Journal of Modern African Studies,* 36 (2), 175-201.

———— (2006), 'The Role of Religion in Development: Towards a New Relationship between the European Union and Africa', *European Journal of Development Research,* 18 (3), 351-367.

————— (2007), 'Religion and politics: taking African epistemologies seriously', *Journal of Modern African Studies,* 45 (3), 385-401.

————— (2009), 'The occult does not exist: a response to Terence Ranger', *Africa,* 79 (3), 399-412.

ter Haar, Gerrie (forthcoming), 'Stephen Ellis: his life and work', in Rufus Akinyele and Ton Dietz (eds), *Crime, Law, and Society in Nigeria: Essays in Honour of Stephen Ellis*. Leiden/Boston: Brill, 2019, pp. 6-30.

Trewhela, Paul (2015), 'Stephen Ellis: a standard of moral courage', *South African Historical Journal* (67), 3.

SECTION ONE

METHOD

WRITING HISTORIES OF CONTEMPORARY AFRICA*

This essay argues that historians need to engage with the history of contemporary Africa both as a way of throwing new light on Africa's more remote past and as a way of understanding the present. The paper discusses two types of problem involved in such an enterprise. The first is the identification of the most fruitful themes for investigation. The second is the sources that may be used.

Key words: Historiography, post-colonial, sources.

Forty years, or nearly two generations, have passed since the majority of African states became independent. This passage of time presses historians to consider how they might write histories of Africa since independence. Not least among those who might find such work useful are historians of earlier periods, if only for the functional reason that every piece of the past forms a context for other pieces of the past. Histories of colonial times, for example, are inevitably coloured by what we think we know about what happened next. Conversely, some keen observers of contemporary Africa, although not motivated by any professional commitment to historical inquiry, nevertheless feel impelled to investigate the recent past as a means of understanding

---

* I am grateful for comments on a previous draft of this paper by David Killingray and by two anonymous referees.

phenomena that are apparent today, in an effort to produce a more convincing explanation than is currently available of how things came to be the way they are.[1] Analyses of this sort may be more relevant to the rest of the world than is generally realized.[2]

In short, both historians and specialists from other disciplines sometimes find unsatisfactory the models of historical explanation that are available to them when they are studying Africa's recent past and its present. This is unsurprising inasmuch as many of the contemporary histories written in the 1960s and 1970s reflected the political preoccupations considered most urgent at that time, using the intellectual models that seemed most convincing.[3] For all their achievement, such works by and large no longer speak to concerns that appear important today, as we shall see, and yet they have not been replaced by a new generation of contemporary histories rooted in more up-to-date themes.[4] If anything, the void has been filled by journalists' accounts, which can be excellent, but which are not quite contemporary history.[5]

This essay considers how a new generation of works on Africa's contemporary history might be written. Most of the examples chosen concern Africa south of the Sahara, but some of the remarks may also apply to north Africa. At times, the essay may seem to refer to contemporary history as though that were synonymous with the period since the golden age of independence, the late 1950s and 1960s. It is, however, an important part of the following argument that the writing of contemporary history sometimes requires going much further into the past than forty or fifty years ago. It is for this reason that some recent general histories of Africa, although necessarily treating the contemporary period as only a small part of a larger whole, are nonetheless rich in their implications for consideration of more recent times.[6] This is further evidence of the seamlessness of all history. Such matters are discussed in the first part of the paper, which briefly considers some of the techniques used in writing contemporary history before going on to discuss particular themes that could be addressed in regard to Africa. Any identification of those aspects of Africa's recent past that are thought to be sufficiently important, interesting or rewarding for historians to use as central themes has to be based on criteria of some sort. It is of crucial importance to consider what these criteria might be. It should not be assumed that the leading themes of Africa's recent history must always be the same as those which are seen as the most relevant by historians of other parts of the world. Africa, like every other place, has a distinctive character derived largely from its particular history, and yet it is also a part of a single world bound together by what people have experienced in common. Assessing the relationship of distinctiveness on the one hand to human commonality on the other is one of the most delicate and consequential of the historian's tasks.

The second half of the essay concerns the sources that historians of contemporary Africa have at their disposal. Here it is argued that, although sources are abundant, they are not always of a type that historians feel comfortable in using. This may have an effect on the way historians insert Africa in the time-scales generally used in world history, just as it is having an effect on the way in which Africans tend to think of themselves in relation to their own past.

Problems of contemporary history

Academic history-writing involves assembling masses of verifiable facts and arranging them in a series, generally a chronological one, or a set of such series. Some historians may immediately recoil at this use of the word 'fact' to describe historical data. The word is used here to designate empirically verifiable events of the past, distinguishable from rumour, myth, memory and fiction (all of which may have a role to play in historical reconstructions, as we will see). The arrangement of such facts in a series is not the only activity undertaken by historians and perhaps not even the most distinctive aspect of their task. What is proper to the work of a historian as opposed to that of a natural scientist who is reconstructing, say, the stages of development of a species of dinosaur, is the effort to penetrate the thinking of those who were implicated in the events of the past.[7] Arranging the data in a sequence and attempting to re-think the thoughts of those involved create a narrative; even a historian who spurns story-telling still creates a narrative in some shape or form, implied by the type of facts selected and the sequence into which they are fitted.

It is in considering history-writing in these terms that it soon becomes apparent why some historians may be suspicious of any attempt to write the history of recent times, for such an enterprise is undertaken by inquirers who do not have a complete sequence of historical data and who are therefore obliged to make premature judgments as to the logic or the significance of the series they assemble. This begs the question of what is meant by a 'complete' sequence of historical data. Strictly speaking, no narrative based on a series of historical facts is ever complete, not only because further information could always be added to the sequence (for example, by finding relevant new data to insert), but also because telling or retelling a story itself adds a new element to the sequence. Nevertheless, it is fair to say that the longer ago the period under discussion, the easier it is to discern a beginning and an end to a given sequence of events and to appreciate the pattern of the whole. In writing the history of the contemporary world, by contrast, the final phase is notably incomplete. No matter how well researched, such a work of history is fated to become obsolete as new events occur that tend to invalidate whatever combinations of facts appeared to have a sequential logic at the time of writing. This is true of all history-writing inasmuch as the historian is bound to see things from the standpoint of present time, but, views change with particular speed in regard to recent history.

Historical research, moreover, ideally consists of something more than sifting the records of the past in a single-minded search for data that have a direct bearing on current concerns. According to some accomplished practitioners, it is important to see the past not just as the embryo of the present, but also as a period in its own right, replete with unfulfilled ambitions and disappointed hopes, ideas that once seemed important but that did not actually result in outcomes that are still with us today. One historian of the European past reminds us that this is not just a story of 'inevitable victories and forward marches'.[8] The same could be said of Africa—or perhaps it would be more appropriate, in view of the streak of pessimism often apparent in writing about contemporary Africa, to turn the proposition upside down by saying that Africa's past is not only a story of tragic failures and retreats. Triumphalist and defeatist histories are merely two sides of the same, devalued coin. Of more worth is an appreciation that the present is 'just one possible outcome of our predecessors' struggles and uncertainties'.[9]

The examination of the past-in-the-present together with the turning-points at which history failed to turn[10] is an original contribution that contemporary history can bring to the literature concerning our world today.[11] It may even be quite urgent for such an approach lest Africa be seen, by the general public and even by professional historians, in Europe and North America especially, as existing in a timeless zone where events are no more than what one British historian notoriously called 'unrewarding gyrations'.[12] There are many accounts of the recent African past produced by politicians, journalists, essayists, biographers and other writers of various sorts that, being ordered chronologically, could be considered histories. In addition, historical material is assembled by specialists in academic disciplines such as political science and anthropology. Historians bring to the same or similar data a particular approach. Their special expertise consists in the techniques they use to recover the record of the past and the precise manner in which they arrange their data in sequences.

Thus contemporary histories may bring a new perspective to Africa's present by viewing it through the prism of its past. They have the potential to change the way that people think about Africa by picking out strands from its past that are sometimes unnoticed, or by combining these threads in new ways. In order best to do this, however, it seems necessary to identify, at least tentatively, the themes that most deserve to be studied.

Historical themes

The golden age of Africa's independence[13] occurred at a time when intellectuals and politicians in both the first and second worlds, as they were then called, were generally convinced that social science had the power not only to provide accurate explanations of political and social phenomena but also to serve as a guide to action. Their colleagues in the third world had every incentive to share their view that societies could be governed, politics regulated and economies stimulated, by a range of techniques that could be identified and implemented by the established methods collectively described as 'modernization'.

This was perhaps the key concept of the ideologies of both left and right extant at the time of Africa's independence.[14] Influential political scientists saw Africa as the site of nation-building and party formation;[15] economists and sociologists considered it ripe for development.[16] The historians who were writing in the first years of Africa's independence, like all historians, swam in the currents of their time, and this was reflected in the attention they devoted to the historical antecedents of what various academic colleagues and political actors and opinion-formers were identifying as the burning issues of contemporary Africa. One experienced African historian has recently noted that members of the profession in the first years of independence tended towards a misguided search for uniformity, intent on mapping a history for each newly-emerged state when they might have been better advised to think in terms of multiple histories.[17] New states required new historical charters.

Independence in most African countries occurred at the mid-point of the period between 1945 and the mid-1970s that witnessed a worldwide economic boom of unprecedented size and scope. It was accompanied by profound changes in the way people lived. This was also the period that saw the birth of African history as an academic discipline. To be sure, people have been writing texts recognizable as histories of Africa since the seventeenth century at least,[18] but it remains useful to distinguish this earlier work from the modern type of history-writing that is dominated by professional academics making systematic use of archives, a technique applied to the history of Africa only since the mid-twentieth century.[19] The first generation of professional Africanist historians created a basic chronological division of Africa's past into pre-colonial, colonial and independent periods, a trinity recalling the conventional European concept of ancient, medieval and modern history. At bottom, the division of African history into these periods was an assertion that the establishment of colonial rule marked a feature in African history so basic that it could be considered a change of era,[20] with the implication that, as Basil Davidson put it in 1959, Africa's history was beginning anew with the proclamations of independence.[21] The rather brief colonial period became the fulcrum around which African history turned, with time stretching backwards and forwards from that point into the infinite 'pre' and 'post' ages, both defined by reference to colonialism.[22]

No one deserves to be castigated for failing to predict the future, but it is legitimate to point out the extent to which social scientists writing thirty or forty years ago may now be seen to have identified the key aspects of the present, as it then was, in features which turn out to have been less durable than anticipated. Political independence has turned out not to have had such a straightforward connection with development as many commentators and analysts once assumed. It seems that it was the belief in a more or less clearly signposted road to modernization or development, so widely held by intellectuals in the west, the socialist bloc and Africa around the time of Africa's independence, that caused many of even the most penetrating analysts of that time to suppose that the features of African life that they identified as being the most dynamic in the 1960s and 1970s were permanent fixtures. Among these was an assumption that African political life was henceforth likely to revolve around the state and other formal institutions in much the same way as it had come to do since the seventeenth century in Europe, so many of whose political institutions had been exported to Africa. Nowadays, forty years later, it is more convincing to argue that sovereign independence, desirable though it was on a variety of grounds, and politically unstoppable, was not a universal milestone, but is in reality a concept largely derived from studies of Europe and North America.[23]

If one seeks to identify points of discontinuity in Africa's history since independence or, to be more precise, in the history of Africa's insertion in the world, it becomes apparent that many ruptures first became visible in the 1970s, when oil crises, currency instability and a series of related events and trends combined to create a comprehensive change in the prospects for African states and societies, and in the forms of their political life. One leading observer of the history of the world in the twentieth century is surely correct in seeing that decade as a time of change more crucial than 1989, the year of the fall of the Berlin wall.[24] One effect of the crises of the 1970s was to render obsolete many of the assumptions that had been unchallengeable only a few years earlier.

Some of the ambitions, fears and aspirations of the 1960s, although still within living memory, now seem so distant as to be barely comprehensible. They have become history. Some opinion-formers and political actors, however, including many African leaders themselves, continue to make rhetorical allusions to the great themes of the independence generation: nation-building, liberation, economic development, pan-Africanism, the struggle against dependence. These ideals are not ignoble. The problem, rather, in intellectual terms is that they have turned out to be less fully understood by social science than was thought to be the case some decades ago, while in political terms they have proved less easily attainable than was once thought likely. One of the sharpest African political commentators noted that a rhetorical insistence by political leaders on the ideals of the past is a way of avoiding the real political debates of the present.[25] Persistent reference to outdated ideals may also be considered as a spurious attempt to acquire legitimacy by speaking the language of revered ancestors.

This rhetorical poverty should not be blamed on politicians alone. Intellectuals too have done little to renew the vocabularies that are at the disposal of politicians both inside and outside Africa. The historian Achille Mbembe is most severe on this point. Regarding the literature of political science and development economics, he writes,[26]

> these disciplines have undermined the very possibility of understanding African economic and political facts. In spite of the countless critiques made of theories of social evolutionism and ideologies of development and modernization, the academic output in these disciplines continues, almost entirely, in total thrall to these two teleologies.

Historians have made their own modest contribution to this unsatisfactory state of affairs by their reluctance to reconsider Africa's contemporary history in terms appropriate to the present state of affairs. To create or repeat a narrative of contemporary history that coheres around the notions of political and economic development in vogue at the time of independence is to continue working in the shadow of the great ideals of forty years ago. Such a narrative risks excluding some key events from the sequences of data it assembles. It is also relevant to note that it is almost certain to produce a story of failure, since what is happening in Africa today is being examined at least implicitly in terms of ideals that are not of this age and whose grounding in African societies is itself in need of greater study. This was observed already in 1987 by a historian who asked, in regard to the previous twenty-five years, 'whose dream was it anyway?'[27]

To be sure, it is legitimate—necessary, even—for historians to reconsider lost ideals and to wonder why things went wrong or whose fault it was. But if this becomes the dominant theme of their writing, then it should be no surprise if their essays are read as expressions of nostalgia or tragedy. It makes all the difference if such an inquiry into the contemporary period is conducted in the consciousness of ideas that are alive in society today in the sense of motivating actual behaviour. This may not result in reading that is edifying, but it will always be relevant. There is, for example, now a substantial literature on the 1994 genocide in Rwanda that, quite properly, examines how such a thing could happen and who was responsible.[28] It is when narratives of contemporary history are couched only in terms of outdated ideals that they risk becoming sterile. They risk misidentifying some features of the more recent landscape by viewing them through an old lens. This has, for example, been a feature of the historiography of African liberation movements, too often seen as harking back to a perceived golden age of revolution and liberation rather than being situated in their own time.[29] It leads to the position where those writers on Africa's contemporary history who take as their starting-points the features of Africa that are visible today risk appearing as pessimists because their stories form a narrative of failure to achieve high ideals, whereas those whose narratives continue to privilege the ideals of a bygone age are liable to be seen as optimists, but romantic and out of touch ones. The ensuing Afro-optimist versus Afro-pessimist stand-off is reinforced by journalists in search of pathos and humanitarians in need of funds.

This surely is an intellectual cul-de-sac. It is perhaps because the prospect of writing Africa's contemporary history in such terms has become so unattractive that there has been a noticeable decline in publication within this sub-discipline since the 1970s. My own count of the articles published in the *Journal of African History* from 1990–1999 and listed in the cumulative index suggests that 65 articles were published on the pre-colonial history of Africa in that period, 118 on colonial history and 18 on general subjects. Only one article unambiguously concerned contemporary history, and that was a historiographical survey rather than a presentation of original research.[30] A rapid search of other leading journals of African history for the same decade suggests some three articles fairly unambiguously addressing contemporary history in the *International Journal of African Historical Studies*. *History in Africa,* being a journal of method, is more difficult to classify by period. This is a straw poll only, since studies of Africa's contemporary history are also to be found in current affairs journals such as the *Journal of Modern African Studies, African Affairs, Cahiers d'Études Africaines, Politique africaine*, the *Journal of Contemporary African Studies* and others. It does, though, underline the point that the main journals of African history appear to have developed a certain reticence in regard to contemporary history, perhaps for some of the reasons suggested here, leading writers in this mode to place their work elsewhere. The lack of much in the way of an authentic historical approach to Africa's contemporary period impoverishes the work of other disciplines too, including political science, which remains driven more often by contemporary theoretical questions than by preoccupations rooted in the historicity of Africa or of its insertion into the world.[31]

The above remarks, amounting to no more than a sketch, do scant justice to the many works that have suggested new fields of contemporary history-writing. These have been particularly innovative in regard to personal relations and the lives of small communities. We may cite some examples. Given the enormous changes that have taken place in family life over the last couple of generations—not just in Africa but in many other parts of the world as well—a new interest in histories of gender and family is entirely welcome.[32] The history of locality, although it has never been absent from the historiography of Africa, has also received a fillip from the anthropological concern with the relation of globality to locality.[33] Histories of health and healing have been illuminating.[34] These and others are worthy additions to the historical literature on fairly recent times but it is evident that few of these notable contributions, opening inroads into contemporary themes as they do, engage with what arguably remains the overwhelming problem of Africa today, and the one most in need of rethinking: how to secure an equitable public order. It is also notable how few of these works have been produced by African writers living in Africa, who surely apprehend the conditions of their continent most directly. The reasons for the latter are connected to the poor condition of many African universities as a result of financial difficulties and the growing dominance of international journals by non-African scholars or by Africans who, based in North America and Europe especially, may become engaged in Euro-American debates, particularly on a range of theoretical issues that do not arise directly out of Africa's experience. In some countries, of which South Africa is the most striking example, young intellectuals and professionals seem uninterested in history to judge from the lack of student enrolment in history degree courses, perhaps regarding it as a dead weight on the present that is best discarded. In these circumstances, one of the most useful signs of what the African condition is, or is perceived to be by those people living in the continent who are best able to make their opinions known, is the flourishing but largely ignored African pamphlet and media literature that will be briefly described in the second half of the present essay.

It seems, then, that the vogue for applying to the history of Africa postmodern theories drawn from philosophy and cultural and literary studies, while it has resulted in many notable achievements, has not always helped in the identification of themes of Africa's contemporary history that are rooted in some of the key preoccupations of Africans today. It is tempting to conclude that, while the idea that Africa is making progress according to the tenets of mid-twentieth century modernization theory has become more or less formally extinct in academic circles, the implication remains that it *should* be modernizing, by reference to many of the same criteria as were current forty years ago. In the last resort, few academic writers are able to escape the supposition that a stable, prosperous and non-violent existence is the aim of all right-thinking people and that this is best ensured by public policy in a well-ordered state, one organized according to the western models that have become just about universally accepted, at least in theory. If this is indeed so, it is a reflection of a belief that goes much deeper than current academic fashion. Europeans and North Americans for the last two centuries or so have generally held that all the world's societies, including those of Africa, ought to be heading in a roughly similar direction and that the most thoughtful and most powerful westerners know what this direction is. Over time, others of the world's elites have come to share this view. This direction for all humanity was known to the nineteenth-century colonizers of Africa as 'civilization', and its lineal descendant today is called 'globalization'. Whatever the name, it is taken to be a progressive movement along a more- or-less identifiable path.[35] Any human society that fails to follow this route, in the view of many leading thinkers and technocrats in the west and elsewhere, is considered to have deviated from the one and only road leading towards human improvement. (The preceding sentence, I would emphasize, is not my own view but my attempt to summarize a common assumption.) The economist Deepak Lal has written that this and many 'so-called universal values' associated with it are 'actually part of a culture-specific, proselytizing ethic of what remains at heart western Christendom', with a pedigree centuries long.[36] This is a point of view in urgent need of further investigation.

For all the radical pretensions of the postmodern movement in the humanities and the social sciences, many of the studies influenced by postmodernism have not been 'post' enough in the sense that they have not engaged in a sufficiently pointed critique of a range of fundamental assumptions made by earlier social scientists about how human societies are ordered. Postmodern thinkers have tended to concentrate on the important fields of discourse and representation, but have devoted far less attention to the crucial and eminently material matters of exchange and coercion in the relations between dominators and dominated. As two critics have written of works of 'post-foundational' historiography with particular regard to India, 'they have as much to do with arguments about the politics of representation in Western intellectual and academic circles, as they do with imposing that manner of representation on the third world's history'.[37]

Emerging themes

According to Geoffrey Barraclough, '*contemporary history begins when the problems which are actual in the world today first take visible shape*'.[38] This definition suggests that the first task of a historian of the contemporary world is to consider which aspects of the present are of prime importance and, most especially, which features distinguish the current period of time from previous ages. Determining what these distinguishing features are is a crucial task since the resulting identification will have a bearing on the choice of historical material to be gathered into sequential order.

A wide variety of opinions is possible about which problems are actual in Africa today. In regard to politics at least, many observers would no doubt agree on such matters as the high number of states unable to fulfil basic functions of security or welfare provision; the high level of international public debt; the number of wars; the extent of ethnic mobilization; the consequences of weak economic performance; the resilience and even revival of religion in public space; and the manner of Africa's insertion in international relations. A historian interested in social matters might identify as important or striking features of Africa today: family and gender; demography; the rise of AIDS and the re-emergence of other diseases; the workings of the informal economy; the growth of cities; patterns of migration. Other subjects could also be listed. It is interesting to note that many of these themes have important antecedents in colonial times or earlier[39] for it is becoming increasingly apparent that the travails of African states are closely related to the fact that the modern state-system was introduced into most parts of Africa only rather recently and that some significant vestiges of precolonial political organization may still be detected in the continent today. This suggests a need for historians of contemporary Africa to devote particular attention to the structures of political and social organization and power relationships as they appear today and to extend the starting-point of their data sequences back into pre-colonial times if necessary, without paying undue heed to the proclamations of formal independence that, while significant, did not always mark the radical break with the past that many observers once took for granted.

The list of research topics in the previous paragraph is no more than a few examples. It may strike some readers as containing a discouraging number of themes that risk representing Africa in an unfavourable light. Why not focus instead on the re-emergence of parliamentary democracy? The flowering of the free press? The changing condition of women? These are, of course, all possible subjects for research. But the point is less to compile a list of interesting research topics than to make the point that almost any given sequence of data can be arranged in a set that suggests degrees of either progress or regression and optimism or pessimism. It is largely a question of where the data start and the patterns into which they are arranged. It is precisely because of the dominance of historical models of state-building and economic and social development influenced by the social science theories dominant in the mid-twentieth century that contemporary histories of Africa, or parts of it, run such a risk of appearing as stories of failure and decay. Other ways of ordering and interpreting data, extending the data-set in some circumstances back to pre-colonial times, could represent Africa as emerging gradually from attempts to oblige populations to submit to structures of domination that were originally imported from Europe, thus portraying a post-colonial Africa groping to reconnect with deeper currents of its own history in which power is organized other than through bureaucratic corporations disposing of a monopoly of legitimate violence.[40] It is precisely the element of chronological depth, in support of an analysis of the origins and antecedents of the features of the world today, which distinguishes the writing of contemporary history from the study of current affairs or from media punditry.[41]

Sources

The ambition of the pioneering generation of academic historians of Africa was to reconstruct Africa's past in chronological sequences primarily (but not only) by locating archives from which verifiable and datable facts could be drawn. This would enable Africa's history to be described in the same way as has been done for the industrialized world since the nineteenth century. One French historian noted in 1962 that if African historians were creating for themselves a history in the conventional north Atlantic mode, by attempting to situate even Africa's most distant past in the chronological patterns held to govern the history of the world, then it was 'a sign that they aspire to play by the rules of the world, which were to a large extent written in the West'.[42] The compilation of a version of the past that will qualify as academic history is dependent on chronology, which in turn depends on the availability of precisely datable sources of the type that bureaucracies produce as a matter of course. This poses an immediate question with regard to contemporary history, for many official archives and private papers do not become available for twenty-five years or more after their redaction, and even then it may take more years before some sort of consensus emerges as to the value of particular archives.

But it is increasingly clear that it is not just a matter of time before Africa's contemporary history is revealed as archives become accessible to scholars. Bluntly stated, it is unlikely that historians seeking to write the history of Africa since independence will enjoy the same quality of documents as their colleagues studying the colonial period. This, it should be said at once, is an unscientific judgement, for there does not appear to have been any general survey carried out on the location or condition of African official archives compiled since the 1960s, the decade of independence.[43] There is certainly a distressing number of archives in the continent that have suffered massively from war damage—the state archives of Liberia for example[44]—or from environmental hazards such as rain, fungus and termites. The comprehensive looting of capital cities including Freetown, Monrovia, Mogadishu, Kinshasa and Brazzaville in recent years bodes ill for the survival of major archives. Anecdotal evidence suggests that in some places government documents generated since the 1960s have not been placed in official archives at all. On the positive side, there are also state archives in Africa that contain abundant material and were reasonably well-organized and well-maintained up to the 1990s at least. Sometimes even local archives contain recoverable material.[45] A useful archive does not just contain large numbers of interesting documents but is also classified, catalogued and generally maintained, all of which requires money that, for many types of state activity, has been in short supply since the onset of a financial crisis in so many African countries, sometimes twenty or more years ago.

In the absence of a systematic survey of African state archives, a tentative impression based on largely anecdotal evidence is that in many African countries official archives for the post-1970 period especially are likely to be increasingly poorly maintained and difficult to use, largely as a by-product of financial difficulties generally, and even when they have not been deliberately vandalized. This is also likely to be generally true for non-state archives. The production of archives by any corporation requires a style of management that places a high value on the maintenance of an institutional memory in documentary form, which may not always be the case in businesses or other institutions in Africa, including many churches, for example. Even some heads of state in Africa operate largely on a basis of orality, preferring spoken rather than written briefings from their aides. Without doubt there are private archives waiting to be identified and used by historians. Individuals can be persuaded to write down their own knowledge.[46] Fascinating material is likely to emanate from collections compiled by churches, international organizations and businesses, or simply from private or family papers, which will throw light on Africa in the 1980s or 1990s. The history of medieval and early modern Europe shows the use that can be made of such sources, the material for brilliant micro-studies of small communities or even of individuals.[47] A comparable African micro-history is that of the South African sharecropper Kas Maine, although this, unlike the European studies cited, was compiled largely through oral rather than documentary sources.[48] Brilliant studies of individual locations or of small groups of people in colonial times have been produced partly on the basis of oral research.[49] But the value of studies such as these is often proportionate to the research that has already been done on matters of wider reach, especially on government and on state politics, so that the biography of a Samkange family[50] or of a Kas Maine illuminates a wider society because quite a lot is already known about the general history of southern Africa in the twentieth century. One implication is that historians interested in mentalities, culture or sensibility in contemporary Africa, even if they are able to locate rich private archives, are likely to find that the value of these holdings is limited in the absence of material about the wider society.

There are many other collections of documents concerning contemporary Africa. There are for example archives produced by foreign organizations, such as diplomatic missions in Africa, the World Bank, humanitarian organizations and so on. Some of these may already be accessed, at least partially or occasionally, especially through the Internet, and in time they may be expected to open their archives more fully. Many collections of papers on development projects are not formally published but exist only in photocopies or as 'grey literature', almost impossible to locate systematically. International legal records can also be a useful source but are similarly difficult to locate. But if an Africanist historian depends heavily on an archive produced by foreigners, who sometimes frankly misunderstand and always give a particular interpretation to what they observe, and who generally have a professional interest in recording certain types of information only, how is one to avoid reflecting the resultant bias in a historical work? Historians of pre-colonial Africa face exactly this problem and have nevertheless produced many excellent works in which archives produced by European traders, missionaries and diplomats have been used to reconstruct events in African societies that produced few written records themselves.[51] Their work surely serves as a model for the historian of contemporary Africa, who, especially where good state archives are unavailable and foreign records therefore take on a larger importance, needs to pay more than usual attention to the cardinal rules of gathering historical evidence, considering who has produced a particular item of information, in what context and for what purpose.

There is, though, at least one major source of African-generated documentation that is available to historians of recent decades in Africa, providing some sort of corrective to the bias of external sources, but that exists only rarely for those researching the distant African past. This consists of accounts of events authored contemporaneously or near-contemporaneously by Africans. This category includes eye-witness accounts by journalists and others in book form, in newspapers and periodicals or on the internet, memoirs and autobiographies, as well as information broadcast via radio, film or video. In some parts of Africa—a continent generally considered a graveyard for academic publishing—there is clearly a market for short books falling within this category, produced by local publishers. To take only one example, West African interest in the 1990s war in Liberia in which regional peacekeeping forces were deployed has resulted in a whole series of firsthand accounts published in the sub-region and clearly intended for the general public—and they are continuing to appear.[52] Similar accounts have been published in the USA especially, where there is a large Liberian diaspora, apparently aimed at a West African public in the first instance.[53]

Such first-hand accounts, being published in world languages in book form, represent a type of source that many historians will find reassuringly familiar. Other forms of information currently being produced may be more difficult to use. In some parts of Africa, such as northern Nigeria and Madagascar, there is a thriving local market in pamphlets written in vernacular languages, often almost unobtainable outside the country of origin. Above all, there are African mass media. It is generally accepted that the most important medium of mass communication in Africa is the radio, which, these days, is transmitted by a wide range of broadcasters, both official and otherwise, and reaches more Africans than do printed media, television or the internet.[54] The most obvious problem for anyone seeking to use radio as a historical source is the transience of the broadcast word, but this can be rectified in part by the use of the printed summaries published by the BBC in Britain (the *Summary of World Broadcasts*) and in the USA by the Foreign Broadcast Information Service, a division of the Department of Commerce. These are important, and much under-used, sources for African history. The internet has a great number of sites where information on current events can be gleaned, although many of the discussion sites especially are of extremely uneven quality and are dominated by contributions from people living outside Africa. More reliable are official websites for governments and organizations that, although often bland, have the advantage of being authoritative. A major obstacle for the scholar is the impermanence of many websites, suggesting that references that are diligently noted may nevertheless have disappeared by the time a learned book or article is printed.[55] Film and video are somewhat less evanescent than the internet, since there are libraries that hold collections of material useful for historical research.[56]

If permanence makes for viable sources, then it is the printed media of magazines and newspapers that provide a more accessible and more comprehensive documentary record for historians. A practical problem consists in locating substantial collections of the massive range of African magazines and newspapers that now exists.[57] But this major source poses problems of interpretation that, in practice, are likely to be among the main challenges facing the historian. It is arguable that historians in general have shown themselves to be rather unskilled in their handling of the press as a source of political history, being rightly sceptical about whether it is legitimate to regard newspapers and magazines as reliable records and often therefore considering them largely as supplements to a staple diet of official archives. It is the case that even a prestigious newspaper highly conscious of its own reputation and obsessive in its attention to detail—the *New York Times,* say—is produced at great speed, which is never conducive to accuracy. If only for this reason, even a so-called 'journal of record', which aspires to produce an accurate periodical account of what has happened and that is of concern to its readers, is liable to make factual mistakes. Perhaps more important still, it is useful to reflect that newspapers and magazines are genres that have their own rules, both written and unwritten.[58] Not all newspapers aim to be journals of record, and even when they do, their styles and traditions vary from country to country. Once again, historians are well advised to follow their basic precepts concerning evidence, asking themselves who has produced a particular document and why. It is particularly useful to bear in mind the often very parochial way in which newspapers and magazines are produced, with small numbers of journalists, editors and politicians writing to a considerable extent for each other, even when their publications have a wide circulation.[59]

In general, few African newspapers can be regarded as 'journals of record'. In the early years of independence, many African states had only one main newspaper, owned by the government or ruling party and committed to development or nation-building, the great mobilizing slogans of the day.[60] At worst, such papers were tawdry propaganda sheets, which does not mean that information cannot be gleaned from them but only that they cannot be regarded as attempting to give a full and disinterested account of significant events concerning a society. Even at best, official newspapers of this type must be regarded as highly partial sources. They are nevertheless invaluable historical sources, since even such things as photographs and advertisements may convey an enormous amount of information of use to historians.[61] Between the early 1960s and the late 1970s, the number of daily papers published in Africa actually fell as the many one-party states strove to establish a monopoly of public information and as commercial operators were driven out by financial problems.[62] Even now, few Africans read newspapers at all: in 1998, only 11 newspapers were produced for every thousand people living in Africa, compared with 96 per thousand for the world as a whole.[63] By comparison, over the period 1994–7, on average 172 per thousand people in sub-Saharan Africa had a radio, and 44 per thousand had a television.[64] This says something about the place of the press in society and therefore about its value as a source. To a certain extent, though, the influence of a newspaper in the society where it is produced is not the key point. It is rather the relative durability of newspapers and magazines that gives them particular value as a source.

It is important for a historian who is contemplating using African newspapers as documents of record to consider the changing orientation of the press. (For that matter, the same consideration applies to non-African newspapers too, according to the principle that all historical sources need to be placed in the context of the time, place and circumstances of their production.) The African press has enormous variety. By and large, African newspapers throughout the 1960s and 1970s, including even the few that were independently owned, had to be mindful of the formidable monopolies of power that many ruling parties had acquired, and therefore to avoid stories or subjects that could be considered hostile to the national government. Important events could go completely unreported. Hence, from a historian's point of view, the press produced under single-party governments cannot be considered an accurate reflection of the political landscape of an African country, but only as a partial record of official thinking, or perhaps that of a faction or tendency within a government. This is valuable enough. It does, however, mean that for a history of unofficial thinking or of events not officially recognized, one needs to look elsewhere. For decades, there have been newspapers and magazines published by Africans or for African readers abroad, such as *Jeune Afrique* in Paris or *West Africa* in London. These too have their particular points of view, often reflecting opinions among the diaspora rather than among people living in Africa. The situation in most African countries changed rather quickly from the late 1980s with the demise of one-party states and a new freedom of expression that witnessed a massive increase in the number of newspapers and magazines.[65]

It has become apparent since the move away from one-party states in the early 1990s that the new, freer, African media do not generally reflect the classic values of the liberal press as these are often considered in the west. But then, even in the west the view of the press as watchdog or teller-of-truth- to-power is based on a highly idealised view of its real nature. In many African countries various forms of government censorship remain, sometimes in the form of press laws or requirements for official registration, but also through the use of libel or similar laws to restrain journalists or simply by way of unofficial initimidation, bribery and manipulation. In the new, fragmented, political landscape, many political bosses have their own newspaper, and there are independent newspapers that can, for a price, be persuaded to carry articles favourable to a paymaster under the guise of news stories or features. According to African journalists themselves, various forms of bribery and of literary terrorism are common practice, variously labelled 'vendetta journalism', 'yellow journalism' and such like.[66] There is even a technique known as 'blackmail journalism', whereby unscrupulous journalists simply threaten to write a hostile story about someone and to desist only if bribed.[67] In short, the intellectual space opened up by freedom of the press in the early 1990s was quickly taken over by the very same entrepreneurs and their associates as constitute the political elites themselves, using often ruthless methods to pursue their interests. This was actually a key part of the process by which existing elites in many parts of the continent were able to neutralize the threat posed to their status by the turn to multiparty systems and to convert the instruments of democracy and freedom into means for the defence of privilege. This makes the African press an outstanding source for analysing the nuances of politics but a generally poor source for anyone seeking an impartial view of events.

Even those African newspapers that do seriously aspire to be a journal of record are severely hampered by the nature of the societies in which they exist, with prevailing low salaries (encouraging journalists, therefore, to seek extra sources of income), poor communications, a 'plurality of publics'[68] rather than a single civic life, few local newspapers to act as feeders of information to the national press, and so on. It is hard to think of a single newspaper anywhere in Africa that could be regarded as a guide to 'All the news that's fit to print', as the *New York Times* claims to be. But none of this disqualifies the press as a prime source for the historian of Africa today. The important thing is to inquire into the nature of a publication, or even of a particular article, before using it as a source. Some African newspapers and magazines have a reputation for being reasonably impartial, although this doesn't necessarily make them accurate, while others might be known as being close to a particular person or party or to be liable to throw their columns open to all comers in return for payment. Particular stories can be evaluated partly by reference to the identity of their author, their position in a newspaper (for example, as features, news stories, readers' letters, question-and-answer interviews, etc.), the sources they cite in support of particular information, and the verifiability of such information by other sources. Handled with prudence, the press can be a prime source not only for political history but for all manner of social history as well.

One of the most intriguing and potentially informative features of the African press is the frequent appearance of articles that purport to be news stories but that, to a reader familiar with European or North American canons of journalism or information more generally, seem no more than rumour, gossip or even fairy-stories. Some of these, such as the many stories about witchcraft, miracles and other quasi-mystical phenomena, may appear deeply eccentric to a reader who believes that all news should consist of empirically verified fact.[69] In some of the most frivolous media, where it is not unknown for journalists to make up stories without moving from their desks, such stories may indeed be discounted, but when they appear in newspapers that are otherwise serious in tone and apparent intent, they provide a means of access to a key source for the history of Africa. Such articles may usefully be considered primarily as written forms of a style of communication that is pervasive in Africa, namely the unofficial, spoken news succinctly described by the French-African expression *radio trottoir* (literally, 'pavement radio') and often rendered in English by the derogatory and inadequate translation 'rumour'. The classic places where *radio trottoir* gathers and disseminates news are markets, places of refreshment, taxis and barbers' shops, but ministerial waiting-rooms and top people's places of leisure produce their own, upper-class, versions as well.[70] It is instructive to learn that in *ancien régime* Paris there were also known places where public rumours were aired, including on political matters, and that the news circulating there was sometimes written down in literary salons in violation of the convention that high politics were 'the King's secret'.[71] In Africa, as in eighteenth-century France, the fact that *radio trottoir* is popular does not therefore mean that it is exclusive to the masses.

At the risk of simplification, it could be said that newspapers and media generally in the industrialized world depend on the convention that verbal information not emanating from an appropriate public authority has no status as 'hard' news: it is considered mere rumour, and indeed an acute study of rumour in western societies points out that it is often analysed in terms of some collective delusion or pathology, using a psychiatric or medical metaphor that disqualifies it as a representation of reality.[72] In Africa, on the other hand, information conveyed unofficially by word of mouth is often taken by the general population, and even by elites, to be more accurate than information conveyed by the government or other formal institutions, which in any case is not always readily accessible due to the poor distribution of newspapers. While there is an abundant literature that laments this state of affairs as a sign of under-development, it could at the same time be seen as evidence of an element of democracy or at least of personal autonomy in Africa that is absent in industrialized countries. Strange as it may sound, Africans, although generally having access to a comparatively limited range of sources of information, are more at liberty than Europeans and North Americans to decide for themselves what is real or true, and less obliged to accept the information offered to them by what one of the founders of modern public relations, as early as 1928, called 'an invisible government which is the true ruling power', engaged in 'the conscious and intelligent manipulation of the organized habits and opinions of the masses [that] is an important element in democratic society'.[73] Control of information is undoubtedly one of the keys to political power in any circumstances, and for this reason African leaders often express their irritation with the popular tendency to prefer the anonymous offerings of *radio trottoir* to those of the state media, asserting, and perhaps even believing, that development is possible only if people accept that proper information is that retailed by a qualified elite of media managers, politicians and technocrats. Cameroon's President Paul Biya expressed this exactly in 1984 in the infamous statement that 'rumour is not the truth. Truth comes from above; rumour comes from below.'[74]

Compared with the inhabitants of industrialized continents, Africans have a tendency, alarming from the point of view of information managers, to believe things they have heard from their friends and neighbours even when official media assure them that these are not true. They can also put their own twist on what they read or hear through the mass media, such as the young people in Bamako who claim 'to have heard on the radio that condoms ... are actually infected with the AIDS virus and are being donated by agencies as part of a conspiracy by the West to control the Malian population'.[75] It is small wonder that governments in all parts of Africa pay enormous attention to *radio trottoir* as a vital barometer of public feeling and a key component of power.[76]

Although much of what is conveyed by *radio trottoir*, being spoken, escapes the historian's grasp, some of its output is written down in tracts or newspapers or in some other form.[77] African newspapers, in fact, can usefully be thought of as written forms of *radio trottoir* in some ways, to the point that these oral and written forms of communication need to be considered in the same bracket. Assembling information from transcripts of *radio trottoir,* it is striking that it shows consistent patterns in each single country and even across wide regions, suggesting the interest historians have in developing a suitable method for studying some of its favourite themes not just as aberrations or evidence of a 'moral panic', but as a royal way to mainstream ideas about society and politics.[78] To take just one example, in Ghana, as in many parts of West Africa, *radio trottoir* frequently reports stories, sometimes also taken up in newspapers, concerning alleged human sacrifices or ritual killings carried out by people in search of wealth or political power. Tracing this backwards in time, we find it recorded that in 1965 rumours were circulating in Ghana that President Nkrumah had caused people to be sacrificed to a deity described as the Goddess of the Volta River, in order to ensure the success of the Volta River construction project.[79] In the colonial Gold Coast too there were stories of people being killed for ritual purposes,[80] and this can probably be connected to various religious practices in the Ashanti kingdom, and indeed in some other parts of pre-colonial West Africa.[81] Nor is it to be assumed that such rumours of killing carried out by people who believe that certain forms of blood sacrifice can serve to enhance their wealth and power always represent some sort of popular illusion or fantasy, since in some cases such stories may be based on actual practice.[82] A similar set of historical antecedents for favourite themes of radio trottoir could probably be compiled for every single African country, and indeed something similar could be done for every country in the world. For the west has its favourite rumours too: the famous alligators-in-New-York-sewers urban legend was first recorded in 1843.[83]

In summary, then, any historian who wishes to study the political or social history of Africa in recent decades needs to consider radio trottoir as a prime source. How to interpret it is the problem. Although there is rather little literature suggesting how radio trottoir may be handled as a historical source, a very considerable amount of academic attention has focused on closely related subjects such as the politics of memory and oral literature, often written by anthropologists or specialists in oral performance.[84] Historians of Africa have also produced an important corpus on oral history. Here, some of the classic works wrestle with how to extract datable historical facts from oral performance. With this ultimate aim in mind, the earlier literature on this subject tried to identify the structure of oral traditions and to understand their inner logic. This, it was hoped, would clear the way for using them as sources of factual information.[85] This was done in the spirit of those historians, Bible scholars and classical philologists who had painstakingly assembled and compared different versions of ancient and medieval texts with a view to identifying copyists' mistakes and deducing the original version of a document. This approach, however, has shown its limitations. To regard a present-day oral performance of stories about the past as though it were a degenerate version of an ancestral original is not without value but it risks overlooking the value of that performance as evidence of how people see things now, and of the nature of historical change as people perceive it. Even in pre-colonial times there probably never did exist in most societies any form of oral performance so pure and canonical that it can best be analysed in this manner.[86]

All of this is useful to bear in mind when listening to, or reading transcripts of, *radio trottoir*. The stories it retails may or may not have a basis in fact, but in the first instance they need to be considered as products of the imagination which are nevertheless believable to those who tell the stories, which have meaning, and which may therefore prompt people into action, as for example with southern and east African stories of vampires,[87] or witch-stories from all over the continent. For the academic historian in search of facts, a secondary operation may consist in regarding these stories as containing the germ of a verifiable fact. But even when a story concerns an action that is in itself perfectly feasible, such as a rumour of a coup attempt, it seems important for a historian to suppose that this should be investigated not only (or not primarily) as a clue to discernible facts but above all as the product of a social attempt to organize reality, which deserves to be analysed as such. A search through the output of *radio trottoir* in an effort to discover allegations that might be confirmed by other, more reliable, sources has value, but it may often not be the most useful way of handling this particular medium. Political events are almost invariably more complex than simple truth or simple lies.[88] African politicians, knowing this and being aware of the nature of *radio trottoir*, make prodigious efforts to convey an image of power through this medium.[89] For as Thomas Hobbes observed, 'Reputation of power, is Power; because it draweth with it the adherence of those that need protection'.[90]

Radio trottoir—unofficial, anonymous—is usually conveyed in a group setting, where information is subject to a degree of control through assent. Also of value to historians are formal interviews with an individual witness to some matter under investigation. These are usually held in private. Interviews can be a source of major importance, with the usual precaution that individual speakers, like other sources, exist in a particular situation and have motives, which makes it imperative to gather material for comparison where possible. It is interesting to note that the biography of Kas Maine, mentioned above, is based on extensive interviews with the subject and members of his family, making maximum use of the often astonishing recall that people educated in cultures of the spoken word are capable of exercising. It is worth recalling that one of the greatest of all historians, Thucydides, worked largely in this way, regarding history as that which he could elicit through skillful questioning from people who could still remember the events he wanted to describe.[91] His example is important for historians of contemporary Africa, while it also serves as a riposte to anyone who maintains that good history can not be written about events that are still recent.

The stories or narratives of people recalling the past are not the same as fiction, although the two certainly have in common their use of imagination.[92] The best historians and the best novelists use an *a priori* imagination, that is, one which is not arbitrary but connects known facts (in the case of historians) or established points of their story (in the case of novelists).[93] It is striking just how accurately African novelists have sometimes taken the temperature of their societies, well before social scientists or other observers based in academic disciplines have reached the same point of understanding. Chinua Achebe, J.M. Coetzee, Ahmadou Kourouma and Ngugi wa Thiong'o are all examples of authors who have written novels that can be used by historians as guides to the political climate and even the political thought of a society at a given moment.[94]

Although historians of post-independence Africa will rarely have the quantity or precision of official documents at their disposal that historians of many other parts of the world can routinely expect, Africanists would be wrong to regard themselves as therefore being the poor relations of historians of industrialized continents. Techniques for analysing perception and meaningful belief in society at large are increasingly needed also in industrial societies, each with its share of unofficial beliefs 'embody[ing] a moral-political message'[95] at odds with the officially proclaimed truth. Above all, as an American media commentator has described the situation in his own country, 'Journalism is becoming less a product than a process, witnessed in real time and public—first comes the allegation, then the anchor vamps and speculates until the counter-allegation is issued. The demand to keep up with this leaves journalists with less time to sort out what is true and what is spin.'[96] A world of shadows where assertion and counter-assertion are plausible, where facts cannot be immediately discerned and the truth of a situation is not clear, extends to the west and not just Africa. The crucial difference is that in the west, where information has become a highly organized commodity, this contest is dominated by an elite group of professional manipulators with formidable technology at their disposal, leaving the public at a very considerable disadvantage, whereas in Africa most people participate on rather more even terms in the struggle to determine what is fact and what it means.

Standards of time

This essay has argued that a new generation of contemporary histories is necessary if Africa is not to be thought of as existing in a temporal black hole. One of the characteristics of western thinking about Africa, according to one leading commentator at least, remains its tendency to think of Africa in terms of timelessness.[97] This may have been compounded by academics, even those with impeccably liberal motives, in the many works they have published on Africa since the 1970s that have been preoccupied by a discussion of what Africa should be or should have become. It is useful for historians to recall that their vocation is to write about what actually happened.

The first step in writing contemporary histories is to identify the character of Africa in its present age, which shows every sign of focusing attention on the 1970s rather than the era of independence as the time of the most significant change. This may then serve as a thread for constructing data-sets that could go back even into precolonial times. If this were pursued, it might in time lead to an identification of historical periods relevant to Africa's past that are more satisfactory than the current ones, setting colonialism into a broader context of the continent's passage through time. At a time when countries are more closely connected than ever (including Africa, despite its reputation for being internationally marginalized[98]), any rethinking of the fundamental changes that can define various epochs of Africa's past needs also to take into account the rhythms of the wider world.

This leads to a crucial point, for not all societies view the past in the same way, and not all live at the same tempo. It is discomforting to wonder whether many parts of Africa have not, since the 1970s, come to adopt a rhythm out of step with the industrialized world, and that one symptom of this may be a decline in the knowledge of history (in its narrowest, academic sense) in African societies. In many parts of the continent there is a decrease in the use of formal archives by corporations, accompanied by a relative absence of the formal education whereby children learn history through a formal syllabus. Little heed is paid to academic history in many parts of Africa, even by people with a high standard of formal education. At the same time, academic writing of Africa's history is dominated by western writers and propagated in channels which barely touch Africa.

None of these assertions about the decline of academic history in Africa should be taken to imply that memories of times past have diminished in their power and importance. But memories of the past, whether or not based on fact, are not the same as history in its narrowest, academic sense. History can only make its weight felt on living generations through mechanisms or repositories of information that can become operational. Hence, it is important to know how Africans themselves perceive and recall their own past. They—like other people—do not act only or at all times in the light of rational choices about the likely outcomes of their behaviour. They also act— again, like everyone else—on the basis of repertoires transmitted from the past in the form of institutions, rituals, language or structure. These repertoires of action are comparable to the grammatical rules that people use to govern the way in which they speak. In countries like Angola that are riven by conflict, different groups of people have different visions of the country's history to the point that they are hardly talking about the same place.[99] A personal impression, which I have never systematically researched but which is based on interviews in many African countries and which seems to receive support from more rigorous research,[100] is that many Africans today view their past much as the ancient Greeks did,[101] as divided into a recent time that may be rigorously and critically examined through discussion with people who remember it, preceded by a period of myth or social memory whose accuracy is untestable. It is possible that the majority of Africans have always thought of the past in this way, but certainly until recently they were governed by elites who had themselves had long exposure to formal, written histories, and by institutions with a bureaucratic memory, relayed by archives. These factors weigh less than they did twenty-five years ago in the substantial number of countries where institutions have eroded or are unable to govern the whole country and where those in power have little interest in bureaucratic rule of this type. If it is indeed the case that many Africans today have less reason and less opportunity than they had a generation ago to be aware of the existence of a 'scientific' history, in the sense of one written in the mode that has become conventional in industrialized countries, then this may contribute to what one of Africa's most thoughtful writers has described as a tendency to identify the past as a quasi-mystical element whose power can be seized by force. 'History', Achille Mbembe notes, 'in the last resort is considered to be part of a vast economy of witchcraft'.[102]

Africanist historians, who created a usable African history not so long ago, need to think hard about the nature of Africa today, and to think anew about the fundamental sub-categories into which its history may be divided now that the colonial period is gone. In doing this they need also to be aware that the object of their study, namely things that people have done in or concerning Africa, appears to be perceived increasingly in a radically different mode by the bulk of Africans themselves, one better understood as religious than as historical thought. This has considerable implications for what the African past and the African present are, and how they can be described. And indeed, it may contain valuable lessons for historians of the world as a whole.[103] The notion that Africa today is post-colonial is hardly satisfactory, not least because of the continuing reference to the colonial past in this epithet. Also unsatisfactory is the suggestion from the South African government that now is the age of the African Renaissance. Nor is the notion that Africa is in the age of globalization of great use.[104] Some other labels that academics have sought to apply to present-day Africa are even less convincing, such as the suggestion by two prominent anthropologists that Africa is entering what they term 'the Age of Futilitarianism', said to be the period 'wherein postmodern pessimism runs up against the promises of late capitalism'.[105] The problem with this formulation, other than its lack of elegance, is precisely its lack of historical precision, whereas Africa needs more than ever a contemporary history that is sensitive to the depth of time.

It is no longer an age of development or national liberation in Africa. The discussion is open as to what sort of an age it really is, in the sense of determining the characteristics that distinguish Africa now from Africa in the last identifiable period. Perhaps one should think less in terms of African history and more in terms of a world history in which Africa has its part. 'All the labels we put on periods are *ex post facto*; the character of an epoch can only be perceived by those looking back on it from outside. That is why we must be content for the present with a provisional name for the "postmodern" period in which we live', Barraclough wrote in 1964, in a strikingly early use of the term 'post-modern'.[106] It is already possible to see a dividing line in Africa's history in the 1970s, and even if the character of the current age is unclear, at least that of the one preceding it should by now have become easier to grasp. But it would be frivolous merely to think of names that, like advertising slogans, are designed primarily to stick in the mind. The main task at hand is to inquire into the nature of recent times diligently and, above all, without the burden of past expectations. It may then turn out that, for all the terrible events and formidable problems of recent years, it is not an age of nihilism.

2

AFRICA'S WARS OF LIBERATION

SOME HISTORIOGRAPHICAL REFLECTIONS

This essay offers some preliminary reflections on the ways in which scholars have considered African wars of liberation, that is to say organised, armed campaigns which have been widely perceived to have as their aim the establishment of some sort of collective assertion of self-choice in government, most often interpreted in terms of the rejection of authority wielded by foreigners, especially European colonialists. As with most subjects in contemporary history, it is not only professional scholars who are responsible for the extant literature on this subject, but also politicians, journalists and others who have influenced one another and have contributed to our overall understanding of liberation wars.

This is a topic on which Rob Buijtenhuijs has made a significant contribution, initially through his work on the 1950s Mau Mau insurgency in Kenya, and later through two books on the Frolinat-led insurgency in Chad.[1] His most recently published works have concentrated on the political processes connected with the introduction of a multi-party system and formal elements of democracy in Chad.[2] During the course of this work he has come to question the very notion that armed insurgents are primarily to be understood as people in rational pursuit of specific ideals, emphasising rather the elements of contingency and confusion which are prominent in times of armed insurrection or civil war.[3] This gradual shift in his thinking suggests that while Buijtenhuijs has maintained the interest in political emancipation which has been such a central feature of his work, he has over the course of time become somewhat disillusioned by the politics of armed struggle. If this is so, then he is certainly not alone in this regard, as we shall see.

For present purposes, a useful way of approaching this subject—which may at first sight appear tangential, but which is of great relevance—is to consider some of the general assumptions which have been commonly applied to African history and which have served as a framework for a great deal of writing about Africa, including in fields which are not concerned with historical reconstruction in the first instance but with other areas of academic inquiry, such as in sociology and political science. This inquiry constitutes the first part of the present paper. The second and third sections consider more directly some of the ways in which scholars have considered the historical significance and even the moral worth of those organised campaigns of violence which, ostensibly at least, have had as their goal the liberation of some part of the population. This discussion comes to the conclusion that there has for some years been a growing perception among writers on the subject that many self-proclaimed liberators in Africa have achieved rather little of what they promised. This scepticism is combined with an alarm in many quarters at the scale of violence in Africa in recent years, and also with an increasing difficulty experienced by many commentators in reaching a satisfactory understanding of the nature or purpose of some recent episodes of large-scale violence. Together, these doubts or uncertainties have resulted in a number of new approaches to writing on wars in Africa. The fourth and last section of the paper suggests some new trends in historical interpretation which have been applied to various parts of the world and which might, it would seem, be usefully applied to Africa as well.

Periods of African history

Although Africa is an ancient continent, in terms both of geology and human occupation, the writing of its history is a strikingly recent enterprise. In fact the systematic study of African history by professional historians—in short, academic history-writing—began only in the mid-twentieth century. To be sure, long before then both Africans and non-Africans had written chronicles, memoirs and travel guides or other texts containing some historical material, and it could be argued that recognisable histories of parts of Africa were being published already in the seventeenth century.[4] The nineteenth century in particular saw some notable attempts both by Africans and by others to write histories of various parts of the continent on conventional chronological lines, such as William Ellis's *History of Madagascar* (1833) or Samuel Johnson's *History of the Yorubas* (1897).[5] Nevertheless, it remains true to say that the production by Africans of serviceable narratives of times past was done almost entirely by word of mouth until well into the twentieth century. Before that time there were rather few Africans who could read and write, and fewer still accomplished scholars with the leisure necessary for historical research. As for foreigners, few had the right combination of time, materials, and inclination to undertake a rigorous examination of the African past, although the early colonial period saw plenty of publications by European scholars and administrators of ethnographic material containing some historical data.

Only in 1984 was the first university post in African history created, at the School of Oriental and African Studies in London, and this event is generally considered to be the first clear evidence that African history was achieving at least a degree of recognition as a legitimate subject among professional scholars, although sometimes in the face of considerable reticence.[6] It was exciting to be one of the generation pioneering the academic study of African history; such, at least, is the impression gained from reading the memoirs of those European historians who were influential in the period and who could be regarded as having created space for African history in professional academic circles.[7] (What African scholars or other Africans thought of this great historiographical venture is less easy to determine since they have been less forthcoming in producing their autobiographies.) Collectively, a relatively small band of professional historians operating from universities in the third quarter of the twentieth century, African and non-African alike, was able to create the outlines of an academically respectable view of the past of what Victorians used to call the Dark

Continent. A great deal of the work of the generation of academic pioneers continues to govern the way in which Africa's history is conceived among scholars of all disciplines and to find reflection in a wider body of opinion.

Perhaps the most basic of all the conventions established by the first wave of professional Africanist historians is the notion that African history may be divided into the precolonial, colonial and postcolonial or independent periods. At bottom, this is no more than an assertion that the establishment of colonial rule marked some sort of major feature in the course of African history, an observation so difficult to refute that even today, forty years after the independence of many African countries, most observers would almost certainly still agree with it. But the fact that it remains helpful to this day to suppose that it is possible to make some sort of meaningful distinction between colonial and precolonial periods of African history should not lead us to regard an intellectual convention as though it were itself a phenomenon of the same type as a specific historical fact. The unearthing of historical data and their attribution to periods of time which are deemed to have some sort of retrospective unity or coherence—the essential activity of academic historians—always tends to apply a layer of ideological interpretation to the actions of historical figures who may not have been aware that they were living in such periods and who, even if they were conscious of it, may have acted as they did in pursuit of objectives quite foreign to the preoccupations of later writers. Just as King Richard III was not aware that he was closing the period of English medieval history when he lay dying at the battle of Bosworth in 1485, so, to take an African example, the great Malinke warlord Samory Touré was not aware that he was creating a reputation as a proto-nationalist freedom fighter when he raided for slaves and forcibly converted tens of thousands of people to Islam through a wide swathe of central West Africa in the 1880s.[8] The imposition of any sort of intellectual order on a mass of historical data always involves some sort of theoretical or ideological assumptions ... if, that is, we are to accept the existence of such things as clear historical facts at all, which some historians are loath to do on philosophical grounds.[9]

In short, we should not forget that the fundamental chronological categories which historians create or identify and subsequently use are in fact later impositions on masses of historical facts. They acquire their significance only with the benefit of hindsight. In practice, however, these classifications tend to gain the status of established truth as they are used and re-used by authors and teachers and their readers or students. To take an obvious example, the widely-used European convention that there exist ancient, medieval and modern periods of history clearly represents some sort of supposition that each of these three periods of time had (or has) some definable qualitative difference, some property peculiar to its own time, which makes it possible and meaningful to distinguish one period from another. To inquire what these properties may be is to plunge into an intellectual current which goes back some two hundred years, characterised by a view that the world has progressed over the centuries towards a higher plane, in the fields of human social and economic organisation as well as in the evolution of species. This has become such a fundamental tenet of belief among most people in the industrialised countries of Europe and North America that it is sometimes assumed to be almost a law of nature.

It is important to note, however, that not all people and not all societies hold a general belief in the progress of humankind. On the contrary, some cultures have tried to keep their world as nearly static as possible,[10] and others have believed that humankind has in fact degenerated through the centuries or that history is cyclical. The idea held by most Europeans and North Americans today that there has been progress from antiquity through the middle ages to the modern period has been an essential underpinning to virtually all categories of Western thought, perhaps since the Enlightenment, and most certainly since the mid-nineteenth century.[11] So firm is this chronological bedrock, and the idea of linear progress contained in it, that it is hardly possible to think in terms of ancient, medieval and modern periods, of history without simultaneously evoking the idea that humankind (or at least Europeans, for whom and in respect of whom this chronology was originally constructed) has progressed over the years in some sense. If more people today than a hundred years ago might question the notion that Europe has seen a moral improvement over time, the vast majority of Europeans would no doubt still subscribe to the notion that an increase in wealth, life expectancy and technology capacity represents progress of some sort.

When the academic pioneers of African history formalised the division of African history into precolonial, colonial, and independent or postcolonial categories, they were endowing their subject-matter with many of the implications of such a linear, chronological categorisation of their material. This is not to imply that these historians were necessarily naive or blinkered for, as one French historian wrote at the time, any history based on chronology in the European tradition inevitably carried certain implications for Africa's insertion in the world. The creation of such a history, Henri Brunschwig noted 'offer[s] to all peoples a rational and critical construction ... If Africans wish to create a history today, it is a sign that they wish to enter into a global system of interactions, the rules of which have to a large extent been written in the West.'[12] It is more than coincidental then, that the creation of a new history of Africa by an elite of professional historians in the 1950s and 1960s was taking place at the very moment that sovereign states were being created in Africa as full members of the recognised family of nations: the historiographical and political elements were connected. A continent which had previously been regarded by Europeans as having no history worth knowing was now claiming its full place in the literate, intellectual, historical imagination of the world. It was not only African leaders and intellectuals or foreign Afrophiles who were keen to see more extensive research and publication on African societies and their history but also university funding committees, research institutes and others in the world's richest countries.

As perhaps the most popular of Africanist historians put it, in a book full of optimism published in 1959, Africa's history was beginning anew with the proclamations of independence.[13] But not all Africanist scholars, by any means, were enthusiasts for the victory of nationalism in Africa, since there were some who regarded the colonial achievements with considerable respect.[14] Many of the new foreign specialists in African studies in European universities were former colonial administrators themselves, who could hardly be expected to renounce half their life's work, like the historian Hubert Deschamps in Paris, or they came from colonial families like his London counterpart, Roland Oliver.[15] Nor were all Africanist historians primarily concerned with the study of what was becoming known as 'the colonial period', and in fact one of the most important achievements of the first generation of professional academic historians of Africa was to produce studies of the distant African past, of a time long before the creation of European colonial administrations.[16] Nevertheless, even a specialist in ancient history like Cheikh Anta Diop, famous for his theories on the African heritage from ancient Egypt,[17] was operating within the conventions governing the modern Western division of historical knowledge into chronological series, subscribing to a common set of rules concerning the nature of historical reality and of time. Once again, these are not universal norms, since other societies have used other ways of conceiving of what their ancestors did. (We may note in passing that the exploration of how oral histories were constructed in Africa was in fact another of the notable achievements of the early academic historians of Africa.[18])

Thus, European, American or (increasingly from the 1950s) African historians; specialists in ancient history or writers on present times; historians, political scientists or other scholars: all of these, using basic Western scientific concepts concerning time and change, tended to subscribe to certain common assumptions about the African past. Prominent among these was that the colonial period had a deep historical meaning in the sense of forming some sort of dividing line in Africa's historical development. Exactly what the historical significance of colonialism might be was a matter for debate, but all commentators were convinced that it marked a watershed of some sort. The concepts of Africa's precolonial, colonial and postcolonial history were established.

The liberation of Africa

History, while making a crucial intellectual contribution, was probably not the most significant academic discipline which interested itself in emerging new fields of study in Africa from the mid-twentieth century onwards, as Africa became the site of over fifty new sovereign states. Nor were historians by any means the only academic observers who developed an interest in, and often a personal sympathy with, the emerging African nationalist movements which, from the mid-1950s onwards, were acquiring control of these sovereign states in the act of independence or decolonisation. Political scientists, naturally enough, were centrally concerned to investigate the nature of these new phenomena, and so too were sociologists and many others, while anthropology remained the discipline most specialised in the analysis of African societies.

Some of the foreign writers most full of enthusiasm for the new political order in Africa employed their talents, in a spirit of deliberate political engagement, to create a scholarship which they intended to be supportive of African nationalism. Basil Davidson, for example, probably did more than any other individual to popularise in the English-speaking world a heroic view of the African past strongly coloured by his nationalist sympathies.[19] As for Africans themselves, some outstanding intellectuals actually became leading politicians, such as the anthropologists Jomo Kenyatta and K.B. Busia or the poets Léopold Sédar Senghor and Agostinho Neto.

If we can understand why many intellectuals, African and non-African, were inclined to see nationalism as a form of progress, it is even more easy to see why the governors of newly created African states might have been interested in the creation of academic historical accounts which could serve as charters of sovereignty and support their claim to respectability in Western intellectual circles. Nor is it hard to understand why, given their use of nationalism as mobilising force, they often wished to emphasise their anti-colonial credentials. More difficult to trace is the influence of the accounts of African nationalism which began to circulate in academic books and journals on the various popular narratives which circulated among African populations who, as in the past, continued to form their historical views largely on the basis of oral tradition. The dialectic between official and popular historical narratives is certainly a field worthy of further study. What influence nationalist historiography had on the mass of Africans remains open to question.

The development of a new academic vision of African nationalism, sensitive to the claims of African nationalists themselves, called into question some views which were then current in European seats of learning. At bottom, the point being contested between enthusiasts for the new vision of African history and others who were less persuaded of its validity was the real meaning of colonialism. Until the 1960s it was widely accepted among European historians that the imposition of colonial rule marked some sort of progress for Africa in the sense of a decisive break with all that had gone before. Those Africans who took up arms to resist the imposition of colonial rule were therefore easily conceived of by imperial historians as having acted in defence of a traditional way of life which was doomed to disappear. Representative of this view was, for example, the account published by Robinson and Gallagher, two eminent British historians of empire, in *The New Cambridge Modern History* in 1962.[20] They considered that the establishment of colonial rule marked a rupture with previous periods of African history so complete that the nationalism which eventually replaced colonialism could only be interpreted as a force without substantial indigenous roots, developed by a new generation of African politicians and intellectuals who had been formed by the colonial powers themselves and who had thereby learned how to operate the colonial systems to their advantage. They were deemed to have little in common with the first generation of resisters of colonial rule, those of the late nineteenth century who had opposed alien rule not in the name of a modern political force but in the cause of tradition.

The most influential criticism of the conventional European notion that African nationalism was a force created by colonialism itself, in the image of the coloniser, was conveyed in a series of works by Terence Ranger, a British historian who had worked in colonial Rhodesia. Expelled from Rhodesia on account of his African nationalist sympathies, this prolific writer and lecturer went on to head the most dynamic school of Africanist historiography within the continent, in Dar es Salaam, before eventually taking a chair at Oxford. A seminal conference on African history held at Dar es Salaam in 1965 resulted in publication under Ranger's editorship of a series of papers on emerging themes in African history, several of which pointed to the significance of armed resistance to colonial rule.[21] Ranger published on his own account a two-part essay on armed resistance to colonial rule in the *Journal of African History*[22] which became an instant classic. In it, he connected the history of what had happened when Europeans first imposed colonial rule on Africa with what occurred two or three generations later at the time of independence, when modern nationalist movements emerged in opposition to colonial or settler rule. Both sets of events he saw as part of one long process of confrontation between African societies and the forces of colonialism. Ranger began his article in the *Journal of African History* with an attack on Robinson and Gallagher, who had represented early resistance to colonial rule as 'romantic, reactionary struggles against the facts', in contrast to modern independence movements which they termed 'defter nationalisms', since they were 'operating in the idiom of the Westerners.'[23] Ranger, rather than emphasising the contrast between older and newer forms of resistance, preferred to see all forms of resistance to colonialism as essentially similar. All were related to nationalism, itself the flowering of the tradition of independence. He labelled the early resisters of colonial rule as organisers of 'primary resistance', and later generations as proponents of 'secondary resistance'. One of the principal tasks for historians was to trace the precise relationship between the two, which would also have the effect of tracing the roots of modern African nationalism back into the nineteenth century.

The view of the historical roots of nationalism sketched by Ranger and others in the late 1960s soon became an orthodoxy among the new generation of politically engaged Africanists who often acted in the spirit of what one acute observer, himself a former member of the history department at Dar Es Salaam, called a 'Committee of Concerned Scholars for a Free Africa'.[24] There were always a substantial number of scholars who remained sceptical of the notion that there existed such a pure nationalist strain of African resistance to colonial rule.[25] This was particularly so among French-speaking scholars, for example.[26.]

If a full-blooded nationalist interpretation of the colonial period gained such popularity in the late 1960s and 1970s, it was perhaps less because of its intellectual persuasiveness than because it gave precise form to a notion much more widely held in society at large, as is often the case with historical orthodoxies. In this particular case, the idea that militant nationalism was the fruition of a spirit of resistance which had been present throughout the colonial period, and which now emerged to claim the leadership of African countries as sovereign members of the international family of nations chimed with a widespread perception that the emergence of African nationalism as a political force marked some sort of progress. Since Africanist historians construed resistance to colonialism to be an act in tune with history itself, those who fought against the imposition of colonial rule in the late nineteenth century, or shortly after, came to appear as protonationalists, sometimes visionary, always on the right side of history. And since colonial rule, in the view of many scholars working on Africa from the 1950s onwards, was self-evidently an injustice, and at the very least an idea whose time had gone, it was tempting to consider Africans who had worked enthusiastically with colonial administrations as 'collaborators', a word loaded with reference to Nazi-occupied Europe, as was noted by a French communist who had lived through the German occupation of France.[27]

The creation or identification of a nationalist history could hardly be other than a politically charged act in years when African countries were gaining their independence, just as its opposite (that is, the denial that such a history existed) would also have been politically charged, if any scholar of standing had been foolhardy enough to undertake the task.[28] Most of Africa after 1960 could take satisfaction in the knowledge that colonial rule proper had gone, but much of southern Africa in particular still awaited its liberation. Since the colonial and settler regimes of that region refused to concede majority rule by negotiation, military campaigns generally referred to as 'armed struggle' began to take place. There was an obvious and simple relation between the sense of history and the moral justification for armed struggle against continuing colonial or settler rule.[29]

Postcolonial Africa

Some of the fundamental elements of an intellectually viable view of African nationalism, as sketched in the previous few paragraphs, were easy enough to accept during the first two decades of independence in most of Africa, since the new nationalist governments were, for the most part, bringing a recognisable system of political order and relative prosperity to their populations and pursuing a commitment to a strategy of economic development which had broad international support. The idea of a triumphant nationalism, poised to move forward, gave succour both to African governments and their international partners; it was in harmony with the international consensus operative after 1945 on the need to govern the world through sovereign political units usually defined by reference to nationality; it appeared to be evidence of progress; and it seemed to explain the rapid speed of decolonisation in the 1950s. As long as these conditions applied, then nationalist historians such as Ranger could hold their own not only against European conservative critics but, more importantly, against those radical pessimists who, in the spirit of Frantz Fanon, regarded African nationalism as a European creation as much as an African one, a vehicle for the transmission of neo-colonial interests.[30]

All of these factors tended to deflect attention from the historical shortcomings of what was, by the 1970s, the orthodox nationalist view of resistance to colonialism. The central weakness of this theory was the danger inherent in the proposition that Africans who took up arms to oppose the imposition of colonial rule at its inception, generally around the end of the nineteenth century, were 'primary resisters', so called because they were forerunners of the 'secondary resisters' or modern nationalists. This made it all too tempting to read history backwards by implying that, since modern African leaders were nationalists, then earlier opponents of colonial government must have been proto-nationalists. This supposition did some disservice to the historical data. In the first place, many early resisters of colonial rule were most probably unaware of the existence of such things as national states, and so it is hardly accurate to consider them as nationalists of any sort. The retrospective identification of them as forebears of modern nationalism is based on an absence of careful consideration of exactly what they themselves thought they were doing when they took up arms. More prosaically, a number of people who emerged at the time of independence as nationalist leaders had in fact worked closely with the colonial authorities at various stages of their careers, typically as government officials, as soldiers or in receipt of official patronage such as scholarships, all of which calls for a nuanced understanding not only of their relationship to the colonial authorities but also that which they had with less privileged strata of the African population. Furthermore, there are many examples of African nationalist leaders of the mid- to late twentieth century claiming as proto-nationalist forebears social groups or sociological strata with which they actually had little connection. This is related to the fact that the anti-colonial struggle itself was rather less than a substantial threat to colonial rule in many cases. Outside Algeria and southern Africa, there were in fact strikingly few cases of anti-colonial armed movements forcing the path to decolonisation. Where such movements did occur after 1945, such as in Madagascar, Cameroon and Kenya, they were defeated before independence and those who led them in the field rarely tasted the fruits of power. In short, the practice common among African nationalists of postcolonial times, of claiming to be the descendants of a long line of doughty fighters for liberation, often looks suspiciously like a revival of the old practice of manipulating genealogies.

This is not to deny that some parts of Africa witnessed constant acts of resistance to colonial rule throughout the sixty or seventy years for which colonial government generally lasted, nor to deny the validity of seeing such episodes as part of a longer sequence of events. Our suggestion is, however, that it is possible to construct such a sequence in various terms other than as a narrative of African nationalism. It is at least theoretically possible in many cases to see episodes of armed resistance to colonial authority as fitting more convincingly into a history of banditry, for example,[31] or at least of some form of localised political action, or as a means of economic accumulation or as a cultural phenomenon.[32] Conversely, it is possible to trace the history of nationalism other than as a story of resistance to colonialism. Nationalism could be construed, for example, primarily as a discourse concerning the centralisation of power or the formation of social classes, as it sometimes was by Marxist scholars,[33] or as a process of imagining.[34] Underlying such perspectives is the question of whether it is most convincing to consider modern African nationalism primarily as the climax of three or more generations of struggle against colonialism. It is a rather pedestrian thought, but perhaps one actually entertained by substantial numbers of Africans today, that modern African politicians might be most accurately viewed primarily as skilled manipulators of power rather than as people driven by a romantic attachment to a particular ideology, and that it is their pursuit of power which sometimes causes them to invoke aspects of the past, real or fictitious or mixed.[35] Approaches of this type could be used to construct an alternative interpretation of the events which, to

73

observers in the 1960s, were most persuasively seen as evidence of the forward march of African nationalism.

If such a change of perspective has some explanatory power, it also underlines some of the risks inherent in the difficult, but necessary, task of writing contemporary history, when historical data are sometimes difficult to determine and, above all, when placing them in coherent sequences or patterns carries risks of misidentification. In retrospect, it appears that a tendency to suppose that nationalism was an unstoppable force, combined with a sometimes uncritical acceptance of the forms it took, blinded Africanist scholarship as a whole to the many cases in which substantial segments of Africa's populations, and legitimate African political interests, were full of foreboding for a future under the particular brand of nationalism which was actually emerging. Some of the events of recent years compel us to reconsider these. Burundi, for example, was only one of several African countries in which a substantial section of organised political opinion in the 1950s argued against an immediate granting of independence, which it feared would be dominated by a minority group, as is clear from the document known as the *Manifeste des Bahutu*. In the light of Burundi's postcolonial history, the fears of what the authors of this text termed 'Tutsi colonialism' cannot be said to have been wholly misplaced. Substantial sections of the population in other countries also had reason to fear their fate under political systems which had inherited the colonial organisation of power into formidable monopolies, as comparable movements in Ghana, Cameroon and Madagascar indicate.[36] Those Africans who, on the verge of independence, actually faced the prospect of government by the particular groups and individuals who had acquired or seized power in the name of the nation, all too often had reason to fear the hegemonic aspirations of their new leaders. The foreign Africanist intellectuals who were so influential in creating the historiography of nationalism, on the other hand, generally had less reason for fear: in most cases, unlike African intellectuals, they were not threatened by the darker side of a Sékou Touré or a Kamuzu Banda or by any of the armed corporations which came to proliferate throughout the continent.

Chad is another country which provides interesting food for thought on the nature of armed struggle in postcolonial Africa and its relation to nationalist historiography, and since it is also the main field of study of the sociologist Rob Buijtenhuijs, it is useful to consider the Chadian case briefly. The territory marked on the map as Chad did not correspond to any stable or well defined political entity in the nineteenth century, but was one of many territories in Africa which acquired the contours of its current political definition in the act of colonisation. It was actually the site of some of the longest lingering resistance to French colonial rule, with expeditions of military conquest or pacification still being launched against armed opponents until well into the twentieth century. When Chad became independent, at the same time as most other African colonies of France, in 1960, it was no more than three decades after all parts of the country had submitted to *la paix coloniale*. Just five years later, in 1965, a series of risings began which soon came to be identified as a campaign led by the National Liberation Front or Frolinat, an organisation which claimed to be fighting for the liberation of the country. Frolinat, allied to radical nationalist governments in Algeria and Libya, was opposed to the Chadian government led by François Tombalbaye, which had been supported by France since independence and which Frolinat qualified as neo-colonial. Frolinat thus purported to be fighting not merely for Chad's formal independence from colonial rule, which had already been attained, but for a political dispensation which would bring a different type of liberation, one identified with freedom from the set of relationships known as neocolonialism and with victory over the various elements of the Chadian population who supported that arrangement.

The Chadian struggle went largely unstudied by scholars, other than by Buijtenhuijs and a handful of others, and little remarked by journalists, at least until violence hit the capital of Chad in the late 1970s, by which time Frolinat had advanced to lay siege to the central organs of the state. Thereafter, the victory of Frolinat, or at least of some of its offspring, set an interesting precedent as it became the first armed movement with a relatively broad social base (as distinct, that is, from a faction in the armed forces launching a classic *coup d'état*) to take power, not from a colonial government, but from a postcolonial African one. This feat was achieved by Hissène Habré, himself a former protégé of the colonial administration like so many nationalists in the first flush of independence, in 1982.

The significance of Habré's seizure of power escaped widespread notice at the time, largely, no doubt, because of Chad's relative obscurity and because of the major role played in the country by foreign powers, especially France, Libya and, later, the USA. It was only when Yoweri Museveni repeated Habré's achievement four years later, by overthrowing the existing government in Kampala, that significant international attention was turned to the new phenomenon of a broad-based armed movement liberating an African country from a home-grown despot rather than from colonial rule. The tortured history of Uganda, the huge attention which the tyrannical Idi Amin had earlier received from international news media, Museveni's own political and intellectual dexterity, and the gradual ending of the Cold War, all combined to make Uganda appear a new paradigm of how an oppressed African people could free itself from a home-grown dictatorship.[37]

This gave a new twist to the historiography of nationalist wars of liberation. For, by the time Museveni came to power in 1986, Mozambique, Guinea-Bissau and Angola had been freed from Portuguese colonial rule, and Zimbabwe's liberation movements had overthrown the settler government of Ian Smith. The only places remaining for liberation, from European colonial or settler rule were Namibia and South Africa. The apogee of African nationalism—the liberation of a whole continent—was nearing its zenith. This was not, however, cause for unalloyed joy, for it was apparent that the commitment of a whole generation of politicians and intellectuals to the idea of the liberation of Africa had not resulted in the progress that had been hoped for, and which indeed was implicit in the very notion of national liberation. In retrospect, one of the most far-sighted essays published in the late 1980s was one by the British historian Michael Crowder, who wondered, concerning the commonly held nationalist view, 'whose dream was it anyway?'[38] Throughout the continent there were signs of a growing disillusion with various nationalist leaders and parties whose sparkle had faded once they were in power, a disillusion so widespread that it could not simply be ignored or explained away with platitudes, as ideologues of nationalist regimes had done so often in the past. Algeria, an inspiration for earlier African nationalists, still ruled by the Front de Libération Nationale (FLN), was engulfed by serious rioting, amounting almost to a popular insurrection, in 1988.

By this time there was a widespread perception, including among African intellectuals, that the giants of African nationalism who had had the good sense to engineer their own retirement, most notably Senghor and Nyerere, had been more far-sighted than those who were still in power, like Kaunda, Banda or Houphouët-Boigny, whose reputations were fast becoming tarnished as their earlier achievements began to appear in a different light. In these circumstances, Yoweri Museveni's National Resistance Army in Uganda seemed to indicate to some observers the possibilities offered by a new type of armed struggle, one freed from some of the illusions or immaturity of the previous generation, endowed with a more thoughtful and educated leadership and a more useful analysis of what precisely needed doing to secure a better future for Africa.

Those who were inclined to view certain movements of armed opposition to postcolonial African governments as new forms of national liberation, were essentially basing their case on an updated identification of who, or what, was the factor inhibiting Africa's progress towards the higher form of political life implicit in the notion of national liberation. Whereas a slightly earlier generation had considered colonialism to be the enemy, the target had shifted to neo-colonialism: substantially the same enemy, but in a different guise. This corresponded to a view of Africa's political economy which was fashionable in the 1970s among many political scientists, namely the 'dependency theory' which held that countries of the third world, being on the periphery of a capitalist economic system which reached throughout the globe, could not hope to advance to any higher stage of political or economic development unless they could decrease their dependency on the industrialised core countries.[39] While dependency theory was in high retreat from academic lecture halls in the West by the time Museveni took power in Uganda, it remained popular among many African intellectuals and continued to inspire a degree of support from Marxist analysts in the face of the neo-liberal theories which were then sweeping through Western academies of learning. Other commentators were beginning to see Africa's fundamental problem as lying in the institutional forms of power, largely inherited from the colonial period. This, according to a prominent strand in Africanist thinking, had imposed on Africa an ill-adapted form of government.[40]

If it were true that Africa was struggling under the weight of imported institutions of government, then it was logical to seek better-adapted forms which were home-grown. Hence, despite the unhappy precedents already set by African leaders (most notably, Mobutu Sese Seko) who had claimed to have discovered an authentically African way of doing things, President Museveni of Uganda was very successful in recruiting international support for his no-party system of government on the grounds that this was a genuinely Ugandan alternative to non-African systems of democracy.

However, by the late 1980s the very notion that an African country could be liberated from an oppressive political regime by force was being challenged as a result of a number of factors at least as important as the demise of certain theories of political economy. Parts of Africa were now home to movements which had many of the hallmarks of guerrilla armies, and could demonstrate at least a fair degree of popular support, but which were difficult to classify. One of these was the União para a Independência Total de Angola. For most Africanist scholars, Jonas Savimbi's UNITA organisation could not be considered a liberation movement since it was opposed to a government which was already held to have liberated Angola, and in any case Savimbi was allied to the illegitimate apartheid regime and the US secret services. Nevertheless, UNITA refused to go away. It constituted an uncomfortable reminder that not all large-scale armed movements could automatically be regarded as forces of liberation even when, like UNITA, they had at least some degree of popular support. This was also a consequence of a strategic choice by the US government under Ronald Reagan (1980–88), or by elements within it, to fight the Cold War by sponsoring a new wave of anti-Marxist guerrillas wherever appropriate, by encouraging movements like UNITA in Angola or the Nicaraguan Contras. How was a person intent on Africa's liberation to distinguish genuine movements of emancipation from bogus ones? By reference to their political programmes? The problem was that such movements invariably claimed that their ultimate goal was some sort of freedom. In practice, observers ended up by judging the merits of various armed movements by reference to their external allies, thus binding African liberation movements inextricably into the politics of the Cold War. This was one reason why Ethiopia posed the biggest puzzle of all: for who were the liberators in a war, growingly severe throughout the 1980s, in which several different guerrilla movements, many having both Marxist and nationalist credentials, were opposed to a home-grown African government, and a Marxist–Leninist one at that?

The burgeoning number of armed movements in Africa seemed increasingly to suggest that the continent was in need not so much of liberation from dependence on the West, as of some form of politics which was marked by real power-sharing, and not merely by the seizure of power by one armed group from another. Even RENAMO, the Resistência Nacional Moçambicana, in Mozambique, considered by Marxist-influenced scholars to be a-political in the sense of representing a form of banditry rather than any constituency with real roots in Mozambican society, or used as a simple front for the South African Defence Force, came to be included in the literature which called out for rethinking on the nature of Africa's liberation from colonial rule, particularly after the path breaking study by the French anthropologist Geffray had revealed that RENAMO gained support from substantial peasant grievances.[41]

Moreover, seismic shifts in global society and politics were changing some previous ideological positions. The astonishingly rapid collapse of the Soviet empire in 1989 raised fundamental questions about the viability of concepts such as liberation and revolution which had been common currency in African political ideology for decades. A wave of political contestation within Africa itself, leading to the overthrow of one-party regimes through largely or entirely non-violent means in Benin and Mali, and the removal from power by constitutional means of the founding father of the nation in Zambia, gave powerful incentives to rethink the particular idea of liberation which had become current since Africa's decolonisation thirty years earlier, and most particularly the frequent supposition that true liberation required force of arms.

In the excited atmosphere of late 1989 and early 1990, with the fall of the Berlin Wall and the release from prison of Nelson Mandela, some influential outside observers were keen to apply to Africa what they believed to be lessons learned from the triumph of capitalism and democracy. Among the most important of those acting thus was the World Bank, which called for the political reform of African countries in a report published, by chance, at the same time that the Berlin Wall was breached.[42] The simultaneous end of the Cold War and the collapse of African one-party states offered to aid donors, so influential in a continent where most governments and even states had become dependent on official loans and grants for their survival, an opportunity to reinforce the programmes of political and economic reform which the main donor agencies had come to believe were necessary for Africa's well-being. It is not irrelevant to note that a substantial part of the academic research done on Africa is financed by these same donors, not merely in the vague sense that many universities in Europe and North America receive funding from their national governments, but in the form of contracts for specific items of research offered by donor institutions to both Western Africanists and African scholars, the latter often trying to survive in universities starved of funds. The foreign ministries and aid administrations of Western governments, developing an interest in such concepts as democracy and civil society in pursuit of their mission to manage the process of change in Africa, invested in research on these subjects and had a considerable influence on some emerging Africanist debates.

The significance of this last observation is to underline that, just as an earlier generation of writers had been inclined to construct a nationalist historiography which could be enlisted in the causes of state-building and nation-building, there were now numbers of consultants, scholars and others interested in examining democratisation and the role of civil society in Africa and re-interpreting Africa's recent past in the service of their purpose, even though writing or rewriting history was not usually their primary objective. Thus, in the early 1990s, democracy was often deemed to hold out the promise of what was sometimes called a 'second liberation' of Africa. This time around, liberation was no longer to be from colonial rule, but from national oppression. To many observers, the struggle to liberate Africa, often clothed in the vocabulary of development, now appeared to require not so much armed force as a combination of parliamentary government, press freedom and civil liberty, the whole compatible with the proposition that an economic revival could be based on free trade.[43]

The demise of Marxism as both political force and analytical tool, and the fashion for liberal theories of democracy and civil society, alas, did not mark the end of political violence in Africa. On the contrary, war in Liberia after 1989 and Sierra Leone after 1991, civil war in Somalia culminating in the disastrous US/United Nations intervention of 1992–4, and, especially, the Rwandan genocide of 1994, all marked major new epicentres of violence. It was now clear to observers of every shade of opinion that armed movements, even where they had some degree of organisation and popular support and claimed to be liberating some group or other, could not automatically be regarded as forces for emancipation or progress as so many writers had been inclined to believe in earlier decades. To be sure, there was an important current of pan-Africanist revolutionary thought which continued to hold that armed struggle still had a place in the emancipation of African peoples, and which even underwent something of a revival under the inspiration of Museveni's achievement. The Seventh Pan-African Congress held in Kampala in 1994, for example, expressed this in a statement to the effect that the first phase of the African revolution had ended with the overthrow of white domination of South Africa, but that this had not solved the basic needs of the people, which required further struggle.[44] But many armed struggles were hugely destructive and appeared to some commentators to have no coherent political programme whatever. Many analysts began to adopt a more anthropological approach to some campaigns, which suggested that some at least might better be understood as complex social phenomena rather than campaigns in support of modern political ideologies.[45] It was not only in Africa that war, in the confusing new world of the 1990s, seemed to have left the realm of political and military studies. A leading British historian in 1993 infamously described the war in Bosnia as 'a primitive, tribal conflict only anthropologists can understand,'[46] a remark rich in implications.

These tumultuous events were bound to have an effect on historiography by causing writers to re-evaluate the meaning of earlier historical events. For, while the world after the Cold War was turning out to be a more violent place than many had hoped or expected, some old champions of national liberation in Africa were still in power. Some movements, and some leaders, whose claim to have liberated their country in the earlier times had been widely accepted, were now beginning to look uncomfortably like oppressors in their turn, in some cases as much so as the colonisers whom they had replaced. This raised a series of questions which had previously been largely avoided in the historical literature about the nature of liberation as a political and social process. Who *precisely* had been liberated by ZANU in Zimbabwe in 1980, for example? A series of pogroms launched by Prime Minister Robert Mugabe in Matabeleland in the mid-1980s, in which thousands of Matabele people were killed on the grounds that they were potential supporters of the political opposition, raised the uncomfortable thought, in a country which had been a shop-window for the cause of national liberation, that the identification of those liberated might be partly couched in ethnic terms.

This last suspicion—that the fruits of power in independent Africa had been distributed partly according to ethnic criteria—opened up a vast Pandora's Box which nationalist ideology had to a large extent managed to keep closed, concerning the exact relationship between nationalism and ethnicity in Africa.[47] Not only was the impartiality of postcolonial governments open to question on ethnic grounds, but some even wondered about their good faith in regard to the concept of development, which had always been claimed as one of the great goals of nationalist policy. Hence, the Nigerian writer Claude Ake wondered whether African governments had ever believed in the notion of development in the first place, or whether they had not just cynically used this notion as a slogan which permitted them to pursue their real agenda, that of acquiring and manipulating power.[48]

Just as Ake questioned the use which had actually been made of the idea of development, so did other observers question other major aspects of the old paradigm of liberation. Some analysts of earlier liberation wars, like Rob Buijtenhuijs, disturbed by the growing violence of the continent and struck by the poor record in power of so many former liberation movements, turned their hopes towards peaceful political change. For them, the second wave of liberation would no longer be through the barrel of a gun, but through the ballot-box. In a similarly prudent vein, the Marxist scholars John Saul and Colin Leys, veteran opponents of apartheid, were concerned in a book on Namibia to ask questions concerning the incoming government formed by the South-West African People's Organisation, SWAPO, which had been guilty of terrible abuses of human rights even before it came to power.[49] Some scholars have come to interpret new political–military campaigns in Africa as forms of warlordism or other types of combat less uplifting than romantically conceived struggles for liberation.[50] In the field of strictly historical study, while Zimbabwe continues to provide one of the richest literatures on nationalist guerrillas, a new note has been sounded by Norma Kriger in her description of the coercive element in nationalist violence. New studies of the apparently inchoate violent movements of the 1990s, such as in Rwanda, Sierra Leone and Liberia, are also appearing.[51]

Although Africanist scholars during the 1980s and 1990s have tended, rather more than the previous generation, to question the credentials of would-be liberators, the vestiges of the earlier notion that Africa could be freed by a liberation movement which marked a radical break with the past have not disappeared, even if the suggestion often made in earlier literature, to the effect that this was achieved most fully by force of arms, has now become less prominent. In an exquisite irony, the notion that African societies may be liberated by radical political action, earlier identified with Marxism, has now been assumed by certain Western administrations responsible for giving financial aid to Africa. Influential US media especially have entertained the notion that there has arisen a generation of new leaders in Africa, of whom Yoweri Museveni is generally seen as the archetype, who have taken power in their own countries by force of arms from postcolonial governments, notably in Uganda, Rwanda, Ethiopia and Eritrea, and who are using their conquest of power to rebuild states along capitalist-friendly lines.[52] The idea of a progressive, US-friendly, second wave of liberation has been enthusiastically taken up by the president-in-waiting of South Africa, Thabo Mbeki, who has turned the notion of an African Renaissance into a corner-stone of his politics.[53] In truth, this was a grotesque proposition even before several of the much-vaunted new leaders of Africa launched a particularly murderous new round of wars in the Horn and in central Africa in 1997–8. Many of those very same new leaders who were courted and praised by the US State Department, the Pentagon and the World Bank are former Marxists who in fact still head political organisations run along recognisably Marxist–Leninist lines: the militarism of Museveni, Afewerki, Meles, Kagame and others suggests that they still retain a robustly Leninist belief in the merits of force. Money may these days come from the West, but power in Africa still comes all too often from the barrel of a gun.

Many of the finest African scholars these days have found jobs abroad, in the USA especially, where they tend to become subsumed in US domestic debates, particularly those concerning multiculturalism and the politics of identity. Some of the best African political thinkers or analysts, including some who previously worked on the historiography of national liberation, have become immersed in the field of postcolonial studies, where some African expatriates have endeavoured to explore aspects of Africa's political ideologies, often in ways distinctly unflattering to the idea of African nationalism.[54] Postcolonial discussions of memory, representation and cultural invention all leave a rather uncomfortable historical question concerning who actually created the earlier nationalist ideologies, in which so many of the most academically influential works were penned by non-Africans, or in fact more precisely by British and Americans. It raises the haunting question of to what extent African nationalism has been, in part, a foreign creation at well as an African one, as Ake thought of Africa's commitment to development. If at least one of the cherished ideologies of African politics could be called into question so brutally as it was by Ake, could not others?

Ideology and history

All ideologies, it is said, share 'the widespread virtue that identifies History with the winning side'.[55] This ideological insistence on maintaining an interest only in those ideas which are with hindsight deemed to have been winning ones was a characteristic of historiography generally during the Cold War, and certainly not just of writing on Africa. A recent attempt to retrace the history of Europe in the twentieth century as far as possible without viewing it through any particular ideological prism, viewing the present as just one possible outcome of our predecessors' struggles and uncertainties, rather than as the inevitable progress of some great historical idea such as democracy or national liberation, is illuminating.[56] It would be useful to apply the same technique to the history of Africa's decolonisation and of the various contests which have been called armed struggles or wars of liberation. In this last section we will briefly consider some possible approaches towards re-reading the late colonial and postcolonial period of African history with a similar lack of any ideological prism.

Perhaps it is first necessary at least to acknowledge the limits of such an approach, for all history-writing, we have said, carries within it suppositions about rationality and time which could be said to be of an ideological nature. This does not, however, mean that all history writing is condemned to be ideological in a narrower sense, or that historians cannot redress their own biases. In fact, they always have the option to resist to the best of their ability the temptation to extend contemporary ideas or concerns back into the past in a single-minded manner. They can strive to recreate the context in which previous generations lived and acted. They can give due attention to those undercurrents of earlier history which were important at the time, but which are neglected by more ideological investigations interested single-mindedly in results. Just as Europe's own tortured history can be better seen as 'a story of narrow squeaks and unexpected twists, not inevitable victories and forward marches',[57] so might it be profitable to see the last fifty years of African political history other than as the triumphal progress of liberation from colonial rule and of nationalism.

In fact, it requires little demonstration to show just how far Africa's recent history has been something less than a triumph, since the period since the 1970s is so widely acknowledged to have been a difficult one. While there are no remaining colonies or white settler regimes in Africa, and in that sense African nationalism may be said to have attained one of its main goals, the heroic vision of African nationalism, connected as it is to the notion of progress, could not be expected to escape the recent travails of African states. This indeed calls for a view which pays full attention to what may earlier have seemed the pools and eddies of history, movements and ideas which did not actually attain power, turning-points where history failed to turn. Perhaps the current vogue for historical studies of culture, subjectivities, identities and everyday life may help in the long run inasmuch as they throw light on the nature of politics 'from below'.

If we are to gain a new understanding of what actually occurred in self proclaimed wars of liberation in the past and in the present, above all more empirical research is needed on how Africans view the historical experience of their societies in the circumstances of distress or even trauma which obtain in places such as Congo, Liberia, Sierra Leone or Somalia, but also in less blighted countries like Nigeria. There is evidence that many people in these countries, while regarding the present period as a difficult one and the future with trepidation, regard its place in history primarily in religious terms.[58] Here historians can benefit from a rich literature on the study of religion in Africa. They can also learn from writers on war in other continents and periods, some of whom have noted the need for new historical research on earlier campaigns of armed struggle, or at least for new ways of thinking about published data. This is so partly because war itself has changed[59] and scholars need new tools to study it. It has been noted that debates on the origins of the American revolution, for example, tend to focus on socio-economic groups while neglecting the role in events of military formations, a subject left to specialist military historians. This seems to stem from a notion that war and revolution, on the one hand, and social and economic developments, on the other, are best understood as separate things requiring separate study. This may have some justification for vast military campaigns like the First World War, but surely one of the main lessons of modern wars is the major effect they have on economics and society. Conversely, those interested in political revolutions need to pay greater attention to the role of armies in those revolutions. To take one example, whereas historians have been quite inclined to interpret forms of public violence which occurred during colonial times as forms of anti-colonial protest, thus constructing a chronological series of data whose outcome is national independence, recent examples of pillaging in African cities might cause one to re-examine some earlier bouts of violence in light of a logic of predation and plunder.[60] We may agree with David Keen on the importance of seeing war as a form of economic activity, for example.[61]

One conclusion which can be drawn from a consideration of the historiography of nationalism, then, concerns the desirability of studying Africa's previous wars in a wide context of social, economic and political history, and not merely with a single-minded concern to assess only their contribution to particular ideologies of nationalism or revolution. With hindsight, it is notable that some of the most striking insights into the questions raised by the exercise of violence, and indeed by the experience of nationalism and independence more widely, have actually come from the pens of novelists rather than those of historians or even of scholars more generally.[62] Perhaps this is because so many of the crucial developments in those decades have occurred in the realm of the imagination, one which historians have, until recently at least, found it more difficult or less interesting to explore than the more concrete sphere of human activity. If it is indeed the case, as we have suggested, that political ideas in Africa today are often embedded in religious forms of expression, then it suggests that historians might fruitfully continue a tendency of recent years to investigate the workings of the imagination. Certainly nationalism, the constitution of imagined communities, lends itself easily to such a project.

Most probably too, historians who consider nationalism will need to reformulate one of the most enduring paradigms used by analysts of Africa, namely the perceived contrast between Africa and the outside, and between what is authentically African and that which is imposed or borrowed from the rest of the world. This has proved a resilient idea, which continues to inform much analysis of Africa and to provide material for reworking by African politicians, as we have suggested. But the observation that African societies have historically been more remarkable for their porous boundaries rather than their strict rules of exclusion, and that political power has for centuries, even before the colonial period, been connected to the successful manipulation of external connections, surely suggests the usefulness of seeking other models which are less dualistic in nature.[63] These are all lines of approach which may in time help us to reinterpret Africa's liberation wars.

While scholars may react in these and many other ways to the unfolding of events in Africa and in the rest of the world, one effect has already been to weaken the consensus which previously existed concerning the 'meaning' of the colonial period in African history and to dent the notion of nationalism as a heroic project whose armed struggles, however regrettable, were inevitable or necessary. Those who write on African politics, or on the history of nationalism, are generally considerably more cautious than they once were, since they are now aware that nationalism was unable to realise all of its promises, or even that nationalism may well be in need of reinterpretation in the light of other, wider patterns in African societies. Yet still, the very spread of the notion of a postcolonial condition inevitably implies the existence of a postcolonial historical period, whatever we may think of the quality of that period, whether heroic or other. In other words, we are still left with the now-classic division of African history into three periods defined by their relationship to colonial rule: precolonial, colonial, and postcolonial Africa.

References

Achebe, C., 1966, *A Man of the People*, Heinemann, Londres.

1983, The Trouble with Nigeria, Heinemann, Londres.

Ake, C., 1996, *Democracy and Development in Africa*, Brookings Institution, Washington DC.

Badie, B., 1992, *L'Etat importé: essai sur occidentalisation de l'ordre politique*, Fayard, Paris.

Bayart, J.-F., sous presse, 'Africa in the World: a history of extraversion', *African Affairs*, 99, 395.

Bazenguissa-ganga, R., 1999, 'The Spread of Political Violence in Congo-Brazzaville', *African Affairs*, 98, 390: 37-54.

Berman, B., 1998, 'Ethnicity, Politics and the African State: the politics of uncivil nationalism', *African Affairs*, 97, 388: 305-41.

Buijtenhuijs, R., 1971, *Le mouvement 'Mau-Mau': une révolte paysanne et anti-coloniale en Afrique noire*, Mouton, La Haye.

――――. 1978, *Le Frolinat et les révoltes populaires au Tchad, 1965-1976*, Mouton, La Haye.

――――. 1987a, *Le Frolinat et les guerres civiles au Tchad (1977-1984), la révolution introuvable*, Karthala, Paris.

――――. 1993, *La Conférence nationale souveraine du Tchad: un essai d'histoire immédiate*, Karthala, Paris.

――――. 1996, 'Rational Rebel: how rational, how rebellious ? Some African examples', *Afrika Focus*, 12, 1-3: 3-25.

――――. 1998b, *Transition et élections au Tchad 1993-1997: restauration autoritaire et recomposition politique*, Karthala, Paris

――――. 1993 (avec E. Rijnierse), *Democratization in Sub-Saharan Africa, 1989-1992: An Overview of the Literature*, African Studies Centre, Research Report n° 51, Leyde.

————. 1995 (avec C. Thiriot), *Démocratisation en Afrique au sud du Sahara, 1992-1995. Un bilan de la littérature*, Centre d'études africaines et CEAN, Leyde et Bordeaux.

Coquery-vidrovitch, C., 1997, 'Réflexions comparées sur l'historiographie africaniste de langue française et anglaise', *Politique africaine*, 66: 91-100.

Creveld, M. Van, 1991, *The Transformation of War*, Free Press, New York.

Clapham, C. (éd.), 1998, *African Guerrillas*, James Currey, Oxford.

Crowder, M., 1987, 'Whose dream was it anyway? Twenty-five years of African independence', *African Affairs*, 86, 342: 7-24.

Coetzee, J.M., 1980, *Waiting for the Barbarians*, Secker et Warburg, London.

Crummey, D. (éd.), 1986, *Banditry, Rebellion and Social Protest in Africa*, James Currey et Heinemann, Londres et Portsmouth.

Cohn, N., 1993, *Cosmos, Chaos and the World to Come*, Yale University Press, New Haven et Londres.

Cooper, E, 1994, 'Conflict and Connection: rethinking colonial African history', *American Historical Review*, 99 (5): 1516-1545.

Davidson, B. , 1970, *Old Africa Rediscovered*, Longman, Londres (original 1959 publication by Victor Gollancz, Londres).

————. 1994, *The Search for Africa: a history in the making*, James Currey, Londres.

Denoon, D. et Kuper, A., 1970, 'Nationalist Historians in Search of a Nation: The "New Historiography" in Dar Es Salaam', *African Affairs*, 69, 277: 329-49.

Deschamps, H., 1975, *Roi de la brousse: mémoire d'autres mondes*, Bergy-Levault, Nancy.

Diop, C.A., 1960, *L'Afrique noire précoloniale*, Présence africaine, Paris.

Ellis, S., 1995, 'Liberia 1989-1994: a study of ethnic and spiritual violence', *African Affairs*, 94: 165-197.

————. 1999, *The Mask of Anarchy: the destruction of Liberia and the religious dimension of an African civil war*, C. Hurst et Co., Londres.

Essack, K., 1994, *The Second Liberation of Africa, Proceedings of the Seventh Pan-Africanist Congress held in Kampala, Uganda, 4-8 April 1994*, Thackers Publishers, Dar-Es-Salaam.

Fuglestad, F., 1992, 'The Trevor-Roper Trap or the Imperialism of History: An Essay', Cambridge University Press

Gann, L., 1993, 'Ex Africa: an Africanist's intellectual autobiography', in Africa 1870-1960, part Ill, pp. 127-166, Cambridge University Press, *Journal of Modern African Studies*, 31 (3): 477-498. Cambridge.

Geffray, C., 1990, *La cause des armes au Mozambique: Anthropologie d'une guerre civile*, Karthala, Paris.

Glassman J., 1995, *Feasts and Riot : revelry: rebellion, and popular consciousness on the Swahili Coast, 1856-1888*, James Currey et Heinemann, Londres et Portsmouth, NH

Gluckman, H.M., 1971, 'Tribalism, ruralism and urbanism in South and History: An essay', *History in Africa*, 19: 309-326-Central Africa', in V.W. Turner (éd.), Profiles of Change : Colonialism

Hansen, H.B. et Twaddle, M. (Eds), 1991, *Changing Uganda* James Currey, Fountain Publishers et Ohio University Press, Londres, Athens OH.

Human Rights Watch, 1999, 'Leave None to Tell the Story': *Genocide in Rwanda*. Washington DC.

Indicator South Africa, 1998, 15, 2.

Jenkins, K., 1991, *Re-thinking History*, Routledge, Londres et New York.

Johnson, S., 1921, *The History of the Yorubas: from the earliest times to the beginning of the British protectorate*, Routledge, Londres.

Keen, D., sous presse, Political Economy of War', in F. Stewart et V. Fitzgerald (éds), *The Economic and Social Consequence of Conflict in Developing Countries*, Oxford University

Kourouma, A., 1970, *Les soleils des indépendances*, Ed. du Seuii, Paris.

Kriger, N., 1992, *Zimbabwe's Guerrilla War: peasant voices*, Cambridge University Press, African Studies Series n ° 70.

Ley S, C., 1996, *The Rise and Fall of Development Theory*, James Currey, Oxford.

Leys, C. et Saul, J., 1995, *Namibia's Liberation Struggle: The two-edged sword*, James Currey et Ohio University Press, Londres et Athens, OH.

Mamdani, M., 1996, *Citizen and Subject : contemporary Africa and the legacy of late colonialism*, Princeton University Press, Princeton.

Mazower, M., 1999, *Dark Continent: Europe's twentieth century*, Penguin Books, Londres.

Mbembe, A., 1991, 'Domaines de la nuit et autorité onirique dans le maquis du Slid-Cameroun (1955-1958)', *Journal of African History*, 32 (l): 89121.

———. 1992, 'Provisional Notes on the Postcolony', Africa, 62 (l): 3-37.

Oliver, R.O., 1997, *In the Realms of Gold: pioneering in African history*, University of Wisconsin Press, Madison WI.

Ottaway, M., 1999, *Africa's New Leaders: democracy or state reconstruction?*, Carnegie Endowment for International Peace, Washington DC.

Person, Y., 1968, 1975, Samori, 3 vols., Institut fondamental d' Afrique noire, Dakar.

Pomper, P., Elphick, R.H. et Vann, R. (Eds), 1998, *World History ideologies, structures and identities*, Blackwell, Malden MA et Oxford.

Raison-Jourde, F., 1997, 'Preface' à Jean-Roland Randriamaro, Padesm et luttes politiques à Madagascar: de la fin de la Deuxième Guerre mondiale à la naissance du PSI), pp. 9-18, Karthala, Paris.

Ranger, T.O., 1968a (éd.), *Emerging Themes in African History*, East African Publishing House, Nairobi.

————. 1968b, 'Connexions between "primary resistance movements" and modern mass nationalism in East and Central Africa', *Journal of African History*, 9: 437-453; et 631-641.

Reno, W., 1998, *Warlord Politics and African States*, Lynne Rienner, Boulder, Co.

Richards, P., 1996, *Fighting for the Rain Forest.War :Youth and Ressources in Sierra Leone*, James Currey et The International African Institute, Oxford.

Robinson, RE. et Gallagher, J., 1962, 'The Partition of Africa', *The New Cambridge Modern History*, vol. 11, chapitre '17, Cambridge University Press.

Suret-Canale, J., 1982, '«Résistance» et «collaboration» en Afrique noire', l'École des hautes études en sciences sociales, Paris.

Toulabor, C.M., 1986, *Le Togo sous Eyadéma*, Karthala, Paris.

Vansina, J., 1961, *De l'histoire orale : essai de méthode historique*, Musée royal de l' Afrique centrale, Tervuren.

Vansina, J., 1994, *Living With Africa*. Madison: The University of Wisconsin Press.

World Bank, 1989, *Sub-Saharan Africa : From Crisis to Sustainable Growth*. World Bank, Washington DC.

Zeleza, P.T., 1997, 'Pasts and Futures of African Studies and Area Studies', Ufahamu: *Journal of African Studies*, 4-41.

3

TUNING IN TO PAVEMENT RADIO

This article is an attempt to describe and define a phenomenon known all over Africa, for which there is no really satisfactory term in English but which is summed up in the French term *radio trottoir*, literally 'pavement radio'. The article contends that *radio trottoir* is a phenomenon worthy of observation and study by scholars, and that it is best understood in the context of the oral traditions and respect for oral culture which modern Africa has inherited from its past.

Perhaps the closest English translation of the term *radio trottoir* is 'bush telegraph', but this is unsatisfactory in that it is an old-fashioned metaphor: the telegraph was superseded decades ago, whereas the radio has for some 30 years been Africa's favourite modern news medium. Moreover, the bush is no longer a place where gossip is really hot, if ever it was. That distinction lies nowadays rather with the urban pavement, bar, market, living-room or taxi-park. That is where Africa's political pulse beats most strongly. So, rather than use an outmoded English metaphor to render the sense of *radio trottoir*, we may refer instead to 'pavement radio'. It may be defined as the popular and unofficial discussion of current affairs in Africa, particularly in towns.

Although pavement radio is a controversial medium, often mistrusted, feared or despised by politicians, journalists and academics, there is no doubt of its pervasive existence. Any inhabitant of Africa, familiar with the fact that the most important political news is often

93

gleaned not from official news media but from conversations with friends and acquaintances, will recognize this. As befits its nature, pavement radio is more often talked about than written about. However, it is occasionally described in serious studies of African affairs,[1] and is treated with dry humour, for example, in a political novel written by a former prime minister of Congo.[2] It is often referred to (albeit indirectly, for reasons which will become evident) in newspapers published by African governments or subject to their control.

Unlike the press, television or radio, pavement radio is not controlled by any identifiable individual, institution or group of people. Of course, individuals may, and do, seek to influence what is transmitted on the airwaves of pavement radio. But it is essentially anonymous and even democratic in that a story cannot be transmitted orally over any considerable distance or for any substantial period unless it is judged to be of interest by a significant number of people.

Pavement radio has certain favourite topics of discussion. It thrives on scandal in the sense of malicious news, and rarely has anything good to say about any prominent person or politician. Transmitters of pavement radio, that is to say ordinary people in Africa meeting in the course of their daily round, delight in casting doubt on the good name of a politician, ascribing improper or dishonest actions. One government minister will be said to have completed a corrupt transaction. Names will be named and sums of money quoted. Explanations will be advanced towards the behaviour of the political elite.

Clearly pavement radio is related to a phenomenon known in all societies at all times and generally called by pejorative names such as 'rumour' or 'gossip'. And it is true that pavement radio includes generous helpings of rumour and gossip. However, an examination of the social role and pedigree of pavement radio in Africa reveals it to be qualitatively different from either rumour or gossip and to have a quite different social and political function from its counterpart in Europe or other societies which have become essentially literate, not just in terms of the numbers of people who can read and write, but in the cultural significance attached to the written word.

The fact that pavement radio in Africa operates within an essentially oral culture causes it to have special features of both structure and content. An African audience gives far more weight to the spoken word than a European one, which generally believes little, and certainly little concerning national politics, that is not written or broadcast on radio or television. Moreover pavement radio is characteristically animated by certain social groups or in certain situations which listeners instinctively recognize as giving increased authority to rumour. The most believable purveyors of information are likely to be those whose jobs give them some access either to top-level gossip, such as government drivers, servants and hairdressers, or people with wide social or geographical contacts, such as market-sellers and long-distance lorry drivers. In Mali, for example, discussion and information on current affairs is especially conveyed in what are called in Malian French *grins*, regular social meetings of friends for relaxation and discussion. [3]

Music and dance remain important for conveying political messages, as they always have been. In a study of popular songs and poetry in colonial Mozambique, Leroy Vail and Landeg White concluded that poetry was seen as a proper form for statements about power, and that even in a generally repressive climate criticism was permissible in the form of songs. The form made the content lawful. [4] If this insight is also true of Zaire, it throws an interesting light on the tough position taken by the government of Zaire, whose Censorship Commission of Music, established in 1967, has to pass all songs before they can be performed in public. [5]

So not all rumours have equal weight. In part, their credibility depends on who recounts them and in what context. Over time pavement radio selects the most credible rumours and repeats them, helping to form popular consciousness.

Some examples of pavement radio broadcasts

African pavement radio is also different from mere rumour, at least sometimes, in its choice of subject, often discussing matters of public interest or importance which have been the subject of no official announcement. To some extent, of course, this is a result of censorship. A person who hears an item of news orally transmitted— or, for those who prefer, who hears a rumour—may find that the broadcast and printed news media are silent on a subject which is being widely discussed among the populace at large, or at least that these same news media offer an inadequate explanation. Popular rumour, for instance, might offer information on a demonstration which has gone unmentioned in the national press, or it might offer information about the causes of the demonstration or of casualties sustained which are at odds with facts and figures announced by the national media of press and broadcasting. Thus an important riot in Madagascar's capital, Antananarivo, is said to have left over 50 people dead in December 1984.[6] It was a riot charged with political implications since many of the dead belonged to a youth organization used as a security force by the ruling party. Following the riot, the government dismissed several leading army and police officials. Yet the events went unmentioned in the government-owned media and received only a belated mention in a Catholic Church newspaper,[7] although thousands of Antananarivo's citizens had witnessed the killings. The riots provided a topic for discussion on pavement radio for weeks.

It seems then that pavement radio's listeners and broadcasters—the two can hardly be distinguished—feel that their medium can retail information of public interest. Politicians and news managers may disagree, but the African public reserves the right to decide what is interesting and important. This can make pavement radio highly subversive.

Some subjects discussed on pavement radio may not be of obvious interest for high politics but relate to tradition and myth, underlining the extent to which pavement radio is a contemporary form of the oral traditions and oral histories which have been the subject of analysis by modern historians. Thus pavement radio sometimes transmits stories about witchcraft and other phenomena which, to a Western observer, can seem irrational or bizarre. These repay closer study in the light of the imagery of popular culture which retains a foundation in African religion, folklore, and oral history.

A specific example of this may be taken from Madagascar again. In Antananarivo, a rumour arose in late 1981 that a number of male corpses had been discovered which had been castrated. The genitals were said to have been used for ritual purposes. The stories were widely believed, the wicked deed being attributed to North Korean military or civilian aid workers in the island, who were generally unpopular.

This bizarre rumour has an interesting pedigree. The theme of a group of foreigners seeking to acquire human organs for mysterious purposes is well-known in Madagascar, and has been recorded by anthropologists. Usually the organ thus used is said to be the human heart, or sometimes the liver. One anthropologist, having encountered the belief that all Europeans are heart-thieves, interpreted it as a cultural metaphor. European culture, perceived as a corrosive influence on traditional Malagasy culture, could steal a person's heart in the sense of turning affections away from the culture of the ancestors and towards an imported European ideology.[8] This may be satisfactory as an academic explanation or decoding. The fact remains that many Malagasy sincerely believe in heart-thief stories and are terrified by them. Moreover the belief is old. The first known reference to it dates from the late nineteenth century, while very similar reports date from as early as 1824, when British missionaries reported that people feared them as kidnappers. They explained it as a result of the slave trade, when foreigners had taken people away, never to return.[9] So an unbelievable story heard on pavement radio may turn out to have a deep meaning and a long history, in this case relating to the way in which many Malagasy consider foreigners and the intrusion of foreign culture.

Such weird stories are not unique to Madagascar. In early 1982, popular opinion in Accra attributed a series of murders in the Volta region of Ghana to the action of government officials, said to be motivated by the desire to harness powerful magic.[10] One source records a spate of rumours in Malawi in the 1960s alleging that corpses had been drained of their blood, which was to be sold to South Africa. This too is an old myth, said to have its origin or functional explanation in the flow of manpower from Malawi to work in the South African mines.[11]

In all these cases orally transmitted rumours are superficially absurd but may be seen to be of political and cultural significance. Their meaning is implanted in local images and metaphors. They are not necessarily archaic in the sense of being marginal to the modern political process. For example, David Lan's remarkable study of Zimbabwe's liberation war, which admittedly relates to a rural environment, shows how supernatural beliefs rooted in tradition can be crucial to modern political developments.[12] Urban rumours too are often based on traditional symbolism.

Rumour, news, myth and politics

Nobody more than African politicians appreciates the fact that pavement radio is widely listened to and believed. In Cameroon, which has a strict official control of information, one coup attempt reported by pavement radio in 1979, almost certainly with some accuracy, appears to have gone unmentioned in any written or broadcast bulletin. Another coup attempt in April 1984 certainly did not go unreported, but provides a clear example of how pavement radio presents a problem to the political authorities. Official accounts of the April 1984 coup attempt were so inadequate, particularly in regard to the precise origins and aftermath of the bloody fighting in Yaounde, that radio trottoir recorded a spate of rumours about the causes of the coup attempt, the number of casualties, and the ensuing hunt for those implicated. The rumours became so widespread and worrying to the government that President Paul Biya felt obliged to mention the subject in a speech broadcast on national radio on 20 September 1984 which is worth quoting:[13]

> As for the truth, many of you confuse it with rumours. But rumour is not the truth. Truth comes from above; rumour comes from below. Rumour is created in unknown places, then spread by thoughtless and often malicious people, people who want to give themselves a spurious importance. Cameroonians, pay no heed to the rumours which are spreading through the country.

President Biya's remarks constitute a remarkably frank appraisal of the political significance of pavement radio by a most authoritative source. That which is not officially sanctioned, President Biya told his listeners, is not true. But information reported from above in Africa, that is from official sources, and which therefore purports to be authoritative, is often insufficiently detached or detailed to satisfy the public. In Ghana, an official survey in 1983 found that citizens were more inclined on principle to believe rumour than official news.[14]

The inadequacy of official news is partly because it is in short supply. According to a United Nations survey, Africa and its offshore islands had 220 daily newspapers in 1964, of which 169 were in black Africa. One estimate was that the 1964 total had fallen to some 156 daily papers by 1977. Of these, Arab Africa accounted for 35 dailies, white Rhodesia and South Africa for 24, Mauritius and Madagascar for 30, and the remaining 36 states had only 67 daily newspapers. Many of those papers were subject to some degree of censorship. The number of readers was some 5 million. There was one newspaper for every 1,000 sub-Saharan Africans. In the same year, 1977, there were only 11 television sets for every 1,000 Africans.[15]

Without doubt, the most important modern news medium in Africa is the radio. Since the invention of the transistor in 1948, and its subsequent introduction to Africa, the ownership of personal radios has increased at impressive speed. By 1977 sub-Saharan Africa was reckoned to contain 630 radio transmitters and 20 million receivers, or 62 radios for every 1,000 people. More recent statistics for East Africa indicate that the total is now much higher. By 1987 Kenya alone, for example, had an estimated 3 million radio sets.[16]

Even so, people do not derive all their news from the radio. The available audience research appears to suggest that many people in Africa listen to the radio primarily for music and general interest programmes. For a variety of reasons, they are less influenced by current affairs or news bulletins.[17] Possibly, the same could be true of listeners the world over.

Even when an African has a radio, and is seeking political news, he or she is unlikely to find fully satisfactory accounts from local radio stations which, as with newspapers, are controlled by governments and which broadcast news which the African public appears to find anodyne. Radio-owners can, and do, listen in large numbers to international radio stations such as the British Broadcasting Corporation, Radio France Internationale, Deutsche Welle, or Afrique No. 1, which are often said to carry more hard-hitting news that appears, to judge from audience response, to rouse strong feelings of hostility or approval in various African quarters. In 1982 Radio France Internationale was reckoned to have some 12 million listeners in Africa, and the other international stations probably have comparable or higher numbers.[18]

Information compiled outside a given country, especially when it is edited and broadcast by a radio station financed by a former colonial power, inevitably acquires a certain slant, as African information ministers and some intellectuals are not slow to point out. Moreover foreign correspondents based in Africa can have difficulty acquiring and filing stories. So, like any news media, international radio stations are liable to transmit only a partial or distorted version of the complex truth. They may make errors of judgement or fact. News producers or editors may even be prevailed upon to transmit information which has been tailored for political purposes.

These remarks on the state of modern mass communication in Africa help explain the reaction of the imaginary African who hears an intriguing rumour from a friend and who is unable to check its truth by other means even if he wishes to do so. Part of the explanation for the importance of rumour in African political life, therefore, lies in the absence of persuasive written or broadcast news. Like the *samizdat* of pre-*glasnost* Eastern Europe, rumour is of great political sensitivity as a consequence.

Governments the world over, of course, manage news as a means of political control. In this respect African governments are no different from those of other continents. However African governments, with exceptions such as Nigeria and Mauritius, exert an official control over the media which is stricter than in many other parts of the world.

This is a sensitive matter to discuss, since it has been the subject of some partisan and sometimes racist comment. African governments and intellectuals have sometimes argued that to call for press freedom is itself an example of Europe imposing its cultural values. They contend that free speech outside a circumscribed political sphere is not an African tradition. It is relevant that this argument, though not devoid of truth, is often cynically used to justify tyranny. But foreign liberals, if they go to the other extreme in championing unrestricted freedom of speech, may be guilty of ignoring some of the subtlety and sophistication of African political culture, or of underestimating the importance for Africa of maintaining political stability.

For present purposes, this argument is intended only to emphasize the fact that it is widely acknowledged that the broadcast media occupy a sensitive political space, and that the role of oral media in this regard has been less often noted.

The repression and manipulation of oral news

The political significance of this conceptual space may be gauged by the attempts made to control it.[19] Several African governments are said to employ rumour-mongers whose task is to place pro-government material in the public domain. Incidentally, my source for this is *radio trottoir.* On firmer ground, many African governments have been known to arrest people suspected of peddling rumours critical of the government, and indeed this is often regarded as a serious offence.[20]

The practice of arresting rumour-mongers on the grounds of subversion has an impressive pedigree. At least one old African law-code designated rumour-mongering as a capital offence.[21] This raises the question of how, in pre-literate Africa, governments distinguished between legitimate oral communication and unlawful rumour. The answer would appear to be: in much the same way as modern Africans distinguish between worthless rumour and important oral information, that is by reference to what is said, by whom and in what context.

All African politicians are acutely aware of the power of rumour. Their predecessors have known for centuries that this can be rendered harmless, or even useful, by carefully channelling its expression. There is a West African tradition that dissident opinions could be spoken into a gourd, where the dissident could vent his feelings without inspiring subversion.[22] A modern variant, whereby the sting is taken out of popular rumour, is that used by the government of Gabon under the name Makaya. This is taken to be the name of an imaginary common man, described as a government driver, someone who is not part of the elite but who overhears some of its secrets. Makaya is, in fact, the archetypal originator of rumours and exponent of pavement radio. The daily column published in the Gabonese daily newspaper *L'Union* is signed by the imaginary Makaya, in fact the pen-name of a senior journalist said to work in the presidency. The column is highly critical of individual ministers, and will often reproduce rumours which are currently circulating on the streets of Libreville. It is the only genuinely popular item in a turgid newspaper. It is notable however that the column never criticizes President Omar Bongo, whom it refers to as '*Le Makaya d'honneur*', implying that he, alone of all the elite, is in touch with the feelings of the man or woman in the street.[23] President Bongo uses very skilfully the populist technique of attacking the government of which he is the head, criticizing its corruption, incompetence et cetera. Thus he succeeds at a stroke both in reducing the power of popular rumour and in keeping government ministers in a semi-permanent fear of denunciation by the press. In June 1986 President Bongo took the Makaya technique still further when he unexpectedly entered a television studio for the broadcast of a programme in which government ministers are questioned by an audience. The president proceeded to humiliate the unfortunate minister of social security by asking him about his salary, his secretary's salary and the functioning of his department. Probably few Gabonese are fooled by these antics. They are aware that nothing happens in Gabon without the implicit or explicit approval of the president. Nonetheless Makaya, and his selective transmission of rumours from *radio trottoir,* is a useful political device.

Pavement radio and oral history

If popular opinion, including urban popular opinion, needs political news, it also needs history in some shape or form. Twenty-five years ago, when Western academics began to study African history in significant numbers, it was fashionable to suggest that oral histories were dying out, and that they were known only to a dying generation of old people who had access to the pre-colonial heritage. Oral history had been replaced by documentary history, just as princes and big men had been replaced by political parties. But the passage of time has demonstrated that popular oral discourse on politics, often in a highly individual form which draws on African images, continues to thrive in Africa's towns.

Pavement radio, in other words, should be seen in the light of oral tradition and treated as a descendant of the more formal oral histories and genealogies associated with ruling dynasties and national rituals. Just as those older oral histories enshrined national constitutions, with king-makers, priests or others able to pronounce upon the legitimacy of royal claims and actions, so does pavement radio, the modern equivalent, represent a populist restraint on government. This perhaps explains why pavement radio so often reports malicious stories about politicians. It is for the same reason that, in less modern communities, gossip and indeed witchcraft allegations often have an egalitarian effect, punishing individuals who threaten to become too much more powerful than their neighbours.[24] In the same way pavement radio cuts down to size politicians who are often perilously unconstrained by paper constitutions which they do not respect. For the poor and the powerless, pavement radio is a means of self-defence. At the same time, it should be noted, *radio trottoir* often expresses admiration for the enterprise and acquisitiveness of the very politicians whom it lambasts for their corruption. This paradox is also found in village politics.[25] It seems to express deeply-held attitudes towards power and wealth wherever it is encountered.

If it is true that pavement radio contains a traditional element of limiting the power of politicians and magnates, then it is likely that modern oral tradition probably contains, or itself represents, a means of remembering history. Little academic work appears to have been done on how the vibrant popular oral culture of modern times assimilates current events into history. The most scientific work available on the subject, done by teams of researchers recording rumours in Malawi in 1959, suggests that pavement radio plays an important role in cementing popular belief in certain ideas and in propagating an enduring view of important political events.[26] There are also some interesting clues as to how this may happen. Roger Koumabila-Abougué has recorded how a popular cult in eastern Gabon in the 1950s grew up around a fetish named after General de Gaulle.[27] A popular interpretation of elite politics, in this case the career of General de Gaulle, was transformed into a politically important anti-colonial movement in religious form. It is said that the late president Kwame Nkrumah is remembered in parts of northern Ghana as a mythical creature who married a water-spirit.[28] This is not only a tradition of a type quite commonly used to account for the origin of new dynasties, but may also relate to the fact that Nkrumah married an Egyptian woman, hence someone from outside the usual frame of reference in northern Ghana. It would be interesting to know how this modern remembrance relates to those stories about Nkrumah which were current in the area thirty years ago.

These last examples from Gabon and Ghana are not of recent date and come from rural areas. But they do hint at the extent to which popular oral culture, which uses pavement radio for its communication, can retain a memory of a political fact and situate it within a mythological framework in an astonishingly short time. Already, to take a more recent example, we hear that the townspeople of Conakry in Guinea do not believe that Ahmed Sékou Touré really died in 1984, but that he left power and is still living elsewhere.

All this suggests that pavement radio transmits more than just idle gossip. Even the most sensational allegations are at least revealing of popular opinion. They must be, to be repeated and considered believable. As anthropologists and politicians have always known, and as historians seem now to accept, these opinions are related in Africa to religious forms and to other quasi-mystical forms of consciousness. C. M. Toulabor's study of the government of Gnassingbé Eyadéma in Togo, for example, is an illuminating and highly original blend of documentary study and information gleaned from *radio trottoir*.[29] What makes it a work of valuable scholarship is the manner in which this is put into the context of local religious cults and the legitimation of power through religion. This is a model of how *radio trottoir* can be used intelligently by scholars. Oral history is not dead. It is alive and living in Africa.

4

RUMOUR AND POWER IN TOGO

The present article describes some of the main political events which took place in Togo in mid to late 1991, at a time when the power of President Gnassingbé Eyadéma was facing more serious opposition than at any time since his assumption of the presidency twenty-four years earlier, and examines how these events were represented in popular discussion in Lomé. By analysing some aspects of the power struggle in that period, and popular perceptions of them, the article aims to shed light on the cultural mechanisms by which Eyadéma sustained himself in power and through which his power could be contested. For, as Patrick Chabal (1992) has recently reminded us, even the presidents of one-party states seek to legitimise themselves in a variety of ways.

Until the 1990s it was difficult to acquire reliable information on the real workings of the political system in Togo, since the security forces had instilled a fear so pervasive as to discourage any discussion of politics, particularly in the capital city (Amnesty International, 1986). This situation changed dramatically during 1990–91, when the circumstances became such as to encourage intense public debate about the nature of Eyadéma's government. There was an abundance of previously unobtainable information, written and oral, describing the techniques by which he had imposed his power on the population. This period therefore constitutes an exceptional point of observation for the political analyst interested in the Togolese political system.

Without doubt the main forum for debate on these matters was the National Conference inaugurated in Lomé in July 1991, which is described in more detail below. Many of the speakers at the National Conference wrote short papers which they circulated during their presentation. Photocopies of these documents were freely available at the time, although they may well have become more difficult to acquire since. There was also published a daily summary of the conference's proceedings, at least in its early stages. It is not clear to the present writer what has become of this record or of the archives of the National Conference in general: this is a matter of regret, since they constitute a valuable first-hand source.

The work of the conference was both supplemented and encouraged by the growth of the free press, as some twenty newspapers appeared in Lomé within a few months in 1990–91, many of them weeklies or monthlies which in fact were published rather erratically. The great majority of the new papers were hostile to President Eyadéma and sympathetic to the work of the National Conference. All the papers—and, indeed, the official press, television and radio, which had been taken over by anti-Eyadéma elements—reported the proceedings of the National Conference at length, adding their own editorial comments to the quoted views of conference-goers. However, within a couple of years many of the new papers had gone out of business as a result of commercial pressures or of physical intimidation by military supporters of President Eyadéma. Thus even some of the printed information which was available during 1991 may not be easily located in future by scholars wishing to study Togo's short-lived attempt to install a democratic government.

As well as these written sources, another source of information was the form of oral communication known in French as *radio trottoir*, a term for which there is no good English equivalent but for which a poor translation would be 'bush telegraph'. It may be defined as the informal discussion of current affairs by the urban public in Africa. It has been argued elsewhere that *radio trottoir*, far from being mere gossip, and of little account, may be considered a modern form of oral tradition (Ellis, 1989). It is of considerable political importance, mainly because it appears to be the principal means by which many city dwellers in Africa acquire information. *Radio trottoir* consists not only of rumours, but also of jokes, puns and anecdotes passed on by word of mouth, and hence it is a field where ordinary citizens play an active role in forming a popular image of the government. Governments and their opponents certainly acquire information by listening to *radio trottoir*, but at the same time they seek to influence public opinion in a manner which, at bottom, is no different from the work of public relations specialists in modern Western politics. *Radio trottoir*, in other words, is a field of political contestation no less vital in its own way than the columns of the daily press or the television news to a modern Western government.

Previous authors have analysed rumours in various parts of Africa in an attempt to discern what these rumours tell us about political events (Musambachime, 1988; Kastfelt, 1989). A few writers have gone further, to analyse how rumour is formed and transmitted in Africa at a time of political tension (Bettison, 1968). Nevertheless, it is fair to say that analysts have generally tended to steer clear of *radio trottoir*, for the good reason that most of the information it conveys is impossible to check and its sources are generally impossible to verify. In fact one may go further and say that quite often rumours reported by *radio trottoir* are patently untrue, at least to the seeker of what may be called 'hard facts', meaning empirically verifiable statements.

Despite these difficulties, the rumours transmitted by word of mouth in Lomé in 1991, like other examples of *radio trottoir*, are worthy of study for the light they shed on the nature of political legitimacy and authority in Eyadéma's Togo, and the means by which they are contested.

President Eyadéma

Gnassingbé Eyadéma, born some sixty years ago in the village of Pya in north Togo, and given the Christian name Étienne, has the dubious distinction of having instigated modern Africa's first *coup d'état*.

In his youth Eyadéma followed the path of many young men from the poverty-stricken north of Togo by enlisting in the French colonial army. When the country received its independence in 1960, its first president, Sylvanus Olympio, refused to incorporate some hundreds of Togolese who had been demobilised from the French army into the national army of the new Togolese state. On the night of 12–13 January 1963 Sergeant Étienne Eyadéma (as he then was) and others discharged from the French forces attacked Olympio's residence. The President was shot dead on the morning of 13 January 1963 as he was attempting to gain asylum in the American embassy next door. Eyadéma claimed to have carried out the deed, although it remains unclear whether he actually killed President Olympio. It also remains uncertain to what extent there may have been French involvement in the affair (Agbobli, 1992).

Following the death of Olympio, Eyadéma became Togo's military strong man and was elevated to the rank of lieutenant-colonel. (His current rank of general came later). On 13 January 1967, four years to the day after the assassination of Olympio, Eyadéma declared the dissolution of the government, soon followed by his own assumption of power as head of state. In 1969 Eyadéma founded his own political party, the Rassemblement du Peuple Togolais (RPT), which was to remain the country's sole political party until 1991.

In many respects Eyadéma's conquest and consolidation of power are a classic example of how a soldier from the lower ranks, having taken power by force, may use a variety of techniques to buttress his rule in a search for the elusive quality of legitimacy. Eyadéma learned much from President Mobutu Sese Seko of Zaire, many of whose methods of control he frankly imitated and whose friend he became. Eyadéma was also an assiduous borrower of political techniques from a variety of other countries. His grip on power was backed by a vicious system of coercion and by pervasive networks of informers. The president took particular care to ensure the loyalty of his original power base, the army, which throughout his period in power has been composed mainly of soldiers from his own region. He became adept at appointing and reshuffling ministers, army officers and senior officials, keeping them loyal with promises of power and wealth interspersed with the threat of prison or worse. There can be no doubt of Eyadéma's ruthlessness even towards those who had been close to him: in 1984 his own former vice-president, Antoine Méatchi, died mysteriously while in prison. It now seems virtually certain that Méatchi was subjected to the *diète noire*, systematic deprivation of food and water until death.

Among his entourage Eyadéma was known simply as *le patron*, 'the boss'. In imitation of Mobutu, Eyadéma introduced a policy of *authenticity* in which sweeping nationalisation of key areas of the economy was accompanied by a requirement that Togolese citizens should renounce their baptismal names and assume instead authentic Togolese names, the president himself having assumed the name Gnassingbé and dropped the Christian name Étienne in 1972. By 1976 all government officials were being expected to join the ruling party and to sport its badge on their lapel, as well as to wear the correct official dress in imitation of that affected by Eyadéma (Amnesty International, 1986: 27). Eyadéma promoted as official government dress a Western business suit, double-breasted if possible. This was seen by many people as an important symbol. As one Togolese journalist wrote (Apedo-Amah, 1991):

> Eyadéma, in the 1970s, when he wanted to give himself a civilised air, following the odious murder of Olympio and to hide his characteristic as a hireling of the colonial army ('un soudard de la coloniale') introduced the business suit into the upper levels of the state apparatus. Even on television, programme presenters had to wear a jacket and tie just to introduce children's programmes! When you were a guest on a television show and you arrived without a jacket and tie there was panic in the studios ...
>
> The history of the suit used as the protocol uniform of the state is simply the will of Eyadéma to become at all costs a civilised man. Naively, he believed that manners maketh man. For him, wearing this civilian uniform which he had exchanged for military khaki is synonymous with the evolution of a primitive sergeant of the colonial army.

A most important aspect of the Eyadéma personality cult was the cultivation of religious and cultural symbols which were calculated to demonstrate to Togolese that Eyadéma was semi-divine and that his government was endowed with supernatural authority (Toulabor, 1986). Although certain aspects of the mystical side of the personality cult were evident enough to observers during the heyday of Eyadéma's rule, the general fear which his rule inspired was so extreme that it was very difficult for inquirers to compile data with which to analyse the bonds which connected ruler and ruled. Nevertheless, even at the height of Eyadéma's power it was possible for people to demonstrate their opposition to the ruling party by the use of puns, subtle parodies of official slogans and songs and general linguistic subversion (Toulabor, 1981). These forms of protest were a constant challenge to Eyadéma's dominance of both public and private expression, which is presumably why the police would sometimes punish people severely for even implied criticism of the government.

Togo, 1990–91

By late 1990 this tyrannical government was under severe pressure. Eyadéma was regarded as a leading member of the group of French-speaking heads of state who had rejected the call for multi-party democracy by President François Mitterrand at the Franco-African summit held in June 1990 at La Baule, France. Nevertheless, under pressure from the political reform movement sweeping Africa, beset by economic difficulties and popular protest, Eyadéma had been forced into a series of concessions to popular demands.

On 5 October 1990 demonstrators defied the security forces to demonstrate on behalf of a number of students who had been detained and tortured for distributing anti-government tracts. The government had for years routinely detained and tortured anyone suspected of opposition and even some who were not, apparently, suspected of any offence but who were tortured simply as a warning to others. This time there was an unprecedented popular outcry. Encouraged, opposition forces began to display greater confidence and pressed demands for institutional reform. In April 1991 the president agreed to permit the foundation of opposition political parties, a key demand, and in June 1991 he yielded to demands for the staging of a national conference, similar to those which had been held in many other French-speaking countries in Africa over the previous eighteen months. Scenting victory, members of the National Conference which was inaugurated in July 1991 promptly declared themselves as constituting a sovereign body and suspended the constitution (Conférence Nationale, 1991). They went on to establish a transitional government which would run the country until full multi-party elections could be organised in mid-1992, intending to leave the head of state, Eyadéma, as a mere cypher while the real power passed elsewhere. The conference pronounced the abolition of the ruling party, the RPT, and of its trades union arm, provoking bitter complaints from President Eyadéma, who accused the conference of going beyond its constitutional powers. On the night of 26–7 August 1991, amid high tension, and sitting in a building surrounded by hostile soldiers, the Sovereign National Conference elected as premier Maître Joseph Kokou Koffigoh, a well known lawyer and human rights activist (*Marchés Tropicaux et Méditerranéens* 2390, 30 August 1991). Some radicals even called for Eyadéma to be put on trial.

The staging of the National Conference and its bold challenge to Eyadéma had an obvious therapeutic effect on the population of Lomé and other parts of the country. Over a period of several weeks people who for years had been obliged to keep their innermost thoughts to themselves gave public testimony to the conference, the proceedings being broadcast on national radio and television. Many gave harrowing first-hand accounts of over two decades of appalling human rights abuses, including illegal detention, torture, murder and exactions at the hands of the ruling party and the army on a large scale. The fear which had been instilled for over twenty years by the president and his supporters in the army and the RPT was broken.

The conference was discussed and reported in the new independent newspapers which had appeared in Lomé during the previous two years and even in the official daily, *La Nouvelle Marche*, once staunchly pro-Eyadéma. Like the multi-party system itself, these newspapers had initially been tolerated by President Eyadéma in an attempt to make concessions to calls for greater freedom while retaining his grip on power. As so often in circumstances of this kind, the emergent press had responded not with gratitude but by asserting its complete independence of his government, often expressed in the form of strong and even insulting criticisms of the head of state (Article XIX, 1991).

However, optimists were premature in believing that they had overthrown a dictatorship and installed a democratic system of government. The situation remained very unstable. The National Conference as a whole, and some individual politicians, had support from the mob which had constituted itself since popular disturbances the previous year and had become an actor in national politics. Power in the streets of Lomé had passed from the security forces to groups of youths who demonstrated, fought the army and police with stones, and attacked police stations or symbols of one-party rule. Prime Minister Koffigoh, inexperienced in politics and without any political organisation of his own to support him, was struggling to impose his authority on the interim administration.

It also became apparent, when the first euphoria produced by the public uprising against dictatorship had evaporated, that the democratic credentials of the transitional government were not beyond question. The National Conference was not popularly elected but was composed of nearly 1,000 distinguished individuals and representatives of various lobbies and political associations. It included a disproportionate number of members from the south of Togo and a relatively small number from the north, Eyadéma's home area. The conference's assumption of sovereign status was self-proclaimed, which enabled Eyadéma and his supporters to question its legitimacy and to represent the events of July and August 1991, as a 'civilian *coup*' against a constitutional government. As Eyadéma pointed out, in law sovereignty could be delegated by the people only by universal suffrage (Eyadéma, 1991). In its haste to claim sovereign authority and to issue its own laws, in defiance of the president's authority, the National Conference may have made a tactical error, since it enabled Eyadéma to use some of the rhetoric of democracy and accountability in order to counter-attack.

To many citizens of Lomé these shortcomings were not at first apparent. In the capital city the National Conference enjoyed great popularity. This disguised the fact that its political base was insecure. When it closed at the end of August 1991 the conference haughtily proceeded to elect a *Haut Conseil de la République*, in effect a parliament which had not been popularly elected or approved by the head of state and whose status was, therefore, not beyond question.

Above all, it was unclear who really controlled the army. The army had been the mainstay of Eyadéma's power since his 1963 overthrow of Sylvanus Olympio. Although Prime Minister Koffigoh now claimed, as head of the government, to be in political control of the army, it was not obvious that the soldiers would obey him. Some three-quarters of the armed forces' estimated 12,000 men came from the president's home region in the north of Togo. Many of these soldiers could be reckoned as unconditional supporters of Eyadéma, who had habitually hand-picked new recruits during the wrestling matches which were traditionally held every year in his home region during the important festival known as *evala*. The army's officer corps contained a sprinkling of officers from every region of the country, but the most sensitive command positions were held by personal protégés of the president, including his half-brother, Colonel Donou Toyi Gnassingbé, and his son, Lieutenant Ernest Eyadéma. Soldiers had for years been subjected even more intensively than the rest of the population to the Eyadéma personality cult, supported by viciously harsh discipline. Other ranks were encouraged to believe that the brutal treatment they received from their officers was not condoned by the general, who was represented as a stern but benevolent father. As an army sergeant put it in 1991, when begging for Eyadéma to reassert his power *(West Africa* 3853, 15–21 July 1991, p. 1159):

> Our action is that of the hands of subordinate officers outstretched towards their only commander, General Eyadéma, the outstretched hands of we your sons ... toward their only father, Daddy Eyadéma, to demand their rights concerning the officers ... [who are] brutalising us, and torturing us morally and intellectually, in the name of military discipline...
>
> Please accept, without a lurking thought of revenge, the expression of these grievances, because you are our father, the only parent that loves us and listens to us with much attention.[1]

The question of who should control the army was unclear even in the legal texts published by the National Conference. The provisional constitution described the president of the republic—who also held the rank of general—as the 'chef supreme des forces armées' (supreme commander of the armed forces'). At the same time the transitional government, in which Koffigoh fulfilled the roles of prime minister and minister of defence, was said to 'dispose[r] des forces armées' ('Have the armed forces at its disposition'). Some observers wondered whether the army was simply out of control. An attempt by a group of soldiers to take over the national radio station on 1 October 1991 and an apparent attempt to assassinate Prime Minister Koffigoh one week later gave rise to varying analyses and explanations. The Haut Conseil de la République on 8 October declared itself ready in principle to

113

accept foreign military intervention in order to combat the army's reluctance to place itself under civilian control. These events demonstrated graphically that the Haut Conseil de la République, and Prime Minister Koffigoh's interim government, for all their bluster, did not have a real grip on the levers of power.

Radio trottoir in Lomé

The hopes, fears and excitement generated by these events, added to the considerable confusion which reigned, naturally encouraged rumours of every description to fly around Lomé. The newspapers were only of limited effect in checking the allegations of *radio trottoir*, since the papers themselves were all to some extent written versions of rumour in the sense that most articles were not based on quoted sources in the conventional manner of newspaper reporting.

A typical example concerned the events of 10 April 1991, when there was a series of violent clashes between crowds of pro-democracy demonstrators and elite army units. On 11 April some twenty-eight bodies were recovered from a lagoon in Be, a popular district of Lomé. A report by the Commission Nationale des Droits de l'Homme (1991b), an official human rights organisation established in 1986 by President Eyadéma but which had been taken over by anti-Eyadéma forces, maintained that the victims were mostly people who had been trapped between two army units on a causeway on the morning of 10 April, and who had jumped into the lagoon to escape. Some had drowned, and others had been beaten to death when they tried to haul themselves ashore. However, there were certain problems in the account compiled by the CNDH. According to one well-placed foreign observer who made extensive enquiries, for example, all the victims were found in the lagoon on one side of the causeway only, whereas if they had all been escaping panic-stricken, from baton-wielding soldiers, it would have been more likely that they would have escaped into the lagoon on both sides of the causeway. Moreover, the news that bodies were found floating in the lagoon did not break in Lomé until the morning of 11 April, whereas the clashes on the causeway had taken place almost twenty-four hours before. Why had the floating bodies not been in evidence immediately after the first clashes on the causeway which crosses the Be lagoon? Were the bodies in fact those of people who had been killed elsewhere, and dumped in the lagoon only on the night of 10–11 April? All that seemed clear was that something nasty had happened, and that the army was responsible one way or another for most or all of the deaths.

Every significant move by the army, such as the 1 October attack on the national radio station, or the 8 October attack on the home of Prime Minister Koffigoh, was invariably said to have been ordered by President Eyadéma in an attempt to sabotage the transitional government. Was it really so? Was this not a simplistic explanation? It had become evident during the National Conference that the army was far from monolithic and some observers even suggested that President Eyadéma might be struggling to keep control of his armed forces.

In fact any occurrence which was not in the interests of the National Conference or of the transitional government it had established was widely said to be the result of manipulation by Eyadéma. Thus any political figure who dared to suggest that it might be in the long-term interest of the country for the transitional government to come to an understanding with Eyadéma on the division of powers risked becoming the subject of rumours that he was on the presidential payroll. The baleful figure of the president dominated discussion of current events, and it could be said that this was itself a form of recognition of his continuing influence over public life.

Certain dates in the calendar also provoked a spate of rumour. It was widely suggested, for example, that some element of the armed forces would attempt a *coup* on behalf of President Eyadéma on 5 October 1991, the first anniversary of the popular demonstrations which had sounded the beginning of the end for the one-party government of Eyadéma's RPT. Another rumour, reported to the author by lower-rank soldiers who had performed guard duty at the presidential palace in Pya, maintained that President Eyadéma was in the habit of performing human sacrifices every year in his home village of Pya on 12 January, the eve of the date in 1963 when, as an obscure army sergeant, he had assassinated the then president Sylvanus Olympio and begun his climb to power. The fact that dates such as this continued to be considered significant presumably gave Eyadéma cause for satisfaction, since it meant that *radio trottoir* continued to hold the official myths of his regime in awe.

In order to counter Eyadéma's influence over the calendar, as it were, there were popular calls for the renaming of streets and buildings named after key dates or places in the career of President Eyadéma, or Sergeant Eyadéma, as his enemies persistently referred to him, in recollection of his humble origins. The Boulevard du 13 Janvier and the Hôtel du 2 Février, respectively a main avenue and the most prestigious hotel in Lomé, both commemorated dates in Eyadéma's rise to power. This struggle to control dates and names was taken so seriously that Prime Minister Koffigoh's interim government devoted attention to the subject at its first cabinet meeting, on 10 September 1991 (BBC, 1991). We may interpret this as an effort by the new government to impose its own identity on the physical space of Lomé, and hence on the psychology of its inhabitants, just as Eyadéma had done in his time.

In general, there was a widespread and spontaneous move to reject the symbols of President Eyadéma's long rule and that of the RPT. In Lomé, where many of the population are Christian, people again began using the baptismal names which had been banned when Eyadéma had introduced a policy of African authenticity in 1974.

Analysing radio trottoir

The constant flow of rumours posed a considerable problem for any observer who wished to respect the conventional techniques of social science or the usual criteria of empirical analysis. There were few clear statements from authoritative sources which could be taken as the basis of journalists' despatches or scholars' footnotes. When there was a clear such statement, as when President Eyadéma appeared on television to deny any knowledge of the military intervention of 1 and 8 October, there were obvious grounds for being sceptical about his claims, but there was no firm evidence to refute him.

People offering information by word of mouth in the form typical of *radio trottoir* almost never cited their sources with precision, and quite often they offered no empirical evidence whatsoever for a theory of causation. They simply asserted an explanation for the cause of an event with no supporting evidence. Conversations with Togolese officials, foreign diplomats and others close to power were hardly different in the sense that such people, too, frequently offered assertions as to the course of recent events without precise sources. It appeared that everybody, from the head of state downwards, both listened and contributed to *radio trottoir*. There existed, in effect, higher and lower forms of rumour which could be measured according to the closeness to power of one's interlocutor. From the point of view of using *radio trottoir* as a conventional source of information, the best that could be done was to assess the accuracy of a rumour by reference to its inherent likeliness, the status of the person reporting it, and the context in which they did so. It could then be compared with other rumours from different individuals from other social groups. Rumours repeated in front of others, who could correct the speaker, had more status than those repeated in private.

It is productive not just to attempt to glean truth from falsehood in *radio trottoir*, but to consider what it says about Togolese concepts of political authority and legitimacy. Lomé is situated in a region that has long been well known for the importance of the cult of *vodu* and for the existence of a complex belief system which supposes the constant influence of religion on the affairs of humankind and which often seeks an explanation for human events in the spirit world (Maupoil, 1943). Belief in the spirit world is not restricted to the domain which might conventionally be called religious, but is also crucial in Togolese politics (Toulabor, 1986: 110–31). Thus during 1991 there were many rumours concerning spiritual phenomena or which supposed spiritual explanations for human actions. Some people in Lomé, for example, still recalled in 1991 that dissidents who had infiltrated the country and attempted to overthrow the government five years earlier had been able to cross the border from Ghana by using magical powers to transform themselves into owls, an animal which, being a carnivore that flies by night, appears to symbolise the darker aspects of power. It is notable that, in other parts of West Africa too, people possessing power are assumed to be able to transform themselves into animals (Gilbert, 1989: 59).

Similarly, *radio trottoir* reported in October 1991 instances in which a powerful politician was able to materialise in two far-apart places at the same time. President Eyadéma seemed to play on this belief by occasionally letting it be known that he was at his presidential palace in the suburbs of Lomé, at other times in his home village of Pya. One could never be quite sure where he was. It was by the use of such techniques that Eyadéma ensured that an element of mystery remained concerning his person, and this in itself helped to bolster his power.

The identification of spiritual and political power, which appears to be at the centre of Togolese political thought, can be looked at from either side of the equation: just as a person known to have political power is presumed also to have power over the spirit world, so a person who successfully manipulates the symbols of spiritual control is assumed also to be in possession of political power. This means that the appearance of being powerful, achieved by maintaining one's prestige and manipulating the appropriate symbols, is at least as important as the possession of a legal right to control the government of the country, or some part of it. In the end, despite his legal destitution, President Eyadéma still had the appearance of power and Prime Minister Koffigoh had not. Public perception was a crucial field in which *radio trottoir* was all-important.

Material and invisible power

It is not surprising to learn that almost every foreign observer confesses to finding Togolese politics to be—if I may borrow a useful image—a wilderness of mirrors. Nothing is sure; nothing can be known precisely. Manipulation and deception are constantly suspected, and the role of what in the West might be called the supernatural is taken to be of prime importance. A powerful person is one who gives the impression of being in control of this complex array of forces visible and invisible. In this respect, it should be said, Eyadéma appeared far more convincing than Prime Minister Koffigoh. In these circumstances, many observers have wondered about the material or empirical basis of certain beliefs or events in Togo. For example, is it really true, as is sometimes whispered, that powerful politicians perform human sacrifices to maintain their power, and hold ceremonies to communicate with the spirit world? Or is it true, as some foreigners have opined, that Eyadéma's fearsome reputation has been based more on appearance than on reality, and that his prisons are not as terrible as people have sometimes supposed?

The staging of the National Conference in July and August 1991, and the events surrounding it, constituted an autopsy of power in Togo. The National Conference revealed empirically satisfactory information, in the form of first-hand testimonies and confessions in public, about the repressive techniques used by President Eyadéma and his RPT government. Such information included evidence of the detention without trial of anyone even suspected of being an opponent of the government. More sensational—and more interesting for the purposes of the present analysis—was the evidence of the number of people killed, tortured or detained for the alleged practice of witchcraft, including considerable numbers of people from the President's native village of Pya (Assih, 1991; Commission Nationale des Droits de l'Homme 1991a). Victims of apparently arbitrary or unjust imprisonment included the president's own adoptive father, who was also the traditional chief of Pya. Other victims in the president's own village included a man who had allegedly been responsible for the death of President Eyadéma's natural father by means of sorcery. Among those illegally detained was a woman who had conceived a child by President Eyadéma. She was detained together with her baby, Eyadéma's own child. There emerged evidence that some of Eyadéma's closest supporters had also used religious symbols in the pursuit of power. When a mob sacked the house in Lomé of the feared former interior minister, Kpotivi Tévi Djidjogbé Laclé, on 8 October 1991, the attackers discovered under his bed a human foetus preserved in a jar, a photograph of which subsequently appeared in a Lomé newspaper (*Courrier du Golfe* 117, Lomé, 130, 10 October 1991). This indicated that even the highest authorities in the land made use of such symbols, not just to impress the public but also in private rituals. This was not surprising to any Togolese, since it is generally believed that people in positions of power sometimes sacrifice children as a means of acquiring or preserving power. This, no doubt, was the source of the rumour circulating throughout mid-1991 that large numbers of children were disappearing. The story could be interpreted as meaning that political power had become unstable, and politicians were seeking spiritual power, by means of human sacrifice, in order to acquire or preserve temporal power. To judge from some of the things which were proved beyond reasonable doubt during the National Conference, it is quite likely that *radio trottoir* was literally true in some of these cases and that some politicians were indeed causing human sacrifice to be performed in their pursuit of power.

It became clear that popular fear of Eyadéma had a solid material foundation in the sense that he had indeed run a cruel and arbitrary system which physically threatened anyone suspected of being an opponent. It was clear too that belief in the President's powers over the spirit world was encouraged by the President himself, inasmuch as he persecuted those alleged to be using witchcraft to harm him or his government.

The public revelation of these things during the National Conference impaired Eyadéma's reputation. No Togolese had ever doubted that he was a cruel man, but laying bare some of the mechanisms of control removed the mystery, and thus part of the force, from his reputation. Power in Togo, it appears, is most awesome when it is exercised secretly. Different forms of power are connected: wealth, political control and spiritual influence all go together. Possession of one strongly implies possession of the others.

Spoken words and visible symbols

It is perhaps not surprising to know that politicians in Togo make frequent use of symbols of power, and that, in deference to the importance of spiritual belief, these symbols also have spiritual significance. Nor is it surprising to learn that sinister dictators make use of symbols which have sinister implications, presumably to cause others to fear them. After all, it may be argued, all politicians make use of symbols understood by themselves and their constituents.

However, examination of Lomé's *radio trottoir* and of the political behaviour which it reports suggests a qualitative difference between the use of symbols by modern Western politicians and their use by many Togolese politicians. In the latter case the role of the symbols is taken much more seriously, to the point where it is possible to assert that the public manipulation of relevant symbols is of overwhelming importance, as it is in many other parts of Africa (cf. Balandier, 1962, 1980; Martin, 1988: 248–81; Raison-Jourde 1991: 239–89). The successful use of the symbols of this power is not just a political tool: it is actually what politics is about.

In such a system symbols are to be found everywhere, even in everyday things such as clothes, food, drink and—above all—words. Names, for example, have very great importance in Togo. Far from representing a mere whim, the systematic substitution of new symbols for old, as in Eyadéma's authenticity campaign of the early 1970s, or as attempted by the Koffigoh government in 1991, is serious power play. In Zaire, where the policy of *authenticité* was first introduced, it was understood by many people as only one measure in a comprehensive policy designed to validate traditional symbols of power, including notably those relating to the spirit world and witchcraft (Roberts, 1988). In the same way, Eyadéma used language as a key field of political control, by obliging people to take Togolese names and naming public monuments after key events in his own life as visible symbols of his power. He borrowed at the same time many of the forms of indoctrination pioneered in Mobutu's ruling party, using the same type of *'animation politique'*, even importing songs and dances originally composed in honour of Mobutu and translating them into Togolese languages (Toulabor, 1986: 161–82).

In Lomé the public have consistently reacted to attempts to turn all public performance into a paean to the president by linguistic subversion, turning official names into obscene word play, designed to demystify and ridicule the government and the man who is officially referred to by a variety of grandiose titles (Toulabor, 1981, 1992). In the same spirit of struggle for linguistic hegemony, *radio trottoir* dubbed the stone-throwing mobs of adolescents who confronted the Eyadéma government throughout 1991 'Ekpemog', a pun on the name of the Economic Community of West African States Monitoring Group (ECOMOG), the West African peace-keeping force in Liberia. 'Ekpe' means 'stone' in the Ewe language (*Jeune Afrique* 1601, 4–10 September 1991, p. 24). The implication was that the mob constituted a legitimate national army loyal to Prime Minister Koffigoh's government, in competition with the Togolese armed forces controlled by General Eyadéma. Eyadéma's government, like many others in Africa, had deployed a vast range of acronyms, particularly those applied to the parastatal organisations which are widely and justly regarded as the reservoirs from which politicians derive their funds or, in popular parlance, where they feed (Bayart, 1989). *Radio trottoir* is immensely inventive in parodying these, and there is hardly an acronym in Togo which has not been co-opted by *radio trottoir* for subversive purposes.

Politicians the world over like to impose their own terminology on political debate, recognising by instinct, experience or deduction the Orwellian truth that language and politics are inseparable. But, as with other forms of political symbolism, the use of language in African *radio trottoir* goes further than this, for the reason that it is the product of cultures which have evolved over centuries without writing. The introduction of large-scale literacy in most of Africa dates only from the middle years of the present century, and it has neither wiped out illiteracy nor, more to the point, eliminated the cultural patterns and mechanisms formed during the times before writing was known or widely used.

It is evident that in oral societies the spoken word has a quite different value from that which it has in literate ones. Such cultures are far more subtle and inventive in the use of the spoken word than are long-literate cultures. Quite apart from any subjective or ideological values which may be attributed to spoken language, it has to serve a variety of uses which in modern societies are fulfilled by writing. Law, history and genealogies cannot be written but can only be remembered. Nevertheless, as Jan Vansina pointed out in his pioneering work on oral history, considerable use can be made of mnemonics, physical devices to aid memory (Vansina 1973: 36–9). In pre-colonial Africa oratory, politics and religion all intertwined, not least because politics in an oral culture require a far more intensive use of symbols to preserve an orderly system of laws and a constitution.

The words and symbols which constitute the basic political vocabulary of Lomé are also the vocabulary of *radio trottoir*. The latter is thus a crucial element in the interplay of forces between state and civil society, or an element of the politics from below described by Bayart *et al.* (1992). It was here, rather than on the official level of written laws or paper constitutions, that Eyadéma sought to find legitimacy with the general public in a city in which the president he had overthrown and murdered, Sylvanus Olympio, had been popular.

In analysing Eyadéma's grasp of power, one is constantly put in mind of Shakespeare's *Macbeth*. There is a direct relation between the exceptionally crude manner in which Eyadéma first assumed power and the lengths to which he was obliged to go to create a myth of his own legitimacy. To cast doubt on that myth was to cast doubt on the regime itself in a manner which could be interpreted only as a direct challenge for power.

References

Agbobli, A.K. 1992. *Sylvanus Olympio: un destin tragique.* Dakar: Nouvelles Editions Africaines.

Amnesty International. 1986. *Togo: political imprisonment and torture.* London: Amnesty International.

———— 1992. *Togo: impunity for human rights violators at a time of reform.* London: Amnesty International.

Apedo-Amah, A.T. 1991. 'Attention à la barrière du protocole', *Tribune des Démocrates* (Lomé) 28, 1 October.

Article XIX. 1991. *Truth from below: the emergent press in Africa.* London: Article XIX.

Assih, 1991. Presentation to the National Conference, Lomé. Unpublished manuscript, July.

Balandier, G. 1962. 'Les mythes politiques de colonisation et de décolonisation en Afrique', *Cahiers Internationaux de Sociologie* xxxiii. 85–96.

———— 1980. *Le pouvoir sur scènes.* Paris: Balland.

Bayart, J.F. 1989. *L'État en Afrique: la politique du ventre.* Paris: Fayard.

Bayart, J.F., Mbembe, A. and Toulabor, C. 1992. *Le politique par le bas en Afrique noire.* Paris: Karthala.

Bettison, D. 1968. 'Rumour under conditions of charismatic leadership and racial political tension', *African Social Research* VI, 413–62.

British Broadcasting Corporation. 1991. *Summary of World Broadcasts* 13 September. London: BBC.

Chabal, P. 1992. *Power in Africa: an essay in political interpretation.* London: Macmillan.

Commission Nationale des Droits de l'Homme. 1991a. 'Rapport de Mission d'Investigation des Déportés de Mandouri', 6 March, Lomé: CNDH.

———— 1991b. 'Proces-verbal d'enquête, d'avis et de recommandations', 16 July. Lomé: CNDH.

Conférence Nationale Souveraine. 1991. Acte No. 1, 16 July.

Ellis, S. 1989. 'Tuning in to pavement radio', *African Affairs* 88 (352), 321–30.

Eyadéma, G. 1991. Letter to Monsignor Kpodzroh, Chairman of the National Conference, 8 August, in British Broadcasting Corporation, *Summary of World Broadcasts*, 16 August. London: BBC.

Gilbert, M. 1989. 'Sources of power in Akuropon-Akuapem: ambiguity in classification', in Arens, W., and Karp, I. (eds.), *Creativity of Power.* Washington, D.C., and London: Smithsonian Scholarly Press.

Kastfelt, N. 1989. 'Rumours of Maitatsine: a note on political culture in northern Nigeria', *African Affairs* 88, 83–90.

Martin, D.C. 1988. *Tanzanie: l'invention d'une culture politique.* Paris: Presses de la Fondation nationale des sciences politiques/Karthala.

Maupoil, B. 1943. *La géomancie à l'ancienne Côte des Esclaves.* Paris: Institut d'Ethnologie.

Musambachime, M. 1988. 'The impact of rumour: the case of the Banyama (vampire men) scare in Northern Rhodesia, 1930–64', *International Journal of African Historical Studies* XXI (ii), 201–15.

Raison-Jourde, F. 1991. *Bible et pouvoir à Madagascar au XIXe siècle.* Paris: Karthala.

Roberts, A. 1988. 'L'"authenticité", l'"aliénation" et l'homicide: une étude sur le processus social dans les zones rurales du Zaire', in B. Jewsiewicki and H. Moniot (eds.), *Dialoguer avec le léopard?* Paris and Quebec: L'Harmattan and Safi.

Toulabor, C. 1981. 'Jeu de mots, jeu de vilains. Lexique de la dérision politique au Togo', *Politique africaine* 3, 55–71.

———— 1986. *Le Togo sous Eyadéma.* Paris: Karthala.

———— 1992. 'La dérision politique d'hier et aujourd'hui au Togo'. Unpublished manuscript.

Vansina, J. 1973. *Oral Tradition.* Harmondsworth: Penguin Books.

Acknowledgements

I am grateful to my colleagues Wim van Binsbergen and Rijk van Dijk for comments on an earlier version of this article, as well as to Murray Last for his editorial guidance.

Abstract

The article describes some of the main political events which took place in Togo in mid to late 1991, at a time when the power of President Gnassingbé Eyadéma was facing more serious opposition than at any time since his assumption of the presidency twenty-four years earlier, and examines how these events were represented in popular discussion in Lomé. By analysing some aspects of the power struggle in that period, and popular perceptions of them, the article aims to shed light on the cultural mechanisms by which Eyadéma sustained himself in power and through which his power could be contested.

5

VIOLENCE AND HISTORY

A RESPONSE TO THANDIKA MKANDAWIRE

Introduction

Last year, Thandika Mkandawire (2002) published an article in the *Journal of Modern African Studies* proposing 'an explanation of the violence against the peasantry' in Africa, referring to people in rural areas who have suffered so much in recent wars across the continent. The article starts by categorising suggestions made by some other authors as to why combatants have used 'extremely brutal and spiteful forms of violence' in such a disturbing number of cases. In the opening section of his paper, Mkandawire takes exception to suggestions I have made concerning the antecedents of the 1990s civil war in Liberia, describing my views as 'essentialist' and 'poorly veiled racist', and alleging that I believe 'there is something fundamentally wrong with African culture' (2002: 183).

These tags are inaccurate to designate my own views on the matters he refers to, which I will shortly describe in more detail. Nowhere in the text that he so dislikes do I actually refer to either race or 'African culture'. 'Culture' I take to be the meanings, changing over time, that are generally attributed in a given community to repertoires of action. I do believe that culture in this sense is a concept that can be used for analytical purposes; it should, like other analytical instruments, be handled with precision. In my view, there can never be anything fundamentally 'wrong' with any cultural pattern, although the political use that is made of certain widely held ideas may be deleterious in any part of the world. The idea that distinct, definable, homogeneous cultures exist is inaccurate. Similarly, 'race' is a social construct—not a biological category—that I have never used. As for an 'essentialist' argument, if, as Mkandawire suggests, it is the assertion that a given group of people have 'culturally encoded genes', which cause them to commit 'atrocious acts', then my arguments do not belong in that category either.

It is not necessary to invoke genetics to explain how patterns of behaviour that have occurred in the past may be reflected in any given society or community. All societies transmit such coded historical knowledge. They do it largely through institutions that transcend the life-span of individual generations—states, for example—which impose on people particular forms of action that can gain widespread social currency. These socially recognised forms of action, although evolving over time, inevitably reflect ideas and practices that were current in the past. Historical patterns of behaviour are inculcated in every child through education, whether formal or informal, through rituals and games, and through learned behaviour in the broadest sense. The mode of transmission may be written documents, but also stories told by word of mouth, moral injunctions, and forms of behaviour that people, through social contact, learn are expected of them. Such knowledge, derived from historical precedents, can also be transmitted through objects that are vested with meaning, such as flags, buildings, religious artefacts, and even landscape. Although nowhere in the paper that Mkandawire criticises do I refer to 'Liberian culture' or 'African culture', as he suggests I do, I would indeed say that all historical knowledge is transmitted in culturally coded form.

My views on these matters are contained not only in the paper on the Liberian civil war (Ellis 1998) that Mkandawire has referred to, but also in a full-length book that, curiously, he has not cited (Ellis 1999). Briefly, my argument is that the civil war in Liberia, or at least the phase of it that lasted from 1989 to 1997, was about money, power and revenge, like most wars. Its causes were complex. But the war was not inevitable, in the sense that its most immediate cause was the greed, miscalculation, insouciance or ruthlessness of various key players including (in alphabetical order) James Baker III, George Bush Senior, Samuel Doe, Moammar Gadaffi, Félix Houphouët-Boigny and Charles Taylor. There was an unusual conjuncture of events that a religious believer might attribute to the hand of God, a conspiracy-theorist to some fiendish plot, and many readers of academic books might regard as bad luck or coincidence—most notably the fact that in August 1990, at the very climax of an uprising against the Liberian president Samuel Doe, Iraq invaded Kuwait, thus diverting the attention of the US government and some other key players, and changing the whole context of the Liberian struggle.

The prime aim of my book *The Mask of Anarchy* was not, however, to examine the causes of the Liberian war, but rather to explain why the violence took certain distinctive forms. Consideration of this question I believe provides an insight into the historical experience of Liberians over a long period. One of the most penetrating writers on violence, the philosopher Walter Benjamin (1986: 284), considers that a failure to consider the moral and historical aspects of violence deprives any specific act of violence of its meaning, and beyond this it prevents the possibility of detecting 'any meaning in reality itself, which cannot be constituted if "action" is removed from its sphere'.

I suggest that the method I have used to analyse the violence of the Liberian civil war could be usefully applied to any violent situation in any part of the world. This could include not only large-scale armed conflict but also, for example, distinctive patterns of 'private' violence, such as that within families. Accordingly, I will first consider Mkandawire's suggestion as to why particular forms of violence occur in African wars, explaining why it is generally unsatisfactory, after which I will consider an alternative method for examining the question of large-scale violence in Africa, one broadly similar to that used in my study of the Liberian war.

City and country

After introducing his paper, Mkandawire moves on to advance his own suggestion as to why so many armed movements in Africa in recent years have tended towards extreme violence. In brief, he argues that many armed opposition movements in Africa have been organised or supported by people from cities. Usually, their aim is to capture control of the state, whose nerve-centre is located in the capital city. But the balance of military power is such that they are generally unable to wage a successful campaign of urban guerrilla warfare. Armed opposition groups of this sort are therefore forced to retreat to the countryside. There, they may have difficulty attracting peasants to their cause. The reason for this is that peasants in Africa, although massively exploited, generally through the mechanism of markets, are at least in possession of the means of production, namely land and labour. Almost nowhere in Africa are peasants oppressed by a landlord class, as they are in some other parts of the world. Although African peasants often take evasive action of various sorts against the state, this tends to fall short of armed insurrection. Hence, rebels find it difficult to generate enough support among the peasantry to mount a Maoist-style, rural-based, guerrilla campaign. 'Retreating to the countryside', as Mkandawire (2002: 181) puts it, 'rebels can rarely swim among the peasantry like Mao's fishes in the sea'. Consequently, often being unable to develop a permanent rural base where they can live in a relationship of symbiosis with the peasantry, rebels may be forced constantly on the move, living from predation. According to an observation made by some analysts of warlords in Chinese history, 'stationary' and 'roving' bandits have very different relations with the peasants whom they move among. 'Stationary bandits are dependent on the prosperity of the communities that they inhabit, and will therefore adopt measures that facilitate such prosperity ... Roving bandits, in contrast, are constantly on the move ... They thus tend to be extremely predatory and destructive' (2002: 199–200). Among the factors that tend to induce rebel movements in Africa to adopt a roving nature are their 'urban origins and agendas'; 'their ideological fuzziness and leadership problems'; the fact that their agendas often do not correspond with those of rural societies; and 'the extreme ethnic fragmentation of the African countryside' (2002: 200). Mkandawire points out that these are broad generalisations, and are therefore not absolutely accurate. Even the most disciplined rebel groups may at times roam the countryside and become predatory, while, by the same token, even essentially roving groups may at times stay in one place and develop some sort of relationship with the peasants they live among.

Mkandawire's explanation for the type of violence used in African wars is unsatisfactory on several counts. Most obviously, the distinction he makes between rural and urban populations, even making allowance for the degree of imprecision inevitable in almost any general statement about a whole continent, does not fit the empirical evidence closely enough to have any explanatory power. For example, some analysts might think that the first of Africa's postcolonial rebel movements to show a consistent pattern of atrocious violence was RENAMO in Mozambique (Vines 1991: 1), and yet this was almost entirely a rural movement. It appears that few of its foot-soldiers or even its leaders had lived for long periods in cities before they became caught up in war. Similarly, one of the most vicious rebel or bandit groups in operation today, the Lord's Resistance Army in northern Uganda, is also a rural movement.

Other movements particularly notorious for their brutality, such as the Revolutionary United Front (RUF) in Sierra Leone and the various warlord armies in Liberia during the 1990s, were probably more complex from a sociological point of view. It has been established that some of the founders of the RUF had been influenced by quasi-Marxist and pan- Africanist ideas current among Freetown-based intellectuals in the 1980s (Abdullah & Muana 1998: 174–6), although very few members of pan-Africanist radical movements actually joined the RUF. During the first stage of its insurrection, the RUF relied heavily on mercenaries or other professional fighters from Liberia and Burkina Faso. No thorough analysis has been made of who precisely the RUF's foot-soldiers and field commanders were, but the available evidence suggests they included both unemployed youths of urban origin, whom some analysts refer to as 'lumpens' (1998), and large numbers of disenchanted youth from rural areas. Quite a few of these were abducted from small towns and villages rather than being volunteers. Others were recruited while they were working as labourers in the diamond fields. Sierra Leone is rather a small country, offering limited possibilities for an armed group to range over wide areas: some districts were subjected to hit-and-run raids, but others were under more or less continuous RUF control for considerable periods of time; the RUF had a simple but efficient command structure based on territorial units. In short, the RUF cannot be accurately described either as an urban movement forced into the countryside or as a collection of 'roving' bandits.[1]

In regard to the Liberian war, when this began in 1989, the invading National Patriotic Front of Liberia (NPFL) was sponsored by a number of professional politicians, who organised its financing and weapons supplies, and supported the fighters in the crucial sectors of diplomacy and propaganda. Its actual field commanders were mostly former professional soldiers like Prince Johnson, Elmer Johnson (no relation) and others trained in Burkina Faso and Libya. Elmer Johnson could accurately be described as an urban intellectual, since he had a degree from Boston University in the USA. Prince Johnson, although coming from a poor rural family, had been raised by an uncle in Monrovia. In any event, the NPFL's core of professional fighters was small.[2] Most of its combatants were rural youths who rallied to the cause. There is every reason to believe the description of the first phase of the war given by Charles Taylor, who was to emerge as the undisputed leader of the NPFL during the course of 1990, when he said that 'As the NPFL came in we didn't even have to act. People came to us and said "Give me a gun. How can I kill the man who killed my mother?"' (Berkeley 1993: 54).

This was the situation of the NPFL during the first year of the Liberian war, which was exactly the period that the international press paid particularly close attention to it, establishing its media reputation as a war of exceptional brutality. Although Western journalists often gave particularly lurid descriptions of the violence they witnessed, and were fascinated by the unusual costumes of many fighters, many West African observers also regarded the war as extraordinarily brutal (e.g. Brehun 1991). Probably 10–15,000 people were killed in the first year of Liberia's war, the vast majority of them non-combatants. Many atrocities were committed by people intent on taking revenge on the government of Samuel Doe. Thousands of Krahn and Mandingo people, considered to be Doe supporters *en masse,* were massacred, even when they were not suspected of having personally worked with the Doe government, on account of their ethnic identity alone. The NPFL fighters who committed many of these atrocities were, at that early stage of the war, subject to very little hierarchical organisation and had had little or no training. The great majority of them were not professional fighters but simply ordinary young men and women, mostly from the rural areas of Nimba County, doing what they believed was right. By the same token, Doe's armed forces also launched ethnic massacres. In the latter case, the victims were Gio and Mano people considered guilty by association with the rebels. Doe's forces, however, had a well-deserved reputation as hardened killers. Many of them had received US and Israeli training, and these professionals were joined by '1990 soldiers', mostly Krahn and Mandingo youths and men who joined up to protect their communities and take revenge for NPFL massacres. After 1990, the original two protagonists, the Doe forces and the NPFL, were to evolve and spawn new militias. The NPFL became much better organised. Although there has been no sophisticated analysis of who exactly composed the numerous warlord armies that emerged in Liberia later in the 1990s, it is clear that they cannot be easily categorised as either urban or rural, nor as stationary or roving. All of them aimed to control a core territory and to derive income from it. All of them were intent on economic exploitation, ranging from individual looting to sophisticated deals with specialist operators, such as foreign firms and professional import-export traders. African, American, Asian, European and Middle Eastern companies or individuals all participated in the war economy in this way (Ellis 1999: 164–80).

These examples from Mozambique, Uganda, Sierra Leone and Liberia could be supplemented by reference to other armed conflicts. Taking into account the literature on armed groups or guerrilla armies in Africa,[3] one could perhaps generalise by saying that it is probable that many rebel groups operating in recent years have been composed of people from both city and village or, more likely, of people who have spent much of their lives in between the two and cannot be easily described as either city people or village people. Some movements are led by people who cannot be accurately regarded as having an urban background. In other cases, it may be that the political representatives of a rebel movement tend to have a different background from field commanders. Again referring to cases from across the continent, it is inaccurate to say, as Mkandawire (2002: 193) does, that 'there are no urban guerrilla movements in Africa in the sense of movements whose fighting terrain is urban'. Bangui, Brazzaville, Bujumbura, Freetown, Kigali, Monrovia and Mogadishu are all capital cities that witnessed pitched battles in the 1990s, as Ndjamena did a decade earlier. Kinshasa has been the scene of massive looting more than once. Provincial cities like Huambo, Hargeisa and Kisingani have also suffered major bombardments. Koidu, the diamond capital of Sierra Leone, was entirely destroyed in the late 1990s. The relationship between cities and their hinterlands in time of war seems to be complex. The leading researcher on successive campaigns in Brazzaville, for example, detects a shift in the pattern of violence between 1994, when combatants were overwhelmingly inhabitants of the city itself, and later bouts in 1998–9, when many were of provincial origin (Bazenguissa-Ganga 1999: 52–4). Fighters from Brazzaville itself, he notes, often sent looted goods to their villages of family origin with a view to preparing a place of refuge in case they had to withdraw to the countryside, while provincial youths were readier to inflict wanton damage on the capital city. The twin city of Kinshasa, also the capital of a war-ravaged country, has, on the other hand, been remarkably unscathed since the start of the current war in the Democratic Republic of Congo in 1996.

In Angola, Liberia, Sierra Leone and doubtless some other war-torn countries, one of the most notable long-term effects of war has been to drain population from the rural areas as people move in search of safety. Other than crossing the nearest international border and becoming refugees according to international law, many people head for the capital city and acquire the unenviable status of 'internally displaced people' (IDPs). This has led to Luanda, Monrovia and Freetown, the respective capitals of these three countries, becoming massively overcrowded as people displaced from rural areas struggle to survive in what may easily turn into a permanent new home in a city shanty-town. It also has the effect of damaging agricultural production but tends to suck in food aid given by humanitarian organisations, which thus become players in the struggle (Duffield 2001). It would be useful to consider at more length the political economy of this pattern, although that is an ambition beyond the scope of the present article. In heading for the capital city of a country like Angola, Liberia or Sierra Leone, many displaced country-dwellers are heading for the places that are home to the very elites who have been complicit in draining the provinces of their wealth over a long period of time. In all three countries, these same ruling elites, although by no means solely responsible for the violence in the rural areas, manipulate that violence in such a way as to derive benefit from it. Moreover, this pattern seems quite old, and not surprisingly there is evidence that rural people often have a highly ambiguous attitude towards their capital city, which they regard simultaneously as an attractive place but also as a source of corruption and exploitation on which, in circumstances of war, they may take revenge by destroying buildings and plundering what country people feel to be rightfully theirs. This was certainly the case in Monrovia in 1990 and Brazzaville in 1998–9, and almost certainly also in Freetown in 1999.

In short, the sharp rural–urban division posited by Mkandawire does not conform to the available evidence, either in terms of the composition of rebel movements or in the patterns of violence and exploitation. Probably one of the main reasons for this is the complexity of the relations between people living in cities and rural areas generally. There is a vast literature suggesting that many people in Africa move between town and country throughout their lives, and that even confirmed city-dwellers retain complex economic and moral relations with the villages that they regard as their ultimate place of origin, perhaps retaining a claim to ownership of land there and aspiring to build a house and be buried in their ancestral home (cf. Bayart *et al.* 2001). In many respects people bring a village style of living to the cities. Investigation of the complexity of these relationships could eventually produce a more satisfactory sociological model of the urban–rural relationship in situations of war. However, even if such a model were to be developed, it may supply only limited evidence as to why the violence used by fighters sometimes seems so extreme or gratuitous. Violence is a subject sufficiently complex, and pervasive, as to defy understanding in any single dimension.

The context of violence

'The phrase "senseless violence" is a peculiarly empty piece of huffing and puffing', according to Noel Malcolm, a historian of the Balkans.

'However repugnant violence may be, the one thing it is not is senseless' (quoted in Blok 2000: 24). According to Anton Blok (2000), reputed for his work on the Sicilian mafia and one of a number of scholars currently attempting to investigate the meanings that people attribute to violence that they themselves perpetrate, of which they are victims, or which they observe, violence may be considered 'as a changing form of interaction and communication, as a historically developed cultural form of *meaningful* action'. For this reason, he suggests, it is important to study violence in its particular context, 'as a historically developed cultural form or construction' (2000: 26). In brief, he suggests that if we wish to study the meaning of a particular act of violence, we must first consider it in the context in which it occurs, since a given act may have a quite different meaning in one time or place than in another. Part of the process of setting an event in context is to examine its antecedents, to see whether it resembles earlier acts or at least is connected to them in some way. Indeed, it seems quite likely that many major acts of violence are committed in imitation of earlier such acts. An obvious example of this concerns modern armies that are in a permanent state of training, generally aiming to perfect techniques of inflicting violence that have been learned from earlier wars, or that have been developed with earlier wars serving as a relevant precedent.

A similar element of imitation may also be present in many acts even of violence that are not organised by a state. As I write, I have on my desk an essay reviewing some recent research on the ghastly subject of lynching in modern American history, which has become the subject of renewed popular attention largely as a result of an exhibition of photographs organised by the New York Historical Society in 2001, currently on display in Atlanta, Georgia (Lewis 2002). Lynching derives its name from one Charles Lynch of Chestnut Hill, Virginia, a justice of the peace during the period of the American revolution who was known for his support of summary executions of supporters of the British monarchy. It may be distinguished from other forms of murder and mob violence by a number of specific characteristics related to the identity of actors and victims and the almost ritual sequence of events. In its early period, lynching was not confined to the southern states of the USA, nor was it directed especially against black people. In fact, we are told, ' protected by masters whose community standing generally could not be challenged, slaves had been virtually immune to the sanctions of avenging mobs in the Old South' (2002: 27). During the first half of the nineteenth century, lynching was often considered to be an American virtue, a form of communal justice meted out to outlaws by rugged frontiersmen. This changed after the civil war of 1861–5 and the abolition of slavery. It was during the restoration of white supremacy in the southern states in a new form after about 1880 that lynching gained the character that has since become so notorious, an appallingly cruel form of mob violence directed especially against black men, most particularly those accused of raping white women. An informed estimate is that some 3,400 blacks and 1,300 whites were deprived of life without due process in the US between 1880 and 1945 (Lewis 2002). While lynching had died out by the 1960s and the era of civil rights, it has left a powerful memory, particularly among African Americans. When Clarence Thomas, a black lawyer proposed by the administration as a candidate for membership of the US Supreme Court in 1991, was subject to particularly hostile questioning by the Senate judiciary committee before confirmation in his post, his most memorable riposte was to accuse his tormentors of perpetrating 'a high-tech lynching'.[4]

Situating lynching in its historical context is certainly not the only useful way of analysing this practice, but it is one of the most useful for anyone whose interest is in detecting the 'meaning' of lynching in the sense of discovering why people did it and what messages they intended to send, and to whom. In its best-known form, it was clearly used as a way of maintaining a social and political order based on subjugation by reference to skin colour in the southern states after the legal abolition of slavery. In this respect, the element of communication conveyed by such an action is of crucial importance, since a similar series of actions carried out in another time and place might carry a quite different significance. Many societies experience killings carried out without due process, sometimes by mobs; not all such episodes of extreme mob violence, however, convey the same message as lynching. For example, a mob in a South African township killing a suspected government informer in the apartheid period, by the form known as 'necklacing', also conveyed a strong message, but of a radically different sort. As Whitehead (2002: 192) observes:

Violence sometimes appears both appropriate and valuable, and is not necessarily understood as dysfunctional and pathological. Accordingly, even careful analyses of Western forms of violence, such as of the Nazi genocide, are not necessarily relevant to the understanding of postcolonial ethnic violence, such as the genocides in Rwanda and Cambodia, precisely because 'genocide' is there mediated through cultural forms with which Westerners are often unfamiliar.

Moreover, the history of lynching illustrates another important principle, concerning the ways in which knowledge of past events can be transmitted from one generation to another, even in the absence of an official institution ensuring such continuity through policy. Lynching was essentially unofficial, even if people holding state office may have participated or allowed it to occur, and it could be perpetuated by informal means even in such a highly developed state as the USA in the twentieth century. The ring-leaders who organised a particular lynching were people who had seen earlier atrocities of the same type, or who had heard or read about them, and were sufficiently aware of what was involved as to give the practice a degree of consistency over time, in spite of its lack of any legal basis.

My own research on violence in Liberia in the 1990s follows a broadly similar approach to what I have suggested about the study of lynching. For that reason, my book on the subject is divided into two quite distinct parts. The first of these is a short history of the Liberian civil war considered as having lasted from 1989 to 1997. The purpose of this section is to situate the mass violence of those years in their political context, which includes, most importantly, its international aspect. Briefly, I describe how deeply Liberia was associated with the USA, having been founded by African American settlers, eventually becoming, in effect although not in law, a US protectorate. It developed a system of government dominated by an elite of settler families living in Monrovia and a handful of other coastal cities. Over time, the settlers extended their influence into the hinterland, developing in the process extensive networks of patronage that reached their greatest extent under the presidency of William Tubman (1944–71), who benefitted from US support and received a substantial income in the form of royalties from foreign mining and agricultural firms. This system began to disintegrate by degrees from the mid-1970s for a variety of reasons, but largely because of changes in the international situation. A military coup in 1980 led to the establishment of a military dictatorship under Samuel Doe, who, in the final phase of the Cold War, received massive financial and security assistance from the USA. When Doe was attacked by a small group of opponents armed and supported by foreign powers, however, he was abruptly dropped by his former patron, the USA, which no longer regarded Liberia as a strategic asset after 1989. The dramatic shift in the balance of power was a main factor in turning the anti-Doe rising into a full-scale civil war. In retrospect, the Liberian emergency was the start of a period of disturbance throughout West Africa that was to lead to war in Sierra Leone and Guinea, and has had an influence on Côte d'Ivoire. Although my book is not primarily concerned with investigating the causes of the Liberian war, these would certainly include the consequences of using government administration and development as a means of individual accumulation (Ellis 1999: 47, 188); social upheaval following a century of rapid and profound change (297) and modernisation (218); the effects of elite political rivalries throughout the West African region and further afield, even in Libya, Europe and the USA (66f); and the activities of foreign firms prepared to make alliances with various rival factions for purposes of their own (Ellis 1999: ch 4).

The second section of the book examines some of the most striking acts of violence, including those that struck many foreigners as particularly odd or otherwise seeming to defy explanation. These include the practice of male fighters dressing in women's clothing, which was not itself a violent act but was often done by fighters preparing for battle; certain forms of mutilation; and documented episodes of fighters eating human flesh. It was not only Western journalists in search of sensation who noticed the latter. For example, a Nigerian officer serving with the ECOMOG intervention force recalled how 'it was not unheard of to see fighters catch a member of an opposing side, especially key personalities, kill and butcher the chest, extract the heart and later eat it, either in cooked or roasted form' (Nass 2000: 157). The same officer also recorded the use of human body parts for what he called 'a wide variety of funny uses' (2000: 158).

Reference to earlier literature shows that these and other patterns of violence in Liberia that seem most in need of explanation had identifiable antecedents, and ones that seem particularly rich in meaning. For example, transvestite dressing is a feature of the transition to adulthood in the rituals of the most widespread initiation societies in Liberia, essentially indicating the perception that a child entering adulthood goes through a dangerous indeterminate zone between male and female identity before finally being confirmed as an adult (cf. Bledsoe 1984: esp. 462–4). Liberians, even those who have never been initiated into one of the traditional societies, are familiar with the symbolism employed by these sodalities, which is shared in many masquerades and popular entertainments. For a young man to dress as a woman at moments when violence is in the air is tantamount to carrying a sign saying 'Look out, I am dangerous' (cf. Moran 1995). One could compare this with the behaviour of English football hooligans in the 1980s; these did not dress in women's clothing, but, on the contrary, used to sport military-style cropped haircuts and boots, often calling themselves an 'army' or a 'squad', thus displaying symbols of martial status and aggressiveness that everyone in their society would recognise. This is comparable with the fighters of the Liberian war in that both were using a widely understood symbolic language to make a point about what they were doing: looking dangerous. Other aspects of the Liberian violence also had clear antecedents in the rituals of the initiation societies that were the mainstays of public order in much of Liberia in pre-republican times and that survived, often in radically altered form, throughout the twentieth century.

The point of tracing these antecedents is to attempt to identify the meaning that Liberians attribute to such acts. In short, I find that some of the most extreme violence of the Liberian war refers to a range of symbols concerning power that are widely understood and historically rooted. The argument is not that Liberia is going backwards in time—which is impossible—nor that Liberians are inherently worse than other people, nor that the violence was some form of religious ritual. It is not an argument that Liberia's culture or cultures are dysfunctional. Nor is it an argument that all the violence in Liberia was traditional, since some of the dramaturgy was clearly copied from Hollywood videos. The main conclusion to be drawn from the finding that some of the violent actions committed in the war bore a distinct similarity to violence committed, or at least suggested, in religious contexts is that there has existed over a considerable period of time a repertoire of action associated with the idea of acquiring power that is widely understood, and that fighters used this repertoire. The fact that many of these actions were terrifying to others served the fighters' purpose. Armies always act in a way that they hope will intimidate others.

One can draw further conclusions from this finding, for it indicates how patterns of religious and political authority have changed in Liberia during the twentieth century. One of the interests of any civil war, from an analytical point of view, is that it offers an exceptional position from which to observe society. A civil war occurs when a society is torn in pieces. It always shows in vivid relief social and political cleavages that may have existed for decades previously but that had not always been easy to perceive. As in many civil wars, in Liberia, once hostilities had begun, individuals also used the circumstances to settle personal scores on a large scale (Ellis 1999: 129). At various stages of the war this inspired ethnic pogroms against specific groups (1999: 74, 86, 92–3, 216). This itself does not tell us much about why the war happened, but it does tell us a great deal about the history of Liberia since the nineteenth century, the nature of the accommodation between Americo-Liberian elites and hinterland peoples, changes in the distribution of power and so on. In so doing, it provides an archaeology of Liberia.

Who are Africa's rebels?

Trying to discover what people think they are doing when they perform acts of violence is by no means incompatible with using the disciplines of social science to anyalse the broader forces affecting their lives. However, the insights of social science are less compelling than they once seemed, for a variety of reasons. Over the last three or four decades, a number of factors have combined to cause a loss of confidence in the ability of social science to offer explanations in terms that are universally valid. Such factors include the failure of social science, in the form of modernisation theory, to offer a reliable guide for policy-makers intent on developing countries they regarded as 'backward', 'underdeveloped' or 'traditional' (to use the vocabulary of the mid-twentieth century). The failure of modernisation theory has been more marked in Africa, on the whole, than in any other continent. Some thinkers have reacted to this and other shortcomings of a broad range of theories offered by social science during the last century by embracing postmodernist approaches that are suspicious of any attempt to articulate universally valid propositions. Others continue to use older methodologies despite the weaknesses that, in the opinion of the Cameroonian intellectual Achille Mbembe (2001: 7), for example, 'have undermined the very possibility of understanding African economic and political facts'.

A creeping lack of confidence among social scientists as to whether they can really provide universally applicable explanations makes it all the more important not to ignore people's own understanding of why they act. In my view, this is best done not from a sense of despair—which may be caused by a perception that understanding general causes is impossible—but in a more positive frame of mind, open to new insights, with a view to adapting older models of social science to accommodate data obtained from a broader study of human histories than was customary in the earlier twentieth century. For this reason it seems rather foolish to call local ideas 'false consciousness' or 'ideological fuzziness' (Mkandawire 2002: 190) without further investigation. What appears most desirable is a two-step approach that consists, first, in understanding local ideas in their own context, and only then considering the light such ideas may throw on established models of behaviour known to the social sciences. Hence, it is persuasive to argue, as Neil Whitehead (2002: 192) does, that 'Thinking of violence as a cultural form reveals that violence is often engendered not simply by adherence to globalised ideologies such as Christianity, Liberal Democracy, Communism or Islam, but through the regional and subregional disputes whose origins are in the complexities of local political history and cultural practices.'

Thus, the ultimate purpose of paying attention to historical patterns of violence in each case, rather than immediately attempting to fit it into models developed from a social science based on Western precepts, is to understand variations better than we are equipped to do at present. Far from implying that cultures are homogeneous and unchanging ensembles, condemned to misunderstand each other for ever, this approach implies a renewal of the tradition of social science as an attempt to reach a general understanding of humans and their actions.

It may be that, as the colonial period fades into history, a growing number of countries once colonised by Europe, or obliged to adopt institutions of governance in imitation of European models, will adopt institutions and codes of behaviour that have roots in their own precolonial history. This has already become a vital area of intellectual and political contestation. Thus, there are politicians and influential academics who claim that certain types of belief and behaviour are proper to particular cultures only. Some, of whom Samuel Huntington (1996) is the most notorious, claim, by this token, that the world consists of major cultural blocs that would be well advised to keep their distance from each other. There are governments, as in Malaysia, China and perhaps these days the USA too, that claim exemption from criticism of their human rights policies on the grounds that these are based on distinctive cultural values. Interestingly, Africans are in increasing numbers making a statement based on a precisely opposite argument by adopting religions that claim to be based on spiritual knowledge of universal value, in the form of the world religions of Christianity and Islam. In considering this, it is instructive to compare current debates about religion and governance with what happens in the field of natural science. In the biotechnology industries, the search for universally valid theories and models has led to an interest in what is known as 'indigenous knowledge'. This refers to knowledge of the natural world that is possessed by people in the non-Western world, but that is not directly accessible to international scientists, since it is not contained in books or on internet sites, but only in the memories of people living in geographically remote areas. It concerns notably knowledge of plants and herbal medicines, considered as a potential boon to the whole of humanity (cf. Juma 1989). If knowledge of a herbal medicine held by people living in a rain forest is found by laboratory technicians in California or Switzerland to be scientifically exact and useful, leading to the eventual manufacture of a patented drug, it ceases to be considered as indigenous knowledge and is reclassified as scientific knowledge. It is then deemed to be of universal value, and becomes universally sellable, thanks to intellectual property regimes. Indigenous knowledge, it could be said, is that which is awaiting discovery by scientific and business elites.

The idea that all human knowledge can be examined by qualified specialists with a view to testing its universal validity is witness to the continuing confidence of natural scientists in their ambition to develop sound models of the natural world. How, it may be asked, does this apply to the knowledge of any particular cultural repertoire, whether it is in North America, Africa, or anywhere else? Social scientists, whose province this is, are less sure than they were even thirty years ago how to consider such knowledge. Anthropologists especially have become far more sensitive then they once were to accusations of arrogance or cultural imperialism, and pay lip-service at least to the right of people to think in whatever ways they want. However, politicians, being more serious about power than academics, tend to be less reticent. Any Western politician who wishes to avoid pressure to become involved in a war that is not regarded as of vital strategic importance for his or her own country is likely to represent it as representing a fixed cultural pattern. When Western politicians refer to conflicts in distant countries as being due to 'age-old hatreds', it is almost invariably shorthand for saying 'I see no reason to intervene'. African politicians also make full use of this cynical device. In Kenya, violence politically manipulated or even organised by the national government under the presidency of Daniel arap Moi was often carried out by thugs who dressed in traditional costume, enabling the ultimate beneficiaries to describe it as 'ethnic clashes', implying that it was an unavoidable consequence of poverty and underdevelopment (cf. Kagwanja 2003). Similar examples could be cited from South Africa under apartheid, from Nigeria, or any one of a large number of countries. Failure to consider the cultural style of the violence perpetrated in such cases allows those in power to get away with murder. Literally.

Understanding violence, then, is not just of intellectual interest but of vital political importance. Social scientists need to investigate this contested terrain. Personally, I maintain that they can best do so in the belief that all human beings have fundamental qualities, tendencies and abilities in common, and on the assumption that it is possible to reach a sophisticated and informed understanding of what these qualities are, exactly. This is made difficult because many social scientists have lost the conviction that they possess the keys to such understanding, but those who think this way are only partially correct.

African wars: A research agenda

Often, the large-scale, organised violence that has occurred in Africa over the last fifty years has been interpreted through the narrow ideological prism of nationalism. It is undeniable that some well-known armed struggles occurring in that time—in Ethiopia, Zimbabwe, Mozambique, Angola and elsewhere—were waged by people who had sophisticated nationalist ideologies. It can be easily demonstrated that such ideologies had some important historical roots in Europe. Quite often, they were related to the philosophy of Marxism, also a European creation. Until the late 1980s, many armed movements aspiring to national liberation received support from one or other Cold War patron who had an influence on their ideological style, on their forms of organisation and on their political and military strategies. Some intellectuals analysed these movements in Marxist terms. During the Cold War, armed movements, particularly if they were ranged against a colonial or settler government, could realistically expect to get super-power support and could realistically aspire to take over government. Indeed, a number did exactly that, from Algeria to South Africa.

Today, analysts are faced with the problem of analysing a generation of conflicts that no longer conform to this type. These new conflicts appear to many observers to have no clear ideological pattern, to use forms of violence that have no obvious military explanation, and to be concerned to a large extent with economic gain. Although Mkandawire (2002) has examined some attempts to analyse this new generation of wars, he has omitted to mention some of those that are most convincing (e.g. Reno 1998; Kaldor 1999) precisely because they attempt to fit Africa's current generation of wars into a changed global context. The Cold War is over, and the nature of government has changed markedly in Africa—and indeed everywhere else—as a consequence. The change in political order is inseparable from the change in warfare, for the two always belong together. Hence, it is of both political and military significance that Europeans over three or more centuries, later joined by the USA, developed a theory and practice of war in which massive violence can be inflicted by very large bodies of men (and these days, sometimes women too) organised by states. This form of war, fought by the trinity of nation, state and army, reached its peak during the first half of the twentieth century. It was exported all over the world, precisely during the period of Europe's expansion that also introduced colonialism. This form of trinitarian war came to form the basis of international rule-making on war, conceived of as a period of intense violence, properly controlled by states, with a clear beginning (such as a declaration of war or a clear act of aggression) and an end (such as a peace treaty or the surrender or collapse of a protagonist state). Wars became conceived of as exceptional interruptions to a state of normality, called peace. Although Western publics are now being introduced to the idea of wars that are not like this, the classical idea of trinitarian war remains strong and continues to dominate international rule-making in this field (van Creveld 1991).

So, although the ideologues of the most prestigious African liberation movements of the Cold War period could conceive of politics as being properly organised by a state, much as did the governments they battled against, this is no longer the case. Politics in many of the world's most troubled countries are no longer state-centred, or at least tenure of state office is used as a strategic site from which to launch a struggle for power that is both political and military. Violence is often used as an instrument to acquire control of markets or valuable resources, or simply as an instrument of mobilisation, or to destroy the power-base of a potential rival (Reno 1998). Many of the movements making use of the most atrocious violence arise in such circumstances, not only in Africa but also in the Balkans, the Caucasus, central Asia and elsewhere (Kaldor 1999).

This observation can usefully serve as the starting-point for future investigations of Africa's current wars, as social and political movements that need to be interpreted in the light of changing conditions in the world and in their local context. This is especially difficult because of 'the dominant conception of violence in modern societies in which the means of violence have long since been monopolised by the state' (Blok 1999: 23). In many cases, in Africa, central Asia and elsewhere, some of the most apparently gratuitous or extreme forms of violence occur in places where states have imploded, but also where the history of state monopolies of violence is short. Countries like Liberia and Somalia (and, for that matter, Afghanistan) and many others have historical experiences of war different from the Western experience of defined periods of massive, state-led violence. In some cases, there are clear indications that even within living memory, committing violence for self-enrichment has been considered morally acceptable under certain circumstances, as indeed it is in many parts of the world. The desire for plunder as a motive for war is not to be underestimated. In the widest sense, the relation of war to trade is common throughout the world, as nearly all wars are about economic gain in some respect. Anyone who doubts this may consider the bellicose policy of the US towards the oil-rich Middle East, for example. This economic aspect, however, takes different forms in countries with different experiences of states or their absence.

Such considerations impel scholars to revisit some earlier struggles, including those that were regarded for decades as the paradigms of liberation struggle in Africa, such as in Algeria and Zimbabwe. Both of these countries were once regarded as paradigms of successful liberation wars, but it is impossible to sustain such a view today. In Algeria, the civil war—if that is the right phrase to describe it—that has marked the country since the 1990s, marked by the most atrocious and indiscriminate violence, cannot be seriously studied without reference to the period of even larger-scale violence preceding independence in 1962, since some of the roots of the current violence reach back to that period (Martinez 2000). Whether the Algerian war of independence was morally justified is perhaps not the first question to be asked: a more urgent historical question is, rather, to establish what exactly the war was about. Recent historiography, notably by Algerian historians (e.g. Harbi 1980), has shown beyond any doubt that the Front de Libération Nationale (FLN) was engaged in a far more complex struggle than that portrayed by nationalist historians. Its leaders were concerned with gaining power, and therefore were more preoccupied with intimidating rival nationalist movements than with attacking the French army. Zimbabwe has been brought to its present state under the leadership of the same party, and even the same individuals, as those who fought against settler rule in the 1970s and turned on rival nationalist movements thereafter.

147

A search for the historical roots of today's violence will require questioning nationalist historiography. This may not be pleasant, and it may involve the deflation of some hallowed myths. But it needs to be done if we are to seek to understand current events, including current violence.

References

Abdullah, I. & P. Muana. 1998. 'The Revolutionary United Front of Sierra Leone: a revolt of the lumpenproletariat', in Clapham, *African Guerrillas*, 172–93.

Bayart, J.F., P. Geschiere & F. Nyamnjoh. 2001. ' Autochtonie, démocratie et citoyenneté en Afrique', *Critique Internationale* 10, 177–94.

Bazenguissa-Ganga, R. 1999. 'The spread of political violence in Congo-Brazzaville', *African Affairs* 98: 390, 37–54.

Benjamin, W. 1986 [1955]. 'Critique of violence', in W. Benjamin, *Reflections*. New York: Schocken Books, 277–300.

Berkeley, B. 1993. 'Liberia: between repression and slaughter', *Liberian Studies Journal* 18: 1, 127–39 (originally published in the *Atlantic Monthly*, 270, 6, Dec. 1992).

Bledsoe, C. 1984. 'The political use of Sande ideology and symbolism', *American Ethnologist* 11, 455–72.

Blok, A. 2000. ' The enigma of senseless violence', in G. Aijmer & J. Abbink, eds. *Meanings of Violence: a cross-cultural perspective*. Oxford: Berg, 23–38.

Brehun, L. 1991. *Liberia: the war of horror*. Accra: Adwinsa Publications.

Clapham, C. ed. 1998. *African Guerrillas*. Oxford: James Currey.

Duffield, M. 2001. *Global Governance and the New Wars: the merging of development and security*. London: Zed.

Ellis, S. 1998. 'Liberia's warlord insurgency', in Clapham, *African Guerrillas*, 155–71.

Ellis, S. 1999. *The Mask of Anarchy: the destruction of Liberia and the religious dimension of an African civil war*. London: Hurst.

Harbi, M. 1980. *Le F.L.N.: mirage et realité*. Paris: Editions J.A.

Huntington, S. 1996. *The Clash of Civilizations and the Remaking of World Order*. New York: Simon & Schuster.

Juma, C.J. 1989. *The Gene Hunters: biotechnology and the scramble for seeds*. London: Zed.

Kagwanja, P. 2003. 'Facing Mount Kenya or facing Mecca? The *Mungiki*, ethnic violence and the politics of the Moi succession in Kenya, 1987–2002', *African Affairs* 102: 406, 25–49.

Kaldor, M. 1999. *New and Old Wars: organised violence in a global era*. Cambridge: Polity Press.

Lewis, D.L. 2002. 'An American pastime', *New York Review of Books*, 21 November, 27–30.

Martinez, L. 2000. *The Algerian Civil War, 1990–1998*. London: Hurst.

Mbembe, A. 2001. *On the Postcolony*. Berkeley & Los Angeles, CA: University of California Press.

Mkandawire, T. 2002. 'The terrible toll of post-colonial "rebel movements" in Africa: towards an explanation of the violence against the peasantry', *Journal of Modern African Studies* 40: 2, 181–215.

Moran, M. 1995. 'Warriors or soldiers? Masculinity and ritual transvestism in the Liberian civil war', in C.R. Sutton, ed., *Feminism, Nationalism and Militarism*. Arlington, VA: Association for Feminist Anthropology/ American Anthropological Association, 73–88.

Nass, I. A. 2000. *A Study in Internal Conflicts: the Liberian crisis and the West African peace initiative*. Enugu: Fourth Dimension.

Reno, W. 1998. *Warlord Politics and African States*. Boulder, CO: Lynne Rienner.

van Creveld, M. 1991. *The Transformation of War*. New York: Free Press.

Vines, A. 1991. *Renamo: terrorism in Mozambique*. Oxford: James Currey.

Whitehead, N.L. 2002. *Dark Shamans: Kanaima and the poetics of violent death*. Durham, NC: Duke University Press.

SECTION TWO

REBELLION AND REPRESSION

6

THE POLITICAL ELITE OF IMERINA AND THE REVOLT OF THE *MENALAMBA*. THE CREATION OF A COLONIAL MYTH IN MADAGASCAR, 1895–1898[1]

One of the most puzzling and fascinating of all resistance movements is that known as the revolt of the *menalamba*. It occurred over a wide area of central Madagascar, mostly in the kingdom of Imerina, in the two years following the French invasion of Madagascar in 1895. The most mysterious aspect of the rising has always been the question of who, if anyone, was its leader. The official version, that reported by the French government in Madagascar, was that the movement was inspired or directed by a number of magnates at the old Merina court.[2] The published evidence is so ambiguous as to have obliged every subsequent author to accept this version,[3] although there was considerable doubt expressed as to its truth at that time. Recent research in previously unopened archives has thrown new light on the question.[4]

The background to the rising may be summarized quite briefly. The French army, on its march to Tananarive, had met no effective opposition but had suffered heavy losses from disease. The Merina government, divided by vicious feuds, was impotent. One faction led by the prime minister's secretary, Rasanjy, was even in secret communication with the invaders.[5] The French themselves were divided as to what to do with the government of Imerina once it had fallen. In fact they settled for the conventional device of a protectorate, established by a treaty signed on 1 October 1895.[6] The queen of Imerina, who also claimed to be the queen of Madagascar, kept her throne; but the essential Malagasy collaborators were to be Rasanjy and another high official, Rainandriamampandry.[7] Despite outbreaks of violence in Imerina and in other regions of Madagascar, both civil and military administrators pronounced themselves to be satisfied with the progress of events throughout the first six months of their administration.[8] They did not realize the extent of the agitation which was in the air all over Imerina, and particularly the strength of the nationalist coalition being formed in the north.[9] When a full-scale rising broke out in March 1896, it took almost every French official by surprise. The rebels, often calling themselves *menalamba*,[10] attacked indiscriminately Europeans and those Malagasy whom they reckoned to be collaborators. Mostly they vented their wrath on churches and on native churchmen. By June the *menalamba* were burning churches within sight of Tananarive, where the French were more or less besieged.[11]

The reaction of the French at times came close to panic, and the existing divisions within their ranks immediately became much more apparent.[12] The most basic split, but not the only one, was between military and civilian personnel. Personal disagreements and policy disputes added fuel to the heat of these arguments. Most soldiers suspected that the rising was supported by one or more of the many political groups among the Merina officials who still remained in Tananarive. They pointed to the fact that from the very day of the occupation of the capital there had been rumours that some of the Merina oligarchy would support an anti-French rising, although no one in a high position had taken the rumours seriously.[13] Only when the intelligence service was taken over by the young and none too tactful Lieutenant Peltier did some sort of evidence materialize. By May 1896 Peltier had amassed from very dubious sources what he considered to be evidence of an anti-French conspiracy, said to involve almost every politician in Tananarive.[14] His story was, on the face of it, utterly fantastic. His reports spoke of secret committees and lamplight messages. One almost expects to read of cloaks and daggers as well. The civilian resident-general, Laroche, calmly dismissed the whole story.[15] And although most of the higher ranks of the administration were at odds with Laroche on other matters, not one of them was willing to support the theory of a high-level conspiracy.[16]

The general consensus of opinion among the best-informed observers was that the Merina political world was split into two main factions which were capable of going to any lengths to destroy one another. One of the factions centred upon the queen and her court. The other was led by Rasanjy and included a relative of the queen called Ramahatra. Rainandriamampandry occupied an uneasy position in between. Not even General Voyron, the commandant of the army, was prepared to support wholeheartedly the allegations of a plot, although he frequently gave his opinion in terms so vague as to be meaningless. His main concern was not to commit himself.[17]

Most of the pressure to take action against the mysterious traitors in Tananarive came from the lower ranks of the army, in fact from young officers very like Lieutenant Peltier. The finger of guilt was pointed at almost every Merina politician, but chiefly at Rainandriamampandry and Rasanjy, who were the best known. Laroche was widely held to have been outwitted by a combination of Merina politicians and British missionaries.[18] In France a similar interpretation gained currency in many circles. Laroche was attacked in the press for his supposed incompetence and his protestant faith.[19] Moreover Laroche's earlier complaints of military brutality had led to an official complaint from the colonial ministry to the war ministry, so that even in Paris considerations of professional pride were involved.[20] There was also a small lobby in metropolitan politics, led by the two deputies for Réunion, which called for Madagascar's outright annexation. The rising in Imerina made their case much more convincing.[21] Accordingly, the island was declared on 6 August 1896 to be a French colony. General Joseph Gallieni was despatched to Madagascar to relieve Laroche of his duties and to set up a military government.

On 10 October Laroche left Tananarive after handing over to his successor. Within twenty-four hours Gallieni had arrested Rainandriamampandry and some relatives of the queen, together with some lesser figures. Some were exiled. Rainandriamampandry and Prince Ratsimamanga, the queen's uncle, were tried for rebellion, found guilty, and shot on 15 October.

Gallieni claimed that he had found important new evidence of the guilt of Rainandriamampandry and Ratsimamanga.[22] Other people disputed this hotly. Of those French administrators who were in a good position to judge and who later published their memoirs, two insisted on the guilt of the accused and one, an associate of Laroche, claimed that the executions were completely arbitrary.[23] But the private papers of the Laroche family include a detailed account of the trial, which has been missing to this day.[24] This omission from the official archives is not to be wondered at as, if Laroche is to be believed, Gallieni deliberately avoided leaving any transcript of the proceedings.[25] Laroche's account was written some years later, and forms part of his unpublished memoirs.[26] It is evident that he felt a strong personal dislike of Gallieni, but there is no reason to doubt the truth of his account of the trial. It corresponds with details from other, less full accounts,[27] and it is plain that Laroche derived some information from a number of people who had actually played a part in the events described.

The proceedings were a parody of justice. The counsel assigned to the defence was none other than Lieutenant Peltier, while Rasanjy was a major witness for the prosecution. The only charge of any substance levelled against either of the accused was that Rainandriamampandry was said to have received a letter from the northern *menalamba* in February or March 1896, although no exhibit was produced.

According to Laroche, Gallieni had decided even before he set foot in Madagascar that heads must roll, and the assertion seems a reasonable one.[28] He needed to choose a member of a noble family to represent the court party and a commoner to stand for the opposition. To this purpose Gallieni had asked Gautier, the director of native affairs, who should be the candidates for the firing-squad. Gautier advised the choice of Ratsimamanga, a nobleman who had been unpopular for many years because of his financial extortions. The other choice was to be Rainandriamampandry because, although he enjoyed a considerable reputation as a politician and a leading protestant, he had no close political friends and might therefore be considered dispensable. Most important was Gautier's advice to retain Rasanjy, the most obvious target, because of his value as an administrator and probably too because of his friendship with the former secretary-general, Paul Bourde, who had friends in high places in Paris.[29] Laroche's account here fits two other pieces of evidence. One of Laroche's colleagues, using a pseudonym, also wrote that the choice of victims was made by 'un fonctionnaire civil qui jouissait alors de sa [i.e. Gallieni's] confiance', although he did not mention any names.[30] If this was indeed Gautier, then his troublesome conscience might explain the extravagant praise which he was to give to Rainandriamampandry thirty-five years later.[31]

The executions achieved some at least of their desired effect. They inspired suitable fear in Tananarive and were popular with French soldiers and many civilians.[32] They were greeted with enthusiasm by the forward members of the colonial lobby in Paris,[33] where Gallieni's action was rightly interpreted as the most spectacular manifestation of a *politique des races* which was intended to eclipse the Merina protestant oligarchy and which, largely through Gallieni and his colleague Lyautey, was to become an important strand in French colonial thought. In February 1897 the queen and another handful of magnates were exiled, but in this case there was no trial and no execution.

While Gallieni was working to dismantle the protectorate, the *menalamba* bands in the countryside were growing weaker from starvation and more susceptible to a negotiated surrender. In the north, where one of the most powerful bands was commanded by a man named Rabezavana, military command was exercised by Hubert Lyautey, recently summoned to Madagascar by Gallieni and eventually to rise to become a marshal of France and a leading colonial theorist. On 12 May 1897 Lyautey received in his camp a Merina official, Rainianjanoro. He was an associate of Rasanjy who had been sent out from Tananarive to secure Rabezavana's surrender.[34] Over the next seventeen days Rainianjanoro succeeded in meeting Rabezavana and discussing with him the possibility of surrender. He persuaded the *menalamba* general to meet one of Lyautey's subordinates, Captain Remond.[35] Lyautey later discovered, much to his annoyance, that throughout the period of this mission Rainianjanoro was secretly and quite unofficially corresponding with Rasanjy, although he was supposed to be acting solely under Lyautey's orders.[36] Only later did it become clear that Rainianjanoro and Rasanjy were in pursuit of a business deal with Rabezavana.[37]

At the same time Lyautey was in possession of highly confidential instructions from Gallieni as to the conditions of surrender which he was to demand from Rabezavana. On 28 May, before Rabezavana had met any of the French or their collaborators other than Rainianjanoro, Lyautey sent to Remond a private note which, he stressed, should not be shown to Rainianjanoro. It is worth quoting at length:[38]

> Le G[énér]al m'a laissé carte blanche, sans détail, tout en m'imposant de garder Rabezavana jusqu'à son retour. (Ceci est strictement confidentiel.) J'ai à demander à Rabezavana des gages que je vous dirai verbalement, qui seront l'épreuve de sa sincérité et d'après lesquels le G[énér]al verra dans quelle mesure il peut, en ce qui concerne la rentrée en grâce, dépasser la vie et la liberté.
>
> Je ne puis lui dire quels sont ces gages que moi-même à Morafeno … Je puis dire que les gages que je demanderai à Rabezavana sont facilement exécutables.

It would be intriguing to know what were the *'gages'* which were so very secret that they could only be told to Remond and could not be committed to writing. A description of Rabezavana's surrender permits us to have a good idea of them. On 29 May Rabezavana made his first contact with a European negotiator when he met Remond. Two days later he came to Lyautey's camp accompanied by Rainianjanoro and Captain Remond.[39] Lyautey duly reported that he had met Rabezavana and that the *menalamba* leader had returned next day with a list of his allies, whose surrender he offered to secure.[40] Lyautey's published account of this meeting, incidentally, is pure fiction.[41] It was not until 11 June that any mention was made of Rabezavana's exact role in the insurrection and of his alleged relations with the executed magnates Rainandriamampandry and Ratsimamanga. Lyautey wrote to Remond:[42]

> Les déclarations que vous a faites Rabezavana au sujet des % [*sic*] qu'il aurait reçues de la cour de Ranavalo et des personnages fusillés Ratsimamanga et Rainandriamampandry ont une très grande portée et présentent un intérêt particulier pour le Résident Général. Il y aurait grande importance à ce que vous obtenez de Rabezavana, s'il en existe et s'il en possède, tous les documents écrits donnant la preuve matérielle de ce fait ou seulement même des indices y relatifs.

Clearly Rabezavana had not yet produced any documentary evidence of his involvement with the court. In fact on 14 June Lyautey reported to Gallieni Rasanjy's underhand dealings, and went on to say that all Rabezavana had done so far was to secure his life. To obtain other concessions he now had to render what Lyautey called 'services effectifs et palpables',[43] Rabezavana wrote down a copy from memory of a letter which, he claimed, had come to him from Rainandriamampandry in January 1896. There exist two versions of Rabezavana's transcription, both the same in substance.[44] One version was in due course despatched by Gallieni to Paris as retrospective proof that the rising had been planned and led from Tananarive. In time all of the main menalamba leaders, when they surrendered, were to produce similar letters said to have come from Rainandriamampandry early in 1896, at the beginning of the revolt.[45]

The description of Rabezavana's surrender enables us to reconstruct the conditions upon which he laid down his weapons. He was neither imprisoned, executed nor exiled. He had been guaranteed his life and liberty and clemency for his followers. In return he had undertaken to obtain the submission of some of his allies. That was never any secret. What then were the orders which Gallieni had given to Lyautey regarding Rabezavana's submission and which were so highly confidential? There is a great deal of evidence to suggest that Gallieni made it the main condition of surrender of all three main leaders of the menalamba that they should supply him with written evidence of the conspiracy of the politicians in Tananarive. Gallieni got his evidence. The menalamba generals were spared. The man who gained the most was Rasanjy, who became unchallengeable as France's chief collaborator, and also added to his considerable wealth. While Rainianjanoro had been officially negotiating Rabezavana's surrender, the two allies, Rasanjy and Rainianjanoro, had been privately arranging a financial coup. They bought several thousand head of cattle from the grazing lands so recently occupied by the menalamba and took them to the under-supplied market of Tananarive, where they were sold for a very handsome profit.[46]

A fraudulent version of the revolt of the menalamba passed into history. There were quite a few Europeans who disagreed with Gallieni's version of events, mostly friends of Laroche or foreigners. Once armed with evidence against the Merina elite, Gallieni could proceed to replace the protectorate with his own controversial *politique des races,* secure in the possession of a weapon with which to discredit criticism. Gallieni's official report on his mission to pacify Imerina maintained that the traitors in Tananarive had begun to foment opposition to France in January 1896, and thereafter continued to encourage the insurgents.[47] In his unpublished reports and his private correspondence Gallieni stressed still further the personal blame attached to Rainandriamampandry as the ringleader.[48] Some people thought that he later felt guilty about the use of Rainandriamampandry in particular as a scapegoat.[49] It is a fact that in 1901, while Gallieni was still governor-general of Madagascar, a subsidy of 86,000 francs was paid to the dead minister's family.[50]

But the proof that evidence was fabricated against Rainandriamampandry and Ratsimamanga does not in itself disprove the story of a high-level conspiracy in Tananarive. There are indications that one or more of the magnates in the capital could possibly have incited a rising without committing themselves to paper. It might therefore be argued that Gallieni, while transgressing the letter of the law, was yet in pursuit of the real chief of the insurrection. In fact Gallieni sometimes hinted that this was the case.[51]

There had been rumours of a mysterious conspiracy from October 1895 onwards.[52] But the first time that there was concrete evidence that someone in government circles might possibly have foreknowledge of an insurrection was the affair of what was called the 'Ambohimanga letter'. On 14 February 1896 the queen and a group of courtiers including Rainandriamampandry showed Laroche a letter written in the queen's name, calling upon the governor of Ambohimanga to organize a revolt. The messenger who had delivered the letter was questioned. At first he claimed that the letter had been forged by Rasanjy, an assertion which the queen supported, but later he changed his story and said that the letter was indeed the product of a conspiracy hatched in the royal palace.[53] It was never proved one way or another who had written the letter. Laroche refused to treat the matter as being of any importance.[54] Some officials took it a lot more seriously,[55] and in time it came to be regarded by the general staff of the army as the first definite evidence of a conspiracy. [56] The most likely explanation is that the letter was not really intended to precipitate a rising but was written by one party as a means of discrediting its opponents. [57] It implies that the courtiers were aware that some sort of insurrection was in the offing. The French themselves had had ample warning of that but had ignored the danger-signals. [58]

Shortly after the incident of the Ambohimanga letter, when it was becoming painfully obvious that there was a genuine insurrection in the countryside, Prince Ramahatra, a friend of Rasanjy, came to the French authorities with yet another compromising letter. [59] It was addressed to Ramahatra himself and signed by Rabezavana under his *nom de guerre* of Ravaikafo, 'the spark'. There seems no reason to doubt that the letter was genuine. The *menalamba* were always anxious to give their movement a focus by using the figurehead of monarchy. Since the queen was guarded by the French in Tananarive, who better to appeal to than Ramahatra, one of the very few courtiers who was popular and probably the person with the best claim to the throne after Ranavalona herself?[60]

In view of the discussion of letters purporting to come from the *menalamba* we should perhaps proceed to a brief review of their value as evidence. It may be argued that it is unreasonable to characterize the Ambohimanga letter as a forgery but to accept the letter from Rabezavana to Ramahatra as genuine. There can be no doubt whatever that there were a number of forged letters in circulation, a fact commented upon by some of the *menalamba* leaders themselves. [61] Broadly speaking there are three categories of false letters. The first has already been met in our discussion of the surrender of Rabezavana. It has been demonstrated that letters were written after June 1897 by former *menalamba,* directly or indirectly at French request, to suggest that Rainandriamampandry and Ratsimamanga had organized the rising. Another type of false letter was that not inspired by the French, but bearing a forged signature in order to incriminate a third party. We have suggested that the Ambohimanga letter was of this type. The third category, by far the most common, is of letters written by genuine *menalamba* using a well-known name in order to attract support. It is not always clear whether such false signatures were intended to mislead the ignorant, by pretending that the rising had more extensive support than was really the case, or whether they were merely a rhetorical device.

Clearly the existence of such a bewildering variety of misleading evidence leads to special problems of interpretation. Although there is evidence that a certain amount of forgery was deliberately encouraged by Gallieni after June 1897, the present study does not assume that this makes all French material suspect. Neither in Tananarive nor in Paris was the government in business to forge evidence, and indeed *menalamba* letters annexed to Gallieni's political reports of 1896 often contradicted his stated opinion of the rising. It has therefore been assumed that most of the statements of evidence or copies of documents placed in French archives were sincerely believed to be genuine, unless there is good reason to suspect otherwise. This does not preclude the possibility that letters captured by French troops and believed to be authentic may have been falsified by a Malagasy for whatever reason. There are two exceptions to this general admissibility of evidence from French archives. The first is cases in which considerable doubt was expressed at that time as to the origin of a document. A good example is the Ambohimanga letter which was so often thought to be of doubtful authorship as to leave the historian no choice but to treat it with scepticism. The second case is with letters which are known to have been written by the *menalamba* after June 1897. There is no evidence that the French solicited any forgeries before that date, and in fact they could hardly be in a position to do so since none of the major *menalamba* leaders had yet surrendered.

The letter given by Rabezavana's messenger to Ramahatra on 18 March does not fit any of the categories of likely forgeries. Suspicion is attached only to Ramahatra's insistence that Rabezavana had sent similar letters of exhortation to other magnates, including Rainandriamampandry.[62] It is highly questionable whether there ever was a letter from the *menalamba* to Rainandriamampandry. None was ever produced; in fact the version of events finalized in official records after the end of the rising was that Rainandriamampandry had solicited Rabezavana, and not *vice versa*. And yet Ramahatra's revelation that he had received a letter from the *menalamba*, and his assertion that Rainandriamampandry had done as well, had a sensational effect in Tananarive. As we have seen, this story was to be the mainstay of the case against Rainandriamampandry at his trial. The whole idea of this letter seems to have been invented by Ramahatra, perhaps with Rasanjy's help, as a means of casting doubt upon an opponent.[63] Perhaps we may even guess that it was repayment in kind for the court party's earlier tactic of the Ambohimanga letter.

There were thus two powerful interests which sought to inflate the rumours of a conspiracy and which eventually were to settle upon Rainandriamampandry as their scapegoat. One was the French army and some of the civilian population. The other was constituted by the Merina factions in the capital, each straining to discredit the opposition by tarring it with the brush of disloyalty. But from March 1896 onwards, French troops operating against the *menalamba* in the countryside constantly reported that the insurgents themselves claimed to have high-level support. The name most often quoted was that of the queen herself, although most French officers were willing to concede that her name was used as a means of claiming leadership among the rebel bands. This only increased the suspicion that someone was behind the rising. Sometimes letters were found bearing the names of the queen or of Ramahatra but which were evidently not signed by them personally.[64] Very rarely was there any remark as to precisely how or why the magnates might be involved with the *menalamba*.

There were several aspects of the rising which tended to point towards a central organization. Although none of the *menalamba* was of really high rank in the old hierarchy, it was nonetheless obvious that the insurgents were quite well organized. Secondly, the rising had broken out in full intensity at the same moment in both the north and the south. Finally there was the evidence of prisoners who spoke of having allies in Tananarive.

To illustrate the problems involved we may cite the example of a letter found on 8 April 1896 which is one of the very few pieces of concrete evidence to suggest how the rising might have been organized and which at the same time illustrates so many of the processes at work in the formulation of the theory of a conspiracy. The letter was undated and anonymous but was addressed to the Malagasy governor of the village where it was discovered in the house of a local pastor. The text is as follows:[65]

Look out for and examine the deeds of the people. And if you discover that many people unite and that there is a command for an attack of all the provinces of Imerina and the coast, let us know. And if the province of Sisaony makes this agreement, it need not fear the fate of Ambodirano.[66]

Colonel Oudri, who discovered the letter, concluded that it provided evidence that the rising had been planned for some time and must be known to some of the Merina officials in Tananarive.[67] Upon his return to Paris, Oudri, now promoted to the rank of general, told the minister of war that the letter he had found proved that 'le mouvement insurrectionnel devait éclater sur un ordre venu de la capitale', and that among the enemies of the French were British missionaries and some of the Merina élite. The most likely candidates for the post of ringleader were, he thought, Rasanjy and Rainandriamampandry.[68] Like many others, Oudri could not believe that the country people of Madagascar were capable of organizing a rising without leadership from high places.

Similar reports of a connexion with the court are so persistent that it is evident that many of the insurgents really believed that their anti-European rising had the support of the queen and some of her principal officers. Even some of those Europeans best acquainted with Madagascar and who were at first sceptical of the conspiracy began to think that there might be something in the notion. Dr Besson, an old Madagascar hand, wrote that the Merina elite 'n'ont aucune espèce d'influence sur les rebelles et leurs chefs' but admitted that he was very puzzled.[69] Only after the execution of Rainandriamampandry did he change his official attitude and maintain that the whole rising had been plotted by the former minister from the beginning.[70] In private he lamented to the end of his days the destruction of a protectorate based on the Merina monarchy.[71] Some Norwegian missionaries believed that 'des gens haut placés dirigent', and even one or two members of the London Missionary Society had their suspicions.[72]

Some of these assertions can be checked against the letters written by the *menalamba* to each other and captured after their surrender. There are still in existence several hundred letters written in various *menalamba* camps between the beginning of 1896 and mid-1897. There can be no doubt of the authenticity of the vast majority of them. Several are in the handwriting of Rabezavana, and many are stamped with the seals which the rebels used to distinguish 'official' letters.[73] The queen is frequently mentioned as the source of the revolt, but in a figurative sense. One letter declares in a telling passage:[74]

> Voici ce que nous vous disons, Messieurs: nous avons reçu une lettre de la reine et du Prince Ratsitiavola, 15e honneur.
>
> Nous vous donnons connaissance, que nous ne sommes pas des fahavalos [bandits]; la lettre actuelle est engagée par le gouvernement lui-même.

The menalamba had a horror of rebelling against legitimate authority, which would have been sacrilege, and they were therefore at great pains to point out that they were not rebels but patriots, because they had the leadership of the queen. They were also adapting for their letters the traditionally spoken form of discourse called a kabary, which always began with an appeal to various authorities. The menalamba therefore began many of their letters with a litany of names, including those of the queen and some of her courtiers. Sometimes the list even included the prime minister's name, although the incumbent of that office was generally agreed to be a French puppet and was only rarely accused of conspiracy.

The names of courtiers in Tananarive occur in a limited number of contexts. Most often they are in a litany of the type used in a kabary, especially when the menalamba issued a public proclamation.[75] They were used whenever a leader wanted to attribute military promotions to some of his followers, so that he could claim they had been brought from the queen.[76] They were most often used by certain leaders: by two who were of very low traditional status, Rainijirika and Ramenamaso,[77] and by Rafanenitra, the leading tactician among the menalamba generals, who would often say that a certain line of action had been ordered by the mysterious figures in Tananarive.[78] The latter, the mythical directors of the rising, always bore the names of Ratsitiavola (or sometimes Rainitsitiavola) and Ratiatanindrazana. Literally, the names mean respectively 'Mr Does-not-love-money' and 'Mr Patriot'. The pseudonyms, standing for any prince or great man patriotic enough to join the rising, continued in use long after the deaths of Rainandriamampandry and Ratsimamanga, which is further proof of their innocence. Indeed, their execution seemed to provoke little except contempt among the *menalamba*:[79]

> Quand vous êtes arrivés, Faratay,[80] vous avez dit: la Reine reste Reine, le Premier Ministre reste Premier Ministre. Et voilà que vous avez tué ce dernier[81] ainsi que les officiers qui étaient à Tananarive et qui, pourtant, vous aimaient.

The names of 'Patriot' and 'Does-not-love-money' are hardly of a traditional type, although it is possible that Ratsitiavola refers to a famous *kabary* pronounced by the great King Andrianampoinimerina.[82] In fact they bear a striking resemblance to the names of the people encountered by Christian in *The Pilgrim's Progress*. Bunyan's great allegory had been translated into Malagasy by British missionaries in the 1830s and had subsequently become so popular in Imerina as to gain almost the status of ancestral wisdom.[83] The pseudonyms of the *menalamba* show how deeply British nonconformist culture had penetrated even among the opponents of Christianity. They also give an insight into the sort of war which the *menalamba* thought they were fighting. Many of them accepted that Tananarive had only fallen to the French because it had been sold by a corrupt oligarchy. Those who collaborated with the invaders were told 'vous faites un idole de l'argent', because they preferred money to justice.[84]

Ratsitiavola and Ratiatanindrazana were no more real people than was the King Ludd of the English machine-breakers. The names were nevertheless important for the *menalamba* in that they enabled them to use in their service traditional authority and the whole panoply of an ancient culture.[85] It was the strength of this tradition, and the real sense of nationality of many Malagasy, including some non-Merina, which enabled the *menalamba* to achieve that degree of co-ordination which baffled Europeans. And although the queen was real enough, her title was used quite without her consent. Furthermore it was neither the first nor the last time that such a thing was to happen. Dissident groups had likewise claimed to be acting in the name of the sovereign in 1863[86] and 1877.[87] A similar phenomenon was to occur in 1947, when Malagasy insurgents claimed to be acting for their deputies in the French chamber.[88] It is most unlikely that any of the *menalamba* leaders believed that there was anyone in the court or the government who was on their side, although to judge from the frequency with which captured *menalamba* told the French that they had support in high places it seems that many of the rank-and-file really did believe it. This was partly wishful thinking, since their whole philosophy required them to believe that the queen must in some sense be on their side. They also appear to have thought that the queen's will could be expressed independently of her person. The true royal will, conforming to the wishes of the past kings of Imerina, was expressed by their leaders, who thus played a part akin to that of a spirit medium.

The *menalamba* in the countryside undoubtedly did have some contacts in Tananarive. There is specific mention in a couple of letters of the need to take a message to someone in the capital.[89] Among the Lyautey papers there exists a letter from the ubiquitous Ratiatanindrazana informing Rabezavana that there are many in Tananarive who are awaiting his arrival. There is no indication of the identity of the author,[90] although some Frenchmen were to claim later that Ratiatanindrazna was the pen-name of Rainandriamampandry.[91] It remains possible, at any rate in theory, that there was someone in a high position in the capital who sympathized with the rebels.

But that is a far cry from saying that the rising was directed from Tananarive, still less that the leaders were Rainandriamampandry and Ratsimamanga. The *menalamba* had a strong contempt for the corrupt politics of the capital, to the extent that a fair number of high-ranking Merina officials were killed by the insurgents.[92] It would be tedious to refute one by one the accusations made against individual magnates, but some of the names quoted as possible conspirators were of people who could have expected little mercy if they had fallen into the hands of the rebels. There were certainly those who used the rising for their own ends, but there was no need to communicate with the real *menalamba* to do that, as Rasanjy showed.

The *menalamba* did include in their number some people who had been fairly highly placed in the old royal administration.[93] But it is very significant that none of these individuals normally lived in Tananarive and none was caught up in the intrigue and corruption of the court. Nor do any of the rebels appear to have been very rich. Lists of goods confiscated from *menalamba* chiefs reveal nothing to match, for example, Rainandriamampandry's fortune of 300,000 francs.[94]

It is clear that the two men cited by Gallieni as the real leaders of the rising of the *menalamba* were not guilty, and indeed that the role of the old oligarchy in the rising was virtually nil. The significance of these findings goes far beyond proving that Rainandriamampandry and Ratsimamanga were morally and legally innocent of the charges against them. The case of Rainandriamampandry—like that of his contemporary, Dreyfus[95]—is much more than a question of individual innocence. It was a point which divided opinion among all the Europeans in Madagascar and stood for a multitude of other issues. Gallieni's ruthlessness was successful in its aim of attracting support among the French community, but it had several unexpected consequences. It strengthened the suspicion already held by many Frenchmen that the revolt was in some way supported by the protestant churches and by Britain. It is true that even under Laroche's administration the attitude of some Malagasy churchmen had been ambiguous, but by and large they were more inclined to collaborate with France than with the *menalamba*.[96] The executions helped to drive protestants and rebels together. Closely connected with this was the belief that Britain, the home of so many protestant missionaries, would intervene to help the Malagasy. As early as August 1896 a captured Englishman had been told by the *menalamba* that 'la reine a donné l'ordre aux chefs de l'insurrection de respecter les Anglais'.[97] The myth of British intervention was encouraged by the execution of Rainandriamampandry, a leading anglophile and protestant. The rumour reappeared after the Fashoda crisis, in 1898 and 1899, and never really disappeared.[98] It emerged once more in 1942 after the Allied landings in Madagascar.[99]

The policy of which the executions were a central part also helped to set off a vicious religious war in the villages of central Madagascar throughout 1897 and 1898. Much of the struggle between collaborators and resisters became channelled into bitter confessional disputes which were battles for the control of individual villages.[100] These disputes were all the more fierce because the fate for a protestant who was out-manoeuvred was often to be denounced as a rebel and shot.[101] None of this was intended by Gallieni.[102] It was a side-effect of a *politique des races* which was never to succeed in its central aim of restricting the influence of the Merina, and especially the Merina of the old oligarchy.[103]

The false history of the *menalamba* was written in official histories and guilty memoirs and thence passed into history books. It helped to make the reputation of Rainandriamampandry as a nationalist hero and a protestant martyr, which is how he is remembered today in Madagascar.

7

MBOKODO

SECURITY IN ANC CAMPS, 1961–1990

No less than four official reports have been published since 1992 by the African National Congress (ANC) into human rights abuses perpetrated by the organization during its years in exile. At least three other organizations have also published reports on the same subject. These documents, plus an abundance of first-hand testimony by former prisoners and officials of the ANC, permit us to reconstruct with some confidence the record of the detention, torture and executions carried out by the ANC in exile, as well as the context in which these events occurred. This constitutes a chapter in the history of the ANC sufficiently important, albeit unpleasant, as to be worthy of further study. In present circumstances, it also has far-reaching implications.

The present article does not attempt to investigate either the legality of the ANC's security policy during its period in exile, nor to compare it with that of other organisations, including notably that of the South African government, whose own human rights record is well known. The article summarises what has been established concerning the ANC's security apparatus in the 1980s, and in particular its response to indiscipline, espionage and widespread criticism by rank and file members of its armed wing, *Umkhonto we Sizwe*, in the period 1981–4. It compares this with an earlier, and less well-documented, wave

171

of unrest in 1967–9. In doing so, it concludes that the nature of the ANC in exile changed markedly in the period due to the organisation's militarization under the guidance of the South African Communist Party (SACP), which after 1969 became the dominant force within the ANC's exile leadership, or the External Mission of the ANC as it was formally styled.

Sources

For many years the conditions inside ANC training and guerrilla camps were not widely known outside the ranks of ANC members in exile. Howard Barrell, a journalist and ANC member who had good access to information on the inner workings of the ANC in exile, has stated that it was common knowledge among ANC cadres that there were security men who inflicted routine beatings on their victims and for that reason were commonly known as 'panel-beaters'.[1] Nevertheless it remains unclear to what extent ANC cadres in exile were aware of the treatment meted out to their own kind in some detention centres, especially in the ANC's Angolan punishment camp known as Quatro (sometimes wrongly rendered as 'Quadro'). Perhaps surprisingly, the South African government, whose intelligence services were clearly well informed about conditions in the ANC camps, did little to make their information public, not even releasing details of the mutiny which took place in ANC camps in Angola in 1984, and which shook the ANC to its foundations. The first lengthy account of the 1984 mutiny was published only in 1990, written by five former ANC detainees.[2] The ANC itself established a commission of inquiry into the 1984 mutiny and its origins as early as February 1984, known as the Stuart Commission after its chairman James Stuart,[3] a veteran member of the ANC who was elected to the ANC's National Executive Committee in 1985. The report of the Stuart Commission, however, was not released by the ANC until 1993.[4]

The first official inquiry on the abuses in ANC camps to be made public was that chaired by Thembile Louis Skweyiya S.C., a senior member of the South African bar, in 1992.[5] His cousin and fellow lawyer, Zola Skweyiya, was himself an ANC official who in exile was given responsibility for investigating human rights abuses within the organization in the wake of the 1984 mutiny, although by all accounts he was able to make little headway in this work.[6] The Skweyiya Commission was constituted as a result of public and private pressure on the organization to give an account of its conduct during the years of exile.[7] Its terms of reference were restricted to the cases of former detainees who had themselves complained to the ANC. It was empowered to investigate complaints relating to 'the conditions of their detention' and to inquire into 'the allegations of their mistreatment'.[8] Its mandate did not include an investigation of cases of murder or execution. Nor was it empowered to investigate other cases of detention reported to it but in which the victim had not personally complained to the ANC. The Skweyiya Commission did not address, other than in passing, the question of where responsibility lay for these abuses, although it did name several senior ANC officials whom it considered to bear some responsibility for the abuses which had occurred.

Partly because of the limits to its terms of reference, the Skweyiya Commission did not bring an end to pressure on the ANC to launch a more thorough investigation. In consequence, the organization appointed another commission, chaired by Dr Samuel Motsuenyane, a well-known South African businessman, which reported in August 1993.[9] Although the Motsuenyane Commission mentioned the names of two senior ANC officials whom it found to have committed errors of conduct, it again avoided determining the question of which senior ANC leaders might by reason of their office, be held responsible for the abuses which had taken place in exile. Yet another ANC commission of inquiry was that chaired by Z.N. Jobodwana which inquired into the death of Thami Zulu, a prominent officer of *Umkhonto we Sizwe* who died in 1989 shortly after being released from a period of 14 months during which he was detained by the ANC on suspicion of espionage. The Jobodwana report, which appears to have been drafted by senior ANC and SACP lawyer Albie Sachs, dates from March 1990 but was released only in 1993.[10]

In the meantime, there were at least three other reports on the question, one published in December 1992 by Amnesty International,[11] and another written by Bob Douglas S.C., a South African advocate who had been commissioned by a right-wing lobby, the International

Freedom Foundation.[12] A third was published by the International Society for Human Rights, an organization which seemed broadly to share the political standpoint of the International Freedom Foundation.[13] By late 1993 there were also dozens of depositions in circulation in photocopy form by people claiming to have suffered at the hands of the ANC's security apparatus or to have intimate knowledge of such abuses. These and other information were the basis of many newspaper articles either by alleged victims or by senior ANC officials reacting to the various allegations made against the organization or against them personally.

There is evidence that some alleged witnesses or victims of abuses in ANC camps, having returned to South Africa in the early 1990s destitute and, in some cases, embittered received funding and material support from political enemies of the ANC, including possibly from South Africa's Directorate of Military Intelligence. Evidence from sources which may have been affected by considerations of political bias or enmity should, like all other historical evidence, be evaluated in the context not only of what is stated, but of the circumstances and motives for which it was compiled. The fact that a given testimony may have been produced at the request of, or with support from, an organization opposed to the ANC does not make it invalid: it is merely a factor which needs to be assessed in its proper context.

Of all this abundant evidence, the most authoritative documents are probably the three widest-ranging reports produced by the ANC, namely the Stuart, Skweyiya and Motsuenyane Commissions, in 1984, 1992 and 1993 respectively. Since these inquiries were commissioned by the ANC itself, they had better access to internal ANC documents and more power to summon ANC witnesses than any other investigation. Moreover, although there are grounds for criticizing all three inquiries, the Skweyiya Commission in particular was generally regarded by observers at the time of its publication as a courageous and fair report, albeit with rather restricted terms of reference, which was path-breaking in its significance. The Stuart Commission has the merit of having been compiled at the height of the armed struggle, within a few days of the 1984 mutiny, and of having been written for internal consumption rather than with an eye to publication. The Motsuenyane Commission, unlike the Skweyiya and Stuart Commissions, was independent in the sense that it was composed of people who were not members of the ANC, but who had access to ANC documents and witnesses.

Of the other reports, that by Amnesty International has the merit of having been compiled by an organization with acknowledged expertise in its subject and which cannot seriously be suspected of ulterior political motives. The Douglas report, in contrast, was commissioned by an organization which has explicit political aims opposed to those of the ANC.[14] The report contains so many unsubstantiated and often wild allegations, combined with a highly polemical tone, as to make it the least satisfactory of all the various inquiries, notwithstanding its author's qualifications as a Senior Counsel.

These various documents, in spite of their strengths, weaknesses and omissions, agree on a good many points which may therefore be regarded as established beyond any reasonable doubt. In brief, the central finding of all of them, supplemented by other evidence, is that the camps run by the ANC in southern Africa to house its guerrilla army, and particularly those located in Angola, were the scene of numerous hardships and administrative abuses from the late 1970s onwards. The Angolan camps were closed in 1989, but others in Tanzania, Uganda and elsewhere remained open until 1992 at least. The conditions in the camps provoked expressions of dissatisfaction which the ANC met with harsh and often arbitrary punishments, particularly at the punishment camp known as Quatro, properly known as Site 32 or, later, the Morris Seabelo Rehabilitation Centre. Corruption, authoritarian administration and other abuses including arbitrary detention, torture and murder, combined to cause great resentment which resulted in the 1984 mutiny known as *Mkatashingo* (or, according to Ronnie Kasrils, *Mkatashini*).[15] Participants in the mutiny were themselves severely punished, including by public execution. Similar abuses, however, continued until 1990, when the ANC was unbanned in South Africa and its members allowed to return from exile. Even as late as 1993, when most *Umkhonto we Sizwe* fighters had been back in South Africa for two years or more, the ANC's soldiers were so angry with the way they were treated by their leaders that it was necessary to hold a special conference where they could voice their complaints. A particular target was Army Commander Joe Modise, the subject of bitter complaint for

25 years or more. The *Umkhonto we Sizwe* conference held in Kangwane in September 1993 may thus be viewed in a long tradition of tension between the *Umkhonto we Sizwe* leadership and the rank and file.[16]

None of the reports gives any credence to the allegation that the 1984 mutiny was directly inspired or organized by South African government agents as Oliver Tambo asserted to the ANC national conference in Durban in July 1992.[17] The ANC's own Stuart Commission stated in 1984 that 'we have not uncovered any evidence that enemy agents organized the disturbances [i.e. the 1984 mutiny] from the beginning'.[18] Tambo's allegation at such a late date must therefore be regarded as a cynical lie.

It is unedifying but, perhaps, unsurprising, to learn that ANC soldiers in Angola lived in poor conditions, and that these gave rise to frustration and indiscipline which, in the circumstances of a military struggle, were repressed with a heavy hand. For present purposes, what is of concern is to establish why the ANC was not able to deal with these problems more effectively, and to assess the significance of these events for what they indicate about the ANC as an organization.

The ANC security apparatus

The most authoritative published information on the evolution of the security apparatus set up by the ANC in exile is contained in the latest of the ANC's official commissions, that chaired by Dr. Samuel Motsuenyane which issued its report on 20 August 1993. Motsuenyane did not receive any evidence on the existence of an ANC security department prior to 1981, but noted that 'it is clear, however, that security and intelligence duties were carried out as part of the operations of the MK [*Umkhonto we Sizwe*]' before that date.[19] The Motsuenyane report stated that the person appointed by Oliver Tambo to head the Department of Security and Intelligence in 1981 was Mzwandile ('Mzwai') Piliso, who selected his own personnel from the ranks of *Umkhonto we Sizwe*. Originally from the Transkei, and related to some leading members of the organization, Piliso was a veteran ANC member. He had joined it in the late 1940s but left South Africa shortly afterwards and became politically inactive. Persuaded by Oliver Tambo to re-enter politics, Piliso threw himself into ANC work and was appointed to the National Executive Committee in the early 1970s. In short, Piliso was a senior member of the ANC leadership, with close personal ties to Tambo and other key leaders, especially those of his own generation who were also from the Transkei. By the late 1970s Piliso was the head of ANC personnel, based in Angola, where he was responsible for setting up training camps to accommodate the large influx of new recruits to *Umkhonto we Sizwe* in the wake of the 1976 Soweto uprising. According to Kasrils, Piliso already headed a security apparatus at this stage, but this appears to be incorrect.[20]

Only in 1981 did an urgent need arise for a new head of the ANC's Department of Intelligence and Security, based in Lusaka. Piliso was considered to have made such a good job of assimilating the influx of new recruits in Angola that he was offered the job. He was reluctant to accept, but allowed himself to be persuaded. As head of intelligence and security, Piliso was chief of a directorate whose other members were the heads of external intelligence, security, and administration. The security organ, one of the three separate structures which fell under Piliso's overall authority, was responsible for running the ANC's places of detention and became known as *Mbokodo,* a Xhosa word designating a stone used for grinding maize, generally regarded as 'a euphemism for the harshness with which the Department treated its victims'.[21] As the head of this whole structure, Piliso reported directly to ANC President Oliver Tambo. At the time Piliso took up his post in 1981, the other members of his directorate are said to have been Peter Boroko (an SACP member, head of intelligence and number two in the Department of Intelligence and Security directorate), Reddy Mazimba (head of security) and Sizakele Sigxashe (head of administration). Sizakele, trained in the Soviet Union, was elected to the Central Committee of the SACP in 1984 and the Political Bureau in 1985, the same year in which he was elected also to the ANC's National Executive Committee.[22]

Motsuenyane is correct in pointing out that the large influx of recruits to *Umkhonto we Sizwe* after the Soweto rising of 1976 greatly stretched the ANC's resources, and that the failure to respond adequately to the demands which this imposed on the organization, in spite of Piliso's best efforts as head of personnel, was one of the factors which led to unrest among the rank and file. However, neither

Motsuenyane nor any of the other reports mentions that *Umkhonto we Sizwe* had experienced similar problems of disaffected personnel and an unpopular leadership as early as 1967–9, and it is useful to consider briefly the history of the ANC's security structures in order to put the later disturbances in context.

The ANC was, as is well known, a non-violent movement for over four decades after its foundation in 1912 and it had no institutional means for enforcing discipline or security within its own ranks. It was only in the 1950s that the organization adopted a strategy of mass mobilization and of defiance of the law, and only in 1961 that it adopted a policy of armed struggle. To be more precise, the ANC did not formally adopt the armed struggle in 1961: rather, many individual members of the ANC, with the tacit (but not yet explicit) blessing of the leadership of their organization, joined their Communist Party allies in establishing an underground army, *Umkhonto we Sizwe*. At this early stage *Umkhonto we Sizwe* did not, technically speaking, 'belong' to either the ANC or the SACP, but was an autonomous unit composed of members of both organizations. None of the three—the ANC, the SACP or *Umkhonto we Sizwe*—had a specific apparatus for ensuring its own security. That was to evolve only in the course of the armed struggle.

In the years immediately after 1963, police repression caused many members of *Umkhonto we Sizwe* to leave South Africa and to find shelter in camps established by the ANC in Tanzania. Some South African Police intelligence, we may note, even at this early date came from spies whom it had succeeded in placing or in recruiting at the heart even of the ultra-cautious SACP.[23] The ANC's four Tanzanian camps became the bases of the *Umkhonto we Sizwe* guerrilla soldiers, a small number of whom had undergone training courses in China, the USSR, or elsewhere. It appears that any problems of either discipline or security within the Tanzanian camps at this stage were dealt with by the *Umkhonto we Sizwe* command under Joe Modise, appointed army commander in 1965.

In 1967, *Umkhonto we Sizwe* launched its first foreign-based offensive, in the Wankie district of north-west Rhodesia, together with soldiers from the ANC's ally, the Zimbabwe African People's Union (ZAPU). The ZAPU/*Umkhonto we Sizwe* forces, using inappropriate tactics and with poor logistic support, were attacked by more mobile

Rhodesian forces and badly mauled. Some of the survivors, eventually making their way back to ANC camps in Tanzania, were highly critical of the leaders who had sent them into Wankie badly prepared and supported, and they spread dissatisfaction to the point of mutiny. Some survivors of the Wankie campaign were detained by the ANC in Tanzania on account of their criticism of the army leadership.[24] Chris Hani, one of the most articulate of the young Wankie veterans, was held several months by the authorities in Botswana after escaping from the Wankie defeat. Returning to Tanzania, incensed by the poor leadership of the army, he submitted an angry memorandum on behalf of the *Umkhonto we Sizwe* combatants, 'charging the then MK leadership with incompetence and complacency'.[25] Modise appears to have been a particular target of Hani's memorandum, which is said to have been penned in early 1969.[26] According to one report, Hani was summarily sentenced to death by the *Umkhonto we Sizwe* high command for this act of insubordination, but later reprieved.[27] In fact there had been a groundswell of dissatisfaction in the ANC camps even before the Wankie campaign, and indeed one of the motives for launching the campaign in the first place was probably to prevent the spread of demoralization through inactivity.[28]

It was largely as a result of pressure from its disaffected soldiers that the ANC held a consultative conference at Morogoroj, Tanzania, in 1969. The conference resulted in sweeping changes in the ANC leadership, with the appointment of a new body to oversee the armed struggle, and with a clearer statement of strategy than had previously existed.[29] There were also major changes in the composition of the ANC's National Executive Committee. In general, the Morogoro conference was the point at which the SACP could be said to have gained decisive influence over the whole of the ANC in exile, asserting its superiority over other factions or tendencies within the ANC leadership.[30] It was in the context of this overhaul of the ANC's apparatus, along lines recommended by SACP thinkers, that the ANC appears to have first established an autonomous Department of Intelligence and Security, at some time in the mid-1970s. One of its first directors is said to have been Simon Makana (later, ANC representative in Moscow and a member of the SACP Central Committee). However, I know of no published source confirming the date of origin of this department.

It was in these circumstances that *Umkhonto we Sizwe* received the influx of new recruits who left South Africa in 1976–7. Barrell estimates that there were some 800 *Umkhonto we Sizwe* guerrillas in 1965.[31] Stephen Davis puts the number of ANC exiles at 1,000 in 1975 and 9,000 five years later, after the influx of fighters from the Soweto generation. A substantial number of these would have been guerrilla soldiers.[32] By 1993 *Umkhonto we Sizwe* was said by its chief of staff to have trained altogether some 16,000 people, of whom 5,000 returned to South Africa after the unbanning of the ANC in 1990, while a further 6,000 still remained in camps outside the country.[33] These figures suggest that the total number of soldiers enlisted in *Umkhonto we Sizwe* at any one time never exceeded 11,000, at most. From 1976 until 1989 the bulk of them lived in camps in Angola, the ANC's main military region, with others scattered in other countries in southern Africa or attending training courses in eastern Europe.

Following the reorganization of the *Umkhonto we Sizwe* command structure in the 1970s in the wake of the Morogoro conference, and after the incorporation of the wave of new recruits in 1976–7, there were the first reported cases since 1968 of the detention of suspected dissidents. As early as 1976 there were cases of *Umkhonto we Sizwe* soldiers being classified as suspected enemy agents by the newly-installed Department of Intelligence and Security and relegated to a permanent administrative limbo as 'suspects', apparently as a result of their attempts to resign from the ANC, or because they had complained about conditions in the camps, or were otherwise regarded as trouble-makers.[34] There was a small number of similar cases throughout the late 1970s. However, virtually all sources agree that the first major purge by ANC security took place only in 1981, the year in which Piliso took control of the Department of Intelligence and Security, and that this was to be one of the root causes of the 1984 mutiny. Again, there is general agreement that the causes of the mutiny were dissatisfaction with the leadership of *Umkhonto we Sizwe* on the part of the rank and file; dissatisfaction with being deployed in battle against the *União National para a Independencia Total de Angola* (UNITA) in Angola rather than against the South African state; harsh punishments by ANC camp commanders, including arbitrary detention and torture, sometimes resulting in death; and poor camp conditions.

Spies and suspects

There can be no doubt whatever that *Umkhonto we Sizwe* actually was infiltrated by South African Police agents in the late 1970s. One such spy, Joseph Tshepo Mamasela, subsequently testified to a South African government commission of inquiry, explaining in detail how he had been recruited by the police to spy on the ANC. A professional car thief, born in 1955, Mamasela agreed to work as a police agent in exchange for an exemption from prosecution after he had been arrested for a criminal offence. He joined the ANC in Botswana, where he was detained by ANC Security in 1981. He managed to escape, returning to South Africa where he was formally enrolled in the South African Police in February 1982.[35] It appears clear that a motive for the 1981 purge—probably the leading one—was the discovery by the ANC's security organ of the existence of Mamasela and other spies, many probably with similar backgrounds. These included a number who had penetrated the organization at a relatively high level. It was this realization which caused the ANC leadership to appoint Piliso to head the Department of Intelligence and Security with a brief to root out the spies.[36] There seems to have been something close to panic in the ANC leadership. The security offensive against suspected spies was accompanied by a general campaign by the ANC leadership to restore discipline. This took the form of fierce repression of any perceived infraction. Minor disciplinary offences, such as drunkenness, and perceived infringements of the military code, such as criticism of the ANC leadership, were equated with espionage. Marijuana-smoking was viewed by ANC security officials as a particularly serious crime.[37] All the commissions of inquiry agree that the 1981 purge resulted in the detention of many *Umkhonto we Sizwe* soldiers who were not seriously suspected of espionage but who were detained in the general atmosphere of suspicion which spread throughout the ANC camps in 1981, during which offences of every kind were turned into an amalgam.

Some sources, however, allege a more specific political motivation for the mistreatment of *Umkhonto we Sizwe* cadres and in particular for the purge of 1981 which lay at the origins of the mutiny. The most explicit of such allegations is made in an article by five former Quatro detainees, who suggest that the first stirrings of protest against the leadership of *Umkhonto we Sizwe* and the ANC may be traced to 1979, when inmates of an ANC camp near Quibaxe in northern Angola known as Villa Rosa or Fazenda, where conditions were harsh, began to criticize their leaders. They allege that the ANC's response was to strengthen the security apparatus, 'which till then had just been composed of a few old cadres of the 1960s', using security personnel recently trained in East Germany and the Soviet Union, and to proceed with construction of the prison camp at Quatro.[38] They go on to suggest that the discovery of South African spies in 1981 was a classic Stalinist purge, using the deliberate manufacture of what they term an 'internal-enemy-danger-psychosis' which was used to condemn any ANC member who called for a conference to debate the movement's problems, as the Morogoro conference had debated the aftermath of the Wankie campaign.[39] According to the same account, security men who refused to implement the purge were themselves punished. Paul Trewhela, one of the editors of the journal which published this account, himself a former member of the SACP and of *Umkhonto we Sizwe* who was sentenced to a prison term in South Africa in 1965,[40] has gone still further in suggesting that the training of the ANC security apparatus by officials of the Soviet KGB and the East German *Stasi* lay at the origin of the purges. The ANC security men, Trewhela implies, were trained by their German and Soviet instructors to apply the methods of East European Stalinism within the ANC's camps.[41]

Certainly, most of the key security personnel in Angola by the time of the 1981 purge were SACP members. The first commander of Quatro, from 1979 to 1982, was Gabriel Mthembu (also known as Sizwe Mkhonto), who had been trained in security intelligence in East Germany. In 1982 he left Angola to attend the Lenin School in Moscow. He returned in 1984 to take up the post of deputy head of intelligence and security for Angola.[42] The first deputy commander of Quatro, Morris Seabelo, also a SACP member, had risen to become regional chief of security in Angola by the time of the 1984 mutiny. Seabelo was a member of the tribunal which sentenced a number of mutineers to death by public execution. The man who coordinated the security crackdown from Luanda was 'Captain' Lentsoe Moeketsi, also a SACP member.[43] Throughout the early 1980s the ANC's national commissar,

Andrew Masondo, filled an important position at the apex of the network of political commissars which the ANC had established on the Soviet model. He was also a member of the Central Committee of the SACP. According to one former ANC intelligence officer, Masondo 'provided the critical nexus between the commissars and Mbokodo. The two were to work in harness as the Praetorian Guard of orthodoxy and "ideological correctness" in the movement. Their task was clearly to defend the movement from both "ideological subversion" and espionage penetration. That was the climate abroad in the camps.'[44]

Senior officials of the ANC confirmed in testimony to the Skweyiya Commission that they knew of torture in the camps in Angola in the early 1980s.[45] Whatever lack of awareness there may have been in the ANC and SACP leadership about the excesses of the security apparatus was dispelled by the 1984 Stuart Commission, which described the conditions in the ANC's Angolan camps accurately and made a number of recommendations for improvement. Although at least one senior official—Andrew Masondo—was explicitly blamed for the abuses, and was demoted, others of the Stuart Commission's recommendations were not adopted or were implemented in theory but not in practice. The arbitrary detention and torture of prisoners continued throughout the 1980s, even after Tambo had personally visited Quatro in 1987.[46] The findings of the Stuart Commission appear never to have been formally tabled before the full National Executive Committee of the ANC or presented to the ANC consultative conference at Kabwe in 1985, and the Stuart report was effectively buried until 1993. People detained during the mutiny remained in detention in harsh conditions until as late as 1990, and the security organ continued to be responsible for numerous abuses of the same sort as those that had touched off the 1984 mutiny, in spite of minor reforms. In 1986–7, the directorate of the Department of Intelligence and Security was suspended as a result of personal conflicts between Piliso and Boroko, and the department was run temporarily by a committee consisting of Alfred Nzo, Joe Nhlanhla (the new head of security) and Jacob Zuma (the new head of intelligence).[47] Both Piliso and Boroko were later redeployed, and Nhlanhla became the new head of the department, introducing a number of reforms.[48] Nevertheless, the catalogue of abuses continued.[49]

Security and politics

All armies confront problems of discipline from time to time. An exiled guerrilla army is certainly no exception, and the fact that similar troubles were recorded in *Umkhonto we Sizwe* in the 1960s could be said to indicate no more than that soldiers living in harsh conditions, frustrated by lack of contact with the enemy whom they have enlisted to fight, are prone to indiscipline which then causes the military command to exact punishment. The first known wave of detentions, in 1967-9, was conducted not by a special security service but by the army command. Thereafter there was a satisfactory political solution to the problem, with the calling of the Morogoro consultative conference at which the rank and file of *Umkhonto we Sizwe* were allowed to air their views and to discuss the shortcomings of the army high command, as a result of which far-reaching changes were implemented. As far as is known, no ANC members were executed or murdered as a result of their expressions of complaint in 1967–9 (although Hani appears to have come perilously close to it) and none was detained for any considerable period.

The situation in *Umkhonto we Sizwe* changed markedly with the influx of new recruits to the organization in 1976–7. The organization's leaders were concerned to impose some form of discipline on the newcomers whose sheer numbers posed a problem of assimilation, and at the same time ANC leaders were concerned—rightly, as it transpired—that the new recruits might contain a number of enemy agents. Since *Umkhonto we Sizwe* was a military structure, it was reasonable that the leaders of the ANC/SACP should wish to establish a security service which would both enforce discipline and act as a counter-espionage service. Many security personnel were rather young, and the fact that many would have had some experience of detention by the South African police before their flight into exile would no doubt have made them prone to take a robust view of the duties of a security officer. Some had certainly undergone training by East European operatives, some of whose methods and views of what constituted dissent they would have assimilated. Certainly there are cases of people being detained in the late 1970s because of their criticism of the ANC's leadership and for calling for a consultative conference. While this may be regarded as circumstantial evidence, it does not fully support the thesis advanced in the journal *Searchlight South Africa* that the purge of 1981 was a classic Stalinist manoeuvre in the sense of being planned with the primary aim of enforcing a degree of ideological correctness. A definitive judgement will have to await study of the ANC and SACP archives, which are at present closed. But the available evidence suggests that, until 1981 at least, such abuses as did occur were the result of a rather unsophisticated approach to the enforcement of discipline and of material shortages rather than of any political decision to purge people judged to be ideologically suspect. The torture methods used by ANC security officials bore little resemblance to the highly bureaucratized repression and surveillance typical of the KGB and the *Stasi*. Only once the security apparatus had been unleashed on suspected spies or dissidents, or other perceived troublemakers of all descriptions, did the ideological and political aspects of the purge become apparent.

In considering this point, it is useful to compare the ANC's response to the troubles of 1967–9 and those of 1981–4. The SACP appears to have thrown its full weight behind the calling of the Morogoro conference in 1969. The importance of this is that it put the SACP on the side of the reformers within the ANC and gave the party a populist position within *Umkhonto we Sizwe*. In the event, the delegates at the Morogoro conference endorsed a range of views advocated by leading lights of the SACP and in so doing inaugurated a major change in the relationship between the SACP and other elements within the broad coalition which was accommodated within the ANC, although not every leading SACP member supported this change. This was to lead to the exclusion from the ANC of any organized faction other than the SACP, and notably in the withdrawal of the so-called Gang of Eight, a group which included both communist and non-communist ANC members who were critical of the leading position taken by the SACP within the ANC alliance.[50] The ANC leadership, however, remained sufficiently broad as to accommodate such an iconoclast as Palio Jordan, who had spent many years in America and had a background in the Trotskyist-inclined Non-European Unity Movement. It is telling that Jordan was not a member of the ANC/SACP military wing, where a military standard of discipline was required, but a holder of a civilian office, and that he was not regarded as leading any sort of faction within the ANC, which allowed him to be tolerated.

The Morogoro conference committed the ANC to a manifesto which Joe Slovo characterized as one of 'revolutionary nationalism', bearing a marked resemblance to the manifesto of the SACP itself, both in its analysis of the South African condition and in its commitment to a particular strategy of guerrilla war.[51] Moreover, for the first time the ANC agreed to allow members of all ethnic groups to sit on a senior committee, namely the Revolutionary Council, which had oversight of the political and military struggle and which immediately became an SACP fief. These changes helped to sharpen the ANC's strategic focus and to render its military bureaucracy more efficient. At the same time, they provide a clue as to why the SACP was able to support grassroots criticism and dissent following the protests of 1967–9, but did not adopt a similarly sympathetic attitude after the mutiny of 1984, by which time it was in control of the ANC and was determined to fight off any challenge to its position from below.

The 1981 purge was not associated with a factional struggle within the leadership along the lines of the great Stalinist purges of the 1930s. On the contrary, the ANC leadership seems to have been united in its failure to give political attention to the abuses it knew to be taking place in the camps and in its failure to halt them, and even when it felt obliged to find a high-level scapegoat in the person of Andrew Masondo, he was not utterly disgraced in the classic Stalinist fashion, but was found alternative employment as the head of the Solomon Mahlangu Freedom College and remained an acknowledged member of the ANC leadership. This means of sidelining a senior official rather than holding him up to public ridicule or exemplary punishment is far more reminiscent of, say, Zambia under President Kaunda than it is of East European Stalinism.

Only in one or two cases could it be said that detention may have been used as a weapon in the in-fighting between ANC leaders. For example, the Jobodwana Commission failed convincingly to dispel suspicions that Thami Zulu, a senior *Umkhonto we Sizwe* commander, was detained as a result of in-fighting between rival factions of the ANC/SACP.[52] But perhaps the most celebrated example of an arrest motivated by in-fighting was that of Pallo Jordan, which also demonstrates how precarious was the ANC's tolerance of such a free-thinking intellectual. According to a source who was at that time a member of the ANC intelligence apparatus, this took place in June 1983, as follows:

Pallo was detained on the orders of Party member and *Mbokodo* chieftain, Peter Boroko. Another member of the Party, Francis Malaya, an official with Department of Information and Publicity (DIP) and a secret informant of *Mbokodo*, complained about Pallo's behaviour. Pallo was accused of exposing the *Mbokodo* informant network within DIP by mockingly referring to Malaya and another man named Ace ... as *Amapolisa*—warning other DIP staffers to be careful of them. On that basis, Pallo was detained and was to spend six weeks in detention. I participated in an informal meeting at Green House (*Mbokodo* HQ) which discussed Pallo's arrest ... During the discussion one *Mbokodo* officer made a chilling remark which seemed to capture the essence of the entire saga. The comment went thus *'eli intellectual lase Merika liijwayela kabi'* —'this American trained intellectual is uppity'—and thus in need of straightening out. Clearly, the arrest had ideological overtones. Pallo's education in the West made him suspect to a group of youngsters brought up to revile and suspect everything the West represented. This was a centrepiece of the Party's anti-Western propaganda which had been imbibed uncritically by these enforcers. The person who made that comment was Samora Gcina (alias Vusi) ... I'm almost certain Vusi was not a member of the Party but like many young men joining the ranks with only a rudimentary high school education, he was susceptible to influence by the virulent anti-West rhetoric of the commissars. This is where the tragedy lay.[53]

Had there existed significant factions within the ANC other than the SACP after the exclusion of the Gang of Eight in 1975, no doubt the security question might have become an important topic of debate within the ANC leadership. In fact there was relatively little difference of opinion on the issue. The non-controversial nature of the security question is indicative of the comprehensiveness with which the SACP, building on its base in *Umkhonto we Sizwe*, had imposed its will on the whole organisation. One of the overwhelming calls of rank and file agitators was for progress in the armed struggle—a consistent theme both in the 1967–9 and in the 1981–4 disturbances. *Umkhonto we Sizwe* soldiers wanted to know why they were kept in boring, demoralizing camps, or deployed to fight in Angola rather than in South Africa. On both occasions they reserved their special contempt for Joe Modise, the army commander, who had a reputation for holding the rank and file in contempt and for incompetence. These charges, if seriously debated, would have called into question the conduct of the armed struggle in the form championed by the SACP and as it was accepted by the ANC at its 1969 Morogoro conference. In this sense the abuses perpetrated by the ANC security organ certainly were political: one of the classic motives for purges in the tradition of Soviet Marxist-Leninism was to provide an explanation for the failure of the leadership to make the progress which it claimed would follow from the application of scientific socialism. If the armed struggle made less progress than was desired, and than the rank and file called for, then an explanation had to be found. And it was found in the agitation of spies. Where spies did not exist, they must be invented. Thus, even marijuana-smoking was regarded as the work of enemy agents.

Jeremy Cronin, a senior member of the SACP who went into exile only in 1987, while acknowledging the excesses of the ANC security organ, has suggested that it would not have made any difference whether the ANC's security personnel had been trained by the KGB, the *Stasi*, or some other security force such as the US Central Intelligence Agency.[54] We may assume that all militarized formations have a need of some form of security apparatus which will use detention as its chief weapon. Bluntly put, the question is: were the excesses of *Mbokodo* a regrettable by-product of the armed struggle, as Cronin and other ANC/SACP apologists suggest? Or were they, as Trewhela suggests, a symptom of the ascendancy of the SACP and of its alliance with the governments of the Soviet bloc? Or should they be understood in some other way?

The crude interrogation methods of *Mbokodo* cannot be specifically related to Soviet or East German training. However, where they may be said to owe something to the Soviet connection, as Trewhela has charged, is in the role of the security service within the politics of the ANC. It was the specific contribution of the SACP during the years of its ascendancy after the Morogoro conference to introduce into the ANC the notion of a single correct ideological and strategic line, a direct input from the scientific Marxist–Leninist method. A Stalinist notion of the correct political and ideological education of soldiers spread to other parts of the ANC, and tended to penalize critical thought even among non-soldiers. In the hands of political commissars and zealous young security officers, persons suspected of failing to conform to this line were equated with security suspects.

All political systems which adopt authoritarian or totalitarian features tend in this direction. In the case of the ANC, the growth of a Stalinist style of political-military discipline was associated with the rise of communist influence in the ANC, particularly after 1969. This gave to the practices of the security organ a coherent ideological justification.

Conclusion: the militarization of the ANC

Whereas there exists a considerable literature on the militarization of African states and on the effect of military regimes, including in regard to the South African state,[55] previous authors have paid little attention to the effect on the ANC of its own militarization after its adoption of the armed struggle in 1961.[56] A banned organization, led from exile, necessarily encounters particular problems which are not faced by a state. The ANC after 1961 aspired not only to be an alternative government of South Africa, but also, like other liberation movements controlling camps or territory, it acted as a state of sorts in regard to its own personnel.[57] Whether in a legally-recognized state or a quasi-state, the effects of militarization are similar. Most notably, the field of political activity is reduced, typically to the pursuit of single goals or slogans. In the case of African military regimes this is typically the 'elimination of corruption', economic development, or national unity. In the case of a liberation movement, it is victory in the struggle to overthrow the target government. Other political issues are subordinated to this single, overwhelming goal. Since the political regime is militarized, military discipline is required and harsh punishments await dissenters. Dissent is characterized as mutiny. These remarks could equally apply to a right-wing or to a left-wing system of militarization, but a system such as that introduced to the ANC in exile, particularly after 1969, identified liberation with a specifically Marxist vision of strategy and ideology introduced to the ANC by its SACP ally. Dissenters, or simply people who clashed with those who governed the movement, were easily equated with saboteurs or spies. The restrictions on critical thought, or on inappropriate behaviour, were all the stronger in the case of members of *Umkhonto we Sizwe*. The longer the ANC's armed struggle lasted, and the more it became apparent that its success was far from certain, the more pressing became the need to find scapegoats, real or imagined.

Just as a period of military government may permanently alter the historical development of a state, so did the militarization of the ANC permanently alter its character during the period of exile. Since its unbanning in 1990 the ANC has been the scene of diverse political and ideological debates and disputes, and the public airing of the abuses of the past via the Skweyiya and Motsuenyane commissions was itself a symptom of such differences. It is apparent that within the National Executive Committee of the ANC and, no doubt, within the Central Committee of the SACP, there have been sharp disagreements between those whose inclination is to air the mistakes of the past in public and those who would prefer to conceal them or to place the responsibility elsewhere. It appears that the first group includes particularly leaders like Nelson Mandela who were on Robben Island during the troubles of exile, backed up by former leaders of the United Democratic Front who had never been in exile. In the second group are ANC security officials and many veterans of the exile leadership.[58]

An evident sign of the factional struggles behind the scenes is the question of personal responsibility. The Skweyiya Commission fairly clearly attached a degree of personal responsibility to Mswai Piliso, who was the head of the ANC's Department of Intelligence and Security from 1981 to 1986 and who 'candidly admitted his personal participation in the beating of suspects in 1981'.[59] However the Motsuenyane Commission, which identified some individuals responsible for specific abuses, made no special mention of Piliso in this regard but instead named in passing army commander Joe Modise and former intelligence chief Jacob Zuma.[60] The ANC postponed investigation of where the full responsibility for these abuses lay, suggesting the constitution of a 'truth commission' which would treat the whole range of crimes and abuses committed during the armed struggle by both the ANC and the South African government.[61]

By the time the Motsuenyane Commission reported, in August 1993, the ANC seemed well on the way to becoming at least the main element in the government of South Africa. ANC headquarters in Johannesburg continued to employ many of the officials of the Security Department who were found to have participated in abuses in Angola and who presumably would be well-placed to hold political or other high office in a future government. ANC security officials had had a number of meetings with their opposite numbers in the South African Police and the South African Defence Force with a view to discussing future mergers of their services and personnel.[62]

One of the more disturbing possibilities of a future South African government is that it will employ in its security departments veterans both of the old South African Police Security Branch and of *Mbokodo*, both of them having a shabby tradition of brutality and of contempt for legality. If so, it will not be the first time in southern Africa that a shared ethos, irrespective of its precise ideological origin, will have overridden old enmities and brought former enemies together after the overthrow of a racist or colonial government.[63] At the time of writing, the ANC had not yet become a party of government in South Africa. Only when it does so will it be possible to see its rich and complex history in a new perspective. In particular, only time will tell the extent to which its armed struggle against a ruthless opponent, which had itself been profoundly militarized, has affected its political nature.

8

THE HISTORICAL SIGNIFICANCE OF SOUTH AFRICA'S THIRD FORCE*

Accounts of South Africa's transition from apartheid differ markedly in the role they attribute to violence. The most influential narratives of negotiations tend to portray the violence of the transition period, including that perpetrated by those networks within and without the security forces which have become known collectively as the Third Force, as a reaction to events, doomed to failure and rather disconnected from the main narrative of history. Newly available evidence shows the degree to which the Third Force was integrated into the policy of the National Party over a long period, and played a crucial role in determining the nature and outcome of constitutional negotiations in 1990– 1994. The consequences of the tactics used by the Third Force, and the legacy of the war for South Africa in general, continue to have an important influence on politics and on society. Analysis of contemporary South Africa can benefit from consideration of the manner in which politics, military activity and crime became enmeshed during a long war.

Most people who lend some attention to South African politics first heard of the Third Force in September 1990, when the phrase was

* I am grateful to a great number of people who have granted interviews or provided me with documents or helped in other ways with research for this article. I am especially indebted to John Daniel and others at the secretariat of the Truth and Reconcilation Commission, where I worked in July and August 1997 and May 1998, and to Phillip van Niekerk.

first used in public by leaders of the African National Congress (ANC) including Nelson Mandela, then just seven months out of prison and already established as the organisation's *de facto* head.

After a brief honeymoon, in which preliminary accords had been signed between the government and the ANC, Mandela had been incensed by a spate of murderous, random attacks on black people, first in the Vaal area and later on the East Rand and on trains running between Soweto and Johannesburg. These attacks, he believed, bore the hallmark of organised, covert government death-squads. There had also been an escalation in the conflict in Natal, notably in the so-called 'Seven-Day War' which ravaged the Natal Midlands in March 1990. Such attacks continued after the ANC had formally announced a suspension of its armed struggle in August 1990. Mandela suggested that a mysterious third party—distinct from the ANC and the National Party, but presumably including members of the security forces—lay behind much of this violence, which President F. W. de Klerk denied.

Although the South African press took to making repeated references to the Third Force after Mandela had first used the phrase in public, and as random attacks such as train massacres and drive-by shootings proliferated, most newspapers were to remain rather vague about the exact nature of the alleged network throughout the period of transition which culminated in the elections of 1994, with the notable exception of the two newspapers which gave most attention to investigating the inner workings of the security services, the English-language *Weekly Mail & Guardian* and the Afrikaans-language *Vrye Weekblad*. Many prominent commentators suggested that, while there certainly were diehards and even organised death-squads in the security forces, the violence in the country was essentially a symptom of rapid political change. Some pointed out that violence was partly, or even largely, the result of the ANC's own previous revolutionary strategy and its earlier call on the people of South Africa to render the country 'ungovernable'.[1] Others saw the violence as stemming essentially from the government's policy towards the ANC and its allies.[2]

Broadly speaking, the views of both politicians and commentators could be situated on a spectrum, at one end of which were those who believed or claimed that the government was doing its best to administer the country peacefully in a difficult period and that official death squads either did not exist or represented isolated acts of indiscipline. This was the point of view adopted by the National Party itself: Hemus Kriel, then Minister of Law and Order, stated in September 1991 that, 'We are in a period of change in our country, of political change, of constitutional change. And history has taught us that whenever something like that happens in a country, it is always accompanied by some sort of instability'.[3] According to this view, the violence in the country was largely the result of social upheavals, the culture of lawlessness among youth particularly, and the handiwork of criminals and opposition parties seeking to make gains at a time of contested authority. At the other end of the spectrum of opinion were the ANC and its supporters and allies, who tended to believe that violence was directly or indirectly caused by units of the security forces directed by a government which was pursuing a secret agenda. At times, ANC leaders suggested that the government was perhaps not in full control of its security forces, and that these were intent on sabotaging negotiations completely or even creating the conditions for a military coup.

Since 1994 especially, new evidence has confirmed that a Third Force did indeed exist. Significant new sources of information have included official or judicial inquiries, notably the commission led by Judge Richard Goldstone, established by President De Klerk in 1991 to investigate allegations of security force involvement in political violence, and the proceedings of the Truth and Reconciliation Commission.[4] Further evidence has come to light through the press and from various other judicial proceedings such as the inquest into the deaths of Matthew Goniwe and others and the trials of Colonel Eugene de Kock and of General Magnus Malan and others. In addition, recently published academic research has shed further light on the Third Force and on the context within which it developed.[5]

It is now clear that the name 'Third Force', in the sense in which it was used by Nelson Mandela in September 1990, is something of a misnomer, since the State Security Council, effectively the most senior organ of government under the presidency of P.W. Botha, began actively discussing the creation of a third force as early as 1985, although in a sense different from that conveyed by Mandela when he first used the phrase in public, as we shall see in due course.

But since the expression 'Third Force' has gained both national and international currency, the present article will continue to use the term to designate a substantial, organised group of security officials or former officials intent on perpetrating violence in the service of a counter-revolutionary strategy.

The versions of events during the transition from apartheid to democracy in South Africa which have been most influential throughout the world are probably those published by the journalists Allister Sparks and Patti Waldmeir.[6] Both these valuable works tend to disconnect the role of violence from the narrative of negotiation. Although Nelson Mandela himself in his best-selling autobiography has indicated that he became gradually convinced of the existence of a Third Force, this occupies only a small section in a generally more edifying account of the transition.[7] A number of academic studies also regard organised violence as a secondary element, somewhat apart from the main narrative, or at least as a factor out of the immediate control of the negotiators.[8]

It is certainly not our intention to belittle any of these works, or still more, the South African achievement in bringing an end to apartheid without plunging the country into a full-scale civil war. Rather, the purpose of the present article is to demonstrate that concentration on the narrative of negotiations, or indeed any account which fails to give due weight to the perpetrators of organised violence including those who constituted the Third Force, implicitly assigns the violence of 1990–1994 to a position somewhat divorced from, or even antithetical to, the pursuit of negotiation.[9] This has deflected attention from the important question of ascertaining the extent to which the agenda and pace of negotiations, and thus the shape of the eventual political and constitutional outcome, were actually driven by proponents of violence who were able to make their influence felt from outside the conference chamber. Moreover, many of the people who perpetrated this violence continue to play an important role in South Africa to this day, and in some cases continue to use violence in pursuit of their aims. A reconstruction of the role played by the Third Force raises questions concerning the emerging polity of democratic South Africa which lives with the legacy of this bloody confrontation. Some questions regarding the connection between the political and paramilitary violence of the past and the current epidemic of crime are addressed in the last part of the paper.

The information now available concerning the Third Force compels us to develop a more nuanced view of South Africa's transition. More than 14,000 South Africans lost their lives in violence between 1990 and 1994, more than at any other period of the war to overthrow apartheid. Hence the history of this period may be considered not only as the moment at which moderation and reason triumphed over violence, but also as that in which the war for South Africa, previously fought most ferociously outside the country's borders, now enveloped South Africa itself.

To be sure, there were a number of political organisations and social groups which perpetrated violence in South Africa between 1990 and 1994, including the ANC, which are mentioned in the present essay only in passing. The state-organised or state-connected covert and clandestine networks known as the Third Force were not responsible for all the political violence which occurred in this period, but there is reason to believe that they were by some way its most important sponsors.

War and politics

It is appropriate at this juncture to justify our use of the word 'war' to describe the competition for control of the state in South Africa over more than three decades. Those most centrally involved in this contest did not doubt that South Africa was indeed at war between the early 1960s and the early 1990s. For, as Thomas Hobbes observed over three centuries ago, 'Warre, consisteth not in Battell only, or the act of fighting; but in a tract of time, wherein the Will to contend by Battell is sufficiently known... So the nature of War, consisteth not in actuall fighting; but in the known disposition thereto'.[10]

Many inquirers, including the Truth and Reconciliation Commission, regard the Sharpeville massacre of March 1960 as the true beginning of hostilities. It was in response to this and other provocations, including the banning of the ANC and the Pan-Africanist Congress (PAC), which then joined the South African Communist Party (SACP) on the list of proscribed organisations, that the ANC and SACP formed an armed wing, Umkhonto we Sizwe. Umkhonto we Sizwe issued a formal declaration of war on 16 December 1961. Thereafter Umkhonto we Sizwe carried out a sabotage campaign for some two years until the arrest of its High Command at Rivonia in 1963. The new leaders of the organisation, now based in exile, came to regard their struggle explicitly as revolutionary in nature, comparable to similar campaigns in Algeria, Vietnam and elsewhere, and they developed a sophisticated strategy of guerrilla warfare. South Africa's National Party government also became convinced that it faced a war of some description. After the mid-1970s, it defined this war as the spearhead of a 'total onslaught', in the words of a 1977 defence white paper, orchestrated by the Soviet Union, which provided military, diplomatic and other support to the ANC and the SACP and to allied governments in Angola and Mozambique. South African army and police officers who had studied the theory and practice of revolutionary warfare, and who became known as 'securocrats' due to their belief that security structures could be used as institutions for managing political change, devised a counter-insurgency doctrine aimed at mobilising every branch of the state in a campaign to defeat the total onslaught which they believed to be directed from Moscow. A document approved by the State Security Council in 1985 stated that 'there is consensus over the view that the unrest has developed into a revolutionary struggle', although it noted that it would be unwise for the government to use such language in public.[11] Counsel for the South African Defence Force (SADF) argued before the Supreme Court in 1988 that a *de facto* state of war existed in South Africa which precluded civil courts from exercising jurisdiction over the state in certain security matters. This argument was, however, rejected by the Court.[12]

The aim of one side in the war was, in the words of the most influential of the military theoreticians on the government side, 'to subvert and overthrow by force the established regime and to replace it with another'.[13] The government's counter-strategy, naturally, aimed to prevent such a thing. Murder, torture, smuggling, forgery, propaganda and subversion were instruments used by both sides in this struggle, but it was the state which brought the greatest resources to bear in these domains. Since Umkhonto we Sizwe could not hope to defeat the SADF on a conventional battlefield, the key to the struggle was to induce the mass of the population to either accept or resist continued government by the National Party. The ANC, increasingly influenced by the SACP's orthodox Marxist analysis, came to consider the black urban proletariat as the most important constituency, and to believe that its own armed struggle could spark a general insurrection or 'people's war'.[14] Theoreticians on both sides suggested that violence, although important, was not the main element in the struggle, although both sides in practice found it difficult to sublimate the use of armed force to clear political strategies. The thinking of the securocrats on this matter was spelled out by the head of the Security Branch, Lt-Gen. P. J. Coetzee, in a speech in 1982. He pointed out that the battle was not fought just with tanks and guns:[15]

> Perhaps even more important is the battlefield of enemy propaganda and terrorist mythology... Our target is the collection of individuals and organisations, operating from within and without, who practice or attempt subversion or revolution. The importance of this task at a time of total onslaught against the Republic of South Africa cannot be gainsaid.

'Lt-Gen. Coetzee', added the reporter of the SADF journal which published his speech, 'said that it was on the psychological rather than the physical battlefield where the struggle would be won or lost'.

In the view of the securocrats, then, the aim of violence was less to destroy the enemy's armed forces than to win the support of the population by a mixture of political action, intimidation, propaganda and the symbolic manifestation of authority. In time, the securocrats added to this list the elimination of those socio-economic grievances which made South Africa fertile ground for revolutionaries. For the securocrats, most of whom were professional soldiers and policemen rather than politicians, this was essentially a matter of management in which the security and welfare functions of government had to be integrated for the overall purpose of preserving the life of the state. This is the ideology of sophisticated military rulers. They believed that it was above all the use of revolutionary violence and propaganda by the ANC and its allies which accounted for the ANC's success in winning support from what they saw as an essentially manipulable black population, as part of what became, after the late 1970s, a classical revolutionary strategy. The securocrats saw the wave of township violence after 1984 as evidence of this. The ANC intended to implement a revolution, the securocrats believed, by proceeding through four phases beginning with the organisation of an underground apparatus and passing through acts of terrorism to a guerrilla war or people's war. The final phase of such a conflict would be mobile or semi-conventional warfare. Accordingly, the securocrats sought to identify the current phase of the war and to turn it back to the preceding phase, using the revolutionaries' own tactics. For, according to another theorist closely studied by the securocrats, 'the solution to the problem of defeating revolutionary warfare is the application of its strategy and principles in reverse'.[16]

The military and police units which were later to be a central part of the Third Force have their origins in the earliest period of the war in the 1960s. In the following paragraphs, we will briefly trace the history of these units. We will then discuss how they were organised for counter-revolutionary warfare inside South Africa in the form of the Third Force and the role they played in South Africa's transition from apartheid. The final section of the essay consists of remarks on some of the consequences of the activities of the Third Force.

South African counter-insurgency

At the beginning of the armed struggle, in the early 1960s, South Africa possessed two significant security forces: the South African Police (SAP) and the SADF. It was in 1961 that B.J. Vorster became Minister of Justice and Minister of Police. Believing that South Africa was seriously threatened by revolution,[17] he introduced new security legislation which had the effect of transforming the Police by equipping the force with extensive powers to detain and virtual immunity from prosecution. The change was summarised by Joe Slovo, himself a trained advocate as well as Umkhonto we Sizwe's leading strategist for two decades. 'However firm the old type of policeman … were [sic], they were not torturers', Slovo later recalled almost nostalgically. 'In a sense up to about 1960–61 the underground struggle was fought on a gentlemanly terrain. There was still a rule of law. You had a fair trial in their courts. Nobody could be kept in isolation. Up to 1963, I know of no incident of any political prisoner being tortured.'[18]

All that changed during Vorster's tenure of the Justice and Police portfolios. Vorster promoted his friend H. J. van den Bergh to become, first, head of the Security Branch of the newly-reorganised police, and later, a US-style national security supremo, combining this post with directorship of South Africa's first modern secret service, the Bureau of State Security (BOSS), established by law in 1969 and largely staffed with officers transferred from the Security Branch of the Police. In the process of reorganising a security apparatus built on the Police, Vorster developed for himself a political fief in a key element of the state bureaucracy which was to stand him in good stead when he was elevated to the premiership, still retaining the Police portfolio, in 1966.[19] He introduced into South African politics a convention whereby any successful political career had to be based on a constituency in at least one element of the security forces. Vorster's own career, his elevation of Van den Bergh, and the primacy of the Police in taking responsibility for the conduct of the war against subversion, were developments so closely associated with one another that Vorster's eventual decline was also reflected in that of the institutions which were so marked by his hand, to the point that BOSS itself was abolished and Van den Bergh forced into retirement when Vorster resigned in 1978.[20] The Police service was to be eclipsed as the paramount security service as a result of Vorster's replacement as premier by Defence Minister P. W. Botha, whose power-base lay partly in the military, whose minister he had been since 1966.

Over the years, the SAP, and most particularly the Security Branch, developed a characteristic view of subversion. To some extent the origins of this lay in the SAP's own evolution from a colonial-style mobile police force.[21] Long before the outbreak of hostilities in the 1960s, and indeed even before the National Party government came to power in 1948, the SAP had developed a strategy for policing African populations, in conformity with the British colonial tradition of indirect rule. The latter was a system of government which aimed to keep Africans as far as possible in rural areas under their own traditional or quasi-traditional rulers. In English-speaking southern Africa, it included provision for rural African men especially to move to the towns as migrant workers who could live in cities and mine compounds for a specified period before returning to their home areas and their families after their contracts had expired. Indirect rule required government officials to identify and promote local rulers, hereditary chiefs if possible, who would govern rural areas as far as practicable by their own devices and according to customary law. The role of the national police force, then, was to ensure that chiefs did not contravene the laws of the central government which applied in those rural areas designated as African reserves, or the later apartheid creations of bantustans or homelands, and to act as a mobile armed force when intervention was necessary. Any significant agitation against a chief regarded by the government as legitimate was interpreted by the Police as a form of insurgency.

The Police continued to apply this policy in the vastly different environment of the urban areas which emerged with South Africa's industrialisation, despite the fact that most black townships were ethnic melting pots with no rulers who could be regarded as traditional. The growth in the African population of the cities left the Police attempting to carry out its traditional task of seeking local strongmen with an ethnic constituency, in the absence of any clear government policy on cultivating political institutions in black urban areas. Not until the 1980s did the government try to develop a coherent policy on the representation of Africans in urban areas, and by that time, control of the townships was being contested by armed revolutionary organisations such as the ANC and the PAC. The Police found it difficult to identify people of influence who would work with them but who could also command respect among the black population, and resorted to cultivating informer networks and repressing anti-apartheid activity with the immense powers at their disposal. At no stage were policemen operating in black urban areas able to dispose fully of the most important element of all successful policing, namely the active support of the local population.

To this tradition was added a corpus of experience gained directly in border wars in Rhodesia and Namibia. In 1967, Umkhonto we Sizwe, now based in Tanzania, developed a new strategy known as 'hacking the way home'. This envisaged a campaign of rural guerrilla warfare in Rhodesia, intended to open up a Ho Chi Minh trail to South Africa. Implementation of this plan depended on an alliance with ZIPRA, the armed wing of the Zimbabwe African People's Union (ZAPU), at that time the premier Zimbabwean nationalist movement. After a joint Umkhonto we Sizwe/ZIPRA force had infiltrated Rhodesia in August 1967, SAP units were sent to work alongside the Rhodesian security forces. By 1975, as many as 2,000 South African policemen were stationed in Rhodesia. A further theatre of rural conflict emerged in the north of Namibia, the South African colony threatened by the guerrilla army of the South West African People's Organisation (SWAPO), based first in Zambia and, after 1975, in newly-independent Angola. In Namibia too it was initially the Police and not the SADF which was deployed.

The key lesson learned by South African policemen on detachment in Rhodesia was the value of intelligence in irregular warfare of this sort. The best and most useful intelligence was that obtained from an active guerrilla who, after capture, could be induced to give information on his unit before it had had time even to register his absence. Once such intelligence had been obtained, it would rapidly become obsolete if passed from an intelligence-gathering unit via the central chain of command to an offensive unit, giving the enemy time to move position. Some Rhodesian commanders advocated the creation of intelligence-gathering units which also had an offensive capacity. The main Rhodesian unit of this type was the Selous Scouts, which specialised in 'pseudo-operations', a technique learned from British forces in Malaya and Kenya and the Portuguese *flechas* or irregular police troops in Mozambique and Angola. The Selous Scouts, using black troopers disguised as nationalist guerrillas, operated in enemy territory, capturing and interrogating guerrillas and using the intelligence gathered to launch an immediate surprise attack. After such an act of treachery, a captive could not return to his guerrilla organisation but could now be induced himself to become a Selous Scout, by which time he had been definitively 'turned'.[22] Such 'turned' guerrillas were called *askaris*, a Swahili word acquired by British forces in the Mau Mau insurgency and transmitted via Rhodesian officers to the South African Police. The Selous Scouts killed more people than the rest of the Rhodesian armed forces put together.[23] They rapidly became a law unto themselves, and Rhodesia's intelligence chief later judged the militarisation of pseudo-operations to be 'the worst mistake I made in the conduct of the war'.[24]

There can be no doubt of the importance of the Rhodesian experience in forming the views of South African counter-insurgency specialists who were later to become key members of the Third Force. Among the South Africans who served in Rhodesia, for example, was Eugene de Kock, who joined the South African Police in 1968 and, as a young constable, served 10 or 11 tours of duty in Rhodesia between then and 1972. He trained with various Rhodesian military units including the Special Air Service (SAS) and the Rhodesian African Rifles. It is notable that, whereas a policeman is in theory employed to uphold the law of the land with the minimum use of force, De Kock was partly trained by a military unit specialised in long-range reconnaissance, sabotage and fighting behind enemy lines. The Rhodesian SAS, originally a squadron of the British SAS, had served in the Malayan insurgency where leading Rhodesian officers such as General Peter Walls, later to become the commander of the Rhodesian army, and Lieutenant-Colonel Ron Reid Daly, commander of the Selous Scouts, had learned the dark arts of counter-insurgency.[25] The lessons he learned in Rhodesia, says De Kock, 'made sense to me. Why keep to the Queensberry rules and fight one boxer when you can kick them in the balls and kill three?'[26]

Like De Kock, many of the policemen who were to emerge at the heart of the underground war against subversion in South Africa served in Rhodesia. They included General Hans Dreyer, the founder of the Koevoet unit. Koevoet, established by Dreyer on behalf of the Security Branch in Namibia in 1979 with officers who had served in Rhodesia, was another formative influence. Dreyer, having begun with the idea of using Koevoet in imitation of the Selous Scouts, soon decided that the intelligence function was secondary, and that 'highly mobile and heavily armed hunter-killer teams were the best way of dealing with insurgents in the thick bush of Ovamboland'.[27] De Kock, a founder-member of Koevoet, recalls that during four years in the unit he was involved in some 350 contacts with the enemy. He left Koevoet in 1983 suffering, he now believes, from post-traumatic stress, a condition which went unrecognised by his superiors. 'There was no such thing as counselling', he recalls, 'they wanted kill-rates'.[28] Particularly alarming, from the point of view of traditional policing, was the practice developed by Koevoet, based on the Rhodesian experience of so many of its officers, of using 'turned' guerrillas as troopers in the security forces without giving them a formal indemnity for their earlier offences. In the long run this could only bring the central principle of the law into disrepute.

Battle-hardened, psychologically and socially divorced from their communities of origin and compromised by their treachery, *askaris* were well-suited to the grisliest acts of war. After De Kock had returned to South Africa in 1983 he was drafted into the C 1 unit of the Police based at Vlakplaas where he became commander in 1985. This unit (later renamed C 10), founded in 1979 by yet another veteran of the Rhodesian war, was largely composed of *askaris*, former fighters from Umkhonto we Sizwe, the PAC, ZIPRA and several other guerrilla armies of southern Africa. After the independence of Namibia in 1990, its ranks were swelled by former Koevoet troopers, some of them originally members of SWAPO, bringing the number of *askaris* under De Kock's command to over 300. From 1979, but especially under De Kock's command, the C 10 unit became a general-purpose death-squad which would be handed instructions to kill specific individuals who had been identified by the Security Branch in various parts of the country as well as acting on the initiative of its commander, who had an effective power of life and death. Like their mentors in the Selous Scouts, the Vlakplaas *askari* commanders developed a sense of immunity and eventually performed all manner of freelance operations, including arms-trading and diamond-trafficking, which their superiors would routinely overlook or cover up.[29] After 1986, various provincial police commands also developed their own *askari* units, such as that run by Colonel Andy Taylor in Natal.

The techniques of counter-insurgency developed by the SAP in Rhodesia and Namibia thus made their appearance in South Africa itself. Colonel Theunis 'Rooi Rus' Swanepoel, the architect of the bloody repression of the Soweto rising of 1976, for example, had taken part in the first counter-insurgency operations against SWAPO in northern Namibia ten years earlier.[30] Swanepoel was one of a dozen policemen who had trained on detachment in Algeria in the last days of French rule. The Police were increasingly ruthless in the use of torture and various techniques learned from other countries including Israel, Chile and Argentina, the latter at the height of 'dirty wars' of their own.[31] In combination with the sweeping legal powers introduced in the early 1960s, these factors created a culture of brutality within the Police.[32]

Many of the Security Police techniques of intelligence-gathering were learned by sections of the military, despite the sometimes bitter rivalry between the two services. Until the 1970s the SADF had been a fully conventional force. The favour which John Vorster showed to the SAP and BOSS prevented the SADF from taking a prominent role in counter-insurgency. Nevertheless a few officers had given some thought to the security problems facing South Africa. The young Magnus Malan imbibed the latest US theories of counter-insurgency on courses in the USA in 1962–1963. Even as a junior officer he was regarded as a rising star in the military due to his father's political connections with P. W. Botha, Minister of Defence after 1966, and due to Malan senior's standing in the Broederbond, the Afrikaner secret society which has played such an important role in National Party politics.[33] Malan took command of the Namibian border in 1966 and later, as head of the Army, established systems of joint counter-insurgency committees in the territory which were to serve as models for South Africa itself. A former Army chief, Lieutenant-General Alan 'Pop' Fraser, wrote two privately-circulated studies of counterinsurgency based on British, American and French experience of low-intensity wars. Fraser, a veteran of the Malaya campaign, was instrumental in disseminating the view which was to prevail among a later generation of securocrats that the basic site of revolutionary warfare is none other than the population itself, and that counter-revolutionary warfare must operate on the same terrain.[34]

In 1975, responding to the imminent independence of Angola, the SADF launched its first major operation since the Second World War, penetrating deep into Angola in an effort to prevent a Soviet-allied government from coming to power in Luanda. Although the South African forces were to get close to Luanda, their intervention was a disaster. The operation failed to achieve its objective of installing a pro-Western government, but instead provoked the intervention of a Cuban expeditionary force, thus internationalising the Angolan conflict and compounding the very problem which the SADF had set out to solve. The catastrophic SADF intervention in Angola in 1975–

1976, stymied by poor intelligence and confused political decision-making, taught the SADF the necessity of coordinating different branches of activity if its military efforts were to be successful. In 1977, the SADF unveiled a doctrine called a 'total strategy' which proposed sublimating every aspect of national life to the defence of the state against subversion. As far as South Africa's immediate neighbours were concerned, this meant using every available means to prevent or dissuade them from supplying the ANC and its Namibian counterpart, SWAPO, with bases.

Henceforth, the SADF preferred to stop short of invading neighbouring countries, other than Angola, where it was too deeply committed to pull out entirely. Instead, the securocrats, who acquired such great power in South Africa after P.W. Botha's elevation to the premiership in 1978, developed a variety of instruments to influence South Africa's neighbours, including the offering of diplomatic and economic inducements and a technique of destabilisation involving the use of economic sanctions, sabotage, sponsorship of anti-government groups, propaganda and other techniques in order to create chaos in the country targeted, with a view to making its government more pliable to Pretoria's will. For these purposes the Department of Foreign Affairs was drawn into the securocrats' ambit.[35]

These aspects of the total strategy were regarded as state secrets and were not revealed to the South African public. Officially, sabotage operations in neighbouring countries, the use of death-squads to assassinate opponents of the government at home and abroad, and the use of torture, did not exist in South Africa. Generally speaking, the more gruesome tasks associated with the total strategy were entrusted to specialist units of the SAP or the SADF. In the SADF, Military Intelligence, the Special Forces (founded in 1974) and auxiliary units such as 32 Battalion were the leading specialists in this type of activity. Within the Police, the Security Branch, and especially C 10, based at Vlakplaas, became specialists in covert or clandestine warfare. Here lay the origins of the Third Force, among professional counter-insurgency specialists with long experience of border wars which, as the years went by, they increasingly applied in South Africa itself.

Counter-revolutionary war abroad and at home

The change of government in South Africa in 1978 cleared the way for military commanders to implement the total strategy outlined in the 1977 Defence white paper. Prime Minister Botha, who retained the Defence portfolio until 1980 when it passed to his protégé General Malan, presided over a thorough overhaul of both the strategy and the machinery of government which gave immense power to the securocrats.

The whole point of the total strategy was that it was not limited to purely military matters. It also concerned, for example, control of information and of strategic industries such as arms production and power generation. In response to, or anticipation of, the imposition of economic sanctions, the securocrats concerned themselves with the encouragement of alternative networks for trade not only in strategic commodities such as oil, but even in the normal products of South African agriculture and industry. Even welfare ministries had a role to play.

All of these matters were coordinated by a National Security Management System which was developed after 1979. (Later, this became known simply as the National Management System after welfare ministries had been integrated into it.) This apparatus was overseen by the State Security Council, a sub-committee of the Cabinet which, after it had acquired its own full-time secretariat in 1979, became more powerful than the Cabinet itself.[36] Thanks to these arrangements the securocrats, led by P.W. Botha, made considerable progress in coordinating the different departments of state and in gaining command of a state bureaucracy which had expanded enormously in the previous two decades. Senior securocrats believed that Vorster's *ad hoc* style of government had allowed the machinery of government to run out of control. Their own military culture caused them to impose a more rigorous centralisation than had previously existed and Botha, a talented administrator as well as a powerful politician, found this to his taste. The State Security Council in effect functioned as the apex of a complex system of committees designed to coordinate the work of security and welfare departments, and even, at times, of civic and business organisations, at every level of government. Every part of the country was overseen by a local Joint Management

Committee, dominated by security personnel, which coordinated the action of government agencies within its area, and even brought some non-officials within its scope.[37] If a township was considered to be under the influence of government opponents, the local Joint Management Committee could identify the ringleaders for arrest or even murder while simultaneously arranging for the improvement of local social services in an effort to stem the conditions which gave rise to political discontent. Hence, a massacre at the small Natal settlement of Trust Feed in 1988, for example, was planned by the local Joint Management Committee, and actually carried out by the secretary of the Committee, Police Captain Brian Mitchell.[38]

By 1979, Botha had installed the basis of this formidable machinery. Responding to intelligence that senior ANC and SACP officials had been on a study-tour to Vietnam, and were developing a new strategy based on the insights of the legendary General Vo Nguyen Giap which would abandon the concept of semi-conventional rural guerrilla warfare in favour of an urban strategy,[39] leading securocrats held a conference at Fort Klapperkop in 1979. Also present was an Argentinian visitor, one General D'Almeida. The conference resolved to develop the SADF's Special Forces wing, shortly to come under the control of General 'Kat' Liebenberg, so as to disrupt the ANC's development of military bases in neighbouring countries.[40] After 1979, the aggressive strategy adopted by the South African government towards its neighbours was reinforced by the presence in the USA and Great Britain of strongly anti-communist governments.

The most thoughtful securocrats were aware that the system of apartheid was at the heart of South Africa's political problems and proposed as a solution a programme of political reform. The centrepiece of this was the new constitution unveiled in 1983, which provided for limited power-sharing with Indian and Coloured South Africans. To this was later added a programme of socio-economic upliftment. The securocrats' hope was that in the fullness of time the integrated policies of repression and improvement would create space for the development of new political forces which would provide the black population with a gradualist view of change in contrast to the revolutionary programme of the ANC, SACP and PAC. By early 1984, the government believed that its strategy was working. The new constitution, although widely spurned even by the Indian and Coloured voters it was intended to woo, was in place and the government had negotiated a treaty with Mozambique, the Nkomati Accord, which would help drive Umkhonto we Sizwe out of striking-distance from South Africa. President Botha, in unmistakably triumphalist mode, observed to members of the State Security Council that the total strategy was one 'which is perhaps not perfect, but which works'.[41]

Within a year, this view was to change radically. In September 1984, a wave of rent boycotts and other protests broke out in the Vaal Triangle and spread rapidly, leading to violent disturbances which were met with brutal counter-methods by the Police. So intense was the conflict in Sebokeng that the SADF was deployed in the township, which did much to sharpen the always latent antagonism between rival security forces. With the United Democratic Front (UDF), the pro-ANC front founded in 1983, having great success in providing a national focus to various local conflicts, the ANC believed that a popular rising was at hand and called on South Africans to make the country 'ungovernable'. The dreaded petrol-filled tyre or 'necklace' made its appearance and became widely regarded as the ultimate weapon of pro-ANC 'comrades'. According to the SADF, between 1984 and 1989, 399 people died as a result of necklacing.[42]

The government was now facing a virtual insurrection more serious even than that of 1976, since this time around the insurgents were better organised, were supported by an armed guerrilla movement and had the support, or at least the sympathy, of substantial parts of South African society and of world public opinion. Government ministers saw the hand of the ANC—and behind it, of the Communist Party—everywhere. Even before the Vaal Triangle uprising, exasperated ministers had expressed their concern 'over the use made by the enemy of the trade unions, the courts, the press, political parties, Parliament and other democratic institutions, with a view to undermining the Republic of South Africa'.[43]

Determined to restore control of the country and to regain the political initiative, the government took a series of radical measures which changed the nature of the struggle and which, importantly for the subject under discussion, gave shape to what was later to be called the Third Force.

In January 1985, the State Security Council approved a major new system of propaganda projects known as Strategic Communication or Stratcom.[44] Although these projects were in theory concerned with the dissemination of information and disinformation, many involved blackmail, libel and manipulation of such a mischievous type that, in situations of acute unrest, they could lead to murder and other bloodshed, as we shall see. Throughout 1985, as the situation slipped from bad to worse, almost every fortnightly meeting of the State Security Council brought new measures designed to restore the government's control. On 18 March 1985, the Council broadly approved a document presented to it by its secretariat on the revolutionary climate in South Africa. Approving a plan to arrest key leaders of the agitation on a selective basis, President Botha said he was concerned that the impression was being given 'that the state's authority is being undermined and that action is not being taken in a sufficiently focussed way'.[45] Reflecting on the matter at the next meeting, Botha announced that he wanted to meet privately with 20 to 22 senior officers of the security forces to talk to them 'about how to fight the revolutionary climate'. He added that the government would meanwhile continue with its reforms, but that there was no question of conceding one person, one vote.[46] When exactly this meeting took place is not known, but one police general who attended said that 'PW gave us hell', and that 'he told us we must take the gloves off'.[47]

By July 1985, the situation had not improved. Deputy Minister of Law and Order Adriaan Vlok told the State Security Council that 'the security forces are doing everything they can but that the unrest situation is continuing and that law and order cannot be restored in affected areas, and that damage and loss of life are on-going'[48] The same meeting decided to impose a partial state of emergency two days later [49] The following month, August 1985, while the world focussed on Botha's botched Rubicon speech, and Chase Manhattan became the first major bank to announce it was leaving South Africa, President Botha became yet more obdurate. He said that the country could not wait for legal proceedings against the UDF to take their course, and that 'order must be restored'. The State Security Council approved an intelligence assessment which noted that South Africa was now fighting a revolutionary war, although this assessment should not be publicised for fear of alarming the population.[50] This amounted to a formal finding that the revolutionary onslaught had now reached the phase of guerrilla war inside South Africa and the securocrats believed, following the tenets of their strategic guides Fraser, McCuen and others, that the appropriate step was to fight fire with fire, organising guerrilla forces of their own for deployment inside South Africa.

It was in these circumstances that the government first began to debate the establishment of a third force. To this end, the secretariat of the State Security Council began assembling academic articles and other material on special anti-insurgency or anti-terrorist forces in Europe and elsewhere.[51] When the State Security Council first considered the subject, in November 1985, it was clear that it was thinking in terms of setting up a special paramilitary unit, more aggressive than the Police but, unlike the Army, devoted to internal security. Over the following months, SADF and SAP representatives differed, with the Police arguing for the creation of a strengthened riot police, and the SADF maintaining that a 'third force' capacity already existed within its ranks, in the Army's counter-insurgency forces such as the Special Forces and the Special Tasks directorate of the Chief of Staff (Intelligence).[52] The former unit had been responsible for many cross-border raids, while the latter was the organisation which ran South African support to the União para a Independência Total de Angola (UNITA) in Angola, and the Resistência Nacional Moçambicana (RENAMO) in Mozambique, as well as overseeing the destabilisation of Zimbabwe and Lesotho. It is significant that one of the main police representatives in staff meetings on the third force was Brigadier J. J. Viktor, the original architect of the Vlakplaas death-squad. President Botha himself was adamant that such a third force must be prepared to be unpopular and even 'feared'. He added that the security forces had to cooperate on the new force 'so that the subversives can be fought using their own methods'.[53]

The Police and the SADF were never able to agree on the constitution of a third force since both argued either that such an agency should be under their control, or that they already had the means to carry out the functions allotted to such an organisation. But both Police and Army were in time to create units, or adapt existing ones, to carry out the job of undertaking internal repression of the robust nature which the government required, noting the State President's repeated injunctions to the security forces to cooperate with each other. Deputy Minister Vlok was detached from his usual functions to chair a Joint Security System housed within the secretariat of the State Security Council. Some time in 1985 or 1986, a high-level intelligence committee known from its Afrikaans acronym as Trewits was established to coordinate intelligence and to designate targets for action: in effect, to sentence them to death.[54] As the highest level of government expressed the conviction that the country was now facing a revolutionary war within its own borders, and as the President bullied and exhorted his security forces to restore order at all costs, the departments of state responded by putting in place the mechanisms of an organised network of illegal repression. In July 1985, Eugene de Kock, one of the most feared and admired veterans of Koevoet, was put in charge of the C 1 death squad at Vlakplaas, and thereafter some provincial police commands established their own *askari* units to carry out murders. In May 1986, the Civil Cooperation Bureau was established as a front company by Special Forces on the orders of senior military personnel and the Minister of Defence, and the following month, the head of Special Forces was ordered to deploy his forces, using 'unconventional methods', in support of the Police.[55] After the institution of a nationwide state of emergency in June 1986, the CCB undertook its own operations abroad and carried out assassinations in support of the Police at home, before establishing a comprehensive internal organisation in 1988. The SADF Chief of Staff (Intelligence) set up a clandestine operation to train 200 paramilitary personnel for Inkatha, while a similar attempt was also made to create a pro-government paramilitary force in the Transkei and Ciskei. In effect, military units, which had carried out the destabilisation of neighbouring countries, were now implementing similar strategies at home, on the instructions of the State President, the State Security Council and the head of the SADF.

In April 1986, the State Security Council had endorsed guidelines for a strategy for counter-revolutionary war which, among other things, emphasised that the forces of revolution should not be combatted by the security forces alone, but also by 'anti-revolutionary groups such as Inkatha ... or the ZCC [Zion Christian Church] as well as the ethnic factor in South African society'. In the following months, specifically ethnic organisations were armed and trained in KwaZulu and Ciskei, while anti-ANC groups in other places were encouraged and armed in the form of *kitskonstabels* or special policemen and vigilantes. This was perhaps the most effective counter-revolutionary tactic of all since vigilantes could fight the comrades of the ANC in their own communities. Most obviously, this took the form of arming potential allies among the black population to fight the pro-ANC 'comrades' who had taken control of some townships.[56] At the same time, this pushed KwaZulu Natal beyond the brink of civil war and brought other areas close.

In September 1986, President Botha ordered General Fraser's handbook on counterrevolutionary war to be translated into Afrikaans and circulated to senior officials with a foreword by the State President in which he expressed the wish for them to assimilate and apply these principles,[57] which were based on the concept that the style of revolutionary guerrilla warfare which was being used against the South African state could be countered only by using the same techniques in reverse. In paragraph 33 of his original work, Fraser noted on terrorism: 'As the goal of modern warfare is the control of the populace, terrorism is a particularly appropriate weapon since it aims directly at the inhabitant'. He went on to caution that it should be used by the counter-revolutionary power only with the greatest circumspection, and only with approval 'at the highest level'.[58] In other words, terrorism, as used by the enemy, could also be used by the state's security forces, provided only that this was done 'with the greatest circumspection' and under appropriate political control.

The ambiguity of command

It is in the nature of hierarchies for the precise conditions on the ground to differ on occasion from the intentions of those making strategic decisions at the top of the organisation. Moreover, the senior officials who ran the National Management System at its upper reaches were familiar with the usual techniques of civil servants, including the use of circumlocutions designed to save their political masters from embarrassment and the studied cultivation of ambiguity which permits a functionary to secure a favourable response to lines of action which he (never she, since no women are known to have held posts at the higher levels of the National Management System) hopes will be approved; this is what a senior British official once famously called 'being economical with the truth'. Nevertheless, instances in which the flow of documents from the bottom of the security hierarchy to the apex of the system have come to light illustrate that the State Security Council was well informed of events within its sphere of responsibility. In the case of a leading UDF and underground ANC activist in the Eastern Cape, Matthew Goniwe, a provincial military commander who also chaired the Eastern Province Joint Management Committee ordered the secretary of this JMC to signal the head of the Strategy Branch of the Secretariat of the State Security Council requesting permission to effect the 'permanent removal from society' of Goniwe and others. The request is known to have been discussed at senior levels of the National Management System. On 27 June, Goniwe and three colleagues from the leadership of the United Democratic Front in Cradock were murdered.[59] A judge was to find that there was *prima facie* evidence that both the Chairperson and the Secretary of the Eastern Province JMC had intended the order to mean that Goniwe and others should be killed. It is now known that the murders were carried out by local members of the Security Police. In another case, when the State Security Council in 1986 gave approval for the SADF to train some 200 military personnel on behalf of Inkatha, the papers submitted to the State Security Council did not mention that these were to be used in an offensive capacity.[60] The provision of an offensive capability was discussed only at a slightly lower level of the bureaucracy. Nevertheless, it must have been apparent to members of the Council that, given the nature of the conflict between Inkatha and the ANC in the province, the provision of trained military personnel to Inkatha could only fan the flames of war in the area. In these and similar cases it is apparent that the securocrats who ran the National Management System had become adept in using exactly the combination of euphemism and ambiguity which was necessary to centralise decision-making while avoiding language which would allow a court of law to convict senior officials and ministers of responsibility for law breaking. Senior Police officers who asked their political masters what exactly was meant by phrases such as 'eliminate', 'wipe out' or 'remove from society' were often told that they knew what had to be done, and that they should take appropriate precautions.[61]

Here, then, was a paradox, for while the state as a whole was being rigorously centralised, there was an increasing tendency for covert units to act on the Special Forces' principle of 'need to know' in order to promote operational effectiveness while minimising the risk that senior officials would be embarrassed.[62] An important consequence of this was that covert operatives acquired greater scope to raise money from their operations. For example, covert military operatives ran ivory, hardwood, diamonds and other products out of Angola through a front company on a large scale from the late 1970s. The operation was personally approved by General Malan while he was still head of the SADF before 1980,[63] and yet neither the financial administration of the SADF nor the State Security Council appears to have been informed.[64] The need-to-know principle generally used in covert operations precluded knowledge of the trade from circulating through normal managerial channels. What happened to the income generated by the Angolan trade remains unknown, but the implication is clear: covert operations not only increased enormously the possibilities of corruption, but covert units had a tendency to fracture into vertically-integrated patronage systems whereby covert operators in the field could carry out illegal operations on the authority of just one senior central official, by-passing various committees designed to coordinate government action. Just as happened with the Selous Scouts in Rhodesia, so in South Africa certain covert units were kept under close control only for as long as their patron had the political will and the necessary means. If the patron found it expedient to distance himself from an operation for political reasons, covert units which had grown accustomed to handling largely unaccountable funds were able to operate with progressively less oversight. Moreover, the contacts which military men made with local government agencies and business people through the network of Joint Management Committees and similar parallel administrations gave them exceptional possibilities to intervene in almost any sphere of life.

One of the main concerns of the National Management System was to minimise the always latent, and sometimes intense, rivalry between competing security services. To this end, the secretariat of the State Security Council was able at an early stage to arrange an effective division of functions between the SAP's intelligence-gathering apparatus, Military Intelligence and the National Intelligence Service, the latter being the former BOSS, now shorn of its offensive capability. This was decided at an important conference held at Simonstown in January 1981. The Police's main role was internal, but it continued to have some external assets. The arrangement made at the Simonstown conference was that, in principle, the SAP would run agents and also offensive operations in Swaziland, while the SADF, in principle, took responsibility for other front line states.

The government was dominated by the formidable State President, a bully but also a man with strong religious beliefs, who demonised, quite literally, what he called 'the enemy'. Interested in the prophecies of the great Afrikaner mystic 'Siener' Nicolaas van Rensburg,[65] he believed that ultimately this enemy could be identified with international communism. He was so convinced of the imminence of a Soviet nuclear attack as to order the building of an underground nuclear-proof command bunker in the heart of Pretoria. Years later, after his old foe Nelson Mandela had been elected president, Botha told an interviewer:

> There is a gradual buildup of two forces in the world. The one is the final return of Christ to this earth and the other is the eventual destruction of Satan himself. I told Mr Mandela when he came here … 'Mr Mandela, I warn you, these forces are going to destroy you'.[66]

Botha's ministers, like Florentine courtiers, vied for the prince's ear. Foreign Minister 'Pik' Botha was widely distrusted by senior securocrats who suspected him of leaking information to curry favour with the US State Department. Some regarded him as little better than a traitor. Military men developed their own lines of communication with the US intelligence services and especially with William Casey, the anti-communist Director of Central Intelligence in Washington from 1981 to 1987.

The military, like the Police, developed specific underground warfare units. The most important of these was that commanded by the Chief of Staff (Intelligence), although the various armed forces—navy, army and air force—still retained their own intelligence services. The Chief of Staff (Intelligence) was a unit of the general staff of the SADF, directly under the head of the SADF. Until 1980, when he became Defence Minister, the head of the SADF was General Malan. He and President Botha soon developed the habit of confiding certain executive tasks to the Chief of Staff (Intelligence) with the result that the position, previously relatively obscure, became a very powerful one since it became divorced from the usual line function and devoted increasing attention to executing covert operations rather than simply gathering or coordinating intelligence. This had several effects which were to leave their mark on the history of South Africa. In the first place, the post of Chief of Staff (Intelligence) became coveted by ambitious officers, since it gave direct access to the head of the SADF and the State President, who seems to have regarded it as his personal operational arm.[67] It also polluted the quality of intelligence since the politicisation of the office created pressures for intelligence estimates to be slanted for political reasons rather than in conformity with the intelligence officer's ideal of impartiality.[68] The number of employees of the office grew to hundreds or even thousands, some of whom had no background in any military corps. One officer described the change in personnel of the office of Chief of Staff (Intelligence) as follows:

> Most of them are civilians, you see. They get a degree, and so on, and he joins the Defence Force and he puts on a uniform and now he's a colonel, or he's a major, or he's a brigadier, or he's a corporal, or whatever. But now he's got status. But he's not a fighter ... CSI is Intelligence, and being Intelligence they are always secret. And when you are secret you can do all sorts of weird and wonderful things without anybody knowing what you are doing.[69]

One section of the office of the Chief of Staff (Intelligence), known as the Directorate of Special Tasks, had the job of running allied armies in the front-line states, including super-ZAPU in Zimbabwe, UNITA in Angola, and RENAMO in Mozambique. After 1986 the Directorate of Special Tasks also developed liaison with Inkatha. In practice, the Chief of Staff (Intelligence) worked closely with Special Forces. This SAS-type arm, founded in 1974, was strengthened by an influx of Rhodesian special forces operatives recruited at the time of Zimbabwean independence in 1980.

Collectively, then, a number of covert units had a licence to break the law at home and abroad. Some, particularly those associated with the Chief of Staff (Intelligence), had political protection at the highest level in a chain of command which by-passed the conventional line of management, and all, in varying degrees, enjoyed opportunities to generate funds in the course of their work. The people manning these units were diverse. Some had largely civilian backgrounds, while others were veterans of wars in Rhodesia and elsewhere. In general, elite units such as Koevoet (Police) and the Reconnaissance Commandos (SADF Special Forces) enjoyed great prestige within the security forces. They developed a distinctive culture which was aggressive, arrogant and utterly contemptuous of the law and of civilians and even of ordinary soldiers or policemen. Such units tended to attract officers with disordered personalities, and long service in them brutalised otherwise unremarkable people.

Officers who had been trained in covert and often illegal work learned to interpret the wishes of politicians who spoke of 'eliminating' and 'taking out' activists, as Minister of Law and Order Adriaan Vlok often did, or of tracking down the enemy wherever he may be, as Minister of Defence Malan often urged.[70] 'I support you in these things', Minister Vlok told a meeting of Security Police officers in 1990, referring to illegal activities, 'but you must know I would be committing political suicide if they ever came to light'.[71] His bluntness made Vlok popular among police officers. Eugene de Kock and other Vlakplaas operatives recall specific occasions on which Vlok and senior Police commanders joined in the drinking sprees and *braais* with which secret operators celebrated successful acts of illegal sabotage and murder such as the 1988 bombing of Khotso House, a Johannesburg office building housing a number of pro-ANC organisations. 'I was amused', De Kock told a court in 1996, 'because now we were talking about terrorism on home ground'.[72] The head of the SAP was later to confirm that the orders to bomb Khotso House came from President Botha.[73] Members of special units interpreted the concept of total war quite differently from the more cerebral of the securocrats, for whom it was all about sublimating military activity and indeed every other branch of state activity to strategic political goals. For the rank and file of the special units, total war meant simply war without rules. None of the operatives seems ever to have imagined that one day they might be held to account for their actions.

The culture of cynicism and illegality penetrated very deep. One police unit, the Brixton Murder and Robbery Squad, developed a particularly sordid reputation for working in league with criminals, taking bribes and even carrying out criminal activities itself. Its members became used to enjoying the 'good things' in life: cars, expense accounts and, for the greedy, the opportunity to earn money on the side in lucrative black market deals.[74] Officers of this unit were recruited en masse into the CCB, the Special Forces' own murder squad which functioned from 1986 to 1990. Several were thereafter recruited by the Chief of Staff (Intelligence) to carry on the covert war against the ANC. Hence, at the lower end of the hierarchy, covert operatives could be criminals and could pass easily from one special unit to another, immersed in the common culture of violence and illegality. Ferdi Barnard, who worked for the Brixton Murder and Robbery Squad, the CCB and Military Intelligence, despite having served a prison sentence for murder, was described by his girl-friend as having become addicted to crack cocaine, which he traded with a senior officer of the Narcotics Squad of the Police.[75] Another operative, a former Special Forces' soldier named Rich Verster, was commissioned in Military Intelligence immediately after serving a prison sentence.

The total strategy increasingly required covert operatives to set up front companies and adopt false identities. This is a form of subterfuge widely used by modern police forces in 'sting' operations in which the aim is to penetrate criminal circles by infiltration. It made its appearance in South Africa in the 1970s originally in connection with the government's efforts to promote propaganda overseas through the Department of Information.[76] Secret servants working on international aspects of the total strategy, such as sanctions evasion, propaganda and intelligence gathering overseas, increasingly made use of this technique, setting up companies which appeared to have no connection with the

South African government but which were in fact controlled by one or another covert unit. Running networks such as these required the export of funds from South Africa, which was often done illegally both to hide the true nature of the operation and to evade the South African government's own foreign exchange controls. The more intricate and large scale the financial manipulations became, the more even the South African Reserve Bank, internationally regarded as one of the few bastions of financial orthodoxy and professional rectitude on the African continent, became an accomplice to law-breaking. The Reserve Bank turned a blind eye to state-sanctioned illegality and provided financial succour to certain banks which had lost money in support of ventures which were more politically than commercially motivated. The Broederbond, via its influence in the Reserve Bank and Volkskas in particular, appears to have played a leading role in coordinating the upper levels of financial manipulation.[77] White-collar criminals, such as the Pretoria lawyer Albert Vermaas, developed close relationships with leading politicians and securocrats whom they helped to organise the more intricate legal and financial aspects of front companies in banking and transport.[78] The possibilities of making money from international fraud sanctioned by the South African state attracted the attentions of highly skilled professional criminals from abroad, even of at least one convicted Italian mafioso.[79] Both these and more legitimate businessmen in search of government contracts developed close relations with securocrats and politicians whom they plied with gifts and invited to weekend *braais* and hunting-parties.[80]

During the 1980s, the number of front companies increased enormously. The SADF, via the Chief of Staff (Intelligence) and the Civil Cooperation Bureau (itself a front company), set up literally hundreds of front companies to carry out covert activities in fields such as peddling political influence, trading weapons and disseminating propaganda. Alongside the SADF-run front companies, there existed a number of state-owned companies, closely integrated into the security establishment, dealing with weapons research and development. Furthermore, ex-soldiers or retired officers of the Security Branch often set up private security companies unconnected to the SADF. A vast private sector arose, employing tens of thousands of people, consisting of either security companies or companies offering such mundane services as risk analysis, transport and so on, run by active soldiers working under cover, or by former security officers who, though no longer on the state payroll or subject to orders, retained contact with their old colleagues. This commercial–military complex became a fertile environment for covert operatives to do their work.

At the same time, after the mid-1980s, a number of elements converged to make the great network of covert units less coherent than they had previously been. The deployment of the SADF inside the townships greatly increased the likelihood of 'turf battles' between rival units, particularly of the SAP and SADF. Moreover, the destabilisation of the front-line states had had the effect of increasing the size of the informal economy on South Africa's own borders since the government of Mozambique, in particular, had virtually lost control of the usual instruments of formal economic policy. This provided new openings for South African covert units to gain influence by infiltrating smuggling and currency-trafficking activities of various descriptions.

The scale of the township uprisings of the mid-1980s persuaded some influential white South Africans, and eventually the government itself, to open discreet lines of communication with the ANC. The chairman of the Broederbond, Professor Pieter de Lange, had his first informal meeting with the ANC's Thabo Mbeki in 1986, and various businessmen and intellectuals also began to develop contacts with the ANC in exile, which the National Intelligence Service soon discovered and discreetly monitored.[81] It was in this same period that the government began to develop its line of communication with the imprisoned Nelson Mandela.[82] Although these communications remained shrouded in secrecy, rumours began to spread, particularly among those on the inside of the security establishment. A sense grew that change was in the air, and with it, some lower-level covert operatives began to suspect that if their political masters were changing tack, then those who moved at less exalted levels should take precautions of their own. In 1989, shortly before Namibia's independence, Eugene de Kock acquired from his old colleagues in Koevoet several truckloads of weapons from the stockpile of Eastern Bloc arms which Koevoet had captured from SWAPO. He transferred these weapons to the Police farm at Vlakplaas, where he henceforth controlled his own private arsenal alongside the official one.[83]

Although most securocrats remained unbendingly anti-communist, and hostile to the ANC, they could not fail to be affected by the changing international environment. The US government, after 1986, was moving towards a new understanding with the Soviet Union, and Pretoria's anti-communist position could no longer command the same support in Washington as it had done previously. A sure sign of this was the formidable squeeze applied to Pretoria by the US government during the negotiations which linked Angola and Namibia and led to Namibia's independence election in 1989.[84] Given South Africa's increasingly precarious financial position, the Pretoria government could not resist pressure of this sort indefinitely. The beginning of the Namibian decolonisation process was the clearest sign to date to all South Africans that change was coming.

It was at this juncture that P.W. Botha was taken ill and the leadership first of the National Party, and later of the government, passed to F.W. de Klerk. De Klerk, on the conservative wing of the National Party throughout his career, never underwent a Pauline conversion.[85] A skilled and intelligent politician, far more subtle than the bullying P.W. Botha, he was quick to detect that the combination of pressures on the government also constituted a major opportunity. His predecessor had begun negotiations with the ANC and had even entertained Nelson Mandela to tea at his official residence. To use a metaphor drawn from the quintessential Afrikaner game of rugby, the ball was passed to De Klerk, and he ran with it.

Transition: The national party ascendancy

'My God, he's got guts.' A senior securocrat, now retired from the army, recalls uttering these words when he sat watching television with other officials of the State Security Council secretariat on 2 February 1990. They were watching President De Klerk deliver the speech to the South African parliament in which he announced the unbanning of the ANC, the SACP and other proscribed organisations.[86] De Klerk appears to have consulted no one, or almost no one, about his true intention. By springing such a surprise he was able to obtain for himself acres of political space and to win the international respect and even admiration which later qualified him for a half-share of a Nobel peace prize.

It appears that few in the security forces actively disapproved of De Klerk's move, followed as it was by the freeing of Mandela amid massive and unprecedentedly favourable media attention. The more thoughtful securocrats had always maintained that their struggle could be won only by political action, and they were realistic enough to know that the ANC had to play a part in this. Further down the hierarchy, seasoned covert operatives had seen enough twists and turns not to be surprised by anything which came their way. Many who had fought in Rhodesia and Namibia had become cynical about politicians. They had understood that ministers are sometimes obliged to say what they do not mean, and to will what they cannot say.

President de Klerk himself had never held a security portfolio, although he had attended most meetings of the State Security Council in the 1980s, and lacked the solid base in the security forces which his two immediate predecessors had both had. One of his chief assets in this rather forbidding environment was the support of the civilian intelligence agency, the NIS. This was itself the direct descendant of the former BOSS which had been thoroughly overhauled and was now manned by academics rather than policemen. Both directly and through the NIS, De Klerk enjoyed a close relationship with the Broederbond, the 20,000-strong secret society which still wielded immense influence among the Afrikaner elite and which in 1983 had been taken over by a reform-minded executive.[87] The President authorised the NIS to spy on certain military and police units, with the result that NIS officers claim to have begun receiving a string of death threats.[88]

While no senior army or police officer would easily have contemplated countermanding a direct order from the government, the security services had become so powerful in three decades of war that they had abundant scope for feeding the Cabinet with information in a particular form and for interpreting instructions in their own way. Sparks mentions an early case which occurred within days of De Klerk's elevation to the presidency, when senior NIS officials who had set up their first formal meeting with the ANC in exile, anxious not to have the new President veto months of preparation, put a request for permission in such coded language that even De Klerk, a lawyer by training, did not realise what it was he was approving. The following text was placed before the State Security Council:

> It is necessary that more information should be obtained and processed concerning the ANC, and the aims, alliances and potential approachability of its different leaders and groupings. To enable this to be done, special additional direct action will be necessary, particularly with the help of National Intelligence Service functionaries.

In accepting this, the President did not realise that he had just approved a face-to-face meeting between the NIS and the ANC.[89]

In similar vein, when a number of secret Strategic Communication (Stratcom) propaganda projects were presented to De Klerk by the Police, their bland descriptions disguised their full import. After a full review of covert projects in mid-1990, a number were approved for further implementation, including one involving payment of a Police subsidy to Inkatha.[90] Far more than his predecessor, De Klerk kept his distance from the details of such covert operations, and he probably did not wish to know exactly what measures some of these entailed.

The most satisfactory explanation of the President's attitude is that, while he was determined to restore the authority of the Cabinet, he also fully intended that the security forces should maintain their grip over the country. In this, he had little room for maneouvre, since not only were the security forces the most powerful part of the state machinery, but Umkhonto we Sizwe and other opposition forces continued on a revolutionary footing, armed and dangerous. For the ANC until August 1990, negotiations were simply 'but another terrain of a number of interrelated terrains of our struggle',[91] including notably the armed struggle. Nevertheless, in retrospect, De Klerk certainly missed opportunities, whether from insouciance, timidity or self-interest, we can only surmise, both to assert control over the murkier recesses of the security forces and to uphold the rule of law. In January 1990, when the President appointed Judge Louis Harms to head an inquiry into government death squads, its terms of reference were such as to minimise its possible effectiveness. Judge Harms was perhaps not the ideal choice if a truly penetrating inquiry had been intended. While many covert operators were amazed that the inquiry was instituted at all, since they had become accustomed to believe that they had absolute impunity, they soon realised its toothlessness. Many witnesses, by their own later admission, lied persistently to Judge Harms and even subjected his inquiry to ridicule. Several members of the CCB testified before him using pseudonyms and wearing dark glasses and false beards. The inquiry was ineffective in bringing death squads under the rule of law.

In an effort to impose his own control over the administration as well as to send a signal to the outside world on which he pinned such great hopes, De Klerk abolished the National Management System, the means by which security officers maintained oversight of the government at all levels through a parallel system of government, and replaced it with a National Coordinating Mechanism with much less power, ultimately responsible to a Cabinet sub-committee.[92] He abolished the State Security Council's powerful secretariat and made a real effort to reassert the paramountcy of the traditional form of cabinet government, which seems to have weakened the coordination of military and political activity.

Government strategists were applying to South Africa some of the conclusions they had drawn from the decolonisation process in Namibia, where the SWAPO share of the vote had been whittled down from somewhere over 70 per cent to just 55 per cent in barely 6 months. This had been achieved by massive and coordinated covert activity including funding of opposition parties, dissemination of propaganda, the creation of covert media organisations and the intimidation of voters, notably by keeping the ferocious Koevoet unit deployed in the field until the eve of balloting.[93] All this had been carried out despite the presence of United Nations monitors and an influx of foreign journalists and observers. It is significant that the military campaign to influence the results of elections in Namibia is alleged to have been overseen by General 'Kat' Liebenberg, a former Commanding Officer of Special Forces who was to head the SADF during the first part of the transition to democracy in South Africa itself.

Many government strategists concluded that similar techniques, if applied over years rather than months, could be even more effective in South Africa. The calculation of the most influential National Party leaders was that, if the transition were protracted, it might even allow the National Party time to form a right-of-centre alliance, in company with Inkatha and a number of minor parties and conservative homeland leaders, which could beat the ANC at the polls. Dr Gerrit Viljoen, Minister of Constitutional Development in the first De Klerk cabinet and a past chairman of the Broederbond, was a leading advocate of this strategy. In March 1990, after describing apartheid as a theory that 'didn't work', Viljoen continued,

> And that is why we went to the electorate and said: 'We want to change our approach completely. We want to include blacks as fellow citizens ...' The whole approach of the government is to shift the emphasis from race to quality of government and the broadening of democracy, in spite of the risks.[94]

This would be achieved, Viljoen maintained, not through universal adult suffrage in a unitary state, but by negotiating full citizenship rights for all in a constitution with strong guarantees for minority rights and a powerful second chamber. We may note, furthermore, that the idea that the National Party could redefine itself 'as the core of a substantial multi-racial conservative alliance' was one which was being mooted by some influential academics at the time.[95]

The strategy of building a multi-racial political alliance opposed to the ANC/SACP depended crucially on Inkatha. The latter, technically a cultural organisation which turned itself into the Inkatha Freedom Party (IFP) in 1990, was the only political party with which the National Party could reasonably hope to build an alliance which both commanded substantial support among black voters and had a strong regional base. Although ANC supporters tended to represent Inkatha as simply a puppet of the apartheid state, it is relevant to recall that Inkatha could claim a long historical pedigree and consistently demonstrated its ability to mobilise considerable numbers of supporters. In Chief Mangosuthu Buthelezi it had a leader who, at least until the emergence of the Transkei's General Bantu Holomisa as an ally of the ANC in the late 1980s, had been more successful than any other homeland leader in asserting his own autonomy. The intensification of armed struggle in the 1980s had pushed him ever closer to the security forces upon which he relied for military assistance against Umkhonto we Sizwe and the ANC-supporting young comrades in Natal.

In many ways the securocrats' military training and culture were ill-adapted to the emerging rules of the political game. One senior securocrat recalls his dismay when he realised just how little value De Klerk attached to long-term planning after the President had admitted that he had no idea in what position the government would be six months hence.[96] In this respect De Klerk was a pure politician, with none of the inflexibility or near-military thoroughness of his predecessor. It was a clash of cultures between the military code— disciplined, hierarchical, averse to risks—and a view of politics as the art of the possible. No doubt many securocrats, like most people in similar circumstances, resented their own loss of influence under De Klerk and were dismayed by the prospect of losing power. Lower down the security hierarchy, some covert soldiers, having been trained to fight the ANC and SACP enemy, assumed that they would continue to do this unless explicitly told by their commanders to do otherwise in terms which brooked no misunderstanding or evasion. Politics was not their business, and middle-level operatives appear to have believed that, if the rhetoric of the government had changed under De Klerk, this was simply in keeping with the current phase of the struggle: the politicians' task was to make political capital out of their continuing military activities. Eugene de Kock recalls noting how the 'politicians talk peace in the newspapers', but that 'amongst the forces there was a culture of resistance. It came from the top'.[97] Even after the unbanning of the ANC, De Kock's unit was kept on full alert and fully armed. By mid-1990, he had more than 300 *askaris* under his command. In July 1990, working with the chairman of the Inkatha Youth Brigade in the Transvaal, Themba Khoza, who was on the Vlakplaas payroll as a police informer, De Kock began selling guns to the pro-Inkatha inhabitants of hostels on the East Rand where local tensions ran high. This was to spark some years of strife on the East Rand which turned some areas into veritable war zones. De Kock claims that he carried out some offensive actions of this sort on his own authority, and others under direct orders.[98]

One former resident of the C 10 farm at Vlakplaas which De Kock commanded recalled the atmosphere at the base during 1990. Day after day, groups of *askaris* would leave by car to sow mayhem at taxi-ranks and among the public generally.[99] Returning from their grisly work to the farm at Vlakplaas, the *askaris* held parties and drinking-bouts long into the night. It was also in mid-1990 that the train massacres began. Former members of the SADF's 32 Battalion were later to seek indemnity from the Truth and Reconciliation Commission for their role in train attacks, and there is evidence that some such attacks may have been the work of Five Reconnaissance Commando, which had worked closely with RENAMO in Mozambique.[100] RENAMO had demonstrated that random killings of this sort had a powerful psychological and political effect. In this case they demonstrated that the ANC's claim to have won the struggle was hollow since it was unable to protect its own supporters and future voters. It became suicidal to wear an ANC tee-shirt in some townships and the ANC's capacity to organise was seriously disrupted.

The assertion by certain senior police officers that they were unaware of De Kock's covert warfare from 1990 to 1993 does not stand up to examination.[101] Since 1989, when the *Vrye Weekblad* newspaper carried its first interview with Captain Dirk Coetzee, one of De Kock's predecessors as commander of the Vlakplaas unit, the whole of South Africa had been able to learn De Kock's name and the function of his unit. And yet his superior officers did nothing to prevent him from continuing in his special field of murder on a larger scale than ever. Officially the Vlakplaas unit was reorganised in 1991 and redeployed to investigate the weapons trade, but this simply provided a perfect cover for selling guns to Inkatha while making money into the bargain. Former members of the unit have described how they would cache guns from De Kock's private arsenal, 'discover' them the next day, and then receive a police reward. When interviewed by the present author, Police Commissioner General Johan van der Merwe was unable to account for how De Kock was able to continue the nefarious activities which made him a mainstay of the Third Force while he was allegedly being 'closely supervised', in Van der Merwe's words, by several Police generals.[102] There is every reason to concur with Judge Goldstone's later conclusion that certain Police generals were accomplices to Third Force activity carried out by De Kock's unit,[103] which is what De Kock himself also maintains.

Both the Police and Military Intelligence operated programmes of military and financial aid to Inkatha, and key Inkatha personnel were on the security forces' payroll. While leaders of the ANC were now frequenting ministerial suites and conference rooms, middle-ranking ANC officials were extremely vulnerable, and many were killed in the burgeoning violence, in some cases the apparent victims of planned assassinations. At the same time, the ANC was inflicting casualties on its own enemies, most notably in Inkatha, which lost almost 300 office holders to violent attack between 1985 and 1993.[104] The Police too were under assault as never before, losing hundreds of officers to acts of violence. Ordinary police officers who risked their lives in war-zones on the East Rand and elsewhere, without themselves being party to any covert activity, naturally enough resented being labelled as instigators of violence by opponents of the government.

Like the security forces, the ANC did not in fact cease its armed struggle in 1990. It was continuing to send personnel abroad for military training and it was smuggling arms into the townships. ANC leaders admitted that they could not always control their own supporters. After the outbreak of the war on the East Rand, the organisation devoted considerable attention to organising Self-Defence Units and arming its supporters there and in other conflict zones. When, in July 1990, the Police discovered Operation Vula, a sophisticated undercover network for arms-smuggling and guerrilla warfare dominated by the SACP, the securocrats accused the ANC and the SACP of negotiating in bad faith and secretly putting in place a network aimed at the armed seizure of power.[105] No professional security officer would cease to be vigilant or would contemplate disarming as long as there was a chance of the opposition launching an offensive.

In short, the security forces were not alone in perpetrating violence in 1990–1994. Nevertheless, both written and oral sources and analyses of the statistics of violence lead to the conclusion that covert units of the state and its Inkatha ally were the main aggressors. In general, the violence of the period is best understood as an intensification of the existing campaign of low-intensity warfare.[106] After mid-1990 it was clear that the unbanning of the ANC had led not to peace, but to a change in the unwritten rules of engagement. South Africa is not the only country in the world where revolutionary struggles have been accompanied at various stages by intensive negotiation. In a contest of this sort, proponents of violence and of peace may exist within the same organisation and the preponderance of one or the other mode of operation may reflect the outcome of factional struggles within the various parties to the conflict as well as between protagonists. Partly for this reason, disclosure, publicity and the quality of media representation can become crucial elements in political-military struggle. Indeed, one of the skills of covert operatives on both sides was to organise their military activities in such a way as to appear to the black South African public as winners while appearing to the international and white South African publics as the innocent party in the war, the one reacting to aggression. Political leaders in these circumstances strive to turn military gains into solid political capital, and in the process to rein in those within their own ranks who are the strongest advocates of military methods. Conversely, perpetrators of violence sometimes intend not just to inflict damage on the enemy, but also to use violence as a means of securing advantage in inner-party factional struggles.

The National Party, the ANC, Inkatha and probably every other main actor understood well the nature of this contest. In each of these organisations there were struggles between advocates of peace and proponents of violence. According to Chris Hani:

> It is our conviction that the National Party government is pursuing a twin-track strategy. This strategy involves negotiating with its major political opponent, the ANC and allies, and at the same time deliberate destabilisation, including violent destabilisation of our forces.[107]

This was an accurate description of what the government was doing. It was also an accurate description of what the IFP and the ANC were doing. Moreover there were plenty of freelance operators, professional criminals and others, or rival armed groups from the Afrikaner Weerstandsbeweging (AWB) to the Azanian People's Liberation Army (APLA), who were taking advantage of the circumstances to launch campaigns of their own. The existence of various security forces established by the state, such as homeland armies and police forces, the National Peacekeeping Force, and the Internal Stability Unit of the Police, further complicated the politics of security and coercion.

The Vlakplaas unit was by no means the only covert unit which was still centrally involved in violence against the ANC on behalf of the state, or in other words which constituted the Third Force, and it was probably not even the most important of them. Curiously enough, the best-known of the military death squads, the Civil Cooperation Bureau (CCB), was responsible for relatively few murders inside South Africa. The CCB was never a very significant force inside the country since its mandate specifically charged it with working abroad. (Hence the deviousness of the terms of reference of the Harms commission, which empowered Justice Harms to study only death squad activities *inside* South Africa!). After the CCB was disbanded in 1990, many of its former members joined other covert units. The most important of these was the office of the Chief of Staff (Intelligence). During the previous decade, this had become the richest and most influential of all covert units, with an awesome offensive ability and experience in destabilisation as well as an intelligence-gathering network at home and abroad. After 1990, many Military Intelligence projects were being carried out by front companies, like International Researchers in the Ciskei homeland. Within the office of Chief of Staff (Intelligence), the Directorate of Special Tasks, the unit which had overseen destabilisation campaigns abroad, was in charge of a special project of support for Inkatha known as Operation Marion. Another section of the office of the Chief of Staff (Intelligence), the Directorate of Covert Collection, was running both offensive and information-gathering projects including specific anti-ANC programmes. Operation Marion is known to have been approved by the State Security Council, and many other projects too were approved in principle at the highest level, at least until 1991. Such veteran securocrats as Adriaan Vlok and General Magnus Malan still retained security portfolios and Malan, in particular, carried great weight in the Cabinet until his demotion in July 1991. One member of the cabinet recalls De Klerk challenging these two without success:

> Every time we would discuss it, they would try to convince us that there was no third force. I was present several times when De Klerk challenged first Vlok and Hernus Kriel. He said to them, "But how do you explain this?" He really got into them. But they always had very convincing answers. I think it was a question of trusting the people who advised him.[108]

Waldmeir comments, rightly, that 'De Klerk's concern for stability was a convenient excuse for doing nothing. He seems to have chosen to remain in a state of negligent ignorance rather than face the impossible choices with which knowledge would confront him.'[109] The veteran covert operative, Craig Williamson, made the same point about De Klerk more harshly: 'He either misunderstood entirely the nature of the machine at his disposal, the machine he was running, or he was deliberately closing his eyes, or he's a liar'.[110]

Until this period, the government as a whole, including the State President, was willing to allow covert war to be waged on a substantial scale provided only that ministers could not be personally held responsible. They did not wish to be informed precisely about what happened on the ground. Given the general atmosphere of violence, it did not require much imagination to suppose a connection between secret projects, no matter how bland their formal description, and the waging of war at ground level. The danger to South Africa was that if the National Party persisted in protracting the transition, particularly if it also allowed covert units to continue making war on the ANC with little check, violence could gain such momentum as to destabilise the political situation entirely.

By early 1991, the government appeared to believe that it was succeeding in its strategy of surreptitiously attacking its enemy while consolidating its political position. De Klerk's international standing was higher than that of the head of any South African government for 50 years. However, the government had to pay a price for its continuing sponsorship of covert warfare. In the first place, the high incidence of violence and the widespread belief among many black South Africans that covert units of the security forces were implicated led to the erosion of the substantial credit which De Klerk had acquired among some sections of the black community, thus limiting the likelihood of the National Party successfully redefining itself as a non-racial party, as it hoped to do. At the same time, his unwillingness or inability to limit these activities suggested to some that he was not in fact in total control of government policy. In other words, the covert use of state violence, rather than projecting an image of strength calculated to cow the population, could also create an image of weakness which had exactly the opposite effect. It undercut rather than complemented the National Party's longer-term political strategy.

Transition: The eclipse of the National Party

In July 1991, the Johannesburg *Weekly Mail & Guardian* and the British *Guardian* newspaper simultaneously revealed the existence of a secret Police project for funding Inkatha. This dealt a major blow to De Klerk's prestige both at home and, perhaps even more significantly, abroad, where he had been almost entirely absolved from blame for any of the violence until this point. The ANC was eventually to seize the advantage in political negotiations largely as a result. In retrospect, National Party leaders may feel that they overplayed their hand in 1990–1991, and failed to capitalise on their political supremacy at that point. That is certainly the view of many former security force commanders, who point out that in that period a total amnesty for security force personnel was on offer but was rejected by an over-confident Cabinet.[111]

In response to the Inkathagate revelations, De Klerk reshuffled his two leading security ministers, Malan and Vlok, and on 30 July 1991 the President ordered a new review of secret projects, known as the Khan Commission. Although the Khan report has never been published, it is known to have investigated at least eleven projects run by the Department of Foreign Affairs, sixteen by the SADF, nine by the Police and seven by the NIS. The Khan commission is said to have noted that the official descriptions of some projects were bland in the extreme and that some were used to 'piggyback' other operations. For example, one SADF operation known as Project Echoes was officially 'aimed at combatting verbal attacks on [SADF] duties and functions. Activity relates to the acquisition of information in relation to MK [Umkhonto we Sizwe] mainly and passing this to the media'.[112] Project Echoes was later revealed to have made use of violence, blackmail and other illegal means. After failing to secure from his senior Police officers an assurance that no further leaks would take place, De Klerk ordered the termination of a number of projects deemed to be of an offensive nature. But he also approved the recommendation of the Khan Commission that certain covert activities, including the SADF's

Project Echoes, should continue. The new Law and Order minister, Hemus Kriel, took a largely hands-off approach to his department, clearly unwilling to risk being compromised but also unwilling to purge covert operatives. Again according to De Kock, police chiefs interpreted the government's distinctly ambiguous signals to mean that they should carry on making war on the ANC but not expect any political cover. There is evidence to support this account as, despite the notoriety of his unit and the continuing violence in the country, and despite being under the 'close supervision' (in the words of the Commissioner of Police) of Police generals, nothing substantial was done to close down De Kock's activities.

The more the Cabinet distanced itself from the covert units, the more the latter used their own initiative. Some covert operators set up informal connections. De Kock, for example, had many acquaintances in Special Forces and in Military Intelligence, as well as in the network of arms companies run by the state-owned arms manufacturer ARMSCOR, and he would meet them from time to time without informing his superiors. He and other covert warriors met frequently at a brothel in Johannesburg run by Military Intelligence as part of Project Echoes. The official function of the brothel was described by its managers as being to provide a safe-house where security specialists could meet each other and could talk to ANC contacts and informers under cover.[113]

The longer the transition lasted, the clearer it became that the days of the National Party government were numbered. It lost that most important and intangible political asset, authority. Beset by problems of this nature, and under pressure from white conservatives to the right of the National Party, in March 1992 De Klerk held a referendum of the white electorate in which he sought a vote of confidence to continue the negotiating process. He misinterpreted the handsome victory which this brought him, evaluating it too much in terms of the old white politics. De Klerk hardened his attitude at the constitutional negotiations known as the Convention for a Democratic South Africa (CODESA), begun in December 1991, which soon broke down in consequence.[114] Some hitherto optimistic commentators and by-standers began for the first time to wonder whether the whole transition process might not collapse irretrievably, and to speculate whether there were not people within the security forces who intended precisely that.

In the absence of negotiations, both sides resorted to demonstrating their strength in the ways they knew best. The ANC declared a campaign of 'rolling mass action', a series of demonstrations which in the circumstances were bound to lead to violence but which were the best available way of demonstrating the size of its support. Then, on 17 June 1992, some people from a migrants' hostel at Boipatong, south of Johannesburg, attacked a pro-ANC township and killed 38 men, women and children during the night. There was an immediate recognition that this massacre was distinctive, not only because of its large scale. Local people were convinced that it was the work of the security forces, and there is circumstantial evidence that it was indeed the work of one or other of the covert units. Above all it took place at a time when negotiations were suspended, on the day after the anniversary of the 1976 Soweto rising. If it was indeed organised by one or other of the state security forces as appears most probable, it was clearly intended as a provocation to the ANC. This is how the ANC interpreted it, and ANC hardliners in their turn canvassed the possibility of what some termed 'the Leipzig option', a reference to the vast demonstrations which had only recently brought about the collapse of East Germany.

It is ironic that the term 'Leipzig option' was used by some people previously noted for their uncritical admiration of the East German government. Among these was Ronnie Kasrils, the former head of Umkhonto we Sizwe Military Intelligence and a leading ANC/SACP radical. When, on 7 September 1992, Kasrils led some 80,000 people in a march on Bisho, the capital of the Ciskei homeland whose government was under the effective control of Military Intelligence, another major massacre occurred. Over 28 people died as Ciskeian security forces fired into the crowd. The South African press attached a large part of the blame to Kasrils's cavalier attitude.[115] The Bisho massacre brought all of South Africa's major politicians to the realisation that they were staring into an abyss of violence.

To judge from his actions over the next three months, President de Klerk was one of those who recognised just how acute was the danger now faced not just by his government, but by South Africa as a whole.

So far had his authority diminished that he now needed the ANC, and particularly the personal support of Mandela, to support the writ of the state and to prevent a slide into anarchy or even civil war. But to secure Mandela's support required a fundamental change in National Party strategy, which had previously been based on the notion of eroding the ANC's power and building an alliance with Inkatha. After the Bisho massacre, the government's whole political strategy was comprehensively and rapidly switched. On 26 September 1992, the National Party and the ANC signed a Memorandum of Understanding which implicitly confined Inkatha to the margins. The National Party's chief negotiator was Roelf Meyer, one of a younger generation of National Party leaders who could hope to continue their careers into a democratic future and who favoured working with the ANC towards a new dispensation. This is a good example of the way in which highly symbolic acts of violence, like the Bisho massacre, could substantially alter the balance of forces not just between rival organisations, but also between factions and generations within one party.

De Klerk, now siding with Meyer and the new generation in his party, took real steps to rein in the Third Force. Already, in August 1992, the President had retired a number of senior Police officers in a move interpreted as an attempt to assert his authority over the force. In October 1992, the powers of the Goldstone Commission were strengthened and the following month, Goldstone's investigators discovered a Military Intelligence safe house in Pretoria, with proof that offensive operations against the ANC, including Project Echoes, were still in force. The State President immediately appointed the SADF Chief of Staff, Lieutenant-General Pierre Steyn, to investigate the armed forces. It is probably no coincidence that at the same time, Eugene de Kock was approached by his superiors and asked to resign from the police force pending negotiations over severance pay.

General Steyn's report to De Klerk remains shrouded in mystery. Steyn himself came under considerable pressure from fellow officers as he went about his investigation; his house was broken into by persons unknown. There has been much speculation as to the exact form his report took. He is said to have briefed the State President on the basis of a series of written reports rather than to have handed over a finished document. He communicated the names of officers considered to have some connection to Third Force activity, but whether he did so verbally or in writing is unclear. In December 1992, shortly after receiving Steyn's briefing, De Klerk fired 23 officers, including two generals.[116] Among those dismissed were the deputy Chief of Staff (Intelligence) of the SADF and the chief of the Directorate of Covert Collection. Some of those fired protested their innocence, claiming they were the victims of bureaucratic intrigues orchestrated by the NIS, which they thoroughly distrusted. Although much remains to be known about this episode, the drift was plain: De Klerk had now hitched the National Party to the ANC and was demonstrating his determination to act against covert units which had constituted the Third Force and which had until now been making war on the ANC. The most careful analysis made so far of violence statistics indicates that, whereas the level of political violence rose steadily until 1994, the types of attack most characteristic of hit-squads declined after mid-1992 when De Klerk began to exert control over the covert units.[117]

One clear implication is that De Klerk could have taken similar action at any time during the previous three years, difficult though this may have been. By failing to assert his authority decisively over covert operatives until late 1992, and in fact by previously approving offensive operations such as Project Echoes, euphemistically described as Strategic Communication projects, De Klerk had contributed to the weakening of his own government's authority and had committed himself to a political-military approach which turned out to be ineffective in securing the government's strategic goals. Foreign governments and local business leaders increasingly saw the government's weakness as the greatest threat to stability and were inclined to modify their own positions accordingly. The ANC, after an initial period of disarray, considerably sharpened its negotiating strategy at the reconvened constitutional negotiations known as CODESA 2, where the formidable Cyril Ramaphosa emerged as the chief ANC negotiator. Ramaphosa and his team, including Joe Slovo, Valli Moosa, Mac Maharaj and others, demonstrated a greater skill than government negotiators in turning events on the ground into political capital.

All of this left the commanders of the armed forces in a difficult position. Officers who had been trained for years to believe that they were fighting a war against communism and subversion, some of whom displayed the hubris of those grown accustomed to power, now saw the ANC heading inexorably towards government. Communication between senior officers and their political masters was extremely poor as the successive ministers of the Police and of Defence who replaced Vlok and Malan after July 1991 either distanced themselves from their porfolios or were simply unable to impose themselves on their officials. Many senior military and police officers by this time had utter contempt for De Klerk and his ministers.

But no matter how much they resented this turn of events, and even if they believed it was their patriotic duty to act against the ANC on behalf of white South Africa or, more precisely, the Afrikaner *volk*, senior military commanders were too experienced, after 30 years of war, to believe that violence alone would solve their problem. It is perhaps for this reason, as well as for reasons of professional self-esteem, that no serious plan for a *coup d'état* is known to have existed within the SADF at any stage, although there were certainly rumours of such. There was no organisation to the right of the National Party with the ability to contest the political ground where the struggle had to be fought. Some former securocrats who had retired from active service tried to build right-wing parties and homeland governments into a grand anti-ANC alliance, most notably in the form of the Concerned South Africans Group (COSAG), and some ex-generals remained in close touch not only with each other but with former colleagues who were still serving in the security forces. Using these contacts, Inkatha began building a major private army, using game parks for training purposes.

As the government grew weaker, the armed forces emerged clearly as the single most powerful bloc in the country. Aware that they could not rely on the political support of more than a small minority of South Africans, the commanders of the SADF nevertheless headed a coherent organisation possessed of a massive capacity to make war. Generally speaking, the generals adopted a low political profile. Their rare public pronouncements, particularly by the shrewd Army chief, Lieutenant-General Georg Meiring, who took command of the SADF in 1993, were generally limited to utterly fallacious but politically meaningful comments that the SADF was a Westem-style force which eschewed politics and served the government of the day. Such comments, although superficially banal, signalled that the SADF could be prepared to accept the constitutional change now taking shape, which would inevitably bring the ANC to power. It is known that after mid-1992 senior SADF commanders, including the Chief of Staff (Intelligence), had a series of discreet bilateral meetings with leaders of the ANC and its armed wing Umkhonto we Sizwe.[118]

SADF generals could be confident of the discipline of their forces, although most seem to have been convinced that the SADF would never obey an order to open fire on white protestors or paramilitaries. Although the SADF could not assert direct control over white civilians, including former Permanent Force members, and could only with difficulty exert influence over members of the Citizen Force when these were not in uniform, SADF commanders nevertheless occupied a strategically vital position. The force continued to benefit from the general respect of the white population, so many of whom had performed national service in its ranks, and to represent the ultimate guarantee against anarchy or unrestrained communist or black government. Covert warfare units abounded inside the SADF, and related networks existed in the Police and among white extremists and their allies generally. If the leadership of the SADF were to cut off all links with these covert operatives, it would find it impossible to control them at all. Eugene de Kock, for example, who resigned from the Police in April 1993, continued to supply arms to Inkatha, with the apparent cooperation of businessmen working for military front companies and other military-run companies. He set up his own private weapons-trading company which immediately became the hub of yet another Third Force-style network. The Third Force broke up into smaller units which were increasingly independent of any central line of command, although individuals were able to communicate with each other via informal channels.

The risk this presented became clear in April 1993 when a group of right-wing conspirators murdered Chris Hani, bringing the country to the edge of disaster once more. It was in these circumstances that General Constand Viljoen, a former commander of the SADF, probably white South Africa's most respected soldier, made a spectacular arrival on the political scene, leaving retirement on his farm with a public promise to lead the right wing. He was supported by Eugène Terreblanche, leader of the Afrikaner Weerstandsbeweging (AWB), who pledged his troopers to the service of Viljoen's Afrikaner nationalist Volksfront. The threat from this source was at its greatest in March 1994, when Viljoen encouraged AWB paramilitaries to travel to the homeland of Bophuthatswana to defend the homeland's anti-ANC president, Lucas Mangope, against a popular uprising. But Terreblanche's men were an undisciplined and ineffective rabble who withdrew in disorder after some of their number had been killed, in view of television cameras, by soldiers of the Bophuthatswana Defence Force. Viljoen distanced himself from the AWB. The Battle of Bop, as it was known, probably marked the closest point to civil war reached during South Africa's transition.

In retrospect, Viljoen's role in the last year of the National Party government may be seen to have been an historically important one in the sense that, while he consistently argued the cause of a self-governing *boerestaat*, he nevertheless kept a significant section of the far right on the constitutional path and eventually participated in the April 1994 elections. Although General Viljoen has denied having orchestrated his plans with the leadership of the SADF,[119] a question remains as to whether serving officers, desperate to prevent a civil war after the April 1993 murder of Hani, prevailed upon him to take the leadership of the extreme right which was threatening to plunge South Africa into chaos.

After 1992, then, the commanders of the SADF, who had wielded such great power in government since the late 1970s, had become the essential arbiters of whether the country would have all-out war or elections and something resembling peace. The generals, as Afrikaner nationalists and as veterans of three decades of war, were no doubt disappointed by many aspects of the emerging constitutional settlement, but on balance it was one they could tolerate. It required considerable political skill, in a situation where large numbers of complex informal relations existed both within and outside the armed forces, to impose this view on the wilder right-wing elements who were pushing for the unilateral declaration of a white homeland, a *boerestaat*. The full details of whatever discreet contacts took place between the leaders of the SADF, the leaders of the ANC, and the far right which, after May 1993, was grouped around a former head of the SADF, General Viljoen, remain unknown. But it can be said that Viljoen's role was crucial in bringing the country through the elections of April 1994. The new President, Nelson Mandela, recognised in Constand Viljoen something of a kindred spirit, a nationalist and a fighter with a reputation for personal integrity. The two men, the icon of black liberation and the last of the old-fashioned Boer generals, became close.

The splintering of the Third Force

The name 'Third Force' is in many ways a misnomer, implying as it does an autonomous force situated between the ANC and the National Party. In reality, the Third Force, in the sense of a nexus of SADF and Police units experienced in covert warfare, was originally organised by the state itself, coordinated in the National Management System through a dense network of committees, and continued to have a recognisable degree of central coordination until late 1992.

The name 'Third Force' was often used by the mainstream media in the period of transition vaguely to designate a group of semi-independent operators who sought to sabotage negotiations through the escalation of violence. Some individual officers may have had this in mind, particularly those below the top level, but it is not a convincing explanation of the motives of those senior SADF and Police commanders, and their political masters, who at least permitted them to perpetrate violence in South Africa in the early 1990s. The evidence contained in the present article suggests that the Third Force was organised from a very high level, certainly until 1989, after which its senior command and control system were gradually eroded until 1992. Thereafter it was effectively privatised. It cannot be considered to have been independent of the National Party government itself. We might add that the most senior people who can be said to have constituted the Third Force, or who at least encouraged it to operate, did not actually wish to halt negotiations entirely.

Middle-ranking officers like Colonel Eugene De Kock and Colonel Joe Verster, the managing director of the CCB, saw themselves as warriors, professionals who had been trained to attack the enemy until unambiguously ordered to stop. They had been brought up to believe that to fight for *volk* and *vaderland* was their highest duty. Throughout careers spent in underground warfare they had learned the arts of camouflage and subterfuge which meant that even disbanding their units was not taken as an unambiguous signal to disarm. They had seen too many ruses of this sort to take them at face value. Many covert warriors had developed a financial interest in war, and this was an incentive to continue. In the last few months of the National Party government many opened informal channels to the ANC, hoping for amnesty under a new government or even reinstatement in the security forces. But, until the end, both the SAP and the SADF remained coherent organisations, and hence it was the senior officers whose views counted most.

The evidence suggests that few senior officers actually wanted to sabotage negotiations for good simply because they knew that this would not help them win the war. If they had wanted to do so it would have been easy enough to sabotage the elections of April 1994. What they did intend was to use violence in such a manner as to secure a political settlement on the terms most favourable to white South Africa. As we have seen, even according to this standard, they seriously miscalculated the political effect of Third Force violence in a period of transition and under-estimated the political skill of the ANC leaders, especially after July 1991. Although every week was crucial in the transition period, and crises occurred too often to enumerate, the truly decisive period was probably that from March to September 1992, during which constitutional negotiations broke down and the Boipatong and Bisho massacres threatened a major unravelling of the political fabric. President de Klerk secured a resumption of progress only by aligning himself with those in his party and in the country who were prepared to deal with the ANC on something like the terms it was offering, which would inevitably mean an ANC-dominated government coming to power in the foreseeable future. Thereafter the principal threat to a constitutional transition came from the possibility of an assassination, which required no more than a lone operator, or the activities of a larger group outside the security forces, like the AWB at the Battle of Bop.

Substantial numbers of white extremists who wanted to stop negotiations at all costs were to be found less in the ranks of the Army and the Police than on the civilian extreme right, outside the security forces, in the form of the AWB and similar groups. After the murder of Chris Hani in April 1993 it appeared that such saboteurs were within an ace of succeeding. What was to stop a right-wing maverick from shooting Joe Slovo, or Nelson Mandela? Few senior SADF officers had anything but contempt for the bluster of the AWB or its leader, the loutish Eugène Terreblanche. The problem was that if they expelled the most aggressive covert operatives from the armed forces, the latter were most likely to make common cause with the AWB and others, thus making a descent into civil war more rather than less likely. It was a case of wanting them inside, where they were at least under observation, rather than outside, where all manner of harm was possible. Once the government had made it clear that it wanted to exert control over the Third Force, which it did after September 1992, it became clear that it had the means to do so, although it was a gradual process. The ANC helped De Klerk to rein in the Third Force by having the wisdom to offer the National Party constitutional terms which were broadly acceptable to the SADF generals, as Afrikaner nationalists, and thus to tempt them into peace, as well as by its political handling of the generals themselves. Even so, the last eighteen months of white South Africa were fraught with danger. Many participants believe that the risk of civil war, particularly after Hani's murder and during the battle of Bophuthatswana in March 1994, was at times very great.

Today, the SADF (now renamed the South African National Defence Force, or SANDF) and the Police (now renamed South African Police Service, or SAPS) continue to serve the state as before. Neither institution can be suspected of harbouring people who have plans to overturn the new order in South Africa. Of the two, the SANDF has the easier task since, despite the central role played by the Chief of Staff (Intelligence) in covert operations from 1978 to 1994, it has emerged from inquiries and from the Truth and Reconciliation Commission less tainted than the Police service. This may be attributed in part to the skill with which the SADF was able to disguise its waging of covert warfare and in part to the political skill with which senior officers played their cards, in effect negotiating with the ANC a soft line on prosecution and various other marks of consideration in return for their support for the new government. Since South Africa is not at war and faces no foreseeable military threat from outside its borders, the armed forces can assume a peacetime role in relative comfort.

A far more difficult task faces the Police, tainted by the outrages which they perpetrated before 1994. The Police actually had a less prominent role in the conception and execution of low-intensity warfare than did the SADF, and yet the Police have generally received the greater share of the blame. In retrospect, it may be said that Police commanders, quite apart from the other mistakes they made and the great crimes they committed, made a bad job of negotiating their political relations with the ANC as the latter came closer to power. A direct consequence of this is the public opprobrium now being heaped upon the Police, justly, by the hearings of the Truth and Reconciliation Commission and the trial of Eugene de Kock. To add to its woes, the police force now faces the task of policing a highly volatile society containing a dangerous degree of lawlessness, compounded by the ready availability of weapons which were so freely distributed by various armed organisations, including notably Military Intelligence and the Police, before 1994. The police force has shown problems in reorienting itself to these major tasks. Morale is said to be low, and the Police authorities admit to the existence of disturbingly widespread corruption. This is one of the legacies of the dirty war.

Many of the people who actually constituted the Third Force have now left the services. Many senior officers who had responsibility for covert units have retired. Some now work for private security companies or elsewhere in the private sector. Of the middle-ranking officers, Eugene de Kock is serving a 212-year prison sentence. Others have become farmers, administrators or businessmen. Some have established businesses in Mozambique. A few ex-Special Forces personnel have even bought farms in Angola. At least one former Military Intelligence brothel is still functioning in Johannesburg, managed by ex-covert operators, apparently as a purely criminal enterprise. As Eugene de Kock told his judges, with only slight exaggeration, a person with a curriculum vitae like his can choose between becoming a drug smuggler or a mercenary.[120] Others combine legitimate enterprises with illegal ones both locally and internationally. It appears that some have established interests in the new weapons and narcotics trades and, given the strategic importance of these trades and the huge sums of money which can be generated by narcotics-smuggling, this is of great significance. Here, Mozambique plays a key role, since the country has effectively become a free-trade area for businessmen and smugglers of every description. As it produces little for export and has only a small domestic market, it is essentially an entrepôt for onward trade. Particularly influential are those former South African covert operatives who are acquainted with Mozambican politicians and officials and who are able to use Mozambique as a centre for offshore transactions involving South Africa itself. Some former members of the CCB are reported to have established a new organisation known as the Binnekring, which combines drug-trafficking and gun-smuggling for profit with activities designed to bolster opposition to the ANC.

While criminal activities of this type are probably carried out largely for profit alone, the fact that some former securocrats remain preoccupied with the long-term future of the Afrikaner *volk* may provide a continuing link between the more strategic thinkers and former covert operatives now turned professional criminals. The possibility remains that criminal networks which cross South Africa's borders, run by ex-security operatives, could in future provide the sinews of new political movements which derive income partly from criminal activities. If this appears far-fetched, it is worth recalling that, since the end of the Cold War, the smuggling of drugs and weapons especially has become connected with new forms of political mobilisation, associated with the use of violence, in many parts of the world.

Occasional incidents cause some observers to wonder whether remnants of the Third Force do not continue to exist as an identifiable series of networks having at least a modicum of political purpose. The fact that still other former covert operatives have found employment in the new, post-apartheid intelligence services, the South African Secret Service and the National Intelligence Agency, further complicates the already complex relationships between former colleagues whose careers have now taken different paths.

Some of the toughest elite troops of the former SADF, including several managers of the CCB death-squad, work for the security company Executive Outcomes Ltd, which has negotiated major contracts for security work with governments in Angola, Sierra Leone and elsewhere. Executive Outcomes is far more than a group of mercenaries. A legitimate company, it employs intelligence analysts and an array of technical staff and, by 1995, it had generated over 30 subsidiary companies throughout sub-Saharan Africa specialising in activities including air transport, video production and mining. It is said to have contracts in Africa, the Indian Ocean and the Middle East.

Other companies which began life in the service of the counter-insurgency strategy of the South African state also continue in business, such as GMR (Pty) Ltd, a company set up by an Italian businessman in the Seychelles and now run by a former naval officer, Willem 'Ters' Ehlers, former private secretary to President P.W. Botha. In 1996, a United Nations inquiry found that Ehlers had sold arms to Hutu extremists in Zaire via the Seychelles. Ehlers is also reported to have traded with UNITA in Angola.[121] The same report exposed some of the links between drug-trading and weapons-trading in which former South African security men play an important part and which are having a major influence on events in central Africa.[122]

Legacies: Crime and politics

South Africa has become a democracy, but the country is now witness to a level of crime which causes deep concern to its citizens and its government. It is said to have one of the world's highest rates of murder. Half the population pronounce themselves in opinion polls to be 'very worried' about becoming victims of crime in their own communities.[123] The notion that South Africa has solved its outstanding political problems while being saddled with a problem of crime is not a satisfactory analysis. One of the conclusions we may draw from a survey of the last 30 years of South African history is that politics and crime are inter-connected and are not always amenable to conventional analyses, one in the discipline of political science, the other in that of criminology. Furthermore, the abolition of apartheid has had the effect of strengthening South Africa's attachments to a region where states have become weak and informal economies are burgeoning. There are indications that some leading members of the current ANC government have established discreet relations with several old securocrat networks and seek advice from them in a private capacity.

In short, the story of South Africa's constitutional transition, inspiring though it may be, is only one of a number of chronicles which have the power to explain the salient features of the country's recent history. The struggle against apartheid mobilised literally millions of people, often reacting to highly local grievances and political patterns.[124] These local struggles gave rise to local narratives of violence which at times became subsumed in the national narrative of negotiation, and at other times became disconnected from it. Thus, although the history of the constitutional transition represents the triumph of reason and moderation over violence and bitterness, some regional struggles continue, most obviously in Natal. The fact that local violence between competing factions is nowadays generally regarded as criminal rather than political in nature should not blind us to the fact that many of the participants are the same as those who were regarded as political actors when apartheid was still in place.[125]

At the local level, particularly in poor black communities, armed militias or gangs today attempt to control territory from which they derive economic benefits. Some reach an understanding with local police officers who are unable to enforce the law fully and who may in any case have developed alliances with various unofficial armed groups over many years. Some such groups develop vertical alliances with national political parties and individual politicians who encouraged violence in various ways over many years, or with businessmen who can import the goods which they most require—guns—and wholesale the goods which they offer for export. Prominent among the latter are marijuana and stolen cars (of which there were 98,000 in 1995).[126] Some criminal middlemen have good connections in politics and the security services, especially those who are themselves veterans of the covert actions of the past. In July 1997, Deputy President Thabo Mbeki claimed in public that a former police brigadier who retired in 1996 was the head of the country's biggest organised crime syndicate.[127] During the cross-border struggle between the South African security forces and the ANC, SACP, PAC and SWAPO, armed groups of all types sprang up throughout southern Africa, and many of the security and intelligence forces of the region have been penetrated by criminal groups in a complex network of relationships. Senior politicians and intelligence officers in Mozambique are widely believed to have interests in smuggling concerns including the drug trade. The same is true of Zambia, Angola, Seychelles and elsewhere. Thus South Africa's national politics remain related to struggles in South African society (including some generally classified as criminal in nature) and to wider patterns of political and informal economic activity in the region which have become, if anything, even more complex than before.

Part of the reason for the changing pattern of crime and its relation to politics is the failure of the security forces in the 1980s and early 1990s to reflect sufficiently on the evolution of crime and politics both locally and internationally. So intent was the Police on the struggle with the ANC and the SACP during the end-phase of the war for South Africa that officers failed to halt an influx of sophisticated professional criminals from abroad who, after 1990, were able to take advantage of the normalisation of the country's foreign relations to base themselves in South Africa. These include sophisticated Nigerian drug-smuggling syndicates and other similar groups from as far afield as Russia and China.[128] These international operators have transformed South Africa in just a few years from a country in which heroin and cocaine were almost unknown to a leading transit-point and a significant market for these products. As in all countries where a significant narcotics trade exists, this has important implications for society and politics.

The countries of southern Africa are closely linked in an economic system constructed by the British government and the great mining houses in the late nineteenth and early twentieth century, with only Angola, of all the countries in the region, standing largely outside this highly integrated trading system. As the outlying parts of the southern African economic system have grown poorer, not least as a result of the war for South Africa which brought about such destruction, so their formal economies have shrunk to be replaced by informal economies and international trades which are technically illicit, but whose existence is widely known. If South Africa remains at the hub of the region's formal economy, it also stands at the centre of this burgeoning smuggling economy and even plays a role in the smuggling networks of the Great Lakes region of Central Africa. It is not only in Mozambique, Angola and Zambia that senior figures in government and the formal economy sometimes play a key role in the smuggling economy as well, but also in South Africa. It was South African Military Intelligence officers who succeeded in establishing Johannesburg as the hub of the ivory and rhino horn trades from the late 1970s, with the personal approval of General Malan, then head of the SADF and later, Minister of Defence.[129] According to the head of the Organised Crime Unit of the South African Police Service, leading gold smugglers are often rich businessmen seeking to export capital in contravention of currency laws.[130] South African mines are estimated to lose some 1.5 billion rands' worth of gold per year to theft, and gold smugglers export this by air or sea to neighbouring countries and thence to Europe. The South African diamond marketing cartel, De Beers, has traditionally had an intimate acquaintance with the gem-smuggling trade due to its concern to purchase stones which are unofficially mined and marketed, as well as the official production of various countries.

South Africa attracts criminals from abroad not only because it constitutes a large market for drugs and fraud, but also because it is an ideal base for operations elsewhere. At the same time its relative prosperity attracts millions of people from countries to the north who are not professional criminals, but are simply desperate to earn a living. Here the economic failure of other parts of southern Africa, which the securocrats did much to create by their policy of destabilisation, shapes South Africa's own underground economy. For example, traders from Zambia and Congo seeking to buy consumer goods in South Africa for resale at home often have no access to a suitable form of cash, since the currencies of Congo and Zambia have no international value. They often acquire small quantities of gems, gold, silver, ivory, rhino horn, local works of art or any other goods which are easily transportable and have an international value. These they take to South Africa as a form of currency rather than as a commodity. In a highly organised trade, cars stolen in South Africa are often exported via Mozambique to points further north as far as Nairobi as a form of easily transportable wealth for settlement of debts contracted particularly in the course of drug transactions. Cars stolen in South Africa have also been traced as far afield as Turkey and New Zealand.

Throughout the 1980s, the South African government ignored some of the key changes taking place in the international system of southern Africa, preferring to see everything through a Cold War prism. In fact, politics and economies throughout southern

Africa, and many other parts of the world as well, were becoming less formal and less dominated by states as a result of profound changes in international relations. The international context is now quite different from that of the 1980s, and the transformation has been accentuated by South Africa's emergence from international isolation into a world in rapid mutation. In much of Africa, powerful factions and individuals increasingly make use of informal economies and the informal political alliances which produce 'shadow states',[131] patterns of politics and trade at variance with the official and formal structures which, in theory, exist to articulate these fundamental human activities. Quite apart from the domestic factors which tend to weaken the state's monopoly of violence and which encourage the development of a criminal economy, South Africa cannot stand apart from the trends taking place elsewhere. Some criminal trades, such as the rapidly-increasing drug trade and the trade in illegal weapons, are international in nature. Large amounts of money are generated by these trades and some of the profits are likely to be recycled in the form of political finance by criminal bosses whose aim is to secure political advantage and protection.

Southern Africa is not the only part of the world where politics and crime have become closely associated and South Africa is not the only state which, in its struggle to mobilise all possible means and all available social forces for its own preservation, has condoned the creation of criminal enterprises by its own intelligence officers. The great majority of South African police officers and politicians are deeply concerned by the incidence of crime and its penetration of the state, and they can at least count themselves fortunate that the process has proceeded less far than in some other countries. The formulation of new power-blocs by professional criminals, secret service officers and senior officials working together has not claimed control of the state itself to the same degree as in Russia, for example.[132] Nor have South African politicians combined tenure of public office with personal enrichment to anything approaching the same extent as in some other important African countries, such as Nigeria and Congo.

In practice, the most pressing question for South Africa is probably to know whether it is possible for criminal activity to be successfully contained in such a manner as to permit the functioning of a conventional political and economic sector, with all that that implies with regard to the rule of law and the security of individuals. Private security guards and fortified suburbs have no doubt become permanent features of South African life, as they have in many other parts of the world. In some parts of South Africa a form of warlordism may have become endemic for the foreseeable future, again like some other parts of the world. This does not necessarily imply the further erosion of the state or even of the conventional business sector since warlordism does not exist in a separate world from official politics but has become an integral part of the political system through the relations between party bosses and the actual perpetrators of violence. The examples of Mexico, Italy and Colombia, to name but three, may well be of relevance to South Africa in showing how a highly developed system of criminal syndicates with connections to political parties and the security forces can co-exist with high rates of economic growth and conventional business activity.

9

LIBERIA 1989–1994

A STUDY OF ETHNIC AND SPIRITUAL VIOLENCE

Many people have noted that the war in Liberia which began in 1989 has been peculiarly horrible.[1] Even professional soldiers from other countries taking part in peace-keeping duties, who may be assumed to be hardened to acts of violence, recoil before the savagery of the Liberian conflict in which cannibalism, random violence and tortures of every sort imaginable have become commonplace. During the earliest phase of the war Western journalists were particularly fascinated by the images which the conflict produced, particularly of young fighters dressed in women's clothing, wearing bizarre accoutrements, such as shower-caps or women's wigs, human bones, and the like. The fact that many fighters were children added another grotesque ingredient. One British newspaper carried a photograph of uniformed peace-keeping soldiers trying to attract their enemy out of the bush by offering them toys and sweets, while another had a picture of a Liberian militiaman looting a large teddy-bear from a Monrovia shop.[2]

A Ghanaian businessman who had lived in Liberia for over 30 years and who was caught up in the violence noted what he called the 'animal' character of the war, and wrote that of all the wars he had heard or read about,

In all frankness the Liberian civil and guerrilla war topped and surpassed [all other wars] in form and character, in intensity, in depravity, in savagery, in barbarism and in horror ...

As far as the men behind the war were concerned, one should be forewarned that the world could be breeding a new species of mankind with no contrite hearts, with no compassion, with no regard for law and order and whose ambitions in life have no bounds at the peril of others.

It has started off in Liberia, but one should beware that there are many more Charles Taylors and Prince Johnsons, the new species of human kind, around not only in Liberia, but in other places, especially in Africa today.[3]

The present article examines how Liberia descended into conflict and why it took such violent form, suggesting that the causes are not only political, but may also be explained in religious or spiritual terms.

The NPFL invasion and the civil war

In some respects Liberia's agony may be traced to 12 April 1980, when a group of lower-ranks soldiers led by Master Sergeant Samuel Doe seized power in a coup. But the civil war itself may be dated more precisely to 24 December 1989, when 100 or more fighters claiming allegiance to the National Patriotic Front of Liberia (NPFL) led by Charles Taylor, an organization hitherto unknown to the outside world and even to most people in Monrovia, advanced over the border from Côte d'Ivoire to attack the town of Butuo in Nimba County.

Faced with this invasion, President Doe, who had civilianized his regime in the manner of an Eyadéma or a Mobutu, at first appeared confident that his armed forces could contain the threat.[4] Remaining in the seat of government, the Executive Mansion in Monrovia, Doe despatched to Nimba County units of the Armed Forces of Liberia (AFL), the government army whose senior ranks were dominated by members of Doe's own Krahn ethnic group. Arriving in Nimba County, the AFL carried out collective punishments against local villagers, killing, looting and raping, singling out people from the Gio and Mano ethnic groups whom they regarded as supporters of the invasion by reason of their ethnic identity alone.[5] There was already a history of enmity between Doe's own Krahn, on the one hand, and the

Gio and Mano on the other, resulting from the politics of the military after the 1980 coup, which had already led to bloodshed in 1985. A report written by a US human rights monitoring group in 1986 made clear how extensive was the hatred of the Krahn generally even by the mid-1980s, and predicted, all too accurately, 'the prospect of massive reprisals against the Krahn if President Doe is violently removed from power'.[6] This was exactly what was to happen after 1989, as Gio and Mano people from Nimba County especially sought revenge, while Krahn soldiers fought to maintain their power.

While Doe seemed to calculate that the best strategy was to sit tight and tempt the rebels into a pitched battle, during the early part of 1990 the NPFL made rapid progress. The core group of NPFL guerrillas, Libyan-trained and supplemented by mercenaries from Burkina Faso supplied by President Blaise Compaore and by internationalist revolutionaries from Gambia and Sierra Leone, distributed arms to the Gio and Mano villagers of Nimba County, knowing that the weapons would be used indiscriminately to attack Krahn and anyone suspected of complicity with the Doe government. So hated was the Doe government that the NPFL attack was welcomed by many Liberians and the violence rapidly spread out of control. Armed bands claiming allegiance to the NPFL launched pogroms against people suspected of being Krahn or Mandingo, another ethnic group regarded as supporters of the Doe government. NPFL war-bands moved into Grand Gedeh County, the Krahn heartland, committing atrocities against people guilty of speaking the same mother-tongue as Doe. By mid-1990, NPFL bands were invading the outskirts of Monrovia. Doe responded by distributing weapons to Krahn and Mandingo civilians and his soldiers killed hundreds of Gio and Mano civilians in the capital, as well as some leading political opponents.[7] Liberia's capital city became the site of a protracted battle, with President Doe and his AFL soldiers holding the Executive Mansion, the seat of government, and areas of the city surrounding it, with the Atlantic Ocean at their backs, while the NPFL held other parts of the city. By the end of the year, perhaps two-thirds of Liberia's 125,000 Krahn had fled the country and tens of thousands of people, not only Krahn, had been killed.[8] Altogether, as many as 700,000 people may have fled the country.[9]

In July 1990, several hundred of Taylor's fighters broke away to form a third group, the Independent National Patriotic Front of Liberia (INPFL), which also occupied a part of Monrovia. The INPFL was led by the psychopathic Prince Yormie Johnson, himself a Nimba County man, a former soldier in Doe's army who had fled abroad in the early 1980s and had subsequently received military training in Libya. Before his split from the NPFL, Johnson had been the NPFL training officer and he took with him the core of experienced NPFL fighters, notably the Libyan-trained Special Commandos, leaving Taylor with few trained men but only thousands of civilians, many from Nimba, who had acquired weapons and joined the NPFL on its progress south. Monrovia was effectively divided into three zones, each infested by a separate group. By most accounts daily life was least affected in Johnson's zone. Although Johnson himself was given to acts of extreme violence, particularly when he was drunk, his men were less desperate than Doe's armed forces, who felt themselves trapped, and more disciplined than Taylor's freebooters.

There were numerous calls for international intervention to stabilize the situation, and there was in particular a general expectation that the USA would intervene in what had long amounted to an unofficial US colony. In June 1990, US warships with 2,000 marines on board anchored off the coast but contented themselves with evacuating US nationals. They went no further to restore order, President George Bush declaring that Liberia was not worth the life of a single US marine. There seems to be widespread agreement that most Liberians, brought up in the shadow of Uncle Sam, would have accepted a US intervention. But at a crucial point, in August 1990, something happened elsewhere in the world which took up all America's attention and definitely ruled out any possibility of US intervention in Liberia: Iraq invaded Kuwait.

Other countries in West Africa were alarmed by the Liberian situation. President Ibrahim Babangida of Nigeria was a personal friend of Samuel Doe. Moreover the Nigerian military government regarded itself as a regional hegemon and, in the first months of the post-Cold War era, saw the Liberian emergency as offering a chance, or a duty, to intervene elsewhere in West Africa and to legitimate itself as a regional peace-keeper, a sub-contractor to the United Nations. There was probably also an element of Nigerian rivalry with francophone West Africa, and particularly with the leading country of the French-speaking bloc, Côte d'Ivoire. The francophone world had recognized the Biafra breakaway in the 1960s, and French policy traditionally had been to regard the existence of the English-speaking countries of West Africa as a threat to the cohesion of the francophone bloc. Since Taylor's NPFL was known to have the backing of Côte d'Ivoire, Burkina Faso and others, Nigeria felt itself challenged. Some sources have also alleged a degree of personal interest in Babangida's decision to intervene in Liberia, suggesting that he had business interests there, but this remains unproven.

Some other countries in the region felt themselves threatened by the NPFL invasion for other reasons. The NPFL was receiving backing from Libya, which had a history of political and military adventurism in West Africa. During visits to Libya probably between 1986 and 1989, Taylor had met a number of Gambians who had taken part in a coup attempt in Banjul in 1981 with Libyan backing and had taken refuge in Libya afterwards. They included Kukoi Samba Sanyang, known to the NPFL as 'Dr Manning'.[10] At the beginning of operations in 1989, Dr Manning was officially listed as Taylor's vice-president, although he soon abandoned the NPFL after being edged out of the leadership by Taylor, and retired to manage a bar in Ouagadougou.[11] Since various Sierra Leonean and some Ghanaian adventurers had also made common cause with Taylor, it was feared by governments throughout the region that a Taylor victory in Liberia would lead to further insurrections or coups elsewhere in the English-speaking countries of West Africa.[12]

Under President Babangida's leadership, and with the encouragement of the USA, the Economic Community of West African States (ECOWAS) hastily dusted off the non-aggression treaty which its members had signed in 1978 and assembled a peace-keeping force whose main component was Nigerian. This intervention force, known as the Economic Community of West African States Monitoring Croup (ECOMOG), arrived in Monrovia on 24 August 1990. From the outset, Taylor opposed ECOMOG, and most particularly the Nigerian element, seeing it as the obstacle between himself and the presidency, which by mid-1990 was within his sight. NPFL forces attacked ECOMOG troops even as they disembarked at the Free Port in Monrovia in August 1990.[13]

On 9 September 1990, President Doe was captured by the INPFL of Prince Johnson, one of the three factions disputing control of Monrovia, when he ventured outside his Executive Mansion for a meeting with ECOMOG. The fact that he was captured while on a negotiation mission, and that it was by Johnson rather than by the NPFL, generated all manner of conspiracy theories. Already seriously wounded during his capture, President Doe was mutilated, tortured and killed by the INPFL in the presence of Prince Johnson in the early hours of the next morning. The ordeal was recorded on video, copies of which Johnson took pleasure in showing to visitors to his headquarters. Copies went on general sale in cities throughout West Africa, and extracts were even broadcast on British television news.

After Doe's murder, the NPFL consolidated its control of the whole of Liberia outside Monrovia while the city itself remained under the control of ECOMOG, with a small area held by Johnson's INPFL. The situation stabilized somewhat. The ECOWAS states agreed to install an Interim Government of National Unity (IGNU) headed by Professor Amos Sawyer, an academic and political activist who had been one of Doe's main political opponents. The IGNU government which was sworn in on 22 November 1990 was not recognized by the NPFL, which formed its own administration of the areas of Liberia under its control, with headquarters in Gbarnga, Bong County, although IGNU received backing from many West African states.

Subsequent developments further complicated the situation. An organization formed in 1991 by Liberians who had taken refuge in Sierra Leone, known as the United Liberation Movement for Democracy (ULIMO), began to participate in armed combat inside Liberia with the backing of the Freetown government. ULIMO included a number of former soldiers of the AFL, as well as other elements, mostly Krahn and Mandingo civilians who had taken up arms in opposition to the NPFL.[14] ULIMO was formed from three existing components. One was a Muslim organization founded in February 1990, the Movement for the Redemption of Liberian Muslims, based in Guinea and led by Alhaji G. V. Krornah, a former Assistant Minister for Information who was playing both with a religious and an ethnic definition of the Mandingo constituency he was cultivating. The second was the Liberian United Defence Force led by General Albert Karpeh, a Krahn, a former Doe minister who had most recently served as ambassador to Sierra Leone. The third element was the Liberian Peace Council established by another former Doe minister, Dr George Boley, also a Krahn. (Boley was shortly to leave the ULIMO leadership). Although ULIMO was officially founded in Conakry on 29 May 1991, it had in fact been born in Freetown some two months earlier as a result of contacts between a group of ex-Doe ministers and the government of Sierra Leone.[15] The latter wanted the support of the Liberian exiles to fight against the NPFL after Charles Taylor in March 1991 had launched a campaign to destabilize Sierra Leone under the nominal leadership of Foday Sankoh and a group called the Revolutionary United Front (RUF), Taylor's aim being to punish the Sierra Leonean government for its participation in ECOMOG.

On 15 October 1992, the NPFL, which had previously been taking part in international peace negotiations, launched a surprise attack on the centre of Monrovia which was defended by ECOMOG with assistance from forces which acknowledged political allegiance to President Sawyer and his IGNU. In its efforts to mobilize all available means to defend the city, ECOMOG rearmed the Armed Forces of Liberia, the remnants of Doe's old army which had been eclipsed since 1990 but which was now relegitimated as the armed forces of an internationally recognized government, the IGNU. The attack, known as Operation Octopus, led to fierce fighting in Monrovia. There was widespread murder, rape and looting by the NPFL as it advanced towards the heart of the city. The NPFL also abducted thousands of people whom it transported to its own headquarters at Gbarnga in the interior of Liberia. During this second battle for Monrovia ECOMOG took a major part in the conflict for the first time. Outraged by Charles Taylor's bad faith in launching Operation Octopus, ECOMOG passed onto the offensive, using aircraft to bombard NPFL positions, which led to civilian deaths.[16] Although ECOMOG was not able to defeat the NPFL decisively, it and its allies did succeed in defending Monrovia, which remained under the formal control of the Interim Government. The INPFL of Prince Johnson collapsed. Some former INPFL members rejoined the NPFL. Johnson himself retired to live abroad. By early

1993 Liberia was in effect partitioned into two zones. Monrovia and its outskirts were controlled by ECOMOG, with formal sovereignty being held by President Sawyer's government, and the other nine-tenths or so of the country, referred to by Charles Taylor as 'Greater Liberia', controlled by the NPFL from its capital at Gbarnga. ULIMO was launching attacks against the NPFL from areas close to the Sierra Leonean border, as well as doing battle with Taylor's surrogates, the RUF, inside Sierra Leone itself. Taylor cultivated all the attributes of a sovereign government, with ministries and even his own currency. A private bank opened its doors for business in Gbarnga, and foreign diplomats including representatives of the French and German governments visited Taylor in his headquarters, in effect treating him as a head of state. Few diplomats had much enthusiasm for Taylor, although some were captivated by his undoubted suavity and intelligence. Others reasoned that since he was the *de facto* ruler of most of Liberia, there was every reason to maintain relations with him. Taylor encouraged foreign companies to do business as usual in territories which he controlled, exporting iron ore, diamonds and timber from his zone in return for taxes which were paid to him personally.[17]

On 6 June 1993, as negotiations were in progress towards agreeing a peace plan and a ceasefire, the attention of the world media was drawn to a massacre of some 600 displaced people, mostly women and children, at a camp in the Firestone Plantation, the world's biggest rubber plantation which had been disputed between the NPFL and the AFL, still legally the armed forces of the government. An inquiry instituted by the Secretary General of the United Nations, and conducted by Amos Wako, attorney general of Kenya, concluded that the Harbel massacre had been carried out by the AFL, although other reports concluded that it was the work of the NPFL, which appeared to many observers to be more likely.[18] It was probably ordered by Taylor as a means of gaining world attention and increasing the pressure for a ceasefire, which he now considered in his interest. If so, the Harbel massacre had the desired effect.

On 25 July 1993, the three main Liberian armed factions, under pressure from the international community, signed a ceasefire in Cotonou, Benin. These three—the NPFL, the AFL, and ULIMO—agreed to cease hostilities and to maintain the positions which they occupied. In the meantime, provision was made for the establishment of a transitional government, which was to contain representatives of ULIMO and the NPFL as well as others nominated by the outgoing Government of National Unity. This was accompanied by a timetable for elections and a return to full democratic government. ECOMOG was to remain in place as a monitoring force. The Secretary General of the UN established a United Nations Observer Mission (UNOMIL) after complaints by the NPFL that ECOMOG was not an impartial force, since it had taken an active role in fighting against the NPFL in the past. UNOMIL's task was to report to the UN Secretary General on the peace process. The Cotonou Accord provided for the disarmament of the three factions which were its signatories to proceed concomitant with the establishment of the transitional government. They were to disarm to ECOMOG.

After some delay due to disputes about its precise composition, the Transitional Government was finally formed on 7 March 1994, under a five-person Council of State. The latter was an unwieldy and probably unworkable construction included in the peace process at Taylor's insistence. Some 3,500 fighters were reported to have delivered their arms to ECOMOG by early July 1994, but there were clear signs that the peace process was in jeopardy. One of the factions, ULIMO, split along roughly ethnic lines after months of tension between rival groups. The immediate cause of the fighting which broke out between the two factions in March 1994 was a dispute about nominations to positions in the transitional government. Both ULIMO factions remained opposed to the NPFL. Moreover a new armed group, Boley's Liberian Peace Council (LPC), which had existed for two years but previously been dormant, appeared on the ground in late 1993 and began to attack areas under NPFL control in the south-east of the country. It appeared that the LPC was resurrected by the Krahn faction within the AFL as a proxy force. The aim was for the Krahn warlords within the AFL to use the LPC to wage war while themselves being seen to observe the letter of the Cotonou Accord. In May 1994 the AFL's own Provost Marshall, Lieutenant-Colonel Amos Garlo, was killed while fighting with the LPC.[19] ECOMOG maintained that it could not take any action in regard to the LPC since the latter was not a signatory to the Cotonou Accord, and that it therefore fell outside the ECOMOG mandate. It seemed that ECOMOG, or at least certain elements within it, far from remaining neutral, was using various Krahn-dominated groups, including the AFL, the LPC and ULIMO, as foot-soldiers in the fight against the NPFL.[20] There were reports of other armed groups springing up in different parts of the country, such as the Lofa Defence Force in Lofa County, and the Citizens' Defence Force in Maryland. Some sources believed that these were in whole or in part the creations of various parties to the Cotonou Peace Accord, designed to carry on the war by proxy. By mid-1994 fighting between rival factions was growing steadily more serious. The future both of ECOMOG and UNOMIL was also in doubt as it became evident that elections could not be held by the specified date of 7 September 1994.

It was possible to perceive certain trends in the progress of political or military events. In the first place it was apparent that the Cotonou Peace Accord had not brought peace but, on the contrary, had led to a multiplication of militias, which themselves were increasingly ethnically based. The faction which gained most from the events of 1993–4 was the Krahn fighters, the remnants of Doe's supporters, who by July 1994 controlled the general staff of the AFL, the LPC and one faction of ULIMO. It did not escape attention that the AFL's Krahn officers, who were said to include eight out of the army's nine generals, seemed to enjoy the sympathy of some of the leading officers of ECOMOG, particularly from the dominant Nigerian contingent. ECOMOG already controlled the ports of Monrovia, where the AFL had its headquarters, and Buchanan. In under a year of fighting following the Cotonou Peace Accord, largely through the medium of the LPC, the Krahn warlords of the AFL, the LPC, and the Johnson faction of ULIMO, had taken control of Liberia's remaining ports with the exception of Harper, thus taking a strategic position for future negotiations. It seemed plausible that the Nigerian army, which could not stay in Liberia indefinitely, was in effect cultivating the Krahn warlords as local collaborators and was not averse to seeing them take control of the country's ports. A year of peace had cost Taylor dear, since he had lost control of a large swathe of territory. He had been unable to make the transition he sought from warlord to politician.

Most estimates put the number of casualties of the period 1989– 1994 at a minimum of 150,000 dead, compared with a pre-war population of only some two and a half million,[21] meaning that as many as one Liberian out of every seventeen may have been a victim of the war, quite apart from those who were injured or suffered other trauma or material loss or the hundreds of thousands who fled abroad. Many survivors sought refuge in Monrovia, where ECOMOG guaranteed security and international relief organizations offered aid.

Despite the warnings made in the 1980s about the level of ethnic hatred which had built up during Doe's tenure of power, it appears that no one—neither President Doe, nor Charles Taylor, nor the latter's main sponsor, President Félix Houphouët-Boigny of Côte d'Ivoire—expected that the December 1989 attack would lead to the collapse of the Liberian state and a descent into anarchy. They seem to have expected that the invasion would lead to a coup of a relatively familiar type. Liberia, after all, is the oldest state in West Africa and one of only two African countries never to have been formally colonized. Certainly until the 1980s, it had been prosperous by African standards, it had the protection of the USA, it used US dollars as its currency, and Liberians were generally regarded throughout the region as rather docile people.

In the following section, we will attempt to examine some of the fault-lines which opened up in the collapse of the state's monopoly of violence after 1989, before going on to trace some of the new dynamics which this has produced.

The causes of collapse

With hindsight, some of the flaws in Liberia's system of government may be traced as far back as the presidency of William Tubman (1944–71), generally regarded as the heyday of the True Whig Party and the Liberian–American elite whose political vehicle it was.

The Liberian state owes its origins to the presence of settlers of American origin, former slaves who began to settle on West Africa's Grain Coast in the 1820s and who in 1847 proclaimed the Republic of Liberia. From then on, as several of the leading historians of Liberia have noted,[22] although Liberia was never formally colonized, its history in many respects was comparable to that of colonies of settlement, with the major difference that the settlers were themselves ultimately of

African origin. Like European colonists in other parts of the continent, the American–Liberian elite regarded itself as culturally superior to the peoples of the hinterland, the 'country people' or the 'tribal people', and dominated the political system. The True Whig Party built up a formidable patronage machine which reached its height under Tubman, who in effect made Liberia into Africa's first 'party-state' and personalized authority more than any of his predecessors, making the presidency 'the ultimate source of individual livelihood … All incomes were perceived to be derived from President Tubman. Accordingly, all praises went to him'.[23] The personalization of authority was both a reflection and a cause of the failure to build autonomous institutions, the result of which was to be fatal when the state later fell into the hands of an individual less qualified to govern the country than Tubman, a lawyer who had emerged through the True Whig political machine. Both Tubman and especially his successor William Tolbert (1971–80) sensed the weakness of their apparently monolithic rule and attempted to open the True Whig national patronage network to Liberians of indigenous origin, the 'country' people. Liberians of indigenous origin had previously been able to rise to prominent positions by attaching themselves to one or other of the important American–Liberian families.[24] But the gradual extension of the True Whig Party's creaky patronage system to a multitude of previously excluded Liberians coincided with the onset of economic problems caused by the oil price rises of the early 1970s, with the result that there was increased competition to obtain slices of a shrinking national cake.[25] Tolbert was eventually to become the victim of the classic dilemma of a reforming government, losing the support of his conservative base without being able to satisfy fully the new constituencies he was wooing, whose political appetite he had aroused.[26]

The army was a key institution, especially as it too was used in the service of President Tolbert's strategy of extending his patronage machine to the 'country' people. From their inception in 1908, the Liberian armed forces were 'an instrument of internal repression',[27] used particularly to enforce the will of the Monrovia government in rural areas which had only recently been incorporated into the Liberian republic. Whereas the peasantry was for many decades the favoured source of rank and file recruits, particularly men from the supposedly warlike 'tribes' of Lofa County, the emphasis under Tolbert turned to recruiting among the urban unemployed, not least as a means of reducing vagrancy. But soldiers of 'country' origin still found their advancement blocked by an American–Liberian officer corps. As Amos Sawyer noted, Tolbert's recruitment policy not only upset the ethnic balance within the armed forces, but also introduced into the soldiery some people from the most alienated sector of society, the urban unemployed, which boded ill for future standards of military behaviour.[28] This became clear to most people only after 1980, when Master Sergeant Doe and his companions from the lower ranks took power. The Doe regime, whether in its initial military guise or in its later civilianized form, was not merely brutal; it had what Sawyer called a 'marauding nature' which he attributed to 'its social basis and historical circumstances'.[29] Writing after six years of Doe's increasingly personalized government, Sawyer characterized the period accurately enough as 'six years of rape and plunder by armed marauders whose ideology is to search for cash and whose ambition is to retain power to accumulate and protect wealth'.[30] Since the state had historically been used as a means of personal enrichment, it was not illogical for Doe to use it for the same purpose. Nevertheless, the speed with which he and his military supporters acquired wealth and the brutality which they employed were of a different order from what had gone before.

At the heart of the Doe government was a man who had no conception of power other than as a display of accumulation and force, surrounded by cronies and lieutenants, many of them fellow-Krahn. These people were simply not interested in investigating technical problems of government or the measures for their solution.[31] Their perspective was generally short-term and, at least after Doe's execution in 1981 of his rival fellow-putschist, Deputy Head of State Thomas Weh Syen, Doe personally was caught in a Macbethian logic which compelled him to spill ever more blood merely to retain power. He certainly could not contemplate leaving power, even if he had been inclined to do so, for fear of reprisals.[32] As we have noted, many Krahn, even the many who had not shared the spoils of government, were afraid of a change of regime for the same reason.[33] Doe, in basing his power on his own ethnic group, was in a sense blackmailing all

Krahn, since they knew that, whatever their personal circumstances, his departure would lead to violence against them.

Doe had abolished the political machine of the True Whig Party and he needed to replace it with another political system of some sort. In its early months the new junta, the People's Redemption Council (PRC), had the support of some left-wing intellectuals who saw it as a means of implementing their own programmes, but that relationship soon ended. In spite of the general short-termism of his government, there is evidence that one of the few areas where Doe thought on a strategic level was in the building of ethnic alliances. He used the immense powers of the presidency which he had inherited, and the patronage attached to it, to create ethnic constituencies since he had neither the time nor the skills to build any other type of political apparatus. In the first months after the 1980 coup, the regime enjoyed widespread popularity precisely because of its ethnic character, since Doe and his fellow-putschists could claim convincingly enough to have struck a blow against the American–Liberian oligarchy represented by the True Whig Party, and thus to have emancipated the 'country' people. However, the construction of a workable political system soon required further definition if it was to attract the lasting support of at least some of those 'country' people whom the junta claimed to represent.

Doe seems to have been conscious of the political possibilities of ethnic affiliation from the moment that, as the most senior of the noncommissioned officers to have staged the 1980 coup, he was appointed chairman of the PRC. His own ethnic group, the Krahn, formed only some five per cent of the Liberian population and did not include significant numbers of wealthy or educated people. Not only were few Krahn equipped to serve in senior government positions, but Doe himself hardly knew how to run a government. He had no relevant experience, spoke poor English and was functionally illiterate. He urgently needed advisors who could teach him how to use the instruments of politics and government, and he found one such in the person of Dr George Boley, one of the few Krahn to have received higher education (a doctorate in education from an American university) and to have been an activist in a national political party. Boley was appointed Minister of State, responsible for political affairs, on the very day of the coup. He later occupied other ministerial positions in the Doe government and he produced a book supportive of the new government.[34] Although Boley was gradually sidelined, and Doe was to take advice on ethnic politics from other intellectuals whom he recruited,[35] Boley's participation in the early months of the Doe government introduced him to the circle of Krahn warlords whom Doe was to create and promote.[36] Doe doubled the strength of the AFL from three to six thousand after 1980, and particularly promoted Krahn within the officer corps. By 1986 the numbers had once more been reduced as he purged rivals from other ethnic groups.[37] Doe's consolidation of his personal power within the junta, and the rapid recruitment and promotion of Krahn within the armed forces, quickly led to specifically ethnic tensions within the armed forces, not to mention an accentuation of clan and lineage divisions among the Krahn themselves.[38] The construction of ethnic patronage systems by rival soldiers, starting from scratch, in the shortest possible time, was probably the single most important cause of Liberia's subsequent collapse.

The crucial conflict within the junta was between Doe and his fellow-putschist Thomas Quiwonkpa. After the coup the latter became commanding general of the Armed Forces of Liberia, while Doe cultivated a more political role as chairman of the PRC. Unlike Doe, who immediately began to cultivate a presidential style although carefully eschewing the title of president for some years, Quiwonkpa continued to live in the barracks and remained popular with the soldiers. He also spoke on occasion about the need for returning the country to civilian rule, which earned him a reputation as a moderate. Like his rival Doe, Quiwonkpa needed both to build an ethnic base and to take advice from someone who knew how to work the levers of government. His ethnic base he found in the Gio and Mano soldiers of his home area, Nimba County. One source of advice he found in a little-known American–Liberian whose wife was from Nimba and was a distant relative of Quiwonkpa. This advisor was one Charles Taylor.[39] A showdown between Quiwonkpa and Doe in 1983 led to Quiwonkpa fleeing into exile and his ill-fated attempt to return at the head of a coup attempt in November 1985.

The personal rivalry between Doe and Quiwonkpa was translated into tension between Krahn and Gio and Mano, their respective ethnic constituencies, within the armed forces, especially since there was a degree of traditional rivalry between Krahn and Gio and Mano as a result of competition for land in the rural areas where both groups lived.[40] After the failed coup of 1985, the struggle spread from the army into society at large, as Doe's soldiers purged Gio and Mano from the armed forces and punished Gio and Mano generally, looting and killing as a form of collective punishment with exceptional savagery.[41]

In addition to promoting Krahn to positions of influence, Doe's creation of an ethnically-based clientele also led him to cultivate another ethnic group, the Mandingo.[42] The latter is the name of a diaspora of traders especially which has its origins in present-day Guinea, but which has over the centuries spread over a considerable area, including throughout Liberia. Virtually all Mandingo are Muslims, and indeed the name Mandingo is generally applied in Liberia to traders of different ethnic origin who take on the appearance of Muslim culture. Despite the length of time that Mandingo have lived in Liberia they are nevertheless perceived by many Liberians as outsiders, not authentically Liberian. This appears to be largely because of their religion and their commercial vocation, both of which provide the Mandingo with a distinctive set of cultural attributes, such as in dress, Koranic education, and gender relations. Mandingo men are generally polygamous, and although they often take wives from different ethnic groups, male family-heads are renowned for their reluctance to allow their own womenfolk to marry into other groups. In many villages in the 1980s, the local trader, money-lender or shop-keeper was a Mandingo.

The two last True Whig Party presidents, Tubman and Tolbert, both cultivated the Mandingo community because of its commercial importance. From the early 1980s, when Doe's ethnic politics obliged him to address the problem posed by Quiwonkpa's cultivation of a support-base in the armed forces among Gio and Mano soldiers, Doe made a conscious effort to build a rival political constituency in Nimba County by favouring the Mandingo, who are quite numerous there. He appointed Mandingo officials to official positions in Nimba County and encouraged them to purchase land. At the national level, Alhaji G.V. Kromah, a journalist by training, became Assistant Minister of Information and began to cultivate a reputation as the Mandingos' national leader, although Mandingo had previously tended to shy away from politics, regarding it as incompatible with their business interests. In 1986, in the aftermath of the Quiwonkpa coup attempt, Doe explicitly recognized the Mandingo to be a Liberian ethnic group, which intensely annoyed many Liberians who persisted in regarding the Mandingo as foreigners.[43]

Quiwonkpa's legacy: The NPFL

In view of Doe's and Quiwonkpa's rival cultivation of ethnic consistencies in 1980–83, it is not surprising that Doe and his Krahn supporters in the army considered Quiwonkpa's 1985 attempted putsch to be backed by Gio and Mano in general, including civilians. Many Gio and Mano soldiers, some of them survivors of Quiwonkpa's coup, as well as civilians fleeing the massacres in Nimba County, fled to Côte d'Ivoire where they received sympathetic treatment from the government of President Houphouët-Boigny, who had himself never forgiven Doe for his execution of prominent True Whig Party officials in 1980, among whom was A.B. Tolbert, a son of President Tolbert who had married Houphouët-Boigny's adopted daughter.[44] The latter, after the death of her husband, became a close friend of Captain Blaise Compaore, later president of Burkina Faso.

Refugees from Nimba County and Gio and Mano soldiers who had fled for their lives in 1985 joined a previous wave of Liberian exiles, remnants of the True Whig Party oligarchy who had left the country in 1980. It was from this common hatred of Doe that the NPFL was born. According to Tom Woweiyu, a long-standing opponent of Doe who was to become one of the NPFL's leaders, the organization was actually founded by Quiwonkpa himself, and Liberian exiles in Côte d'Ivoire particularly supported it, although it appears to have had little formal structure until 1989. Only in the late 1980s did Charles Taylor come to be regarded as its leader.[45]

Taylor is an American–Liberian, born in 1948, who had gained a degree in economics in the USA, where he became prominent in the Liberian students' movement before returning to Liberia shortly before the coup of 1980. He was, and is, a man of boundless ambition. As soon as the coup took place, Taylor, largely through his wife's family relations to Quiwonkpa, succeeded in ingratiating himself with the new junta which was in dire need of managerial talent. Cleverly, instead of seeking a minister's portfolio, Taylor successfully lobbied for the directorship of the obscure General Services Agency, a government procurement office. By arguing that economies of scale could be made by ordering equipment in bulk rather than through individual ministries, Taylor centralized government procurement in his own hands and was able to take commissions from each contract in such a manner as to amass a fortune within a very short time. He was also, briefly, Deputy Minister of Commerce. In 1983, under investigation for a $900,000 fraud, and seeing the career of his military patron Quiwonkpa in decline, Taylor fled to the USA, where he was arrested by the police under an extradition treaty with the Liberian government. He succeeded in escaping from a maximum security prison in Massachusetts by paying a bribe, allegedly of $50,000.[46] He then passed through Mexico, Spain and France before settling in Accra in late 1985 or 1986. On his travels Taylor acquired a working knowledge of French.

Once back in West Africa, Taylor was able to make contact with other exiled opponents of the Doe government and, together with them, he sought international backing for an armed resistance movement. In the context of the Cold War, this posed a delicate problem: since the USA was a confirmed backer of the Doe government, the US government was excluded as a source of support. To turn to the Soviet bloc in these circumstances was out of the question since the USA would never allow a Soviet client to take power in Liberia. So committed was the USA to supporting the existing government of Liberia that for some years it actually gave Doe more financial help than it gave to any other government in sub-Saharan Africa, despite his appalling human rights record.[47] Taylor, as a fugitive from US justice, had little to lose by seeking help from other sources whereas most American–Liberians valued their rights of entry to the USA too highly to risk dabbling with anti-American governments. In Accra Taylor befriended the Burkinabè ambassador, Memunu Ouattara, at a time when Captain Thomas Sankara of Burkina Faso and Chairman Jerry Rawlings of Ghana were close friends, and both had quite close relations with Libya. It was largely because of his dabbling in revolutionary politics that Taylor was twice detained by Ghanaian security. (He was also, at various times in the 1980s, detained in both Sierra Leone and Guinea).[48] Taylor's companion Agnes Reeves and other Liberian exiles in Accra succeeded in contacting the new ruler of Burkina Faso, Blaise Compaoré, who prevailed upon the Ghanaian authorities to release Taylor into his own custody. Compaore had close relations with President Houphouët-Boigny, and also, like his predecessor Sankara, with the revolutionary government in Libya. Taylor was able to travel to Tripoli and make direct contact there. The Libyan government, smarting from its defeats in Chad, was seeking new avenues to extend its influence in West Africa, and cultivated its relations with both the government of Burkina Faso and with Taylor. Taylor, a most persuasive talker, was able to convince the Libyan government of his revolutionary credentials.

By these means Taylor was able to build international support from the unlikely trio of Côte d'Ivoire, Burkina Faso and Libya, providing the group of exiled Liberians with the international backing which they had previously lacked. Colonel Gadaffi's Libya was the focus for revolutionaries and adventurers of every type and there, and in Burkina Faso, Taylor met a number of West African revolutionaries. He was able to arrange for a small group of Liberians to receive military training in Libya and then resettle in Burkina Faso, most of them former farmers or soldiers from Nimba County who had fled the repression after 1985. One of the most influential of these was Quiwonkpa's former aide-de-camp, Prince Johnson. It was Taylor's leadership of this group which enabled him to claim to be chairman of the NPFL. Thus Charles Taylor, an obscure former official of the Doe government who was known, if at all, as a fugitive from criminal justice, succeeded in becoming the head of an exiled combination of Nimba County farmers and soldiers and members of the American–Liberian elite which had ruled the country before 1980, the whole purporting to be a pro-Libyan revolutionary movement.

The emergence of the warlords

In response to the NPFL's 24 December 1989 attack on Butuo, it was not only AFL soldiers who went to fight against the insurgents. Alhaji Kromah, striving to secure his ambition of becoming the national leader of Liberia's Mandingo community, travelled to Nimba and, sporting a military uniform and a gun, urged Mandingo people to support Doe's forces and called on Muslim businessmen to help finance the war. This was to be fatal for thousands of Mandingo. When NPFL forces succeeded in occupying Nimba County, they extracted a terrible revenge on Mandingos.[49]Taylor was unable to control his fighters and to prevent the spread of widespread massacres and atrocities,[50] although he was also to encourage massacres in some cases for political reasons. Taylor exploited the violence he had unleashed to cement his own position as the leader of the NPFL, making skillful use of his satellite-telephone to conduct interviews with the BBC's Africa Service, a vital asset as Taylor once admitted publicly,[51] and by the formation of the Small Boy Units, squads of adolescents or pre-teens, many orphaned by the AFL's counter-insurgency activities, whom he formed into a personal guard, inculcated with his own cult of personality in a way which was harder to achieve with units of adult fighters. Taylor was soon to build up a formidable personal power, which cowed other NPFL leaders, and he did not hesitate to assassinate potential rivals within the organization, especially politicians with a following among the Gio and Mano, and most notably Jackson Doe, presumed to have been the real winner of the rigged presidential election of 1985 and thus a potential president of Liberia.[52]

During 1990 large number of Krahn and Mandingo fled to Sierra Leone to escape the massacres taking place, and began to regroup there, starting their own movement in exile, ULIMO, as we have described. An internal struggle within the fledgling ULIMO led to the murder in obscure circumstances of General Karpeh in Kenema, Sierra Leone, in May 1992, and later of Major Solomon Kamara, a prominent Kromah supporter. In effect ULIMO became the site of a struggle between Mandingo elements led by Kromah with support in Conakry, and Krahn politicians, who had support in Freetown, a rivalry of which Karpeh and Kamara were victims.

The factional rivalry within ULIMO was to erupt into major bloodshed only in March 1994, when rival ULIMO war-bands began raiding each other's territory, especially in Cape Mount county along the Sierra Leonean border. Although the power-struggle which emerged into the open in March 1994 did not represent a fundamental Mandingo–Krahn rivalry, it led to territorial raiding. As with the Krahn–Mandingo/Gio–Mano rivalries, the Krahn–Mandingo split in ULIMO did not have its origins in any generalized ethnic hatreds, but in the factionalism of ambitious politicians seeking to carve themselves a following. Once small groups of combatants, identifying themselves by ethnic labels, had begun to fight, and their activities had been reported in the media or by word of mouth, it easily led to more generalized suspicion of one group towards another.[53] All of Liberia's current ethnic feuds started at the top and spread downwards. To a great extent, all have been manufactured by people hungry for power, using violence as a means of political recruitment. Victims of militia violence from various part of Liberia, interviewed in July 1994, reported that war-bands in fact were generally composed of people speaking various Liberian languages. This supports the view that the ethnic labels generally attached to the various militias are ideological representations used by politicians as a means of creating constituencies. They then acquire a certain political substance over the course of time. It is interesting to note, moreover, that the warlord who failed most spectacularly—Prince Johnson—did so precisely because he neglected to cultivate an ethnic base, that is to say a political constituency.

The misconceived Cotonou Peace Accord of July 1993 served only to encourage the mobilization of ethnic constituencies by warlords. At the time of the Cotonou Peace Accord, Taylor appears to have reasoned that violence had secured for him as much as it could, and that a political strategy would yield greater fruits in the future, by legitimizing his *de facto* control of nine-tenths of Liberian territory, and would enable him to undermine the fragile political institutions in Monrovia from within, by planting his own placemen within a transitional government in what was widely perceived as a 'Trojan Horse' strategy. Although opinions on the subject differ, a persuasive interpretation is that Taylor genuinely wished to respect the Cotonou Peace Accord as he perceived that a new political phase would deliver to him the prize he craved but had not achieved by violence alone: the presidency. It seems likely that some of the other signatories or parties to the Accord had no such aim and envisaged instead a two-track strategy of signing a peace treaty while pursuing a military goal through surrogate forces constructed on an ethnic base. Hence, there was abundant evidence that the Krahn faction within the AFL, backed by others possibly including some elements of ECOMOG, decided to use the Liberian Peace Council as a means of continuing the war.[54]

By mid-1994 it had become clear that not only had the Cotonou peace process broken down irretrievably but that, in the absence of any real political trust or commitment, it had had the effect of splintering the existing armies. The AFL had spawned the LPC and itself showed signs of internal divisions between Krahn and non-Krahn elements.[55] ULIMO was split into two ethnically-defined factions, one loosely owing allegiance to Alhaji Kromah and consisting largely of Mandingo fighters, the other largely Krahn under one Roosevelt Johnson. On the side of the NPFL, Taylor had encouraged the creation of a Lofa Defence Force, also as a means of waging surrogate war. Within the NPFL some of Taylor's key lieutenants defected after they had arrived to take up posts in the Transitional Government in Monrovia, denouncing Taylor and singing the praises of ECOMOG. Probably the most important of these were Sam Dokie, Interior Minister in the Transitional Government, and Tom Woweiyu, Taylor's former defence chief. Dokie was from Nimba County and Woweiyu from Grand Bassa County. Both had personal followings among segments of Taylor's fighters, dangerously separating Taylor, the American–Liberian, from his fighters, many of them Gio and Mano. There were vague reports of still other armies, such as the Citizens' Defence Force in Maryland County, the Bassa Defence Force, and so on.

Not only were the militias becoming increasingly ethnicized all over Liberia, but it was apparent that to a large extent, violence had become divorced from politics in any normal definition of the word. The nominal heads of several militias—Alhaji Kromah of ULIMO: Mandingo, George Boley of the LPC, and Charles Taylor of the NPFL—had all been senior officials of the Doe government who had learned there the deadly skills of ethnic politics built on clientelism and violence. But they had only tenuous control of the actual fighters. Taylor was even unable to stop some of his most senior commanders from doing battle with each other.[56] The United Nations estimated in 1994 that there were some 60,000 Liberians under arms,[57] of whom few had received any formal military training and none of whom (with the partial exception of the AFL) was paid. The fighters were mostly not soldiers at all, but armed civilians, sometimes very young, who lived by the gun, stealing what they needed or wanted. This produced its own *logique de guerre*. War-bands based themselves in any area where there were exploitable resources, especially diamond-producing areas, or where villagers were still producing crops, or places where humanitarian convoys could be looted. They would defend these strategic positions against all comers while raiding the territory of rival militias with the aim of looting, damaging the enemy's core population, and commandeering slave labour, in a way probably akin to the mode of warfare practised in the days of the slave trade.[58] This has produced a mosaic of militia zones of control, where civilians have some degree of protection but must pay tribute in kind to the local warlord, and constantly shifting frontier zones in which civilians are liable to raiding from all sides. The aim is control of people and acquisition of booty more than it is to control territory in the conventional military manner. Armies prey upon the unarmed civilian population, looting their belongings, stealing their food, and forcing them to head-load the victims' own goods back to the militias' base areas. Already by late 1990, some of the original core of NPFL fighters, originally dispossessed farmers from Nimba County, had made enough money through looting as to leave the army and return home with their booty.[59] By 1994, Nimba County was said to be remarkably peaceful, possibly the most peaceful part of the country, and many of the original Libyan-trained NPFL fighters had settled down as shop-keepers and businessmen, having had successful careers as fighters. 'You wouldn't know that was where the war started', one government minister commented in July 1994.[60]

In conventional military terms, none of the various armies in Liberia was very formidable. Displaced people from Cape Mount County, victims of raids by ULIMO:Kromah faction, reported a typical pattern of attack. War-bands up to 40 strong would reconnoitre a village often using a local youth whom they had persuaded to inform them of the lay-out of the village and, above all, of which people had possessions worth looting. The war-band would then attack, instilling the maximum fear in unarmed villagers by perpetrating some acts of exemplary violence. They would then assemble the people and read out lists of names of those whom they knew to have goods worth looting. A common tactic was to capture women, and threaten to kill them unless their husbands paid ransom-money. Having looted everything worth taking, the war-band would then abduct some men to act as porters. Attempted escape would be met by instant death.[61] Refugees from LPC attacks in Grand Bassa County reported being attacked by smaller groups, of perhaps 10 men, who would systematically torture them, typically by beating and by branding them with heated matchets. They would then take all the goods they could find and force men to head-load the booty to their base.[62] In all cases, rape, including gang-rape, and other gratuitous violence, were commonplace.

In the core-zones under NPFL control, Taylor largely allowed people to go about their normal business, taking a tax on external trade which he supervised personally and demanding levies of young men for his army, in a manner strikingly reminiscent of pre-19th century war-leaders.[63] Farmers liable to attacks from the various war-bands fled to the relative safety of the main cities, especially Monrovia. Only rarely did the militias attack each other head on. For the most part, they preyed on civilians. At the same time, senior commanders, who were adults, preyed on their soldiers. As one junior NPFL fighter put it, 'you go to dey front, you fight, anything good you get, dey take it from you, dat why you see some of those boys to the front dey don't want to come to Gbarnga because if dey bring anything good, dey will take it from them'.[64] On occasion rival warlords from the same militia would fight over the division of spoils of war.[65] A veritable mode of production had evolved in which the main aim was enrichment through looting, and wealth was sucked upwards within the militias' rudimentary hierarchies, from fighters to their officers. All the armed factions included a sprinkling of ex-soldiers from Doe's old AFL who had defected at some time or other. Just as Doe's government had had, in Sawyer's phrase, 'a marauding nature',[66] so too did the armed groups which eventually succeeded it and which it had in fact spawned.

The international peace-keeping force, ECOMOG, showed signs of demoralization and had itself taken on 'a marauding nature', looting where possible, and even wholesaling stolen goods looted by some Liberian militias. There are indications that some factions, and also some ECOMOG soldiers, have taken to international drug-trading.[67]

Liberian concepts of power

Many Liberians, or probably most Liberians, have tried to understand what has happened to their lives by reference to religion. Paul Gifford has demonstrated how, already during the Doe years, there was a spectacular growth in evangelical churches during the 1980s.[68] Whereas Gifford interprets this phenomenon as a flight from reality, a refusal to take real political action by seeking refuge in a world beyond, there is room for advancing other interpretations for the growth in evangelical and spiritual churches.

Although the political culture of Liberia is not uniform, and there are significant variations between different language groups, there are nevertheless some general comments which one might make. In addition to Liberia's modern, secular institutions of government, imported by the 19th-century settlers and articulated officially in the English language, there exists another political culture, or other cultures, with deep historical roots. As Amos Sawyer points out, the political culture of the peoples living in Liberia in the pre-modern period (that is, the complex of symbols and attitudes concerning power which constitute the country's 'governmentality'[69]) was rooted in spiritual beliefs closely associated with the occupation and cultivation of land.[70] Among the Mande-speaking peoples who constitute perhaps half the country's population, the most evident aspect of governance which has survived in institutional form at the local level is the Poro and Sende secret societies.[71] Although the Poro and Sende as such are strongest in the western and northern parts of Liberia, similar secret cults exist in other parts of the country. Even Liberians of American origin have created their own secret societies, like the Freemasons and the United Brothers of Friendship, which became veritable cults of a type familiar to pre-settler Liberian culture.[72] Perhaps the only major population group which does not participate in Poro or similar cults is the Mandingo, whose Muslim identity excludes them from the Poro and Sende or similar societies, although the Mandingo generally are widely regarded as experts in magic and various forms of esoteric religious knowledge.

The Poro and Sende are ancient, dating from before the 17th century. In many parts of Liberia the Poro represented the most important political institution certainly until the mid-20th century,[73] with chiefs being purely civic authorities subject to the real control of the Poro. While the rise of Tubman's party-state certainly eroded the power of the Poro, Presidents Tubman, Tolbert and Doe all found it necessary to have themselves proclaimed supreme authorities of the Poro as a buttress to their power. A good definition of the Poro is that of Harley:

> The Poro may be thought of as an attempt to reduce the all pervading spirit world to an organization in which man might contact the spirit world and interpret it to the people, where men became spirits, and took on godhead.[74]

The designation of Poro (for males) and Sende (for females) as secret societies is in some respects rather misleading, as every adult Mande-speaker is in principle a member of the appropriate society. As Bellman explains, the secrecy attached to Poro ritual is less an attempt to keep knowledge restricted than to transmit certain messages to members in an esoteric form. Since boys are initiated into the Poro in order to become men, the essence of the message encoded in the Poro rituals concerns the proper understanding of the power of manhood, including one of its immanent features, violence.

At the heart of Poro initiation is a ritual of death, represented as the act of being eaten by a wild spirit, and rebirth in adulthood. The initiation rituals include the infliction of physical pain and are designed to cause the maximum effect on the impressionable adolescents who undergo them, by enacting a theatre of terror. Elders of the society wearing spirit-masks abduct future initiates from their house at the beginning of the period of ritual confinement. The power attributed to the spirits of the bush, represented by masked officers of the society, is both terrifying and morally ambiguous. Inherent in the understanding or acquisition of the power represented by the bush-spirits is that of sacrifice and the eating of human flesh and blood, represented symbolically by animal sacrifice and often by the ritual scarifying of an initiate, symbolizing his spiritual death and resurrection. Thus the Poro initiation rituals, as well as educating boys in the duties of manhood, also demonstrate that the power of the wild and dangerous spirits of the bush has been tamed and made socially productive by the Poro, and that it has been domesticated to underpin political order. Within the Poro are other, more exclusive, societies which include cults of ritual murder.[75] Although there does not exist such rich documentation on other masking societies or cults of symbolic violence in non-Mande areas of Liberia, they appear to use a rather similar symbolism.[76]

In many respects this popular and deeply-rooted political culture has been inadequately discussed in the literature on Liberian politics, probably because it does not conform to the modern, secular political institutions which have earned the country its place in the international community of nations. The Poro and similar cults have appeared to many writers to be provincial rather than national, and archaic rather than modern. Political analysts have tended to concentrate their attention on the modern and elite political institutions represented by the national government rather than such institutions as the Poro society, which were felt to be material for study by anthropologists or other specialists. And inasmuch as anthropologists have studied the Poro and similar societies, it has tended to be without reference to national or 'modern' politics.[77] Before 1980 at least, elements of this occulted aspect of Liberian political culture were visible to outside observers only at particular moments or in specific contexts.

Perhaps the point at which it was most evident that, behind the apparent transparency of Liberia's official, written, legal institutions of government, there lay other systems of political symbolism, was when occasional reports surfaced of human sacrifices carried out by politicians in the pursuit of power. Although this is a subject which, in the past, has been difficult to investigate and to document, many Liberians today claim that some candidates for senior political office during the years of True Whig government would routinely seek magical aid from so-called 'heart men' or spiritual experts. Quite how frequent such consultations were is impossible to ascertain precisely, but certainly there were occasional publicly-known cases, and it seems to have been widely believed in Liberia that the search for great power, such as that wielded by a government minister or even a member of parliament, could be facilitated by the sacrifice of a human being, on the advice of a ritual expert. One way of analysing this would be to say that the metaphors of the Poro society and similar cults had been adopted even by the American–Liberian national political elite,[78] in the sense that it had become generally believed that the consumption of the vital organs of a human victim, especially the heart, could impart great power. In 1979, in a celebrated case, some prominent figures from the True Whig Party in Maryland County, Tubman's old fief, were convicted by a court of law for committing a ritual murder of this type. A beleaguered President Tolbert allowed the sentence of death to be carried out. Indeed, there are grounds to suppose that the exceptionally public nature of this case was a reflection of divisions within the True Whig Party between the conservatives and the new elements, especially 'country' people whom Tolbert was courting, which were to hasten Tolbert's downfall.[79] Ten years later, Defence Minister Gray Allison, a man raised in an American–Liberian family, was sentenced to death for a similar offence, at a time when a spate of ritual murders was reported.[80] The available evidence suggests that these cases were exceptional only in being brought to court and exposed to the scrutiny of the modern institutions of government represented by the national laws.

Doe, an uneducated man and one with a rural Liberian culture rather than the American–Liberian background of his predecessors, was well known for his unrelenting search for supernatural power. He attended both church and mosque.[81] Sawyer notes Doe's penchant for personal audiences with people claiming to have supernatural inspiration, and his imprisonment of those he believed to be false prophets.[82] In the spiritual as in the political realm, Doe had destroyed the system of his predecessor by sacking the imposing Masonic Temple which, from its hill-top site, physically dominates Monrovia, and thereafter he had to improvise a means of spiritual control. On the first anniversary of the 1980 coup, Doe erected a monument on the road outside the Executive Mansion, one of the main arteries of Monrovia, known as the Tomb of the Unknown Soldier. The monument consists of a plinth displaying an inscription commemorating the liberation of Liberia, by soldiers of the AFL, from decades of government by what is termed a 'clique', meaning the American–Liberian elite of the True Whig Party. On top of the plinth is a statue of an AFL soldier with rifle at the ready, bayonet fixed. Monrovians are convinced that Doe inaugurated the statue with a human sacrifice, burying alive an AFL trooper beneath it. True or not—and it would certainly be in keeping with what is known of Doe's methods to have taken such a precaution—many Monrovians are convinced that this was the case. When, in 1990, NPFL forces had invaded the University of Liberia, a few hundred yards from the Executive Mansion, where Doe was besieged with hundreds of his soldiers, the NPFL fighters believed that the statue which stood in the no man's land between themselves and Doe's men in the Executive Mansion constituted a powerful magical protection for Doe and that he could never be defeated while it stood. The military under Doe generally cultivated what Sawyer refers to as a 'magico-super naturalism', believing that their possession of the powerful technology of modern warfare endowed them with spiritual power.[83] So great was Doe's reputation for cultivating occult forces that his suite of rooms in the Executive Mansion remained sealed and undisturbed even after the IGNU had occupied the building in 1990.[84] The Mansion was, in a manner of speaking, haunted by the terrible spirits which Doe had invoked in the years that he lived there.

As Byron Tarr, a former government minister, has commented, Liberians have an 'eschatological belief that God or a spirit brother would solve their problems'.[85] But if virtually all Liberians have an abiding belief that the problems related to worldly power (which we might call political problems) can be understood only by reference to the world of spirits, then, according to this logic, there has been a problem for some time, and certainly since 1980, in that the spirit world is itself disordered. Tubman and Tolbert both adopted spiritual policies analogous to their political strategies, using imported, American-style institutions or systems of symbolism (Christianity, Freemasonry and the True Whig Party) as the most obvious bases of their power, but also using the conventions of indigenous symbolism such as the Poro. Since 1980 it has become increasingly difficult to play in these different registers simultaneously as the various systems of ritual mediation have fragmented. There has been a multiplication of churches, as Gifford has noted, many of them placing great emphasis on spiritual healing, in effect assimilating some of the symbolic language of older Liberian cultures. Islam has also spread since 1980, with non-Mandingo increasingly being converted.[86] The power of the Poro society has over a period of decades been eroded by the actions of national governments and the churches. These days there is a bewildering variety of individuals—prophets, priests, marabouts, preachers, healers and 'heartmen'—who claim to have expertise in the spirit world. None at present can make a convincing claim to have tamed the violence of the spirits which made itself apparent in the 1980s and, most particularly, after 1989. Doe, true to his 'marauding' nature, attempted to acquire protection from experts of all sorts without ever lending his influence to the construction of any ordered system of spiritual power. The evidence that power in Liberia has temporarily escaped all institutional control—the essential purpose of both religion and government—is there for all to see.

There can be no doubt that most Liberians have interpreted the violence which has ravaged their country since 24 December 1989 in terms of movements in the spirit world as well as in other terms.[87] This emerges from some testimonies, as well as from a reading of the symbolic actions of those involved. In some cases, the appalling atrocities committed by fighters, particularly the practice of cannibalism, contain direct references to the symbolic language of Poro or similar cultic rituals. Charles Taylor himself has been reported, probably accurately according to some who know him well, to have drunk the blood of sacrificial victims. A former associate has stated that Taylor and his closest aides form an elite society known as the Top Twenty, which practices a cult of cannibalism.[88] Naturally, first-hand evidence of such events is rather difficult to acquire, but credible documentary sources exist nonetheless. The number of those who have seen convincing evidence of acts of cannibalism and similar ritualized violence includes both Liberians and foreigners, including generals, bishops, United Nations officials, aid workers and others. There are eye-witness accounts by professional journalists and other trained observers of incidents of public cannibalism after the Quiwonkpa coup of 1985,[89] including a Nigerian journalist, for example, who saw Quiwonkpa's body being used in 'a macabre cannibalistic ritual by some of Doe's soldiers who, astonishingly in these modern times, still believe that by eating bits of a great warrior's body, some of that greatness would come to them. The heart, of course, was the prize delicacy and it is traditionally shared on a hierarchical basis'.[90]

The extreme violence of these ritualized acts is not incompatible with modernity. On the contrary, the modern technology of communication serves to strengthen and amplify the symbolic language involved. The most obvious example of this is the video made by Prince Johnson of the torture and murder of Samuel Doe in September 1990, which Johnson showed to visitors to his headquarters, no doubt calculating that it would enhance his prestige as a warrior. One ULIMO commander, Stephen Dorley, had photographs of himself taken committing atrocities including killing and mutilating prisoners. He proudly displayed these photos on the wall behind his desk to impress visitors with his power. One of the photos is of Dorley and some of his fighters standing over a corpse whose heart has been cut out.[91] Incidents of cannibalism have been documented by the respected Catholic Justice and Peace Commission.[92] The observation that there is a 'cultic' element to violence of this type does not imply that the militias fight primarily as a form of ritual behaviour. Clearly the prime motive is to gain wealth and power through violence, with the cultic aspects being a means of spreading terror and also of psychologically strengthening fighters, using a lexicon of symbols which is widely understood. Moreover it is not new for individuals who have become prominent through their pursuit of wealth and the size of their armed following to found their own cults. The historic Grand Gedeh 'big man' known as Old Man Krai appears to have done such a thing, and it is in fact from him that the name Krahn is said to be derived.[93]

Before 1980, when greater order prevailed in Liberia, cultic violence of this nature was largely contained and ritualized by the Poro, the Freemasons and similar societies, and by the mainstream churches which were dominated by the American–Liberian elite. Even before 1980 such cults were used, or perhaps abused, by politicians and others seeking power through occult, but nevertheless ordered, rituals in which the power represented by violence and the capacity to dominate are represented symbolically, including sometimes by human sacrifice. It may be argued that, since all power is indeed morally ambiguous in the sense that it can be used for good or evil purposes, secret societies like the Poro play a crucial role in expressing this fact while maintaining a monopoly of acts of lethal violence. A system of socially legitimated control of violence is, after all, essential to order. This ritual control of violence allows civic authorities to forbid and to prosecute acts of violence committed outside the bounds of ritual control or, in other words, to maintain a monopoly of violence which is one of the defining characteristics of a coherent political order. In Poro and other masking rituals, the various violent bush-spirits who symbolically eat their victims are represented by society officials wearing masks. To be more precise, it is not the wearer of the mask who represents the spirit. Rather, the spirit lies in the mask itself, which then possesses its wearer as part of a ritual which imparts order to human society and provides civic authorities, such as chiefs, with their legitimacy. We may note that, although Christian churches are of course opposed to human sacrifice, this did not prevent prominent Christian laymen in the past from performing such gruesome rituals, including Presidents Tubman and Tolbert, who are both said to have performed ritual murders but were both prominent lay churchmen: Tolbert was president of the Baptist World Alliance.[94] The symbolic language of the masking societies is easily assimilated into Christian belief as a manifestation of the absolute struggle between the Holy Spirit and the forces of Satan. The Roman Catholic cathedral in Monrovia is dedicated to the Sacred Heart and is dominated by a vast mural showing the Sacred Heart of Jesus emanating rays of light. While the spiritual churches have assimilated much of the vocabulary of pre-Christian cults, they have used it in the service of a theology of moral absolutes.[95]

In the civil war, in a world grown anarchic, acts of violence are daily performed in the familiar language of the secret society rituals, but now out of control. Ritual murders are no longer carried out by officers of established cults, but by unqualified adolescents. Whereas cultic violence is properly performed by society elders wearing masks, in Liberia today young fighters improvise masks with any objects they have to hand: dark glasses, women's wigs, shower caps, and so on, which they use to alter their spiritual character. Having committed atrocious acts of violence they routinely—and quite literally rather than metaphorically—eat their victims' vital organs and drink their blood and emerge reborn as warriors, using war-names in place of their given names. Just as an official of the Poro is possessed by a spirit when he puts on the appropriate mask, effectively becoming that spirit for the duration of the ceremony and therefore absolved of personal guilt,[96] so is a fighter possessed by spirits as he commits his acts of violence. The effect is no doubt enhanced by the consumption of alcohol, marijuana, amphetamines and other drugs which is commonplace among fighters.

The dangerous spirits which are believed to infest the world, and which in normal times are under the ritual control of qualified people, such as the elders of the Poro, are stalking Liberia and may enter anyone at any time, even children. All that is required is to have a gun.

Re-establishing order

By the middle of 1994 it seemed that there would never be an end to Liberia's agony. The peace process represented by the Cotonou Peace Accord had run out of steam, leaving no prospect of any political solution to the country's anarchy. Moreover the multiplication and ethnicization of the various militias seemed to preclude the possibility of any military solution. ULIMO was split clearly into two factions, one Krahn-led, the other Mandingo-led. The AFL was increasingly divided into Krahn and non-Krahn, as was its surrogate the LPC, and the NPFL was also split along ethnic lines, with Taylor mistrusting anyone outside his inner circle of American–Liberians. There were reports, difficult to verify from Monrovia, of the creation of new ethnic militias such as the Bassa Defence Force, the Citizens' Defence Force, and others.

Some well-qualified observers, including Liberians whose family origins are in Lofa County, agree that the Lofa Defence Force, a militia which arose in late 1993 after the Cotonou Peace Accord, is organized by the Poro society, which is particularly strong in Lofa. In November 1993, the LDF occupied the town of Zorzor, a centre of the Poro society. Observers were divided in their opinion as to the degree to which the LDF was merely a surrogate for the NPFL. In Lofa County, many peoples' view of NPFL administration appears to be less negative than their opinion of ULIMO. There are no particular antagonisms between the NPFL's Gio and Mano fighters and the peoples of Lofa County, with the important exception of the Mandingo who were quite numerous in Lofa County before the War. When the Mandingo-dominated faction of ULIMO under Alhaji Kromah began to raid NPFL territory in Lofa County in 1991, in revenge for NPFL attacks in Liberia and Sierra Leone, the raiders committed appalling atrocities and also desecrated Poro sites and cult objects, in effect declaring war in a spiritual as well as a military sense. In response, the Poro society was able to organize its own militia, its grassroots structure providing a perfect infrastructure for military activity, as it had in the Mande rising against British colonial rule in Sierra Leone in 1898.[97] Fired by revenge, there seems little doubt that the LDF is preparing to rid Lofa County of Mandingo and to desecrate the latter's mosques, in revenge for the humiliations inflicted by ULIMO:Kromah, in a bout of ethnic cleansing.

The emergence of the LDF, although difficult to document or identify precisely, may mark a significant development in Liberia's recent history. Unlike the other militias, it is not organized in the service of members of Liberia's national political class in search of a clientele, but by village elders owing their allegiance to a structure deeply-rooted in rural life. Its aim is not to obtain for its leaders a seat in a national government, and thus a chance to take a share of the 'national cake', but rather to rid its territory of outsiders and raiders of every sort. If it should succeed in this aim and spread to areas outside Lofa County, it holds the distant promise of bringing back stability to some rural communities at least. If so, it provides a hope, however slight, of ending the vicious circle of impoverishment and violence. Many observers believe that the majority of Liberia's 60,000 or so fighters are demoralized by the violence they have lived through and inflicted but lack opportunities to demobilize, having no means of livelihood other than looting and being afraid to go back to what remains of their families, or having no social context to which to return. A system of local self-defence might help in that regard.

The Poro society is essentially a system of socio-political control based on communication with the invisible world. We may differ with Gifford in suggesting that mediation with the invisible, rather than being a desperate irrelevance, is the precise opposite: it appears to offer the only realistic solution to Liberia's crisis. The country's spiritual anarchy underpins its other forms of anarchy, political and social, and in practice it may require to be reordered first.

As Ken Wilson has noted in a study of comparable violence in Mozambique,

> It is highly significant that cults of violence and their associated magic can be countered not only by other cults of violence. Where military

and political power is not promulgated on the basis of *de facto* strength, but through hegemony rooted in ritually established inequality and intimidation, a movement that can reject such authority can be extremely powerful.[98]

A movement which is able to convince large numbers of Liberian civilians that it is possessed of spiritual power not only has a chance of encouraging the victims of militia violence to resist, but could also provoke large-scale desertions, given the widespread view that many of the fighters are disillusioned with their existence. As other writers have noted, religion is after all a ground for political discourse in the sense that it constitutes clusters of symbols which enable people to form 'a generalizing and productive political language'.[99] Thus the construction of a coherent system of spiritual communication may accompany the building of a coherent political order. In these circumstances representations of power expressed in a spiritual register may be seen not as a-political, but as the necessary accompaniment to a political project.[100]

What a new political order will look like remains to be seen, of course. Despite all that has happened, the Liberian state has not disappeared. It is striking that, despite the years of civil war and ethnic division, none of the warlords proposes secession or the construction of a separate state. There remains a sense of Liberian identity expressed in language ('Liberian English') and in culture, although it is likely that the Mandingo, for example, precisely because of the degree to which their culture and their religious identity has been used for political purposes by first Doe and then Kromah, risk being excluded from that definition in future. But so profound is Liberia's crisis that it seems unlikely Liberia will ever be restored in its pre-1980 form and, given the structural flaws of that system, in particular its personalization and centralization of power, nor would that be a recipe for success.

Probably the one external power which has the means and, potentially at least, the motive to stabilize Liberia—the USA—has no Liberia policy at all. It seems unlikely, given the isolationism of US public life and the general marginalization of Africa in US foreign policy, that the US government will develop a coherent and effective Liberia policy in the foreseeable future. The solution to Liberia's problems, in these circumstances, can only come from within. The national political structure which reached its apogee under the True Whig Party has collapsed. The ethnic politics introduced by Doe has led to disaster.

Healing, in these circumstances, lies in the spiritual field at least as much as in the political one, and at the local level rather than the national one. The spirit world is the only domain in which constructive action is still detectable, and in this a leading role may fall to the churches. Unlike the Poro society or other traditional cults, they are universal in orientation, having the potential to incorporate all Liberians. In their own symbolic language, the Holy Spirit is pacific and universal in nature and can enter anybody. The Christian God can forgive any crime, no matter how terrible.[101] In the case of the international and former missionary churches, they also have the connections and even the material resources to help in this process. Their greatest disability is the unwillingness to come to grips with the anarchic spiritual world of Liberia which may well necessitate assuming more of the symbolic language of Liberian spirituality than is the case at present.

SECTION THREE

RELIGION

RELIGION AND POLITICS*

TAKING AFRICAN EPISTEMOLOGIES SERIOUSLY

Religious modes of thinking about the world are widespread in Africa, and have a pervasive influence on politics in the broadest sense. We have published elsewhere a theoretical model as to how the relationship between politics and religion may be understood, with potential benefits for observers not just of Africa, but also of other parts of the world where new combinations of religion and politics are emerging. Application of this theoretical model requires researchers to rethink some familiar categories of social science.

Introduction

Nine years ago, this journal published an article (Ellis & ter Haar 1998) in which we argued that politics in Africa cannot be fully understood without reference to religious ideas that are widely shared in societies south of the Sahara. Subsequently, we developed this hypothesis into a book, *Worlds of Power* (Ellis & ter Haar 2004), that presents a theoretical model for analysing the relationship between religion and politics in sub-Saharan Africa, showing at length how this can aid understanding of a wide range of social and political phenomena. We embarked

---

* Co-authored by Gerrie ter Haar.

on this exercise simply because we found the existing models for understanding the relationship between religion and politics to be unsatisfactory. All the models in common academic use are based on the assumption of a structural distinction between the visible or material world and the invisible world, whereas such a rigid distinction does not reflect ideas about the nature of reality that are prevalent in Africa. The development of a new theoretical model intended to explain the relationship between religion and politics in Africa reflects more than a striving for scholarly precision. It promises to be of much wider usefulness at a time when religious movements are occupying public space in so many ways and in so many places: neo-pentecostal, charismatic and Islamist movements, but also neo-traditional movements like Kenya's *mungiki* (Wamue 2001), or difficult-to-categorise phenomena such as the Lord's Resistance Army in Uganda (Van Acker 2004).

The purpose of the present article is to revisit our theory regarding religion and politics, nine years after its first formulation, in the light of various reviews and critiques that it has encountered. Our theory proceeds from the proposition that the religious ideas held by so many Africans—hundreds of millions of people—need to be taken seriously, and should be considered in their own terms in the first instance (Ellis & ter Haar 2004: esp. 16–21). Yet it is striking how many reviewers and other readers choose to describe such ideas as manifestations of 'superstition' or 'the occult'. This is significant because, as Harold Turner (1976: 13) noted in regard to African-initiated churches, ' our approach to any range of phenomena is both revealed and influenced by the names we bestow upon it'. In fact, this observation may aptly be applied to religious phenomena in general. In Africa, the latter are grounded in distinctive modes of acquiring knowledge about the world, characterised by a holistic approach in which the sacred and the secular can be said to constitute one organic reality (Ilesanmi 1995: 54). Philosophers routinely make distinctions between different kinds of knowledge. African modes of thought, we suggest, are neither more nor less than epistemologies that include ways of acquiring knowledge not normally considered within the scope of social science. We suggest that such epistemologies have validity, meaning that not only do all people have a right to think about the world in whatever way they choose, but that modes of perception unfamiliar to Western observers may—in theory, at least—be of universal application.

If this is so, it means that African ideas about religion and its relation to politics are important not only for understanding Africa, but may have the potential to inform our understanding of religion and politics more generally, in a world that is presently characterised by new alignments of these two fundamental elements. This is a capital point, which distinguishes our approach to the study of religion and politics from the many studies that, however excellent they may be, are based on the supposition of a separation of the religious and secular realms. Such studies almost invariably translate religious data (assumed to be a second order of truth at best) into sociological terms (assumed to correspond to reality). We argue for a different point of departure. In order to understand the relation between religion and politics in Africa, we suggest, it is more fruitful to take Africans' own views of reality as a starting point. Generally speaking, these include both material and immaterial realms.

A new theory of religion and politics

All the evidence points to the fact that most Africans—like most people on the planet, for that matter—understand and interpret the world partly through the prism of religion. In other words, religion, whatever else it may be, is a mode of apprehending reality. Much, of course, depends on what is meant by 'religion'. There is a wide variety of definitions in existence. For present purposes, we have argued, the best way to proceed is not to assume that religion has the same meaning in all times and places, nor to use whatever definition the writer personally finds most pleasing. A better approach, we suggest, is to study the range of social phenomena observable in Africa, and only then to formulate a definition of religion that incorporates features relevant to its specific context. This then constitutes a working definition—not an attempt to classify religion in general, but a tool adapted for the purpose at hand (Ellis & ter Haar 2004: 13–16). A working definition has the advantage of being provisional in nature, meaning that it can be adapted in future as new data become available (Platvoet & Molendijk 1999). Such a definition will then proceed from local epistemologies. Among the most salient features of African epistemologies, we have argued on the basis of empirical research, is a conviction that the material and immaterial aspects of life cannot be separated, although they can be distinguished from each other, much as the two sides of a coin can be discerned but not parted. To judge from the available evidence, religion in sub-Saharan Africa is best considered as a belief in the existence of an invisible world, distinct but not separate from the visible one, that is home to spiritual beings with effective powers over the material world. This is the definition that we used in *Worlds of Power*.

Another distinctive feature of religion in sub-Saharan Africa is its use of what may be termed a 'spirit idiom'. This refers to the widespread belief that the immaterial forces perceived to be operating in the material world consist of, or are controlled by, individual spirits. These spirits are often imagined as having a name and a personality, and to have their abode in an invisible world. This spirit world is perceived to contain power, and for those who believe in it, this power is real. Belief in the existence of immaterial forces is common pretty much everywhere in the world, although these forces are often imagined in secular terms, for example as social or economic ones. No serious social scientist thinks that because something cannot be seen, it therefore does not exist. Furthermore, as we have argued, a social scientist or other analyst does not have to be a religious believer in order to study or understand religion. Our own analysis is not written from the point of view of a religious believer. However, for many observers, taking African religious ideas seriously requires thinking about religion in terms different from those with which they are most familiar.

The historical record suggests that what we term 'religion' has always existed in every part of Africa, and that it has been changing continuously. We do not believe that there exists an authentic Africa that stands outside time and that incorporates a primal view of the cosmos. Simply, Africa, like other parts of the world, has a history. It is possible to reconstruct, at least partially, what people in Africa have thought about the world in the past and how their ideas have changed over time (cf. Collingwood 1993: 228). Any analysis that places distinct phenomena in historical context implies a greater or lesser degree of continuity. In the present case, the historically grounded theory that we propose tends to emphasise continuities rather than ruptures. Hence, we see current charismatic and neo-pentecostal or 'born-again' Christianity, for example, as a recent development in a long-existing mode of thinking about the spirit world rather than as a major historical rupture. This is in spite of the fact that 'born-agains' often make extravagant rhetorical claims to have made a complete break with the past (Peel 2006). In other words, the claim of a born-again Christian to have broken with the past is to be understood as an emic statement, as distinct from the etic position adopted by an academic analyst. Thus, the neo-pentecostal movement in Africa reflects the times we live in, on the one hand, but, on the other hand, it can also be situated in historical context. Religion is a symbolic language, whose evolution may be compared to that of other languages. Like them, it reflects and communicates people's ideas about the world they live in. All languages change over time. Individual items of vocabulary disappear and new ones appear, invented on the spot or borrowed from abroad. Languages, however, also have a grammar, a structure that changes only slowly. Religion, too, has a vocabulary and a grammar, both of which change over time and at different speeds.

Taking religious ideas seriously—the heart of our endeavour—challenges the academic disciplines in which the study of contemporary Africa is most often conceived. The basic reason for this is that social science has been developed over generations on the assumption of a separation between the secular and the religious realms. Other writers (e.g. Lal 1998) have pointed out that this separation reflects the historical experience of Europe, but not necessarily that of the rest of the world. The proper reaction to this awareness is not to reject social science as irredeemably Eurocentric, but to adapt its techniques in such a way as to encompass worldviews that are a product of histories different from those of European countries (Chakrabarty 2000).

With regard to Africa, taking religious ideas seriously seems particularly to challenge the disciplines of anthropology, development economics and political science. If we deal with the latter first, we may observe that political science has no difficulty in accepting our proposal to understand politics as a field of activity that is not associated only with state power, but that can be found in a wide variety of social settings, in the form of politics 'from below'. If this is a rather uncontroversial observation, it is no doubt because it is a theme that has been quite widely studied in the literature on politics in Africa for over 20 years (Bayart *et al.* 1992). Far more striking is the problem caused to political scientists by the subject of religion, which, at least until the post-9/11 period, they often omitted from their scope entirely. When political scientists have focussed on religion, with some notable exceptions, it has tended to be on its institutional aspects rather than the ideas and social practices that permeate the institutions (e.g. Haynes 1996). This is rather odd, since there is overwhelming evidence that institutions borrowed from elsewhere or imposed on a particular society by outsiders rapidly gain a distinctive flavour through assimilation into local repertoires of ideas, to the extent that states are individually formed through a multiplicity of procedures (Bayart 1991). Development economists, too, largely ignore religion, although there are signs that a number of research-funding institutions are beginning to reflect on the importance of religion in African societies, and this may lead to new angles of vision in due course (ter Haar & Ellis 2006). Anthropology, on the other hand, has a long record of considering African religions, but has tended to do so as cultural artefacts rather than as 'real' religions. Furthermore, anthropology has often considered African societies in an ethnographic present rather than in historical terms. Although many anthropologists nowadays would claim that these problems have been rectified, and that they do now place the phenomena they analyse in historical context, such an assertion remains open to question. It has become quite fashionable for anthropologists to take as objects of study topics related to religion. Prominent examples include the study of pentecostal movements and of witchcraft. Both of these are expressions of religious thought and practice. Pentecostalism is universally acknowledged as a particular form of religion, but is often treated by anthropologists with only scant regard for its global history and theological content. Witchcraft is usually studied without reference to religion at all—although, being concerned with a belief in mystical forces, witchcraft falls within the scope of religion (ter Haar 2007) according to the definition we use. Some influential anthropological studies emphasise the role of these phenomena as modes of negotiating modernity (e.g. Comaroff & Comaroff 1993; Geschiere 1997; Meyer 1999), despite the fact that modernity is not a concept of great analytical value (Ashforth 2005: 116–21). Moreover, analysing religious phenomena in terms of negotiating modernity overlooks the fact that, in Africa, religion has historically been a language for interpreting the world.

Any project of taking African epistemologies seriously, and attempting to incorporate them into a formal theory with the power to explain a range of social and political phenomena, is not an enterprise that concerns Africa alone. It is for this reason that our book *Worlds of Power* (2004) is interspersed with comparative material from other parts of the world. Given the extent and depth of new alignments or realignments of religion and politics throughout the world, it is possible that a theory developed on the basis of data from Africa could also provide new insights for analysing developments in other parts of the world, including notably Asia and the Middle East. Scholars therefore have a rare opportunity to show that Africa is not disconnected from world affairs and that the study of Africa can help in developing a better understanding of these. Religion and politics are undoubtedly forming new patterns in many parts of the world. This does not mean, however, that a religious revival is taking place worldwide, as is often suggested. The new patterns of religion and politics discernible in Africa and other places are of course affected by phenomena such as state failure, globalisation and economic crises, as many commentators have pointed out, but that is not the heart of the matter. The heart of the matter, rather, is that many people in the world, just as in sub-Saharan Africa, consider power as having its ultimate origin in the invisible world. This, we argue, has a marked influence on the conduct of politics and on political attributes such as authority and legitimacy.

Religion remains a prism through which many people view the world. *Worlds of Power* investigates this proposition in detail in regard to sub-Saharan Africa. We show that, for those who believe in it, spiritual power constitutes real and effective power. Thus, religion and politics become two facets of power that are in constant interaction. This is not always evident to observers of African politics, as African countries since colonial times have been officially governed through institutions based on a Western model of separation of church and state. This institutional architecture of government has tended to obscure the reality of spiritual power in Africa's public life. Like politicians the world over, Africa's political leaders spend most of their time in the pursuit or distribution of material resources, and their cultivation of spiritual power is usually more private than public. But, in any event, cultivating spiritual power is a vital component of a political career, as is widely attested by the popular media and *radio trottoir*.

This is why no study of African politics can afford to ignore the religious factor. A prime advantage of adopting our suggested definition of religion is that it enables us to consider religion and politics within a single field of power.

Some issues of method

Writing about religion and politics in the way we suggest has certain methodological implications. Among other things, it entails writing about religion in Africa in a manner that is objective, in the sense of not containing hidden assumptions about its ontological and moral status.

The latter requires particular attention to terminology. We have already noted (see above) that many reviewers of *Worlds of Power* assign to such categories as 'superstition' and 'magic' a range of phenomena that we prefer to classify as 'religious'. Reference to 'superstition' and 'magic' amounts to making unscholarly judgements as to what constitutes proper or 'real' religion, as opposed to improper types of religion. In similar vein, many anthropologists writing on Africa today use 'the occult' as a category to include various phenomena that we describe as 'mystical'. The word 'occult', although having a primary meaning of 'hidden', has a pejorative implication when applied to religious matters. All these labels carry a heavy ideological burden that should be set in historical context: for centuries, outsiders have tended to judge religious ideas and practices in Africa as both wrong and morally inferior. The use of such labels as 'magic', 'superstition' and 'the occult' implies that certain phenomena which in other parts of the world would be classified as religion, are better described by different terms in the case of Africa. This amounts to a form of exceptionalism, suggesting that a special vocabulary is needed for analysing Africa by reason of its supposed uniqueness. It is ironic that the charge of exceptionalism is sometimes made against our approach by anthropologists, who, we maintain, continue to struggle with the implications of the ethnographic method that has been so foundational in their discipline (e.g. Green 2006).

To be sure, it is inevitable that social scientists will attribute data to categories of their own choosing as part of a process of analysis. However, the choice of categories is neither arbitrary nor innocent. In matters of religion, we maintain that scholarly analysis is best done in two stages, known as emic and etic modes of interpretation. This means that the starting point for analysis is to consider religion in a subject's own terms of expression, before analysing it in terms of social science at a later stage. Following a two-stage process of interpretation of religious data implies a translation of the symbolic language of religion into the secular language of social science. In the case of Africa, this process may well involve the literal translation of key concepts from an African to a European tongue. In the end, therefore, analysts can never escape the demands imposed by the language in which they write. Whatever terms they use will always carry some historical and ideological charge, even such apparently universal terms as 'religion' and 'politics' (Meyer 2004: 466). The knowledge that this is so does not, however, absolve analysts from their obligation to take due precautions in making cultural translations of all types (Crick 1976: 109–27), defining, wherever necessary, any category that is being used for analytical purposes (Platvoet & Molendijk 1999).

African epistemologies often pose a particular challenge to academic categorisation due to their tendency to work on the basis of addition or incorporation rather than replacement. In other words, people show a marked preference for adopting innovations by assimilating new elements into existing repertoires, without necessarily making a choice between ideas or practices considered in Western epistemologies to be mutually contradictory. The tendency in African religious traditions to innovate through incorporation rather than exclusive selection does not in itself pose a conceptual problem, but it does require attention from social scientists used to categorising by reference to distinct typologies. It is relevant to note that the social science literature on Africa has often been marked by an insistence on filtering data by reference to dualistic categories of analysis or binary oppositions, including notably tradition/modernity and African/non-African, whereas, in African epistemologies, ideas or institutions can belong to several of these categories simultaneously.

A final comment on method is to ascertain whether sub-Saharan Africa constitutes a viable category for analysis of the matter at hand. Opinion seems divided on this issue, with some reviewers of *Worlds of Power* objecting to the inclusion of material from outside Africa on grounds of relevance, or arguing that Africa is in any case too diverse to fit a single model of analysis. Others, meanwhile, warm to our suggestion that no aspect of African religion is so unusual that it cannot be understood by reference to universal categories suitably defined, and that a model of religious-political interaction developed on the basis of African data can perhaps be usefully applied to other parts of the world. It is not unusual to take one sub-continent, one continent, or even the entire world as a unit of analysis, depending on the matter under consideration. Few people seem to object to the idea of analysing economics or development in pan-African terms (as implied, for example, by the existence of NEPAD, the New Programme for Africa's Development). The question is whether the great variety of religious practices and ideas to be found in sub-Saharan Africa has enough in common as to support this level of generalisation.

In our view, sub-Saharan Africa has at least four common elements that make it a viable analytical unit for our purpose. These are, first, that religious cultures throughout the region show a marked tendency to posit the existence of a spirit world. Second, all of sub-Saharan Africa has a robust oral culture, notwithstanding the use of writing for religious purposes, in some places for many centuries. Third, African religious cultures have a strong idea of evil as a transcendental force. Fourth, all sub-Saharan countries have undergone a similar experience of colonialism in some shape or form, even Ethiopia and Liberia. All four factors have been significant in shaping people's religious ideas. It should go without saying that within an area of some 600 million people, there will always be a great variety of opinions—including, in this case, the existence of professed atheists—and that any given religious idea is always liable to be associated with different material outcomes, depending on various factors. Taking an entire sub-continent as a unit of analysis is therefore not unusual, nor does it amount to 'cultural essentialism' (Green 2006), in other words identifying a cultural element that has remained unchanged over time. On the contrary, the identification of common elements over a variety of societies permits comparison, while insistence on the historical processes that have affected Africa indicates that religious change has always taken place there.

In summary, then, we maintain that religion in Africa is grounded in modes of acquiring knowledge that both reflect and shape the ways in which people have viewed the world, past and present. If only for this reason, religion has an important bearing on politics, and indeed politics in Africa cannot be fully understood without taking its religious dimension into account. Although African epistemologies involve concepts that may be unfamiliar to many Europeans and North Americans, there is nothing in them that cannot be analysed by the conventional methods of social science, provided both the scope of investigation and the terms of analysis are considered with sufficient rigour.

Religion and development

Up to this point, we have considered the relation between religion and politics in Africa as a purely theoretical matter, striving to avoid terms that imply either approval or disapproval of the data at hand. The question arises, however, how a theory of religion and politics might be applied to specific situations.

Some observers seek to go beyond a consideration of the theoretical relationship between religion and politics and its close relative, economics. Interested in practical solutions to real problems, they want to know whether particular religious trends help or hinder development. For example, it is sometimes argued that the emphasis on deliverance found in neo-pentecostalism diminishes individuals' sense of personal responsibility for their own financial circumstances, as does the rhetoric of miracles. The religious views of charismatics—the argument goes—do nothing to encourage productivity or a work ethos. The spiritualisation of politics can thus play into the hands of the worst dictators, who are able to use religion as a channel of political support (e.g. Gifford 1993, 2004). 'In what way have religious revivals affected resources or made life more successful, and how could one show that?', Gifford (2005: 247) asks in a review of *Worlds of Power*. 'Are modifications of religious ideas in fact leading to Africa's economic and political progress?'

These questions cannot be answered satisfactorily without prior consideration of what the people concerned—in this case, Africans—understand to constitute 'progress' and 'development' (ter Haar 2006). It is a mistake to assume, as some authors do, that an improvement of material and institutional conditions would necessarily reduce 'the hegemonies of the spirit' (Green 2006) that are apparent in Africa, and would instead stimulate the language of liberal secularism. Nor can the symbolic language of religion be reduced to a cultural tradition reflecting the continuation of certain ancestral practices. Rather, a religious mode of apprehending reality (even one couched in a spirit idiom) constitutes an epistemology that is simultaneously traditional and modern, capable of updating and renewing itself as times change.

African epistemologies, then, include religious perspectives affecting popular understandings of concepts such as progress and development, but also justice, prosperity and others (ter Haar & Ellis 2006). Consequently, Africa's economic and political progress should not be considered exclusively in terms of technical criteria such as macroeconomic indicators, nor should all the standard formulae of development be taken at face value. Nor should the ways in which Africans debate these matters be assumed to be apolitical because they are expressed in spiritual idioms. One example is 'good governance', an expression widely used in development circles, but which serves poorly as an analytical concept due to its implicit value-judgement. The word 'good' in this expression invites judgement in regard to technical excellence, but it also conveys a moral concept. For many Muslims, for example, good governance implies a society that is ultimately ruled in conformity with divine law. Among both Muslims and non-Muslims in Africa, the moral nature of power depends on the manner of its exercise, as we have suggested in *Worlds of Power* (Ellis & ter Haar 2004: ch. 7). Charismatic preachers preoccupied with Satan are not necessarily externalising responsibility for the misfortunes of the society they live in, but may rather be considered as condemning the actual presence of evil within their society. Such criticisms are typically expressed in a spirit idiom and are often extended to national politics, as we have demonstrated at length in *Worlds of Power*. The Nigerian scholar Ogbu Kalu (2006) has pointed out how Western opinions on these matters contrast with the analyses of African scholars. These include Matthews Ojo (2006), Kwabena Asamoah-Gyadu (2005) and Asonzeh Ukah (forthcoming). This underlines the importance of taking into account studies by scholars living and working in Africa.

Development, from a religious perspective, is more than a set of technical benchmarks. For many religious believers, the road to development is at least as important as the final destination. For them, development is an integral process that implicates the full range of human existence, including its perceived spiritual dimension. In such a view, lasting and effective social change is dependent on the inner change or transformation of individuals. This is clearly an opinion shared by charismatic Christians and by Islamists, for example, both of them representing important and popular movements worldwide, and not just in Africa. As one observer has noted, many of the major flaws in the development process arise from a failure to consider the metaphysical questions concerning human life (Tyndale 2001: 3). In investigating the connection between religion and development, therefore, the first requirement should be to understand what religious believers are saying and thinking about the nature of society and its defects, and what ideas they have about its possible improvement. Academic researchers should scrutinise these issues within the context of religious actors' worldviews. Only then is it helpful to investigate the matter from a social science perspective, and to investigate, for example, whether a given religious group has issued a statement on development or human rights or any associated matter, or has taken money from a corrupt head of state.

Within the development business, there are signs of a growing acceptance of the possibility of different paths to political and economic development. It has been noted that the success of many East Asian countries was achieved largely by ignoring the advice of the international financial institutions on specific economic policies (Stiglitz 2002: 91). More importantly, it was also achieved by some creative marriages between the technical requirements for development and local political resources that invariably express themselves in cultural form

(Bayart 1994). The realisation that development has an inescapable cultural dimension has, over time, helped to mellow some of the rigid and even dogmatic theories of modernisation that were current in the middle of the last century. This is not to suggest the existence of fixed, development-friendly or development-unfriendly cultures, but only to underline that political choices affecting development contain a cultural dimension.

In recent years the relationship between the macro-economic aspects of development and the social processes involved has been articulated through the concept of human development, now widely used by both policy-makers and theorists. According to the United Nations Development Programme (2006), human development, 'is about creating an environment in which people can develop their full potential and lead productive, creative lives in accord with their needs and interests'. It thus refers to people's resources beyond any purely material aspect. Many policy-makers today accept that sustainable development can be achieved only if people build on their own resources, including the quality of relationships in society, often construed as 'social capital'. In Africa, we have noted, communication with a perceived spirit world is common religious practice. In other words, social relationships extend into the invisible world and the latter hence becomes part of people's 'social capital'. For those who believe in its existence, the invisible world is another human resource. For analytical purposes, religious resources may be divided into four major categories. Religious ideas (what people believe) are one such category. Others are religious practices (what people actually do on the basis of such belief), religious organisation (how religious communities are formed and function), and religious—or spiritual—experiences (such as the subjective experience of inner change or transformation) (ter Haar 2005: 22–7). All of these elements produce knowledge that, in principle, could be made beneficial to the well-being or the development of a given community.

No person or institution has thus far been able to identify mechanisms for eliminating corruption or injustice, or for improving the quality of governance in Africa, so effective that they cannot be subverted. Effective action to improve the quality of governance, and thus of economic performance, can come only from a variety of factors that include a widespread moral commitment to this goal. The latter can take a religious or a non-religious form: the overwhelming preference of Africans seems to be to express these matters in a religious idiom. In any event, improvements of this nature do not come from legislation alone, but from a changed moral climate (Wraith & Simpkins 1963). This is a point where religion and development may meet.

Spiritual knowledge and history

Conclusions as to how religion may either help or hinder development can be situated on a continuum. At one extreme is the proposition that Africa has to adopt specified institutional forms if it is to achieve the 'good governance' considered necessary for development. This is a point of view favoured by aid donors and by the international financial institutions, which generally base their ideas about the types of institutions suitable for their purpose on models drawn from an idealised reading of European and North American history. At the other end of the spectrum is an opinion that indigenous institutions and epistemologies can potentially adapt themselves to a wide variety of purposes, and that development is indeed most likely where the fundamental technical skills or qualities required have been incorporated into local social patterns. However, whether indigenous or of foreign origin, all institutions depend crucially on the mental dispositions of those who staff them (Douglas 1986).

It is useful in this regard to consider the widespread sense of powerlessness that is often said to pervade African populations. Several sources—from Achille Mbembe (2000: 25–6) to the US National Intelligence Council (2005)—have noted the importance in Africa of the belief that the continent is threatened by vast forces that amount to something resembling a cosmic conspiracy. It is undeniable that Africa is indeed threatened by some massively destructive forces that can be quite precisely identified, including disease, debt and underinvestment. At the same time, however, many Africans also consider these conditions in a spirit idiom, seeing themselves as beset by evil forces that have a known material cause but that also have a spiritual dimension (Ellis & ter Haar 2004: ch. 3). The roots of this conviction that economic and political power has a dangerous spiritual aspect, which Africans can no longer control, can be located in the continent's history. Ultimately, this perceived lack of control dates from the colonisation and evangelisation of the nineteenth and twentieth centuries, that regarded indigenous spiritual forces as harmful, backward or demonic. A combination of ignorance and prejudice caused European colonisers and missionaries to despise many indigenous concepts of the spirit world (Ilesanmi 1995: esp. 54). It is rather disturbing to note that many secular analysts today appear to react in a comparable way, displaying bias or intolerance regarding manifestations of an interaction between sacred and secular aspects of reality as it is perceived by many Africans.

One consequence of this history is that many traditional spiritual experts have lost prestige and are often regarded as unable to deal with the evil forces threatening the African continent today. While vast numbers of people continue to consult local healers, the feeling is widespread that they cannot provide effective remedies for the key problems of modern times (ter Haar 1992: ch. 4; Ashforth 2005: esp. 295–300). The quest for effective healing is evidenced by the enormous variety of priests, clerics, prophets, diviners or self-proclaimed experts that exists, contributing to what we term a 'spiritual confusion'. By this, we mean a situation in which spiritual forces are considered powerful, but where there is little consensus on what precisely these forces are, and how they may be channelled or controlled. This is one main reason why religious or spiritual healing continues to have such importance in Africa.

As an illustration of what spiritual confusion can lead to, we may take the Rwandan genocide of 1994. Some reviewers of *Worlds of Power* wondered how a theoretical model of a political world that is deemed inseparable from the religious realm might help explain arguably the greatest tragedy of the late twentieth century. The extensive research carried out on the Rwandan genocide (Des Forges 1999) has revealed the extent to which it was planned and implemented with a high degree of bureaucratic efficiency by a political and administrative elite associated with President Juvenal Habyarimana and his wife Agathe. However, research making use of Kinyarwanda-language sources and popular iconography indicates the overwhelming importance in the genocide of ideas about the nature and proper use of power that are derived from the sacred kingship of pre-colonial times (Taylor 2004). In the circumstances of the early 1990s, many Rwandans were inclined to believe that their country was not able to enjoy the prosperity and fertility that, according to local religious and political ideas, emanated from the mystical force of *imaana,* traditionally channelled through the government. The work of the *génocidaires* associated with the army and the ruling party consisted in persuading many Rwandans to accept that the blockage of the necessary flows of virtue and fertility, simultaneously political and spiritual, was the fault of political opponents of the government. The interest of this point is not that it suggests an alternative explanation for the 1994 genocide. Rather, its importance is that it adds an extra dimension to explanations that are normally couched in uniquely secular–political terms. Ordinary Rwandans were moved to acts of genocide, spurred on by propaganda and fear, because they believed their society to be threatened not only by political and military upheaval, but by malevolent spiritual forces also. Only by taking this spiritual dimension into account does it become easier to understand the awfulness of genocide: why otherwise 'good' people are moved to do unspeakably evil things (Juergensmeyer 2003).

* * *

We hope to have demonstrated in this article that the theoretical model concerning the interaction of religion and politics that we have set out in our in book *Worlds of Power* has the power to explain a wide variety of political phenomena, not only in the conventional sphere of state politics, but in African societies at large. The main obstacle to the use of this model as a tool for analysing African politics in the broadest sense appears to be the novelty of some of its analytical categories, which are drawn from African epistemologies rather than from mainstream social science. In our view, this presents no insoluble problems to social scientists—it only requires them to adopt some new angles of analysis and reflection. Moreover, we maintain that such a theory of religion and politics may well be useful for analysing societies in other parts of the world in which these two forms of power are recomposing in ways that do not accord directly with the classical models of social science. There is an urgent need for analysts to consider how spiritual power works as a political force in contemporary societies.

Religion is the emerging political language of our time. Already, in our original article (Ellis & ter Haar 1998: 201), we noted that African politicians were challenged to use this language in a manner comprehensible to outsiders. We also noted that non-Africans needed to learn this language. This remains truer than ever: as with any language, learning to understand a spirit idiom takes time and application, but it can be done.

References

Asamoah-Gyadu, J. Kwabena. 2005. *African Charismatics: current developments within independent indigenous pentecostalism in Ghana.* Leiden & Boston, MA: Brill.

Ashforth, A. 2005. *Witchcraft, Violence, and Democracy in South Africa.* Chicago, IL & London: Chicago University Press.

Bayart, J.F. 1991. 'Finishing with the idea of the third world: the concept of the political trajectory', in J. Manor, ed. *Rethinking Third World Politics.* London: Longman, 51–71.

Bayart, J.F., ed. 1994. *La Réinvention du Capitalisme.* Paris: Karthala.

Bayart, J.F., A. Mbembe & C. Toulabor. 1992. *Le Politique par le Bas en Afrique Noire: contributions à une problématique de la démocratie.* Paris: Karthala.

Chakrabarty, D. 2000. *Provincializing Europe: postcolonial thought and historical difference.* Princeton, NJ: Princeton University Press.

Collingwood, R.G. 1993 [1946]. *The Idea of History.* Oxford: Clarendon Press.

Comaroff, J. & J. Comaroff, eds. 1993. *Modernity and its Malcontents: ritual and power in postcolonial Africa.* Chicago, IL: Chicago University Press.

Crick, M. 1976. *Explorations in Language and Meaning: towards a semantic anthropology.* London: Malaby Press.

Des Forges, A. 1999. *'Leave None to Tell the Story': genocide in Rwanda.* New York: Human Rights Watch.

Douglas, M. 1986. *How Institutions Think.* Syracuse, NY: Syracuse University Press.

Ellis, S. & G. ter Haar. 1998. 'Religion and politics in sub-Saharan Africa', *Journal of Modern African Studies* 36, 2: 175–201.

Ellis, S. & G. ter Haar. 2004. *Worlds of Power: religious thought and political practice in Africa.* London: C. Hurst & Co. and New York: Oxford University Press.

Geschiere, P. 1997. *The Modernity of Witchcraft: politics and the occult in postcolonial Africa.* Charlottesville, VA: University Press of Virginia.

Gifford, P. 1993. *Christianity and Politics in Doe's Liberia*. Cambridge University Press.

Gifford, P. 2004. *Ghana's New Christianity: pentecostalism in a globalising African economy*. London: C. Hurst & Co.

Gifford, P. 2005. Review of Ellis & ter Haar, *Worlds of Power, Journal of Religion in Africa* 35, 2: 246–8.

Green, M. 2006. Review of Ellis & ter Haar, *Worlds of Power, Review of African Political Economy* 110: 779–80.

Haynes, J. 1996. *Religion and Politics in Africa*. London: Zed Books.

Ilesanmi, S. 1995. 'Inculturation and liberation: Christian social ethics and the African theology project', *The Annual of the Society of Christian Ethics*. Baltimore, MD: Georgetown University Press, 49–73.

Juergensmeyer, M. 2003. *Terror in the Mind of God: the global rise of religious violence*. Berkeley, CA: University of California Press, 3rd edn.

Kalu, O. 2006. 'A book on pentecostalism', *USA/Africa Dialogue* 94: http://www.utexas.edu/conferences/africa/ads/94.html

Lal, D. 1998. *Unintended Consequences: the impact of factor endowments, culture and politics on long-run economic performance*. Cambridge, MA: MIT Press.

Mbembe, A. 2000. 'A propos des écritures africaines de soi', *Politique Africaine* 77: 16–43.

Meyer, B. 1999. *Translating the Devil: religion and modernity among the Ewe in Ghana*. Edinburgh: Edinburgh University Press.

Meyer, B. 2004. 'Christianity in Africa: from African independent to pentecostal-charismatic churches', *Annual Review of Anthropology* 33: 447–74.

National Intelligence Council. 2005. 'Mapping sub-Saharan Africa's future'. https://www.dni.gov/files/documents/africa_future_2005.pdf

Ojo, M. 2006. *The End-Time Army: charismatic movements in modern Nigeria*. Trenton, NJ: Africa World Press.

Peel, J. 2006. Review of Ellis & ter Haar, *Worlds of Power, African Affairs* 105, 418: 145–6.

Platvoet, J. & A. Molendijk, eds. 1999. *The Pragmatics of Defining Religion: contexts, concepts and contests*. Leiden: Brill.

Stiglitz, J. 2002. *Globalization and its Discontents*. New York: W.W. Norton & Co.

Taylor, C. 2004. 'Deadly images: king sacrifice, President Habyarimana, and the iconography of pregenocidal Rwandan political literature', in N. Whitehead, ed. *Violence*. Santa Fe, NM: School of American Research Press and Oxford: James Currey, 79–105.

ter Haar, G. 1992. *Spirit of Africa: the healing ministry of Archbishop Milingo of Zambia*. London: C. Hurst & Co.

ter Haar, G. 2005. 'Religion: source of conflict or resource for peace?', in G. ter Haar & J. Busuttil, eds. *Bridge or Barrier: religion, violence and visions for peace*. Leiden: Brill: 3–34.

ter Haar, G. 2006. Review of Gifford, *Ghana's New Christianity, African Affairs* 105, 420: 486–7.

ter Haar, G., ed. 2007. *Imagining Evil: witchcraft beliefs and accusations in contemporary Africa*. Trenton, NJ: Africa World Press.

ter Haar, G. & S. Ellis. 2006. 'The role of religion in development: towards a new relationship between the European Union and Africa', *European Journal of Development Research* 18, 3: 351–67.

Turner, H. 1976. 'The approach to Africa's new religious movements', *African Perspectives* 2: 13–23.

Tyndale, W. 2001. 'Towards sustainable development: a shift in values', *Commentary: International Movement for a JustWorld* 1, 8: 1–4.

Ukah, Asonzeh F.K. forthcoming. *The Redeemed Christian Church of God: Nigeria's new paradigm of pentecostal power*. Trenton, NJ: Africa World Press.

United Nations Development Programme. 2006. http://hdr.undp.org/hd/

Van Acker, F. 2004. 'Uganda and the Lord's Resistance Army: the new order no one ordered', *African Affairs* 103, 412: 335–57.

Wamue, G. 2001. 'Revisiting our indigenous shrines through "Mungiki"', *African Affairs* 100, 400: 453–67.

Wraith, R. & E. Simpkins. 1963. *Corruption in Developing Countries*. London: Allen & Unwin.

11

RELIGION AND POLITICS IN SUB-SAHARAN AFRICA*

There is a thriving literature of religious tracts in Africa. The few formal bookshops, and the far more numerous market-stalls and itinerant hawkers who sell books, offer for sale pamphlets and popular works on religious subjects in every country of the continent, it would seem. Some are theological inquiries into aspects of the Bible or the Koran. Others contain moral lessons derived from these sacred books. Perhaps the most common category, however, is testimonies of personal religious experiences. Much of this literature hardly makes its way outside Africa and is only rarely to be found in even the finest Western academic libraries.[1]

The most puzzling genre, at least for anyone educated in modern Western academies of learning, is that of the numerous works on witchcraft and other perceived forms of evil, sometimes in the form of a description of a personal journey into a world of spirits. While many pious works on Christianity on sale in Africa are authored by American

    * Co-authored by Gerrie ter Haar. Respectively a historian at the Afrika-Studiecentrum, Leiden, and a scholar of religion at Utrecht and Leiden Universities, both in the Netherlands. We are grateful to numerous people who have commented on earlier drafts of this article, notably during a presentation at the African Studies Association of the USA annual conference in San Francisco in November 1996 and at a conference on religion and politics organised by the University of Copenhagen, Denmark, 1–3 Oct 1997.

evangelicals and published in America, popular books on witchcraft and mystical voyages are almost invariably written by Africans and published locally. Similar material is circulated through churches, sometimes in the form of video recordings. This is also true of African- led churches in the diaspora, among African communities on other continents. It is impossible to know with certainty how many people give any credence to stories like these, but the indications are that very many do so. Not only do pamphlets describing mystical journeys appear to circulate in large numbers,[2] but such accounts may clearly be situated within an older tradition of stories about witchcraft and journeys into the underworld which is to be found in collections of folklore and even in the literature of high culture.[3] Studies of churches and of healers in almost any part of Africa indicate that incidents of perceived witchcraft and of shamanism or near-death experiences are relatively common, and probably have been for as long as it is possible to trace. Such evidence may be drawn not just from studies of the pentecostal churches which have attracted so much scholarly interest of late,[4] but also of many other sorts of church including African independent congregations, of Muslim communities and of indigenous religious traditions. Thus, the popular literature written by people who claim to have experienced spiritual journeys or to have expert knowledge of witchcraft is not, we believe, an ephemeral genre but rather represents a modern form of an important tradition of mysticism in Africa.

It is perhaps helpful to note that many such texts are treatises on evil. They may be read as expressions of deep concern about the moral confusion which reigns in societies where people are no longer able to distinguish easily between that which is good and that which is evil. In the considerable number of African countries in which political institutions have largely broken down, religious discourse can be seen as an attempted remedy by means of a reordering of power, as will be discussed in due course. To this extent these popular religious texts reflect the preoccupations of Africans concerning the way in which power is exercised in their societies. If it is often difficult for analysts operating in the Western academic tradition to penetrate the meaning of such works, this is for reasons which, we will assert, derive from some common misapprehensions about the nature of religion and politics in Africa south of the Sahara. Since the texts to which we refer are concerned with power in African societies, or to be more exact, with the dangers which can arise when power is not properly organised and controlled, they can be considered a commentary on a world in which power is seen as being too often an instrument of evil people who use it to destroy peace and harmony. To that extent, they are also an oblique criticism of government or of misgovernment. Hence they cast an interesting light on the way in which religion and politics in Africa act upon each other.

There is widespread evidence that many Africans today continue to hold beliefs derived from traditional cosmologies which they apply to their everyday activities, even when they live in cities and derive their living from jobs in the civil service or the modern economic sector.[5] Contrary to what an older generation of Western scholars was inclined to believe, such views have hardly diminished with education. Religious belief operates at every level of society in Africa. Popular priests and prophets work in areas where the poor live, while the rich may have their own more exclusive spiritual advisors. Some religious leaders minister to both rich and poor. In most countries plural religious allegiance is common at all levels of society, so that an individual may be a member of several religious congregations simultaneously, and in many parts of the continent may even practice religious rituals regarded in the West as belonging to different systems of belief, such as Christianity and Islam, or Christianity and 'traditional' religion, or Sufism and reformed Islam, as in Sudan.

The present article, then, is an attempt to sketch a theory which we hope will clarify the relationship between religion and politics in Africa. We propose to proceed by steps from a discussion of what religion is, and how it may best be studied, to a brief analysis of a couple of popular religious texts chosen by way of illustration, before passing on to some further observations on the way in which power is organised and perceived in various African societies. Our text has been written with sub-Saharan Africa in mind, although it is possible that the theory which we outline is at least partly applicable to North Africa, and indeed some aspects may be of interest to observers of other parts of the world, for reasons which should become clear. It has also drawn examples mostly from the literature on Christianity rather than Islam simply due to lack of knowledge on our part.[6]

Since politics is generally supposed to be concerned with the distribution of power in society, religious texts which discuss the latter are at least implicitly political in nature. However, we emphatically do not argue that the many popular texts about encounters with witches or about hidden universes of evil are simple allegories, critiques of politics written in code in order to avoid prosecution or other retribution. That has become hardly necessary in the last ten years, during which time most of Africa has acquired a remarkable press freedom which removes most need for criticism of a government to be oblique. It is rather that any discourse on the morality and organisation of power, even if such a discourse is written in religious idiom, has political implications in a continent where all power is widely believed to have its ultimate origin in the same source, namely the invisible world. Religious discourse thus has implications for states which certainly cannot be described as weak or in crisis, like South Africa. But the fact is that many African states do show symptoms of acute political fragility and in some dramatic cases, such as Somalia, Congo, Sierra Leone and many others, the conventional apparatus of the state functions hardly or not at all. Again, for the sake of clarity, we will state what we are not arguing: we do not contend that the emergence of new religious forms or new religious tendencies, including those Muslim and Christian movements sometimes labelled 'fundamentalist', is always a response to what has often been described as state collapse. On the contrary, it is clear that certain widespread religious trends, such as Islamic renewal and pentecostal revival movements, affect many parts of the world,[7] and in this sense Africa is merely undergoing a similar experience to that of some other continents. What we do point out is that such movements are not devoid of political significance in an African context, where there are deeply rooted concepts of power which tend to merge the religious and the political, and that such movements acquire a specific public role when the institutions of state have rotted away.

The short, highly readable religious texts which are so popular in Africa are not, then, conscious or even unconscious attempts to broadcast political messages in the conventional meaning of the word 'politics'. On the contrary, there is no reason to doubt that the authors of such texts believe themselves to be recounting true stories or discussing real occurrences, no matter how puzzling these may seem to those who do not believe that witchcraft or journeys to the underworld can possibly be real. Their meaning is to be sought less in a refined deconstruction of their symbolism, although the symbols used are indeed informative, than in considering how entire cultures come to consider reality in specific ways, including in terms of interaction between the visible and invisible forces which they believe to constitute the world and to determine its evolution. In short, we believe that the analysis of these religious texts should be based on one vital assumption: that the authors intend what they write to be taken literally, however unlikely it may seem.

Interpreting religion

The interpretation of popular religious literature (and, *a fortiori,* of the oral expression of religion) in Africa poses problems for conventional modes of analysing both politics and religion.

The disciplines most widely used for writing on public affairs in Africa are political science and economics.[8] Neither of these two is equipped to encompass the belief, so widespread in Africa, that there exists a continuum between visible and invisible worlds, or that mankind shares its environment with spirits of various types which have a determining influence on the outcome of mundane transactions and with which direct communication is possible. Western analysts who attempt to study the role of religion in African politics often adopt an institutional approach which can hardly consider how religious ideologies come to have a bearing on the ways in which political power is actually perceived and exercised.[9] The work of those historians who have made the most interesting attempts to reconstitute past relationships between religion and politics[10] has made relatively little impact on the literature on contemporary politics and public affairs. An important exception, however, is a francophone school of political science, strongly influenced by a wider literature of philosophy, history and anthropology, which has succeeded rather better than the anglophone tradition of political science in incorporating religion in its frame of analysis.[11] Meanwhile, the most influential of all economic analysts of Africa, the World Bank, has incorporated certain insights from political science into its own analysis, maintaining that the root cause of Africa's economic problems actually lies in the nature of the continent's political institutions and the political culture of the people who officiate in them, or, in the World Bank's formulation, in 'a crisis of governance'.[12] In recent years this has given rise to an extensive literature on governance in Africa.[13]

If the study of African politics is mainly in the hands of political scientists and economists, the academic study of religion in Africa, meanwhile, is largely in the hands of anthropologists, the more so as the influence of writers trained in the disciplines of theology, church studies and the like has diminished in proportion as theology has lost the central place it once had in Western academic curricula. Anthropology was created as a formal intellectual discipline as a result of the expansion of European interests in Africa and Asia particularly. The earliest anthropologists of Africa were concerned above all to systematise the indigenous practices and beliefs which flourished in rural areas, where tradition was felt to exist at its most pure.[14] Many classic anthropological texts were based on the study of local institutions and cultures conceived of as traditional or closed systems which seemed destined to be eroded by the forces of modernisation. This approach continued to have a significant effect on anthropological views of African religion for decades. Only in more recent times have anthropologists studied the religious beliefs of Africans from a wider perspective, incorporating into their field of study, for example, new Christian communities,[15] and extending their inquiries to the ways in which religion and politics combine in contemporary Africa.[16]

At the same time as anthropology has widened its scope, however, it has often failed to consider the central point of religion, which is, we have suggested, communication with a perceived spirit world. While fashions in anthropological analysis of religion come and go— Marxism, postmodernism, cognitive anthropology—many works on religion in Africa have in common the implicit supposition that religions are fallacious as representations of reality.[17] Some authors go as far as to consider religious thought a vehicle for almost anything except religion.[18] In short, contemporary anthropologists tend to consider religion as a metaphor expressing other fundamental elements in human societies. All analysts seem to agree, however, that there has existed in Africa, for as long as history is able to detect, a widespread belief in the existence of invisible beings which, to greater or lesser degree, influence human destiny. Such a belief is widely regarded as a basic definition of religion.[19]

One critic, Robin Horton, divides anthropologists of African religion into three categories: the Symbolists (those who see religion as a form of representation, comparable to poetry or music); the Fideists, 'who like to think of all religious life as the expression of an autonomous commitment to communion with Spiritual Being', and the Intellectualists, in which category Horton places himself, who understand religion in Africa as 'a system of theory and practice guided by the aims of explanation, prediction and control'.[20] Although there have been new developments in writing on religion in Africa since Horton first made these distinctions, his basic categorisation remains a viable one. Perhaps the main feature of the Intellectualist approach is its propensity to consider statements on religious matters in the first instance in the believers' own terms before attempting to translate these into a vocabulary more appropriate to other branches of learning. To borrow a word derived from linguistics, it is useful to describe religions in 'emic' terms, that is, those derived from the believers' own point of view, before doing so in 'etic', or more detached, terms which correspond more closely to a Western approach based exclusively on the rational method of determining objective truth. It is important to note that this does not imply that an analyst who adopts the 'emic' form of analysis in the first instance has to share the religious beliefs of the people he or she studies; it implies only that the observer must initially suspend judgement by allowing the believers being studied (in this case Africans) the right to express matters in the terms they think appropriate. This is the approach which we will follow here.

Modern Africans, then, tend to believe in the existence of invisible forces which share the world with visible ones and to that extent they may be described as religious.[21] Among the evidence for this assertion is the rapid growth of movements of religious renewal or revival which are to be found in all parts of Africa today.[22] Some dynamic Christian and Muslim movements are often described as 'fundamentalist', a term which has become more misleading than useful and which we will try to avoid.[23] Among the common characteristics of new religious movements, including Christian charismatics and Islamists as well as others, are a highly visible occupation of public space, in the form of public ceremonies and parades; a frequent concern with combatting evil which often takes the form of rooting out perceived impurity; and a physical multiplication of places of worship such as churches and mosques which are springing up in bewildering number in towns and villages throughout the continent. There are entirely new movements such as the Unification Church or Moonies, introduced from Korea;[24] and there are revivals of traditional forms such as in witch-finding movements, which have reached epidemic proportions in South Africa.[25] Only in North Africa and Sudan has religious renewal taken on a distinctly political form in the shape of the well-known Islamist movements. Elsewhere, Christian and Muslim revivalists and followers of other movements seek less to create theocracies than to effect a change of heart in individuals or to purge society of evil and sickness. However a religious preoccupation with evil is not devoid of political implications, as we may see by taking some specific examples.

The journey of Evangelist Mukendi: A brief exegesis

At this point, we will turn to an example of one of the popular religious texts referred to in the introduction to this article which provides an illustration of the belief that the modern world is infested by witches and other persons who make use of spiritual powers for malign purposes. In spite of its mystical form, this text is replete with political meanings due to its preoccupation with the extent of evil in society.

The text, published in English and Swahili, is by a Congolese Christian preacher who is well known in the west of the former Zaire. The preacher, Evangelist Mukendi, tells the story of his life from the time he was weaned by a mermaid and pledged to Satan by his father, himself a witch. Mukendi, now born again in Christ, records the appalling experiences he had in his years as a witch. He describes how he travelled throughout the witches' underworld which, he claims, contains complexes of modern institutions created and used by witches, including universities and an international airport in Kinshasa. In this extraordinary treatise on the underworld of sorcery, he records how 'every town or village in the world has some hidden human activities under the water nearby'. Here, the spirits of people who in life were controlled by the fallen angels, the agents of evil, congregate and communicate with the 'witch doctors, sorcerers and magicians' still living in the town.[26] In their underwater lairs, the agents of the Devil feast on human flesh. They 'promote sorcerers, magicians and witch doctors' to high positions in the towns above ground, in the visible world. They manufacture diabolic objects underground, including 'cars, clothes, perfumes, money, radios and television sets' which they peddle above ground to try and 'distort and destroy the lives of those who purchase such items'. There are even underground scientists employed by the fallen angels. The ultimate purpose of all satanic activity of this type is 'to steal, kill and destroy'.[27] According to Mukendi, who claims personal experience of these matters, some major underground cities are located in former Zaire, one near the Inga dam and another near Matadi. Here there are diabolical underground conference centres 'where many decisions affecting the countries and continent of Africa are effected'. These are on a large highway which connects them to other parts of Zaire and to the other side of the Atlantic Ocean.[28] Zaire even has a 'very busy international airport for all sorts of sorcerers and magicians, flying in and out'.[29] Some of the users of the witches' airport are African witches who transform themselves into white people.

> These false white persons will then get out of their 'planes' and enter into bigger ones awaiting at Mukamba Lake [the international sorcerers' airport], destined to Europe, America or any other countries of the world. Their purpose is to acquire jobs in those countries posing as specialists or expatriates, to earn big salaries to be used for the international organization of sorcerers of the world.[30]

Mukendi claims to have taken part in such trips while he was a witch. The witches have a government, organised just like a visible government except that those in charge are women. There are witches' universities, with lecturers and staff.

This text is an investigation in religious form and using religious imagery of a fundamental problem of human life: the meaning of evil. In some respects it is highly traditional, since in western Zaire, as in some other parts of Africa, access to the spirit world is often said to pass through water,[31] and the figure of the mermaid or female water-spirit is a familiar one, which is itself a subject of popular literature and, increasingly, of academic study.[32] Nevertheless, this is by no means a tale from folklore. On the contrary, it purports to be an autobiography which represents the agents of the Devil as fully modernised and as operating in the central institutions of society. They are said to have their own universities, scientists and airports, and to infiltrate international organisations. In fact this text comes close to suggesting that the world of consultants and development experts has been infiltrated by evil-doers. This may be inferred to include employees of the World Bank, for example, international experts on Africa *par excellence,* who would probably be shocked to know that they are considered agents of the Evil One.

This is not an isolated example of prophecy, testimony or other writing in contemporary African religious mode which discusses manifestations of evil said to infest the main institutions of Africa's governance, including heads of state and aid donors. By way of comparison we may cite the prophecy of a Ghanaian preacher, Reverend Ernest Pianim, who is well known as the administrator of a leading Christian charismatic movement in Ghana. Pianim has written a booklet in which, using the well-known Christian model of the Book of Revelation, he foresees the rise of Ghana from its current woes after the reign of the Antichrist. He identifies the Antichrist as none other than the European Union.[33]

Another comparison is a work on demonology published in Nigeria by a young pentecostal preacher, Reverend S.N.I. Okeke, a university student of economics. The particular interest of Okeke's text, for present purposes, lies in his use of military jargon. Okeke describes in detail the attempted rebellion by Lucifer, the fallen angel, against God, whom he refers to as the commander-in-chief of heaven. Jesus he describes as God's second-in-command, while Lucifer, before his fall, had the rank of general officer commanding (GOC) the host of angels. The following is Okeke's account of the battle in heaven when Lucifer launches his coup;[34]

> The day for the coup came. Lucifer and his followers got more than they bargained for. Their logistic and strategic plans failed. They were defeated almost before the coup execution started!

The announcement was brief. A group of dissident angels led by Lucifer, the commander-in-chief of the heavenly angels, had attempted to overthrow the kingdom of our Lord. The dissidents have been rounded up. All peace loving angels should go about their normal duties as every situation is under control. There would be no need for curfew as all the dissidents were arrested at less than the first second of the coup. The prince of peace is in firm control of every situation.

The description is adapted to a Nigerian public only too familiar with hearing normal radio broadcasts interrupted by martial music and a coup announcement. The assertion that all evil originated in a military coup in heaven has rich implications for any reader who contemplates the origins of the many evils which are so evident in contemporary Nigeria, whose governments have been often installed through military coups.

Evangelist Mukendi's text from the former Zaire, then, is not unique. All over Africa there is a flourishing business in the publication of similar tracts which describe experiences of evil or which deliver precepts for the combatting of evil. Generally speaking the value of these accounts lies in the fact that they are first-hand testimonies produced by Africans for other Africans, rather than the accounts given to us through the mediation of social science. Here are the voices of at least some Africans concerning the condition of their societies, or to be more precise concerning the problem of evil in their societies.

Some analysts may consider expressions such as those briefly cited here to be metaphors, but the writers of such texts clearly do not. They do not regard the spirit world as a metaphor for the 'real' or visible world, but as an integral part of reality, in fact its most important part. In this sense the evolving political language of Africa tends to regard politics as a metaphor for movements in a spirit world rather than vice versa. Evangelist Mukendi and comparable authors believe that the ultimate cause of human suffering lies in the spirit world. By the same standard, they also believe that the eventual source of human prosperity is situated in that same place. Indeed this is the main purpose of religious communication, such as prayer or other forms of ritual behaviour, which is intended to persuade beings in the spirit world to grant the supplicant's wishes. Those who claim to know the world of spirits may therefore suggest in all seriousness that what is required is an alliance of forces—governments, priests and healers—to combat evil on the plane where it operates, which is a spiritual one. The logic of their argument is that African societies will not find stability unless they find spiritual stability. Hence active debates on the nature of evil take place at all levels of society in Africa in a form which most Europeans or North Americans would regard as religious. This is reflected not only in the views of authors such as Mukendi, Pianim and Okeke, but also in those of leading politicians and their constituents. An interesting example is Kenya, whose head of state, Daniel arap Moi, established a presidential commission to inquire into the Cult of Devil Worship. President Moi, however, refused to publish the report of this body although he did attack the activities of Satanists in his country, implying that they were to be found in the ranks of opposition parties.[35] Meanwhile, some Kikuyu were convinced that the real location of Satanism was in the government itself.[36]

Religion in public space

Religion and politics have been linked throughout African history. In all known pre-colonial African political systems and states public religious performance played an important role. Perhaps it should be said at once, then, that since there is no reason to suppose that religious belief has ever declined in Africa, it is incorrect to speak of a revival. It would be most accurate to refer to the revival of public religion, or the revival of religion in the occupation of political space. Many of the most dynamic expressions of religious activity at present take the form of the renewal of Islam, most obviously in North Africa, sometimes inspired by Muslims who have studied in the Middle East or fought in Afghanistan and have returned home full of zeal to create a new political order. In Christian communities, such expressions often take the form of born-again movements which reflect the remarkable growth of pentecostalism worldwide.[37] In some places there is a noticeable renewal of traditional religion, such as in southern Nigeria.[38] Whatever the precise form this new religious dynamism takes, it is a tendency so marked as to require some explanation. This demands some prior consideration of the nature of religious belief in Africa in relation to public power.

In many societies of pre-colonial Africa rulers were endowed with sacred duties, such as causing rain to fall and crops to grow, and charged with upholding the cosmic order generally. In such societies any major disorder in the invisible sphere was held to have a probable or even an inevitable effect on the physical fortunes of the community of believers. By the same token, any major event, such as a war, a famine or an untimely death, was believed to have its root cause in the invisible world. Even in the so-called stateless societies of old Africa, where village chiefs or councils of elders were responsible for the routine administration of government, real public authority actually lay with ritual experts who mediated between the visible and invisible worlds. An example of this is the Poro society of Sierra Leone, Guinea and Liberia.[39] Even in North Africa temporal rulers were expected to possess *baraka,* a power which came from the invisible world and which alone would ensure worldly success. In Madagascar a similar quality associated with the spiritual aspect of public power was (and still is) called *hasina.*

The connection between religion and politics or between religion and concepts of the state is thus rooted in history. The particular form which this takes varies from place to place, according to particular history, culture and circumstances. It is possible, and even necessary, to consider the connection between politics and religion partly in mechanical or managerial terms, since this is a large part of the actual stuff of politics. It is clear that, all over the continent, political elites make use of religious communities for purposes of mobilising voters, creating clienteles or organising constituencies. There are numerous examples. It is easy for us to understand why South Africa's President P. W. Botha should wish to address the Easter gathering of the Zion Christian Church in 1985, or why some years later the same event was attended by F. W. de Klerk, Nelson Mandela and Chief M. G. Buthelezi, all competing for political support. In Senegal, the influence wielded by marabouts or Islamic holy men belonging to the main Sufi brotherhoods has been recognised as a source of political influence for decades.[40] During the liberation war in Zimbabwe, the advice of mediums said to be possessed by the spirits of ancestors played a vital role in securing the support of the population.[41] These brief references are only some of the very many cases in which religion has served as a vehicle of political mobilisation. But if powerful temporal rulers can make use of religious clientelism, it is also the case that they can become alarmed by religious leaders who become too popular, as has happened in Zambia, for example, on more than one occasion.[42]

There is nothing peculiar to Africa about politicians seeking to make political capital out of displays of religious allegiance or respect. Politicians in almost every part of the world sometimes visit places of worship, especially during election campaigns, for the purpose of winning votes. This does not mean that they are necessarily believers themselves. In Africa, however, unlike in Europe or North America, there is reason to believe that political elites do not use religion solely as a means of increasing their base of popular support but that in many cases they also believe that access to the spiritual world is a vital resource in the constant struggle to secure advantage over their rivals in political in-fighting. This can be done by conventional techniques of communication with the spirit world, including the use of sacrifices and protective objects or through divination. President Felix Houphouët-Boigny, widely considered one of the most successful and enlightened African heads of state and known as a staunch Catholic, used such methods in private throughout his career.[43] Only in his last years, however, when he devoted enormous resources to the construction of the great basilica in his home town of Yamoussoukro which was designed to perpetuate his power over generations as yet unborn, did his spiritual preoccupations become fully public.[44]

Many other heads of state are known to employ religious experts in their personal entourage to whom they turn for advice on matters far removed from what, in modern Western thought, would be considered religious affairs. Kenneth Kaunda, for example, when he was president of Zambia, retained the services of an Indian guru, Dr Ranganathan, whom he consulted on a wide range of issues and whom he recommended to those within his immediate circle.[45] A more controversial choice was that of President Mathieu Kérékou of Benin, who retained the services of Mohamed Amadou Cissé, nicknamed 'Djine' or 'the Devil', a Malian marabout who was known to have held a ceremony in which he publicly espoused the Devil,[46] and who had previously worked for other heads of state including President Mobutu of Zaire and President Bongo of Gabon. Cissé was appointed a minister of state in the Beninese government, responsible for the secret services. He was eventually convicted of fraud in a major trial.[47] Other heads of state have founded esoteric cults which play an important role in rituals for their inner circle, such as President Didier Ratsiraka of Madagascar, whose palace included an extravagant temple dedicated to Rosicrucianism,[48] President Paul Biya of Cameroon, also a Rosicrucian,[49] and President Joaquim Chissano of Mozambique, a follower of Transcendental Meditation.[50] While it is good politics for a politician to make a public profession of religious allegiance in order to win popularity, there is thus abundant evidence that heads of state also practice religion in private for no obvious clientelist motive. Quite simply, they, like most of their constituents, believe that real power has its roots in the invisible world and that therefore the cultivation of spiritual power is vital for their continued political existence.

Heads of state with spiritual advisors or private cults appear to believe that the weight of the affairs of state requires them to have access to esoteric forms of power from which the mass of the population is excluded. All elites tend to cultivate their own exclusive institutions, in Africa and elsewhere, in which they may socialise with their peers. African heads of state, the evidence suggests, tend to believe in the importance of the invisible world just as their subjects do, but seek higher forms of power commensurate with the importance of the positions they seek to defend and of the burdens which they have to discharge. It is common to tenure of great power in all cultures that it imposes on its holders choices weightier than those facing most of their subjects, and that this takes power-holders into an exclusive moral realm.

In fact, the religious practices of the mighty in Africa, esoteric though they might be, are usually known to the population. In the days before press freedom became general in the continent in the 1990s, elite activities of this sort were favourite subjects of popular debate through *radio trottoir*.[51] Ordinary people understand well enough the role played by religion in elite struggles since many use techniques similar to those of their leaders to solve the problems of their daily lives by consulting healers, spirit mediums, priests, prophets, diviners and marabouts, by seeking the blessing of the ancestors or by attending religious services of every variety.

One consequence of the frequency with which members of the elite seek advice on their most intimate spiritual problems is that those marabouts and other spiritual experts who include politicians among their clientele themselves become brokers of power in the most mundane sense. The marabouts of the elite become repositories of highly confidential information, since those politicians who resort to their services will divulge their innermost ambitions in a bid to attain the power they crave. In this way a leading marabout may acquire inside knowledge of planned coups and other secrets of his elite clients, as did Amadou Cissé in Benin. Another marabou, Amadou Oumarou 'Bonkano', also the chief of a national intelligence service, himself attempted a coup against his patron and employer, President Seyni Kountché of Niger.[52] In fact a spiritual expert who is frequented by members of the elite bears a close resemblance to the head of an intelligence service because of the confidential information he acquires. Thus a ruler who takes such a person into his service acquires access to a valuable source of worldly information as well as to invisible power. By the same token a ruler who refuses to frequent such people deprives himself of a vital source of information and of the influence of a perceived medium of supernatural power. This was one of the reasons, for example, for the downfall of Benin's President Nicéphore Soglo and the astonishing political comeback of Mathieu Kérékou, the born-again Christian who was once considered by certain of his countrymen as a Satanist.[53]

If the spiritual experts who frequent the palaces of the elite acquire worldly power through their activities, so in a different way do those popular religious leaders who acquire mass followings. Leading priests and prophets become important people in a political sense simply by reason of the number of their followers. They are not the only leaders from what is fashionably called civil society who may become influential by heading some sort of non-government association such as a professional association or a trade union. However, the influence wielded by a popular religious leader in Africa is different in many respects from that exercised by any other leader emerging from the non-state sector. A trade union leader, for example, may be able to articulate demands for higher wages or more jobs which a government can deal with by the conventional techniques of modern government and politics. A religious leader, on the other hand, is endowed with power perceived as stemming directly from the spiritual world, reflecting a world view which is foreign to norms of government based on the classical Western separation of religion and politics into distinct systems of thought and action. The leader of a secular organisation may be placated with gifts of patronage or intimidated with the threat of exclusion or the application of coercion, but a president finds it more difficult to identify techniques for dealing with, for example, an epidemic of possession by evil spirits.

Temporal rulers attempting to govern populations who believe that their daily life is affected by powers stemming from the invisible lack institutional means of control. When the Zambian Catholic Archbishop Emmanuel Milingo carried out his healing ministry by exorcising evil spirits and calling upon the Holy Spirit to fill his parishioners, he was mediating invisible powers believed by Zambians to exist but over which the recognised political authorities of the country had no control. In the end this caused such political disquiet as to cause President Kaunda to become an accomplice to Milingo's removal by the Vatican. [54] Spiritual leaders who develop a mass following in this way are particularly difficult for governments to deal with, even when they have no political ambitions. Even if religious leaders do aspire to play a role in government, they find it difficult to acquire political power on the basis of a purely spiritual authority. This may be one explanation why so many of the national conferences held in Africa in the early 1990s chose bishops as their presidents, people who could appeal to sources of power unavailable to discredited politicians but were unlikely to turn their office into the base for a presidential campaign. [55]

Even in the heyday of one-party states, when heads of state controlled virtually every organ of associational life, the spirit world was always more elusive. Some rulers, like Presidents Mobutu of Zaire[56] or Eyadéma of Togo,[57] established quasi-religious cults of their own in what it is permissible to interpret as an attempt to revive systems of sacred kingship, but always with limited or short-lived success. For while secular government and politics may be managed with appropriate doses of patronage and coercion, the spiritual world is less easy to govern, particularly in a continent where belief in prophecy and spirit possession is widespread and where access to spiritual power is believed to be within the reach of all. In principle anyone can communicate with the world of the spirits and receive messages from that source. People believed to be possessed by spirits, prophets with privileged access to the spirit world, or people who use potent instruments of religious communication to express their wishes and aspirations all have access to power in a form which may pay little respect to the social or political norms in vogue. This poses a constant threat to the ideological order and thus to political stability. This was also the case in colonial times, as many examples testify.[58] It is not a peculiarity of recent decades.

Power and institutions

Religious revival movements of various sorts have had an increasing impact in the public realm of many African countries over the last twenty years. This roughly coincides with a decline of the formal apparatuses of state and government over the same period. The same period has also witnessed an explosion of the type of popular religious literature which we have earlier discussed. While it would be too simple to regard this as a simple case of cause and effect, there are reasons to believe that these two factors are connected.

Africa, of course, is not alone in seeing the emergence of new religious movements in the last two decades, some of which have become political forces, as examples from Asia and America will testify.[59] Hence it would not be correct to argue that new religious movements have emerged in Africa solely in order to fill a vacuum in public life. Moreover, dynamic new political movements have emerged also in African countries where the state cannot be said to be heading towards crisis, such as South Africa. Our observation is simply that such religious movements are rarely devoid of political implication and that when they do emerge in a country where the state is unable to fulfil its expected functions in regard to the law and public order, religion can take on a specific importance.

Before examining this matter further, it is useful to dwell briefly on the travails of African states and the ways in which these are normally described. Probably the most influential analyses of the malaise of African states, which has been increasingly evident since the early 1980s, have been in the field of economics. This is partly a reflection of the fact that the dominant academic mode of contemplating Africa in the years since independence has been in terms of economic development. More specifically, the World Bank and the International Monetary Fund, both of which are dominated by economists, have acquired enormous weight in African affairs since 1980.[60] These institutions have produced an important corpus of literature on Africa and have had a substantial influence on the way in which the continent's public life is analysed both in the academic world and by policy-makers. Today, inasmuch as the industrialised world has a coherent view of Africa, it is that African countries need to enact political reforms which will create public institutions better able to design and implement rational policies conducive to stability and economic growth.

The institutions of state which have decayed so markedly in Africa in the last two decades, and which the major donors are now struggling to restore to working order, are those originally established by European colonial powers in conformity with the norms applying in Europe itself at the time.[61] Briefly, colonial administrators supposed that government should be through modern, bureaucratic organs of a state of which the proper function is to uphold a rational system of law and to design and implement rational policies. These policies, generally speaking, depend on material inputs of resources for the satisfaction of specific aims deemed to be in the common good. The identification of this common good is made, in the last resort, by political authorities. In the colonial times these were situated in European metropoles but these days they are located in Africa's capital cities. It is noteworthy that this conception of government introduced in colonial times is almost identical to the concept of 'good governance' so much in vogue among donors today.

The religious revival in Africa can be said to reflect a concern with poor governance, expressed in a different idiom, inasmuch as new religious movements are often centrally concerned with the problem of evil in society and are looking for alternative sources of power. Even in countries with states which remain strong, the emergence of new religious movements can reasonably be seen as attempts to locate new sources or forms of power. In effect, many forms of religious revival challenge the very bases of legitimacy of states which operate through institutions and norms of governance originally created in colonial times. In this regard Islam, unlike Christianity, offers a specific view of government in the form of theocracy. In general, many new religious movements in Africa can be seen as attempts to revive a known source of power. Spiritual power, unlike political power, is situated not in institutions themselves, nor in the will of the people, but in the world of the invisible.

It is helpful to consider the revival of religion in relation to the dysfunction of states in this light. In the large number of African examples where religion is strong and states prove unable or unwilling to uphold a monopoly of violence or the rule of law, spiritual belief offers access to an alternative form of power and provides a social cement. In this sense the resurgence of religion is directly connected to the erosion of secular state apparatuses in cases where the latter has occurred. This may be described as the revival of tradition in a radically changed context. Unlike in pre-colonial times, every part of Africa is now directly linked via money economies to world markets and via electronic media to world sources of information. It is striking that the present forms of religious revival are generally those of the world religions of Islam and Christianity, which thus link Africa to worldwide cultural systems. They also reflect the literacy which is now widespread in Africa where, less than a century ago, it was rare indeed.

Religion and politics are both systems of ordering the power inherent in human society, in the process of which elements of authority and hierarchy tend to emerge. As such, religion and politics are closely related. In the modern Western tradition these two systems of harnessing or manipulating power have been subject to sharp organisational and intellectual distinctions which conform to the separation of politics and religion or church and state. Colonial governors and missionaries attempted to reorganise the language of power into similar political and religious idioms. However, it is clear that a large number of the world's people continue to regard these two spheres of power as impinging upon one another or even, in some circumstances, of being virtually indistinct from one another. This is true not only of Africa but also for example of China, which has a long tradition of religious risings intended to rid the empire of demonic influence at times of acute disorder.[62] Thus, while the present essay concentrates on Africa, our observations may be situated in a broader debate on the way in which many peoples in what used to be called the Third World are reordering the systems by which power is acquired and distributed in their societies in the aftermath of a century and more of subjection to institutions originally imposed on them by Europeans or otherwise acquired as a result of Western influence.[63]

The moral value of power

Power is usually defined as the ability of a person to induce others to act in the way that he or she requires.[64] Many writers throughout history have expressed the conviction that the possession of great power tempts its holders to immorality or at the very least confronts them with dilemmas which require them to make profound choices concerning good and evil, normally considered the prerogative of gods. Or, as Nietzsche noted, 'every high degree of power always involves a corresponding degree of freedom from good and evil'.[65]

Politicians, being powerful, have the capacity to make choices of great consequence, and the less they are trammelled by constitutions or some other apparatus of restraint, the more dangerous this can be. However, there is evidence from different parts of Africa that the relative latitude enjoyed by the powerful in this respect is merely a reflection of a much wider confusion concerning public institutions regarded as having the legitimate authority to regulate power in both the political and religious spheres. In the absence of such institutions the abuse of political and religious power can create moral confusion and even panic. In small communities, such as a village or a family, this may take the form of witchcraft accusations,[66] but related forms of moral confusion may occur in a larger community, even within a nation.[67] Distinguishing between good and evil and understanding the nature of evil are major preoccupations of the popular religious tracts to which we have referred throughout the present text.

Modern Africa in many cases lacks entrenched protocols of power in both the political and the spiritual fields. To take a common enough example, a politician who arrives in power unconstitutionally through a *coup d'état* may emerge as a generally benign ruler, but it is more likely that he will not, since experience shows that the use of illegitimate violence in the formative act of taking power may well lead to the commission of further acts of violence in its exercise. Similarly the purpose of religious performance may not be clear until its results become apparent in the absence of a generally acknowledged structure of religious authority. Just as a politician who proclaims himself to be the saviour of the nation may turn out to be no such thing, so may a self-proclaimed prophet or healer turn out to be a charlatan or to bring disaster in their wake.[68]

In popular imagery evil-doers are often associated with small, exclusive and secret groups which perform their actions at night, one of the perceived characteristics of witches. Just as political and religious power are comparable, so too are the actions of covens of witches and exclusive groups of plotters and putschists. Their exclusivity and selfishness are signs of their evil intentions. In Zaire, for example, the government of President Mobutu was sometimes considered to be an elite conspiracy of witches, who consulted marabouts of sinister reputation at night in an effort to enhance their power.[69]

In view of this, it is relevant to discuss why certain heads of state have consciously sought recourse to individual experts, or to cults, widely believed in Africa to be fundamentally evil in origin, such as Rosicrucianism.[70] The answer seems to lie in the precariousness of power in Africa. A ruler who has struggled and fought, often literally, to achieve power, and who is conscious of the danger of violent overthrow, is even more likely than a constitutional ruler to require special power to survive. In such conditions any source of additional power becomes attractive. In many traditional African religions instant earthly power is believed to be obtainable through sacrifices, by the spilling of blood. In the Christian tradition the ultimate source of all power lies with God. However, the granting of earthly power and wealth is also considered one of the principal assets of the Devil, the incarnation of evil. One of the effects of Christian evangelisation in Africa has been to demonise certain traditional religious beliefs, notably concerning blood sacrifice. Hence, the spilling of blood for whatever purpose has in many places become associated with evil, considered to be the realm of Satan. Since God, the source of all good, is deemed by Christians to grant power only in his own time and for benign purposes, a politician desperate for instant power and wealth may see little alternative other than to perform an act which will be widely viewed as diabolic, and whose consequences may therefore be anticipated as malign. The former archbishop of Lusaka, Emmanuel Milingo, one of Africa's leading demonologists,[71] records that he has often been approached by politicians who have literally made diabolic pacts in order to secure the earthly wealth and power which Satan can bestow in return for possession of a supplicant's soul.[72]

We have noted that the academic literature on Africa in recent years has been dominated by studies of the deficiencies of public life and public institutions, and that these analyses have generally been written in the idiom appropriate to such academic disciplines as economics or political science. There is reason to believe that many Africans, in pondering questions regarding the vagaries of power, phrase the question and its response in a religious idiom in preference to, or in addition to, the idiom of conventional Western discourse. This becomes particularly clear in the idiom of witchcraft, as may be seen in both academic and popular literature. Many modern Cameroonians, for example, have come to the conclusion that the rapidity with which political careers rise and fall is explicable only by reference to witchcraft.[73] Both during and since the colonial period many countries have witnessed witch-finding movements inspired by a widespread belief that witches are at large and that, since the government offers no solution or may be itself infested with witches who have grown powerful and rich on their illegitimate assumption of power, ordinary people must improvise their own defence.

Religion as a political idiom

In discussing this matter, we encounter a difficult semantic problem. While the vocabulary applied to religion in the modern English language is reasonably adequate for technical descriptions of prayer or ritual, it is inadequate for discussion of more subjective matters such as the positive or negative, or good or evil, purposes of religious action. Writers are obliged to have recourse to terms such as 'witchcraft' and 'sorcery' to describe ideas whose fluidity and nuances may be significantly different in African languages and African thought.[74] Even ritual experts schooled in the Western tradition, such as priests and theologians trained in missionary seminaries, seem to experience difficulty in articulating religious experience in terms which are familiar to African worshippers. This is certainly an important reason why, in Christian communities in Africa, there has been a marked movement away from the missionary-instituted or mainline churches towards African-initiated ones.[75] A major attraction of African-initiated churches is the fact that these churches openly address matters of spirit possession, spiritual subversion or witchcraft, and healing. In this regard the career of Archbishop Milingo is both significant and exemplary. Milingo's success, and his downfall, were his ability to articulate people's problems in terms which they understood exactly. In the classical Western lexicon, some of these problems might be termed medical, others psychological, and others political or economic. Milingo was able to address all of these in a religious idiom of words and action.[76] There are many other examples of religious healers or prophets who have been successful in addressing what we might regard as political or economic or even military problems by religious discourse and action. The Naprama cult of counter-violence in Mozambique was, at least for a brief period, an effective antidote to the cult of violence espoused by RENAMO.[77] Economic problems caused by drought have also given rise to religious movements whose object is to make rain fall, one of the duties expected of public authorities in traditional cosmology but also in modern ones, in Mozambique for example.[78]

Some leading authors have contemplated the formation of idioms or systems of discourse which are, or can be, effective in African politics as 'a generalizing and productive political language'.[79] Such a language is in fact emerging in the idiom of religion. This is particularly apparent in the case of born-again Christians who seek to change society by transforming every individual, and Islamists who aspire to do the same by creating a theocracy. Both Christian and Muslim movements of renewal have important antecedents in African history but they often consciously reject many of their own country's religious traditions, considering them at best as irrelevant to their project or at worst as so much evidence of the Devil's work. Many Christian revivalist movements today, while they appear to some observers as pure American imports,[80] are more accurately seen as simply the latest generation in the century-old tradition of African-initiated churches, all of which may be located in the longer history of evangelicalism. Many of these new churches regard the older generation of 'spiritual' or 'white garment' churches as following practices drawn from traditional African religions which they associate with the work of the Devil. This is a sign of just how preoccupied they are with combatting evil. Similar generational trends are observable in Islam, whose current reforming zeal in Africa may be usefully compared with the nineteenth-century revival movements of Usman dan Fodio and El Hajj Omar. African Islam has been subject to periodic waves of renewal, particularly in West Africa where missionaries with purified beliefs acquired in foreign centres of Islamic learning have preached reform, sometimes combined, as in northern Nigeria, with the construction of new political systems.[81]

Modern religious radicals often argue in favour of a break with popular practices of combining imported and indigenous religious traditions. In doing this, such radicals are also making a statement about the way in which public power should be organised and about the immorality of present systems. They aim to cut through the prevailing moral confusion by making a clear distinction between what they perceive as good and what they perceive as evil. In effect they are attempting to construct a new and simplified system of belief out of the mass of traditions and institutions existing in Africa by reinterpreting life in dualistic categories. They are proposing a new basis for the legitimacy of public power, including that exercised by a state. Hence it is small wonder that many leaders, whether declaring themselves to be born again in Christ like Zambia's President Frederick Chiluba or Benin's President Kérékou, or whether by multiplying the outward signs of personal piety like almost all the leaders of the continent, attempt to bestow religious legitimacy on themselves. In countries where the state apparatus has been eroded to an alarming degree, such as Congo, Somalia, Sierra Leone and others, religious movements in the long term may offer not just a new basis for legitimising power, but even a means of restructuring some sort of apparatus which will fulfil the functions of government.

There is a risk that, if the process of turning religion into an idiom of politics develops along the present lines, African politics will become increasingly incomprehensible to outsiders. Discourses on witchcraft and on the unseen world of evil, like that of Evangelist Mukendi, who declares himself to have been saved from Satan by the power of Christ, may be relevant to many Africans but they are not easily understood by others. A challenge to Africans is to develop a new language of politics which incorporates the role of public authorities as upholders of cosmic order while also being comprehensible internationally. The challenge to academics is to understand this language of public affairs not as a symptom of a new form of exoticism, but as a debate on the proper function of power in Africa.[82]

12

THE OCCULT DOES NOT EXIST*

A RESPONSE TO TERENCE RANGER

In 2007, *Africa* published a review article by Terence Ranger (2007) concerning 'medicine murders', 'child witches' and the construction of 'the occult'. Ranger frames his review with remarks concerning a murder inquiry by London's Metropolitan Police that was set up after the discovery in the River Thames of the dismembered corpse of a young boy of probable West African origin, whom the police dubbed 'Adam'.

Briefly, Ranger admonishes the British police for making use of a crude stereotype of Africa in their inquiry. He goes on to present his own views by way of a critique of a number of recent works on religion in Africa. Ranger does not explain what he means by 'the occult', but it is clearly the category to which he consigns such anti-social and violent or vicious practices as 'medicine murders' and 'witchcraft'. Ranger distinguishes between 'religion' and 'the occult' without explicitly stating what the difference between them is, although in another publication (Ranger 2006: 351) he concedes that it is 'very important, though extraordinarily difficult' to distinguish between religion and certain closely related elements, among which he names 'magic' and 'witchcraft'.

The present article challenges Ranger's argument concerning 'the occult' on the grounds that 'the occult' is one of many concepts and

---

* Co-authored by Gerrie ter Haar.

expressions used in Western academic writing that carries a heavy ideological baggage. Other common expressions falling in this category include 'magic' and 'witchcraft', both of which are indelibly marked by their colonial usage.[1] Continued use of these terms is flawed by their association with a long tradition of thinking of Africa as a continent stuck in a traditional past, to be understood only in terms different from those applied to the rest of humanity today. The choice of language by academics is a matter of great importance. As Harold Turner long ago noted in regard to African-initiated churches, 'our approach to any range of phenomena is both revealed and influenced by the names we bestow upon it' (1976: 13). Our point is not to argue that 'magic', 'witchcraft' or 'the occult' do not deserve to be debated, but that they cannot be understood in their proper historical and moral context as long as the debate is couched in a language that is so heavily loaded.

Religious phenomena—even those that one may personally find repugnant—are best described in neutral terms. This implies that, if scholars are to break with the tradition of regarding Africa as an exceptional continent, they need to describe practices and ideas by applying categories that can also be used, at least in principle, in regard to any other human society. If we take this as a point of departure, it is apparent that many of the phenomena that Terence Ranger considers to fall into the category of 'the occult' are better placed within the purview of religion more generally. This, of course, depends on how one defines religion—something that Ranger neglects to do, just as he does not define any of the other key concepts he uses. It is not a matter of choosing a favourite definition of religion from among the many dozens on offer. What is required is to formulate a definition that emerges from the context under study. Elsewhere we have proposed a working definition of religion in Africa as 'a belief in the existence of an invisible world, distinct but not separate from the visible one, that is home to spiritual beings with effective powers over the material world' (Ellis and ter Haar 2004: 14). This is a working definition, elaborated with a view to incorporating the entire range of religious practices and ideas in Africa. In passing, we may note that it applies to many other parts of the world, too. It is deliberately couched in terms that are morally neutral and value-free. It allows for the inclusion of a broad range of mystical beliefs and practices, irrespective of whether observers consider them to be positive or negative. The latter is precisely what Ranger (2007: 276) objects to in our approach. However, spiritual power, a concept that is crucial to understanding religion in Africa, can be employed for both socially constructive and destructive purposes. This is a capital point, but one that Ranger avoids, apparently on account of his own moral position.

Connections between religion and morality are historically formed; they are not the same in all societies. As we discuss below, a specific connection was developed in early Christianity that still colours the views of many authors today. In this regard, Terence Ranger appears to be one of the many writers who have come to think of religion as something that is (or at least should be) concerned with whatever is good and life-affirming. Adopting such a view leaves no room for ideas and practices relating to a perceived invisible world that are destructive or anti-social. These are precisely the sorts of beliefs and practices that Ranger does not consider to be part of religion, but that he instead consigns to a separate category of 'the occult'.

Hence, Ranger's review article raises important theoretical problems that we propose to address. We begin this task by examining the genealogy of some key ideas concerning the concept of religion. This, we believe, takes us closer to constructing a suitable theoretical framework for discussing such matters as Terence Ranger places within the category of 'the occult'. This is a term widely used by evangelicals in the USA to designate 'bad' religion (Jenkins and Maier-Katkin 1992: 62) that has been popularized by Jean and John Comaroff (1999) as a quasi-technical term, notably in regard to Africa. Although Ranger tells us (2006: 360) that he dislikes the term 'occult', he continues to use it to designate beliefs and practices that are socially destructive.

'Good' and 'bad' religion

So deep has been the historical effect of European practices of labelling and categorization that even the terms 'religious' and 'religion' require some elucidation. For these words, too, carry a historical burden, having been introduced by Europeans in reference to a wide range of practices that they encountered in other parts of the world in early modern times. A major problem arises from the way in which, over a long period, Europeans imposed on other societies, or at least attributed to them, ideas that derived from Europe's own particular history. There exists a substantial corpus of literature, produced notably by academic specialists in the study of religion, that investigates the long historical pedigree of the term 'religion' as it is presently used. This literature reveals the relationship between political power, intellectual authority and social practice in the formation of new, globalized, ideas of religion in recent centuries (for example, Asad 1993; Masuzawa 2005).

European writers in mediaeval and early modern times considered that there were four types of religious observer: Christians, Jews, Mohammedans (as Muslims were then known as), and 'the rest' meaning all others deemed to be attached to some form of idolatry (Masuzawa 2007: 181). This characteristic, fourfold division of religions persisted into the early nineteenth century. By that time, it had become apparent to European intellectuals that a more complex classification was necessary, not least in order to accommodate the sophisticated beliefs enshrined in Buddhism, which possessed all the hallmarks of what a European intellectual of those days could regard as a 'real' religion as opposed to a mere superstition. Indigenous African religious practices, meanwhile, remained consigned to a residual category that included—to use the vocabulary of the nineteenth century—polytheists, animists and idolators.

In sub-Saharan Africa, the introduction of a new vocabulary regarding the invisible world was part of a far more general imposition of new administrative arrangements and practices of power of Western origin or inspiration. Among the novelties of the age of colonialism was the identification of religion and politics as two distinct realms, which should properly be subject to institutional and intellectual separation.

This new vocabulary and conceptual order gave a new meaning to ideas and practices in African societies concerning the invisible world, cutting across existing categories and thereby distorting the empirical reality of indigenous religious experience as well as its various expressions. It is for this reason that many African scholars in the field of religion have reacted against the vocabulary and some of the conceptual categories that were introduced in the nineteenth century. As David Westerlund (1985: 87–8) has noted:

In the works of African scholars there is often sharp criticism of Western terms designating different aspects of African religion. Many of these terms are considered to be inadequate and derogatory. For instance, words like 'animism' and 'fetishism' are considered inappropriate as general labels of African religion, and it is stressed that they have been used by Western scholars in order to ridicule this religion.

In the light of the above remarks, the concept of 'the occult' may be seen to be a recent addition to the stock of labels designating those aspects of African religion that observers find bizarre, distasteful, or, in any event, that they do not consider to be part of any 'true' religion.

The identification of ideas and practices deemed worthy to be included in the category of 'religion', as opposed to those of a supposedly lesser order disqualified for inclusion in this same category, has a long history. The distinction between 'religion' and less worthy forms of practice, often glossed as 'superstition', may be traced back through early modern times to the classical Roman tradition of distinguishing *religion* and *superstition* (Pagden 1986: 168–9). Awareness of how these terms have evolved throws considerable light on the European penchant for distinguishing 'true' from 'false' religion, or 'good' from 'bad' religion.

For the ancient Romans, *religio* was an organized and controlled activity of the patrician class. *Superstitio*, by contrast, was the religious practice of the lower orders of Roman society, associated with perceived social and intellectual disorder (Momigliano 1977: 141–59). In regard to the twin concepts of *religio* and *superstitio*, Italo Ronca (1992: 43) has observed that 'neither the terms themselves nor their negative correlation are cross-cultural universals to be reckoned with in all cultures or at all times: in many areas not influenced by Christianity there is no equivalent to such conceptual terminology'. Modern connotations of 'religion' and 'superstition', as well as their semantic polarity, he argues (1992: 44), are the result of a long theistic tradition. The meaning of these terms is historically conditioned, as are their correlative semantic fields.

The identification by European thinkers and administrators of certain practices as being either religious or superstitious in nature has had a formative effect not only on Africa but on societies in many parts of the world. Some of the effects of these processes of categorization have been well described by the Korean scholar Chin Hong Chung (2007). He notes that before the late nineteenth century the Korean language had no equivalent to the word 'religion'. It was an alien term that entered Korea as part of a more general process of modernization, in this case transmitted via Japan. According to Chung (2007: 206):

[t]he concept of religion never succeeded in incorporating our experience fully, and it has been utilized as an inappropriate measure and criterion in the description and understanding of our traditional belief culture. It is unavoidable, therefore, to reach the point where the empirical reality of traditional religious experience and its expression is distorted, devalued, and confused by such a newly enforced word as 'religion'.

In Africa, a similar process took place to the one outlined by Chung in regard to Korea. In Africa too, many or probably most languages appear to have had no ready translation for the word 'religion' prior to evangelization by Christian missionaries, and no equivalent experience.

Writing on religion in Africa

J.D.Y. Peel has noted (2000: 88–122) in regard to the Yoruba that a wide range of what would now be regarded as indigenous religious practices were originally subsumed in an expression used by West African speakers of English in the nineteenth century, 'making country fashion'. How indigenous practices in relation to an invisible world have subsequently been construed by writers, clerics, politicians and officials as either 'religion' or 'superstition', or how they have been labelled by some other name, is a process that has had a great bearing on local perceptions of spiritual power and on the moral value attached to attempts to access such power. In order to illustrate this more fully, a brief summary is helpful.

Generally speaking, one may identify two phases in the history of the study of religion in Africa (Platvoet 1996). The first of these can be described as 'Africa as object', referring to an early period in which religious data were studied by scholars from outside Africa, many of them amateur ethnographers. This cohort of early foreign collectors, antiquaries and observers established many of the basic approaches, methods, concepts and labels used subsequently. A second phase is that of 'Africa as subject', when similar data were also being studied by professionally trained specialists, including African scholars, most recently based in African universities. Accompanying this change of phase from Africa-as-object to Africa-as-subject was a change in the moral value that observers ascribed to religion in Africa. In the high Victorian period, missionaries and colonizers generally considered indigenous African religious practices to be pretty much uniformly contemptible because they did not constitute 'true' religion, with a partial exception being made only for Islam. Early Christian evangelists often considered indigenous religious practices as 'a kind of absence', as Peel (2000: 12) has noted in regard to Nigeria. In other words, they were not perceived to have any real substance.

In general, it was only after the institution of colonial rule that opinions like these tended to change somewhat. Some colonial officials, spending long periods in Africa, came to see the complexity and subtlety of African religious ideas. If only for administrative purposes, they had to learn to understand the relationship of indigenous religion to justice, land tenure and other matters affecting the social and political order. The colonial period also witnessed the arrival of professional anthropologists in Africa, who tended to view African religious ideas and practices in functional terms, as the cultural epiphenomena associated with specific social and political complexes bearing an ethnic label. Thus was the concept of ethnic religions formed, with a plethora of books on Zulu religion, Yoruba religion, and many others. This was of a piece with the view characteristic of European administrators and scholars until quite late in the colonial period that Africa was best understood as being divided into thousands of discrete ethnic communities, each having its own culture and its own religion. There also emerged texts from African intellectuals trained in European methods, who were able to describe in the academic vocabulary of their day the religious and cultural systems that they knew from within (for example, Kenyatta 1938).

By the time African countries gained political independence, from the late 1950s onwards, the colonial administrations that were then disappearing, and the expatriate colonial society associated with them, included quite a few individuals who had come to appreciate the subtlety and social usefulness of African religious thought. They found common cause with African intellectuals who were, by this time, able to express their ideas in print more easily than before. African theologians of the generation of Bolaji Idowu (1962) and John Mbiti (1969) turned colonial values on their heads, much as nationalist ideologues were also doing, by claiming that certain elements of Africa's cultures previously condemned by Europeans as negative should in fact be considered positively. Many writers in this genre, European or African, were themselves practising Christians or, at least, had undergone a church or missionary education that had impressed on them the basic tenets of Christian religion.

African theologians in particular in the mid- to late twentieth century articulated what may be called a 'theology of continuity' (Westerlund 1985: 89). This refers to a process of interpreting African religious ideas and practices in the light of Christianity, in such a way as to identify elements of African indigenous religions that appear to resemble or anticipate aspects of Christian belief. Typical of this enterprise was the construction of African Traditional Religion—in the singular, and with capital letters—as a system of belief comparable to other major religions. One result of this change of perspective was to suggest that the African sub-continent is not divided into autonomous areas, each with its own distinctive religion corresponding to an ethnic identity, as earlier generations of Europeans had often supposed. Instead, commentators now tended to discern some of the similarities between religious ideas and practices over wide tracts of Africa, for example in regard to healing, noting that certain cults may mobilize people over very wide areas, creating a religious geography that transcends political boundaries (Ranger 1991).

The nationalist discourse of the mid-twentieth century, in both political and theological forms, aimed at restoring the dignity of African culture (quite often in the singular rather than the plural) after the indignities and misrepresentations heaped on it by European scholars and colonialists. Terence Ranger has been a distinguished contributor to this work of rehabilitation in both religious and political fields, being a pioneer in the re-evaluation and reinterpretation of African religious ideas and practices (for example, Ranger and Kimambo 1972) and a leading historian of African nationalism (Ranger 1967). For more than four decades, Ranger has remained faithful to a vision of religion in

Africa as essentially a search for harmony, a point he expresses in his review article (Ranger 2007: 276) when he refers to the importance of individual and collective healing, rain making, peacemaking and environmental protection as key elements of African religions.

These are indeed distinctive elements of African religious practices. They fit easily into a view of African religions that represents religion as fundamentally a search for what is 'good' and positive, reflecting current translations of key Christian ideas. However, such a framework of analysis, rooted in Christian theology, pays little heed to religious ideas that underlie practices less appealing to a liberal sensibility. It leaves no conceptual room for religious practices that are not easily assimilated into a view of religion as a personal and social good. It makes no allowance for inclusion of beliefs and practices that are not concerned with such demonstrably useful or socially constructive matters as healing and reconciliation. It reflects a perspective that descends in an unbroken genealogical line from the early modern categorization of the world that we have summarized above, distinguishing 'true' or 'good' religion from 'false' or 'bad' religion or superstition. A similar approach is replicated in anthropological views of religion in Africa inasmuch as these have tended to consider religion primarily in terms of social practices and institutions, to be judged by its social utility. This has diverted attention from the intellectual dimension of religion in Africa.

In other words, there exists a tradition in social science of considering religion in Africa as primarily something that binds people together, a means of social cohesion.[2] At this point we find ourselves once more drawn back to a very old debate at the heart of Christianity, namely that concerning the original meaning of 'religion'. It is often suggested that the English word 'religion' derives ultimately from the Latin *religare* meaning 'to re-bind'. However, no less an expert than the pre-Christian orator Cicero was clear in stating that *religio* was derived from *relegere/religere,* meaning 'to re-trace, to re-collect', referring to the practice of divination as one of the three pillars— together with prayer and sacrifice—of Roman religion. It was later Christian authors, notably Augustine of Hippo (354–430), one of the founding fathers of the Church, who were intent on regarding *religio* as that which binds man to God by means of love, insisting on deriving the word from *religare* (Ronca 1992: 52–3). This marked a decisive shift from the classical Roman view of religion as a human response to a continuous stream of revelatory messages from an invisible world (as it was seen by Cicero and other pre-Christian authors) to a Christian articulation of religion in terms of a bond between man and God. From a Christian perspective, the nature of the latter relationship was held to have been fully revealed through the person of Jesus, which made further revelation unnecessary, such as through divination.

The interest of this brief reference to debates in early Christianity is the insight it provides concerning the historical transformations in the concept of religion in European history. Here, some of the problems in applying the term 'religion' to Africa become apparent. Since the expansion of Europe in early modern times, Europeans have imposed a Christian interpretation of the concept 'religion' on other parts of the world, ignoring the deeper history of 'religion' in those places, and even in the ancient history of Europe itself. The emergence of a secular social science has made little difference in this regard, as social scientists have, apparently unknowingly in many cases, continued an old Christian apologetic by supposing that the true meaning of religion lies in its binding force.

We see here that nothing much has changed since colonial times other than the normative value attached to specific African practices. What is constant is the insistence that good and bad do not belong together in 'true' religion.

The problem of 'the occult'

The working definition of religion that we have provided is placed in a broad theory of religion and politics (Ellis and ter Haar 2004) that corresponds to paradigms concerning the relationship between the visible and invisible worlds that are widespread among Africans. Political power is widely perceived as originating in the invisible world. This is one reason why many African politicians devote serious attention to the spirit world. As Max Weber (1946: 123) observed in one of his most celebrated essays, 'he who lets himself in for politics, that is, for power and force as means, contracts with diabolical powers'. This resonates in Africa, where religious activity is most persuasively understood as a search for spiritual power rather than in terms of an Augustinian theology. It is important to note in this regard that in African histories, ideas about the power of good and evil have typically been contained within a single mental framework. Many Africans regard power as morally ambiguous, and appear to have done so for centuries. This means that healers are also seen as potential killers due to the morally ambiguous nature of the spiritual powers that they are deemed to possess. The mystical powers attributed to them are not thought of as literally supernatural, but as *natural* forces.

What Terence Ranger and others call 'the occult' is therefore best understood in terms of mystical power. The central element in the identification of certain practices as 'occult' seems actually to be the experience of evil (cf. Ranger 2006: 355). However, the experience of evil is not limited to certain societies only. The main problem with using 'the occult' as a separate category is thus that it deprives analysts of sophisticated tools for thinking about culturally embedded notions of evil. Practices of the type labelled by Ranger as 'occult' do exist. The problem is how to understand them.

Social scientists tend to respond in one of three ways to reports of 'occult' events in Africa, such as violence motivated by witchcraft beliefs or killings carried out to obtain body parts. A frequent reaction is simply to avert one's gaze, considering such occurrences as aberrations that it would be distasteful or unjustifiable to include in any mainstream social analysis, or to question whether such things really happen. Terence Ranger seems to come close to this position, implying that the British police were wrong even to consider that the killing of the boy Adam, whose corpse they found in the River Thames in September 2001, might conceivably have been perpetrated in an attempt to acquire spiritual power. A second response is to interpret such matters as explicable in terms of specific cultures, an approach that few academics are likely to adopt nowadays. A third point of view, much in vogue in recent anthropology, is to regard such behaviour as expressions of economic forces, construed as so-called 'occult economies'. This last point of view is criticized quite effectively by Terence Ranger in his review article (2007). However, none of these three ways of reacting to 'occult' events is satisfactory, or at least not without considerable clarification and nuance.

We do not know, for lack of evidence, why the boy Adam was killed. Whether he was killed by someone in search of spiritual power is unknown. What is clear, though, is that killing in order to obtain spiritual power does take place. Where there is evidence that such an event has occurred, in our view any analysis has to begin by considering what the perpetrators might have had in mind. This is because '[t]he insider's perception of reality is instrumental to understanding and accurately describing situations and behaviours' (Fetterman 1989: 30). Hence, the pursuit of spiritual power falls within the category of religion, as suggested by our working definition. This is an operational definition that proceeds by 'taking African epistemologies seriously' (Ellis and ter Haar 2007), in other words by taking African modes of thought as a point of departure. Socially positive and socially harmful practices both exist within the field of religion. Referring to a specific act or practice as 'religious' does not imply any definite moral value since, academically speaking, religion itself is neither good nor bad, but morally ambiguous. Placing so-called 'occult' practices within a broader religious field helps us to understand the full range of their moral, social and political meanings.

Conclusion

The review article by Terence Ranger published in *Africa* is not centrally concerned with Scotland Yard's investigation of the supposed murder of the boy known to the British police as Adam. Really, what Ranger does is to use the story of the murder inquiry as a literary device, a peg on which to hang his discussion of the academic literature on 'the occult' in regard to Africa. He proposes his own method for investigating 'the occult', emphasizing the importance of context, the crucial need to disaggregate data, and the significance of history (Ranger 2007: 282). Putting things into context and sifting data carefully, however, no matter how skilfully done, will not get us much closer to the goal of understanding if this process is itself based on categories that are unsound. This, we have argued, is the case with the concept of 'the occult'.

Perhaps Ranger believes that the killing of people for ritual purposes, such as to obtain body parts, does not actually occur, or only very rarely. Yet there is overwhelming evidence that such practices do occur and have important social and political consequences. In Nigeria, according to official estimates, there were as many as 6,000 so-called 'ritual murders' between 1992 and 1996, although this figure does not seem to be the result of careful gathering of statistics (Harnischfeger 2006: 61). Archbishop Peter Akinola (2007), leader of Nigeria's 20 million practising Anglicans, has described how he himself came close to being killed in his youth by an uncle who 'was going to sacrifice me for a ritual to make money'. Akinola attributes his own religious vocation to the trauma of this experience. In the trial currently taking place in The Hague of Charles Taylor, the former President of Liberia has been alleged by former associates to have headed a group that regularly carried out such activities for the purpose of acquiring spiritual power (Marzah 2008: 6087–159). Comi Toulabor (2000) has written a brave essay on killings carried out by politicians in West Africa in pursuit of spiritual power. Regarding body parts, in the late 1980s and early 1990s, the township of Umlazi in Durban, South Africa, experienced a *'muti* murder' about once a fortnight, and some nearby settlements as many as six times per month (Evans 1992: 51). This suggests that the number of such killings in KwaZulu-Natal alone ran into dozens per year. In Tanzania, in April 2008 President Jakaya Kikwete publicly condemned the killing of albinos for body parts; nineteen killings had reportedly taken place in the previous year (BBC 2008). As for witchcraft accusations, the large number of these in some countries is well attested, for example in South Africa, where hundreds of people have been killed on these grounds (Ralushai Commission 1996), as well as in other parts of Africa (ter Haar 2007). In some African diaspora communities also, there have been accounts of serious crimes being committed for reasons connected to a belief in spiritual power. These have led for example to prosecutions of people accused of assault in regard to beatings they have inflicted on children suspected of witchcraft (Dodd 2005).

It may be noted that we have drawn examples from southern, eastern and West Africa here, as well as from outside the continent. One of the objections that Ranger has made in regard to the methods of the British police is precisely that they have lumped data from different parts of Africa, failing to disaggregate and specify. We emphasize that our purpose is not to suggest that there is 'an aggregated African occult' (Ranger 2007: 277) in the sense that acts shown to have occurred in one place are therefore liable to take place throughout the subcontinent. Our point is to suggest that such practices do actually occur with some frequency in separate parts of Africa and that they are in fact religious actions in the sense that they emanate from the belief in an invisible world inhabited by spiritual forces deemed to have effective powers over the material world. They reflect religious ideas that are quite widespread in Africa, although of course with regional variations. The authors of probably the most detailed historical study of so-called medicine murders, in regard to colonial Lesotho, have no doubt that 'medicine murder was, and is, a hideous reality' (Murray and Sanders 2005: 290). Moreover, they explicitly suggest a framework for comparison with other countries within the southern African region and also find the idea of a comparison with West Africa to be admissible (*ibid.*: 299–310, 443, note 3).

We should be clear about the point of listing these examples of religious practices associated with criminal acts. The widespread acceptance by Africanist scholars of 'the occult' as an analytical category appears to have caused some of them to dismiss from the outset reports of crimes allegedly carried out in pursuit of spiritual power. Consequently, they may feel little need to examine empirical data at all. Thus Ranger has made no effort to investigate the death of the boy Adam beyond commenting on reports of the police investigation. He has not carried out significant research into the actual occurrence or non-occurrence of the practices alleged. Furthermore, some academics (for example van Dijk 2001), equipped with theories of questionable value concerning 'occult' economies, disqualify other sectors of society altogether as legitimate interpreters of reality. Those dismissed in this way include not only European police forces but also, most importantly, African communities both in Africa and in Europe. Yet these so-called 'occult' practices are also forms of serious crime, in some cases involving killing, people trafficking, and so on. They surely demand empirical investigation in the first instance. Finally, as we have noted elsewhere (Ellis and ter Haar 2004: 149–50), social scientists who discuss beliefs and practices of this sort outside their proper context fail to appreciate their seriousness in moral terms, as threats to human life and human rights.

References

Akinola, P. (2007) *The Times*, 5 July, interview with Ruth Gledhill.

Asad, T. (1993) *Genealogies of Religion: discipline and reasons of power in Christianity and Islam*. Baltimore MD: Johns Hopkins University Press.

BBC World Service (2008) 'Tanzania in witchdoctor crackdown', 3 April, (http://news.bbc.co.Uk/2/hi/africa/7327989.stm), accessed 15 June 2008.

Chung, Chin Hong (2007) 'Religion-before religion and religion-after religion' in G. ter Haar and Y. Tsuruoka (eds) (2007) *Religion and Society: an agenda for the twenty-first century*. Brill: Leiden.

Comaroff, Jean and John L. (1999) 'Occult economies and the violence of abstraction: notes from the South African postcolony', *American Ethnologist* 26 (2): 279–303.

Dodd, V. (2005) 'More children "victims of cruel exorcisms"', *The Guardian*, 4 June, p. 10.

Durkheim, E. (1912) *Les formes élémentaires de la vie religieuse: le système totémique en Australie*. Paris: Alcan.

Ellis, S. and G. ter Haar (2004) *Worlds of Power: religious thought and political practice in Africa*. London and New York NY: C. Hurst and Co. and Oxford University Press.

——— (2007) 'Religion and politics: taking African epistemologies seriously', *Journal of Modern African Studies* 45 (3): 385–401.

Evans, J. (1992) 'On brûle bien les sorcières: les meurtres "muti" et leur répression', *Politique Africaine* 48: 47–57.

Fetterman, D.M. (1989) *Ethnography, Step by Step*. Newbury Park CA: Sage Publications.

Hamischfeger, J. (2006) 'State decline and the return of occult powers: the case of Prophet Eddy in Nigeria', *Magic, Ritual, and Witchcraft* 1 (1): 56–78.

Idowu, E. Bolaji (1962) *Olódùmarè: God in Yoruba belief*. London: Longman.

Jenkins, P. and D. Maier-Katkin (1992) 'Satanism: myth and reality in a contemporary moral panic', *Crime, Law and Social Change* 17 (1): 53–75.

Kenyatta, J. (1938) *Facing Mount Kenya: the tribal life of the Gikuyu*. London: Seeker and Warburg.

Marzah, J. (2008) 14 March Testimony in the trial of Charles G. Taylor. (http://www.sc-sl.org/Transcripts/Taylor/14March2008.pdf), accessed 15 June 2008 [no longer available].

Masuzawa, T. (2005) *The Invention of World Religions: or, how European universalism was preserved in the language of pluralism.* Chicago IL: University of Chicago Press.

———— (2007) 'Theory without method: situating a discourse analysis on religion' in G. ter Haar and Y. Tsuruoka (eds) (2007) *Religion and Society: an agenda for the twenty-first century.* Brill: Leiden.

Mbiti, J. S. (1969) *African Religions and Philosophy.* London: Heinemann.

Momigliano, A. (1977) *Essays in Ancient and Modern Historiography.* Oxford: Basil Blackwell.

Murray, C. and P. Sanders (2005) *Medicine Murder in Colonial Lesotho: the anatomy of a moral crisis.* Edinburgh: Edinburgh University Press for the International African Institute.

Pagden, A. (1986) *The Fall of Natural Man: the American Indian and the origins of comparative ethnology.* First paperback edition. Cambridge: Cambridge University Press.

Peel, J.D.Y. (2000) *Religious Encounter and the Making of the Yoruba.* Bloomington IN: Indiana University Press.

Platvoet, J.G. (1996) 'The religions of Africa in their historical order' in J.G. Platvoet, J.L. Cox and J.K. Olupona (eds), *The Study of Religions in Africa: past, present and prospects.* Cambridge: Roots and Branches.

Ralushai Commission (1996) 'Report of the Commission of Inquiry into Witchcraft Violence and Ritual Murders in the Northern Province of the Republic of South Africa'. Pietersburg: The Commission.

Ranger, T.O. (1967) *Revolt in Southern Rhodesia, 1896–97: a study in African resistance.* London: Heinemann.

———— (1991) 'African Traditional Religion' in S. Sutherland and P. Clarke (eds), *The Study of Religion, Traditional and New Religion.* London: Routledge.

———— (2006) 'African religion, witchcraft and the liberation war in Zimbabwe' in B. Nicolini (ed.), *Studies in Witchcraft, Magic, War and Peace in Africa: nineteenth and twentieth centuries.* Lewiston NY: Edwin Mellen Press.

———— (2007) 'Scotland Yard in the bush: medicine murders, child witches and the construction of the occult: a literature review', *Africa* 77 (2): 272–83.

Ranger, T. and I.N. Kimambo (eds) (1972) *The Historical Study of African Religion: with special reference to East and Central Africa.* London: Heinemann Educational.

Ronca, I. (1992) 'What's in two names: old and new thoughts on the history and etymology of *religio* and *superstitio*' in S. Prete (ed.), *Respublica Literarum: Studies in the Classical Tradition* 15 (1): 43–60.

ter Haar, G. (ed.) (2007) *Imagining Evil: witchcraft beliefs and accusations in contemporary Africa*. Trenton NJ: Africa World Press.

Thomas, K. (1973) *Religion and the Decline of Magic*. London: Penguin.

Toulabor, C. (2000) 'Sacrifices humains et politiques: quelques exemples contemporains en Afrique' in P. Konings, W. van Binsbergen and G. Hesseling (eds), *Trajectoires de Libération en Afrique Contemporaine: hommage à Robert Buijtenhuijs*. Paris: Karthala: 207–21.

Turner, H. (1976) 'The approach to Africa's new religious movements', *African Perspectives* 2: 13–23.

van Dijk, R. (2001) '"Voodoo" on the doorstep: young Nigerian prostitutes and magic policing in the Netherlands', *Africa* 71 (4): 558–86.

Weber, M. (1946) 'Politics as a vocation' [Politik als Beruf] in H.H. Gerth and C. Wright Mills (eds). *From Max Weber: essays in sociology*. New York: Oxford University Press: 77–128.

Westerlund, D. (1985) *African Religion in African Scholarship: a preliminary study of the religious and political background*. Stockholm: Almqvist and Wicksell International.

Abstract

In recent years, it has become common for academic writers to use 'the occult' as an analytical category to which are assigned various types of mystical belief and activity that are quite widespread in Africa, including those often described as 'magic' and 'witchcraft'. It is notable that all these concepts generally go undefined. The present article argues that much of the current academic vocabulary used to describe and analyse the invisible world that many Africans believe to exist is tainted by an intellectual history associated with colonialism. Instead, we propose that much African thought and action related to the invisible world should be considered in terms of religion, with the latter being defined contextually as a belief in the existence of an invisible world, distinct but not separate from the visible one, that is home to spiritual beings with effective powers over the material world.

13

WITCH-HUNTING IN CENTRAL MADAGASCAR
1828–1861*

There was a time when historians and social scientists seemed close to agreement about the study of witchcraft. Techniques drawn from the anthropology of Africa were applied to Tudor and Stuart England to explain the rise and decline of witch-hunting.[1] Authors produced general studies in which European and African evidence appeared side by side.[2] Edited volumes placed papers on witchcraft in early modern Europe alongside analyses of Africa and other parts of what was then called the Third World.[3] It was often implied that witchcraft was some sort of gauge of social strain, although Mary Douglas, introducing one such volume in 1970, made a withering critique of the 'superbly untestable' assumption that witchcraft accusations were 'a symptom of disorder and moral collapse'.[4]

Since the 1970s, studies of witchcraft in different ages and continents have drifted apart. Some influential studies have considered European witchcraft belief as a form of discourse in the first instance, to be understood in the context of the mentalities of a particular time and place.[5] Perhaps this reflects the growth of a general doubt about the ability of social science to propose theories, analogous to those

---

* I am grateful for comments on an earlier draft of this paper by Gerrie ter Haar. Translations from foreign languages are my own unless otherwise stated.

of natural science, that can be applied universally. As far as Africa is concerned, however, some recent studies by anthropologists continue to see witchcraft, in the words of one critic, as a set of 'shifting and versatile practices and idioms deployed within local communities in response to wider social forces', and most particularly as a way of contesting or appropriating modernity.[6]

One of the main features of many recent anthropological studies is their tendency to view witchcraft as an element of culture (which indeed it is), but not as a religious belief (which it also is). If we define religion as a belief in the existence of spiritual forces that may have an effect on human life,[7] then a belief in the existence of a malign mystical force that can be used or abused by human agents, such as is designated by the word 'witchcraft', needs to be situated in the first instance within the wider field of religious thought. The need to study religious beliefs as a coherent whole was long ago noted by Clifford Geertz. The 'anthropological study of religion', he wrote thirty-six years ago, is 'a two-stage operation: first, an analysis of the system of meanings embodied in the symbols which make up the religion proper, and, second, the relating of these systems to social-structural and psychological processes'. Geertz went on to express his 'dissatisfaction with so much of contemporary social anthropological work in religion' at that time, not because it was concerned with the second of these two stages, but because 'it neglects the first, and in so doing takes for granted what most needs to be elucidated'.[8] A recent study of witchcraft in South Africa notes that belief in a malign, mystical force perceived as being channelled through human agents is, like other forms of belief in 'invisible powers and mystical processes', impossible to prove or disprove by scientific means. Hence, empirically based research can neither verify nor falsify the existence of 'witchcraft'. Another essay based on fieldwork in Africa reminds us that witchcraft cannot be seen only as 'symbolic politics', and that witchcraft accusations in particular must be seen as actual political processes.[9] The same could be said of any society in which witchcraft accusations create political and social effects. The implication of these remarks is that the social sciences and the humanities can study the content of witchcraft belief and can also explain why some people may accuse others of practising witchcraft, but that this is indeed an operation in two stages.[10]

The effect of these preliminary remarks is to distinguish between witchcraft as a category of religious belief, on the one hand, and the accusations that may be made on the basis of such a belief, on the other. Different methods of analysis are required for each.

I: Methodological considerations

This article concerns an extended campaign of witch-hunting in a country—Madagascar—that lies off the coast of Africa but that has assimilated over the centuries ideas and technologies from many parts of the Indian Ocean and also from Europe. For present purposes, it is regarded as legitimate to analyse the suppression of alleged witches—that is, people accused of being the human agents of a mystical force that the persecutors suppose to exist—as a form of political action. The comparison of the methods used to suppress the perceived practice of witchcraft in different times and places, while fraught with difficulty, is both feasible and useful. In short, the reasons for considering the suppression of practices considered as witchcraft as a form of political action are as valid now as they ever were, although with two major qualifications.

The first of these is that any study of witchcraft should concern in the first instance the nature of the belief in such a phenomenon, and its relationship with other associated ideas in their original context. It cannot be assumed that beliefs extant outside Europe, which bear a superficial resemblance to witchcraft as it was perceived in Europe in early modern times, are necessarily the same as the historical European version. The apparent similarities between European and non-European variants may be due largely to the way scholars—especially British ones—have thought about certain types of religious belief in Africa. Thus one anthropologist wrote regarding the literature on Africa:

> It is most likely that witchcraft may have become a separate topic for anthropology because of its appearance in the history of our own [that is, British] society. This occurrence, by supplying us with a ready-made

term, would be sufficient to destroy those cautions we observe in the translation of culture in connection with other problems.[11]

Some scholars have cited as an example the intricate theologies of the Yoruba of Nigeria concerning the soul, destiny and the moral self, that have sometimes been labelled as 'witchcraft' by authors writing in English.[12] The term 'witchcraft' is hardly appropriate in this case because it risks producing in the reader a set of assumptions about the moral nature of Yoruba beliefs and their place in a putative evolutionary scheme. By the same token, the enduring Malagasy belief in the existence of a virtuous mystical force known as *hasina*, and of its malign counterpart known as *mosavy*, cannot be assumed to correspond precisely to beliefs recorded in European history. The first half of the present essay sets out these religious ideas in their historical context in old Madagascar, using this local vocabulary for the sake of clarity; an explanation of how they formed the basis of political and social action then follows.

A second qualification concerns the assessment of the political and social aspects of witchcraft suppression. It has become apparent from the study of African history over the last fifty years that specific events which occurred in Africa cannot automatically be assimilated into 'categories of analysis ... drawn from Europe', such as building European-style states, the growth of capitalism[13] or, indeed, the spread of modernity. Although Madagascar, with its distinctive history, cannot be considered typical of Africa as a whole, the same point holds good. Hence a particular narrative concerning the suppression of the supposed human agents of a cosmic force of evil has to be examined in the first instance in its own terms.

There is abundant evidence in many societies that people have believed in the existence of forms of mystical harm which can be inflicted by some human beings on others, with or without malice aforethought. In English these perceived forms of evil are most commonly called 'witchcraft' or 'sorcery'. The classic definitions of these terms are offered by E.E. Evans-Pritchard, the founder of modern anthropological studies of the subject. He describes sorcery as 'magic that is illicit or is considered immoral', a mystical weapon that can in theory be used by anyone, whereas witchcraft emanates from a quality believed to be innate in some people only.[14] But beliefs in forms of mystical evil that can be employed by human agents do not always correspond to the two distinct forms identified by Evans-Pritchard in his studies of the Azande of Sudan.[15] Above all, not all societies maintain a theological or philosophical distinction between radically opposed metaphysical forces of good and evil in the same way as orthodox Christians and Muslims do. It is relevant to note that some key items of religious vocabulary in Africa today reflect the habit, in the quite recent past, among European missionaries, of regarding all forms of indigenous religion as suspect, and possibly even satanic—a tendency which caused them to label a whole set of beliefs as 'witchcraft'. Included in this category are many varieties of initiation, divination and healing. Some of the best recent studies of witch persecutions in Africa point out how the performance of actions or rituals that were once respectable, or at least permissible, may, under the influence of a dualistic Christian theology, be perceived as witchcraft, which, in turn, may be seen as a form of lethal, radical evil inspired by Satan.[16] The history of Christian conversion, together with the use on a world scale of languages originating in Western Europe, has led to a Babel of misunderstanding. We cannot be sure that an English-speaking African who uses the word 'witchcraft' today is referring to the same type of thing as was meant by English-speakers four centuries ago when they uttered this same word.

For these reasons, 'witchcraft' cannot be used straightforwardly as a technical term that, like other items in the lexicon of social science, is supposed to describe something of universal application. Belief in forms of malign mystical force cannot be compared between one society and another without further inquiry. Some such comparison is necessary, however, if studies of the African continent and its islands, in ancient or modern times, are not to be assigned to an exotic category where comparison is considered possible only with other African cases, and never with European or other instances. If this were to happen it would be tantamount to a suggestion that witchcraft belief today is a phenomenon existing in Africa, but not elsewhere. Indeed, some recent literature on 'witchcraft' in Africa comes uncomfortably close to this position. Perhaps it was something akin to the problem this presents that Evans-Pritchard was thinking of when, according to one of his colleagues, he mused, 'there's only one method in social anthropology, the comparative method—and that's impossible'.[17]

Hence, I approach the object of study in the first instance by defining briefly what the people concerned—the inhabitants of central Madagascar in the eighteenth and nineteenth centuries—meant when they spoke of *mosavy*, a form of mystical evil generally translated as 'witchcraft'. I then proceed by considering why massive, successive, bouts of persecution of people accused of this offence took place in the mid nineteenth century. It is argued that persecutions of people deemed to be anti-social in terms of the dominant style of discourse of any particular time and place can be compared if suitable precautions are taken.

II. Pre-colonial Imerina and Madagascar

The perennial combat against metaphysical evil in Madagascar was for centuries associated with the nut of a small, deceptively attractive, tree that is native to parts of this enormous island, two and a half times the size of Great Britain. The tree and its nut are called *tangena* in the Malagasy language, which is spoken throughout the island in various dialects. *Tanghinia venenifera*—the nut's botanical name—is bitter and highly poisonous.[18] In the past Malagasy people sometimes administered shavings of *tangena* nuts to people suspected of having engaged in forms of spiritual subversion called *mosavy*, and sometimes to those accused of other offences.

The Malagasy have generally believed in the reality of *mosavy* as a force for the destabilization of the proper order of society since the seventeenth century at least, when the first relevant historical records were being produced.[19] Many of their ideas about *mosavy* no doubt came originally from East Africa, as the word itself is of Swahili origin.[20.] The use of poison ordeals to detect the presence of *mosavy* in humans was probably also of African origin, perhaps introduced by Madagascar's first inhabitants. These consisted of groups of people originating in what is now Indonesia, but many of these, before moving on to Madagascar over a thousand years ago, had settled in East Africa, where they incorporated local vocabulary into their Austronesian language and acquired some African technologies.[21] Poison was one of several types of ordeal employed by Malagasy to investigate people suspected of using mystical forms of evil. When *tangena* was used, the poison was often administered to an animal deemed to represent the person accused: if the animal died, the person was considered guilty and could be punished by other means. From a relatively early period, the poison ordeal was occasionally applied in some parts of the island to whole families, sometimes even at their own request in cases where people wished to establish their innocence of *mosavy*, the most anti-social of crimes.[22]

At the turn of the nineteenth century, Madagascar came to be dominated politically by a kingdom known as Imerina, situated in the densely populated central highlands.[23] Under this government, a person suspected of spiritual subversion, and sometimes even of theft or other mundane offences, had to drink a solution of *tangena* shavings in water, followed by pieces of chicken-skin. Vomiting the latter was taken as a sign of innocence. Some people thus tested died from the effects of the poison. Others failed to vomit the chicken-skin, in which case they were considered guilty and liable to be executed. Oral traditions and memories first written down by Malagasy in the mid nineteenth century suggest that the application of the poison directly to humans had become a general test of guilt in Imerina less than a hundred years previously, and that use of the ordeal as a technique in the administration of justice was regulated by Imerina's founding king, who assumed the name Andrianampoinimerina on gaining power.[24]

After the unification, in around 1800, of the minor principalities previously existing in the highlands, successive rulers of the kingdom of Imerina, allying themselves with British power in the Indian Ocean, aimed to conquer the whole of Madagascar. The Anglo-Merina alliance, sealed by treaty in 1817, was to dominate the island until the acquisition of Madagascar as a colonial possession by France in 1895–6.[25] Merina rulers began to refer to their state as the kingdom of Madagascar, and were in time recognized by key European powers as sovereigns of the island, although they were never able to exercise effective control over the whole of it. The main British interest at the outset was to enlist the king of Imerina as an ally to stamp out Madagascar's slave exports. King Radama I (reigned 1809–28) welcomed missionaries from the London Missionary Society (LMS). They were highly impressed by Imerina and by the hospitality offered by this personable, ambitious and ruthless young monarch, an admirer of his contemporary, Napoleon Bonaparte. But the course of the Anglo-Merina alliance was anything but smooth after the initial period of intense co-operation. From the mid-1830s until 1861, the government of Radama's successor, Queen Ranavalona I (reigned 1828–61), avidly continued to adopt Western techniques new to Madagascar, including a literate bureaucracy and a standing army, and to import Western firearms, used for some two centuries already in those parts of the island with access to international trade. At the same time, government policy under Ranavalona I was to prevent the queen's subjects from receiving baptism. All but a handful of foreigners were refused permission to settle in the royal dominions. British missionaries were expelled from the island from the mid-1830s, and the small Malagasy Christian community existed clandestinely, suffering sporadic bouts of persecution.[26]

When Queen Ranavalona I died in 1861, Madagascar was again opened to foreign traders, diplomats and missionaries. After a later queen and her consort, the prime minister, had themselves received baptism in 1869, large numbers of loyal subjects converted to Christianity. Madagascar became a focus of interest for British evangelicals. Informed by the publications of the LMS and other missionaries, who had a vested interest in emphasizing the most successful aspects of their work, a section of British opinion considered the self-proclaimed kingdom of Madagascar to be a brilliant example of Christian conversion accompanying economic and social development. Only in the decade before French colonization did British missionaries cease deluding themselves about the extent to which the Church and the government were actually the tools of a Merina elite intent on self-promotion and enrichment.

In effect, Queen Ranavalona I's accession to the throne in 1828 was the result of a military coup organized by a clique of generals and officials able to exploit the establishment of a standing army. This military-dominated expansionist government, unfriendly to missionaries but enthusiastic for foreign technology, was to oversee administration of the deadly *tangena* ordeal on a very large scale until the queen's death in 1861. At times the poison was applied to entire population groups on an unprecedented scale. A French Jesuit,

Father Marc Finaz, who visited Madagascar from 1855 to 1857 and received much information from his compatriot, the adventurer Jean Laborde (who had spent years at the royal court and spoke fluent Malagasy), has left some especially vivid descriptions of the *tangena* ordeal in his unpublished diaries. '*Tangena* is used on the slightest pretext and even without any pretext at all', he noted.[27] Finaz, a careful observer, thought that almost every adult in Imerina had undergone the ordeal, some of them more than twelve times. It is clear that the poison ordeal was not always fatal, because individual nuts might vary in strength, victims might expel most of the poison by vomiting, and—not least—the officials who administered the poison could adjust the dose.

Imerina proper had a population of perhaps five or six hundred thousand in the mid nineteenth century, in an island with a total population of perhaps two to three million.[28] The Reverend William Ellis, writing in the 1830s slightly before the worst excesses, used information compiled by the first generation of LMS missionaries in the island to calculate that one-tenth of the population of Imerina took the poison at least once in the course of their lifetimes, and that a fifth of these died as a consequence. 'And thus', he estimated, 'a fiftieth part of the population is carried off by this most formidable instrument of destruction'. He put the number of deaths at some three thousand per year.[29] Estimates made by other contemporaries, Malagasy and European, range from two hundred thousand to four hundred thousand deaths over the thirty-three years of Ranavalona I's rule.[30] Such high numbers for deaths from the poison ordeal are treated seriously in a modern study of historical demographics.[31]

These figures may well be overestimates, as there were periods of relative inactivity in between major national purges. Both foreign missionaries and later Malagasy Christian authors had a tendency to portray the traditionalist government of Ranavalona I in a dark light. Moreover some slaves who failed the ordeal were revived by their owners, 'by giving them copious draughts of water, in which certain herbs have been boiled', after which they were discreetly sold in distant parts of the island, so as not to lose their value.[32] Nevertheless, it can hardly be doubted that very large numbers of people died through the application of the poison ordeal, and that the 'kingdom of

Madagascar', as the government styled itself, oversaw a redoubtable regime of destruction of human life. To determine why this was so requires first a brief survey of the role of religious belief in Malagasy statecraft over a long period.

III. The polities of old Madagascar

The first sources for a reasonably precise political history of Madagascar are the writings of the earliest European travellers to the island—slave traders and missionaries who left written accounts from the sixteenth century onwards.[33] They described an island containing some clusters of population whose political institutions European contemporaries recognized as states or kingdoms. These Malagasy political formations appear to have taken shape over centuries through the evolution of techniques of domination and subordination as they circulated from one part of Madagascar to another. Ideas and technologies such as literacy in the Malagasy language transcribed in Arabic script, regarded as a potent religious instrument, were imported from an early period by, among others, Islamized settlers and traders from the South-East Asian islands, the Persian Gulf and East Africa. Once Madagascar had become a port of call for European and American East Indiamen and slave traders, Europe also exercised a considerable influence on the evolution of Malagasy kingdoms which imported silver coin and firearms in exchange for slaves. During the seventeenth century, and until the rise after 1750 of slave-importing sugar economies in the islands today known as Mauritius and Réunion, the most powerful of Madagascar's kings lived on the island's west coast, the one most visited by Europeans. The material assets acquired by these rulers supplemented the ideological and spiritual attributes that were the basis of enduring authority. It would be wrong, however, to surmise that this represented a gradual replacement of the religious base of power by a secular command of wealth and coercion, for all these were inextricably linked.

European travellers composing a systematic description of any particular Malagasy polity often devoted chapters to government, religion and various aspects of custom in an early form of ethnography.[34] They had only a limited aspiration to reflect the worldview of the

Malagasy themselves, whose concepts of power, authority and legitimacy were sometimes very different from those of their European chroniclers.[35] This is clear both from a careful reading of the European sources of the period and also from later sources which provide greater insight into key aspects of Malagasy traditions of thought, most notably the texts partly or wholly authored by Malagasy in the nineteenth century.[36] Among other particularities, Malagasy before colonial times were generally more inclined than their European contemporaries to suppose that spiritual forces suffused all aspects of their lives and of nature rather than being restricted to the sphere corresponding to conventional European notions of religion, now or even then. This is not to say that the Malagasy struck most European visitors as people of an especially ethereal character, since they were also known for their hard-headed attitudes towards war and commerce in general and the slave trade in particular.

For the Malagasy, ritual practices intended to communicate with the invisible world were inseparable from all life and action, and did not belong to an identifiable category of the 'religious', in so far as that is possible given that the Malagasy language did not have any word corresponding to 'religion'. Some early European authors, such as Étienne de Flacourt, an official of the French Compagnie des Indes, thought that the Malagasy actually had no religion. This was not because Flacourt was ignorant of Malagasy customs, but rather because he could identify no sphere of ritual oriented towards a deity and no dogma or caste of priests that, in the opinion of a contemporary European, qualified as religious.[37] Malagasy people were inclined to believe that all power—the very breath of life as well as power in a political sense—was derived from spiritual forces. These could include not only the invisible spirits of the ancestors or of previous kings, but also the spirits of such highly visible but (in Western science) inanimate objects as running water, rocks and mountain-tops, and the earth itself, all of which were believed to be sources of an essence that had the potential both to enhance life and to destroy it. The nut of the *tangena* tree was thus understood to be animate, containing an inherent power evidenced by the alarming effects produced by eating it. A surviving manuscript written by one of the religious specialists at the court of Ranavalona I includes a transcription of the prayers used in administering the poison, in which the nut was addressed as a living being, and requested to do its work of discerning metaphysical evil present in a person or animal.[38] As one Malagasy put it at a later date, 'people imagined that the *tangena* contained a sort of spirit which could sound out the human heart and which entered the stomach of the accused person with the poison, punishing the guilty while sparing the innocent'.[39] The spirit of the nut had a name, Manamango. In Malagasy societies without widespread literacy,[40] familiarity with such forces was not derived from texts but was instead transmitted through action and speech.

Common to those kingdoms in old Madagascar which succeeded one another, rising and declining in the extent of their influence, was the notion of *hasina*.[41] This designates the invisible essence of power and fertility that can be channelled to human beings, particularly through ancestors. Maintaining this life-force demands respect for ritual obligations and taboos that in effect bind members of a family or a community to each other, to nature, and to the land. The foremost principle of political authorities throughout the island was that they should embody *hasina* and bestow it on their subjects. Various customs and institutions deemed to be of ancestral origin were associated with the transmission of such power. Some of the most fundamental Malagasy ideas concerning political hierarchy arose from the prestige associated with a person or family considered to be a channel of exceptional virtue by reason of her, his or its ancestry.[42] Mystical power of this type, when applied for the negative purposes of destroying order and fertility, was tantamount to *mosavy*, which is, therefore, *hasina* in reverse.[43]

The oldest ideas of political authority must have been brought to Madagascar with the first settlers, and were then constantly enriched with new inventions and imports.[44] The concept of *hasina* is certainly older than the quite extensive political units that European writers from the seventeenth century onwards regarded as corresponding reasonably well to their own notions of kingdoms. The rulers of the many polities of pre-colonial Madagascar were transmitters of this metaphysical essence, which was more crucial than any powers they might have as organizers of labour and repression or redistributors of wealth. All Malagasy political authorities, from kings to simple family heads, channelled *hasina* by invoking the invisible forces of the world through word and ritual gesture, by securing the services of diviners, and by arranging their affairs, in details ranging from the shape of their houses to the naming and treatment of their children, in conformity with what they believed to be the pattern of the cosmos.

The fundamental task of a Malagasy king was to reign: to dispense blessing, notably through the practice of appropriate rituals, to ensure fertility, to prevent the subversion of the natural order, and to channel the *hasina* of his[45] ancestors to his subjects. These core religious aspects of political authority were no doubt always associated with certain forms of material benefit and coercion, but it was the advent of the European slave trade that radically increased the scope of possible enrichment through trade and war and contributed to the development of a more formidable monarchical power. Successive Sakalava kings on Madagascar's west coast in the seventeenth and eighteenth centuries acquired substantial armed followings and wealth in coin, thanks to their relations with European, Swahili and Arab traders, enabling them to exercise influence over large areas.[46] Various polities, situated in different parts of this huge island, succeeded in asserting their influence as the patterns of the slave trade shifted, and as princes rose and fell. Memories of the major polities and dynasties survive in the form of today's ethnic labels, such as Sakalava, Betsimisaraka and Merina, originally names applied to whoever owed allegiance to a common authority rather than being ethnonyms in a modern sense.[47.] The increase in the command of material resources reflected in the history of these polities did not detract from the fact that the core of political legitimacy lay in the ability to channel the spiritual quality of *hasina*. Hence Toakafo, the Sakalava king of Boina in north-west Madagascar, a slave trader and warrior (and a ferocious consumer of liquor!), probably the most powerful king in the island at the time, was described by a Dutch slave trader in 1715 as 'honoured and feared as a god by his subjects'.[48]

The combination of religious authority with material aspects of domination was evident in the kingdom that emerged in the late eighteenth century under Andrianampoinimerina (reigned *c*. 1783–1809), the most famous king in Madagascar's history since he was the founder of the Merina kingdom that was later to attempt the conquest of the whole island. It is telling that, in the kingdom which he founded, one of the sovereign's titles was 'God visible to the eye', while the death of a sovereign was often referred to as 'Heaven and earth turned upside down'.[49] King Andrianampoinimerina (whose own name means 'the prince at the heart of Imerina') was, like his successors, at the centre of a system thought to mirror the cosmos, with the king being the articulation between heaven and earth. In the Merina kingdom he established, royal authority acquired an extraordinarily pervasive domination of a society where the sovereign was involved in the daily life of every subject. This was in spite of the monarch's lack of much resembling a bureaucracy. Behaviour and thought were governed by intricate rules, conventions and gestures having a force derived from their spiritual aspect which was reflected in everyday relationships and actions. Royal subjects absorbed such ideas from birth, making this a society with a high degree of social integration and political control. It was through ritual that royal power penetrated local communities that were in many respects self-governing.

We should resist the notion that the religious practices which existed in Madagascar before the nineteenth century were 'ethnic' in nature, in the sense of defining and being proper to a bounded group defined by speech or culture. It would be more accurate to say that many religious practices and ideas were current over wide areas and in different polities, while a feature of the most successful rulers was their ability to innovate in ritual matters. A successful ruler, by definition, was one who succeeded in transmitting *hasina* throughout his reign, as measured by fertility and harmony. Sovereigns therefore strove to control the instruments for the transmission of *hasina*, essentially the religious systems of ritual and divination. Queen Ranavalona I was perhaps unique in attempting to create an ethnic religion, in a conscious attempt to underpin the new state institutions established in imitation of European models by her predecessor King Radama I. Her ministers aspired to employ certain conventions that, they had learned, were regarded by Europeans as having international application, such as an obligation on all residents to obey the law of the land.[50] Partly as a result of contacts with British Protestants and French Catholics, Ranavalona and her ministers deliberately set about creating a Merina national religion from existing elements such as the practice of circumcision, transformed into a ritual in which the whole kingdom was represented as a single descent-group stemming from the royal ancestors.[51] A uniform corpus of religious ideas and rituals was therefore imposed on the queen's subjects.

The religious cosmologies of Madagascar were highly dualistic, possibly as a result of the degree of Islamic influence in the island since the twelfth or thirteenth centuries.[52] The ancient Malagasy notion that the cosmos had an exact and regular design, reflected in topography and astrology, generated a series of negative concepts twinned with positive ones. Thus, the complex systems of taboo and divination which guided correct behaviour, typical of Malagasy religious practice, also served to identify incorrect or sacrilegious behaviour. Such ideas were current in all parts of Madagascar and could be as binding on sovereigns as on their subjects: the Dutch slave trader who described King Toakafo of Boina in 1715 noted that this king killed those of his own children who were born on a Sunday or a Tuesday, days which were considered inauspicious by his diviners.[53]

IV. Merina political ideology

Andrianampoinimerina, the unifier of Imerina who died in 1809, has been represented in most Merina oral traditions as an almost superhumanly wise lawgiver and ruler. However, it is clear Andrianampoinimerina owed his success in part to some base political skills, starting with the manipulation of popular grievances in the town of Ambohimanga that enabled him to overthrow its ruler. The Malagasy historian Raombana, writing in the 1850s with access to excellent sources, describes this in detail.[54] The slave trade was growing fast in response to demand from the French sugar-colonies Mauritius and Réunion. Having won power with the support of a faction with interests in the slave trade, Andrianampoinimerina cornered the main slave markets throughout the central highlands, drove up prices, and secured a better supply of guns than any other Malagasy ruler.

Merina political ideology, as we have seen, considered historical reality 'not as the product of human agency, but of ancestral beneficence, *hasina*, which flowed downwards on obedient Merina from long dead ancestors in a sacred stream'.[55] Andrianampoinimerina, a political entrepreneur with a questionable right to rule, became legitimate only gradually, as he was seen to transmit this *hasina* effectively. This he did by carving himself a role in religious rituals considered to bestow this vital force. Various groups under his subjection had their own religious symbols, known as *sampy*. These were cult objects credited with channelling power from the invisible world for collective rather than personal use, likely to be used both aggressively as well as for protection. *Sampy* were made mostly of vegetable matter, sometimes decorated with bits of silver or crocodile teeth, for example. They were considered receptacles of a spiritual power with a personal character, rather like the *tangena* nut.[56]

As he expanded his area of rule, subjecting numerous self-governing groups, Andrianampoinimerina took control of the most potent *sampy* and outlawed those liable to be used by his enemies. 'He plucked from obscurity local or tribal amulets to turn them into the official protectors of all the Merina', noted one French colonial official and scholar; the king thus codified their accompanying rituals and made them obligatory. He often entrusted these powerful objects to his leading generals, 'creating, so to speak, a state religion' based on a national pantheon.[57] To the British missionaries who arrived in Imerina only a couple of decades later, the *sampy* were 'idols', products of ignorance, superstition, and even charlatanism. One LMS missionary, noting that the king 'did repeatedly convene the population to witness the consecrating or setting apart of several of the present national idols', asserted that Andrianampoinimerina 'is said to have acted thus solely from political motives, having their foundation in the conviction that some kind of religious or superstitious influence was useful in the government of a nation'.[58]

This last description implies a distinction between religious belief and realpolitik that would surely not have been shared by the person it describes. For Andrianampoinimerina as for his subjects, the *sampy* were as powerful in their own way as guns. It was normal that the king would seek to control them and to prevent his subjects from honouring other *sampy*. People who refused to respect the king's sacred objects, or who harboured others, were suspected of undermining the order Andrianampoinimerina had now established. The surest method of detecting such disruptive people was through the use of the *tangena* poison ordeal, usually applied to an animal taken as representative of the person under suspicion but also applied by Andrianampoinimerina directly to people suspected of mystical subversion.[59] Such people could be identified collectively as well as individually, in keeping with prevailing notions about the collective aspect of people's identity. 'For now and then', wrote the historian Raombana, who for privacy's sake made a point of writing in the English he had learned at a nonconformist academy in Manchester, '[Andrianampoinimerina] orders the *Tangena* ordeal to be administered to the whole population of Towns and villages (with the exception of children) for to discover those who in his opinion had magics and witchcrafts, and awful to relate, a great number of them dies through this horrible Test'.[60]

The most ruthless rulers in central Madagascar, including the very king deposed by Andrianampoinimerina when he took power, sometimes sold for export as slaves people accused of using subversive mystical force.[61] By this means, wrote a French slave trader, 'the powerful chiefs … make an object of speculation out of this [*tangena*] ordeal'.[62] There is evidence that the practice of selling into foreign slavery people considered guilty of spiritual subversion spread throughout Madagascar during the boom years of the slave trade.[63] The very conditions that made possible the creation of a united kingdom also permitted the emergence of enterprising individuals suspended, as it were, between the strong levelling ethos of their descent-groups and their patron, the king. The resulting jealousies and suspicions were fertile ground for accusations of *mosavy* not just from the king, but also from within their own families.[64] Before Andrianampoinimerina, it was common for families engaged in petty feuds to capture members of rival groups and hold them to ransom, a practice encouraging circulation of the very limited supplies of silver coin. Andrianampoinimerina's interdiction on civil war and on the export of his loyal subjects made this custom obsolete, thereby probably encouraging the growth of accusations of *mosavy* as an alternative arm for the waging of internecine war.[65] Malagasy rulers routinely believed themselves to be surrounded by political opponents in secret possession of powerful charms. It was logical that an expansion of royal power would take the form of searching for possible dissidents with dangerous, unlicensed amulets that represented unofficial, and therefore potentially subversive, channels of the cosmic force *hasina*.

The social dislocation caused by an expanded slave trade made more urgent the task of rooting out dissidents.

To an extent, then, political unification through a monopoly of armed force implied a displacement of political rivalries into related areas of struggle, namely accusations of spiritual subversion that could undermine the king's duty of dispensing *hasina*. Andrianampoinimerina therefore took central control of the poison ordeal, the key element of royal justice, announcing a list of charms and cult objects that would henceforth be regarded as illegal, possession of which was considered evidence of *mosavy*. He forbade anyone to administer the poison other than a group of officials belonging to the noble category called Andriamasinavalona, and even then only in the presence of judicial officers whom he created.[66]

While it is useful to make an analytical distinction between King Andrianampoinimerina's religious practice and other aspects of his rule, it is important to recall that the sovereign's function as the channel for the transmission of blessing was not considered by Malagasy to be distinct from his activities as warrior, trader and politician. The same was true of his immediate successor, Radama I, who was often considered by nineteenth-century British observers to be an enlightened ruler because of his abolition of slave exports and because of the scant respect he showed to the oracles and religious instruments inherited from his father.[67] Radama, urged to abolish the *tangena* poison ordeal by the Irish sergeant whom the British governor of Mauritius had sent to advise him in the wake of the treaty signed in 1817, is said to have replied that 'if I were to abolish the *tangena* ... I would regret it my whole life long. If this form of judgement ceased to exist, the most terrible anarchy would prevail throughout the island'. He did, however, tell Sergeant Hastie that he thought the use of *tangena* was 'barbarous', and at one stage decreed that it should be used on animals only.[68] According to Raombana, educated in England, the king 'disbelieved in the virtues of the *Tangena* ordeal'.[69] Such 'disbelief', though, is better understood as a choice about how power could best be channelled rather than as a crisis of conscience. Radama was encouraged by Europeans to reject the religious form of rule developed by his father. An intermediary between heaven and earth, and only a teenager at the time of his accession, he asserted his independence from the counsellors and officials he had inherited from his father. As a demi-god Radama felt unconstrained by tradition or custom. Impressed with the superiority of British power, transmitted through such ritual objects as Bibles and books, he based his power on the creation of a standing army, officered by men from various parts of Imerina and beyond, with British and French instructors. At his death, his army commander was actually a Jamaican sergeant, James Brady, seconded from the British army.[70] Radama's policy was to shift his father's old elite into the new category of civilians, especially appointing them as judges.[71] Members of this older elite displaced by Radama conspired to put their own candidate on the throne when Radama died in 1828 and were to triumph in the in-fighting that followed.

Despite the disrespect with which he treated religious customs, so potent was the *tangena* ordeal that not even Radama dared abolish it entirely. 'Literally speaking', Raombana wrote in relation to a slightly later period, 'the *Tangena* ordeal is the sovereign of Madagascar'.[72] The noble Andriamasinavalona group that Radama's father had charged with the administration of the poison consisted of certain families enjoying high rank and privilege inherited from their royal ancestors. Traditionally, families classed as Andriamasinavalona, although having high prestige, were not always wealthy and did not always enjoy political power. They were more like a Hindu caste[73] than a European feudal nobility. Andrianampoinimerina, seeking a means of ruling his enlarged kingdom, tried to turn the Andriamasinavalona into a nobility of service, incorporating conquered kings into the group and giving them authority to administer the *tangena* poison in tandem with his judicial officers. Over time, a deep hostility was to arise between these noble families and the coterie of military chiefs who had fought King Andrianampoinimerina's wars, who were mostly from commoner families in his home territory, and who drew most benefit from the political in-fighting after 1828.

As expansion and European contact opened up unprecedented new opportunities, it was overwhelmingly the commoner generals who grew rich on war and slave trading. When Radama's armies conquered Madagascar's main sea-ports, the centralization of power enabled rival factions at the royal court in Antananarivo to recruit personal retinues of clients, dependants and military retainers throughout the provinces. Thus, the bitter rivalries between various families present at the royal court, some of elevated traditional status and others having risen to prominence only recently through the slave trade and success in war, some newly classified as military and others as civilian, were transmitted throughout the kingdom. Added to a general hostility between high-rank families and the new generation of generals were bitter rivalries between senior military men themselves.

V. The tangena ordeal under Ranavalona I

From the military coup of 1828 until Madagascar's conquest by France in 1895, the real arbiters of power were a handful of generals, most notably from a family known as the Andafiavaratra ('on the north side', so called from the position they occupied at court), who ruled from behind the throne. During the reign of Ranavalona I, before the definitive opening of Madagascar to Europeans, the poison ordeal came to play a key role in factional conflict at court, in the manipulation of political power more generally, and in the government of a state which had expanded to include population groups historically independent of any ruler based in Antananarivo.

Queen Ranavalona was under the influence, noted the Reverend David Jones of the LMS, of 'a number of superstitious men who did put her on the throne and who were the ministers of Radama's father'.[74] Since the poison ordeal was regarded as the surest means of detecting *mosavy*, and had been turned by the founder of the united Merina kingdom into the key instrument of royal justice, it may be understood that a restoration of the system of governance through traditional religion, spurned by Radama I, required the general use of *tangena* once more. Radama I's innovations, moreover, had created all manner of social conflicts likely to stimulate accusations of *mosavy* from below, through the creation of a standing army and the division of families that this involved, the expansion of forced labour and the arrival in Imerina of massive numbers of slaves. French ships, attempting to restore France's position in the Indian Ocean, bombarded ports on the east coast, creating fears of an invasion in Antananarivo. It was in this febrile atmosphere that the queen ordered her first general administration of the *tangena* poison ordeal to all civilians, in an established procedure neglected by Radama I, whereby each district was required to use a ballot to identify a number of people suspected of *mosavy*, as a way of cleansing the kingdom.[75]

The group of conspirators who had brought Ranavalona to the throne was quite extensive, however, and included one of Radama's technocrats, Andriamihaja, 'a brilliant young man who knew English and French, very handsome, skilful, immaculately dressed, and very accomplished in European ways', according to later tradition.[76] Missionary sources agree that he was 'the principal man in all the events that conducted Ranavalona to the throne'.[77] The queen appointed him as her army commander, took him as a lover and conceived a child, almost certainly by him. This debonair general was much resented by other courtiers and generals who had lost ground but who had useful connections outside the army, notably through the networks of religious functionaries and family and district heads whom Radama had increasingly placed in charge of the religious duties that he himself disdained. Andriamihaja's main rivals were two brothers, Rainiharo and Rainimaharo, who, using their influence with the keepers of the *sampy* and the chief diviners, succeeded in convincing the queen that Andriamihaja was plotting against her. He was excluded from court and charged with *mosavy*. Among his accusers were the son and grandson of an official Andrianampoinimerina had appointed to conduct the poison ordeal thirty years earlier. Realizing that he had been outmanoeuvred and that the deadly poison would be administered in such a way as to ensure his death, Andriamihaja refused to submit to the ordeal, whereupon his enemies had him stabbed to death.[78]

Through its use in the death of the army commander and royal consort, *tangena* had become not only an instrument of government but also a weapon of elite rivalry. Thus the brothers Rainiharo and Rainimaharo, now in effective control of the army, soon discovered that rivals with influence among the civilian corps of judges and among leading noble families were prepared to make full use of this resource: it was the judges and the Andriamasinavalona nobles who had the authority to administer the poison ordeal, though all manner of senior officials could bring their influence to bear through intrigue. Probably the main supporter of the *tangena* was Rainijohary, a rival politician with particular support among the old nobility and some of the civilian judges empowered to administer the *tangena* ordeal.[79] Thus, even though Rainiharo was the effective prime minister, he was unable to prevent his own wife and sister-in-law, two sisters, and a female cousin falling victim to an accusation of sorcery. All five were subjected to the poison ordeal and failed to vomit the pieces of chicken-skin they had swallowed, as was required for proof of innocence; all were strangled. According to the Malagasy-speaking French courtier Jean Laborde, this episode served to temper Rainiharo's enthusiasm for the *tangena* ordeal.[80]

There are known to have been at least three general applications of the poison using the ballot system during the reign of Ranavalona I. These were in 1829, 1843 and 1860,[81] the general administration of 1843 being intended to clean the kingdom for performance of a national circumcision ceremony.[82] Beyond these three general ordeals, the use of *tangena* against local officials was reported from various parts of the island and in a great variety of circumstances. In 1836 the government sent out an order to arrest any of the queen's Merina subjects who had gone to other districts of the island to trade without a permit. Many of those arrested were forced to undergo the poison ordeal, allowing a handful of senior officials and army officers to create trade monopolies for themselves.[83] Rival military leaders with extensive patronage networks sometimes accused district heads loyal to their rivals of disloyalty to the queen, forcing them to undergo the poison ordeal. Queen Ranavalona's private secretary—the same Raombana who was secretly writing a history of his times—wrote that the poison ordeal was used by leading army officers to attack the client-networks of various rivals and to acquire slaves, cattle and goods from those they accused.[84] The son of one of Jean Laborde's slaves later described how, when the queen went on a provincial tour to visit the Frenchman's workshops in 1850, she was afraid of travelling through a district notorious for harbouring unofficial charms. She had the entire area encircled by troops; its people were forced to undergo the poison ordeal, and the result was thousands of deaths.[85]

There was a wide range of circumstances in which people might accuse each other in ordinary disputes, even cases of theft, resulting in the visit of judges and administration of the poison ordeal.[86] Slave-owners were allowed to administer the poison to their own slaves, and routinely did so if they suspected that an illness or death in the family was caused by malefice, but even if found guilty, slaves were quite often sold rather than executed.[87] The old convention that persons making unsuccessful accusations of witchcraft must themselves undergo the poison ordeal seems to have disappeared, at least in the case of accusations emanating from royal officials. What remained was the practice of dividing the goods of a victim between the accuser and the government.[88] Visiting the royal court of Imerina, the Austrian traveller Ida Pfeiffer noted the blatant self-interest which seemed to motivate so many accusations, since government officials were able to confiscate the goods of those condemned.[89] Great numbers of accusations were due, according to Finaz, 'to the most base passions, to hatred, vengeance, and an insatiable cupidity'.[90] The queen or one of her officials would periodically command a particular village or region to deliver up any unofficial amulets in their possession (taken to include Bibles and other Christian objects), ordering suspects to be tested with the *tangena* ordeal.[91] Some people even denounced themselves. One of the incentives for doing this was that it would save their families from being reduced into slavery, the normal procedure in cases where conviction followed denunciation by a third party.

The surviving archives of the old Merina government, housed in the modern Malagasy national archives, contain no known records of trials involving the use of *tangena*.[92] There is not enough information to say much about the incidence of applications of the ordeal in terms of age, gender, locality, status and so forth, except to say that it seems to have been administered more in central Imerina than on the fringes of the kingdom, and both as a result of accusations from the general population as well as from officials. Probably proportionally more freemen than slaves died from the ordeal.[93] There is no obvious distinction between men and women.

In a case from 1857 recounted by Finaz, the people of one small area had been given one month to produce anyone guilty of an offence. When not enough suspects were forthcoming, the government gave them another month, on pain of administration of the poison ordeal.[94] Fourteen soldiers were burned alive, sixty-five condemned to death by stabbing, 1,237 people were sentenced to chains, and five thousand were sold into slavery.[95] Finaz compared the atmosphere to the French terror of 1793, which was still just about within living memory:[96]

> No one dare leave the house, for fear of never returning. No one dare stay at home, for fear of being dragged from there to a place of execution when least expected. Men tremble for their wives and children, for these are sold and all their possessions confiscated if the head of the family is accused, which is to say if he is condemned; for the slightest hint of denunciation is enough to warrant execution, without the victim even being informed of the grounds on which he is condemned.

VI. Explanations and comparisons

Belief in some form of metaphysical evil exists in many societies, bearing at least some resemblance to what was known as witchcraft in early modern England and English-speaking North America. Hence, it is not surprising that writers in English have consistently translated as 'witchcraft' the belief that we have until this point referred to by its Malagasy name of *mosavy*. No technique of social science can determine whether witchcraft and *mosavy* 'really' exist. They are among the many moral artefacts that societies produce, 'a construction of the real', in the words of one American author, 'no more or less intellectual than its analogues in [American] society—"race", the "value" of gold, the "self" and its cognates'.[97]

In the introduction to this article it was claimed that it is desirable to compare African and non-African beliefs, but that precautions need to be taken as one may not be comparing like with like. Where the comparative approach seems most incisive is in the study of how the consequences of such belief may be translated into social and political action, for here we are dealing with events that can be recorded, visible actions rather than invisible beliefs. This occurs, for example, when one person accuses another of being a witch. A great variety of societies maintain some category of officially labelled deviance, to which are consigned 'those who commit acts perceived as transgressing the fundamental moral axioms on which human nature, and hence social life, is based'.[98] The behaviour of such dangerous and antisocial wrong-doers is often thought to be the mirror-image of that which is desirable in terms of sex, eating habits and ideological orientation.[99] Since such categories of infamy are conceived within a dominant ideology or discourse that may or may not be religious in the sense of supposing the existence of invisible, spiritual forces, then it is in theory possible to compare the way in which people are consigned to such a category of infamy in different places and times, or in other words to write a comparative sociology of scapegoating. An authoritative account of Stalinist purges in the 1930s Soviet Union, for example, explicitly notes the 'many similarities' between that pursuit of people deemed existentially evil and earlier European witch-hunting.[100] A study of the persecution of people perceived as sexual deviants in modern Britain makes a similar analogy.[101] Although neither of these last-cited cases concerns so-called 'witches', both are comparable inasmuch as they concern the use of power to label certain people as deviants and to hound them, often to their deaths. It appears that if those who wield power in a given polity or community believe or construe it to be necessary, or perhaps simply in their interest, to eliminate such deviants, then the resulting purge will inevitably be imagined and described in whatever ideology or discourse is paramount in a particular time and place. Societies in which the invisible world has a high importance—such as that of old Madagascar—are likely to perceive such threats in terms of spiritual subversion.

In old Madagascar, the precise manner in which the life-force known as *hasina* could be acquired was the very stuff of politics. The revolution which occurred in the central highlands in the late eighteenth century and which led to the formation of the Merina kingdom was also a process of centralizing the institutional forms through which *hasina* was channelled. We have seen that King Andrianampoinimerina assembled a pantheon consisting of the protective devices of various groups whose allegiance he had secured. These group protectors—*sampy*—were, in the language of social science, both religious and political symbols. The Malagasy of that time hardly distinguished between these two fields. Royal control of the sources of spiritual power entailed a concentration of control over the means of coercion and material reward. The circumstances were such as to create exceptional opportunities for individuals to gain wealth and power that, moreover, tended to escape regulation by traditional procedures. Some of these became collaborators of the king while their relations to their own kin, to whom they were joined by strong bonds of solidarity, became deeply ambiguous.[102] The social hierarchy became unstable at the top, where heaven and earth were joined through the sovereign, and at the bottom, where farmers were bound to the soil.

Andrianampoinimerina's successors continued the work of centralizing power through innovations that included the standing army, mission-schools, an expanded system of forced labour, and the beginnings of a government bureaucracy. Still, power remained embedded in webs of social relationships of obligation and dependency that took visible form in ritual actions and objects and audible form in words. Merina sovereigns assumed, like their subjects, that the proper order of the cosmos was always vulnerable to subversion by unruly forces articulated by human agents, the *mpamosavy* or witches.

King Radama I pursued his goal of island-wide control through alliance with Great Britain, encouraging LMS missionaries to found Christian schools and awarding key administrative positions to his own favourites rather than to the supporters of his late father. This was accompanied by a suspension of royal favour towards the national pantheon of *sampy*, such a key instrument of his father's rule. Among the conspirators who masterminded the *coup d'état* of 1828 were leading figures associated with the national pantheon who had lost power in the preceding decade. Thereafter, the government of Queen Ranavalona I, while continuing to import Western technology and to centralize power, found it prudent to restore the national pantheon.

In short, the kingdom of Madagascar as it emerged over several generations was governed by an elite whose ambition was to create an island-wide state, but which struggled to locate forms of control and legitimacy appropriate to this ambition. The semidivine figure of the sovereign was the obvious focus. With only a brief interlude when King Radama I experimented with new forms of domination which soon led to an acute political and social reaction, the government used the language of ancestral religion to justify itself until the 1860s, when the opening to Europe entailed the establishment of an alternative political and religious vision. Previously, the idea of an alternative power had been unthinkable except as a form of subversion, necessarily spiritual in nature; no political thought was permissible outside the scope of the ruling power. Traditional *mosavy* beliefs became incorporated into a quasi-nationalist ideology in which religious heterodoxy became a political crime.[103] This is a process very similar to what has been observed by some historians of early modern Europe concerning the conditions in which the witchhunts of those times occurred.[104] Accusations of *mosavy* and, in consequence, application of the *tangena* ordeal, became a redoubtable weapon in competition among factions of the national elite. With the grandees of the royal court recruiting partisans and clients country-wide, this process affected every level of power as rival groups struggled for advantage. Accusations and subjection to the poison ordeal escaped the control of any particular person or faction. Courtiers accused each other, local officials accused other officials, people accused neighbours out of fear, greed or revenge. All the jealousies and rivalries of any society (but in this case, one undergoing profound changes associated with the centralization of government, large population movements, a massive death-toll from war, poison and disease,[105] and the accumulation of impressive fortunes by oligarchs) risked being subsumed into accusations of witchcraft. The effect was deadly.

During the process of centralization associated with the rise of the Merina kingdom, with its rulers' ambition to dominate all of Madagascar, notions of the proper order and of its possible subversion changed markedly, partly through European influence. In general, the European visitors, missionaries and military advisers who stayed in Imerina in the early nineteenth century actually wrote rather little about sorcery or witchcraft as these might be identified in local religious practices, and were far more concerned to combat other forms of 'wrong' religion which they often labelled as 'superstition' or 'idolatry'. The writings of early nineteenth-century missionaries to Madagascar support the view that it was a later generation of European travellers to Africa that identified Africa generally as 'the heartland of witchcraft and magic', as opposed to other forms of supposed religious error.[106] Of greater influence in the witch-purges of the mid nineteenth century was the European tendency to identify the sovereign as an absolute monarch, an idea deliberately supported by very active British diplomatic and military aid to Radama I and unintentionally stimulated by missionary teachings concerning the King of Heaven. 'Is Andriamanjaka and Andriananahary (King and God) the same?', some LMS missionaries were asked in 1823. 'Yes', they replied 'but one is in heaven and the other upon earth'.[107] The translation of Christian ideas and the Bible into Malagasy gave new meanings to existing concepts. While these strengthened in many ways the old Malagasy idea of the sovereign as the monarch at the centre of the earth, they also introduced an expectation, profoundly threatening to the oligarchy that ruled half of Madagascar, of a millennial reign when justice would prevail on earth.[108] The queen herself described Christianity as 'the substitution of the respect of her ancestors … for the respect of the ancestor of the whites: Jesus Christ'.[109] Those who formally accepted Christianity were seen as devotees of a foreign dynasty rivalling the sovereigns of Imerina.

The kingdom remained founded on a conception of power as a metaphysical force channelled to the living. The *tangena* poison ordeal, in spite of its extensive use (or abuse) by courtiers, enjoyed a high degree of legitimacy as a political and religious instrument. One of the set forms of application of the *tangena*, in fact, was known as *horon'ondrin' ny mpianakavy*, in which it was administered to an entire family or clan at their own request.[110] Raombana wrote that the people were so convinced 'of the sacredness of the *Tangena* ordeal … that in law-suits they prefer their cases to be decided by it'.[111] A missionary agreed that '[o]ne of the most remarkable things in connection with this ordeal was the implicit faith of the people generally in its supernatural power'.[112] Queen Ranavalona I herself was so terrified of becoming a victim of sorcery that she routinely caused the poison ordeal to be administered to servants on entry into her service as a form of screening, and whenever she was ill or had bad dreams.[113]

To cease using *tangena* without adopting some other form of anti-witchcraft prophylactic in its place was, in the opinion of many nineteenth-century Malagasy, an invitation to disaster. 'Now is the reign of the sorcerers', one Merina villager told a European missionary in 1880, explaining that the abolition of the *tangena* and other aspects of traditional religion by a government now officially converted to Christianity had deprived people of the main defence against spiritual subversion.[114] And indeed, the Christian government that continued in power from the conversion of Queen Ranavalona II and her prime minister to Christianity in 1868–9 until the annexation of the island by France, was unable to maintain whatever political integrity Imerina had previously had. It could not enforce the extraordinary degree of social control which had been achieved by its predecessors in Imerina in the early nineteenth century, and perhaps in some other regions of the island at earlier periods. Nor has any subsequent government of Madagascar, colonial or post-colonial, been able to achieve the same.

The control of perceived witchcraft was itself a form of government in old Madagascar. Like all forms of government, it could be used for purposes of narrow self-interest, as noted by a missionary who described the poison ordeal as 'this convenient method for the removal of prominently obtrusive members of "the opposition",[115] But to describe the mid nineteenth-century witch-hunts as political is not to imply that the people who engaged in them had no belief in what they were doing. It is probably more accurate to think of this particular cosmology as an inclusive language which governed private thoughts as well as public discourse.

Since the mid nineteenth century this religious construction has been dismantled, first by the conversion of Queen Ranavalona and her prime minister to Christianity in 1868–9 and, later, by the creation of a secular state by the French colonial administration. Nevertheless, nowadays most Malagasy probably still believe that *mosavy* exists and that measures need to be taken to guard against it. Although post-colonial governments have occasionally tried to turn elements of traditional religion into political capital, and elements of it remain important in daily life, they have never been officially incorporated into the structures of the state.[116] And so, the fight against witchcraft takes place in a private and piecemeal fashion.

In retrospect, the great witch-hunts were intrinsic to the articulation of a religious and political power that proved unable to endure, not least because of the vast inequities and ambiguities with which it was associated. For power does not reside in persons or things, but 'in the interstices between persons and between things, that is to say *in relations*'.[117] This, too, is precisely where the artefact we call witchcraft is perceived to exist.

SECTION FOUR

CRIME

14

THE NEW FRONTIERS OF CRIME IN SOUTH AFRICA

In warfare, according to the British field-marshal Lord Montgomery, 'the first principle is to identify your enemy accurately' (quoted in Prins and Stamp, 1991: 32).

South Africa today has no foreign enemies. Its government enjoys overwhelming national and international support. President Nelson Mandela is probably the world's most admired living politician. And yet the state, in the face of a multiplicity of armed groups, is incapable of enforcing the monopoly of legitimate violence which is its most fundamental responsibility, and this poses such a substantial threat to national security and stability that Montgomery's dictum remains relevant. Exactly who or what is responsible for the wave of crime which is affecting the country? An essential task of political analysis in these circumstances is to define the relationship between politics and the practices of illicit violence and illicit enrichment which we call crime.

It should be said at the outset that even a cursory examination of the recent history of South Africa indicates that organized crime has ceased to be a phenomenon at the fringes of political and economic society, the place traditionally allotted to it in the social sciences (cf. Waller and Yasmann, 1995: 277). South Africa is said to have the highest incidence of murder of any country in the world not at war. Half the population pronounce themselves in opinion polls to be 'very worried' about becoming victims of crime in their own communities

(South African Police Service, 1996: 1). In just two years, 80 per cent of more than 2,000 households surveyed by the banking group Nedcor had had some experience of crime (Johnson, 1996). Sections of some black townships are effectively under the control of unofficial armed groups, sometimes in the guise of self-defence or self-protection units claiming allegiance to the African National Congress (ANC) or the Inkatha Freedom Party (IFP), or they are threatened by *tsotsis*, gangsters with no political ideology. Gunmen carrying illegal weapons and operating on the margins between party militias, self-defence units, comrades and crime gangs are known, in the rich vocabulary of South African politics, as 'com-tsotsis', 'comrade-gangsters'. Weapons are readily available. An AK-47 assault rifle can be bought on the black market or even hired by the day, with or without bullets. The country's middle classes increasingly tend to live in enclaves patrolled by private security companies, behind high walls topped by razor wire. Free of the unwelcome attentions of armed militias, they are frequently worried by burglary and particularly by the high rate of vehicle theft—98,000 vehicles in 1995—sometimes carried out by armed hijackers who lie in wait by the garage doors of suburban houses. In the countryside, many white farmers use two-way radios to operate their own rapid-response networks against stock-thieves and burglars.

Many white South Africans regard violent crime as being essentially an activity carried out by certain of their black compatriots, and fear of crime is used by white-led opposition parties and white journalists as a euphemism for fear of black rule, the traditional white South African fear of blacks (*'swart gevaav'*) in a new guise. Black township-dwellers, who in fact are more likely to suffer from crime than people living in suburbs, often blame the upsurge in crime on immigrants from elsewhere in Africa, who have flocked to the country since the opening of its borders in 1990. The South African Police Service, demoralized and ill-adapted to deal with the transition from apartheid to democracy, often appears overwhelmed. Police spokesmen admit that elements of the force have themselves been penetrated by organized crime. Police commanders are acutely aware of the new international dimension to organized crime, particularly in regard to the drug trade, which has increased dramatically in recent years and has prompted the government to appeal for help to the US authorities. It is a fact that South Africa has become the target of major international criminal syndicates, notably from Nigeria, but also from as far afield as Russia and China. South Africa is a leading producer of marijuana and in just a few years has become a leading importer and re-exporter of cocaine and heroin,[1] as well as an attractive location for money-laundering and sophisticated business fraud. South Africa, in fact, has become Africa's capital of organized crime, with a total criminal turnover reckoned at some R.41.1 billion per year (Johnson, 1996). Criminals from abroad are attracted by the existence of a market for drugs and fraud, but equally important is the country's first-class transport infrastructure and banking system and the world's tenth-biggest stock exchange, which make it an ideal base for intercontinental operations and money-laundering.

The crime wave is particularly disappointing to the considerable number of people who assumed that violence generally would decline in South Africa after the abolition of apartheid. To be sure, the variant of national socialism introduced in 1948 in the form of apartheid had a profoundly destabilizing effect on South African society, including in the form of crime, and no serious observer believed that its effects would cease the instant a democratic government was installed. But what has become clearer since the election of an ANC government in 1994 is that crime in South Africa is not only, and perhaps not even primarily, the result of poverty. It is a social and even a political artefact.

The national security and intelligence services, and particularly the South African Police Service, are themselves part of the problem. For decades, the police concentrated so single-mindedly on the threat of communist subversion that it ignored the deep changes taking place in the political economy of crime in southern Africa and indeed world-wide. Far from concentrating their resources on combating crime, the police sometimes regarded important criminal syndicates as allies in the fight against the ANC and its partner and *alter ego,* the South African Communist Party (SACP). For as long as the country existed in its Cold War deep-freeze, it was relatively insulated against major international trends such as the narcotics trade. The normalization of foreign relations after 1990 opened the country to a flood of fortune-seekers from elsewhere, including some sophisticated criminal syndicates which were far more knowledgeable about the techniques of international crime than the country's law enforcement agencies. Boycotted by much of the international community, isolated from many conferences and exchanges, excluded from Interpol, the South African Police did not even have a unit to combat organized crime until 1993. By mid-1996, South Africa still had no laws against money-laundering,

Revolution, crime and security

That South Africa was indeed at war between the early 1960s and the early 1990s, and not merely undergoing particularly acute political difficulties, cannot be doubted.[2] During this period leaders of the ANC and the SACP, the most important organizations of armed opposition, based in exile, explicitly regarded their struggle as revolutionary in nature, comparable to similar campaigns in Algeria, Vietnam and elsewhere. By and large the ANC and SACP were prevented by the effectiveness of police measures from undertaking substantial activity in South Africa between 1964 and the early 1980s, but their intention was plain. South Africa's white government, particularly after the mid-1970s, interpreted this revolutionary war as the spearhead of a 'total onslaught'—in the words of a 1977 defence white paper— orchestrated by the Soviet Union, which provided military, diplomatic and other support to the ANC and the SACP and to allied governments in Angola and Mozambique. South African army and police officers who had studied the theory and practice of revolutionary warfare, and who became known as 'securocrats' because of their belief that security structures could be used as a basis for managing political change, devised a counter-insurgency doctrine aimed at mobilizing every branch of the state in a campaign to defeat the total onslaught which they believed to be directed from Moscow. Murder, smuggling, forgery, propaganda and subversion were instruments used by both sides in the struggle, but it was the state which brought the greatest resources to bear in these domains.

Like many modern wars, it was less about locating and destroying the enemies' armed forces than about inducing the bulk of the population to accept a given political dispensation whose legitimacy could be accepted by international observers. It was, according to the securocrats, a struggle which was 80 per cent political and only 20 per cent military. Only in Angola between 1975 and 1989 did the war for control of South Africa take the form of conventional battles between rival armies. Strategists within both the South African Defence Force (SADF) and the ANC–SACP guerrilla army, Umkhonto we Sizwe, realized at an early stage that the outcome of the struggle would depend largely on achieving hegemony in local communities. This would be accomplished by constructing a political clientele among diverse social groups, particularly in the townships where the majority of South Africa's black urban population live and which both sides recognized as the key site of the struggle. From the mid-1980s the two principal state security forces, the South African Police and the SADF, adopted a strategy of systematically arming various social groups for use as auxiliaries, often called 'vigilantes', who would combat ANC supporters in society at large (Haysom, 1986). State-sanctioned vigilantes of this sort came from sections of the population opposed to the young comrades acting in the name of the ANC, and included established criminal gangs as well as individual convicts released from prison for the purpose. In 1986 the SADF secretly and illegally trained some 200 members of the Inkatha organization, the forerunner of the Inkatha Freedom Party, in counter-insurgency warfare. This decision was made by the government's supreme security organ, the State Security Council chaired by State President P. W. Botha, and these 200 later formed the nucleus of Inkatha's own private army. Violence in KwaZulu-Natal increased measurably in 1987 when the 200 trainees were thrown into the struggle against the ANC and SACP. There can be no doubt that the state itself fanned the flames of war in the province.

The policy of arming vigilantes was itself a reaction to the strategy of the ANC and SACP, who were smuggling guns into the townships and urging South Africans to make the country 'ungovernable' by refusing to pay rents and service charges and by murdering policemen, municipal councillors, suspected police informers and anyone else whom ANC sympathizers regarded as collaborators with the government. It was in 1985, during the explosion of popular anti-state violence which had started the previous year, that the method of lynching known as 'necklacing' was invented, a particularly terrifying form of execution since it was not only agonizingly painful, but also believed by many South Africans to destroy the soul as well as the body of the victim, preventing them from becoming an ancestor. The ANC and SACP urged on the lynch-mobs and only belatedly, and somewhat unconvincingly, condemned the use of the necklace. At the same time the most thoughtful ANC and SACP strategists were surprised and concerned by the resourcefulness and ruthlessness of the security forces when they began organizing popular counter-revolutionary violence to combat that encouraged by the ANC. Joe Slovo, for many years the chief of staff of Umkhonto we Sizwe, admitted ruefully to having underestimated 'the fact that the counter-revolution learns from the revolution' (Slovo, 1986: 25). Indeed, this was so. The SADF's approach was to study the techniques of guerrilla warfare used in Malaya, Algeria, Vietnam and other classic cases, and to employ the same techniques on behalf of the state with a view to throwing the insurrectionary campaign into reverse. 'The solution to the problem of defeating revolutionary warfare', asserted one author much studied by the securocrats in South Africa,' is the application of its strategy and principles in reverse' (McCuen, 1966: 77).

The strategy elaborated by the ANC and SACP in 1978–9, after a study-tour by a group of leaders to Vietnam, envisaged a combination of political and military activity. In the first phase military activity would take the form of 'armed propaganda', the execution of military activities designed less to destroy the enemy's capacity to make war than to advertise to the people of South Africa the presence of Umkhonto we Sizwe and its ability to strike. Among the best-known examples of such activities carried out in the phase of 'armed propaganda' were the sabotage of oil installations at Sasolburg in 1980, a rocket attack on the military base at Voortrekkerhoogte in 1981, and the planting of a car bomb outside Air Force headquarters in the heart of Pretoria in May 1983. These were highly effective in boosting the ANC's standing among radicals. The intention of the High Command of Umkhonto we Sizwe was eventually to proceed to the next stage of the struggle which they called 'people's war', a generalized, revolutionary uprising in which trained guerrillas would play a strategic role, but in which most of the activities would be carried out with a high degree of spontaneity by ordinary civilians.

It was in this light that the ANC and SACP interpreted the outbreak of a popular uprising which began in the Vaal Triangle area in 1984 and soon spread to other parts of South Africa. Like the earlier insurrection in Soweto in 1976, the 1984 rising arose from an essentially local cycle of violent incidents and repression. It was not organized by any specific group. The ANC, believing that the last phase of struggle, 'people's war', was now close at hand, welcomed the rising and aimed to stoke the fires of revolution by propaganda, by developing its political connections inside the country, and by infiltrating guns and trained guerrillas into the townships. Although the uprising was not organized by the ANC, and nor were the leaders of popular militancy in regular contact with ANC headquarters in Lusaka, the presence of ANC guerrillas and the spreading of ANC slogans and propaganda served to legitimize a wide variety of acts of violence in the eyes of young radicals especially and to convince the comrades that their actions were indeed political ones.

The fact that the ANC explicitly encouraged the spread of popular violence during the 1980s has caused some commentators to argue that its call to render the country ungovernable was the main cause of the culture of violence and lawlessness which has become widespread among South African youth in particular (Kane-Berman, 1993). It was undoubtedly a contributing factor, and it is ironic inasmuch as the ANC today is responsible for a problem which is at least in part of its own making. However, it is both one-sided and superficial to attach the main responsibility for the spread of a popular culture of violence to the ANC, the SACP or any other anti-apartheid organization. In the first place, the South African townships had a long history of violence occasionally taking the form of local uprisings, even as far back as the 1940s. The main cause of this no doubt lay in the very fabric of modern South African history, in the destruction of the black peasantry and rapid and chaotic urbanization. Moreover, the state itself could be said to have precipitated violence by banning certain political parties including the SACP in 1950 and the ANC in 1960, at a time when neither of these organizations had adopted a policy of armed struggle. The Sharpeville massacre was perpetrated by the police in 1960, over a year before the ANC's own turn to violence. However, once the armed propaganda of Umkhonto we Sizwe had started to become effective in the early 1980s, and once the ANC and SACP had endorsed the strategy of making South Africa 'ungovernable', spontaneous popular violence in a variety of forms became a political act. The fact that this was countered by the government's arming of counter-revolutionary elements meant that, in effect, both the ANC and the security forces were competing for years to turn many of the country's black communities into armed camps. This they did in order to tip the national balance of power in their favour. The crime and the popular violence which are rooted in South Africa's long history of conquest and shorter experience of industrialization, and in the apartheid system by which it was governed, were also given a political complexion as a result of decisions taken by specific political actors.

Politics and crime in South Africa: A brief history

The agency of the state responsible for combating crime in South Africa is the police force founded in 1913, which played such a leading role in the long struggle against the ANC and the SACP.

Throughout its history, the South African Police—to use its former name—has had a semi-military nature. Long before the outbreak of hostilities in the 1960s, and indeed even before the National Party government came to power in 1948, the South African Police had developed a specific view of how to police African populations. The origins of this lie in the British colonial tradition of indirect rule. As practised throughout British colonies in Africa, indirect rule was based on the aim of keeping Africans as far as possible in rural areas under their own traditional or quasi-traditional rulers. In South Africa, where the mining economy required large amounts of cheap labour, exceptions were made to allow rural African men in particular to move to the towns as migrants who would come to live in cities and mine-compounds for a specific period before returning to their home areas and their families after their contracts had expired. They were discouraged from settling permanently in urban areas and from developing political institutions there. The key to indirect rule was for government officials to identify and promote local rulers, hereditary chiefs if possible, who would govern the rural areas as far as possible by their own devices and according to customary law. The role of the national police force was to ensure that chiefs did not contravene the laws of the central government which applied in those rural areas designated as African reserves, or the later apartheid creations of bantustans or homelands, and to act as a mobile armed force when intervention was necessary. Any significant agitation against a chief regarded by the government as legitimate was interpreted by the police as a form of insurgency, and when, in the 1950s, there were several major cases of rural disturbance in South Africa arising from protests against the stringent apartheid laws then being introduced, and to some extent articulated by nationalist movements such as the ANC and, later, the Pan-Africanist Congress (PAC), this was perceived by police chiefs as a form of crime. Indeed, after the banning of the ANC and the PAC in 1960, mere membership of these organizations was a crime, as membership of the SACP had been since 1950.

The formal outbreak of guerrilla war in South Africa in 1961 took the form of an urban sabotage campaign organized by an underground ANC and SACP leadership based in the cities. This was comprehensively defeated by the police in 1963–4. Thereafter, while the PAC remained ineffective, the ANC and the SACP, based in exile in Tanzania and, later, Zambia, turned to a new strategy, called 'hacking the way home'. It envisaged a campaign of rural guerrilla warfare, beginning with campaigns in Rhodesia in 1967–8, intended ultimately to open up a Ho Chi Minh trail to South Africa. South African Police units were sent to Rhodesia to work alongside the Rhodesian security forces to counter this threat. At the same time a further theatre of rural conflict opened up in the north of Namibia, the South African colony threatened by the guerrilla army of the South-West African People's Organization (SWAPO), based first in Zambia and, after 1975, in newly independent Angola. In keeping with the old colonial tradition, South African policemen regarded these major incidents of armed insurgency as a particularly serious form of crime rather than as a political matter or a war in the conventional sense (Cawthra, 1993: 14–19).

It is notable that it was the South African Police and not the SADF which was deployed in Rhodesia and, initially, in Namibia. Officers from the Security Branch of the police who had worked in Rhodesia later established a special counter-insurgency unit in Namibia,

Koevoet, which was to have a considerable influence on South Africa itself. The main function of Koevoet was the identification and elimination of suspected insurgents, contrary to the main principle of policing, which is to detect, arrest and prosecute wrong-doers in conformity with the law, using minimum force. Its officers were preoccupied with kill-ratios and body-counts. Particularly alarming, from the point of view of traditional policing, was the practice developed by Koevoet of inducing captured guerrillas to work for the security forces, a process known as 'turning'. They were then used as troopers in the security forces without even being given a formal indemnity for their earlier offences. In the long run this could only bring the central principle of the law into disrepute. 'Turned' guerrillas, known as *askaris,* made particularly fearsome killers. Battle-hardened, they were psychologically and socially divorced from their communities of origin, rather like the slave armies of history. Former Koevoet officers were later to form special death-squads organized by the South African Police, largely composed of 'turned' former guerrillas from SWAPO, the ANC, the PAC and several defunct guerrilla armies of southern Africa. Some Koevoet officers, such as Colonel Eugene de Kock, commander of the C-l unit of the South African Police, the leading police death-squad, became deeply involved in weapons smuggling and other forms of serious crime, both as police officers and on their own account. One of De Kock's most faithful lieutenants, an Angolan, had actually been trained in China in the 1960s, embarking on a revolutionary path which eventually led him to membership of an apartheid death-squad.

The techniques of counter-insurgency developed by the South African Police in Rhodesia and Namibia soon made their appearance in urban areas. Colonel Theunis 'Rooi Rus' Swanepoel, the architect of the bloody repression of the Soweto rising of 1976, for example, had taken part in the first counter-insurgency operations against SWAPO in northern Namibia ten years earlier (*ibid.:* 19). By 1975 there were over 2,000 South African policemen serving in Rhodesia, and they brought their experience to bear on the home front. Tactics learned in the border wars in Rhodesia and Namibia, including techniques of disinformation, pseudo-operations and the use of 'turned' captives, gradually made their appearance in urban areas of South Africa. To this was added a growing ruthlessness in the use of torture and sweeping legal powers, as well as other techniques learned from other countries including Israel, Chile and Argentina, the latter at the height of 'dirty wars' of their own (*ibid:* 19, 27).

The absence of any political strategy or even full administrative recognition in regard to black urban areas until as late as the 1980s put the police in a difficult position. At best, they were expected to enforce apartheid laws which, like the Pass Laws and the Group Areas Act, became steadily more unworkable as the police were overwhelmed by the sheer numbers of people living in illegal situations. Since the government itself insisted, in the face of all evidence to the contrary, that black people were living only temporarily in the cities, it was not possible for them to develop sensitive approaches to policing black urban areas or techniques which relied on the essential element of all successful policing, namely the co-operation of the public itself. In keeping with the traditions of indirect rule, according to which the politics of quasi-traditional chieftaincies were the only legitimate political arena for black communities, they continued to regard all forms of nationalist activity, or even of protest about living conditions, as tantamount to crime. At the same time they made relatively little effort to prevent or prosecute everyday forms of crime in black townships, tending to concentrate ordinary domestic policing in white South African areas, intervening in the townships only inadequately or when crime threatened to take on a recognizably political form, such as if people perceived as troublemakers threatened to make common cause with banned or suspect organizations such as the SACP or the ANC. The lack of an effective strategy for policing black urban areas was compounded by the lawlessness produced by rapid urbanization, which bred crime of a conventional type in the form of criminal gangs specializing in racketeering, rape and theft.

The old colonial tradition of indirect rule combined with the exigencies of policing rapidly growing and poorly administered black urban areas to produce a constant search for individuals or social groups who could help the police with their most basic functions of information-gathering and, as the years went by, identifying and arresting nationalist agitators. The police, drawing on their rural experience, continued in an urban environment their search for local strong men who could govern the particular ethnic units into which, according to their analysis, black South African society was divided. Since there were no hereditary chiefs with authority in the townships, the search sometimes encompassed informal associations or even criminal gangs, particularly when these were composed of rural migrants with conservative honour-codes and strong roots in the countryside, who despised the indiscipline of the township youths whom they equated with criminals or *tsotsis* (Bonner, 1993). Such groups, like the famous gang called the Russians which flourished in the 1950s in townships on the Reef, sometimes appeared to the police to be stabilizing elements in a chaotic social milieu. Even in the 1950s the police sometimes tolerated such groups and permitted them to set up quite extensive systems of control, with their own system of kangaroo courts (Freed, 1963: 78, 116).

If the South African government continued to regard black Africans as posing the greatest problem to the security of state and society when they moved to towns where they risked becoming politicized by nationalist organizations, the ANC and SACP themselves came to a broadly similar conclusion. After their unsuccessful foray into semi-conventional rural guerrilla warfare in Rhodesia in 1967–8, they decided that the struggle for South Africa was overwhelmingly urban in nature. Influenced by the SACP's classic Marxist–Leninist approach, South Africa's premier anti-apartheid organization concentrated its efforts on mobilizing the urban working class in the struggle. Like their opposite numbers the securocrats, the ANC and SACP leaders saw political and military activity as a seamless web. And so, when the government belatedly began to recognize the reality of black urban life, and encouraged the creation of local political structures there, the populations of the largest black townships became the site of a struggle for control between the state's attempt to set up black town councils which would provide the black urban areas with self-government, and informal social groups whom the ANC encouraged to take a revolutionary path, themselves countered in turn by government-sponsored vigilantes.

From the mid-1980s until as late as 1994, both the security forces and the ANC-SACP were arming their supporters in the townships in pursuit of this strategy. This is the provenance of many of the weapons used by South African criminals today.

Narratives of violence, local and national

During the wave of popular insurrections which began in 1984, the network of pro-ANC activists called the United Democratic Front (UDF) was remarkably successful in persuading people from different sections of society, living in a wide variety of situations, that their local or particular grievances were ultimately caused by the existence of apartheid. The variety of social groups eventually included in the broad front represented by the UDF was diverse in the extreme: Christian activists and liberal intellectuals, trade unionists, unemployed youth, township thugs and Marxist revolutionaries, but also rural youth mobilized against chiefs and even against witches (Van Kessel, 1995). People from all of these groups operated under the banner of the UDF, itself loosely affiliated with the ANC leadership in exile with which it was forbidden by law to communicate openly. So successful was the popular front led by the UDF that the National Party government and its security chiefs eventually came to the conclusion that the state could not withstand resistance on such a scale indefinitely, even if the security forces were able to prevent its physical overthrow. Once the leaders of the National Party had drawn this conclusion, the unbanning of the ANC was a logical consequence. While the negotiations which began officially in 1990 and the elections of 1994 helped to eliminate political violence at the national level, they made far less impact on the many local struggles which underlay the national contest, which continue to follow a logic of their own to this day in a very different national and international context (du Toit, 1993).

Complex social struggles which are rooted in local communities, particularly when they have been militarized by the action of armed revolutionaries and state security officers, do not end when the formal organizations contesting state power declare an end to hostilities. Thus, many of the social groups which participated in the struggle for South Africa continue to pursue their factional interests by violence. Today, this is generally labelled as criminal rather than political violence, but the change of vocabulary should not blind us to the fact that the actors remain largely the same. Whereas the UDF was so successful in persuading many South Africans that apartheid was the root cause of their various factional or local grievances, the change in the political landscape since 1994 has made this rallying call obsolete, leaving the ANC government bereft of a political message which can unite the dispossessed of South Africa and crusaders for justice as the revolutionary slogans once did.

Just as it is ironic that the ANC must now deal with the violence which it once encouraged, so the security forces now have to struggle against forms of violence which they originally organized in the shape of former allies or auxiliaries who have access to firearms originally procured for them by Military Intelligence or other organs of the state. Some former guerrillas who are unable to find work have become professional criminals or have joined the numerous informal militias which have sprouted throughout the country with only tenuous links to political parties. Whether or not they adopt political labels, local gangs or militias all too often provide a living for young men who have few other prospects of finding a job; there is a thin dividing line between the gangsters who operate protection rackets within their territories and the militias which raise taxes from every household in their area on the grounds that this is necessary to pay for community self-defence. Local militias which develop links with whichever political party governs their area may derive further benefits in the form of protection from prosecution and access to some of the spoils of public office, such as jobs or, for local businessmen, licences to run bottle stores and taxi companies. The feuds between rival taxi operators, which sometimes give rise to deadly gun battles, are closely linked to local politics in this way. In some areas, particularly of KwaZulu-Natal, control of a taxi firm not only brings profits but enables a local militia boss to regulate the weapons and marijuana trades locally and to supervise population movements in his area. It is in KwaZulu-Natal that violent competition between local militias continues on the greatest scale and is so clearly connected to national political rivalries as to constitute a low-level civil war.

Political clienteles, we may reflect, are built not only by the distribution of patronage, but also by coercion and persuasion. At the beginning of the war in the early 1960s the government controlled most systems of patronage and had an effective monopoly of legitimate violence. As the years went by, and it progressively lost control of these instruments and found itself losing the propaganda war as well, the government's response was to increase its use of coercion. As we have seen, this was done not only by the increasingly ruthless methods of the security forces themselves, culminating in the formation of official death-squads, but also by arming certain groups in the black population, which served the purpose of simultaneously making war on ANC sympathizers and helping form new clusters of political allies among the black population at minimum risk to white lives. The creation of ethnic militias was a technique learned by police officers with counter-insurgency experience in Rhodesia and Namibia, as well as by military men who had learned from Portuguese experience in southern Africa and from other colonial wars. The most successful such attempt at forming an ethnic 'contra' force was in regard to Inkatha, whose support was solidly rooted in the rural areas of Zululand.

Before 1990, while the police could not entirely prevent revolutionary organizations from disseminating propaganda, it could largely prevent them from building a formal base. After the unbanning of these organizations in 1990 this too became an impossible task. Since the ANC's election victory of 1994, local ANC branches have had access to some of the resources of government, enabling local party chieftains to build a real patronage network to buttress their power. In KwaZulu-Natal, this is contested by Inkatha Freedom Party bosses who aspire to do the same, using the resources of the only province which the IFP governs. The police, having lost their ability to crush such networks and being now under the tutelage of an ANC minister, watch nervously. Much depends on the personality and resourcefulness of the local police commander, who has to become something of a diplomat in order to keep peace in his area.

The security forces are not, and never have been, impartial as far as most black South Africans are concerned. Not only has history left a legacy of distrust between the police and supporters of black-dominated political parties, but some explicitly criminal gangs have developed close relations with the security forces. This has produced within some sections of the security forces a highly ambiguous attitude towards certain types of crime. During the last phase of the guerrilla war some police and army officers even developed criminal enterprises of their own, such as in the weapons, gems, ivory and marijuana trades, partly for their own profit and partly as a covert means of providing arms and funds for informal militias opposed to the ANC and the SACP. The range of state-sanctioned law-breaking included sophisticated smuggling operations and currency frauds which brought the government's own secret services into business relationships with major smuggling syndicates, Italian Mafia money-launderers and other operators in the international criminal underworld (Ellis, 1996a). Even the august South African Reserve Bank turned a blind eye to currency fraud committed on behalf of the state (Potgieter, 1995: 147–9). It was in this culture that the so-called Third Force arose, a network of security officials who organized violence, both with and without the formal approval of government ministers, in an effort to alter the balance of power in negotiations between the National Party and the ANC between 1990 and 1994. This further complicates the relations between political parties, party-aligned militias, criminal gangs and the police at the local level today.

Cross-border conflict and trade

The war for control of South Africa was also fought abroad, especially in Mozambique and Angola. Whereas the ANC and the SACP, the PAC and others attempted to establish guerrilla bases in neighbouring countries within striking distance of South Africa, the South African security forces attempted to counter them by direct attack, by destabilizing (Hanlon, 1986) neighbouring states and by using networks of professional smugglers as sources of intelligence and instruments of subversion. It was the strategy of destabilizing neighbouring states which first brought South African intelligence officers into complicity with the smuggling networks which, from the 1970s onwards, were an increasingly important resource in the political economy of the region (Ellis, 1994). At the same time, the application of international sanctions against South Africa caused a variety of government departments to become engaged in the international smuggling of major goods and commodities, including oil and weapons. As South African intelligence officers became smugglers and money-launderers, some individuals developed criminal relationships for purely personal enrichment, and some such liaisons have survived the change of government in 1994. Intelligence officers ordered or encouraged to smuggle and defraud in the name of national security found it progressively easier and more tempting to do this on their own account as they saw the power of the National Party inexorably slipping away and as they began to think hard about their own financial future and that of their families after apartheid. Corruption in the public service increased rapidly as a result of the 'total strategy' of counter-revolution. Since the early 1990s, considerable numbers of those very counter-insurgency officers who developed close connections with professional criminals in the course of their work have left government service to work in the private sector. Many have become conventional businessmen, farmers or administrators or work for private security firms. Some at least combine legitimate enterprises with management of prostitution and arms-trafficking both locally and internationally. It appears that a handful have established interests in the new narcotics trade.

Some of the toughest of the elite troops of the former SADF work for a security company called Executive Outcomes Ltd which has negotiated major contracts for security work with governments in Angola, Sierra Leone and elsewhere. The directors and managers of Executive Outcomes enjoy the active support of some senior members of the erstwhile enemy organization, the ANC, and wield considerable influence in other parts of Africa; at one time they virtually kept the government of Sierra Leone in power, for example. Executive Outcomes is far more than a group of mercenaries. A legitimate company, it employs intelligence analysts and technical staff, and by 1995 had generated over 30 subsidiary companies throughout sub-Saharan Africa specializing in activities including air transport, video production and mining. It has contracts in East Africa, the Indian Ocean and the Middle East. Several of Executive Outcomes' senior personnel previously worked for a South African Special Forces' death-squad known as the Civil Co-operation Bureau. Other companies which began life in the service of the counter-insurgency strategy of the South African state also continue in business, such as GMR (Pty) Ltd, a company set up by an Italian businessman in the Seychelles and now run by a former naval officer who served as a private secretary of President P.W. Botha. GMR sold arms to the Rwandan government in the months prior to the 1994 genocide in Rwanda and continues to trade with the UNITA organization in Angola (Ellis, 1996a: 170–8).

In short, certain types of illicit activity in South Africa are linked to international trading networks both legal and illegal through the activities of sophisticated operators who have access to large amounts of capital. Some of these operators have high-level connections in politics and the security forces, and they are able to broker transactions between powerful factions inside South Africa and abroad. Particularly important in this respect is Mozambique, whose own state infrastructure was largely eroded during a long war in which the SADF played an important role. Mozambique today has effectively become a free trade area for businessmen and smugglers of every description. Since the country produces little for export and has only a small domestic market, it is essentially an entrepôt for onward trade. Especially significant are those former South African military intelligence operatives who have influence with Mozambican politicians and officials and who are able to use Mozambique as a centre for offshore transactions involving South Africa itself.

The political economy of crime

Crime in South Africa is rooted in the country's history, including that of apartheid. The particular forms it takes have been shaped by the war against apartheid at a number of levels. At the local level, particularly in poor black communities, armed militias or gangs attempt to control territory from which they derive economic benefits. Some reach an understanding with local police officers who are unable to enforce the law fully and who may in any case have developed alliances with various unofficial armed groups over many years. Some such groups develop vertical alliances with national political parties or individual politicians and with businessmen who can import the goods which they most require—guns—and who will buy the goods which they offer for export, notably marijuana and stolen cars.

Some middlemen have good connections in politics and the security services, especially those who are themselves veterans of the covert actions of the past. During the cross-border struggle between the South African security forces and the ANC, SACP, PAC and SWAPO, armed groups of all types sprang up throughout southern Africa, and many of the security and intelligence forces of the region have been penetrated by criminal groups in a complex network of relationships. Senior politicians and intelligence officers in Mozambique are widely regarded as having interests in smuggling concerns including the drug trade. The same is true of Zambia, Angola, the Seychelles and elsewhere.

The countries of southern Africa are closely linked in an economic system constructed by the British government and the great mining houses in the late nineteenth and early twentieth centuries, with only Angola, of all the countries in the region, standing largely outside this highly integrated trading system. As the outlying parts of the southern African economic system have grown poorer, not least as a result of the war for control of South Africa which brought about such destruction, so their formal economies have shrunk to be replaced by informal economies and cross-border trades which are technically illicit, but whose existence is widely known. While South Africa remains at the hub of the region's formal economy, it also stands at the centre of this burgeoning smuggling economy. It is not only in Mozambique, Angola and Zambia that senior figures in government and the formal economy sometimes play a key role in the smuggling economy as well, but also in South Africa. It was South African military intelligence officers who succeeded in establishing Johannesburg as the hub of the ivory and rhino horn trades from the late 1970s, with the personal approval of General Malan, then head of the SADF and later Minister of Defence (Kumleben, 1996). According to the head of the Organized Crime Unit of the South African Police Services, the leading gold smugglers are often rich businessmen seeking to export capital in contravention of the currency laws.[3] South African mines are estimated to lose some 1.5 billion rands' worth of gold per year to theft, and gold smugglers export this by air or sea to neighbouring countries and thence to Europe. The diamond marketing cartel, De Beers, has traditionally had an intimate acquaintance with the gem-smuggling trade because of its concern to purchase stones which are unofficially mined and marketed as well as the official production of various countries.

South Africa attracts criminals from abroad not only because it constitutes a substantial market for drugs and fraud, but also because it is an ideal base for operations elsewhere. At the same time, its relative prosperity attracts millions of people from countries to the north who are not professional criminals, but are simply desperate to earn a living. Here the economic failure of other parts of Africa shapes South Africa's own underground economy. For example, traders from Zambia and the Democratic Republic of Congo seeking to buy consumer goods in South Africa for resale at home often have no access to a suitable form of cash, since the currencies of Congo and Zambia have no international value. They sometimes acquire small quantities of gems, gold, ivory, rhino horn, local works of art or any other goods which are easily transportable and which they take to South Africa as a form of currency rather than as a commodity. In a highly organized trade, cars stolen in South Africa are often exported via Mozambique to points further north as far as Nairobi as a form of easily transportable wealth for the settlement of payments agreed particularly in the course of drug transactions, although they have also been traced as far afield as Turkey and New Zealand.

The growth of a regional economy of crime from the 1970s, and later of social movements which contested incumbent governments throughout southern Africa in various forms from religious revivals to campaigns in favour of democracy, was misinterpreted by South African security officers who overestimated the degree to which political and social disturbances throughout the region were due to Soviet aggression. And, while the Soviet Union did indeed acquire, via the SACP, very considerable influence over the ANC, the latter never achieved real control of the array of social forces inside South Africa which it claimed as its supporters. Meanwhile the very relentlessness of the securocrats' reaction helped to confirm the popular belief that apartheid itself was the source of all social problems. The government was prepared to murder people like Steve Biko and many others who were not communists or agents of Moscow and had not taken up arms in opposition to the government, but were simply unofficial spokesmen for substantial sections of black society or, in other words, were politicians. Their murder made them into martyrs and narrowed still further the political ground which the National Party government hoped to contest. The fact that these murders were perpetrated by the government's own security forces jeopardized the ability of the organs of public safety and public protection to uphold the law in future.

Throughout the 1980s the South African government ignored or underestimated some of the key changes taking place in the world, preferring to see everything through a Cold War prism. In fact, politics and economies throughout southern Africa, and many other parts of the world as well, were becoming less formal and less state-dominated as a result of profound changes in international relations. Within South Africa the extra-parliamentary politics of the 1980s represented civic action by a vast array of social groups motivated by a wide range of grievances. These the state continued to regard as illegitimate and even communist-inspired. The securocrats were aware of the political nature of their struggle but, being overwhelmingly military men, were incapable of analysing politics other than as top-down systems of command, patronage and coercion. The National Party itself remained shackled to the white electorate which had brought it to power and sustained it for decades, and when it did finally turn itself into a non-racial organization after 1990, the change was too late to make much impact.

Just as not all threats to the South African state in fact stemmed from Soviet activity, as the government asserted, so, too, apartheid was not the unique cause of evil. The social changes which helped to produce illegitimate violence and crime generally were also the consequences of larger changes which are fairly typical of industrializing countries in general. These include the decline of the rural economy and of the peasantry, the disruption of family and social life associated with labour migration, and the decline of older systems of moral economy. South African society has for decades, even before apartheid, been prey to a high incidence of social problems expressed, among other ways, in the form of broken families, domestic violence, and criminal violence without any form of political intent, particularly in urban areas.

In a healthy multi-party political system such as South Africa aspires to today, it is necessary for social grievances to find non-violent forms of expression both within and outside the political field. Here it is worth mentioning the curious transformation of the ANC itself. Because of its banning in 1960, the ANC did not develop at a crucial period of its history as a conventional political party as it might reasonably have been expected to do. Under apartheid it became the legitimizing element for all manner of social struggles whose actual organizational forms were those of civil society unable to find proper political expression.

There can be no doubt of the ANC's deep popularity among South Africans, but one effect of its becoming a party of government has been to call into question the nature of its relationship as a political organization with South African society more generally. It is noticeable that some of the great dynamism of South African social movements, notably those enlisted in the struggle against apartheid in the 1980s, has evaporated since the ANC entered government, not because the fundamental problems of South African society have disappeared, but because the most talented organizers of social movements have now taken on public office and become administrators of the public good rather than militants for social justice. It remains to be seen to what extent the ANC in government can remain attentive to the social causes which it championed when it was an umbrella for social opposition to apartheid. Conversely, it remains to be seen to what extent South Africa has indeed become ungovernable by any government at all, at least temporarily, and whether citizens are able to redress their grievances by means of social and political action through the range of legal institutions which now exists.

The international context is now quite different from that of the 1980s, and the transformation has been accentuated by South Africa's emergence from international isolation into a world in rapid mutation. In much of Africa formal political institutions and formal economies have declined in importance, as powerful factions and individuals increasingly make use of informal economies and the informal political alliances which produce 'shadow states',[4] patterns of politics and economics at variance with the official and formal structures which, in theory, exist to articulate these fundamental human activities. Since the abolition of apartheid, South Africa is more than ever before tied to the region in which it is located. Quite apart from the domestic factors which tend to weaken the state's monopoly of legitimate violence and which encourage the development of a criminal economy, the country cannot stand apart from the trends which are in evidence elsewhere. Some criminal trades, such as those in drugs (increasing rapidly), and in illegal weapons, are international in nature. Large amounts of money are generated by these trades and some of the profits are likely to be recycled in the form of political finance by criminal bosses in search of political cover.

Southern Africa is not the only part of the world where politics and crime have become closely associated and South Africa is not the only state which, in its struggle to mobilize all possible means and all available social forces for its own preservation, has condoned the creation of criminal enterprises by its own intelligence officers. The great majority of South African police officers and politicians are deeply concerned about the incidence of crime and its penetration of the state, and they can at least count themselves fortunate that the process has proceeded less far than in some other countries. The formation of new power blocs by professional criminals, secret service officers and senior officials working together has not claimed control of the state itself to the same degree as in Russia, for example (Waller and Yasmann, 1995). Nor have South African politicians combined tenure of public office with personal enrichment to anything approaching the extent in some other important African countries, such as Nigeria and former Zaire.

In practice, probably the most pressing question for South Africa is to ascertain whether it is possible for criminal activity to be successfully contained in such a way as to permit the functioning of a conventional political and economic sector, with all that that implies with regard to the rule of law and the security of individuals. Private security guards and fortified suburbs have no doubt become permanent features of South African life, just as in many other parts of the world. In some parts of South Africa a form of warlordism may have become endemic for the foreseeable future, again like some other parts of the world. This does not necessarily imply the further erosion of the state or even of the conventional business sector, since warlordism does not exist in a separate world from official politics but has become an integral part of the political system through the relations between party bosses and the actual perpetrators of illicit violence. The examples of Mexico, Italy and Colombia, to name but three, may well be of relevance to South Africa in showing how a highly developed system of criminal syndicates with connections to political parties and the security forces can co-exist with high rates of economic growth and conventional business activity.

References

Bonner, P. (1993) 'The Russians on the Reef, 1947–57: urbanisalion, gang warfare and ethnic mobilisalion' in P. Bonner, Pi Delius and D. Posel (eds) *Apartheid's Genesis*. Ravan and Witwatersrand University Press, Johannesburg.

Cawthra, G. (1993) *Policing South Africa: the South African Police and the transition from apartheid*. Zed Books, London and Atlantic Heights, NJ.

du Toit, A. (1993) *Understanding South African PoliticalViolence: a new problematic?* Discussion Paper No. 43, United Nations Research Institute for Social Development, Geneva.

Ellis, S. (1994) 'Of Elephants and Men: politics and nature conservation in South Africa', *Journal of Southern African Studies* 20 (1): 53–70.

Ellis, S. (1996a) 'Africa and International Corruption: the strange case of South Africa and Seychelles', *African Affairs* 95 (379): 165–96.

Freed, L. (1963) *Crime in South Africa: an integralisl approach*. Juta, Cape Town.

Hanlon, J. (1986) *Beggar Your Neighbours: apaltheid power in Southern Africa*. James Currey and Catholic Institute for International Relations, London.

Haysom, N. (1986) *Mbangalala: the rise of right-wing vigilantes in South Africa*. Occasional Paper No. 10, Centre for Applied Legal Studies, University of the Witwatersrand, Johannesburg

Johnson, Angela (1996) 'The Real Facts on SA Crime', *Weekly Mail Guardian*, 7–13

Kumleben, Justice M.E. (1996) *Commission Qf Inquiry into the Alleged Smuggling of and Illegal Trade in Ivory and Rhinoceros Horn in South Africa*. State Printer, Pretoria.

McCuen, J J. (1966) *The Art of Counter-Hevolutionary War: the strategy of counterinstngency*, Faber & Faber, London.

Potgieter, De Wet (1995) *Contrabancl: South Africa and the international trade in ivory and rhino horn* Queilleriet Cape Town.

Prins, G. and Stamp, R *91 Top Guns and ToxicWhales: the environment and global security*. Earthscan, London.

Slovo, J. (1986) https://digitalarchive.wilsoncenter.org/document/118082.pdf?v=8b70511a8cfbfbb43290fa89c594b125

South African Police Service (1996) *Report on the Incidence of Serious Crime During 1995*. National Crime Information Management Centre, Pretoria.

van Kessel, I. (1995) «Beyond OurWildest Dreams»: the United Democratic front and the transformation of South Africa'. PhD thesis, University of Leiden.

Waller, J.M. and Yasmann, V.I. (1995) 'Russia's Great Criminal Revolution: the role of the security services', *Journal of Contemporary Criminal Justice* 11 (4): 277—97.

15

AFRICA AND INTERNATIONAL CORRUPTION

THE STRANGE CASE OF SOUTH AFRICA
AND SEYCHELLES

The subject of corruption has emerged at the top of the agenda in recent dealings between African governments and the Western donors on whom many are heavily dependant. It is notoriously difficult to define corruption,[1] but it is generally understood to entail the use of an official position for purposes of private enrichment or illegitimate advantage. During the 1970s and 1980s, there was a stream of books on corruption in Africa[2] or on closely related concepts such as neo-patrimonialism,[3] prebendalism[4] and kleptocracy.[5] Particularly since a World Bank report in 1989 explicitly spoke of a 'crisis of governance' in Africa south of the Sahara,[6] much of the discussion of corruption south of the Sahara has been subsumed in a wider debate on governance.

The literature on corruption or on governance in Africa more generally tends to adopt a national perspective, investigating how national elites use corruption or manipulation of public policy to enrich themselves and maintain themselves in power.[7] It is rather less frequent, at least in the academic literature, to encounter detailed studies of the relationship between corruption in various parts of Africa and that in industrialized countries.[8]

The present article is an attempt to trace the development of corruption in one part of Africa in a global context. It demonstrates how the ease with which capital can be transferred and commodities bought and sold and the speed of modern communication in general have given considerable impetus to the linking of corrupt practices across borders, and that this process of trans-national corruption was considerably encouraged by the Cold War. The main focus of study is Seychelles, a small country but one which has the merit—if that is the right word—of providing interesting data on the subject under discussion. After independence in 1976 Seychelles was subject to intense international diplomatic and military activity, often of a covert nature, due largely to the islands' strategic location, which made them an asset both in US–Soviet rivalry in the Indian Ocean and in the more localized patterns of conflict stemming from South Africa's drive to assert its hegemony in southern Africa, notably by destabilizing or manipulating neighbouring states. This led to attempts to subvert or influence the islands' government by bribery and by force, while more powerful governments and business interests associated with political parties as far afield as Italy manipulated Seychelles' status as a sovereign state in order to perform various transactions of dubious legality. There is some evidence also that the islands were used for financial transactions by arms-dealers and as a staging-post for drug- trafficking. These various interests became intertwined with each other and with the Seychelles' government's own policies, having a demonstrable effect on governance in the islands.

It should be emphasized at the outset that not all the transactions, individuals or circumstances described here can be described as corrupt. On the contrary, one of the principal conclusions which can be drawn from the present essay is that grand corruption, sometimes masquerading as *raison d'état*, shapes the environment in which individual politicians, diplomats and business people are obliged to operate.

Seychelles

The Republic of Seychelles consists of over a hundred islands scattered over a wide area of the western Indian Ocean. Most of its population—a mere 60,000 people at independence in 1976, and less than 100,000 today—is concentrated on just two islands. For a century and a half Seychelles was a remote and insignificant part of the British Empire. Only in 1971, as Britain renounced its colonial presence in the Indian Ocean, did the British government endow the islands with an international airport which was to transform their economic and strategic position by providing easy physical access to the rest of the world.

Britain's strategy for decolonization in the western Indian Ocean from the 1960s entailed divesting itself of colonies while detaching from the colonial administrative territories strategically useful islands which could become the sites for air and naval bases politically easier to manage than bases in more populous territories.[9] As Seychelles became independent, Britain at first attempted to retain its influence by supplying the country's first president, Sir James Mancham, with covert political finance and security assistance.[10] But Britain's political role in the region rapidly declined as Britain lost its ability to project its power world-wide. As the Indian Ocean emerged as a major site of Cold War strategic interest,[11] it was the United States which tended to take over former British assets in the area. The US government built its principal air and naval base in the Indian Ocean a thousand miles to the east of Seychelles, on the island of Diego Garcia, a former dependency of Mauritius whose entire population the British government deported before leasing the island to the US.[12] As part of its global military communications network the US government also built in the Seychelles an important satellite tracking station.

President Mancham was staunchly pro-Western in his foreign policy and seems to have envisaged attracting Middle Eastern petro-dollars for the economic development of his country, most notably through his highly public friendship with the Saudi businessman and arms dealer Adnan Kashoggi.[13] But within one year of his election, on the night of 4–5 June 1977, President Mancham was overthrown in a coup by his prime minister, France Albert René. René's coup was aided by the government of Tanzania, and the new president soon took Seychelles into the left-wing camp in African politics. It became a one-party state. Nevertheless René continued his predecessor's policy of encouraging the creation of a tourist industry in the islands, and this has helped to make the country today an economic success by African standards. President René, realising that Western holiday-makers were Seychelles' most obvious customers and source of foreign exchange, strove to maintain correct relations with Western governments as well as with the socialist countries where his personal political sympathies lay.

Much of the world's oil cargoes pass through the Indian Ocean, and in a period of turbulence in the Middle East and of Soviet ambitions to create a naval presence in the Indian Ocean, and especially after the 1979 revolution in Iran and the Soviet invasion of Afghanistan, the whole of the western Indian ocean rapidly increased in strategic importance.[14] Seychelles was sufficiently important in Cold War strategic planning for the US government to be concerned by the pro-Soviet sympathies of the islands' government after the 1977 coup. France too had strategic ambitions in the Indian Ocean which caused it to take an interest in the islands; the government of Seychelles seems to have suspected the French government of being connected with a coup plot uncovered in the islands in 1979, expelling French military advisors and replacing them with Tanzanians and Algerians.[15] The Soviet Union maintained a large embassy staff in Seychelles and for several years the Soviet ambassador was Mikhail Orlov, regarded by Western intelligence agencies as a senior KGB officer, said to have previously worked as the chief of the important KGB station in Turkey. Soviet warships paid courtesy calls to the islands and the Soviet Union also proffered other forms of assistance. Moreover by the early 1980s there were more than 100 North Korean military advisors in the islands.[16] Another country interested in Seychelles was South Africa, whose government was concerned to prevent the Soviet Union from extending its influence in southern Africa, and which saw the Republic of Seychelles as a potential asset in South Africa's own ambition of regional hegemony.

Within a short time of its independence in 1976, then, Seychelles had become of considerable strategic interest to the two super-powers and to a number of lesser powers—France, South Africa and others— all of which sought to exercise influence in the islands. The country was exceptionally vulnerable to the pressures which larger governments could exert, largely because of its small size and tiny army, and perhaps also because its tourist industry was reliant on Seychelles' being able to maintain an image of tranquillity and unspoiled beauty in order to attract holiday-makers. One might add that the manner in which President René took power in 1977 was a significant cause of instability, for, like most other coups, it had established a precedent for the transfer of power by unconstitutional means which was to put into question the government's legitimacy in years to come.

Beset by the attention of foreign secret services and by plots from within, President René turned for help to a friend, Giovanni Mario Ricci, an Italian businessman who had been living in Seychelles since shortly before independence. Due to the influence he had with René, Ricci was to become an important intermediary for foreigners wishing to cultivate commercial or political relations in Seychelles, as we will shortly describe in more detail. Mario Ricci was born near Lucca, Italy, in 1929. Convicted of fraud in Italy in 1958, he had gone to seek his fortune abroad. He was convicted a second time, in Switzerland, this time for possessing counterfeit currency.[17] Ricci lived in Mexico and Haiti before making his way to Somalia where he set up a business exporting grapefruit. He was expelled from Somalia for reasons unknown around 1974, moving to settle in Seychelles.[18] He was a distinctive figure in the islands, instantly recognizable by his long beard, grown white since he first went to live in Seychelles.

Ricci became President René's friend and unofficial financial advisor. In 1978 he set up a company, the Seychelles Trust Company, in a joint venture with the Seychelles government. The government granted to the Seychelles Trust Company sole rights to incorporate off-shore companies and to act as resident agent for foreign companies and foundations registered in Seychelles, which could operate free of tax. The granting of this right to a private company was unique in that it made the Seychelles Trust Company the only private offshore business registration company in the world, and, in effect, Seychelles became the world's first socialist tax haven.[19] In 1981 the government sold its shares in the Seychelles Trust Company, leaving Ricci in sole control. The cost of registering a foreign company, payable to the government, was a mere 1,500 rupees, or $300.

It was to Ricci that President René turned for help after an attempted coup in 1981 (which is discussed in more detail below) had convinced him of the need to improve his government's security. At the President's request, Ricci hired private detectives to keep the exiled opposition under surveillance.[20] In 1982 a private detective employed by Ricci succeeded in planting a recording device in a London hotel room being used by Seychellois exiles to plot a coup against the government, and the tape was handed to the British press.[21] Both the single party and the government of Seychelles came to rely on Ricci for various financial services, and accepted cash from him, in President René's words 'when [the government] needed to finance something for which we didn't immediately have the money'.[22] Ricci in turn received privileged treatment from the government, and when one of his companies was nationalized, he was paid in cash, whereas other companies in a similar position received only government bonds.[23] President René later stated that he had taken the precaution of asking the Italian authorities whether Ricci had a criminal record, but 'they told us that they had nothing on him.'[24]

Ricci was associated with some distinctly unusual companies in addition to the Seychelles Trust Company. In 1982 he was listed as a director of an entity immodestly entitled International Monetary Funding, or IMF, for short, not be confused with the International Monetary Fund.[25] In 1984 he was accredited to Seychelles as a diplomat representing the Sovereign Order of the Coptic Catholic Knights of Malta which, it emerged, was a commercial company incorporated in New York.[26] Seychelles was the only state in the world to recognize the order.[27] President René later claimed that his government had granted Ricci diplomatic status in the mistaken belief that Ricci's Knights of Malta was in fact the Sovereign Order of Saint John, Knights of Malta, the well-known Vatican order of chivalry. Through his accreditation Ricci gained the right to use a diplomatic pouch and a diplomatic passport, and eventually he was to become the doyen of the diplomatic corps in the islands. President René also confided diplomatic missions to him, such as the improvement of relations with Somalia, where Ricci had once lived and where he still had useful contacts.[28]

Ricci increasingly used one of his many companies, GMR (named after his own initials), as a flagship for various interests. According to GMR's own company brochure it was 'a conglomerate of companies which operates throughout the world' and was 'managed from the operational headquarters in the Republic of Seychelles'.[29] At various times GMR's management, consisting mostly of Ricci and members of his and his wife's families, claimed to control companies in as many as 24 countries, including several in southern and eastern Africa as well as in more conventional business locations such as Britain and Switzerland, and tax havens including Panama, Liechtenstein and Luxembourg. This and Ricci's other companies in the islands were registered and run in conformity with Seychelles law. Already by the early 1980s, Ricci had acquired a reputation as someone who could be approached by anyone who wished to transact some form of business in Seychelles. Although having no official government position, he was diplomat, unofficial head of security, businessman and financial advisor to President René all rolled into one.

South Africa

Among the countries which had developed an interest in Seychelles was South Africa. At the time of the islands' independence in 1976, South Africa's National Party government was already feeling the impact of diplomatic isolation and of the gradual development of a military threat to its security. The government in Pretoria placed increasing importance on securing influence and the capacity to exercise force both within and outside its borders by clandestine means, notably through the development of its secret services (especially the Bureau of State Security, established in 1969) and the Department of Information. For as long as Namibia remained a South African colony, and Rhodesia, Mozambique and Angola remained under colonial or settler rule, South Africa itself was insulated from external aggression, but the situation changed rapidly with the independence of Angola and Mozambique in 1975 and the Soweto uprising of 1976.

The Department of Information was an agency of the South African government whose tasks included the covert distribution of government monies—in other words, bribery—to buy influence at home and abroad. This included in Seychelles. During Sir James Mancham's brief tenure of the presidency Seychelles was regularly visited by South African secret servants carrying '[bags full] of bribe money to secure South African interests', the editor of the Johannesburg *Sunday Express* later recalled.[30] In 1978 the Department of Information's role was exposed in a political scandal known as 'Muldergate' or 'Infogate', in which it was revealed that the Department had not only bribed journalists and secretly bought newspapers at home and abroad in a bid to secure better public relations, but that senior civil servants and politicians in South Africa had abused the Department's lack of parliamentary accountability for purposes of personal enrichment—in other words, corruption.[31] The Muldergate scandal became closely associated with the struggle to succeed the ailing Prime Minister, John Vorster, and to supplant the influence wielded by the Bureau of State Security (BOSS), which was headed by a political appointee, the prime minister's friend and confidant General H. J. van den Bergh. The favourite to succeed Vorster, Dr Connie Mulder, was disgraced as a result of the scandal and lost his claim to the premiership.

The person who emerged victorious from the political in-fighting surrounding the Muldergate scandal to become prime minister of South Africa in 1978 was the Defence Minister, P. W. Botha, who had powerful support from the generals of the South African Defence Force (SADF). The military men resented van den Bergh's and BOSS's pre-eminence in security manners and believed that the changed situation in southern Africa necessitated a complete overhaul of security policy under military direction. The security chiefs, the 'securocrats' as they came to be known, were to acquire great power under P. W. Botha's premiership and later presidency. They unveiled a comprehensive new strategy whose centrepiece was the defence of the South African state in the face of what the government saw as a comprehensive threat, a 'total onslaught' in Prime Minister Botha's words, orchestrated by the Soviet Union.[32] Seychelles had a minor but distinct role in this strategy. The islands offered not only potential military facilities but also possible use as a base for clandestine trading purposes in the face of economic sanctions, especially after the Iranian revolution of 1979 had threatened South Africa's main supply of oil. South Africa in fact was to acquire most of its oil after 1979 from Saudi Arabia and the Gulf states.[33]

Due to a combination of the new defence strategy in Pretoria and the change in government in Seychelles in 1977, the South African secret services decided that bribery was no longer the most effective means of acquiring influence in the islands. In 1978 Seychellois exiles in South Africa, acting on behalf of ex-President Mancham, began discussions with officials concerning a coup attempt to be launched in Seychelles. The BOSS case officer who became most closely concerned with this scheme was one Martin Dolinchek.[34] As plans for the Seychelles' coup developed the SADF lobbied to acquire control of the project, and the operation became the subject of an intense bureaucratic struggle between the military and the civilian intelligence service, the National Intelligence Service (NIS). The NIS was the direct descendant of the former BOSS, which had been disgraced in the Muldergate scandal and subsequently overhauled and twice renamed. Prime Minister Botha was more sympathetic to the military men than he was to the civilian intelligence service. In the end the government allocated planning for the Seychelles' coup operation to Military Intelligence, while the protests of the civilian intelligence service were mollified by the appointment of Martin Dolinchek as a liaison officer on behalf of the NIS.[35] In order to provide a screen of deniability to the Seychelles' coup attempt the operation was entrusted to Mike Hoare, an Irish mercenary soldier who had made his name in the Congo but was now living in South Africa as a civilian. Hoare was later to testify that the coup plans were approved by the South African Cabinet and that weapons were provided by South African Military Intelligence.[36] Most of the 45 or so people selected to carry out the coup were members of South African special forces, several of them former Rhodesian soldiers, some with earlier experience in the British army.[37]

On 25 November 1981 Hoare and his men landed at Seychelles international airport disguised as tourists, members of a drinking-club called the Ancient Order of Frothblowers. After a customs officer had found weapons in the luggage of one of the purported tourists, the invaders fought a brief gun-battle at the airport and escaped aboard an Air India jet which happened to be on the tarmac and which they hijacked. They left behind five soldiers, a female accomplice and also Dolinchek, the intelligence man.[38] The Seychelles' government arrested and tried the six men, acquiring from them full information on the planning of the coup. Four of the six were sentenced to death. Hoare and some others were tried on their return to South Africa.

The Pretoria government, severely embarrassed, opened negotiations for the return of the six convicted mercenaries, and they were eventually returned to South Africa in mid-1983. The conditions for their release were not publicized, and only gradually did it become apparent that in the course of negotiations the South African government had not only paid to President René a ransom of $3 million,[39] but that this was part of a broader understanding with President René personally. His cabinet was not informed of the progress of the talks nor of the ransom payment.[40] President René, alarmed by the succession of coup attempts against him, asked Mario Ricci to help improve his security service. He realized that in order to survive he needed to adjust his foreign policy to accommodate South African interests, at least in some measure. The government also took a series of steps designed to mend fences with both South Africa and the US, whose own Central Intelligence Agency (CIA) had had foreknowledge of the coup attempt,[41] and there was a notable shift in Seychelles' voting record in the United Nations and other international fora.[42] The advent of a socialist government in France in 1981 also helped to ease the pressure on the islands' government, since France maintained an interest in the region notably through its possession of the island of Réunion and military base in Djibouti. For its part, in 1983 the South African government uncovered a further coup plan which was under discussion and expelled from its territory Seychellois opposition activists including Gérard Hoarau, a former seminary student who had been detained in Seychelles in connection with the 1979 coup plot and had gone into exile.[43] Hoarau was a cousin of René's wife and, speaking fluent Italian, had previously been a friend of Ricci.

It appears to have been in the aftermath of the 1981 coup attempt, during negotiations for the release of the six South African mercenaries, that the South African secret services first came fully to appreciate Ricci's significance as a potential intermediary with President René. At that time the number two person in section A, the foreign desk of the South African Security Police, was Craig Williamson, the country's best-known spy. Recruited by the Security Police while he was still at university in South Africa, Williamson had posed as a left-wing student activist and gone into exile, where he succeeded in infiltrating the ANC. In 1979 his true allegiance was revealed and he returned to Pretoria to take up a post at Security Police headquarters. To compound the damage inflicted on the ANC, he absconded from the organization with substantial funds in his possession. These he had turned over to the Security Police, and the ANC's money was later used to buy a farm near Pretoria which was to become a base for operations by Security Police death-squads.[44] In 1985 Williamson resigned from the Security Police and publicly announced that he was going into business. It was not announced that he had at the same time been commissioned as a colonel in South African Military Intelligence. Williamson later explained his resignation from the Security Police on the grounds that 'I decided to get involved in proper intelligence work, especially on the international scene'.[45]

By the mid-1980s Williamson and Ricci had developed a close relationship. In 1986, the year after Williamson's resignation from the police, Ricci's GMR company was registered to do business in South Africa and Williamson was appointed managing director of GMR South Africa and vice-president of GMR world-wide. In GMR's own company literature, the GMR conglomerate was henceforth said to be 'controlled from the executive offices based in Switzerland and South Africa.' The company prospectus represented GMR as a holding company which owned various companies world-wide. Some GMR subsidiary companies, it said, were local acquisitions made in the hope of being able to resell them again at a profit. Other subsidiaries it described as 'parked', dormant companies which could be activated to deal with specific transactions if necessary.[46] Williamson assisted Ricci in acquiring permanent resident's status in South Africa.[47] He scoffed at pointed questions from journalists about Ricci's mysterious background, suggesting that any debatable points in Ricci's curriculum vitae could be explained quite easily. 'There is no hot money, or mafia money, in the GMR operation,' Williamson declared to the press.[48] There is no evidence that Ricci was aware of Williamson's commission in Military Intelligence, but he must certainly have known of his earlier career in the Security Police.

The opening of GMR in South Africa, and the appointment of Craig Williamson as its managing director, gave Ricci access to business opportunities in South Africa, and by the same token it gave Williamson access to the GMR empire and to Ricci's business connections. Williamson hinted to journalists that his purpose was to use Seychelles and the GMR company to avoid the trade sanctions which were being applied with increasing severity to South Africa. 'I would like to assist South Africa in the economic warfare facing it', Williamson was quoted as saying, when asked about his new career as the chief executive of Ricci's GMR company. Williamson described GMR as 'flexible' and talked about how it could be used as a front by other companies seeking to do business with South Africa. 'If [GMR] is faced with anti-sanctions laws,' he said, 'it will restructure its activities to avoid any inhibiting laws.'[49] On another occasion Williamson divulged: 'we are involved in trade in strategic commodities. I don't want to go into details, but GMR has a background in oil.'[50] In effect, although Ricci himself had virtually no experience in the oil business, he had earlier helped to introduce to Seychelles some Italians with extensive expertise in the oil business, to whom Williamson may have been referring. This will be discussed further below.

Williamson, cultivating his new persona as a trader, gave seminars to South African businessmen looking for new markets in the Far East and lectured on how to evade sanctions.[51] He seemed intent on creating a political niche for himself as well, and his political ambitions clearly had support from the very top of the ruling party. In 1987 he stood for parliament as a candidate for the National Party in a suburb of Johannesburg but failed to secure election. Not to be thwarted, President Botha appointed Williamson a member of the President's Council.

By this time, South Africa's relationship with Seychelles was thoroughly ambiguous. Seychelles was often represented in the South African press, and the Western press generally, as pro-Soviet and anti-apartheid. In reality, Pretoria had developed closer relations with the government in Victoria in the months after the 1981 mercenary coup attempt and had expelled Seychellois opposition leaders from South Africa, but the South African secret services at the same time conspired with a group of coup-plotters based in Britain through a diplomat at the South African Embassy in London.[52] The South African secret services eventually betrayed the coup plot to the Seychelles government in August 1986 and in effect aborted the plan. It seems that the South African strategy was to cultivate all sides in Seychelles with a view to cementing its own influence. After the August 1986 coup plot, South Africa's Military Intelligence had the Seychelles government under effective control, largely through Williamson and the relationship he had established with Ricci. GMR South Africa shared its Johannesburg office with another company controlled by Williamson, named Longreach, which acquired responsibility for government security in Seychelles after 1986. Years later, after the African National Congress had come to power, Williamson was to admit that Longreach was in fact secretly owned by Military Intelligence.[53] Seychelles was all the more useful as a Military Intelligence asset because of its government's pro-Soviet reputation. In matters of strategic deception, the South African secret services had made considerable advances since the ham-fisted bribery of the Department of Information and the 1981 mercenary fiasco.

Although Longreach purported to deal mainly in risk analysis, claiming officially to be advising businessmen on conditions for investment in southern Africa, particularly in Mozambique, Uganda and Burundi,[54] it in fact operated as an agent of Military Intelligence both inside and outside South Africa. Williamson once admitted that the company had engaged a French mercenary to carry out the attempted murder of President Lennox Sebe of Ciskei.[55] This, it transpired, was part of an operation by South African Military Intelligence aimed at incorporating Ciskei into a larger new homeland.[56]

South Africa's transition to democracy after 1990 did not mean the end of the covert networks established in earlier years, including those in Seychelles. Senior South African ministers continued to visit Seychelles: in April 1991 Defence Minister Magnus Malan visited the islands, following Foreign Minister Pik Botha who had also been on a visit earlier in the year.[57] In 1994, the press reported that a South African naval officer, Commodore Willem 'Ters' Ehlers, who had succeeded Williamson as chief executive of GMR in South Africa, had negotiated with the Zairean government the purchase of some $40 million of arms. These weapons were almost certainly intended for eventual transfer to Rwanda. Ehlers had worked as a private secretary to President P. W. Botha and it was in this capacity that he had first met Mario Ricci.[58] After Botha's retirement, Ehlers had gone to work for GMR, apparently from 1990 until around 1992. A spokesman for GMR said in 1994 that both Williamson and Ehlers had ceased to work for the company.[59] Williamson had indeed resigned on 31 December 1988 and Ricci in November 1991.[60] A leading US human rights organization, Human Rights Watch, repeated the allegations the following year.[61]

This was one of several cases in the 1990s indicating the extent to which the South African state arms company ARMSCOR remained a major international arms dealer even after the end of the armed struggle for control of South Africa, both selling arms manufactured in South Africa and brokering third-party deals.[62] In Africa today arms-dealing is a lucrative business, and also one with obvious political implications. Even since the demise of the National Party government in 1994 ARMSCOR continues to be something of a law unto itself, still largely staffed by the personnel of the apartheid era carrying out secretive weapons deals, some of which have embarrassed the ANC government, and making use of commercial networks created in earlier years in both public and private sectors. As with all modern weapons-deals, ARMSCOR's commercial sales have political implications. This is true of every country with a weapons-exporting industry. In the case of South Africa, however, the question is to know to what extent arms sales are under effective government control.

Covert operations and corruption

GMR and Longreach were only two of the hundreds of companies set up or acquired by the South African security establishment in pursuit of the strategy of counter-revolution. Some of these companies were used to trade in products subject to international sanctions, including oil, but also in less legitimate products such as ivory and rhino horn.[63] One of Longreach's original board of directors, James Anthony White, a former member of the Rhodesian Selous Scouts, was reported to have an interest in the ivory trade.[64] Front companies were used to channel weapons or supplies to South African allies in Angola, Mozambique and elsewhere. Some, like the network run by the main SADF death-squad, the Civil Co-operation Bureau, were used to carry out assassinations, and others for money-laundering or for peddling political influence. Another Military Intelligence front with which Williamson was associated, the International Freedom

Foundation, succeeded in enlisting senior members of the Republican Party in the US, including Senator Jesse Helms, later to become chairman of the Senate Foreign Affairs Committee, in the campaign to defend apartheid.[65]

The securing of influence in Seychelles was very useful for various activities of this type. Thus, Chieftain Airlines, a front company used by the South African secret services which was later investigated for corruption, applied to the South African National Transportation Commission to fly Boeing 737s between Johannesburg, the Comoros and Seychelles.[66] The Comoros too were used by South Africa for clandestine arms shipments to the Middle East, and from 1979 South Africa paid the French mercenaries who were to run the islands' Presidential Guard until 1990.[67]

Pretoria's 'total strategy' required massive resources to implement and it required the people who managed it, the securocrats, to become interested in spheres of activity which are traditionally outside the scope of the military. Some of this was done openly; some of it required deception, either in the form of secret operations, or the establishment of secret organs of government, or the use of covert activity, meaning actions whose real purpose is other than the apparent one. The total strategy implied centralization of power and decision-making and a great expansion both of the role of the state and of the military and security branches within it.[68] This had obvious political and constitutional implications for South Africa, and the increasing use of covert or clandestine operations in the service of the total strategy also had implications for the accountability of government and, hence, its tendency towards corruption.

Any sort of covert operation has numerous ramifications. If a military unit is secretly to channel arms to an ally, such as was actually done by the SADF in Angola and Mozambique, it must first procure the necessary weapons and ammunition. That means either manufacturing, capturing or purchasing them. Since the supply of these weapons is to be secret, the first option is not be recommended, as the weapons must not be traceable to the actual supplier if they fall into the wrong hands. It was far better for the SADF to capture Soviet-supplied weapons in Angola and then supply them to RENAMO in Mozambique, or even to buy them from Warsaw Pact countries on behalf of their clients, than to supply RENAMO and UNITA with standard SADF equipment. Whatever the source of the weapons, a covert armourer must establish a safe channel for their delivery, probably requiring aircraft and pilots, possibly ships, or at least trucks and drivers. Again, in the interests of secrecy, it is best not to use aircraft of the regular air force or army vehicles for this purpose, since that would make the operation too easy to trace back to the supplier government. Far better to use a front company, an airline or transport company which, like Chieftain Airlines or like the Frama company in Namibia,[69] is apparently in the private sector, but is in reality controlled by the secret services. Pilots and truck-drivers are often men with families, and they require salaries, insurance and pensions, which must also be arranged discreetly since the operatives are not officially on the government payroll but on that of a front company.

All of this means extra work for civil servants who must be employed for the purpose. It also requires money, which, to preserve confidentiality, can come from the secret budget of the state or from other sources. The latter are preferable since private-sector funding is less easy for hostile politicians, journalists and others to trace back to the government. The latter, in fact, is precisely what happened in the Muldergate affair, in that the funds used were relatively easy to trace and implicated politicians in decisions which they later found it impossible to deny with any degree of plausibility. Sometimes it is possible to 'launder' state funds destined for a clandestine operation so as to make them appear as if they emanate from the private business sector, or perhaps genuine businessmen can be induced to finance projects which are primarily of strategic interest. Again, these were all features of the financing of the Muldergate operation in the 1970s.[70] Some front companies may actually generate commercial profits, which can be either diverted or ploughed back into the operation. If money is to be generated from clandestine trade or illicit business, it must be laundered or cleared through the banking system in such a way as to disguise its origin and destination, and this may involve breaking the banking laws, possibly of several countries. A pliable bank, or even a bank secretly controlled by the secret services, is an asset. Hence Chieftain Airlines was associated with a bank established in the Ciskei homeland which took unlicensed deposits and engaged in currency fraud.[71] The bank's owner, a friend of Cabinet ministers Magnus Malan and Pik Botha, was in business with one Vito Palazzolo, an Italian who had worked as a money-launderer in the US and Europe for the important 'Pizza connection' mafia syndicate and had subsequently settled in South Africa.[72]

The difficulties inherent in money-laundering, it is relevant to note, are only one of several problems which secret servants intent on undertaking covert or clandestine operations share with drug-traffickers and other professional criminals. The creation of secret or covert networks, maintained with secret funds, inevitably attracts the attention of professional criminals and tempts otherwise honest people to steal, since the funds involved are publicly unaccountable. So it was in South Africa. Some companies set up by the secret services took illegal commissions or 'kickbacks' on otherwise legitimate contracts awarded by the government. This was particularly common in the South African homelands or bantustans, where there was little effective legal supervision of public works contracts and where corruption was rife.[73] Other branches of the South African government used intermediaries to import oil, since South Africa's international isolation sometimes meant that a middleman had to be employed to disguise a transaction. This cost money in the form of the agent's commission and offered opportunities for official corruption.[74]

Front companies are commonly used by secret services operating in pursuit of state interests, and familiarity with their functioning is clearly part of the tradecraft of intelligence officers and specialists in low-intensity conflict. Politicians are necessary to any such operation, since their authority is needed to legitimize any covert operation, and in fact the element of political authority in such circumstances is crucial since it is political responsibility alone which constitutes the dividing line between a state-sponsored covert or clandestine operation and a purely criminal affair, carried out for private interest by professional criminals or by secret servants who have crossed the line to become rogue elements, disowned by politicians and liable to criminal prosecution. If a dishonest politician, whose authority is needed to provide top cover for an operation, demands a percentage of the financial transactions taking place within his or her sphere of interest, their demands can hardly be resisted. This was clearly the case in South Africa, as Dr Eschel Rhoodie, a senior official responsible for covert funding in the 1970s, has testified.[75]

The recent history of South Africa shows clearly how the pursuit of state interests by covert or clandestine means, and the provision of funds or the implementation of plans which are not publicly accountable, encouraged the growth of corruption in South Africa and elsewhere. The system developed into a complex set of relationships in which secret services directly or indirectly developed commercial interests, and made increasing use of violence as well. In effect the secret services became associated with a spectrum of commercial and military or political activity. At one extreme were ventures such as the 1981 mercenary attack on Seychelles which were entirely military in nature. At the other end of the spectrum were legitimate commercial companies such as GMR. All of these had in common the presence of the South African secret services and, in particular, Military Intelligence. From the relatively straightforward bribery of the Department of Information there was a direct line of progression to the complex of commercial relationships in airlines, companies and legitimate or illegitimate trade in ivory and, according to at least one authoritative source, drugs.[76]

It was only after it had suffered severe embarrassment from the attempt to take over the government of Seychelles in 1981 that the South African secret services settled on subtler means. It was in this way, as the South Africans looked for ways of securing influence with President René's government, that they came to appreciate the advantages offered by Mario Ricci's position in the islands and his contacts elsewhere.

Political finance and corruption

Others too were interested by Ricci's position in Seychelles. In 1980, a friend of Ricci's, the Roman banker Roberto Memmo, learned of Ricci's rights to incorporate offshore companies in the islands and established an offshore bank there, Roberto Memmo Investment Banking.[77] Although it was not publicly known at that time, Memmo was a member of the Italian masonic lodge P-2, a secret organization of leading figures in Italian business, the security and intelligence services and politics, which, when its existence was revealed, caused a sensation in Italy. A parliamentary commission of inquiry in Italy established that the lodge had been closely connected with right-wing politics. In effect, during the 1970s P-2 and the Italian secret services had conspired in a strategy aimed at preventing the election of a communist government in Italy, including by inspiring acts of right-wing terror such as the 1980 bombing of Bologna railway station. Leading members of P-2 had also succeeded in infiltrating the finances of the Vatican.[78]

The full extent of corruption in Italian public life was to be fully laid bare only by the *mani pulite* ('Operation Clean Hands') investigations of the 1990s. At the heart of politics in Italy for several decades, it has now been proven, was a system whereby the main political parties received kickbacks in return for the awarding of public contracts from businesses and particularly from Italian parastatal companies over which politicians were able to exert influence. Secret networks like P-2 enabled obscure figures, such as the Venerable Master of the P-2 lodge Licio Gelli, to influence or even to blackmail politicians and government officials and also to negotiate with other important elements in Italian life, including the mafia and the Vatican.[79] The illicit payments negotiated through such networks between businessmen and politicians were illegally transferred to the bank accounts of various operators of the system and of individual politicians, usually through an elaborate series of transactions involving paper companies established for the purpose, and often by using offshore facilities in Switzerland, the Caribbean and elsewhere. The amounts of money involved were huge. One of the parastatal companies most deeply involved in this process was the Italian state oil company, the Ente Nazionale Idrocarburi (ENI), which was eventually found, as a result of the *mani pulite* judicial investigations, to have channelled over a billion and a half dollars to Italian political parties in illegal payments.[80] As part of the political spoils system, Italy's leading political parties had also divided along geographical lines the political oversight of the large Italian development budget, with the Italian Socialist Party taking Somalia, for example, and another party, Mozambique. Each party thus took its cut of kickbacks from contracts given to Italian companies, as did the relevant officials and politicians in Africa itself.[81] This system of political financing produced regular scandals in Italy whenever elements of the country's clandestine system of power-broking were made public. It was only in the early 1990s that circumstances permitted Italian judges to move against the political parties and influence-peddlers. Among the most prominent scandals produced by this system was the 1982 collapse of the Banco Ambrosiano with unrecoverable loans of some $1.3 billion, at that time one of the largest bank collapses in history, and the mysterious death of the Bank's chairman, Roberto Calvi, found hanging beneath London's Blackfriars Bridge. The bad loans had been made to shell companies actually controlled by Calvi and by the Vatican bank, the Institute of Religious Works. A considerable amount of the money, perhaps $250 million, had been siphoned off by the Venerable Master of the P-2 masonic lodge. The Institute of Religious Works lost some $500 million of Vatican money through its transactions with Banco Ambrosiano.[82]

A number of people closely associated with the Banco Ambrosiano, with ENI, and with the illicit provision of public funds to Italian political parties had dealings in Seychelles in the 1980s. Roberto Memmo, for example, worked as a commercial agent for ENI.[83] A significant figure in Italy's political and financial underworld, Francesco Pazienza, arrived in Seychelles, on the run from the Italian police, in 1983. Pazienza was well-known in Italy, and his name had already been associated with several major scandals. Pazienza had been a protégé of a chief of Italian military intelligence, General Giuseppe Santovito, who fell into disgrace when his membership of the P-2 masonic lodge became known, and Pazienza had been employed as a personal assistant by Roberto Calvi at a time when the Banco Ambrosiano chairman was desperately seeking financial support from the secret networks of Italian finance to cover the huge hole in his accounts. It was Pazienza who was in fact the originator of the Sovereign Order of the Coptic Catholic Knights of Malta, the company which Ricci was to represent as a diplomat in Seychelles, and it was from him that Ricci acquired the company.

Pazienza's extraordinary range of contacts in the fields of business, politics and intelligence extended to the US, where he had at one stage worked with a number of Americans associated with Ronald Reagan's 1980 election campaign. While Pazienza was an inveterate liar and fabricator of tall stories, it does appear that he had helped the Reagan campaign by supplying intelligence material calculated to embarrass Reagan's opponent, the incumbent President Jimmy Carter.[84]

When he arrived in Seychelles in 1983, Pazienza was wanted for questioning by the Italian police in connection with various affairs including the collapse of the Banco Ambrosiano.[85] His ambitions were dazzling. He met Ricci and members of the government and shared with them his ideas for turning Seychelles into an entrepôt and operations centre for commodity transactions of various kinds, using the off-shore rights held by Ricci. He claimed to have the support of leading financiers in the US and elsewhere, and indeed many of those he named did not deny knowing Pazienza. Among the schemes which Pazienza claims to have conceived were plans to sell fishing-rights to Mexican interests and to use the islands as a base for dealing in cut-price Mexican oil.[86] In November 1984 Pazienza learned from a government minister that two Italian policemen were on their way to Seychelles to arrest him and he hastily left the islands, travelling on a genuine Seychellois diplomatic passport. He was later arrested in the US and extradited to Italy.[87]

Following Memmo and Pazienza to Seychelles came another Italian connected to both ENI and the Banco Ambrosiano, the financier Florio Fiorini.[88] Fiorini was the former finance director of ENI who had resigned after he was revealed to have prepared without proper authorization a scheme to use ENI funds in a bid to save the Banco Ambrosiano, shortly before the bank's collapse.[89] During his career at ENI Fiorini had become a leading figure in the jungle of Italian political finance and had demonstrated a remarkable talent for financial manipulation. After leaving ENI he had gone on to build up a business empire on his own behalf. His main vehicle was a company called Société Anonyme Suisse d'Exportations Agricoles, known as SASEA.[90] SASEA was an obscure Swiss agricultural products company, part-owned by the Vatican, which had little to recommend it other than a listing on the Geneva stock-exchange. Shortly after the collapse of the Banco Ambrosiano and his own departure from ENI, Fiorini assembled a consortium of businessmen, many of them previously associated with both ENI and the Banco Ambrosiano,[91] who acquired and recapitalized SASEA. The company's chairman was no less than Nello Celio, a former president of Switzerland. In effect, Fiorini and his colleagues transformed SASEA into a merchant bank, buying, asset-stripping and selling companies and financing acquisitions in Europe and North America, while continuing to work closely with Italian politicians. Fiorini had especially close contacts with leaders of the Italian Socialist Party, especially Prime Minister Bettino Craxi and Foreign Minister Gianni De Michaelis,[92] both of whom were to be convicted of corruption in 1995. (Their conviction is currently pending an appeal).

Fiorini visited Seychelles for the first time in 1983 or 1984 and met both Mario Ricci and President René.[93] Fiorini had the idea of acquiring an oil-trading facility in Seychelles, and he and SASEA worked with President René to nationalize the Shell oil company in the islands. In 1985 the government nationalized Shell and replaced it with the Seychelles National Oil Company (SNOC), which also took a share-holding in a number of SNOC subsidiary companies. An Italian oil firm, a shareholder in SASEA with close associations with ENI, obtained a contract to manage the Seychelles' government's new oil interests.[94] The government and Fiorini explained the nationalization by saying that it would enable Seychelles to sell fuel to aircraft and ships visiting the islands. Pazienza, by this time in detention, alleged that it was in fact the realization of his idea of using the islands to trade oil on the world market.[95]

It was probably this development of Italian-run oil interests in Seychelles which prompted the South African Military Intelligence officer, Craig Williamson, to suggest in 1986 that he was joining GMR because of what he called its 'background in oil'.[96] After Williamson's entry into GMR, there were rumours that the government of Seychelles and its parastatal oil companies were used as a cover for South Africa to import embargoed oil. This has never been proven, and oil traders and shippers did not report any extraordinary tanker movements to Seychelles. Nevertheless, a senior Seychellois diplomat has confirmed that, within a couple of years of Williamson's entry into GMR, Seychelles had come to occupy a place in South African sanctions-busting networks, apparently using paper transactions rather than physical transhipment of oil.[97] It is noteworthy that Fiorini's former employer, ENI, developed such a system in the 1970s for selling Arab oil to Israel via front companies and paper transactions in the Bahamas, Malta and elsewhere.[98] SASEA may also have entertained other ideas to make money from the boycotts imposed on South Africa. A private airline which inaugurated a weekly service from Nairobi via Mahe to Singapore, Ligne Aerienne Seychelloise, included at least one shareholder with close links to SASEA. It was planned to join this to a Botswana–Seychelles link.[99]

Among SASEA's acquisitions was a dummy company registered in Seychelles' offshore facility called the Seychelles International Bank, which Fiorini often called SIBANK and which appears to have developed from the earlier Roberto Memmo Investment Banking. The Seychelles International Bank did not have a full banking licence and, indeed, hardly had a physical existence. Fiorini transferred the bank's official headquarters to Switzerland, although such transactions as it carried out were actually performed from a small, shabby office in Monte Carlo. SASEA issued cheques on the bank in an effort to buy shares in an Italian insurance company.[100]

Fiorini went from strength to strength for as long as he enjoyed the patronage of leading Italian politicians. Through a series of companies, Fiorini, together with a partner, Giancarlo Parretti, who had only a few years earlier been convicted of fraudulent bankruptcy,[101] eventually succeeded in a major business coup, acquiring the Hollywood film company MGM-United Artists for the sum of $1.3 billion, after they had earlier been frustrated in an attempt to purchase the French film company Pathé. These acquisitions were made with massive loans from the Netherlands subsidiary of the French state-owned bank Crédit Lyonnais.[102] A French parliamentary commission of inquiry in 1994 failed to reveal any sound commercial reasons for the size of Crédit Lyonnais' lending to such dubious financiers as Fiorini and Parretti.[103] The commission's rapporteur, a deputy from a party opposed to the French Socialist Party which then held the French presidency, gradually put together a picture of political influence-peddling linking SASEA, Fiorini and Parretti with socialist politicians in Paris, where Parretti had been the accredited representative of the Italian Socialist Party, Rome and even Spain.[104] Using Crédit Lyonnais Bank Nederland loans, the two Italians acquired a cinema chain in Britain and the Netherlands on behalf of the Italian media tycoon (and later prime minister) Silvio Berlusconi.[105] They consistently managed to engineer major acquisitions not only with loans from Crédit Lyonnais Bank Nederland, but also from their own Seychelles International Bank. For the MGM acquisition they also appear to have been supported by letters of credit issued by the Sovereign Order of the Coptic Catholic Knights of Malta.[106] Seychelles International Bank was at the heart of Fiorini's and Parretti's finances. Where it acquired its funds from remains unclear.

SASEA was eventually to go bankrupt with debts of 2.7 billion Swiss francs, about $1 billion.[107] Tracing exactly what happened to this money will probably be no easier than it was in the case of the Banco Ambrosiano. Crédit Lyonnais was left with ownership of MGM-United Artists, probably worth considerably less than what Fiorini and Parretti had paid for it, and with a loss of 6–9 billion French francs on its 1993 accounts, much of it stemming from the bad loans incurred by Crédit Lyonnais Bank Nederland.[108] It appears that Fiorini and Parretti, having learned their trade in Italian political finance and enjoying excellent relations with leading members of the Italian Socialist Party, had gone some considerable way to extending the Italian system of political financing to other countries, notably France, although this is a matter which requires further investigation.

The US connection

Some influential figures in the US, too, had formed an opinion of the ease with which the Seychelles' government could be swayed and of the influence enjoyed in the islands for some years by Mario Ricci.

US security and foreign policy in the early 1980s was a bone of contention not only between competing bureaucracies—at the White House, the State Department, the CIA and the National Security Council—but also a myriad of unofficial interests loosely attached to the political entourage of President Ronald Reagan and his Director of Central Intelligence, William Casey. This was the tangle which was to produce the Iran–Contra affair, which came to public attention in 1986.

As CIA director from 1981 to 1987, William Casey actively supported a network of unofficial contacts which, in his view, would assist in the ultimate aim of securing US security interests in the world. He enjoyed the unusual status for a Director of Central Intelligence of having cabinet rank and, in the opinion of some, he was to become the most important figure in the Reagan administration second only to the President himself.[109] Casey was an old intelligence hand who had served in the Office of Strategic Services (OSS), the forerunner of the CIA, in the Second World War. A visceral anti-communist, he took up the post of CIA chief determined to restore America's capacity to fight its foes around the world which, in his opinion and that of many in the Republican Party and in the CIA itself, had been undermined by misguided efforts, particularly under President Jimmy Carter, a Democrat, to impose restrictions on the Agency. This, thought Casey, had had a disastrous effect on the CIA's effectiveness and morale. Casey and other Cold Warriors in the Reagan administration encouraged an array of informal contacts to build a private-sector network which could deliver help to America's friends and allies around the world without having recourse to what they considered the emasculated CIA or the fickle, Democrat-dominated, US Congress. The revelation of illicit deals with Iran and the Nicaraguan contras was eventually to expose the existence of other secret wars fought by Casey and the CIA extending to parts of the world other than Iran and Nicaragua, and arms-dealing links with South Africa.[110] Casey's basic purpose was to get money and guns to any of America's allies who needed them in order that they might inflict damage on America's enemies, and principally the Soviet Union and its allies. The South African government clearly came into the Cold War category of friends of America. It was a bastion of anti-communism in Africa and it was the main conduit to the UNITA organization in Angola.

Just as South African anti-communists saw the strategic possibilities offered by Seychelles, so did some in America. Some of Casey's associates, notably in the influential World Anti-Communist League, became interested in the islands, encouraging propaganda against its socialist government, depicted in a series of articles in the US and British press in the early and mid-1980s as a Soviet client, and fraternizing with the exiled opposition. In the wake of the 1983 US invasion of Grenada, it was not unrealistic to imagine the US government, or at least William Casey's fellow-travellers on the extreme right, backing a coup in strategically important, and allegedly Marxist-dominated, Seychelles. The US Department of Defense was concerned about the Seychelles' government's pro-Soviet tendencies and had its own connections to Defence Minister Ogilvy Berlouis, who was received at the Pentagon in 1985.[111] It appeared that some in the US security establishment saw Berlouis as a potential future president of the islands, recognizing in him an ambitious man with no ideological baggage despite his tenure of a senior post in the René government. The coup plan aborted in August 1986 (described above) had the active support of the South African intelligence services and claimed support from prominent US anti-communists and from the British secret services.

Perhaps the greatest controversy surrounding the Iran–Contra and associated networks was the precise role played by the two senior members of the US executive, President Ronald Reagan and Vice President George Bush. The latter was a former Director of Central Intelligence and, unlike Reagan, an expert in foreign policy. Both during the Reagan administration and during his own presidency, Bush had to fight to deny having had any role in the Iran-Contra affair or in other affairs related to the US government's covert or semi-privatized diplomacy and secret wars.

In view of this, it is noteworthy that one of Bush's closest aides became associated with Mario Ricci in Seychelles. In February 1985, a partner in the US law firm used by Mario Ricci, former US Deputy Trade Secretary David R. Macdonald, travelled to Seychelles to discuss with Ricci and President René how the Seychelles government could best be represented in Washington. He then discussed the matter with Vice President Bush's press secretary, Peter Teeley. Teeley resigned his position at the White House on 1 March 1985 to open a public relations practice in the private sector. Within a week of his resignation Teeley had agreed to represent the government of Seychelles in Washington jointly with Macdonald, and the two of them undertook to introduce Seychellois ministers in Washington at whatever level they desired.[112] The bill for these services, $6,000 per month, was not paid by the Seychelles government but by Mario Ricci personally and correspondence concerning this lobbying arrangement was addressed not to the Seychelles' government but to Ricci personally.[113] In the circumstances, it is unlikely that Teeley would have resigned a senior position in the White House to take on this consultancy without informing his employer, Vice President Bush. It is testimony not only to the importance for the US government of developments in Seychelles at that time but also to the influence which Mario Ricci was acknowledged to have. It seems likely that senior US officials wished to cement their country's influence in Seychelles but also to outflank the more extreme anti-communists such as those of the World Anti-Communist League.[114] Neither the South African government nor mainstream US agencies actually sought to overthrow President René by the mid-1980s, and certainly not after the failed coup of August 1986, since they already had him under control. They were probably most afraid, by this time, not that Seychelles was becoming a Soviet client but that it would be destabilized by extreme anti-communists working with William Casey. This threat from the extreme right was to disappear after exposure of the Iran–Contra networks in America and after South Africa had aborted the 1986 coup. The ending of the Iran–Iraq war was later further to reduce the sensitivity of the western Indian Ocean.

American and South African interests in Seychelles were quite similar. The various arms of the US security establishment were generally agreed on the need to support the Pretoria government in the context of the Cold War, although it was not politically acceptable for Washington to state its support for the apartheid government in Pretoria unequivocally. There were also more complex aspects to this relationship. The US and South Africa were both on the same side in the Angolan war, and needed to cooperate in the supply of UNITA. In the Middle East, the US was determined to prevent an Iranian victory in the Iran–Iraq War and was supplying massive quantities of arms to Iraq but was also arming Iran in secret in order to secure the release of US hostages in Lebanon. Since the South African weapons industry was selling weapons to Iraq and being part-paid in Iraqi oil,[115] the Americans had an interest in monitoring the flow of weapons from Pretoria to Baghdad so as to ensure the desired strategic balance between the two Middle Eastern rivals. At the same time Washington did not wish to disrupt Pretoria's oil supplies from Saudi Arabia and other Gulf states which supported Iraq in the Gulf War. As Indian Ocean islands, Seychelles and the Comoros stood in the middle of the sea-lanes and air-routes carrying weapons from South Africa to the Gulf and oil in the opposite direction.

Some effects in Seychelles

As bureaucrats and businessmen hammered out these strategic arrangements in offices in Washington, Geneva, Pretoria and elsewhere, and in business meetings in hotels all over the world, and as vast amounts of money changed hands, an atmosphere of intrigue and skulduggery settled on Seychelles and among some Seychellois exiles. There were occasional political assassinations or 'disappearances' in the islands, which although few in number, had an unsettling effect in such a small community.[116] Gérard Hoarau, the most effective of the Seychellois exiles, published a series of detailed, well-documented and highly embarrassing allegations concerning corruption by the Seychelles government and promised further revelations[117] which were never forthcoming: in November 1985, Hoarau was machine-gunned in a quiet London suburb. His killer, apparently a professional assassin, was never identified.

There were constant rumours that the islands were being used for heroin- and currency-trafficking. In late 1984, in the US, the New Jersey police found the mutilated bodies of two local drug-traffickers, apparent victims of a gangland killing. One of the two had in his pocket an address book which contained the name and address of Florio Fiorini and the name and private phone number of President France Albert René. The circumstances in which he had come to write these numbers in his address book were a mystery. The US ambassador to Seychelles at the time recalls that when he gave this information to the President, René went pale with apprehension. It was the only time that the ambassador recalls seeing René truly startled.[118] Important international crime syndicates seem to have infiltrated much of the region: in London Francesco Di Carlo, a Sicilian convicted in 1987 of heroin-trafficking on behalf of a mafia crime family in a major trial, was shown to have regularly visited Mombasa, Kenya, where some casinos were said to be used by the Italian mafia for both money-making and money-laundering on a significant scale.[119]

Between the inception of Seychelles' private offshore tax haven in 1978 and 1992 some 40 companies registered to make use of the facility.[120] According to Finance Minister James Michel, speaking in 1995, some of them 'have been engaged in illegal activities and were being investigated by Interpol and the US State Department'.[121] In a court case in France in 1986, for example, it emerged that a company registered in the Seychelles' offshore facility had been used to transact major arms deals, possibly in an effort to acquire nuclear material for Libya.[122]

Finance Minister James Michel's acknowledgement in 1995 of the abuses of the Seychelles' tax haven and measures taken by him to reform the way in which the system worked do not signal an end to the islands' involvement in money-laundering. In November 1995, the Seychelles national assembly amended the constitution in order to open the way for legislation guaranteeing immunity from criminal prosecution for any foreign businessman investing a minimum of $10 million in the islands. The Economic Development Bill provides immunity from prosecution for all investors meeting these requirements 'for all criminal proceedings whatsoever except criminal proceedings in respect of offences involving acts of violence and drug trafficking in Seychelles'.[123] The director of Britain's Serious Fraud Office commented that it was 'the perfect present for drug barons, fraudsters and money launderers'.[124]

The Cold War and global corruption

The fact that South African secret servants, Italian businessmen and others were able to exert such pressure on the government of Seychelles, and indeed the influence which these people had in their countries of origin, should be considered in the context of the Cold War. It was the perception of a total onslaught against the government in Pretoria which led South Africa's politicians and secret services to adopt increasingly ruthless measures throughout the region and, as we have seen, these entailed a rapid escalation of corruption in South Africa itself. The same was broadly true of Italy, for the growth of corruption in Italian public life was directly connected to the fear in certain high circles of the Italian Communist Party coming to power in Rome. Organizations like P-2 were pledged to assure that this would not happen, and they were able to commit all manner of crimes, including massive corruption, in the name of anti-communism. For four decades Italian businessmen and voters and Italian politics itself were hostages to this system.[125] It is no coincidence that the end of the Cold War was to encourage an extraordinary wave of political reform not only throughout Africa, including both Seychelles and South Africa, but also in Italy, where magistrates were at last able to indict politicians and others suspected of corruption.

Corruption on this scale, once entrenched, is hard to eliminate. A good example of this is provided by the maze of companies and organizations set up or acquired by the South African intelligence and security officers in their fight to defend apartheid. Front companies established by intelligence operatives are difficult to trace and difficult to close, not least since their existence may be quite legal and their formal ownership may be no longer vested in the state, but in nominees who cannot legally be dispossessed by administrative decree. Such companies are capable of transforming themselves, if necessary by acquiring a new name but continuing in the same business, as a snake sheds its skin. In this way the arrangements made in or concerning Seychelles in the 1970s and 1980s have produced a longer-lasting infrastructure of personal connections and institutions designed to evade national laws and to perform illicit transactions. There is evidence that illicit trade arrangements set up in southern Africa originally for military reasons survive in the form of networks engaged in the ivory, currency, diamond, drug and weapons trades.[126] These trades have now become a major threat to the security of South Africa and they are an important feature of the political economy of various regions of Africa. This legacy is complicated by the fact that secret service and special forces operatives who have acquired expertise in covert operations have shown themselves capable of using their skills to mount totally independent ventures in the private sector. There are many examples of this, but an important one for the present discussion is the South African security company Executive Outcomes Ltd., which has worked in Angola, Sierra Leone and elsewhere and which has generated a wide array of front-companies in fields from air transport to video production.[127] In a similar vein, successive companies manipulated or controlled by Italian political financiers have shown a similar tendency to resurface in new forms.

In general, the Cold War encouraged the development of relations between crime, politics and intelligence activity, largely because secret services and politicians who purported to be acting for the greater good of the West were prepared to tolerate or even to promote politicians of dubious morality and to do deals even with professional criminals, particularly in the Third World but also in the industrialized world. The longevity of the Italian mafia and the growth of the world narcotics trade are both in part consequences of bargains made by Western politicians and secret services with foreign governments or even with criminal elements in their own countries and sustained over considerable periods of time.[128] The growth of transnational crime and of the corruption associated with it, often seen nowadays as an emerging security threat to the nations of the West, grows out of the Cold War itself.

If a government or an individual politician in an African country is offered unaccountable funds by foreign governments, and is made to understand that refusal can entail violent attempts to overthrow the government, it becomes more understandable why some politicians may come to see international politics as a jungle, in which richer governments ruthlessly pursue their perceived national or factional interest at the expense of smaller and poorer ones. Not all African governments are subject to the same pressures as those applied to Seychelles, but there are certainly many blandishments and threats which are never publicly reported and are not assimilated in academic analyses of corruption and governance. In the case of Seychelles, and no doubt in many other cases also, many of the pressures or promises offered from abroad were articulated by various secret services. While there is an enormous literature and an array of specialist journals on secret services, academic studies of intelligence and security services have devoted little attention to Africa in general, with the partial exception of South Africa.[129] The evidence of the present study suggests that intelligence services play an important role not only in the politics of some African states but also in relations between rich countries and Africa and that, not surprisingly, they are often charged with the more delicate or less acceptable tasks of diplomacy. If the case of Seychelles is anything to go by, intelligence services in developed countries are largely concerned with carrying out aspects of foreign policy which are to be concealed from the domestic public rather than any other function.

If this observation is correct, the inferences which follow apply at least as much to the wealthier nations of the world as to African governments. And if analysis of the activities of major intelligence agencies in Africa tells us something about the nature of governance in some of the world's older and wealthier democracies, it also tells us something about the nature of the political enterprise in those same democracies. Much of the unorthodox or illicit financial activity in Seychelles directly or indirectly was connected with the funding of political parties or individual politicians. This was so not only in the case of funds used for Seychelles' own ruling party, but also in regard to Italy. SASEA's extraordinary relationship with Crédit Lyonnais suggests the existence of a particular relationship with Italian political parties and perhaps also with the French Socialist Party. Political parties in modern advanced democracies, it seems, are permanently in search of funds in excess of what they can obtain from domestic party members or sympathizers. The competition for political power is such that they may be prepared to seek such funds from unorthodox or illicit arrangements with business, or with their own secret services, or a combination of the two. Money can be laundered in real-estate transactions and leveraged buy-outs of the type undertaken by SASEA, in which political support is crucial. It can also be laundered in some circumstances through the media industry, and here the attempts of Florio Fiorini and Giancarlo Parretti to buy film companies and newspapers meshed with the interests of politicians in acquiring influence with the media. Media magnates-cum-politicians such as Silvio Berlusconi are products of this tendency.

Inasmuch as Africa is a field where the governments of powerful countries can pursue factional or personal interests virtually unchecked, Africa may be a more significant factor in the politics of some Western countries than is generally imagined, due to the relative ease with which unaccountable funds can be obtained or laundered there.[130] The globalization of capital movements makes it all the easier and more tempting to carry out such transactions abroad, and here small and easily manipulable states like Seychelles are an obvious attraction. Political job-men and money-launderers come into contact with professional drug-smugglers, and streams of business, political and criminal finance may merge. Africa's role in the international narcotics trade, we may note, is increasing rapidly, not as a producer but as an intermediary for products consumed in North America and Europe.[131]

In this way problems of political funding, crime and governance more generally in the rich world become inseparable from related problems in Africa itself. The networks thus established may become independent of their political instigators, creating power blocs with enduring interests which survive changes of regime in, for example, Rome, Paris or Pretoria. The impression gained by the French Member of Parliament François d'Aubert, chairman of the Anti-Mafia Commission of the French National Assembly and rapporteur of the Commission of Inquiry into Crédit Lyonnais, is worth citing as a description of the nebulous political-financial networks in modern democracies:[132]

> I observed a shadow area, a zone of contact between legality and illegality, between the licit and the criminal, between clean money and dirty money, between honest people and out-and-out crooks. It is a no-man's-land dominated by a demi-monde of intermediaries of every kind, of corrupters and corrupted enjoying complete impunity for laundering money in investments which are clean, safe and profitable.

In South Africa, the growth of political corruption was associated with a very special factor, namely the protracted struggle to defend apartheid. South Africa and southern Africa may feel the effects of methods used in the service of the total strategy for years to come as Pretoria's former secret servants continue their careers either inside or outside the public service. Trans-border trafficking of drugs and weapons is frequently seen by commentators, and by the South African government itself, as a major security threat in an age, and in a part of the world, where conventional wars between states seem to have become obsolete and to have been replaced by armed conflict carried out by factional interests, often associated with international trades in illicit products, including narcotics. Funds gained from enterprises of this type can be channelled into political finances, and in South Africa, as in Italy and elsewhere, the dividing lines between secret services, organized crime and political parties may be seen to have become blurred to a considerable degree.

In much of tropical Africa, the decline of state power in recent years has resulted in the emergence of networks of long-distance trade in high-value commodities including gems, weapons and drugs which are both sources of wealth and vectors of political–military conflict, such as in Liberia, Angola, Somalia and elsewhere.[133] This is an important development in which anti-corruption or good governance campaigns are of little relevance, since either these trades are outside the control of collapsed states, or the political powers which are emerging depend on them for their own finances. Such long-distance trades are producing new patterns of politics in Africa in which secret services or privatized security organizations like Executive Outcomes are playing an important role. There are examples of major banks which launder drug-money and facilitate more traditional forms of corruption such as bribery and capital flight for governments and for individual clients but which are also tolerated by major Western intelligence agencies which find it convenient to observe, but not to denounce, the illicit flows of financing for states, drug barons, political parties and terrorist organizations. BCCI, the Bank of Credit and Commerce International, whose collapse marked the biggest bank failure in history, is the best-known example.[134] The detailed reconstruction in the present article may serve as a contribution to a deeper understanding of the origins and nature of these contemporary phenomena which are inextricably associated with general questions of governance and politics.

16

THIS PRESENT DARKNESS

A HISTORY OF NIGERIAN ORGANISED CRIME

Introduction

You have probably received an email like this one that arrived in my inbox some time ago:

> We are pleased to inform you of the result of the STAATSLOTERIJ NL Email Winners International programs held on 7th day of September.... Your email address have [sic] been selected as one of the lucky winners in the 3rd category, therefore you have been approved for a lump sum payout of 920,000.00 Euro (Nine Hundred and Twenty Thousand Euro).

It seems that, without even buying a ticket, I had been randomly selected by the Dutch state lottery to receive almost a million euros.

> To file and claim your winning, please contact our claim-processing department for the processing of your winning particulars with the contact information's [sic] below.

The contact person is one Gert Gilbertson. His phone number is listed, but it's a mobile, not a fixed phone line. Gilbertson's email address is contactgertgilbertson@gmail.com, which doesn't look like that of a state lottery company. Then there are the small grammatical errors that draw attention to the fact that this message may not be quite as official as it purports to be. Something is definitely wrong here.

If I were to respond to Mr Gilbertson's communication, he would no doubt inform me that several fees are required for bureaucratic or legal purposes before the transfer of €920,000 to my account can take place. It's quite likely he will ask for my bank account details also. He might invite me to meet him in person in order to discuss my amazing lottery win. The meeting will probably be held in a public place, perhaps the lobby of a smart hotel or of a leading bank in Amsterdam. In any event, were I to pursue this matter I could end up paying out hundreds or even thousands of euros without getting a cent in return.

Ever since money was invented, there have probably been dishonest people perpetrating advance-fee frauds—requesting payment upfront for goods or services that do not exist or that they have no intention actually to deliver. However, this particular hoax has some of the hallmarks of a Nigerian scam. Nigerian scammers are generally regarded as pioneers in the sending of mass letters, messages and emails seeking to defraud any recipient foolish and greedy enough to fall for their tricks, although all the signs are that the practice has now spread worldwide. Nigerians call scams like these 'Four One Nine', so called by reference to Article 419 of the country's criminal code, which concerns fraud. Four One Nines are not the only field in which Nigeria and Nigerians have established an unfortunate reputation for fraud or crime more generally.

If I were to fall for this trick, I would be joining the five or six Dutch people who, every week in the early years of this century, responded to a message like the one above and ended up parting with substantial sums of money to Nigerian fraudsters. At that time scams like these regularly featured on a true-life crime show called *Opgelicht* ('Conned') broadcast on Dutch television. Journalists have filmed interviews with Four One Nine victims or even, wired for sound, have themselves met the conmen and have recorded fleeting conversations with them. The gangs seem to consist of Nigerians and Dutch fraudsters working together.[1] The Nigerian embassy in the Netherlands has repeatedly issued warnings to the public to be on guard against these frauds which, it says, began in the 1980s.

According to the Dutch police, Amsterdam was at one point a favourite European operations centre for Nigerian fraudsters. After a police clampdown many of the fraudsters moved to Madrid, where they set up a gigantic scam aimed at fooling victims into believing that they had won the Spanish state lottery. It was said to be the biggest fraud in the world at that time.[2] In 2005, the Spanish police arrested over 300 Nigerians in connection with the fake lottery scam, by which some 20,000 people were said to have been swindled by means of some six million missives per year, bringing in an estimated €100 million per year to the organisers. During this wave of arrests the police seized €218,000 in cash, nearly 2,000 mobile phones, 327 computers and 165 fax machines.[3] Three years later the Spanish police again made a mass arrest, this time holding 87 Nigerians suspected of defrauding at least 1,000 people to the tune of some €20 million.[4] Yet, despite the move of some major Nigerian fraudsters to Spain, by 2012 the Dutch police were still estimating that 90 per cent of advance-fee fraud perpetrated in the Netherlands was the work of Nigerian criminals.[5]

Colin Powell, the urbane former United States Secretary of State, once told an interviewer that 'Nigerians as a group, frankly, are marvellous scammers', adding by way of explanation 'I mean, it is in their natural culture'.[6] I have often met police officers outside Nigeria who have expressed more or less the same idea.

Can culture be an explanation for such behaviour? In any case, how does a specific culture come into being? Didn't the experience of colonial rule play some part? These and many other questions concerning Nigerian crime are discussed later in the chapters that follow.

How to read this book

Nigerian crime gangs, like all human organisations, have a history. To continue with the case of Nigerian Four One Nine scams, this practice has a longer pedigree than many people realise. The first properly documented Four One Nine letter in the history of Nigeria dates from 1920 and was written by one P. Crentsil, who called himself a Professor of Wonders. He was duly prosecuted under section 419 of Nigeria's criminal code. 'Professor' Crentsil's story is told in Chapter Two. But it was only in the 1980s that Four One Nine fraud became the vast international activity that it has now become. In those days, most scam letters emanating from Nigeria were written on headed notepaper belonging to a government office, or possibly a firm of lawyers or accountants, and purported to offer the possibility of sharing in funds embezzled from a government account. In the 1990s, more and more messages of the same sort began to arrive by email rather than letter or fax, and increasingly often purported to be on behalf of firms or individuals situated outside Nigeria. Where Four One Nines were originally the speciality of Nigerian conmen, these days there is no knowing who writes them, or from what location.

Thirty years before the emergence of mass advance-fee fraud, Nigeria had the misfortune to acquire a political elite and a political system that were shot through with practices of fraud and embezzlement, not to mention illicit violence. So pervasive and systematic were these practices that they led a group of soldiers to launch the country's first military coup in 1966, which the putschists justified by saying they were going to root out official corruption. Most Nigerian practices of organised crime, including document fraud, embezzlement and large-scale smuggling, originate in politics and the state itself, or at least have important and durable connections to the state. This is not the place to examine different definitions of organised crime[7] other than to say that most of them imply that to qualify for this label criminal activity has to be associated with an identifiable group of people existing for a substantial period of time. This description actually fits the Nigerian state better than any other group.

It is in order to trace the political origins of organised crime in Nigeria that this book starts with a description of the country's government during colonial times, that is to say from the early twentieth century until Independence in 1960. A British official in 1944 found that 'the number of persistent and professional criminals is not great.... Crime as a career has so far made little appeal to the young Nigerian'.[8] I nevertheless believe that we need to study the colonial experience of Indirect Rule if we are to understand the origin of later practices of organised crime and corruption. So, to those readers who finish Chapter One without finding any mention of organised crime, I say: carry on reading, and you will see what I mean.

Oddly enough, one of the prerequisites for analysing crime in Nigeria is an understanding of the spirit world. Nigerians have thought, and generally still believe today, that wealth and prosperity have their ultimate origins in the spirit world and that no one can succeed in their career, whether in crime or in some legitimate profession, without securing blessings from the spirit world. That is why I begin this book with an epigram quoting St Paul on the spiritual nature of evil.

Here too I advise readers who see crime as a series of purely material activities to persist with reading. It is only by delving into the spirit world that we can hope to understand what causes people to act the way they do—in this case, to investigate some of the psychology of Nigerian organised crime.

A note on sources

In reconstructing the early history of Nigerian organised crime, that is to say from Nigeria's creation in 1914 until Independence in 1960, I have relied on the usual sources used by historians writing on that period, namely state archives and contemporary publications as well as the substantial secondary literature concerning Nigeria under colonial rule. In particular, I made several visits to the National Archives of Nigeria at Ibadan. The organisation of Nigeria's state archives reflects the colonial division of the country into three administrative regions, with headquarters at Enugu, Ibadan and Kaduna. However, the Ibadan archives are particularly rich inasmuch as they contain not only material relating to the former Western Region, but also documents from the central administration, making this the most important of the three main national repositories for present purposes.[9] Unfortunately I have been prevented by ill health from visiting branches of the national archives elsewhere, most particularly at Enugu and Kaduna, and from looking for other depositories of either state or private papers.

The key reality concerning historical research on the post-Independence period, however, is that none of the state archives contains any substantial collection of records generated by government ministries and departments. In many cases it is quite unclear what has happened to such papers. In any event, it has obliged me to turn to other sources of information. In this regard the US national archives held at College Park, Maryland,[10] and the National Archives of the United Kingdom held at Kew, Surrey,[11] have been invaluable. Their holdings of diplomatic and consular material have been especially useful. These records tend to concern elite politics rather than analyses of social developments, but this gap can to some extent be rectified by access to Nigerian newspapers that I was able to view at the excellent press clippings library at the Nigerian Institute for International Affairs in Lagos. Moreover, Nigeria is home to a number of publishing companies that have produced a stream of essays, memoirs and other works that provide insight into contemporary social realities. Many Nigerian publications do not find their way into foreign libraries, but I am fortunate to have worked for twenty-five years at the Afrika Studiecentrum, Leiden, that is home to one of the world's best Africana libraries. Regarding the most recent historical period, the Internet has become an endless mine of material that has helped me compile documentation on my subject, including not only online versions of newspapers but also a great variety of reports, blogs, conference papers, home pages and other material.

In regard to interviews, it is obvious that few criminals are willing to speak openly about their activities—and even if they were to do so, it would be hard for an interviewer to know whether the information being provided was accurate. To be sure, this applies to interviews of all descriptions, as all interviewees, no matter how honest, convey information that reflects their particular experience and personal insights rather than any corpus of 'objective' knowledge. Nevertheless, over more than a decade I have sought out people who can claim to have some expert knowledge of Nigerian organised crime, including law enforcement officers both in Nigeria and abroad. I have attended some invitation-only conferences that were most helpful in this regard, notably one held in Bangkok on 16–19 May 2005 at which law enforcement officers from many countries in Asia and elsewhere presented papers on Nigerian organised crime. I should also acknowledge that there are many organisations that publish regularly on this subject, most notably the United Nations Office on Drugs and Crime (UNODC) but also official bodies with more specific terms of reference, such as the Drug Enforcement Administration of the United States.

Rules of law

Zungeru in Niger State—one of the thirty-six states that today compose the Federal Republic of Nigeria—is a neglected town, hot and dusty. Far away from Nigeria's most vibrant city, Lagos, and from its modern capital, Abuja, Zungeru is not often visited by foreigners. Yet this is where Nigeria began.

When Nigerians were gearing up to celebrate their country's centenary in 2014, a newspaper printed a photo of the very house where the document was signed that brought Nigeria into existence, revealing it to be no more than a sad ruin.[12] It was in this building that the British official Frederick Lugard, better known as Lord Lugard, put his signature to an order that various British-ruled territories were to be merged into a single unit called Nigeria. At that time, Zungeru was the headquarters of colonial administration in the Northern Protectorate, and it briefly served as the capital of the new country overseen by Lugard in the office of governor-general. It was Lugard's wife, the former journalist Flora Shaw, who actually invented the name of the new colony, using it in a newspaper article in 1897.[13]

Lugard signed the document amalgamating the British-ruled territories of the Northern and Southern Protectorates into a single colony and protectorate of Nigeria on 1 January 1914. A military parade was held to mark the occasion. The small population of Zungeru, mostly railwaymen and civil servants working for the colonial administration and their families, turned out to watch. It is very likely that one of them was a nine-year old boy called Nnamdi Azikiwe. Although Azikiwe was from the Igbo people[14] whose homeland is southeast Nigeria, he was born at Zungeru in the North after his father had moved there to work as a clerk for the colonial government. 'Zik', as the boy was to become nationally known, was eventually to become Nigeria's first president.

There is a recording of Lugard's speech declaring the amalgamation of the former protectorates into the single new entity of Nigeria. This record reveals him to have had a rather high-pitched voice and to have spoken with the clipped accent and strangled vowels characteristic of the British upper classes in the age of empire. 'His Majesty the King has decided that ... all the country ... shall be one single country', he told the small crowd in Zungeru.[15] He made it sound as though Britain's King George V had personally made the decision to merge the various British possessions clustered around the Niger valley, whereas the King, being the ceremonial figurehead of a parliamentary system of government, actually had little to do with it.

Technically speaking, the creation of Nigeria was the result of an order-in-council made by the British government. It was a measure that Lugard had lobbied for with the invaluable assistance of Lady Lugard, the former colonial editor of the London *Times,* the newspaper of Britain's top people. Her network of connections was impressive. The key person who had to be convinced about the creation of a new colony was the Secretary of State for the Colonies, Lewis Vernon Harcourt, today little remembered although his name is carried by Nigeria's leading oil town, Port Harcourt. The main argument in favour of amalgamation was based on administrative convenience, as it would allow the governor-general to create a single budget for all the territories acquired by the British Crown in bits and pieces since 1861, when it had annexed Lagos as a base for the Royal Navy's activities against the slave trade. If all the British possessions were treated as a single unit for fiscal purposes, customs and excise duties from the South of the country, where there was a lively import-export trade, including in spirits that could be heavily taxed, could be used to subsidise spending in the landlocked North, where raising revenue was proving more difficult.

Nigerians generally look back at Lugard's 1914 announcement with mixed feelings. Amalgamation marked the inauguration of a country that at Independence in 1960 seemed destined to become an African superpower, not least because it has the biggest population of any African country, today somewhere around 175 million people. But many Nigerians, reflecting on their country's chronic inability to fulfil its promise, see the amalgamation decree as a fatal design error because it enforced cohabitation between populations that had little in common or were even enemies. Years later, the British colonial expert Lord Hailey called Nigeria 'perhaps the most artificial of the many administrative units created in the course of the European occupation of Africa'.[16] A leading colonial theorist, the Oxford academic Margery Perham, referred to it as an 'arbitrary block' carved out of Africa.[17]

One thing that nearly all Nigerians can probably agree on is that the foundation of their country was the result of a decision carried out solely in the British interest. 'God did not create Nigeria', a later politician quipped. 'The British did'.[18]

The civilising mission

Lord Lugard, GCMG, CB, DSO, was an imperialist of the old school. With his handlebar moustache, he looked the part. Born in India, educated at public school and at the Sandhurst military academy, he began his career as an army officer serving in campaigns in Afghanistan, Sudan and Burma. He worked for more than one of the commercial chartered companies that in Victorian times administered various bits of the world in the British interest before being appointed High Commissioner of the Protectorate of Northern Nigeria in 1900 at a time when the independent emirates of Hausaland still posed a military threat to British control of the region. Lugard was responsible for subduing them in a series of short military campaigns. He fell in love with Northern Nigeria and stayed in Nigeria throughout his subsequent career, except for a brief interlude as governor of Hong Kong.

Underlying all Lugard's work was his belief in the colonising genius of Britain in the hands of its great imperial administrators. It was this that gave to Britain 'a kind of divine right' to rule, as a later colonial official described Britain's self-evident authority to take control of various parts of the globe.[19] The assumed right to colonise is as difficult to understand today as the claim made by European kings four centuries ago that they had a divine right to rule their countries. Like other British imperialists of his time, Lugard believed that his country possessed a moral superiority that, combined with the organisational skills of public servants like himself, would introduce law and justice where none had existed previously. And, like other European colonisers too, the British thought most highly of themselves when they were suppressing customs that they found morally repugnant, such as the slave trade, the use of ordeal by poison to detect guilt in criminal cases, the infliction of cruel punishments, the killing of twins, and the slaughter of servants to accompany a dead master to the other world as well as other killings perpetrated in the name of religious duty or custom.

Prior to the assertion of British control, southern districts of Nigeria were—in Lugard's own words—'populated by tribes in the lowest stage of primitive savagery'.[20] The only real exception was the western region of Yorubaland, where complex hierarchies and a long history of self-governing city-states suggested a higher degree of sophistication, although here too rulers had been addicted to what Lugard described as 'many barbarous rites'.[21] The North was more promising for someone intent on introducing a colonial bureaucracy, as the area was governed by a string of Hausa–Fulani emirates and the Bornu kingdom, all of which had 'an elaborate administrative machinery, though it had become corrupt and degraded'.[22]

Lugard and other officials of his generation thought that the superiority of the new colonial order would be perceived by any Nigerians not themselves corrupted by their own vested interests. Victorians often believed that chiefs in Africa were intent on exploiting their people by selling them into slavery and that a coloniser with a higher moral conception had a duty to protect the people from their own leaders. It was on account of this perception that British officials had chosen to govern their original colony at Lagos directly, in the years when it was little more than a collection of fishing villages grouped around a lagoon. The system of justice was 'the principal organ of local government'[23] in Lagos colony in the late nineteenth century, before Nigeria itself was willed into existence. But once British authority had spread beyond Lagos, incorporating the valley of the mighty Niger River, the main artery for trade from the interior to the coast, the idea of establishing British courts in such a vast area became unappealing, as apart from anything else, it would be hugely expensive.

It was at this juncture that Lugard arrived in the region. Having overseen the conquest of the Northern emirates, he needed to take stock of the existing systems of justice in the territory for which he was now responsible. In Northern Nigeria the system of government before colonial times was the consequence of the jihad led by Usman dan Fodio at the beginning of the nineteenth century. Zealous Islamic reformers, intent on imposing a purer form of religion on the Hausa emirs of the Sahel, had taken control of the area by force and established a caliphate at Sokoto. Since that time, a century before the British takeover, central authority in the emirates had been transmitted through fief-holders, with justice being administered by judges trained in the Maliki school of Islamic law. However, there were many parts of the North where Muslim law codes were hardly used and communities continued to draw on their own traditions for settling disputes. The Sokoto caliphate and its affiliates were one of the world's last great slaving states,[24] making regular raids for human plunder into the territories further south into the region that the British dubbed the Middle Belt. Stamping out slave-raiding was one of Lugard's most urgent tasks.

As for the Southern Protectorate, where the jihad had not reached and there were relatively few Muslims, Lugard wrote that the entire region was 'deprived of the instruments on which the ultimate enforcement of all law … depends'.[25] The city-states of Yorubaland had elements of a rational bureaucracy but Lugard found the administration of justice there to be rife with 'corruption and bribery'.[26] All the institutions of public administration were liable to subversion by members of the Ogboni secret society that was very influential in Yorubaland and were affected by what Lugard regarded as native superstition.[27] Lugard didn't make explicit exactly what he meant by corruption, which is generally defined as the abuse of entrusted power for personal benefit. Presumably he was referring to the habit of supplicants bringing gifts to bearers of public office, applying a distinction between the public and private realms that did not exist in Nigeria in the way that it did in his own country, Britain.

The circumstances in which colonial power had been established seemed to many British officials to have an effect on the subsequent success of their administration. Lugard, who had personally supervised the military campaigns that overcame the emirates of what was soon to become Northern Nigeria, knew that colonial rule in the North reposed on conquest. It was clear who was in ultimate control. In the South, this was not quite so obvious. British rule there had been inaugurated in hundreds of individual agreements signed with local authorities, and Lugard found that there was consequently some lack of clarity about precisely what executive powers were vested in the colonial government.[28] Beyond Yorubaland, vast tracts of Southern Nigeria lacked even a semblance of central authority and seemed to the British to be the most backward of all the territories in Nigeria.

Here, British penetration had been 'reluctant, uncertain, and rather haphazard', according to Margery Perham, whereas in the North it had been 'confident and rapid'.[29]

One of the most common forms of authority in Southern Nigeria was what British officials referred to as a 'secret society', a group of initiates usually classed by age, whose activities and deliberations were not communicated to those outside the group. In the south and southeast of Nigeria there were communities without any centralised state structure at all, not even a chief. These are sometimes called 'stateless societies'. The anthropologist Robin Horton, who has lived in Southern Nigeria for forty years, lists four features shared by stateless societies such as those that British colonisers found in Igboland and in the Niger delta:[30]

1. There is little concentration of authority. It is difficult to point to any individual or limited group of people as the ruler or rulers of the society.
2. Such authority roles as exist affect a rather limited sector of the lives of those subject to them.
3. The wielding of authority as a specialised, full-time occupation is virtually unknown.
4. The unit within which people feel an obligation to settle their disputes according to agreed rules and without resort to force tends to be relatively small.

Indirect rule and law

Lugard's solution to the problem of governing a vast country composed of such a great variety of communities and polities as Nigeria was a system he called Indirect Rule. This was something he had encountered in India, where it was a key technique of British control. The core idea of Indirect Rule was that the colonial authority should confirm the tenure of indigenous rulers where they existed, subject to direction from a British official who would ensure that the native rulers would govern justly and without recourse to methods the British considered barbarous, such as enslavement and cruel forms of execution. Native rulers were forbidden to sign agreements with representatives of foreign powers. In places where there were no such rulers, the government would appoint them.

Indirect Rule was well suited to British needs in the North, which was ruled by a Muslim aristocracy whose sense of conservatism and hierarchy was appreciated by Lugard and other British officials. The British found the system in the North so useful that they went as far as to keep Northern Nigeria administratively separate from the South in many respects, even after the amalgamation of 1914, and to restrict the work of Christian missionaries in the interests of retaining the rule of the Muslim establishment. While this seemed an ideal solution in the short term, in the longer term it created a major problem. The lack of a corpus of mission-school graduates literate in English meant that the colonial administration in the North had to import English-speakers from other parts of Nigeria, which was exactly how Nnamdi Azikiwe's father came to be living in Zungeru. Small Yoruba and Igbo communities sprang up in the main Northern cities, notably in the ancient trading hubs of Kano and Kaduna. Indirect Rule was less easily implemented in the South of Nigeria, which had fewer centralised institutions and was considered by the British to be at a lower stage of historical evolution. However, Christian missionaries had been at work in parts of the South for decades already and had produced a small number of school graduates literate in English and attuned to the ideas they had picked up from their teachers.

Thus, the precise effects of Indirect Rule differed widely from place to place. In the Northern emirates, still governed by the descendants of conquering jihadists, but now accompanied by a British Resident on the model developed by the British in India, old patterns of rule were preserved in a rather artificial isolation. In the South, British administrators at first tried to create chieftaincies out of nothing, but later tried to make the doctrine of Indirect Rule work through existing institutions that lacked the clear hierarchy of the emirates.

North or South, under Indirect Rule every individual Native Administration was responsible for raising taxes with which it would pay its officials, replacing 'the unlimited exactions on which they had previously lived'.[31] The British in Nigeria, like colonial governments elsewhere in Africa, claimed legitimacy not only on the basis of laws that they had written but above all on the grounds that they were

457

bringing progress, as defined by their own notions of order, justice and knowledge.

Lugard thought he had created a system that would preserve indigenous culture and would as far as possible prevent Nigerians from acquiring pernicious foreign ideas that were liable to lead to political problems. Nigeria would to a large extent be run by Nigerians, with British officials being needed only at strategic points. Indirect Rule was inexpensive, since it was locally financed, and by 1939 the cost of administering Nigeria was lower than in any British colony in Africa except Nyasaland.[32] However the whole edifice depended on native rulers who knew their place. Lugard had a deep dislike of educated Nigerians, especially lawyers who could use arguments from English law and Western philosophy to argue against colonial rule and who even had the gall to criticise their own natural leaders, the chiefs.

Lugard wrote extensively about some of the more theoretical aspects of Indirect Rule,[33] and such was his prestige within the colonial service that his version of it was to become the foundation stone of colonial government not only in Nigeria but also in British colonies further afield. Most British officials were sure that their system, designed to preserve indigenous systems as far as possible, was better than that in French colonies, based on a desire to instill French culture and methods into the natives.[34] When African colonies became independent in the 1960s, former colonial officials were still arguing about whether Lugard's method or the French method was better.[35]

Law in the protectorate territories—all of Nigeria except for the original colony of Lagos—was based on powers derived from the Foreign Jurisdiction Act passed by the British parliament in 1890.[36] This gave the British Crown the authority to create a legislative body or to authorise the governor to issue ordinances. Colonial rule instituted the rule of law in the sense that the executive was assumed to have no powers entitling it to take action against individual liberty or property, other than such as were covered by statute or common law.[37] As in other European traditions, British officials were powerfully influenced by their own country's history, which they took to be the norm of historical development, and above all by the convention that law is derived ultimately from a written authority.

In Britain, as in the rest of Europe, the idea that law emerged from divine revelation[38] had evolved over centuries into a secular convention whereby law is seen as the rules of a political community that governs itself (or, in the case of a colony, is governed by a foreign power). Law in the colonial system was an expression of power in that it resulted from a command; it was not based on any perception of truth held by the indigenous population. For the vast majority of Britain's new colonial subjects in Nigeria, the colonial law code, when people were aware of its existence at all, did not represent a body of rules that had to be followed because of their inherent legitimacy, but only because they were enunciated by an authority able to impose punishment. If people respected the colonial law, or even just pretended they did, it was because they were in awe of the people who proclaimed the law rather than for any other reason. White people in general enjoyed great prestige. Obafemi Awolowo, later to be a leading nationalist politician, recalled how, as a child in the 1910s, he had thought of the white man as 'a superman'. The mere glimpse of a white person filled him with wonder.[39]

With the exception of the Muslim emirates of the Sahel, which made limited use of law based on the scriptural authority of the Qur'an, in most of Nigeria the introduction of written law was a revolutionary innovation. In contrast to the European tradition of law-making introduced by colonial officials, the customary law previously existing in hundreds of communities all over Nigeria was based on principles of natural law in the sense that indigenous lawmakers enacted rules that they thought conformed to the principles of cosmology applying in the invisible world,[40] the home of spiritual beings with effective powers over the material world. They perceived the spiritual and material worlds as two distinct but related spheres. Religious experts were expected to have a refined knowledge of the properties of things, animal, vegetable or mineral, each of which was thought to have 'its own natural law, as well as its own essence'.[41] Justice was usually the prerogative of a ruler or of a committee or an assembly acting in accordance with whatever could be represented as tradition, based on precedent. It was generally inseparable from the spiritual knowledge articulated by ritual experts or priests, who in effect constituted checks and balances and legitimised political rule.

Most importantly, law before colonial times was generally unwritten. 'Prior to colonialism', a Nigerian criminologist has observed, 'Africans primarily saw crime as a threat to religious morality and responded with rituals for the purification of the community for the benefit of all'.[42] This may sound naively benign to a modern sensibility, but legal regimes of this sort were more ruthless than they appear, since a threat to religiously based morality could arise from the breaking of a taboo, such as the birth of twins. The punishment for an offence of an essentially ritual nature could be enslavement or death, in keeping with the gravity of breaking rules that were considered to reflect the cosmic order. Punishments this severe could take place on a large scale, as Lugard recorded when he wrote to his wife in 1912 that he had just dealt with a file concerning 744 'murders by ordeal'.[43]

Other than in Muslim communities, religious knowledge was itself based not on written dogma but on the assumed efficacy of communication with an invisible world. Attainable through ritual, the spirit world could be shaped to the requirements of an individual religious actor. The extraordinary intimacy and closeness of the spirit world in the societies that were incorporated into Nigeria is something quite difficult for modern Europeans or Americans to grasp, as their own ideas about what constitutes religion are so different. For people living in the communities that became part of Nigeria in 1914, and even for their descendants today, religion was neither a corpus of dogma nor a search for meaning in life. Rather, it consisted of a belief in the existence of an invisible world, distinct but not separate from the visible one, that is home to spiritual beings with effective powers over the material world.[44] Nigerians then and now maintain a dialogue with the invisible realm, in effect trying to shape their own well-being through a process of negotiation with the spirit world. This is not as strange as may seem: after all, even convinced atheists believe in invisible entities or forces, such as social structure or capital (not to be confused with money, which is visible), that they try to manipulate in order to achieve particular outcomes. The invisible world that most Nigerians believe in is one populated by specific spirits with their own names. Divination, which has always played an important part in religious communication in West Africa, is perhaps closer to the modern practice of psychiatry than anything else, as it involves an individual shaping her or his own destiny in a dialogue with the spirit world via a skilled intermediary. In other circumstances consultation might be via a shrine or an oracle, often involving a physical object that is thought able to transmit mystical powers. Nigerians often refer to an object of this sort as a juju.

In considering the nature of religion in West Africa, it is helpful to bear in mind some of the particularities of the history of Christianity in Europe that have done so much to shape Western ideas about the world. As the French philosopher Marcel Gauchet has pointed out, all monotheisms tend to consider the divine as an otherworldly realm. Christianity in particular, by locating the promise of personal fulfilment in the inner recesses of the human soul, emphasises divine authority as something exterior to creation. Gauchet has shown the effect this has had on Europe's history, as the kings who founded absolutist states in early modern times inadvertently presided over a transition in which political authority ceased to be regarded as an incarnation of the divine (since Jesus alone could be that) but rather as emanating from the will of individuals. When authority in politics changed to coming from below, from the people, rather than streaming downwards from heaven to earth, the notion of a social contract emerged.[45]

Some of this ideology was transmitted via colonial administration to Nigerians during the earlier twentieth century, and subsequently by the free flow of ideas associated with an international legal order, but it has met resistance from other ideas deeply entrenched in local societies. The dual religious heritage resulting from the encounter between Europe and Africa has shaped Nigerians' ideas about law and morality. Whereas in the European tradition law is derived from a written authority, and individuals are expected to adhere to a fixed moral code, in the older African tradition a morally correct course of action is not deduced from a written source, but is formed in the process of consulting the invisible world. As we shall see, this affects people's ideas of right and wrong to the present day.

A school for deception

Generally speaking, the most important effect of Indirect Rule in Nigeria was to make local rulers less accountable to their subjects, since whatever traditional means existed to remove an overbearing chief had become less effective.[46] The fact that there were twin sources of authority in the form of the colonial government on the one hand, and local custom on the other, gave astute chiefs room to play the two against each other. When it suited them, they claimed to be acting in conformity with colonial law, and also when it suited them, they could act in contravention of the law on the grounds that they were upholding the real traditions of their people. They could continue using traditional mechanisms of rule informally, even when these were technically outlawed. In the early years of colonial rule, there were even cases of people masquerading as local officials of the colonial government in order to enrich themselves, setting up pseudo-courts that purported to have the backing of the colonial authorities but that were no more than personal creations. One such entrepreneur issued false summonses demanding heavy fines from his victims. A former shrine priest, 'he was got up to represent a District Commissioner, giving out that he was opening a new District for the Government. He had his own police, court messengers and prison warders; all sufficiently like the real thing to deceive the ignorant population with whom he had to deal'.[47] A benevolent way of interpreting this incident was that a shrine priest was simply trying to continue his traditional authority in a new guise, which required a claim that he represented the colonial government along with all its accoutrements of police and messengers. But one could also consider such a person to be a charlatan or a confidence trickster, a breed that could flourish in Nigeria as people learned to manipulate the symbols of colonial authority.

The nationalist leader Obafemi Awolowo was one of those educated Nigerians whom Lugard so despised, whose legal training equipped him to identify some of the key defects of Indirect Rule. Awolowo was not impressed with the argument that an administration run by traditional leaders was always best for the people. He thought that corruption was 'the greatest defect of the Native Court system', although, he claimed, 'Government Officials and Administrative Officers always pretend it does not exist'.[48] Corruption, he wrote, most commonly took the form of bribes, but it could also involve the use of social connections or political office for personal benefit.[49] In private, British officials also found Native Administration authorities in many parts of the country to have a distressing tendency towards corruption, although they were so determined to make Indirect Rule a success that they did not like admitting its shortcomings to a politician like Awolowo—precisely because arguing politics outside the sphere of the traditional rulers could only undermine Indirect Rule.

In debates like these, corruption was rarely defined, but the practices to which Awolowo and others referred were to some extent the continuance of older habits in a new context. Thus, in the North there had long existed a 'spoils system' whereby 'an incoming Emir turned all the relatives and supporters of his predecessor out of office and replaced them with his own'.[50] In Igboland, honour required that a wealthy person would make gifts to shrines and distribute money among village elders in order to obtain titles that bestowed prestige. In Yorubaland, officials were accustomed to keeping a proportion of the tax revenue collected on its way from the taxpayer to the central government. To the British all of this represented 'corruption, waste, inefficiency, and extortion'.[51] A more sympathetic analysis emphasises the degree to which ex-gratia payments articulated conceptions of honour. 'Africans and their leaders were concerned with honour in its older forms', a leading historian tells us, 'practising gift-exchange and rarely distinguishing between public and private wealth, at a time when rulers had lost many sources of revenue, numerous activities were for the first time monetised, and bureaucratisation multiplied opportunities for impersonal extortion'.[52]

British colonial officials generally showed a high level of probity despite occasional incidents of theft or fraud.[53] If colonial rule could be considered as corrupting, it was not because of the misdeeds of individual officials but because it was based on extracting wealth from Nigeria and transferring it to foreigners. The entire system of colonial rule was aimed at raising enough tax revenue to pay for itself at the same time as it worked to create commercial opportunities for British companies and to provide raw materials for British industries.

All over Nigeria, when people had disputes in need of regulation, they continued to use tried and tested techniques rather than going to the colonial courts. In the North this could mean attending the Sharia courts, which had British approval. In the South, where secret societies, shrines and oracles were in theory made irrelevant or even illegal by colonial laws banning the administration of oaths and ordeals on the grounds that they were 'repugnant practices',[54] these institutions often continued in existence unofficially.[55] 'It is difficult for the average European to understand the significance of an "oath by blood" to an African', one group of petitioners explained. 'It is the highest form of oath in African Social Institutions and an African bound by oath of blood to carry out any principle scheme is prepared to sacrifice his life for the maintenance of the said principle for tradition has it that a breach of an oath by blood meant instant death and damnation in the spirit world; also all initiated men both living and dead will war against the descendants of such victims who breaks an oath by blood.'[56] However, when oaths were manipulated by local rulers who were able to use both local tradition and colonial law in their own interest, oath-taking became 'a parody of traditional practice'.[57]

It was in southeastern Nigeria that British officials were most concerned by the conduct of people appointed as local agents of the administration. The main reason for this was the lack of centralised authority in many local societies in that area. At first, the British tried to rule Nigeria's southeast via local officials selected by themselves, known as Warrant Chiefs, but they found these government-appointed chiefs to lack legitimacy and often to be dishonest and self-serving. Interpreters, messengers, clerks and other categories of native official gained an odious reputation among the population.[58] After serious disturbances caused by dissatisfaction with local government had spread throughout the region in 1929, the British tried to apply Indirect Rule using 'mass collections of family heads gathered in unwieldy councils.'[59] This too was never very satisfactory.

In the south of Nigeria especially, the traditional religious authorities and practices that were such an important part of political power were changing in ways that were not always conducive to honesty in government. Moreover, the South continued as a field of action for Christian missionaries, as it had been since the mid-nineteenth century, and missionaries continued to offer to Nigerians not only new cosmological and religious insights, but also education. Many students perceived mission schools as though they were a new version of the societies into which youths were traditionally initiated, and mission schools represented an intrusion on 'the familiar political space of the secret societies'.[60] Despite the small number of colonial officials, in parts of Southern Nigeria the system of Indirect Rule was the unwitting cause of a genuine social revolution.

Conversely, in the North, where the Native Authorities had been much stronger to start with, being based on the conquest states that had emerged from Usman dan Fodio's jihad, Christian missionaries were highly restricted. This resulted in a lack of Western education. The outcome was a lack of social movement most obvious in the fact that mission-school graduates from the South had to be recruited to fill various clerical posts, creating islands of Southerners in the sea of Hausa–Fulani authority.

The differing experience of Indirect Rule in North and South was to mark the future Federal Republic of Nigeria in many ways, not least in the patterns of criminality that emerged. It is hard to identify much in the colonial period that could reasonably be called 'organised crime' in Nigeria, although older ideas in regard to slavery could be said to constitute a historical reality from which contemporary people-trafficking emerged at a later stage. More generally, however, the actual experience of Indirect Rule in Southern Nigeria especially involved such a high degree of deceit and manipulation as to amount to a training in subterfuge for anyone who had close experience of it. As we will see in the next chapter, this stimulated specific practices of self-representation and deception, sometimes deliberately targeting foreigners, that we could see as early contributions to a culture of corruption.

17

WEST AFRICA'S INTERNATIONAL DRUG TRADE

Since the publication in 2007 of a report on West Africa's role in the illegal cocaine trade from Latin America to Europe, considerable media attention has focused on Guinea-Bissau in particular as a country infiltrated by drug interests. However, West Africa has a long history of involvement in the international drug trade, that has been dominated by Nigerian interests especially. Consideration of this history may help stimulate a debate in historical sociology that will illuminate both the nature of involvement in the drug trade itself, and also larger questions about the long-term formation of the state.

A report published by the United Nations office on drugs and crime (UNODC) in December 2007 has drawn unprecedented international attention to West Africa's role as an intermediary in the cocaine trade between Latin America and Europe.[1] Major newspapers have carried full-page articles on the subject.[2] But law-enforcement officers have long been aware of the reach of West African drug-trading networks, and the UNODC and other official bodies have for some years been observing a sharp rise in cocaine exports from Latin America to West Africa. The roots of the current collaboration between drug traders in these two sub-continents in fact go back for more than a decade, as this article will demonstrate.

According to the UNODC's estimate, about a quarter of Europe's annual consumption of 135 to 145 tonnes of cocaine,[3] with a wholesale value of some $1.8 billion,[4] currently transits via West Africa. In addition to the cocaine trade, West Africa is also a transit point for much smaller quantities of heroin exported from Asia to North America, as well as being a producer and exporter of cannabis products and perhaps amphetamines.

Needless to say, this trade is entirely illegal, and yet the proceeds are so great as to have a considerable impact on West African economies.

A major change in the global cocaine trade is taking place. South American cocaine traders are reacting against the saturation of the North American market, the growing importance of Mexican drug gangs, and effective interdiction along the Caribbean smuggling routes. These factors have induced them to make a strategic shift towards the European market, making use of West Africa's conducive political environment and the existence of well-developed West African smuggling networks. Some leading Latin American cocaine traders are even physically relocating to West Africa[5] and moving a considerable part of their business operations to a more congenial location, just as any multinational company might do in the world of legal business. Most recently, since a coup in Guinea in December 2008, there have been reports[6] of Latin American cocaine traders moving in significant numbers to Conakry, where some relatives of the late President Lansana Conte have an established interest in the cocaine trade. Some observers believe that the next step for Latin American cocaine traders might be to commence large-scale production in West Africa. Some African law-enforcement officers are deeply concerned by the likely effects of the drug trade and drug money on their own societies,[7] and indeed there is evidence that drug money is funding political campaigns and affecting political relations in several West African countries. Diplomats and other international officials worry that some West African countries could develop along similar lines to Mexico,[8] where drug gangs have a symbiotic relationship with political parties and with the state and drug-related violence results in thousands of deaths every year.

Research by the present author shows that Lebanese smugglers were using West Africa as a transit point to transport heroin to the USA as early as 1952.[9] A decade later, Nigerian and Ghanaian smugglers in particular began exporting African-grown marijuana to Europe on a scale large enough to attract sustained official attention. By the early 1980s, some had graduated to the global cocaine and heroin business. Since then, successful Nigerian and Ghanaian drug traders have established themselves in most parts of the world, including other West African countries, where they work with local partners in Benin, Côte d'Ivoire and elsewhere. Very large shipments of cocaine from South America to West Africa have been recorded for the last ten years. In short, West Africa's role in the international drug trade has historical roots going back for over half a century and has been a matter of significant concern to law-enforcement officers worldwide for decades rather than years. Latin American traders who see some benefit in moving part of their operations to West Africa can find local partners with well-established networks who provide them with safe houses, banking, storage space, and a host of other facilities in return for a suitable financial arrangement or for payment in kind.[10]

Not only is West Africa conveniently situated for trade between South America and Europe, but above all it has a political and social environment that is generally suitable for the drug trade.[11] Smuggling is widely tolerated, law enforcement is fitful and inefficient, and politicians are easily bribed or are even involved in the drug trade themselves. Many officials throughout the region are deeply concerned by the effects of the drug trade, but are often confronted by people and networks more powerful than they, with other priorities. The recent emergence of a sophisticated financial infrastructure in Ghana and Nigeria is a further reason for the enhanced importance of West Africa in global drug trafficking. All of the above draws attention to a point made by Jean-François Bayart and others more than ten years ago,[12] namely that expertise in smuggling, the weakness of law-enforcement agencies, and the official tolerance of, or even participation in, certain types of crime, constitute a form of social and political capital that accumulates over time.

The origins of the West African drug trade

It is sometimes said that West Africa was introduced to the cultivation of cannabis and consumption of the plant's leaves by veterans returning from military service in Asia at the end of the Second World War. Yet a pioneering article published in *African Affairs* in 2005 by the historian

Emmanuel Akyeampong[13] pointed out that a small trade in cannabis products from West Africa existed in the first half of the twentieth century. In Nigeria, later to emerge as the hub of West Africa's illicit drugs trade, the colonial authorities in 1934 were experimenting with the cultivation of the coca plant in the botanical gardens in Calabar and at various other stations in the south of the country.[14] By the mid-1950s, there were occasional arrests of farmers in south-west Nigeria for growing cannabis,[15] and small quantities of locally grown marijuana were being shipped from the region to Europe and the USA. At the same time, Nigerian marijuana smokers were also buying small amounts imported from South Africa and the Belgian Congo.[16]

The first documented use of West Africa as a staging post for heroin smuggling dates from 1952, when US officials noted that parcels of the drug were being transported by a Lebanese syndicate from Beirut to New York via Kano and Accra, using couriers on commercial airlines.[17] One of those implicated at the Beirut end of the pipeline was reported to be an Italian intelligence officer; it was not clear whether he was operating with the approval of his superiors. The US consul-general in Lagos was told by a Lebanese source, described as 'a competent narcotics and diamond smuggler',[18] that the existing 'heavy dope traffic' from the Near East to the USA via Europe was being diverted to Nigeria 'to an increasing extent' to avoid the attention of law-enforcement officers on the European route.[19] Given the use of West Africa by Lebanese smugglers in more recent times, it is an intriguing question whether there has been a highly discreet narcotics pipeline linking Lebanon and West Africa to the consumer markets of North America and Western Europe in continuous operation for more than fifty years. The presence of a murky official element in the person of an Italian intelligence officer is also of interest, as narcotics smuggling the world over seems to have become intertwined with the work of secret intelligence agencies from an early period.[20]

Generally speaking, however, the roots of West Africa's emergence as a major transit point for a more broadly based trade in illegal drugs may be traced to the 1960s. This was the era of the Beatles, youth rebellion and Swinging London, when a mass market for illicit drugs was developing in the United Kingdom and some other parts of Europe. Marijuana was particularly fashionable. It was in this context that the first reports emerged of locally grown cannabis being exported from Nigeria to Europe in significant quantities. In 1966, Nigeria's first military government took this problem seriously enough to decree ten-year jail terms for persons found guilty of exporting cannabis, although it is not clear that anyone was actually convicted under the terms of this legislation. In 1971, Nigeria's Federal Commissioner for Health, Dr J.O.J. Okezie, described marijuana smuggling from Nigeria and other African countries as 'rampant'.[21] By the end of the decade, a Nigerian Federal Ministry of Information official claimed that drug smuggling had become so common that 'Nigerian travellers are often subjected to rigorous search each time they travel abroad.'[22]

Early West African marijuana traffickers seem to have been mostly individuals travelling by air to the United Kingdom in particular, carrying relatively small quantities of the drug hidden in their personal baggage or in cargo. A Nigerian government information leaflet concerning trade in cannabis 'across the border and overseas' claimed that some smugglers made use of unwitting couriers by persuading innocent passengers to carry parcels on their behalf, not revealing the true contents of the packages.[23] Significantly, among Nigerians arrested for smuggling cannabis in 1972 were pilgrims travelling to Saudi Arabia for the *hajj*.[24] This is important for the light it throws on an aspect of Nigerian drug trafficking that appears to be almost completely unresearched, as most reports on West African drug traders over the last forty years, whether by law-enforcement agencies or emanating from other sources, have concerned the supply of consumer markets in North America and Western Europe. The West African trade route to these destinations appears to have been largely in the hands of people from southern Nigeria from its inception. It is therefore interesting to note that, in the 1980s, Saudi Arabia already figured prominently on the list of countries where Nigerians had been arrested for drug offences, in third place behind the USA and the United Kingdom.[25] The transport of illegal drugs by Nigerians to the Middle East, including under cover of the *hajj,* is far more likely to involve people of northern Nigerian origin than the North Atlantic trade, given the historic links between northern Nigeria and the Muslim world.

A significant case from the early period of West African marijuana trafficking concerns the conviction by a court in the United Kingdom of a 33-year-old Nigerian woman, Iyabo Olorunkoya, found guilty in 1974 of importing 78 kilograms of marijuana. The woman, said to be well-connected in Lagos high society, named as her accomplices two Nigerian army officers.[26] One of the two was Brigadier Benjamin Adekunle, known to the Nigerian press as 'the Black Scorpion', a hero of the federal army during the Biafra war. He was suspended from duty on account of the case, although his alleged role was not proved.[27] He never resumed his military career.

The smuggling of relatively small quantities of marijuana by individual traders, some of whom may have had connections to senior officials, was the precursor of the narcotics trade that emerged on a much larger scale in the early 1980s. This too appears to have been largely the work of individual Nigerian and Ghanaian traders, who penetrated the international narcotics market with extraordinary speed. They travelled to South America or Asia to buy small quantities of cocaine or heroin that they could carry to West Africa in their personal luggage for onward transmission to the consumer markets of the North Atlantic, or they took up residence in producer countries and recruited couriers to carry the packages for them. They developed the technique of swallowing cocaine and heroin sealed in condoms, soon to become a hallmark of the West African carrying trade. The large-scale involvement of West Africans in the cocaine and heroin trade is often said to have begun when West African students living in Europe and North America failed to receive payments of their study grants.[28] The US Drug Enforcement Administration has claimed that the trade was pioneered by Nigerian naval officers undergoing training in India, who bought heroin at source and sent it back to West Africa with couriers whom they had recruited from among Nigerian students there.[29] Whatever the exact origin, it is certainly the case that, in the early 1980s, there were already individual West Africans—overwhelmingly Nigerians, plus a few Ghanaians—who were settling in the main areas of narcotics supply. Nigerian smugglers were sending heroin by air courier from Pakistan to Nigeria, where it was repackaged and reexported to the USA.[30] One Pakistani heroin dealer was reported in 1985 as saying that he had made regular sales of heroin to a locally based Nigerian for eight months.[31] There was also a small Nigerian community resident in Bangkok. This early cohort of heroin and cocaine traders was presumably ignorant of the fact that a Lebanese syndicate had been doing something similar a generation previously.

'Prior to 1982', the US embassy in Lagos stated, 'Nigerians played an insignificant role in the marketing of narcotics and dangerous drugs in the United States.'[32] That year, US authorities arrested 21 Nigerians for narcotics offences, with figures rising rapidly thereafter.[33] A similar pattern emerged in Europe, where an official of the West German Interior Ministry reportedly stated in 1983 that Hamburg was importing significant quantities of drugs from West Africa, including one and a half tonnes from Ghana (presumably of marijuana), and that a ship from Nigeria carrying cocaine, heroin, and marijuana had also docked there.[34] A year later, the director of West Germany's customs service, Georg Wolt, stated that Nigeria was one of the top six importers of cocaine to his country.[35] Also in 1983, Thailand witnessed its first known case of a Nigerian convicted of possessing heroin.[36] The great advantage of West African smugglers in the early days of this trade was that European and North American law-enforcement officers were not expecting heroin and cocaine to be imported from West Africa, since it was not a producing area. However, the reputation of Nigeria in particular soon changed, to the extent that, by 1985, British customs agents were said to be systematically searching, and sometimes strip-searching, Nigerians entering the country.[37]

A small market for cocaine soon emerged in Nigeria itself, to the extent that a Nigerian newspaper in 1983 reported the existence of what it called 'a tiny cocaine world' in fashionable Lagos society.[38] In view of this, it is interesting to note persistent reports as early as 1983 that one very senior military officer, married to a high society lady, had developed an active interest in narcotics trafficking.[39] The drug connection was already becoming a factor in Nigerian politics. A coup on 31 December 1983 brought to power the austere General Muhammadu Buhari, who justified his assumption of power, in the customary manner, with the claim that he was going to clean up corruption in Nigeria with military rigour. Within months, the new military junta introduced a decree making drug trafficking punishable by death, and by the end of 1984 a number of minor drug smugglers had been publicly executed by firing squad in Lagos. In general, the reaction of the Nigerian public was not favourable to the severe penalties decreed by General Buhari's military government. Those West Africans who had heard of cocaine and heroin at all appear to have regarded them as luxury products that were consumed in the rich world. In Nigeria at least, little social stigma was attached to people who simply transported them from one part of the world to another in an effort to earn a living. To this day, Nigerians often say that, since the drug trade involves willing sellers and willing buyers at every stage of the chain, it is essentially a legitimate form of commerce. As for the fact that it is illegal, Nigerian drug dealers often 'view the black market as the only way to redistribute wealth from the north to the south, arguing that mainstream commercial channels are effectively occupied'.[40]

The 1980s were years of rapid economic decline in West Africa, including in Nigeria, the region's only major oil producer at that time, where problems were compounded by the corruption and incompetence of the civilian government in office from 1979 to 1983. Most West African countries, in financial difficulties as a result of the global convulsions of the period and their own profligacy in earlier, more favourable times, were obliged to borrow money from the International Monetary Fund and the World Bank and to undergo the process of economic liberalization known as structural adjustment. This required deep cuts in public expenditure and the sacking of public employees. Whether imposed by the international financial institutions or from domestic necessity, drastic reductions in public budgets plunged many people into acute financial difficulty, and this was undoubtedly an incentive to some to make money by any means possible. Those who went abroad in search of new sources of income tended not to be the poorest members of society—generally people from rural areas or without education—but rather those who had lived in towns and, being relatively well educated, spoke good English and were familiar with the workings of state bureaucracies. 'Let us call a spade a spade,' said Nuhu Ribadu, Nigeria's later top anti-corruption official, referring to his country's Second Republic of 1979–83. 'This is the period when we started hearing about 419,[41] it is the period we started having drug problems.'[42] It was indeed a critical moment in West Africa's insertion into global patterns of crime, even if Nigeria in particular had developed a role in the international marijuana trade well before the financial crisis of the early 1980s.

While General Buhari's decree of the death penalty for drug trafficking was regarded by many Nigerians as too severe, his campaign against crime and corruption seriously threatened the interests of some in the military, including the small group with interests in the drug trade. Another coup in August 1985 introduced a less stringent regime. The new head of state, General Ibrahim Babangida, revoked the death penalty as a punishment for drug trafficking and replaced it with life imprisonment. His period in government is recognized as having marked a transformation in Nigeria's already notorious corruption, turning it into a generalized instrument of government. '[D]irect disbursals and administrative favours were increasingly supplanted by politically-influenced arbitrage in a variety of domestic markets', according to one analysis, in a process more simply described as 'Zairianization'.[43] Nigeria became more than ever a literal kleptocracy, a system of government by theft and bribery. The word 'kleptocracy' had been invented some years earlier by the brilliant Anglo-Polish sociologist Stanislav Andreski, who taught for some years at a Nigerian university.[44]

Among the many scandals of the Babangida years was the murder by parcel-bomb of the newspaper editor Dele Giwa. It is widely believed in Nigeria that Giwa's death was connected to his investigations into elite drug trading. Specifically, he is said to have been targeted as a result of an interview he had conducted with a former drug courier, one Gloria Okon, who had worked for principals in very senior positions of the state bureaucracy or for their families. Years later, when Nigeria staged its own truth commission, one of the country's leading human rights lawyers and one of its most senior journalists jointly petitioned the members of the Human Rights Violations Investigation Commission, popularly called the 'Oputa Panel', requesting this body to charge General Babangida and others with murder.[45] It was also during the Babangida period that the Bank of Credit and Commerce International, which had arrived in Nigeria in 1979, became integrated into a practice of financial corruption and money laundering that was 'systemic and endemic'.[46] The chairman of BCCI (Nigeria) Ltd was Ibrahim Dasuki, one of General Babangida's closest associates, whom the head of state later appointed as Sultan of Sokoto. By the end of 1987, BCCI had no less than 33 branches in Nigeria.[47] When BCCI subsequently collapsed, in what was then the world's biggest-ever bank failure, the full extent of its criminal dealings became known.

In the general atmosphere of corruption and manipulation that characterized General Babangida's years as head of state, from 1985 to 1993, the country's role in the global narcotics trade grew. Nigeria was home to what a US government official called 'a vast commercial sector, immune to most regulations and well suited to illegal activities'.[48] When the head of the Ghanaian drug police visited Bangkok in 1986, he found 'a lot of Ghanaians and Nigerians' in prison for drug offences.[49] By 1988, some 2,000 Nigerians were reported to be serving sentences for drug offences abroad.[50] US authorities reportedly arrested 851 Nigerians for drug offences between 1984 and 1989, and reckoned that 55 percent of the heroin arriving at New York's John F. Kennedy airport was being carried by Nigerians.[51] In 1991, Nigeria's own Ministry of Justice reported that 15,433 Nigerians had been arrested worldwide for drug offences since 1984.[52] Of these, 4,802 had been convicted.[53] According to a statement attributed to the deputy director-general of the Ministry of External Affairs, Nigerians were the leading nationality arrested for drug offences in India, Pakistan, Saudi Arabia, and Thailand.[54]

Nigerian traders showed great ingenuity in switching their smuggling techniques and routes, for example exporting from Thailand overland to Malaysia or by sea to Taiwan or Hong Kong for onward transmission to Europe and North America.[55] Professional drug traders were constantly adapting and improving their methods. The Nigerians' commercial skills were also attracting the attention of fellow-traffickers from other continents. Scrutiny of arrest figures suggests that the Colombian drug cartels, reacting to the saturation of the US market, had begun seeking relationships with West African traders even by the late 1980s,[56] interested in using the West Africans' highly developed marketing channels as a way of penetrating new areas, notably in Europe. Among Nigerians involved in the drug trade were figures of privilege and influence, as became clear in 1989 when a former member of Nigeria's Senate was arrested in New York for heroin trafficking and subsequently convicted. He had previously offered $20 million of his own money, purportedly as a patriotic gesture, to pay a debt owed by Nigerian Airways that had caused

French authorities to impound a Nigerian Airways airbus. Although this scheme did not succeed, his intention had apparently been to use the plane to transport drug cargoes. For some time thereafter Lagos heroin dealers referred to their product as 'senator'.[57] A later member of the upper house of Nigeria's legislature, who had previously held a senior position in the police, once alleged that the Senate was infested with ex-419ers and drug traders.[58] Even the law-enforcement agencies were not immune to the lure of drug money. A head of the Nigerian Drug Law Enforcement Agency (NDLEA), a unit established in 1990 largely as a concession to US pressure, reportedly stated in 1994 that 'those charged with the responsibility of eliminating drug trafficking are by far more interested in drug trafficking than the professional traffickers'.[59] One of his predecessors had acquired a particular notoriety in this regard.[60]

The regional pattern

Nigeria was not alone. From the late 1970s there were reports of individuals in various West African countries importing narcotics for eventual re-export. Many traffickers appear to have been acting on their own initiative or at any rate without the support of extensive networks. Some powerful external interests also discovered the commercial potential of small West African states that attracted little international attention, and whose authorities could be bought or manipulated. In Sierra Leone, the most prominent members of the commercially powerful Lebanese community in the mid-1980s found themselves under surveillance from Israeli security officers responding to their role in funding various factions in Lebanon's civil war. They were confronted with a sudden influx of mobsters from the Soviet Union, some of them with connections to Israeli intelligence.[61] The most formidable of the newcomers was Marat Balagula, who later migrated to the USA, where he became a pioneer of Russian mafia influence, serving a prison sentence before being murdered in March 2008. Balagula and his colleagues used Sierra Leone as a freeport facility, smuggling in diamonds from the USSR and swapping them for heroin from Thailand for onward transmission to the USA. They also managed President Joseph Momoh's election campaign.[62]

Trafficking networks with high-level government connections emerged in other countries too. One example involved a group of Ghanaians and a diplomat from Burkina Faso, the latter providing members of the syndicate with diplomatic passports. This team imported heroin from Mumbai to Abidjan for onward transmission to Europe. One of the Ghanaians involved, a certain Emmanuel Boateng Addo, revealed some details of this operation in 1993 after his release from a French prison.[63] The Burkinabe diplomat at the heart of this syndicate was also a close associate of Charles Taylor, subsequently to become president of Liberia. In 1986–7 Taylor was one of several Liberian exiles living in Ghana and plotting against the Liberian government. He was twice detained by the Ghanaian government on political grounds. On the second of these occasions, it was his friend the Burkinabe diplomat who secured Taylor's release from prison.[64] A Ghanaian who shared Taylor's prison-cell in Accra recalled Taylor's opinions on the drug trade:

> In one of our numerous, prolonged arguments whilst in cells he was critical about what he called unwarranted vigilance and the arrest of drug traffickers in Ghana. I begged to differ from him but he insisted that the major concern of African governments should be the prevention of domestic consumption of hard drugs. Once people are exporting such drugs from Africa, they should be allowed. He further stressed that we should think of cultivating coca and marijuana in Ghana as major exports. He was particularly peeved about the fact that African governments complain of lack of capital when they have the easy option of granting banking facilities to drug barons who have billions of dollars for laundering.[65]

Charles Taylor achieved his ambition of becoming head of state when he became President of Liberia in 1997. True to his earlier ideas, he proceeded to associate with professional criminals from a wide variety of countries.[66] His predecessor, Samuel Doe, had allowed Liberia to be used for drug trafficking, as an earlier government may also have done.[67] Other West African heads of state said by police sources to have been implicated in drug smuggling include the late president of Togo, Gnassingbé Eyadéma.[68]

Over the years, West Africa's most prominent traffickers, the Nigerians, developed footholds in many other countries where imported narcotics could be stored and repacked for onward travel. From the early 1990s South Africa became one such base, as it offered the advantages of an excellent transport infrastructure and a good banking system. Before 1990, the drug trade in South Africa was largely confined to mandrax and locally produced marijuana. The South African police, preoccupied by political matters, were extraordinarily inattentive to the risk posed by international traffickers, who flocked to the country from Eastern Europe and from the rest of Africa especially. By 2005, there were between 40,000 and 100,000 Nigerians living in South Africa, as many as 90 percent of them illegally. The drug dealers among them were described as 'the most prolific of the organised crime groups operating in the country'.[69]

Nigerian traders also established operational centres in Cotonou and Abidjan, which were home to Beninese, Ivorian, and other nationals who had entered the narcotics business. In March 1998, the US government described Nigeria as 'the hub of African narcotics trafficking', noting also 'traffickers' expansion into bulk shipments into Nigeria's neighbours'.[70] After Nigeria had dispatched a peacekeeping force to Liberia in 1990, under the auspices of the Economic Community of West African States (ECOWAS), some members of the Nigerian expeditionary force developed interests in the narcotics trade. Their control of Liberia's seaports and of its international airport provided ideal transport facilities. A further attraction was Liberia's use of the US dollar as an official currency.[71] The Nigerian military, in power almost continuously for three decades, had by this time developed a high degree of impunity. In 1998, NDLEA director Musa Bamaiyi complained that his agents were not allowed to search military barracks, despite the fact that, according to him, 'a lot' of military officers were involved in the drug business. He had sent a list of names of military suspects to the presidency.[72] Bamaiyi, generally well regarded by international law-enforcement agents with whom he collaborated, had himself served in the Nigerian peacekeeping contingent in Liberia.[73] Being also a brother of his country's chief of army staff, he was particularly well placed to make such a judgement about the Nigerian military's involvement in drug trafficking.

Nigerian traders especially were truly global. They took over heroin retailing in Moscow. According to one veteran journalist, 'the Central Asians ... were being displaced from 1997 onwards by Africans, especially Nigerians, who have established efficient and well-concealed networks for selling heroin and cocaine in Moscow's student living areas and university residences'.[74] Nigerians were particularly prominent in the North American heroin trade until being displaced in recent years. In 1999, the US Department of Justice said it was looking for two Nigerians who were said to be running a network importing 'up to 80 percent of the white heroin entering the USA from southeast Asia'.[75] This high figure is less noteworthy than might appear at first sight, as the US market for Asian heroin has lost ground to imports from Latin America. In 2002, Dutch customs officers, in a controlled experiment, for a period of ten days searched every Nigerian arriving in Amsterdam from Aruba and the Dutch Antilles, a route used by many of the 1,200 drug couriers arrested annually at Schiphol airport. They found that of the 83 Nigerian passengers using this route during that period, no fewer than 63 were carrying drugs.[76] In the same year, Nigeria's NDLEA arrested two Nigerians and one foreigner with 60 kilograms of cocaine, the agency's largest-ever cocaine find, on board a Brazilian vessel at Tin Can Island wharf in Lagos.[77] Substantial though this haul was, perhaps its chief significance lies in the evidence it presents of direct seaborne transport from Latin America.

There was evidence that knowledge of the drug trade was being passed from one generation to the next. Also in 2002, a twelve-year-old Nigerian boy with US citizenship was reportedly arrested at New York's John F. Kennedy airport with 87 condoms of heroin. He was the son of one Chukwunwieke Umegbolu, who had been convicted in 1995 for his part in importing more than $33 million of heroin in a period of more than a decade.[78]

By the mid-1990s, thus, some Nigerian drug traffickers in particular had not only developed the means to invest in bulk shipments of narcotics, but had also become fully global, having business associates in both producing and consuming countries as well as other facilities in countries outside Nigeria. The same was true on a smaller scale of traffickers from other West African countries, notably Ghana. By the same token, non-African traffickers had become interested in the commercial advantages offered by West Africa. Lebanese smugglers, Soviet gangsters, and South American drug syndicates were among a variety of external interests attracted to the region on account of its usefulness as an entrepot.[79] In 2003, Senegal expelled a senior member of the Sicilian mafia, Giovanni Bonomo, who was subsequently arrested in Italy. A known money launderer and drug trafficker, he was said to have visited South Africa and Namibia regularly.[80]

The structure of the Nigerian drug trade

A senior US anti-drugs official, Robert S. Gelbard, described Nigerian drug networks as 'some of the most sophisticated and finely-tuned transshipment, money-moving and document-forging organizations in the world'. He pointed out that 'they are sought out by both Asian and Latin American drug producers' on account of their commercial skills.[81] The Nigerian drug trade is characterized by a distinctive business structure that has developed over decades, and which gives depth to the emerging cooperation with traders from other countries and continents.

Crucial to the success of Nigerian drug traders is their highly flexible mode of operation, as those involved constantly form and re-form their business relationships from among a wide pool of acquaintances. This modus operandi closely resembles a so-called 'adhocracy', able 'to fuse experts drawn from different disciplines into smoothly functioning ad hoc project teams'[82] in a way that, according to some management gurus, is particularly suited to the modern business environment. It stands in contrast to the more corporate-style relations of classic American 'mafias' that have exerted such a powerful influence on popular ideas about how organized crime works via films like *The Godfather* or the TV series *The Sopranos*.

The following paragraphs will briefly describe the classic structure of the Nigerian drug trade, starting at the top of the ladder, so to speak, by considering the category often labelled drug 'barons'. In the words of a senior Nigerian drug law-enforcement officer,[83] a Nigerian drug baron requires at least three assets. First, he, or she, needs to be able to buy drugs cheaply at source. As we have seen, from an early date, there were Nigerians who travelled to producer countries in South America and south-east Asia to buy drugs. In 2003, some 330 Nigerians were said to be serving prison sentences in Thailand for drug-related offences.[84] Hundreds of Nigerians were living in Bangkok, notably in the city's Pratunum district that is home to an African community some 500–800 strong. Many of these are occupied in the textile or jewellery trades, but a significant number are alleged to have interests in crime.[85] There are also substantial Nigerian communities in the south Asian subcontinent, with over 2,000 Nigerians in Mumbai alone.[86] There is even a small Nigerian community in Afghanistan. A drug baron who lives in one of these locations or has stayed there long enough to build excellent local contacts is well placed to buy heroin. Sometimes, a baron who has the wherewithal to buy a large quantity of cocaine or heroin at source may sell this to a syndicate of smaller operators pooling their resources for such a major purchase. In December 1997, John Ikechukwe, a Nigerian who had emigrated to South Africa and become rich working the South American route, was murdered after cheating some fellow-traders in such a scheme. According to the South African police, 28 Nigerians were killed in Johannesburg alone in the first quarter of 1998.[87]

A second requirement for a drug baron is a good contact in the receiving country, generally North America in the case of heroin, or Europe in the case of cocaine. North America and Europe have substantial Nigerian communities, some of the millions of Nigerians who live outside their own country. Even if most of these people live blameless lives, earning their keep in respectable occupations, the existence of this diaspora nevertheless constitutes a medium in which traffickers can move. Many Nigerian drug barons keep a very low profile in order not to attract attention. The third necessity for a drug baron is a substantial supply of capital to finance operations. This poses little problem to anyone who has already made a couple of successful transactions. An example is Ekenna O, first arrested in 1995 and sentenced to one year's imprisonment, and rearrested in October 2005. At that point, his assets were over 500 million naira, or $4.16 million. He owned three properties in Nigeria and several companies.[88]

For purposes of transportation, a drug baron works with a second layer of operators, known as 'strikers'. This word is used in Nigeria in regard not only to the drug trade, but also to a range of other criminal enterprises in which a high degree of logistical expertise is necessary.

A striker is someone who can strike deals, quite likely a former courier who has entered the business at the lowest level and worked his way up, acquiring an excellent network of contacts. Many strikers are middle-aged, from their late thirties upwards. A striker knows exactly who is the best person to approach for forged documents or who is an expert packer of drugs. He receives a fee for performing this type of service on behalf of a baron, and will typically work with several such barons while remaining essentially self-employed. One of the striker's most important tasks is the recruitment of couriers, and one of the features of the Nigerian system that makes effective police detection so difficult is that the use of independent specialists provides a vital cut-out between the top level of operation and the humble courier. A courier is normally ignorant of the name, or even the very existence, of the baron who is the real initiator of a drug transaction. If a courier is arrested, he or she therefore cannot be prevailed upon to give vital information to police officers. For this reason, strikers often try to recruit a stranger as a courier, although friends and family may also be approached. A Nigerian striker based in South Africa, for example, may recruit South African nationals, or even better, South Africans with British passports. Gambia is a useful transit point because of the existence of a substantial tourist trade, which makes it easy for a courier to travel with a planeload of tourists, or to recruit a holiday maker and persuade or trick them into acting as a courier. The favourite recruits for strikers based in Nigeria itself are fellow-countrymen who have residence permits for European or North American countries, or Nigerians who possess foreign passports, the more prestigious the better. Having recruited a courier, a striker will stay with the person until the point of departure, a period often between a couple of days and a week, to make sure they do not lose their nerve. In some cases, couriers are escorted to religious oracles during this period to swear an oath. Relatives or home-boys who have been recruited, and made to swear a solemn oath of loyalty, do not easily betray their associates. They can also speak on the phone in 'deep' dialects of African languages, difficult for foreign police services to interpret if the conversations are intercepted.

The lowest level of transportation is the couriers or mules, mostly people in desperate need of money. Couriers recruited by Nigerian barons, via a striker, usually carry a small parcel of drugs on their person, in return for cash payment. There are also freelancers, individuals who try their luck at buying and smuggling drugs on their own. The 21-year old Iwuchukwu Amara Tochi, who was hanged in Singapore on Friday 26 January 2006 after being caught in possession of 727 grams of diamorphine, was one such unfortunate. He was just eighteen at the time of his arrest. He had gone to Asia in the hope of pursuing a career as a professional footballer, but had been recruited as a courier by a fellow Nigerian for a fee of $2,000.[89] Of 316 people arrested at Lagos international airport in possession of cocaine or heroin between January 2006 and 5 September 2007, according to a Nigerian police report,[90] no less than 69 percent were so-called 'swallowers', people who had ingested condoms filled with hard drugs. Only 31 percent had packed them in baggage. Of the fifty-five people arrested at the same airport for similar reasons in the third quarter of 2007, most were in their thirties. According to police analysts, this is a vulnerable age because it corresponds to people losing the support of their parents and having to make major life choices. The preferred destination for couriers in recent times is Spain, on account of its relatively lax residence rules. An applicant can get a temporary residence permit after just six months, which makes him or her far less likely to be searched on entry as it is assumed that adequate checks have been made. Thus, between January 2006 and 5 September 2007, out of 273 people arrested in Nigeria on suspicion of exporting drugs, 29 percent were heading for Spain.[91]

Various attempts have been made to profile Nigerian drug traffickers. There is a general consensus among those who have attempted this that the Nigerian narcotics trade is dominated by Igbo people. The Swiss police are reported to have produced a more exact profile, even down to villages of origin, via an analysis of patterns of arrest. Among Igbos themselves, it is sometimes said that most narcotics traffickers come from one particular local government area. Ninety percent of those arrested are male.[92] However, the profiles that are widely used by European, North American and south-east Asian authorities do not appear to include data from the considerable number of Nigerians arrested for drug offences in Saudi Arabia, which may well reveal a different social background.

The ethnic concentration of Nigerian drug traders is not unusual, as some other illegal trades, as well as many legal ones, are also notable for being dominated by people of just one geographical origin, such as the trade in prostitutes from Nigeria to Europe, which is overwhelmingly in the hands of people from Edo State, just one of Nigeria's 36 states.[93] In many legal businesses too, an individual entrepreneur, when he or she needs assistance, often turns to someone from their home area. This may be someone to whom they are related either closely or more distantly, or it may be someone who has property in the same village of origin, or a former school classmate. Entrepreneurs compete with one another but are also able to cooperate when circumstances require this.[94] Social networks that refer to a village of origin are sustained even when people live in Lagos or further afield, with the village remaining a moral point of reference. It is for this reason, too, that when an important bargain is made, including in regard to commerce or politics, the parties to the deal may swear a solemn oath on a traditional oracle, such as the Okija shrine that gained national attention in Nigeria in 2004.[95]

Igbos themselves often explain their general prominence in trade by reference to the civil war of 1967–70, alleging that they have subsequently had a semi-detached status within Nigeria that obliges them to seek their livelihood outside the ambit of the state. However, the Igbo ethos of enterprise also has older roots, in an area once known both for the productivity of its agriculture and for its role in the Atlantic slave trade. The establishment of colonial government and missionary education in the early twentieth century opened an avenue of economic advancement and social promotion for Igbos, whose political organization was traditionally republican, without powerful chiefs or any aristocratic class. During the past hundred years, the population of Igboland has increased dramatically, and the exhausted soil can no longer support even those who stay behind and farm. Still, it remains the ambition of many Igbo men to make money and buy land and build an impressive house in their home village as a mark of their success. 'Rich cocaine pushers' who hold extravagant parties to celebrate the acquisition of a chieftaincy title are a recognizable social type.[96] According to Nigerian police officers, those Igbos who dominate the drug trade do not normally choose this career in order to become professional criminals in the Western sense, but primarily as an avenue to wealth and social esteem. Their use of both traditional oracles and Christian rituals is thought to favour the drive to personal achievement and social success.

The employment by Nigerian drug traders of large numbers of couriers carrying small parcels of cocaine or heroin endows them both with a high degree of 'vertical' integration of their marketing channel from purchase to sale, and with the means to penetrate any customs service in the world. However, this method involves a high human cost, and not only in the sense that it supplies drug users who may have their lives ruined or cut short, as the growing numbers of addicts in West Africa testifies. The courier system also carries a high risk of arrest for those who actually transport drugs through customs controls. The number of West Africans sitting in jails all over the world after being arrested in possession of illegal drugs is probably disproportionate to the volume of narcotics seized, in consequence of the human-wave tactics often used by drug barons.

The new bulk trade

The first recorded case of a Nigerian smuggler transporting heroin in bulk is that of Joe Brown Akubueze, who imported some 250 kilograms of heroin from Thailand by sea, packed in water coolers, in December 1993. He was arrested in Nigeria after a tip-off, and sentenced by a court to 115 years in prison, of which he served ten years before being released.[97] In retrospect, this was an early indicator of a move towards very large shipments by air and sea, although the classic Nigerian courier trade still remains as strong as ever. From the late 1990s, there were growing reports of 'very large consignments' of drugs heading to West Africa 'by ship or commercial containers', according to a police officer working for the UN.[98] In 2000, Cape Verdean authorities reported the interception of a ship in the Caribbean heading to their country with 2.3 tonnes of cocaine.[99] In 2003, a massive cargo of 7.5 tonnes of cocaine was intercepted on a ship en route to Spain via Cape Verde and Senegal.[100] In 2004, six people were arrested in the Ghanaian port-city of Tema in possession of 588 kilograms of cocaine from Colombia via Venezuela.[101] This was a particularly notorious case because of the action of a judge who, amazingly, granted bail to the accused, raising suspicions of corruption. In 2006, a boat was intercepted heading for the Canary Islands, 80 miles from the coast of Senegal, with 3.7 tonnes of cocaine from Colombia, apparently belonging to a Dutch syndicate and destined for the British market.[102] Major Dutch criminals had long had an interest in Liberia and Sierra Leone, in particular for the trans-shipment of hashish cargoes from Asia.[103] This particular shipment had travelled from Venezuela via the Dutch Antilles. On 31 January 2008, 2.4 tonnes of cocaine were on board the *Blue Atlantic* when it was intercepted by the French navy off the Liberian coast, en route to Nigeria.[104] Cargoes of comparable size have been detected in or close to the offshore waters of Cape Verde, Senegal, Mauritania, Guinea-Bissau, Guinea, Liberia, Sierra Leone, Ghana, and Benin.

An authoritative view is that of Antonio Mazzitelli, a senior UN drug law-enforcement officer in West Africa, who sees 2005 as the year in which a major change of scale became visible. He lists the total seizures in West Africa of cocaine as going from 1.2 tonnes in 2005 to 4.3 tonnes in the first seven months of 2007.[105] The UNODC has given higher figures, reporting that the Spanish and British navies seized 9.9 tonnes of cocaine on five ships in international waters off West Africa in 2006, and that 5.7 tonnes were seized in West Africa in the first three quarters of 2007.[106] In June 2007, Venezuelan authorities seized 2.5 tonnes of cocaine on a private plane about to take off for Sierra Leone.[107] None of these sources appears to include a case from 2006, when Nigeria's drug police, the NDLEA, was reported to have seized no less than 14.2 tonnes of cocaine located in a container on a ship, the *MSV Floriana,* berthed at Lagos's Tin Can Island port. According to press reports, the ship had originally come from Peru via the USA and Cameroon. However, several features of this case as reported by the press are puzzling.[108]

By most accounts, the West African country that has become most completely immersed in the drug trade is Guinea-Bissau. A Nigerian drug law-enforcement official has stated that the Bissau-Guinean army cooperates with drug traffickers to the extent of using military premises to stockpile cocaine awaiting shipment to Europe.[109] The UNODC has recorded private planes flying into a military airstrip.[110] In April 2007, two Colombians, Juan Pablo Rubio Camacho and Luis

Fernando Arango Mejia, were arrested in connection with the discovery of a large consignment of cocaine. According to US law-enforcement officers, both men are officials of the FARC, the Revolutionary Armed Forces of Colombia.[111] (Other sources confirm only one of the two as a member of the Colombian guerrilla force.) Both suspects were released on bail; both subsequently disappeared, and are presumed to be at liberty once more. The former head of Guinea-Bissau's judicial police, Orlando Antonio da Silva, says that he was reprimanded by his boss, the country's Interior Minister, and fired on account of his investigations into this case. The country's Attorney-General has received death threats, and also confirms the army's interest in the drug trade.[112] Political upheavals, infighting between rival security forces, and attempted coups in Guinea-Bissau throughout 2008 testify to the effect of the drug trade on the country's politics.[113]

Guinea-Bissau is not the only country in West Africa where Venezuelan and Colombian traffickers, including even FARC operatives, have taken up residence. Similar reports come from Accra, Conakry, Monrovia, and other capital cities. Throughout the region, the Latin Americans' key local partners are often Nigerian drug traffickers who have longstanding connections in South America, and who are paid for their logistical services with cocaine in lots of up to 200 kilograms. The Nigerians can then use this to operate their traditional courier service to European markets. Thus, in December 2006, 32 cocaine mules travelling from Guinea-Conakry via Morocco were arrested at Amsterdam airport. No fewer than 28 of the 32 were Nigerians.[114] Ghana, often seen by donors as a 'virtuous' state (high growth rate, freedom of speech, and democratic politics), has been extensively penetrated by drug money. According to Ghanaian law-enforcement officers, many of the country's politicians have interests in the drug trade, and some of Accra's impressive building boom is being financed with the proceeds of drug deals.[115] On 12 November 2005, US officials arrested a Ghanaian Member of Parliament, Eric Amoateng, in possession of 136 pounds of heroin. He was convicted in 2007.[116] There are reports of drug refining taking place in Ghana on a small scale, with precursor chemicals being imported from South Africa.[117]

In the Niger Delta, the home of Nigerian oil, local militias smuggling crude oil to tankers moored offshore are paid not only with cash and weapons, but also with cocaine.[118] Some of the cocaine imported into Nigeria in this process is consumed by foot soldiers in the militias that have sprung up in the Niger Delta, and towns like Warri and Port Harcourt have now become drug centres. However, it is improbable that all the cocaine imported into Nigeria by this relatively new route is consumed locally. It is likely that some at least is sold on or bartered in the complex international trade in oil, arms and drugs that is now connecting centres all along the Gulf of Guinea, from Luanda to Dakar.

Nigerian middlemen are also playing a leading role in the development of a trans-Saharan route for smuggling cocaine into Europe, using Tuareg guides. In early 2008, Malian authorities seized 750 kilos of cocaine at Tin Zawatine in the middle of the Sahara.[119] Intelligence officers of various nationalities claim that the Algerian armed opposition groups today known as Al-Qaeda in the Islamic Maghreb 'earn their living' from taxes on this route.[120] Once cocaine has reached North Africa, established Moroccan hashish smugglers can take it to Europe. A US investigation codenamed Operation Titan unravelled a Lebanese-dominated syndicate that linked members of the Lebanese diasporas in North and South America and Nigeria with partners in their Mediterranean homeland, together involved in the transport of hundreds of millions of dollars' worth of merchandise to the USA.[121] In this case, an element of continuity in the drug trade becomes apparent, since it was a Lebanese syndicate that was first recorded using West Africa as a transit zone for heroin over fifty years ago.

The drug trade and the long term

The UNODC has pointed out[122] that the relocation of a substantial part of the Latin American cocaine business to West Africa, including even some senior management functions, is not best understood as a consequence simply of comparative advantage in pricing. A more important reason for this development, which has been taking place for over a decade, is the exceptionally favourable political context offered by ineffective policing, governments that have a reputation for venality, and the relative lack of international attention given to West Africa. A pliable sovereign state is the ideal cover for a drug trafficker. The Colombian economist Francisco Thoumi states that '[p]rofitable illegal economic activity requires not only profitability, but also weak social and state controls on individual behavior, that is, a society where government laws are easily evaded and social norms tolerate such evasion'.[123] In short, '[i]llegality generates competitive advantages in the countries or regions that have the weakest rule of law'.[124] Drug production is not primarily to be explained by prices, but by reference to 'institutions, governability and social values'.[125] This is consistent with the 'new' international trade theory, which emphasizes the role of technical knowledge, public infrastructure, and the qualities of institutions in encouraging trade, supporting the view that 'institutional and structural weaknesses and cultural aspects determine the competitive advantage in illegal goods and services'.[126]

As the present article has shown, the development of the drug trade in West Africa has quite deep historical roots and has been enmeshed with politics in some countries for many decades. When the executive director of the UNODC, Antonio Maria Costa, sounds an alarm about the risk of drug money 'perverting economies and rotting society'[127] and of drug profits possibly financing insurgency,[128] he is really describing an existing state of affairs rather than some future nightmare. Liberia, to name just one example, was already a fully criminalized state under Charles Taylor, the country's head of state from 1997 to 2003. The financing of insurgency appears to be an established fact, in the case of both the Sahara and the Niger Delta. It is not hard to see why powerful people may nonetheless tolerate the drug trade in West Africa. For countries as poor as Guinea-Bissau or Guinea-Conakry, it makes a huge, though unofficial, contribution to national income. The UNODC, however, warns that crime hinders development, which it defines as 'the process of building societies that work'.[129] Crime is said to destroy social capital, and therefore to be anti-development.[130]

In purely technical terms, the emergence of the drug trade in West Africa over a period of fifty years or more is an astonishing feat. West African traders, with Nigerians in the forefront, have created for themselves an important role in a business characterized by competition that is cut-throat—literally—and by high profits. They have penetrated drug markets in every continent. Their success, and their growing ability to cooperate with organized crime groups elsewhere in the world, is inextricably linked not only to globalization and new patterns of international migration,[131] but also to specific experiences of rapid economic liberalization in the late twentieth century. Nigerians especially were playing a significant role in the illegal drug trade in the 1970s, before the era of structural adjustment. Subsequently, the manner in which new financial and economic policies were implemented in West Africa in the 1980s contributed greatly to the formation of what has been called 'a shadow state', in which rulers draw authority 'from their abilities to control markets and their material rewards'.[132] Dismantling large parts of the bureaucratic apparatus inherited from colonial times, and the formal economic activity that went with it, rulers became intent on identifying new shadow state networks, sometimes drawing in foreign investors.[133] West Africa's 'shadow states' are thus relatively new, but they draw heavily on older traditions. These include not only the existence since pre-colonial times of initiation societies that are sites of power, but also the colonial practice of indirect rule, which sometimes resulted in local authorities operating unofficial networks of governance rooted in local social realities, hidden from the view of European officials whose attention was focused on the official apparatus of government.[134]

The emergence of shadow states with networks that have become globalized through commerce and migration opens up an important debate in historical sociology concerning the degree to which a turn to predation in the last quarter of the twentieth century was the consequence of a specific context in the 1980s, and the extent to which its historical roots go much deeper.[135] The recent emergence of China as a major diplomatic and business operator in Africa, and the arrival in the continent of substantial numbers of Chinese expatriates and even settlers, adds a further element to this chemistry. Chinese crime gangs have a long history in Africa. Their enhanced presence in the continent can be expected to result in collaboration with African interests, and the development of new illicit markets in China itself.[136]

SECTION FIVE

PUBLIC ENGAGEMENT

18

HOW TO REBUILD AFRICA

Liberia is just one example on a long list of African states that have spent years on the brink of collapse (or have long since succumbed) despite international efforts to help them. Together, these countries (the list also includes Sierra Leone, the Democratic Republic of the Congo, and Somalia) point to a stark truth: the conventional approach for helping Africa's failed and failing states does not work. Part of the problem involves the way that the international community understands failed states in the first place. The conventional view relies on a misleading mechanical metaphor, which leads policymakers to suppose that, like broken machines, failed African countries can be repaired by good mechanics. In fact, dysfunctional governments are more like sick people. Keeping this in mind, a better approach to dysfunctional states in Africa would begin with a diagnosis that takes full account of their individual characters and does not assume that the same therapy will work on all of them.

The Lords of misrule

This past March, a UN panel revealed that Liberian officials had signed a secret contract with an obscure European company, giving it a virtual monopoly on mining diamonds in the troubled country—even though Liberia has been banned by the UN from selling its diamonds since 2001. The arrangement, it was disclosed, had involved members of the new transitional government operating under the (supposed) scrutiny of a large UN mission.

The discovery should not have come as a surprise. Liberia's new government, supposedly a model of national reconciliation, is largely made up of former militia members. During 15 years of war, armed gangs ravaged Liberia, turning it into a classic example of a failed state. Since the fighting stopped in August 2003, the erstwhile warlords have been quick to set aside their differences—at least when doing so helps them acquire more loot. The mining deal was just one in a long series of similar scandals perpetrated by senior members of the transitional government, who are rapidly signing away their country's future in return for personal financial gain.

It did not have to be this way. The new regime was established in October 2003 as part of a peace agreement brokered by West African states and supported by Washington—and backed up by a powerful UN peacekeeping mission. The UN force, originally led by Jacques Klein (a former U.S. diplomat with strong military credentials), has worked to disarm local fighters, build a working bureaucracy, organize democratic elections, and establish a basis for lasting peace. Preparations for presidential and parliamentary elections are proceeding on schedule, with voting expected to take place in October.

Unfortunately, the interim government has used the time to make things worse. Liberian warlords and politicians have found it easy to outmaneuver the UN and the international community in the conduct of what locals, with their habitual grim humor, call 'business more than usual.' Despite claims that they are struggling for peace, democracy, and reconciliation, the warlords and their henchmen continue to use the country's institutions for personal profit. Even if one of the few respectable candidates wins the presidential election in October, there is little chance that he or she will be able to rectify matters. And if the UN starts to wind down its mission after the elections, as it currently plans to do, the most likely outcome will be a resumption of politics-as-plunder and war. Nothing worthwhile will have come of the hundreds of millions of dollars poured into Liberia by international donors or of the hundreds of lives lost by foreign peacekeepers.

Liberia is just one example on a long list of African states that have spent years on the brink of collapse (or have long since succumbed) despite international efforts to help them. Together, these countries (the list also includes Sierra Leone, the Democratic Republic of the Congo, and Somalia) point to a stark truth: the conventional approach for helping Africa's failed and failing states does not work.

Part of the problem involves the way that the international community understands failed states in the first place. The conventional view relies on a misleading mechanical metaphor, which leads policymakers to suppose that, like broken machines, failed African countries can be repaired by good mechanics. In fact, dysfunctional governments are more like sick people. Like humans, states fall ill in a variety of ways, can continue to function (after a fashion) even when sick, and do not all respond to treatment the same way. Some illnesses can be treated quickly, whereas others require long-term care. Most important, serious illnesses often leave their victims—whether people or governments—permanently changed, unable to return to their former condition. Keeping this in mind, a better approach to dysfunctional states in Africa would begin with a diagnosis that takes full account of their individual characters and does not assume that the same therapy will work on all of them. The international community cannot get heavily involved in all of Africa's problem countries anytime soon. However, there are a few places, such as Liberia, where the outside world is already deeply entangled. New efforts should be focused in these states.

Achieving real gains will take time, however, and the international community must start thinking about how to help African states in more than just three- to five-year increments (the current lifespan of most UN mandates). International actors should be prepared to spend ten years or longer on Africa's hardest cases. A new approach will also require new institutional frameworks that draw in all interested parties, including some of Africa's more capable states and regional institutions. International financial bodies, especially the World Bank and the International Monetary Fund (IMF), must also be brought on board.

In some cases, a form of international trusteeship will be required. This idea, anathema since the end of colonialism, deserves rehabilitation. Done properly, it need not involve the wholesale dismantling of national sovereignty, a precedent that would rightly worry many parties. Instead, trusteeship should entail a new, enhanced form of international responsibility.

Not all African states will need such radical intervention. The continent's countries lie along a spectrum of effective statehood. At one end are South Africa, Botswana, and Mauritius—the few sub-Saharan success stories in terms of both governance and economics. At the other end lie the abject failures, including Liberia, Sierra Leone, and Somalia. And in between fall the majority. Notwithstanding the optimistic talk of international development officials, the vast bulk of Africa's countries are doing just about enough to get by. A few, such as Uganda, have pulled themselves back from the brink of ruin. Several others—including Benin, Ghana, Kenya, Mali, Mozambique, Senegal, and perhaps Malawi and Zambia—are functioning democracies that may be on the road to recovery. Still, of the African Union's 53 members, eight or nine could currently be described as war zones, and there are plenty more—such as Chad, Togo, and Guinea—that could go that way at any moment. It is past time that the world's leading states found a better way to help them.

Defining deviancy down

Although they vary in their details, dysfunctional states share two key characteristics: they cannot guarantee law and order throughout their territory, and they cannot fulfill certain critical international obligations. Of these two problems, the former tends to matter most to the state's own citizens, since they are the primary victims. But the latter creates the most widespread concern.

The attacks of September 11, 2001, made it very clear just how dangerous failed states can be for the rest of the world. The U.S. government has discovered that even the most obscure country can become a base for America's enemies—a notion underscored in late 2001 when it was disclosed that Charles Taylor, Liberia's then president, had sold diamonds to al Qaeda. This discovery—made not by a U.S. intelligence agent but by a reporter from *The Washington Post*—highlighted the way that even nonideological leaders may cooperate with dangerous anti-Western forces. Even when they want to, moreover, dysfunctional states are often unable to comply with

Washington's counterterrorism efforts (or with any other policy, for that matter). In such cases, providing military assistance (as the United States is doing in some parts of Africa) only makes matters worse. Aside from these basic failures, no two problem states are exactly the same, and it helps to break them down into categories more nuanced than simply 'working' or 'failing.' Nine years ago, the political scientist Jean-Germain Gros proposed a useful typology that the international community should adopt. He identified five types of dysfunctional states: 'anarchic' states, such as Somalia, which lack a central government; 'phantom,' or 'mirage,' states, such as Congo (formerly Zaire), which exercise only a semblance of central authority and can manage just a few core tasks (such as protecting the president and his circle); 'anemic' states, which are enervated by an insurgency or where, as in Haiti, 'the engines of modernity were never put in place'; 'captured' states, such as Rwanda, where a strong centralized authority has been taken over by an insecure elite that is primarily concerned with defending itself against rival elites; and 'aborted' states, such as Angola, which failed before they were ever consolidated.

This framework underscores the fact that not all problem countries are amenable to the same treatment. Somalia, for example, may work better without a real state than it did with one, since the lack of a central government there has prevented any one warlord from capturing all the resources and aid money for himself. Rwanda, meanwhile, remains a problem not because its government is feeble, but because the paranoid Tutsi political elite regards any moderation as weakness. Crafting a strategy for dealing with these enormously varied situations might seem impossible, but it should not cause officials to despair. There are a number of African states that are now good candidates for international attention, and they should be made the focus of outside help.

Three strikes

Before explaining how best to provide aid, it helps to understand why past efforts have not worked. Large international state-fixing missions are currently under way in Burundi, Côte d'Ivoire, Congo, Liberia, Sierra Leone, and Sudan. These ventures share three major inadequacies.

The first problem is with their time frames: healing a seriously troubled state requires a comprehensive medium-term strategy, not a quick fix. 'Medium term' here means longer than the four-year policy cycle typical in Washington; fixing dysfunctional African states can take ten years or more. Thinking in long time frames is not easy for Western governments, but they can do it when they have to, as they have shown with energy policy. And where Africa is concerned, there is little alternative; too many outside interventions have been undermined by the expectation of instant results.

The second flaw in the current approach is its historical imprecision. Foreign officials tend to talk as though they can restore African states to a degree of efficiency that existed at some vague time in the past. But much of Africa never enjoyed anything like what is now considered good governance. Before 1980, for example, Liberia was run by a few families who claimed U.S. ancestry, under a system analogous to apartheid. It would be a terrible mistake to resurrect such a system today, and Liberians would never accept it. What period, then, should Liberia aspire to reproduce? Even in its heyday, Monrovia never functioned well.

Although Liberia, which was never formally a colony, has an unusual history, its story is similar in important respects to those of many other problem states in Africa. In the majority, colonial administrations ruled for decades, relying on village chiefs and other rural notables to keep the masses quiet. Only from the 1940s onward did most colonial governments begin to try to develop their territories economically and to endow local administrations with some democratic credentials. When most African countries gained independence in the 1960s, they had very little experience with management or governance.

Still, independence came during the height of the Cold War and at the midpoint of the longest and widest economic boom in the modern history of the world (lasting roughly from 1945 to 1973). Prices for agricultural commodities were high, outside aid was easy to attain, and the development community felt very optimistic and very generous. Conditions have obviously changed since then.

This is not to say that African countries can never regain the sense of optimism and progress they enjoyed in the mid-twentieth century, or that their public administrations can never gain a reasonable degree of efficiency and honesty. But in order for them to do so, they must first face up to modern realities. Prices for many agricultural commodities have declined and may never return to their 1960s or 1970s high point. Most African states have shown themselves unable to industrialize and incapable of absorbing capital; instead, outside money has been used to enrich tiny political elites and their partners abroad. Today, many African governments are further than ever from being able to finance themselves through their own resources, and they rely on permanent subsidies from donor countries for their very existence. Population growth has changed the relationship of people to the land, in both economic and cultural terms. Many of the most dynamic and best-educated Africans have emigrated to Europe or North America. Young people express little hope for a better future. And HIV / AIDS is cutting a cruel swath through the continent, with long-term implications that are hard to predict.

Outsiders also tend to ignore the historical roots of today's conflicts. Virtually since independence, much of Africa has been consumed with warfare—in the Great Lakes region and Sudan since the 1950s, for example, and in Liberia since the 1980s. Today's strife is not just the product of the end of the Cold War or the withdrawal of military funding by the superpowers. Many of Africa's current conflicts are just the latest twists in a long and bloody history that goes back to the circumstances of decolonization. Understanding this history is essential for rebuilding today.

The third and final weakness of current attempts to rebuild Africa is that most are too narrowly oriented toward individual states. This was one of the mistakes made by the World Bank and the IMF in the 1980s, when prescriptions for economic reform were given to neighboring countries with little thought of their cumulative consequences. In a similar fashion, Africa's wars are today often erroneously understood as internal, rather than interstate, conflicts. The truth is that most combatants receive support from neighboring governments, making Africa's wars regional in fact if not in name. Indeed, Congo's 'civil' war—a conflagration that has persisted, in one form or another, since 1997 and has claimed more than three million lives—has involved forces from at least eight countries. And the ongoing chaos in Liberia has helped to destabilize neighboring Sierra Leone, Côte d'Ivoire, and Guinea.

To have a chance at success, peacemaking efforts and rebuilding strategies must take these regional dynamics into account. Regionwide cooperation is also necessary on economic issues, such as facilitating cross-border trade and ensuring that people can travel, work, and own property outside their home countries. Achieving such cooperation may require the creation of international customs administrations, for example, and pooled revenue arrangements.

Test cases

No African state has been undergoing major repairs for longer than Sierra Leone. As a result, it has become something of a laboratory experiment in state sickness and remedy. And it serves as a good test case for just what is wrong and what is right about the international approach to Africa.

Sierra Leone started out as colony under British auspices in 1787, serving as a refuge for homeless black people from the streets of London (many of them veterans of the wrong side of the American War of Independence). After the British departed in 1961, the new country quickly succumbed to corruption and misrule under the long reign of Siaka Stevens (1968–85). War broke out in 1991 and began to taper off only after British troops arrived in May 2000.

Since then, the international effort to reconstruct Sierra Leone has been intense. Under UN and British auspices, its army and police force have been reorganized and retrained, law courts and police stations have been rebuilt, and a government has been democratically elected. Many officials in the new government, however, have murky pasts— including ties to a militia that committed atrocities during the war. They and their colleagues have shown little interest in making more than a rhetorical commitment to good governance. Many officials are also highly corrupt and have paid scant attention to the deep social problems (such as bad education and unemployment) that led to war in the first place. Government ministers and senior officials seldom venture outside the capital city, Freetown, where they drive around in luxury SUVs paid for with international aid money. Meanwhile, nothing has changed for the impoverished veterans of Sierra Leone's vicious wars—or for their victims. Some former fighters say they would pick up arms again at the first opportunity; at least the militias provided them with jobs. If the UN and the British leave Sierra Leone in the near future, there is every reason to believe the state will once again collapse.

The same goes for neighboring Liberia, which is now a wreck—despite having boasted the world's second-fastest-growing economy during the 1950s and having been home, more recently, to the largest UN mission in the world and a recovery process to which the United States is estimated to have contributed some $750 million.

In both countries, as in many other parts of Africa, ruling cliques have developed a vested interest in disorder and show little interest in seeing an efficient state emerge. This is not a problem of education: Africa's elites include people with degrees from leading universities around the world. Many of Liberia's warlords studied in the United States, for example, and the president of Sierra Leone, Ahmad Tejan Kabbah, is a former UN official.

And the problem goes deeper than crooked officials. Countries such as Sierra Leone, Liberia, and Somalia, which have suffered through fighting for almost a generation now, lack not just honest, competent leaders but also clerks and bureaucrats. Not enough people have been educated or trained for effective government work. An entire range of social and economic institutions also needs fixing. Reconstruction will take a minimum of ten years and could require as many as 50.

None of these problems can be solved by simply throwing more cash at Africa. Many on the continent have come to see foreign aid as nothing more than a cow to be milked. Unfortunately, much of the international community has yet to recognize this. Consider *Our Common Interest*, the report published earlier this year by the Commission for Africa (convened by the British government). While it cites the need for reform, the report also recommends a major injection of new aid—as if Africa's main problem was a lack of capital. The commission did not adequately consider why that formula has failed so badly, and so often, in the past.

Now the G-8 (the coalition of the world's leading industrialized powers) has made a similar mistake. At the recent summit at the Gleneagles resort in Scotland, leaders promised to increase by 2010 official development assistance to Africa by $25 billion a year, doubling current totals. But Africa's real problem is not a lack of money. In fact, new aid from the West will only make matters worse unless it is integrated into a strategy that also involves much more incisive political input from donor countries.

Tough love

Instead of more money, what Africa really needs is governments that are responsible to their own voters, that are largely self-financing, that are internationally respectable, and that can attract home some of the hundreds of thousands of talented Africans who currently live in the West. New infusions of aid would likely just perpetuate the kleptocratic regimes that have slowly strangled the continent since independence.

Healthier states will need to reflect the actual politics of their societies, including some unconventional arrangements. In Somaliland (a region in the north of Somalia), for example, a relatively competent though still-unrecognized independent government has sprung up, funded by local business leaders and remittances from abroad—which turn out to have a much more salutary effect on government than does foreign aid. Premature recognition of Somaliland could kill it by turning it into another aid junkie. But the territory deserves some form of legal status to recognize its impressive development and to take it out of its present limbo.

Of course, providing basic security remains an essential first step in any rebuilding effort. Africa's lack of security—physical, political, and economic—has wreaked such psychological havoc that it will be hard to redress through conventional government techniques. Few Africans can muster the confidence to invest in their countries, whether financially, professionally, or personally. Persuading them to reengage will require providing military and economic security; only then will the climate improve enough to permit the training and retention of professional and administrative personnel.

But traditional peacekeeping is not enough. Even well-meaning international efforts can do more harm than good. As the academics Denis Tull and Andreas Mehler have pointed out, often the worst violence in Africa has occurred after the outside world intervened to create power-sharing deals between rival elites; think of the slaughter in Angola in 1992, in Burundi in 1993, and in Rwanda in 1994. What was missing, in each of these cases, was enough international pressure and outside resources to keep fragile and sometimes misconceived peace treaties in place.

To craft a better approach to Africa, one other problem must be confronted head-on: effective intervention is going to occasionally require overriding traditional national sovereignty. Certain African governments have never managed to create durable working administrations. In these countries, sovereignty has become a mere legal fiction, one that provides cover for all sorts of internal abuses. For too long, legitimate worries about infringing on Africa's independence have stymied international efforts to address this problem.

Fortunately, there is now a growing body of international jurisprudence defining the circumstances in which the international community is justified, or even required, to bypass such nominal sovereignty in order to protect people who have been abandoned or abused by their governments. And several African governments, most notably Nigeria's and South Africa's, have started to signal a new flexibility on this question, as have the leaders of the new African Union (AU). All seem to agree that in some cases, when states are unable or unwilling to prevent massive human rights abuses, intervention is appropriate—whether local powers like it or not. Intrusive outside meddling often smacks of colonialism and is thus a bitter pill for African nationalists to swallow. But sometimes there is simply no alternative.

This understanding should allow for a new form of international engagement in Africa: namely, trusteeships for certain failed states. No one is advocating a return to the UN's old trusteeship system. Under the new paradigm, locals would remain full partners in any arrangement. What is called for now are multilateral joint ventures in which certain countries and institutions share control over key operations. In such missions, the UN should still play a fundamental role (although not an administrative one), since it alone can confer the kind of legitimacy critical to such projects. In this regard, it would help enormously if the UN Security Council were expanded to include a representative from sub-Saharan Africa, since this would give Africans a sense that they were full partners in the body.

The most obvious current candidate for such a trusteeship is Liberia. Congo and Sudan might equally need help, but they are too large in political, economic, and population terms, and have too many self-interested outside actors involved to allow a novel international arrangement to succeed. Liberia, by contrast, has far less to lose and fewer outside influences and allies. Liberians are also so deeply attached to the United States that many locals would likely support a U.S.-led effort.

Any trusteeship established to oversee the country should include representatives of the U.S. government, as well as of the other parties to the international 'contact group' on Liberia, which was formed in September 2002 to track the country's progress (the group also includes representatives from the UN, the EU, the AU, the Economic Community of West African States [ECOWAS], France, Morocco, Nigeria, Senegal, and the United Kingdom). The IMF and the World Bank should also be included, as well as whoever is elected as Liberia's president in October.

One of the main priorities of the trusteeship of Liberia should be to encourage some of the many Liberians living abroad to return home. These returnees and other exiles could be organized into a continent-wide international corps of administrators who could be deployed wherever in Africa they are needed. The international community, however, must avoid simply giving control of all aspects of the country's public administration to the new trusteeship. To ensure that Liberia starts to govern itself effectively, foreign administrators should concentrate on securing the boundaries of the political field while allowing new local arrangements to emerge. This can best be accomplished by taking control of the main sources of revenue and ensuring that money is then passed on to the Liberian Treasury on agreed terms. A comparable system has been pioneered for oil revenues in Chad, an example that should be studied for future cases. Another option is the arrangement some analysts have proposed for Congo: requiring both local and international businesses to pay taxes not to the central government but into a series of provincial trust funds jointly run by locals and foreigners. Such innovations could be very useful for these countries and many others throughout the continent.

Although the trusteeship idea might sound complicated and costly, the sums of money involved in restoring African states to health will be small—far less than what is now pouring into Iraq or is given as aid to a range of other countries. In many cases, the new paradigm would involve no new allocations, but would simply spread out over longer periods what has already been budgeted. Expensive, large-scale peacekeeping forces would not generally be required, certainly not for the long term. Where peacekeepers are needed, the best approach would be to copy the Sierra Leone model: use a small number of Western soldiers (800 British troops were deployed in Sierra Leone) to spearhead a larger force of regional peacekeepers (such as the West African troops deployed in Côte d'Ivoire or the AU forces sent to Burundi and, more recently, to Darfur). The AU has expressed interest in creating an African standby force, but this may take years to assemble and organize.

Such forces should not occupy whole territories, but simply guarantee effective military intervention in defined circumstances—such as if a legitimately elected government is threatened by a coup or if a troubled country is threatened by invasion. As the British armed forces have shown in Sierra Leone, the credible threat of a deployment by an 'over the horizon' force serves as an effective deterrent when part of a wider political strategy.

A new Africa

One of the few hopeful developments to come out of Africa's many dysfunctional states is the way power vacuums have been spontaneously filled by new structures with deep roots in Africa's history. These institutions, such as Somalia's subclans or West Africa's initiation societies, do not figure in textbooks on government and sometimes play a negative role. In other cases, however—as in the self-governing Somaliland—they have made a positive contribution. At present, UN administrators tend to ignore such networks and often spend an entire tour of duty patiently rebuilding formal new governments without noticing the alternate structures already in existence right under their noses.

Administrators should learn to take advantage of such indigenous political institutions. Over the next few decades, governance in many parts of Africa must be substantially reinvented, and the more solidly it is grounded, the better. Not all local institutions that have a historical pedigree should be preserved. But because certain deep-rooted local structures are not going to disappear, it makes sense to think about how they can play a role. Some self-defense and vigilante groups, for example, could be incorporated into local police forces or national guard units.

With every month that goes by, it becomes clearer that the chapter of African history that opened in 1945 has now closed. The golden age of decolonization and nationalism in Africa did not lead, in most cases, to successful sovereign states. This fact may be hard for Africans to admit, but it is even harder for them to live with.

Too often, Westerners ask only whether Africa's problems affect their security and, learning that they do not, decide to ignore them. Such short-term thinking must now change, especially given the new, global threats that have emerged since September 11. The West should adopt a new, enlightened form of self-interest and be open to engaging in new sorts of involvement in Africa. Sick states there cannot be restored with the medicines and surgical techniques of a bygone era. What is required instead are international joint ventures as discussed above. These arrangements would avoid the evils of colonialism and the errors of more recent peacekeeping and state-building efforts. The outcome—a healthier, more stable, and more secure Africa—would benefit everyone, on the continent and around the world.

19

THE ROOTS OF AFRICAN CORRUPTION

'In broad swaths of Africa many types of corrupt practice are not the deviant behavior of a small minority—they are a standard mode of transacting political and financial business.'

It is easy to imagine how you could smuggle a diamond. A diamond is small enough to be held in the hand, carried in the body, or hidden in the seam of a jacket or the heel of a shoe. It is considerably less easy to imagine how someone smuggles a tanker-full of oil. Yet that is an everyday occurrence in Nigeria, one of the world's leading oil producers. Clearly, it can be done only with the collusion, at the very least, of very senior government officials and officers of the armed forces, the navy in particular.

Corruption is notoriously hard to measure or even to define, and therefore it is impossible to say for certain whether corruption in Africa is increasing or whether it is worse than in other places. What can be said is that it has become astonishingly brazen in recent years, with senior officials and even heads of state quite openly flouting their own countries' laws and a range of international diplomatic and legal conventions.

In the early 1990s, officials in Kenya succeeded in forging their own national currency. Senior Kenyan officials also have been implicated in the so-called Goldenberg scandal, named after a front company that was used to defraud the public treasury of some $600 million by claiming government subsidies for nonexistent exports of probably nonexistent gold and diamonds. Among those recently recommended for prosecution are a former head of Kenyan intelligence, a former governor of the central bank, and a former head of the treasury. One of the main architects of the scam has testified that he gave the head of state, Daniel arap Moi, suitcases full of money; and that he 'never visited Moi empty-handed.'

When Kenyans eventually voted Moi's party out of office in 2002 in favor of a government pledged to ending corruption, the new team used exactly the same technique. Last year, the administration of President Mwai Kibaki was exposed by its own anticorruption chief, the courageous John Githongo, as having paid millions of dollars to fictitious companies or to real companies that were inflating invoices for government contracts. This was done with the full knowledge of key ministers who are themselves suspected of pocketing a big share of the proceeds. Githongo reported his findings to President Kibaki. The president has done precisely nothing.

In Liberia, the transitional government that ran the country until the end of 2005 is believed to have presided over the theft of some $100 million per year, compared with an annual budget of a mere $80 million, even while it was being monitored by a very substantial United Nations mission. In other words, this was a government that stole more than it put into the state treasury—and this at a time when Liberia is widely recognized as having its last chance to lay the foundation for a decent system of government after 15 years or more of war and mayhem.

These and a distressing number of other examples suggest why, when it comes to graft, some African countries have earned a reputation for excess, and even for being beyond caring what others may think. No doubt this is why the 'corruption perceptions index' prepared by the watchdog group Transparency International consistently places African countries among the worst offenders. A grim joke in Nigeria—which for some years was the second most-corrupt nation on the Transparency International list—held that the country had avoided being ranked as the world's most corrupt by bribing Bangladesh to take over the slot.

510

The unlawful state

Not only is there no consensus on precisely what corruption is, but some of the more monstrous cases of corruption can also be called by other names. If a head of state bribes soldiers from the army or officers from the intelligence service to murder his personal enemies, this may indeed be corruption, but it is also conspiracy to murder. If, as in the Goldenberg scam, a businessman with excellent links to government officials colludes with them in securing payments for nonexistent services, it is not only corruption, it is also fraud.

Some African heads of state do not limit themselves to demanding kickbacks for awarding state contracts, which is probably the most common form of official corruption, or extending their protection to professional criminals in return for payment. A handful have gone beyond forms of collusion like these to become the main organizers of syndicates that are smuggling drugs, guns, or other illicit goods on a large scale. They bring to this business all the advantages of state sovereignty: diplomatic bags, diplomatic passports, access to central banks for laundering money, exemption from prosecution, and much more.

In situations like this, observers need to ask themselves what precisely they are dealing with. Is it a problem of corrupt practices among public officials? Or is it a case of professional criminals having taken control of a state, and using it simply as a tool of the trade?

Pursuing this line of thought may lead to historical reflections on the difference between a state and a criminal conspiracy. This reflection need not be unduly cynical. The sociologist Charles Tilly has pointed out that the states that emerged in Europe three or four centuries ago did so largely because of their single-mindedness in organizing armies. To do this, they required finance, which in turn involved raising money from their people. Crudely put, early modern states proposed to their subjects a deal no different from a mobster's unrefusable offer: pay us money, and we will protect you; fail to pay us, and we will rob you.

Associated in European history with the rise of strong states with formidable powers of coercion are countervailing struggles for democracy, freedom of speech, and human rights. The law of habeas corpus and the principle of no taxation without representation were not granted by benign rulers out of the goodness of their hearts, but were negotiated after hard-fought contests. States became both leviathans that could crush dissent and the guarantors of contracts between rulers and ruled. Those who refused the agreements they offered became rebels or criminals.

In light of this view of Western history, it becomes still less clear what the exact nature of corruption is in Africa, a continent where modern states have other origins and the struggles of rulers and ruled have taken different forms. In Africa today, ordinary people regularly give bribes to obtain the services they should in theory receive from the state for free, or to police officers who shake down travelers as a matter of course. In Kenya it is estimated the average urban resident pays 16 bribes per month. Junior officials in many countries routinely take bribes to compensate themselves for ludicrously small salaries. Politicians raise money corruptly to fund their campaigns. International businessmen collude in these practices to obtain the contracts they want. Corruption becomes a way of life, a mode of business and politics. 'It is simple,' a West African civil servant once explained, 'the government pretends to pay us, and we pretend to work.'

Standard practice

None of these practices is unknown in the United States, of course. Their particularity in the case of sub-Saharan Africa is not a matter of scale: the biggest African scams are puny in comparison to Enron, the Texas energy corporation that engaged in massive fraud. Rather, it is a question of context. The word 'corruption' implies deviation from a norm, a falling away from accepted standards. Hence, when certain types of illicit transactions become normal to the point that people do not bother to hide them, it is not satisfactory simply to label them as 'corruption' or even 'crime.' This is especially so when the people who run the state are themselves the main organizers of such activity. As we have seen, evidence from Nigeria and Kenya suggests that outrageously corrupt practices have become routine at the very heart of government in some of the continent's most important countries.

Even in South Africa, which has the biggest economy in Africa and is generally regarded as the leading power south of the Sahara, there are signs that corruption exists deep inside the institutions of state. In

1998, no fewer than 10,000 of the country's 140,000 police officers were under investigation for bribery, theft, or involvement in organized crime. These figures are related to the fact that South Africa's transition from apartheid in the early 1990s made it temporarily vulnerable to sophisticated professional criminals from other parts of the world, who found it a convenient location both to organize their activities and to launder their profits.

Overall levels of recorded crime in South Africa have declined slightly in recent years, but according to a survey in 2003, petty corruption is now the most common offense after housebreaking. And yet international diplomats and businesspeople continue to see South Africa as one of Africa's few 'normal' states—in the sense that it has a functioning government, a central bank and financial institutions that are able to offer a conducive business environment, and a legal system that, creaky though it is, is capable of producing satisfactory and enforceable judgments in commercial disputes.

The observation that corruption is entrenched in such leading countries as Kenya and Nigeria, and that it remains a definite problem even in South Africa, makes it still more disturbing to contemplate what this suggests about the continent's more obviously dysfunctional states, those commonly considered as 'failed' or 'failing.' It is important to recall that even these countries have legal codes, at least on paper. The problem is that the laws in Africa's dysfunctional states are rarely enforced, or only very selectively. Worse, the authorities theoretically responsible for their implementation may themselves break these same laws continuously and routinely.

This is really what Africa's so-called failed states are—not so much places where the state has ceased to exist, but where the formal trappings of statehood serve purposes of strategic deception, rather like the stage-sets in a theater. In one of these countries, you would have to be naive to believe that the law, the police, or the central bank really fulfills the role in theory allotted to it. The Democratic Republic of Congo, the Central African Republic, Guinea-Bissau, and dozens of other African states cannot be regarded as functioning according to international norms. But each one nevertheless has an actual, substantive system of politics and governance—not to be confused with the formal system, although the real and the legal are intertwined.

Anyone who wants to live or do business in a failing state needs to learn the real rules. In each case, the actual conventions of economic, political, and even social life will certainly involve patterns of activity regarded by many international observers as corrupt. In broad swaths of Africa many types of corrupt practice are not the deviant behavior of a small minority—they are a standard mode of transacting political and financial business.

The history of graft

To understand the real political economy of corruption requires an appreciation of moral repertoires, which inevitably requires making historical inquiries. Situating corruption within a specific historical context suggests that certain illicit practices, even if they are formally outlawed, may be considered morally permissible by large numbers of people in some circumstances. (Americans should know this as well as anyone, after the experience of Prohibition in the 1920s.) The law and popular perceptions of morality do not always coincide in their views.

Probing how people's understandings of particular types of action change over time has been made more difficult by the popularity of the dangerously simplistic 'clash of civilizations' theory made famous by Samuel Huntington, which suggests that cultural blocs are rather impervious to change. In reality, cultures are both more complex and more fluid than that. In the case of Africa, an investigation along these lines throws a good deal of light on the phenomenon of 'failing' states, showing them to be not only derogations from international models of good governance, but also places shaped by their individual pasts.

A leading historian, John Lonsdale, once made the striking observation that 'the most distinctively African contribution to human history could be said to have been precisely the civilized art of living fairly peaceably together *not* in states.' This remark may remind us that it is indeed possible for people to live together in reasonable harmony without modern states—although whether that is possible in the twenty-first century is another question.

It also provides clues to the historical trajectory of various types of transaction that are often classed today as corrupt. In many cases, these activities have historical antecedents in practices deeply rooted in African societies. Examples include the accumulation of political power and social prestige mainly through patronage; an expectation that rich people will redistribute wealth to their family and other dependents; and a long history of 'extraversion'—the habit of seeking external resources to build political power within African societies.

Culture in Africa has long been a political battleground. During colonial times, European officials claimed a right to rule Africa on the grounds that their culture was superior. Europeans knew how to organize the type of literate bureaucracies that are at the heart of modern government, whereas Africans had had little or no prior experience with this kind of rule.

Slightly later, the claims of African nationalists that they had a right to govern themselves were often based on a simple inversion of the colonial prejudice that Africans were unfit for self-government for cultural reasons. African intellectuals could reply that Africa, like every other continent, had its own genius that should be celebrated rather than being a source of embarrassment. After the establishment of the United Nations and a world order based on a system of sovereign states, African leaders could also riposte that every nation in any case had a right to sovereignty.

More than 40 years after most African countries acquired sovereign status, these cultural disputes still resonate. Indeed, so politicized does the concept of culture remain with regard to Africa that the mere mention of it risks causing immediate misunderstanding. Of course, observing that a practice has historical roots—in other words, that roughly similar things have occurred previously—does not automatically make it acceptable in our own times. European and American histories are full of examples of historically existing practices that were once considered legitimate but are now seen as distasteful, unrespectable, or illegal. It does not require more than a few moments' reflection to come up with examples. The same should be true of Africa—were it not that Africa is so often thought by both its admirers and its detractors to exist in a timeless present of African authenticity.

Some practices considered as corrupt occupy a prominent place in such a schema, and corrupt politicians are not above invoking an imagined authenticity to excuse their behavior. According to the

Liberian writer Emmanuel Dolo, people who have served as state officials are expected by their own families to enrich themselves through corruption. Otherwise, he writes, they are accused of failing to do what he calls 'the cultural thing': to steal money from the national treasury, an action they may justify on cultural grounds.

In short, corruption has deep roots. If we are to understand it and various related phenomena, including state failure, it is urgent to investigate what has happened over time. In Africa's case, the matters to be considered include a history of power organized on a basis rather different from that in Europe or North America. A moment in Africa's history that is particularly relevant for the present discussion was the imposition in colonial times of territorial, bureaucratically governed states that aspired to establish the rule of law.

The rule of law

At this point, it should be made clear what is meant by the establishment of the rule of law in colonial times. Emphatically, this does not mean that colonial government was a just order. It is no more and no less than the observation that colonial government was based on the idea that a centralized state apparatus should be responsible for promulgating a code of laws and associated rules, usually in written form, that have a binding force on society and even on the state itself. This, we may note in passing, makes thinkable the idea of a state crime.

Nor does the colonial establishment of the rule of law mean that public life has been governed ever since by the consistent application of written laws. The point is that from colonial times, and up until today, African countries are *in theory* governed by the consistent application of written laws. This point is important in part because it allows African politicians and power brokers and their foreign partners or collaborators to manipulate the gap between theory and reality to their advantage.

The preceding observation on the rule of law should also not be taken to suggest that African societies before colonial times were chaotic because they lacked the rule of law. In Africa's case, European colonial officials and a couple of generations of anthropologists tried to identify the authentic rules of African societies in the form of so-called customary law or tradition that they described in ethnographies. It has emerged, however, that the characteristic colonial view of custom or tradition in Africa as a static, codified corpus was not altogether accurate. It implied that African societies had been frozen in time and ruled by unchanging custom, but there is every reason to doubt that this was ever so.

What we call 'tradition' in African societies before colonial times was not so much a body of rules as a way of justifying change. Justice was not in reality dispensed by the application of a fixed code of traditional laws. It was the prerogative, rather, of a ruler acting in accordance with whatever could be represented as tradition. In almost every case, the correct application of 'tradition' was inextricable from spiritual beliefs articulated by ritual experts or priests. The latter thus in effect had a role as guarantors of constitutional checks and balances on a ruler, since they could legitimize or disqualify a ruler's actions by pronouncing them as traditional and, therefore, just.

It was precisely because law in precolonial African societies often turned on individual actions and not on a fixed code—and rules were indistinguishable from rituals—that it was unsuitable for European purposes in the late nineteenth century. The globalization of the *belle époque,* the period that ended in 1914, produced a new breed of bankers and businessmen prepared to loan or invest money anywhere in the world. Large Western corporations found it inconvenient to do business with the ever-shifting population of African kings and big men. Diplomats and bankers increasingly needed a world governed by rules that were enforceable by institutions. They wanted to see Western-style jurisdictions with fixed boundaries established everywhere, opening the whole world to business. Where public authorities of this type did not exist, they had to be encouraged.

In Africa, the establishment of colonial territories fulfilled this need. Bankers could lend money to colonial governments that, unlike individual big men, would guarantee the security of a loan over long periods. Investors could seriously contemplate putting money into mines and railways, safe in the knowledge that these assets were located in a specific territory that was party to international legal conventions. These are the conditions necessary for capitalist investment and production.

In search of authenticity

Colonialism endowed Africa with legal-bureaucratic government in the many places where nothing fitting this description existed before, and it strengthened the legal and bureaucratic elements in cases where these already existed, such as in areas ruled by Muslim sultans. Today, some analysts see this form of government as a Western transplant that, being imposed from outside, never really took root in the African soil or coexisted with the supposedly authentic African way of doing things. This is a romantic point of view; it is also inaccurate.

It is true that every European colonial power did indeed set up a centralized administration in each colony and, to greater or lesser extent, incorporated African rulers in systems of indirect rule. It is now clear that in most cases this involved freezing many of the dynamic processes of local government and, also in many cases, permitted local rulers to dispense with many of the more subtle checks and balances that had traditionally operated, producing what the African scholar Mahmood Mamdani refers to as 'decentralized despotisms.' But, however cruel, none of this was an assault on African authenticity, a figment of more recent imagination. The originators of authenticity were intellectuals of the colonial period, both African and foreign. The leading political exponent of the concept was Mobutu Sese Seko, the infamously corrupt dictator of Zaire.

The institutions of legal-bureaucratic government, introduced in most of Africa by colonial rule, are now being hollowed out to produce the façade states that we witness today. This process, often labeled 'state failure,' is certainly a cause of reduced efficiency in governance. From a politician's point of view, however, it offers increased opportunity to exploit a gap between two measures of reality.

On the one hand is a legal view, defined by national and international law and norms, the basis on which formal diplomatic relations are conducted. On the other hand is the reality of political bargains made between a leader in Africa and those whom he (very rarely she) seeks to represent, include, or assuage, paying particular attention to sectors where capital is produced and reproduced. It is because of the resulting gap between appearance and substance that Northwestern University professor William Reno refers to the existence of a 'shadow state' in

Africa, a rather imperfect comparison inasmuch as it is the shadow in the metaphor that actually contains most of the substance.

The creation of political capital out of the gap between legal and social reality, already perceptible in colonial times, has increased in importance since the 1970s primarily because of the lack of resources available to the official state apparatus. It is here that the hollowed-out institutions of an African state may become part of wider circuits of deception used by international operators who for one reason or another wish to hide their activities behind a screen of formality and law. These include powerful secret services, money launderers, offshore bankers, corporate lawyers, sanctions busters, drug traffickers, arms smugglers, and others.

Ten years ago, I published an article in the journal *African Affairs* showing in detail how this can work in the case of one small country, the Seychelles. There, in the 1980s, Italian money-launderers with connections to the mafia and to Italian political parties made common cause with drug traders, American covert warriors, South African sanctions busters, and Middle Eastern political fixers, all under cover of a sovereign state—in fact, one with a relatively decent reputation for what is nowadays called 'good governance.' In the process the Seychelles became one of the few African states to become literally criminal, in the sense of drafting laws designed to evade both its own and international legislation.

Confidence and con men

In what many Africans think of as happier times, there were examples of politicians who, while being massively corrupt, were nevertheless able to use the possibilities offered by their strategic situation and historical legacy in the service of political projects of general interest. A good example is Félix Houphouët-Boigny, president of Ivory Coast from 1960 to 1993, who for some two decades oversaw what was known as 'the Ivorian miracle,' a period of spectacular economic growth and development. Yet Houphouët-Boigny also diverted state resources on a huge scale, using them, for example, to build an imitation of the Vatican's St. Peter's basilica in his home village. He boasted openly about his Swiss bank accounts.

René Amany, a former head of Ivory Coast's cocoa marketing board, attempted to explain the paradox—a corrupt president who governed with conspicuous success—when he recalled nostalgically in a 2004 newspaper interview how Houphouët-Boigny 'used money as a means of advancing his political project, not politics as a way of making money.'

The corrupt use of a public position to make money, which is then invested in political activities, has also been noted in regard to Nigeria. Writing in the May 2005 issue of *Current History,* the Nigerian author Ike Okonta described how politics there is 'itself a struggle for control of the country's oil largesse, which, once secured in the form of loot, is used to further and consolidate political ends. In this struggle, the state and the means of violence at its disposal are the ultimate spoils.'

It is interesting to speculate why the corruption practiced in Ivory Coast during the 1960s and 1970s could be part of an internationally acclaimed political and economic success story, whereas twenty-first century Nigeria is widely regarded as a potential giant tragically handicapped by corruption. The essential difference between the two cases seems to lie not so much in the existence of corruption—present in both cases—as in the political uses to which it is put. To be successful, any political project has to inspire its supporters with genuine hope and confidence. These are qualities in short supply in Africa since the late 1970s, when the bright vision of progress turned dim in so many of the continent's countries.

Arguably, it is the loss of hope and confidence that makes corruption the scourge it is today. Africans keep an estimated $150 billion of capital offshore, money that could be used to develop the continent if its owners had the confidence to invest at home. Seventy thousand highly qualified Africans leave their continent annually, excluding students going abroad to study. Across much of Africa, a get-rich-quick and enjoy-it-while-you-can mentality prevails—an attitude fatal to stability, prosperity, and long-term investment.

Africa in recent decades has become poorer, which is an important incentive to corruption. But perhaps more important, it has lost faith in the various projects of modernization and development that promised Africans a better life in the mid-twentieth century. Many mistook the outward signs of material progress for the substance of development, at a time when politicians in need of funds could milk cold war rivalries. The disastrous economic and political decline of the past 30 years has left Africans correspondingly shocked and disillusioned. Here too lie some of the roots of today's corruption, as people grasp at anything that will help them survive the next day, month, or year in a world that seems empty of longer-term hope.

Those states with something to sell—especially oil—risk becoming what have been called 'successful failed states,' places that show all the symptoms of failure but that are able to continue indefinitely to the benefit of a corrupt ruling clique and its friends overseas. According to the US National Intelligence Council, 'many African leaders believe that the international economy is still rigged so that Africans will never prosper.' As long as this mood prevails, corruption in Africa will continue.

20

SOUTH AFRICA AND THE DECOLONIZATION
OF THE MIND

Inaugural lecture delivered upon accepting the position of VU
University Amsterdam Desmond Tutu Chair holder in the areas of
Youth, Sports and Reconciliation, at the Faculty of Social Sciences of
VU University Amsterdam on 23 September 2009.

Mijnheer de Rector, dames en heren,
It is an honour to be appointed to a chair bearing the name of
Desmond Tutu. Archbishop Tutu received his Nobel prize in 1984, but
he is probably most famous for his later chairmanship of South Africa's
Truth and Reconciliation Commission. This body was established
shortly after what was, by common consent, the most dangerous
period in South Africa's recent history. I am referring to the four years
between the unbanning of the African National Congress (ANC) and
other anti-apartheid organizations in 1990 and South Africa's first
democratic election in 1994. Thousands of people lost their lives in
that span of time as a result of violence that was more or less closely
connected to the formal political process that led to a successful
transfer of state power from the National Party to the ANC.

I can recall a conversation I had with a leading Western ambassador
in South Africa in 1990. Describing South Africa's transition, the
ambassador told me it was Africa's last chance to join the real world.

Being an academic, and therefore pedantic, I cannot fully approve this formulation, since the world is what it is, and not what any one of us thinks it ought to be. No country can ever join or leave the world, but can only conform to or differ from an ideological representation of it. Still, I think I understand what the ambassador meant. He was referring to a perception that the countries south of the Sahara, over the decades since most of them acquired sovereign status in the 1950s and 1960s, have generally failed to find political stability or to fulfil their economic potential. They have become a permanent concern of the international community, which, collectively and via bilateral relations, provides them with development aid. South Africa, the ambassador was implying, has the means to lead the rest of sub-Saharan Africa out of the hole into which it has fallen.

We are now nineteen years further on from that conversation, and fifteen years from the inauguration of the first ANC government in South Africa. No serious observer has any doubt that the country has seen specific improvements since 1994, too numerous for me to list here. Yet South Africa has not lived up to all the hopes raised when it endowed itself for the first time with a government elected by the whole adult population. The country's high levels of poverty and its growing inequality have been a matter of comment for some years. Moreover, it remains a violent society.

Last year, anti-foreigner attacks did considerable damage to South Africa's image worldwide. In fact, one-third of the 62 people killed as a result of these violent assaults[1] were not foreigners at all, but South Africans generally from rural areas, in many cases killed because they were not perceived as having full rights of residence in urban settlements where competition for houses and space is intense. That brutal outburst confirmed what has been evident for some time, namely that South Africa is not the rainbow nation that Desmond Tutu prayed for. In effect, many South Africans do not perceive citizenship as homogeneous, but as a series of layers, like the skins of an onion.[2] Some citizens are believed to be at the inner core, with real rights, while others are deemed to have lesser rights, because of their geographical or ethnic origin. Poor immigrants from the rest of Africa have the fewest rights of all.

Conflicts fuelled by differing perceptions of citizenship are only one issue requiring reconciliation, the process of persuading the people who live in South Africa to exist in peace, accepting the realities of their past and the responsibilities that flow from such acceptance. Here we encounter another aspect of the vision dear to Desmond Tutu: the idea that South Africa's long season of violence would pass with the election of a democratic government and the promulgation of a non-racial constitution. This, too, is open to question. The hope that a formal political agreement between all the main political parties would end South Africa's violence was often based on a misidentification of the nature of that violence. In the last years of apartheid, strategic thinkers from both the state security forces and the anti-apartheid camp broadly agreed that their country was at war. From the mid-1970s, the South African Defence Force was conducting a conventional military campaign in Angola and launched commando raids on some other countries. Within South Africa itself, the war was never of a conventional type. Much of the violence that occurred there was socially rooted, shaped by the country's history of conquest and segregation. Both the ANC and other insurrectionary organizations and the state's counter-insurgency forces aimed to use this socially-grounded violence for their own purposes. As a leading military strategist wrote in a manual adopted by the state security forces at the height of repression in the 1980s, 'the objective for both sides in a revolutionary war is the population itself'.[3] Accordingly, it was the population at large that bore the brunt of the violence.

South Africa's transformation

Appreciating the degree to which the war for South Africa was rooted in society throws some light on subsequent violence. According to the most recent available statistics, 18,487 murders were reported to the South African Police Service[4] in the twelve months to March 2008, not to mention other types of serious violence. The number of murders before 1994 was often lower than this.[5] In other words, more people may be being murdered in South Africa at a time of peace than when the struggle for liberation was at its height.

South Africa is no longer involved in a conventional war or even a guerrilla war, but it is, as one recent author put it, a country at war with itself.[6] This expression reflects a paradox that was already apparent to observers of Archbishop Tutu's Truth and Reconciliation Commission as it struggled to disentangle political from non-political motivations in the violence perpetrated by individuals. The apartheid years had thrown up such grotesque cases as that of Barend Strydom, the self-proclaimed *wit wolf*,[7] a white supremacist who shot seven black people dead in a random attack in 1988. These murders were carried out as expressions of a racist ideology that had been personally embraced, and not at the behest of any organization. Nevertheless, Strydom was eventually released from prison. Four young Africanist militants who, five years later, killed an American anti-apartheid activist, Amy Biehl, in the mistaken belief that she was a white South African, were granted amnesty by the Truth and Reconciliation Commission on the grounds that they had been incited by militant political speeches.[8] These are extreme cases, but it was in mobilizing emotions and inciting people to violence that both the struggle to overthrow apartheid and the counter-insurgency campaign deployed by the apartheid state took shape. Political and military strategists aimed to subsume conflicts that were socially generated into grand narratives of the state and the nation. Actions that in other circumstances might have been interpreted as non-political thereby became politicized. A murder or a car-hijacking could become a political act. The installation of a democratic government in 1994 removed the legitimacy previously accorded to many acts in contravention of the law that had earlier been hailed as political, but without redressing the social processes from which they had sprung.

To place the relation between politics and crime in proper context it should be appreciated that the system of government that existed in South Africa before 1994 was based not only on the control of the state apparatus by a particular political party, but on a social order in which each person was designated by law as belonging to an ethnically defined population group. Each group was deemed to have its proper place. Various types of social or even personal relationship thereby acquired a political complexion. One of the great achievements of opposition political activists in the 1980s was to persuade a broad swath of the South African public, not to mention world opinion, that the system of apartheid underlay all social tensions. It might have been more accurate to express matters another way, however, by noting that social tensions arising from a difficult past underlay successive forms of oppression, of which apartheid was the most recent and most pervasive. In various parts of South Africa, Dutch and British colonial regimes and a self-governing dominion had already enacted laws that effectively took land away from the country's earlier inhabitants. The formation of labour markets and hierarchies of authority generated further conflicts. South Africa had already been a self-governing country, under white minority rule, for over three decades before the National Party came to power in 1948 and proceeded to implement the policy it called apartheid.

The long negotiations leading to South Africa's first democratic elections in 1994 changed the relationship between the social and political spheres. Yet, the formal change of political authority that abolished apartheid did not itself bring about the deeper transformation of society to which many South Africans aspire. Eighteen thousand, four hundred and eighty-seven lives lost in just one year[9] are an indication that violent struggles continue, now in a form divorced from any conventional definition of politics. Some murders are so banal, such as when people are killed for their mobile phones, that they cannot be dignified with the description of a political act. The fact that they are accompanied by other forms of violence, domestic and sexual, strengthens the impression that violence constitutes a complex social fact that cannot convincingly be viewed as a crude form of class struggle.[10] In this sense, South Africa's political transformation—here meaning the transfer of political control over the state—is one component of a more diffuse set of struggles, social in nature.

This situation is not, in principle, unusual. All societies have their share of conflict, major and minor. Appeals for the state to implement a complete social transformation must therefore be regarded with some scepticism, as such a project can never lead to a final stage of total harmony, but only to new forms of struggle. As Archbishop Tutu recognized long ago, what is most important for South Africa is to achieve a degree of equilibrium through mutual acceptance by people who are destined to live with each other. But as Archbishop Tutu has also pointed out, reconciliation means more than saying sorry for past wrongs. It implies restitution. The ideological and even spiritual aspects of reconciliation cannot be divorced from its material aspects.

The fact that white South Africans continue on average to enjoy a higher standard of living than their black compatriots therefore constitutes a continuing reminder of the legacies of past injustices and of the limits of reconciliation.

The notion that South Africa's transformation remains incomplete is held by people at different points of the ideological spectrum. For the South African Communist Party, now more influential than at any time since 1990, the country's first democratic election was the expression of a national revolution that still has to be superseded by a second phase that communists believe to be inevitable, namely a socialist revolution. Many white South Africans and quite a few of the 'coloured' population, meanwhile, perceive that policies of black empowerment are depriving them of the equal political rights that are guaranteed by the constitution. From both these points of view, the political transformation that occurred in 1994 has not been pursued to its logical conclusion. This is hardly surprising inasmuch as the settlement of 1994 and the constitution entrenching it were based on a compromise, and compromises require people to renounce pursuit of their interests or convictions to the bitter end.

The African context

Let me now return to the ambassador who told me in 1990 that the South African transition was Africa's last chance to join the real world. He was alluding to a longer phase of African history, from the late 1940s onwards, encompassing the period of decolonization and subsequent attempts to mould disparate political communities into nations while building efficient public bureaucracies that could play a role in the mass reshaping of society.

South Africa does not fit easily into a pan-African chronology that is determined by reference to the period of formal colonial rule. The colonization of South Africa began rather early, when the Verenigde Oostindische Compagnie (VOC) established a supply station in Table Bay in 1652, that grew into today's Cape Town. Legally speaking, South Africa ceased to be a colony in 1910. Still, it is not hard to understand why the South African Communist Party and the ANC invented the expression Colonialism of a Special Type to designate the

South African condition under apartheid, referring to a situation in which a sovereign state was ruled by a local political party, but one that represented a particular section of the country's population only, defined by skin colour.

If we are better to understand some common elements that link South Africa to the rest of the African continent, it is useful to approach the issue not in constitutional terms, noting when a certain territory became a European colony and when it acquired international recognition of its sovereignty, but in terms of a longer history of the insertion of the whole continent of Africa into global relations of diplomacy, trade and production. An early form of globalization came into existence in the sixteenth and seventeenth centuries when European traders used South American silver to finance their expeditions to Asia, transporting slaves from Africa to America to work in their mines and plantations. This was the context in which the original VOC station at Cape Town was established.

As Europeans came to exert control over increasingly large parts of the globe, they developed a particular view of their own place in history. Many Europeans, and Americans too, came to believe themselves to be the possessors of the most advanced institutions and systems of government the world has ever seen. They have often thought these systems so good that they should in principle be applied everywhere. Reasoning along lines dictated by a particular concept of progress, it was common until quite recently, and among the European and American general publics perhaps even now, to suppose that Africans are living not just in another continent, but in another phase of historical time, one that Europe and America have long outgrown.

It was at the peak of the Atlantic slave trade, in the late eighteenth century, that the anti-slave trade movement was established in Great Britain. In one of the first campaigns to mobilize public opinion in something like our modern sense, the anti-slave trade activists, many of them with roots in the evangelical revival of their age, persuaded the British parliament to abolish the slave trade in 1807.[11] Anti-slave trade and anti-slavery movements arose in other European countries also.

The association of Africa with the Atlantic slave trade and the abolition thereof marked the emergence among a significant number of people in northern Europe especially of a conviction that they had a moral duty to lift Africa, the victim of the slave trade, to a higher condition. At that time, this was generally expressed as a mission to bring 'civilization' to Africa.[12] This term was used by nineteenth-century Europeans to designate a transfer of European technical expertise and, usually, Christian religion. Together, it was believed, these could transform whole populations and bring them into the world of capitalist trade and, eventually, within the international concert of states. Missionary societies were founded in many European countries with a view to converting Africans and bringing them into a more advanced phase of history. Africa has occupied a particular role in the Western moral imagination ever since. Britain's prime minister Tony Blair, for example, famously referred to Africa as 'a scar on the conscience of the world'.[13]

It was after 1945 that this longstanding moral commitment to Africa acquired the form of a technocratic concept of 'development' that is familiar to us today. The United States' president Harry Truman, articulating a strategy of global economic expansion that was intended both to outflank communism and to avoid a post-war economic depression, declared in his inaugural address on 20 January 1949: 'We must embark on a bold new program for making the benefits of our scientific advances and industrial progress available for the improvement and growth of underdeveloped areas'.[14] Twinned with an ideology of political emancipation, this policy of global development was profoundly unsettling to European colonial empires. The Soviet Union enthusiastically endorsed the same principle of global political and economic upliftment as long as its own official myth—to the effect that it was a union of emancipated peoples rather than a Russian empire—was not questioned. In time, the Soviet government came to consider hegemony over the third world as the key to a global victory in the cold war.[15]

In brief, this was the international environment in which African development in its contemporary sense was born and in which colonial territories in Africa acquired sovereign status. In most African countries, development came to mean legislating sovereign states into existence and equipping them with the bureaucratic apparatus regarded by the international community as standard and with a supply of capital necessary to raise growth rates and to pay for essential nation-building projects. In South Africa, it was clear that this process posed an implicit threat to white rule, and from the 1950s onwards, South Africa's apartheid government generally tried to convey the impression that the country was part of Africa in a geographical sense only. In most other respects, the National Party government portrayed itself as a distant outpost of the North Atlantic world and therefore a natural ally of the West in the Cold War. Any suggestion that South Africa could be lumped with the rest of Africa, such as was made by British prime minister Harold Macmillan in his famous speech to the all-white parliament in Cape Town in 1960, warning that a 'wind of change' was blowing through the continent,[16] was not welcomed by supporters of apartheid. One strand of the South African government's reaction to the new discourse of African freedom and development was to articulate the policy known as 'separate development' in regard to those of its own rural areas that it deemed to be Bantu homelands, mimicking within its own sphere the policy of world powers in regard to Africa as a whole.

In political language, the historical rearrangement of Africa's political structures and legal status after 1945 is often subsumed under the terms 'decolonization' and 'liberation'. It is a process that is generally considered to have come to a formal conclusion, or at least the end of a major phase, with South Africa's first democratic elections in 1994. All over Africa, the development that was explicitly bound to projects of national liberation meant obliging communities that were overwhelmingly agrarian to make more systematic use of money and exhorting them to become more productive. Systematic attempts were also made to encourage individualism and literacy, using techniques of social engineering[17] based on prevailing theories in sociology, political science and development economics. These measures were applied in a continent that had in most places been quite thinly populated throughout its history, and only modestly productive in economic terms. Most African societies had been governed throughout their existence without reference to political entities that we would today recognize as states, and indeed without the use of writing. In fact, according to the historian John Lonsdale, '[t]he most distinctively African contribution to human history could be said to have been precisely the civilized art of living fairly peaceably together *not* in states'.[18]

Africa's experience of development bears comparison with the histories of many other parts of the world in the twentieth century. What they have in common are attempts to improve society by the bureaucratic application of policies based on ideologies, theories and techniques conceived in the mode of social science. The American political scientist Zbigniew Brzezinski, who has also served as his country's national security advisor, uses the term 'coercive utopias' to designate these schemes based on purportedly scientific principles to improve the human condition. The twentieth century witnessed an unprecedented toll of lives 'deliberately extinguished through politically motivated carnage', as he puts it,[19] connected to attempts to create coercive utopias. The sociologist Manuel Castells makes a similar point when he warns us that 'to put it bluntly, all Utopias lead to Terror if there is a serious attempt at implementing them'.[20] The great irony is that these same coercive utopias have resulted in a huge increase in the number of human beings on the planet, and in the ability of a significant minority among them to enjoy unprecedented wealth and comfort.

In short, the development attempted in Africa from the mid-twentieth century onwards may be described as a coercive utopia. Development in Africa has brought such benefits as increasing the numbers of children in school. By improving health care, development policies have been closely associated with the massive increase in population that Africa has witnessed over the last six or seven decades, 'of a scale and speed unique in human history' in the opinion of one leading historian.[21] On the other hand, the failure to achieve some of the goals of the hugely ambitious policies of social engineering implemented in Africa in the name of liberation and development since 1945 has led to the implosion of some states amid widespread social upheaval. (It should be said in passing that this is not true of the whole of Africa, and nor is it true of Africa alone, as the same has occurred in some other parts of the world.)

Coming to terms with history

For African nationalists, South Africa's democratic election of 1994 was a milestone in the liberation of their continent. The way was now clear for Africa to rediscover its true identity. Peace, they believed, could come to societies that had been fundamentally destabilized by the colonial experience or its offspring, apartheid. Thabo Mbeki, already in effect South Africa's premier and shortly to become its president, began to speak of an African renaissance. He was expressing the idea that a continent that had once been colonized and humiliated was now ready to face the problems of its time by drawing on its own traditions, in full self-confidence, no longer overshadowed by foreigners. The South African poet Breyten Breytenbach, no admirer of the current ANC government, expresses this aspiration as 'an African modernity nourished from African roots and realities'.[22]

But the late 1990s did not witness an African renaissance in this sense. One of the great hopes of the African renaissance was that the fall in 1997 of the notorious dictator Mobutu Sese Seko in what is now the Democratic Republic of Congo would liberate the continent's heartland. In fact, Mobutu's enforced departure turned into a period of war and misery in central Africa that has cost more lives than any international conflict since the Second World War. Not even South Africa has found true peace and reconciliation, but has become a society at war with itself, as we have mentioned.

If we are to wonder whether and how Africans, including those in its southernmost country, can regain the self-confidence necessary to face the future in the spirit of realism suggested by Breytenbach and others, we need to reconsider the role of the colonial period in Africa's longer history, as I have suggested. It is also necessary to situate the matter in a broader geographical context. This can usefully be done by referring to Asia. Perhaps the most common assertion made by commentators on world affairs today is that China has truly become a great power, with India close behind. It is also sometimes pointed out that this is not such a remarkable occurrence as may at first appear, as China and India are merely reoccupying something like the position they had relative to Europe before the nineteenth century, in terms of economic performance, population size and other forms of measurement.[23] Not least, the rise of some Asian countries as major economic powers signifies the degree to which their intellectual, scientific and bureaucratic elites have mastered a corpus of technical knowledge that emerged to a large extent in the West. Yet Asian elites have generally continued to find a notable degree of inspiration in their own histories and philosophies. The historian Dipesh Chakrabarty is one of many scholars to have argued that the West has too often believed that, during the period of its own extraordinary hegemony, Europeans were the only historical actors whose ideas and actions mattered in the sense of having lasting influence on the world. Chakrabarty's argument is not a nihilist statement to the effect that we should pay no heed to the writings of dead white men, as the cliché goes. Nor is it a crude assertion that Asia must remain true to something called Asian values (another cliché). On the contrary, he argues that the ideas of the great European thinkers have become the property of all mankind.[24]

The proposition that key Asian countries have been able to pick up a historical thread by assuming responsibility for their past, including its colonial phase, may be extended to the world more generally. We have noted that colonial territories all over the world became sovereign states after 1945. This resulted in an increase in membership of the United Nations from 51 states at its inception to 192 today. In regard to Africa specifically, commentators and analysts advance various reasons why so many of these new states have failed to fulfil their potential, varying from neo-colonialism and the ruthless self-interest of great powers to homegrown errors and flaws and combinations of all of these.

In retrospect, we can see that when African countries acquired sovereignty, the new regimes, although now presided over by Africans rather than Europeans, continued to make abundant use of the practices, routines and mentalities of their colonial predecessors. These postcolonial states became a platform for a more ambitious form of political monopoly than anything European colonial officials had attempted. But this state of affairs proved to be of short duration.[25] Various crises of the 1970s and 1980s produced pressures, external and internal, for the economic and political reconfiguration of Africa's postcolonial states. Deprived of the superpower support they had enjoyed during the cold war, by the 1990s some of them had lost their state-like quality to the extent that talk emerged of 'collapsed' states[26] or 'failed' states, a phrase popularized by US secretary of state Madeleine Albright,[27] and today more generally known as 'fragile' states. All of these terms designate a renewal of informal politics as local societies adapt to the diminished presence of the bureaucratic state together with the services it can provide. The perceived fragility of many African states today is characteristic of a new historical phase superseding the two decades that might usefully be labelled as 'postcolonial'.

In some respects, then, Africa has been thoroughly decolonized. Formal sovereignty has been enhanced by a partial acquisition of financial power. Yet the most important sort of decolonization remains still to take place. This is the decolonization of the mind. Although this phrase is not mentioned by Chakrabarty, it could be used to describe the argument used by him and some other scholars.[28] The key to decolonizing the mind, I suggest, is for all concerned not to reject their past but to assume responsibility for it. It should be recognized that Africans were not entirely passive throughout the processes of colonization and deepening dependency, and that these were phases in a much longer history of insertion in global affairs that began long before colonial times. Furthermore, there is not, and never has been, an authentic Africa that is unchanged by time, outside history, waiting to reawake from long sleep. This is actually a myth of European Romanticism that has been taken over by African nationalists. Encouraging the belief in an authentic Africa that is a permanent victim of history makes it very hard to think of twenty-first century Africa other than as a place that is failing to develop, unless it is by arguing that the continent is poised to achieve a stunning breakthrough, as development experts often do in an effort to show that it is not their policy, but reality itself, that is defective.

By the same token, we Europeans must do something similar for ourselves. We too still live with a myth that was generated by the experience of world domination, namely that every society must sooner or later follow the Western path of development if it is truly to reach the modern age. The rise of Asia, including by its acceptance of intellectual cosmopolitanism, implies that ideas of Asian and African provenance not only have their own validity, but also have the potential to become relevant to Europe.

I may go to the heart of the matter by quoting Martin Luther King, an honorary doctor of this university, who referred in a speech on 4 April 1967, exactly one year before his death, to 'the Western arrogance of feeling that it has everything to teach others and nothing to learn from them'.[29] For two centuries or more, European thinkers have developed a view of the world that purports to be universal but that is in fact based on an idealized reading mostly of their own history. I suggest that it is precisely this arrogance of feeling that we will have to renounce as a consequence of the resurgence of Asian powers in particular, and that if we do this, we will come to see Africa too in a new light.

If we Europeans are to understand the world now emerging, it is in our own interest to accept that not all of the ideas that we have distilled from a reading of our own history are signboards to be passed by all mankind on its journey into the future. We will have to judge the histories of countries outside Europe partly by criteria derived from their own readings of their past. Further, we may even have to review aspects of our own history in that light. We will then be able to interpret Africa's current problems in terms other than as a botched decolonization or a liberation that is always incomplete. In the case of South Africa, we will be able to conceive of its current state and future prospects in ways that are not determined by a failure to be like us. Exactly what these new ways will be no one presently knows. They will emerge from how South Africans interpret their own history.

This is not a call for us to abandon our most cherished ideals in a spirit of despair, for example in regard to human rights and basic liberties, but rather to reinvigorate them by paying far more attention to data drawn from outside Europe than we have done, and by respecting the authority of thinkers formed in other traditions. Increasingly, we will have to appreciate the ways in which others see the world, not only for purposes of comparison and insight, but simply to understand how the world has become what it is. We should cease believing almost instinctively that ideas emanating from Africa must be wrong, since our underlying assumption is that they are destined to be replaced with ideas made in Europe. This will break the habit of decades, even centuries.

We Europeans, too, have to decolonize our minds.

Mijnheer de Rector, ladies and gentlemen, this seems an appropriate point at which to close. But before doing so, I must recognize and thank at least some of those who have made this occasion possible, including Archbishop Tutu himself and the College van Bestuur of this university.

I would also like to thank the Faculty of Social Sciences and especially the dean of the faculty, Professor Bert Klandermans, who has made me feel so welcome in my new job. So too have my colleagues in the Culture, Organization and Management group headed by Professor Marcel Veenswijk. However my most immediate colleagues, and those with whom I am in the closest contact since we all share the same office, are the staff of the South Africa—VU University Amsterdam—Strategic Alliances office, SAVUSA, headed by Dr Harry Wels. Included in this category of closest colleagues are my fellow Tutu professors Eddy Van der Borght, Chris Elbers and Geert Savelsbergh. I would also like to thank Professor Leo de Haan, director of the Afrika Studie Centrum in Leiden, for allowing me to share my time between that institution and this one. Last but not least, I would like to thank my life partner, Gerrie ter Haar, herself a professor, from whom I have learned so much.

Thank you all.

Stephen Ellis

Professor Stephen Ellis is the Desmond Tutu Chair Holder for the Faculty of Social Sciences. He is a historian by profession who obtained his PhD at the University of Oxford. His specialization is contemporary African history. He is also a senior researcher at the Afrika Studie Centrum in Leiden where he has taught in the research master course of African Studies. He has published several books and over a hundred articles on aspects of history and politics in West Africa and Madagascar, as well as on South Africa. He was formerly coeditor of the journal *African Affairs* and sits on the editorial boards of several journals.

Desmond Tutu Programme (DTP)

The VU University Amsterdam Desmond Tutu Programme (DTP) was launched on 4 December 2008, in a festive ceremony in which Archbishop Em. Desmond Tutu himself addressed the audience. During this ceremony, the four Desmond Tutu Chair holders were installed.

The DTP focuses on the themes of Youth, Sports and Reconciliation. Its aim is to strengthen cooperation between VU University Amsterdam and its six partner institutes in South Africa while at the same time contributing to capacity building at campuses in South Africa. Four faculties will host a Desmond Tutu chair for an initial period of five years: the Faculty of Social Sciences (FSS), the Faculty of Economics and Business Administration (FEWEB), the Faculty of Human Movement Sciences (FBW), and the Faculty of Theology (FTH).

The holders of the VU University Desmond Tutu Chair (DTC) will stimulate, and contribute to, academic cooperation between the Netherlands and South Africa, through the (joint) supervision of South African PhD students, through teaching Bachelor and Master students at and exchange students between VU University Amsterdam and South African universities, particularly, but not exclusively, focusing on our six partner institutions in South Africa with which VU University Amsterdam has a Memorandum of Understanding (MoU) on an institutional level. For more information, see www.savusa.nl

AFTERWORD

STATE AND RELIGION IN AFRICA, OR TWO OR THREE THINGS THAT STEPHEN ELLIS TAUGHT ME

Jean-François Bayart

Translated by
Andrew Brown

Stephen Ellis died as he had lived: as a philosopher, a man of faith, a perfect gentleman. Ethnically speaking, he was a historian, and in spite of his successive changes of professional skin he remained one right to the end, in his scrupulous attention to sources and the diversity of those on which he drew. Thanks to the different posts he occupied throughout a particularly successful and varied career, his social skills, his human warmth and his absolute discretion, he probably had one of the best address books a specialist in African affairs could boast of: in it, leading lights in the international scholarly community rubbed shoulders with civil servants of all nations, activists, journalists, bankers, brokers, ex-mercenaries, business figures sometimes with a background in armed struggle, priests and pastors, environmentalists, diamond merchants, and a host of anonymous people he had met in the course of his travels, especially in Africa, to whom he evinced a respect which did not cloud his clear-sightedness. Working with Stephen was a pleasure, but also a necessity, as his erudition was always so valuable for the research of all of us. I experienced this myself on several occasions, especially when I wrote, with him and Béatrice Hibou, *The Criminalization of the*

State in Africa. Although I personally learned a great deal from him for my own books, other people are better placed than I am to salute his activities as a historian of Madagascar and the Republic of South Africa, his contribution to an understanding of the civil war in Liberia, and his decisive work—with Gerrie ter Haar—on the study of religion in Africa.

Having derived such benefit from it, I am, on the other hand, well qualified to express the gratitude of Africanists for his generosity to his colleagues and students, on whom he lavished advice, information, bibliographical leads, and contacts—that famous address book again! Stephen was a sharer. He was active in many collective endeavours— including being a co-editor of *African Affairs* for many years—to the detriment of his personal projects. Nor did he ever hesitate to offer his French-speaking peers the services of his superb English, without regard for his own schedule.

But as our sorrow might otherwise lead us to forget it, I would like here, if I may, to mention one aspect of his personality that lay at the basis of his professional integrity and that I particularly valued, especially in the course of the long field work we undertook while working on our *Criminalization of the State in Africa*: humour. Stephen enjoyed a good laugh, and knew how to make others laugh too. People will object: 'is this so unusual in a Briton, especially a man so British as Stephen?' The fact is that his laughter was not just a sign of decency and distance with regard to the cruelty of the world which saddened his humanism. His laughter was subversive—a guarantee of his freedom of thought.

And it is this philosophical attitude, this 'style', as the great historian of Late Antiquity Peter Brown would put it, that now gives us the strength to follow in Stephen's wake as we continue to share our thoughts on African political societies—in this case, on their complex relationship with the religious sphere. Not in order to 'discuss' his work, his assumptions, or the debates they have engendered in the academic community (an exercise that would be somewhat pedantic and even out of place), but to carry on ploughing the same furrow with the ironic modesty which our colleague and friend always embodied, and which remains a deep source of inspiration for anyone trying to understand the 'intrinsic logics' of faith analysed by Max Weber, without falling into the errors of 'religious over-interpretation' denounced by Paul Veyne.

The following pages were written in the last months of Stephen's life and the months following his death. They were first published as *État et Religion en Afrique* (Paris: Karthala, 2018);[1] I then continued to work on them for this volume dedicated to Stephen's memory at the IHEID Geneva, where I have held the Yves Oltramare Chair in 'Religion and Politics in the Contemporary World' since 2015, and where the teaching draws so much on Stephen's intellectual heritage.

That heritage is more important than ever now, since never, *perhaps*, has the interaction between the sphere of religion and that of politics been so evident in Africa. The 'perhaps' needs to be emphasized because, in this regard, the optical illusions of the current news and the distorting prism of emotions are not good guides.[2] Nevertheless, the jihad of Al-Shabaab in Somalia, Al-Qaida in East Africa, AQIM in Mali, and Boko Haram in Nigeria, the shadow cast by Da'esh over the eastern half of the continent, General Sissi's coup against the Muslim Brotherhood in Egypt, the importance of the religious factor in many electoral consultations—not only in North Africa but also in various sub-Saharan countries such as Benin and Nigeria—and the role of the Christian fundamentalist element in the radicalization of the political crises in Côte d'Ivoire in the 2000s, and in the Central African Republic since 2010, are there to remind us that in this part of the world, as elsewhere, it is each man for himself, and God most definitely for everyone.

More generally, the religious boom that has been perceptible since at least the 1980s has been sustained. Its main manifestations remain, on the one hand, the mobilization of fundamentalists both Christian and Muslim, and on the other, the spread (or the feeling of a spread) of practices of the invisible, if we include these in the sphere of religion; this gave rise to the well-known debate between Stephen Ellis and Gerrie ter Haar, on the one hand, and Terence Ranger, on the other.[3]

From all these facts there immediately emerges one first conclusion, or rather one first confirmation, as the scholarly literature has been prolix and convincing on this point: the phenomenon of religion meshes with its time and produces social transformations rather than incarnating the weight of tradition, except that it often proceeds, by way of an 'invention' of tradition, to invent modernity, in accordance with the still heuristic paradigm of Eric Hobsbawm and Terence Ranger.[4] The various forms of fundamentalism as well as witchcraft are indeed powerful illustrations of this, as they appeal to origins or ancestors to give change a more glamorous appearance.

Faced with these obvious African facts, two remarks can immediately be made. In the first place, there is nothing specifically 'African' about this. On the contrary, the vitality of the religious phenomenon on the continent testifies that religion is part of 'world time',[5] and has been for countless years. Africans' religious practices and representations of the Africans hybridize with those of other continents by appropriating them, as the figures of the Indian divinities or of the Virgin Mary attest in the cult of Mami Wata, the irruption of industrial technology into the invisible, and the proliferation of Asian sects south of the Sahara. There is nothing new under the tropical sun. As early as the 1970s, Peter Geschiere had detected the presence of Baha'i preachers in the Maka country in the depths of Cameroon.[6] And the ancestral cult of Mami Wata, or at least its symbolic imaginary, seems to have arisen from the encounter between the peoples of the Atlantic coast and the Portuguese navigators in the sixteenth century, to be later enriched by figures from the Hindu pantheon.[7] Today, it is the charismatic American preachers of the Awakening, or their equivalents in the Pakistanese Tablighi Jamaat, who are all the rage in Africa.

In this process, the religious phenomenon in Africa is not disconnected from the general transformations and flows in the 'global' religious field, as we say today. In this case, it now takes the form of 'market' religions,[8] including Egyptian TV evangelists and their Christian counterparts on the Atlantic coast, the so-called 'Wahhabist' pious merchants of the Sahel, the neo-liberal economic orientation of the Islamic parties in Tunisia and Morocco (and, as far as there has been enough time to observe it, in Egypt), as well as the Gospel of Prosperity of the Pentecostalists—these are all expressions of religion well-known to anthropologists and sociologists. In any case, the privileged relationship between religious practices and money, their contribution to the monetarization and commercialization of the continent, had already prepared the ground. By observing these developments, we are not on any different planet than, say, Indonesia,

Turkey, or Houston, the centre of neo-liberal Christian management whose lessons contemporary Muslim actors have not disdained to learn.[9]

Secondly, the prominence of the religious phenomenon in Africa must not make us fall into the trap of religious 'overinterpretation'.[10] Admittedly, religion lends politics its own words to express obedience, resistance, and 'self-understanding' or 'sense of self' (*Eigensinn*),[11] and thus gives shape to presidential cults, as in Marshal Mobutu's Zaire and General Eyadéma's Togo, and to millennial, semi-prophetic, semi-revolutionary uprisings, of the kind with which northern Nigeria is familiar, but of which the Congolese rebellions of the 1960s also provided paradigmatic examples, inspired by the Christ-like figures of Patrice Lumumba and Pierre Mulele. But it must be acknowledged that religion has not been at the forefront of the political mobilizations that have swept across Africa in recent years. Islamists won elections and surfed on the tide of an Arab Spring that they themselves had not launched. In Senegal, rappers held the upper hand during the change of government in 2012; and in Burkina Faso, in 2014, it was not faith that drove the grassroots movement known as Le Balai Citoyen, whose name means, precisely, 'the *civic* broom'. The main contribution of religion to the sphere of politics may in fact come from its 'everydayness', its 'humdrum' quality, its 'universal ordinariness', the 'conformism' it represents for the mass of believers, who are 'pious in the same way that they wear clothes: to behave in a respectable fashion'.[12] Even more than the words of radicalism, of distance from or submission to power, religion proposes the words of respectability and the dignity that goes with it—not an easy task on a continent where laying claim to dignity has been an inherent part of the anti-colonial struggle and the emancipation of minors, captives and slaves. This care for the self, found both among the nobility and the petty bourgeoisie, is something that Terence Ranger eloquently described in his colourful depiction of the Samkange Christian family in Rhodesia/Zimbabwe.[13]

Hence the importance of religion as a method of life, which lies at the heart of Max Weber's argument, and in which fundamentalists excel—they are all 'Methodists', 'sticklers' in matters of the soul.[14] It must be borne in mind, as Weber does, that the ideal-type of charismatic authority does not exclude the 'becoming like

543

every day' (*Veralltäglichung*) of the behaviour of the faithful and the bureaucratization of the social institution in which they recognize themselves; in short, the ideal-type of rational-legal legitimacy.[15] In Africa, this is confirmed by the Christian and neo-Christian movements of prophetic origin that are soon erected into denominational churches and nowadays increasingly 'NGO-ified', and the different branches of the Murid Senegalese brotherhood under the aegis of a *general* caliph and sheikhs who no longer hesitate to 'recruit' their disciples, like Sheikh Modou Kara.[16]

Any analysis of the relationship between religion and politics in Africa must also take into account the respective differentiation of the two orders of reality. The political field has become autonomous through its institutionalization, its constitutionalization, its rational-legal bureaucratization, and its own ideological inspiration. In some societies, this process goes back well before colonization, in the Ottoman provinces of North Africa, for example—with the possible exception of Cyrenaica and Tripolitania—and in Morocco (Islam does actually maintain a distinction between religion (*din*) and state (*dolat*), contrary to a common misunderstanding). The same was also true in several sub-Saharan kingdoms and empires, such as Ashanti and the Wolof kingdoms. Nevertheless, colonization extended the differentiation between the two spheres of religion and politics to societies (especially lineage societies) which did not practise it and were in fact unaware of these as separate categories of thought. Colonization generalized and systematized this difference thanks to the resources of writing, capitalism and industrial civilization.

This process of differentiation is not the unequivocal product of secularization—*or, more precisely, secularization often springs from religion itself as much as from politics or the state*. In other words, Islam and Christianity have played a full part, in Africa, in the social and mental transformations that have led to the autonomization of the political sphere, if only because they themselves have been key areas for bureaucratization, the market, the lessons of the Western episteme and the recognition of the legitimacy of the state, even if this involves challenging the latter's policies. In this respect, Africa turns out to be, once again, perfectly ordinary in historical terms. For things were no different in the Europe of the Middle Ages and the Modern Age, or, more recently, in Iran: in the former case the papacy, in the latter the Islamic Republic promoted the state and the *raison d'état* by separating them from the religious sphere or subordinating this latter to themselves—something they could accomplish all the more effectively because they had the spiritual legitimacy to do so.[17]

At the same time, the experience of faith remains irreducible to political reason—and to the reason of the social sciences of the political, which can only take note of it. Stephen Ellis understood this much more clearly than did many others. Religion retains its 'intrinsic logics',[18] as is attested by the 'planes of immanence' of prayer, anointing, visions, aggressive witchcraft, and even jihad. These 'intrinsic logics' of religion are sometimes constitutive of the political considered in its own autonomy. Ruth Marshall, for example, draws on the Foucauldian concept of 'political spirituality' to analyse Nigerian Pentecostalism as a phenomenon of faith. She views it as constituting a 'revolution', and rejects any utilitarian, functionalist or materialist interpretation of it.[19] Similarly, in Senegal, it was paradoxically the disjunction between the Islamic and mystical preoccupations of Sheikh Amadou Bamba and the secular and political aims of the French administration that made possible the strange compromise between the brotherhood of the Murids and a French Republic anxious to maintain the separation between religion and the state—a 'social contract' whose 'success story' has continued to the present day, even if its scope has been relativized or complicated.[20] Where the colonial authorities were obsessed by the necessities of public security and the spectre of the holy war that would not fail to be triggered by the Ottoman Sultan, Caliph of the Muslims, in the inevitable war between France and Germany to which Europe was marching, the Senegalese marabout's thoughts were focused on Salvation, including that of Islam, and he left it to his entourage to sort out the practicalities of such matters as elections, land, banking and military affairs.

In a way, the 'silent dissent' of the Moroccan ulama against a monarchy that was inventing its tradition as 'commander of the believers', with the help of international legal consultations and finally constitutionalizing it thanks to the Arab Spring in 2011, is cut from the same cloth.[21] Finally, the contemporary history of Africa is rich in escapist episodes, both internal, as with the Kitawalists in the

Democratic Republic of Congo, Salafist and Christian Quietism, the Jehovah's Witnesses, and Zionists in Southern Africa, for example, and external, as with emigration. The latter, admittedly, is generally secular, except for jihadist conscripts—who also bring us back to known territory, that of the 'practice of the break',[22] of sectarian departures for the New World and the various problematics of Refuge which prevailed in Europe in the sixteenth and seventeenth centuries.

This leads us to the practices of the invisible, which, by the way, confirm the universality of Africa even though they are generally mentioned in order to categorize it as exotic. To be sure, what we too hastily call witchcraft permeates most social and therefore political events, at least south of the Sahara, while preserving its irreducibility (that of the night) to the trivial affairs of the day. But its namesake, in the Europe of the modern age, also shaped, albeit implicitly, state formation, without being completely reducible to it (as Carlo Ginzburg demonstrated with regard to the 'night battles' of Friuli in the sixteenth century); it has not disappeared from the contemporary social landscape, as Jeanne Favret-Saada has noted with regard to the French Bocage.[23]

The paradigm of the cult city

However, the differentiation between the religious and the political cannot be apprehended in the binary mode of their mutual exclusivity, as the hackneyed themes of 'Religion and Politics' would have it when it is applied in a uniform way to every conceivable situation, or in the positivist and historicist terms of secularization. The overlaps, the synergies, the effects of osmosis between the two categories are too systematic for us to remain content with this vision of things. Hence the paradigm of the cult city (*cité cultuelle*) that I proposed in 1993, based on François de Polignac's research into ancient Greece.[24]

Moreover, the Roman Church—and particularly the papacy—of the Middle Ages and the Renaissance in Europe provide us with an even more heuristic model, since they fostered the formation not of the ancient city, but of the modern state whose domination has been universalized by globalization for two centuries.[25] Their historians now see 'the Church/State relationship no longer as a report of otherness dominated by conflicts of power and jurisdiction or compromises between two opposed and rival units, but as a much more complex relationship in which the modern state, in this period of gestation, penetrates the institution of the Church, even in its most impenetrable nucleus, the papacy, while being in turn permeated by it, assuming some of the characteristics and functions of the medieval Church'.[26]

Having reached this point, we need to define the spirit of the comparativism on which we are drawing. As we know, comparativism acts as an 'operator of individualization' that describes the specific historicity of the societies it embraces rather than reducing them to supposedly universal generic categories.[27] Thus understood, the comparative approach consists in generalizing questions, and not answers.[28] In addition, comparativism, when understood diachronically, is far from any evolutionary historicism. To compare the cult city in contemporary Africa with mediaeval, reformed or Tridentine Christianity does not of course mean that Africa is 'still in' the Middle Ages or the sixteenth century, and that it will 'later on' reach the great light of secularization! It consists in constructing a paradigm and viewing the phenomenon in the light of it, in the hope that the process will be fruitful. Now, it seems to me, this paradigm does indeed make it possible to grasp the historicity of the continent taken in all its ordinariness, i.e. in its comparability.

First of all, it gives us the opportunity to remind ourselves of the extent to which Christianity was rooted in Africa long before the continent was partly Islamized. Africa was a major land of ancient Christianity, to which it gave many of its outstanding figures, starting with St. Augustine, and it was home to a powerful movement of hermits in the Nile Valley. It is useful to keep this in mind if we are to free ourselves from the distorted prism of colonial times, even though Islam later swept away this Christian presence with the exception of the Copts of Egypt and the Ethiopian Orthodox Church—especially as there is another Christianity that was present before the missions embedded in colonization, a Christianity that sprang from the Portuguese explorations, the slave trade, and then the demand for the abolition of this trade. The Catholicism of the Kongo Kingdom, a Catholicism which, as historians point out, survived the collapse of the latter; Methodism in the Fante lands, on the Gold Coast; Anglicanism in the Yoruba territories, including in its relationship with the Afro-Brazilian diaspora: these are all examples, among others, of an African Christianity prior to the European occupation.[29] The same remark can pertinently be made about Islam, in opposition to the culturalist ideology that is inclined to emphasize that Islam does not really belong in sub-Saharan societies, and is thus inauthentic or superficial when it is found in them. Even though Islam greatly benefited from the colonial period and spread to parts of the continent previously foreign to it, or where it occupied a marginal position, over the *longue durée* the religion of the Prophet shaped Africa's Mediterranean coast, the Sahara, the Sahel and the shores of the Red Sea and the Indian Ocean. How many centuries of presence does it need before the Department of Orientalisms will deign to issue certificates of native belonging?

Recalling these chronologies helps us to understand the fact that the *three* monotheisms belong, equally and with the same rights, on the continent (since the Jews were major actors in trans-Saharan trade, including the book trade, especially between Morocco and the Western Sahel, and remained present in Ethiopia under the name of the *falasha*).[30] African Islam is not a cheapened form of Islam, however 'Black' it may be, and the oases of the Sahara and the towns of the Sahel have been places of knowledge that met the requirements of the umma (whereas the spiritual influence of Africa's eastern coast has been secondary). Even today, Mauritanian ulama and preachers are well known figures with a high degree of visibility in mosques or on television screens in the Gulf.[31] Moreover, Africa represents large contingents of global Christianity, playing a part in its evangelical vein as in its political and doctrinal conservatism, particularly in the synods of the Roman Church. As for the prophetism of the so-called independent churches, this is less a sign of any cultural particularism than of the latter's religious universality: the prophet is a major figure not only in the Old Testament, but also in Christianity as a whole.[32] Finally, the many secular movements of piety, such as the Legion of Mary in the Catholic sphere and many informal devotional groups (*Gemeinde*), are the expression of a mass Christianity already prefigured by its appropriation in the colonial era; it needs to be compared with the way historians now study similar movements during the Middle Ages and the Early Modern period.[33]

A twofold lesson emerges from these perspectives. The study of the religious and its relation to the political cannot be confined to the study of its institutions 'from above'. Moreover, it must not treat heresy, deviance, syncretism and 'independence' (or 'indocility', to quote Achille Mbembe[34]) with the undeserved academic respect that has long skewed the history of Christianity in Europe.[35] Terence Ranger notes that the so-called 'independent' churches have never been more 'African' than those of the colonial Christian establishment, which he rehabilitates from a scholarly point of view.[36]

This being admitted, the problem is now to think of the relations between religion and politics no longer in a binary mode, but as a set of combinations and permutations, a 'generalized mutual interaction', as Otto Bauer's definition of the nation puts it—an interaction in which God and Caesar are often thick as thieves.[37] This applies to the point of view of the state, which the religious sphere provides with its vocabulary, its imaginary and its institutional techniques: in an irony of History if ever there was one, Bourguibian and neo-Bourguibian reformism is, for example, a graft of nineteenth-century Islamic reformism (and, by the way, the Ennahda Party is an avatar of Ottoman, colonial and Bourguibian reformism). And this is also true of the point of view of religion, which 'does not exist' (unlike God, perhaps) outside its historically situated relation to the state, the market, and their civilization,[38] and which plays no part in describing different forms of behaviour, since it is impossible to 'define what is "religious" in any practice'.[39]

This set of combinations and permutations can be grasped either in terms of the general process of state formation, or of the mobilizations and practices to which it gives rise in different sites.[40] Without pretending to be exhaustive, we can explore six perspectives that seem, *inshallah*, to refine our paradigm of the cult city in Africa.

Perspectives

In the synergy between the flows of globalization and the formation of the nation-state, the mediation of the religious sphere is crucial, in Africa as elsewhere.[41] In the long run, both Islam and Christianity (or their derivatives, such as prophetic and millennialist movements and jihadist programmes) have been factors in the continent's cultural and commercial unification—a unification also effected in the dimension of the invisible, for example in the form of trans-societal rumours or by the circulation of the imaginary figures of witchcraft.[42] But these movements, which are now described as transnational—not without reason, since the nation-state has been an effective graft—have become embedded in this same nation-state to whose emergence they have contributed.

This is the case of Islam, which can count on representative institutions in most states, either because the political authorities wish to control or at least monitor it, or because its leaders seek to wield influence in the political arena and even absorb it, as in the example of the High Islamic Council of Mali.[43] The Caesaro-Papist trajectories that prevailed in a post-Ottoman context in Algeria, Tunisia, Egypt and (in a post-protectorate context) Morocco reproduced the framework of the nation state. Political Islam, whether parliamentary or revolutionary, does exactly the same when it pays lip service to the umma but is actually a new avatar of nationalism, as demonstrated by the Muslim Brotherhood in Egypt, Ennahda in Tunisia and the Justice and Development Party in Morocco, just like Hamas in Palestine, Hezbollah in Lebanon and the AKP in Turkey. It is inadequate to object that new forms of jihad—such as AQIM in the Sahara, or even Boko Haram in northern Nigeria and Cameroon, like Al Qaida or Da'esh in the Middle East—undermine the territorial status quo. Until proven otherwise, the strength of the reaction not only of the states concerned, but also of the regional and international system of states into which they are incorporated, keeps such extremist movements in check. Any challenge to the state in the name of a principle supposed to transcend it will, on the state's part, trigger repressive, redistributive or co-optative government policies that validate or even reinforce state power, as happened in Algeria in the 1990s.[44]

South of the Sahara, the same applied to Christianity. It is organized into churches that claim to be universal, like the Catholic Church—even when the churches are national, like the Anglican Church or the Reformed churches in Europe associated with state-regulated denominational worship in and after the sixteenth century.[45] During the colonial period, a form of missionary multilateralism (and multiculturalism) prevailed in the different imperial territories, a multilateralism which created tensions with the European authorities administering these territories but remained subject to their logic; indeed, it educated and socialized the local nationalist elites that would eventually take over.[46] The universal churches in Africa are implanted and organized on a national basis—as with the Conferences of Bishops in each of the states, as far as Catholicism is concerned—and the so-called independent churches have assumed the shape of veritable Gallicanisms, as is clear with Kimbanguism in Congo-Kinshasa or Harrism in Côte d'Ivoire, an example of particular interest in that this prophetism is of Liberian origin.

In the end, the conflicts of sovereignty or competence between national authorities and supranational churches in the aftermath of independence have also worked to strengthen and legitimize states, even when these tensions have taken a dramatic turn, in particular in regimes that claimed to be socialist or flaunted a radical nationalism. These disputes focused on national issues—the need for institutions and public authorities to respect religious freedom and human rights, the fate of denominational education, etc.—whose validity and territorial extent they confirmed. That the Vatican is itself a sovereign state playing an interstate game through its diplomacy and nuncios is a major factor in this recognition of the phenomenon of the state by Catholicism. If need be, the Vatican contributes to national unity, albeit through a transnational movement of laypeople such as the Community of Sant'Egidio, which has been involved (with varying degrees of success) in the peace negotiations between the protagonists of civil wars in Mozambique, Burundi, Angola, Côte d'Ivoire, and the Casamance crisis in Senegal. Such a synergy between supranational churches and the institution of a system of nation-states is quite typical: in the Middle Ages, the papacy, or certain religious orders—above all the Cistercians—were the incubators of the Westphalian and denominational Europe of the seventeenth century; the Council of Trent had ratified the definitive renunciation of any unitary government based on the idea of the mediaeval *republica Christiana*.[47]

But the contribution of religion to state formation has more precisely concerned one of its modalities, namely that of its 'privatization', as understood by Béatrice Hibou—a privatization of the state which can lead to its criminalization, including through the intermediation of the so-called secret societies to which Stephen Ellis devoted some of his best discussions.[48] The colonial state was a 'minimum state' which entrusted many of its prerogatives to private operators, and a variable share of its public policies in the field of health and education to Christian missions, depending on the empires and the territories concerned. After a period of post-independence tension and conflicts of competence, in a climate of acute nationalism, the economic liberalization of the 1980s, and in particular the systematic destruction of public health and education on the pretext of structural adjustment, gave the initiative back to religious organizations. There was one difference: their intervention was often delegated to a new type of actors, namely denominational non-governmental organizations, and Islam in turn benefited from this systematic 'discharge' by the state of its prerogatives, thanks to the scope of the financing agreed to by the petro-monarchies of the Gulf, the political and diplomatic support these latter gave Islam in conjunction with national authorities, and the religion's own modernization. In addition to structural adjustment programs, the AIDS pandemic was another windfall for the 'function of substitution'[49] that religious forces now assume vis-à-vis the state. These forces have endeavoured to respond to the health crisis as they can count on international aid, now more often granted to NGOs than to government bodies.[50]

At the same time—and there is no contradiction if we bear in mind Max Weber's view that what we have here is a total social phenomenon encompassing both the private sphere and the public sphere, and the market as well as the state—religion has become inextricably involved in and with the bureaucratization of African societies. In the case of Christianity, it has adopted the ecclesial model, including independent churches, following the paradigmatic example of Kimbanguism.[51] In the case of Islam, brotherhoods and ulama have themselves become bureaucratized, as has been shown by the various aforementioned studies of Morocco and Senegal. And in the case of 'civil society', denominational NGOs have fostered this process of bureaucratization, inseparable from the formation of the state and the market. It bears repeating: rational-legal legitimacy is perfectly compatible with the charismatic authority of the prophet or the marabout, as Max Weber pointed out.[52]

In Africa, the contribution of religion to state formation has, for the most part, followed a conservative path. South of the Sahara, it has not escaped the weight of the 'politics of the belly'.[53] Here and there, Christian authorities have been directly associated with the authoritarian exercise of power, sometimes beyond all decency as in Togo or Rwanda at the end of the 1980s and in the early 1990s.[54] The Vatican, meanwhile, has been careful to quell the potential outbreak of any African rehashing of Liberation Theology, and it has succeeded all the more easily in that Christian criticism of postcolonial power has been confined to restricted circles such as those of the 'theology under the tree' promoted by Jean-Marc Ela in Cameroon, or, more importantly, 'Contextual Theology' in Southern Africa and the Black Consciousness of Steve Biko in South Africa. It should be noted that the charismatic movement is still subject to this influence, although it may offer new modes of political subjectivation, as Ruth Marshall has remarked of Nigerian Pentecostalism.[55] In Mozambique, the Universal Church of the Kingdom of God forged a *de facto* alliance with Frelimo as soon as the latter liberalized religion along with the economy, and set up its offices in the building of the Frelimo central committee, while displaying a certain sense for business.[56] In North Africa, the majority of ulama also supported the nation-states' 'passive revolution', in Morocco and Algeria as well as in Tunisia and Egypt, or else were subordinated to it, at the price of being restricted to their own 'self-understanding' (*Eigensinn*). Rather, it has been Islamist secularists—the Muslim Brotherhood in Egypt and Abdessalam Yacine in Morocco—who have promoted dissent. But most of the time this did not stop them being subsequently co-opted into the state religious apparatus, nor did it prevent their plans for revolution being pre-empted and defused by the political authorities.[57]

From this point of view, revolutions have shed a cruel light on the situation. Faced with democratic protest south of the Sahara, the Vatican emphasized the need for stability. As early as 1982, it recalled to Rome the Archbishop of Lusaka, Mgr Milingo, whom President Kenneth Kaunda suspected of wanting (or being able) to become the spiritual head of the political opposition, an assumption which also worried John Paul II, as did Milingo's support for the American charismatic sensibility.[58] At the beginning of the 1990s, he quickly dropped Monsignor Monsengwo, the overly popular president of the National Conference, in Zaire and worked for the diplomatic rehabilitation of Marshal Mobutu, receiving him at a time when the Western powers seemed to have abandoned him. On the ground, the bishops posed as conciliators—not only in Zaire, but also in Benin and Congo-Brazzaville—but the trompe-l'oeil democratization of the one-party regimes consisted, at best, in a liberal avatar of the postcolonial 'passive revolution', in an authoritarian decompression, and, at worst, in a frank authoritarian restoration, sometimes at the price of a civil war—all developments which they ended up supporting even if only half-heartedly. The Burkinabe revolution in November 2014 did not bring any change to this trend: the Archbishop of Ouagadougou accompanied Lieutenant Colonel Isaac Zida to see the King of the Mossi to cement the 'transition'.[59] In North Africa, the 'Arab Springs' of 2011 demonstrated the same conservative appetite for God: the Islamists did not take the initiative here, even if they reaped the benefits, at least initially, and once they had arrived in government they gave these benefits a neoliberal twist.[60]

In short, religion meets revolutionary passions with a conservative response, which does not necessarily preclude its contributing to democracy, if we follow the provocative thesis of Guy Hermet according to which, 'paradoxically, (...) the best strategists of democratization are not always the most convinced democrats, while those who cause democracy to fail in many cases rank among its most zealous heralds.'[61] In this context, religion can provide models of civic subjectivation, as Xavier Audrain has shown in the case of Senegal and Ruth Marshall in that of Nigeria.[62] Religion is also able to absorb the political field and monopolize public debate when the collusive transactions of the ruling class have emptied them, as in Madagascar and Mali in the 1990s and early 2000s.[63]

However, religion can also be a vector of social emancipation. First, this can be a universalist emancipation from the identity-based categories of ethnicity. And second, it can be an emancipation from the categories of status or social class.[64] Most scholars of Christianity in Africa insist on the place occupied by women, a long neglected question. The case of the Beti in southern Cameroon is paradigmatic. In this polygamous society, where social elders exercised a strong, and in particular a symbolic domination over their younger siblings, the 'second sex' was in a situation of obvious subalternity, though this did not preclude the exercise of true counter-powers, particularly in the field of the invisible. Catholicism, which placed the Virgin Mary at the heart of its devotion, gathered together the faithful of all genders (and all ages), mingling in the same space of worship, that of the church; it imposed the wearing of clothes (of western manufacture, to boot), when nakedness was the sign of social dependence, and met with enthusiastic support from women, although the missions exerted on their flock an iron discipline of an economically rather self-interested nature.[65] But this example is far from unique. The same trend was found in South Africa, in the very different context of a mining and industrial economy and a segregationist political regime.[66] The sociology of Pentecostalism also confirms this situation.[67] It is less commonly claimed that Islam is no exception here, but the fact remains that there is a true Islamic feminism, 'under the veil'.[68]

On the other hand, religion has contributed to the emancipation of these same slaves whose captivity it had endorsed and sometimes aided 'spiritually', as on the Angolan coast in the eighteenth century. Christianity played a part in the abolitionist movement, and in the field its missions were often refuges for fugitives. As for Islam's poor reputation in the matter of slavery, it needs to be relativized. While Muslim states played a crucial role in the slave trade—particularly the Zanzibar Sultanate in the Indian Ocean—many ulama and marabouts challenged this trade, especially when it took their fellow believers as victims. This was the case, for example, in the nineteenth-century Wolof kingdoms. In the colonial context, and thanks to the 'modern moment' of Islam,[69] some of its manifestations took the form of true social movements for the liberation of captives, such as the pioneering Murid penetration of peanut-growing farms at the beginning of the twentieth century, even if this dimension of the brotherhood has been qualified by several authors.[70]

More generally, and more trivially, religion can be a social elevator thanks to the petty-bourgeois respectability and education it provides. After all, the religious school is one school among others, and its teaching opens the doors to bureaucratic power within the state. Largely educated by Christian missions, the sub-Saharan nationalist elite soon understood this, and even today the seminary is a path of social elevation for children of modest condition. Similarly, Al-Azhar attendance has facilitated access to the political and administrative responsibilities of an 'Arabizing' intelligentsia that pursues the reform of Islam in the Sahel.

Above all, the relationship of religion to individuation is ever clearer in societies undergoing profound social transformations. Africans follow personal 'religious itineraries'—to use the notion of 'therapeutic route' that sociologists and health anthropologists have popularized—and 'gather pollen' from different beliefs, denominations or practices.[71] These mobilities relativize so-called 'primordial' affiliations of an ethnic or family type. South of the Sahara, religious pluralism is frequently found in the diachrony of life or in the synchrony of relations of kinship and neighbourhood. Even after the mass departure of Jews to Israel and France, it is even sometimes found in the northern part of Africa, either in the form of the tension between the Islam of the ulama and that of the brotherhoods, or through matrimonial alliances and even conversions, despite the criminalization of apostasy, or as a result of the settling there of sub-Saharan migrants won over by Christian charismatic movements and the echoes, in the societies they left, of the experiences of those who have emigrated to secularized and even thoroughly secular European countries. Some will see such personal journeys and inter-religious compromises as further evidence of the superficiality of Africans' faith or their propensity for spiritual shopping around. But is should be remembered that, in *The Protestant Ethic and the Spirit of Capitalism*, Weber emphasized the fungibility of denominational affiliations and beliefs in the Methodism of Anglican origin, Calvinist-inspired Pietism, and Lutheranism in Europe between the sixteenth and eighteenth centuries; and the Reformation was not, in its beginnings, the kind of bloody Western that was constructed for *political* purposes later on.[72]

And Christianity and Islam are universalist religions whose believers are, among themselves, 'brothers' and 'sisters', placed on an equal footing—at least theologically speaking—within each of the two sexes (though between men and women, things are obviously more complicated, and still a matter of fierce controversy for both Catholics and Muslims). Fundamentalisms are very punctilious on this point and derive much of their success from their rigour. The observation of the matrimonial scene shows that God willingly blesses socially mismatched unions, especially through marabouts who make these marriages their bread and butter.[73]

More radically, there is the question of the 'planes of immanence', and thus the 'lines of flight' opened up by the practices of prayer, possession, trance, and vision.[74] And then there is the even more disturbing question of the challenge to a Western hegemony born of colonization, reproduced in the aftermath of independence, heavy with overexploitation, symbolic domination and violence, sometimes on a massive scale, whose episteme itself is questioned in millenarian or armed terms which, indeed, often go together. This is the meaning of the great uprisings of the nineteenth and twentieth centuries, up until the Congolese revolts of the 1960s and Boko Haram, movements that are depoliticized and condescendingly seen as outbursts of mere barbarism, but which attacked a colonial form of reason that has imposed cruel economic, social and political costs on the vast majority of the continent's population over the past two centuries. This is also the message that Fabien Eboussi Boulaga derived from prophetism.[75]

This so-called religious violence, which is actually more of a social or political nature, like the 'wars of religion' of the Early Modern period in Europe, needs to be seen in the light of the denominational pluralism that prevails in most African societies—going back a long time, in fact, since many political formations of bygone days were able to compromise with men of God or of Allah who did not have the same beliefs as their sovereigns. Religions should not be understood as monads that are consistent and closed in on themselves. They are dependent on the peaceful or conflictual relations they form between themselves. In other words, they form a set of combinations and permutations. This is how we need to interpret, for example, the confrontation between Christian and Muslim fundamentalisms in Nigeria: as true 'complementary enemies' that proceed from the same historical moment.[76] Once again, the works of the historians of European Christianity provide us with a heuristic detour when they complicate the chronologies of the shift from the Middle Ages to the Renaissance and establish a triangulation between the Protestant Reformation, the Catholic Reformation and the Counter-Reformation, a Counter-Reformation which was directed against the latter as much as against the former.[77] Similarly, the fight against AIDS has exacerbated the tension between Christian fundamentalism and so-called traditional religions.[78] Nevertheless, it is today impossible to know if, in Africa, the cult city—the relation between religion and state formation of the state—will assume a denominational form as it did in the Europe of the modern age, although its contribution to 'social discipline' seems to be proven, in particular under the magisterium of fundamentalisms and as a result of its 'becoming like every day' (*Veralltäglichung*).[79] And, in response to those who are worried about this omnipresence of God in the garden of Caesar, it must be remembered that the religious division of the Old Continent, in the sixteenth and seventeenth centuries, ultimately consecrated the shift from a problematic of heresy to one of schism—a problematic which finally yielded to the state the 'capacity to be the referential unit for all'.[80] In other words, the cult city can engender the secularization and empowerment of the state, in accordance with the inscrutable ways of the Lord.

By way of conclusion

The combinations and permutations of politics and religion in Africa lead us to take up again the question of the continent's dependence. This is partly an economic and political dependence, one which has been studied at length, and which, as we now know, has never been an unambiguous submission, but has instead consisted of complex and ambivalent strategies of extraversion.[81] But it is also a cultural and thus religious dependence, also in line with this same logic of extraversion. 'Religious dependence'[82] is at once epistemic—something which Boko Haram vehemently denounces—insofar as the Christian ecclesial institutions and their Islamic counterparts are dependent on Western and Arab foreign funds; and it is political, as the Vatican, the 'North Atlantic'[83] missions and the main Muslim centres in the Near and Middle East often keep the spiritual authorities of the continent in a subordinate position, with the implicit approval of academics who tend to discuss Africa (as well as Asia) in terms of an Islam of the periphery or a Christianity of the tropics.

However, the analysis of Africa's religious dependence, only one facet among others in the tremendous complexity of faith and its practices on the continent, is the royal road to a better understanding of the historicity of its societies, and the interweaving of 'durations', in both Braudel's and Bergson's senses, which is constitutive of this historicity. The religious scene in Africa is a 'creative evolution' whose 'duration', as non-serial and non-spatial time, 'is composed of moments within moments', of 'interpenetrating moments'—the polar opposite of the historicist and linear representation of social change.[84] It is undoubtedly the prophetisms of Central Africa that best illustrate this concatenation of social 'durations'.

Religion is therefore in itself, and in its relation to the state, a historical phenomenon. Michel de Certeau described the way in which 'Christianity shifts as modernity is formed' in Europe in the sixteenth and seventeenth centuries.[85] From one duration to the next, from one moment to another, Islam, the so-called traditional religions, and Christianity are indeed endlessly 'shifting' in Africa. These displacements maintain dialogical relations between themselves that are often traumatic, witness the persistence of the slave trade, the Crusades, colonization and, no doubt in the future, the jihad of Al-Shabaab, AQIM and Boko Haram.

Through this historicity, this 'creative evolution', and also this dependence that in no way cancels them, religion, including in its relation to politics, is a clear sign that Africa belongs to universality, if we study it with the instruments of historical sociology, far removed from culturalist and orientalist arguments which here see a pretext for labelling its identity with terms such as Africanity, exoticism, the subalternity of belief, and the periphery of monotheisms. The 'paradigm of the cult city' is an 'operator of individualization'[86] that makes it possible to think simultaneously of the singularity of the manufacture of the politico-religious domain in African societies, its 'particular development' (*Sonderentwicklung*) as Weber would have said, and its ordinariness from the comparative perspective.

From this point of view, it would be fruitful to return to the religious practices of lay people, secular believers (or their Muslim counterparts), and in particular their institutional initiatives. We know how important the creation of orders and brotherhoods was, as a counterpoint to the hierarchical ecclesial structures of the papacy, in Roman Catholicism, both in the Middle Ages and in the Early Modern period:[87] these new groups owed allegiance to the church's structures, but were either connected with the social institutions of the modernity of their time, such as colleges, schools and hospitals during the Reformation and Counter-Reformation (as with the Jesuits, the Barnabites and the Camilians), or on the contrary developed alternative modes of integration into society, like the Capuchins who stayed away from those institutions and chose rather to move into a territory and adopt the condition of poverty, through their practice of receiving alms.[88]

As long as we keep in mind the attention which the 'politics from below' approach pays to social intermediation—contrary to the way it has sometimes been interpreted[89]—we can admit that this approach remains useful for an apprehension of the cult city beyond the macrohistorical process of state formation as seen through its various effects. The appropriation of religion by its faithful through their concrete practices (even in the world of the invisible), and also their institutional creations, including churches, cults, devout or even violent and militant groups such as Boko Haram, AQIM, Al-Shabaab, and Mungiki in Kenya, so-called secret societies like the Poro of Liberia and Sierra Leone, or associations engaged in the struggle against witchcraft such as the Croix Koma in Gabon and Congo-Brazzaville, are a crucial dimension in the production of the polis. Remember the part played in Africa's history, over the last century, by the so-called independent and, today, charismatic churches, the brotherhoods, the associations of the faithful devoted to piety and the service of others, and the armed movements dedicated to the propagation of the faith. Let us refer to this institutional event by resorting to the concept of 'group' or 'community of the faithful' (*Gemeinde*); Weber, of course, saw such groups as a site of the 'becoming like every day' (*Veralltäglichung*) of styles of life.[90] And let us see it as a part of the 'civil society' which is so lauded today, and which is not the polar opposite of the state, as the neoliberal common sense of 'governance' would have it, but society in its relation to the state.

Several colleagues have already embarked on a new research project, first and foremost among whom was Stephen Ellis. The work to be done is still huge, but it will mean we have a more accurate vision of state formation in Africa, and the role that religion plays in it. In particular, the diversification of religious structures, the 'intrinsic logics' of faith in which they dwell, and the latter's 'planes of immanence' foster specific historical durations, including that of Eternity, which are constituent parts of the polis. If we take them into consideration, says Walter Benjamin, we will be able to 'brush history against the grain', and 'make the continuum of history explode', something which alone can constitute the 'historical object'.[91] Michel de Certeau, who declared himself to be a 'historian of spirituality', showed that the mystical experience, an 'irrational' mode of subjectivation, went hand in hand, in the Europe of the Modern Age, with the institutionalization of the rational-legal bureaucratic state. After all, the great Habsburg, Ottoman, Safavid and Mughal emperors themselves had a Messianic vision of the world.[92] And in eighteenth-century France the Jansenist convulsionaries fostered the idea of nationhood.[93]

Thus envisaged, the study of the relations between religion and the political, one of the most classic subjects of political science, can reinvigorate its problematics, if only because it must confront, on a radically new basis, the thorny questions of the colonial encounter and social subalternity, which both lie at the heart of the African dialogue between God and Caesar.

NOTES

PREFACE

1. Stephen Ellis, *This Present Darkness: A History of Nigerian Organised Crime*. London: Hurst & Co./New York: Oxford University Press, 2016.
2. Stephen Ellis, *The Rising of the Red Shawls: A Revolt in Madagascar, 1895–1899*, Cambridge: Cambridge University Press, 1985.
3. Stephen Ellis, 'Colonial Conquest in Central Madagascar: Who Resisted What?' in J. Abbink, M.E. de Bruijn, and K. van Walraven, *Rethinking Resistance: Revolt and Violence in African History*. Leiden: Brill, 2003, pp. 69–86.
4. During the interwar period, anticolonial movements in Madagascar were mainly dominated by militants struggling to transform the colony into a French *département* and its inhabitants into French citizens. The iconic leader was Jean Ralaimongo.
5. Stephen Ellis (ed.), *Africa Now: People, Policies and Institutions*. London: James Currey, 1996.
6. Stephen Ellis and Tsepo Sechaba, *Comrades Against Apartheid: The South African Communist Party and the ANC in Exile*. London: James Currey/Bloomington: Indiana University Press, 1992.
7. Stephen Ellis, 'Tom and Toakafo: The Betsimisaraka Kingdom and State Formation in Madagascar, 1715–1750', *Journal of African History*, 48, 3 (2007), pp. 439–55.
8. Stephen Ellis, *Season of Rains: Africa in the World*, foreword by Archbishop Desmond Tutu. London: Hurst & Co./Auckland Park: Jacana, 2011.

INTRODUCTION

1. Stephen Ellis—obituary—a cool observer of Africa who took on big themes, by Richard Dowden for African Arguments, 30 July 2015. https://africanarguments.org/2015/07/stephen-ellis-by-richard-dowden/
2. *In memoriam Stephen Ellis*, by Ineke van Kessel. https://web.archive.org/web/20170718052758/http://afrikastudies.nl/in-memoriam-stephen-ellis/
3. See the funeral speech available on the ASC website: http://www.ascleiden.nl/sites/default/files/speech_gerrie_ter_haar.pdf/

4. Jos Damen, *Stephen Ellis Bibliography*, 2nd revised and enlarged edition, Leiden: African Studies Centre, Leiden University, 2018 [ASC Occasional Publication].

5. Tribute to Stephen Ellis for *African Affairs*. <https://www.dropbox.com/s/8s2wm629ogyau7g/Tribute%20to%20Stephen%20Ellis.docx?dl=0>

6. Note that this appears to be a (probably posthumous) misquote. In the original, Powell speaks of 'national culture'.

1. WRITING HISTORIES OF CONTEMPORARY AFRICA

1. E.g. Mahmood Mamdani, *Citizen and Subject: Contemporary Africa and the Legacy of Late Colonialism* (Princeton, 1996).

2. Florence Bernault, 'L'Afrique et la modernité des sciences sociales', *Vingtième Siècle,* 70 (2001), 127–38.

3. This includes much of the work of Basil Davidson, for example, probably the best-selling historian of contemporary Africa in English over a long period. On the key themes of the 1960s, Terence Ranger (ed.), *Emerging Themes in African History* (Nairobi, 1968).

4. I have analysed this in more detail with regard to one important subject of contemporary African history, namely liberation war: Stephen Ellis, 'Africa's wars of liberation: some historiographical reflections', in Piet Konings, Wim van Binsbergen and Gerti Hesseling (eds.), *Trajectoires de Libération en Afrique Contemporaine* (Paris, 2000), 69–91.

5. Among recent best-sellers in this genre are Philip Gourevitch, *We Wish to Inform You That Tomorrow We Will be Killed with Our Families: Stories from Rwanda* (New York, 1998); Bill Berkeley, *The Graves Are Not Yet Full: Race, Tribe and Power in the Heart of Africa* (New York, 2001).

6. E.g. John Iliffe, *Africans: The History of a Continent* (Cambridge, 1995).

7. R.G. Collingwood, *The Idea of History* (1946; edn. with introduction and editorial material by Jan van der Dussen, Oxford, 1993), 228.

8. Mark Mazower, *Dark Continent: Europe's Twentieth Century* (London, 1999), xii.

9. *Ibid.*

10. A phrase borrowed from A.J.P. Taylor, *The Course of German History* (London, 1945), 68.

11. For a discussion of method, see Geoffrey Barraclough, *An Introduction to Contemporary History* (New York, 1964), especially ch. 1.

12. This phrase was originally used by Hugh Trevor-Roper, Regius Professor of Modern History at the University of Oxford, in 1963 during a series of lectures at Sussex University which was also broadcast by BBC Television. It later appeared in a book, *The Rise of Christian Europe* (London, 1965), 9–11. For a full exegesis, see Finn Fuglestad, 'The Trevor-Roper trap, or the imperialism of history. An essay', *History in Africa*, 19 (1992), 309–26.

13. The period from the mid-1950s until the independence of the former Portuguese colonies in 1975. Only Seychelles, Zimbabwe and Namibia gained independence (and Eritrea seceded from Ethiopia) later than this.

14. Naomi Chazan, Robert Mortimer, John Ravenhill and Donald Rothchild, *Politics and Society in Contemporary Africa* (2nd edn., Boulder, 1992), 15–17.

15. Classic studies of the period include e.g. James S. Coleman, *Nigeria: Background to Nationalism* (Berkeley, 1958); David Apter, *The Gold Coast in Transition* (Princeton, 1955, a subsequent edition of which was retitled *Ghana in Transition*); James S. Coleman and Carl Rosberg (eds.), *Political Parties and National Integration in Tropical Africa* (Berkeley, 1964). During the early 1980s the *African Studies Review* published a series of excellent guides to the literature by discipline, which provides useful summaries of the works that had been most influential in the preceding decades.

16. A good summary, from a Marxist perspective, is Colin Leys, *The Rise and Fall of Development Theory* (London, 1996), 3–44.

17. Arnold Temu, 'Not telling: African history at the end of the millennium', *South African Historical Journal,* 42 (2000), 2–10. A similar point is made by Frederick Cooper, 'Africa's pasts and Africa's historians', *African Sociological Review,* 3 (1999), 1–29.

18. Jan Vansina, *Living with Africa* (Madison, 1994), 40–59.

19. For an overview of the development of Africanist history-writing, Joseph C. Miller, 'History and Africa/Africa and history', *American Historical Review,* 104 (1999), 1–32.

20. For a more extended discussion, see Ellis, 'Africa's wars of liberation', esp. 68–78.

21. Basil Davidson, *Old Africa Rediscovered* (London, 1970; first edn. 1959), 266–8.

22. Cf. the remarks in Hannah Arendt, *Between Past and Future* (1961; Penguin edn., London, 1993), 67.

23. Achille Mbembe, *On the Postcolony* (Berkeley and Los Angeles, 2001), 9–11.

24. Eric Hobsbawm, *Age of Extremes: The Short Twentieth Century, 1914–1991* (London, 1994), 6.

25. E.g. Claude Ake, *Democracy and Development in Africa* (Washington DC, 1996), 1–17.

26. Mbembe, *On the Postcolony,* 7.

27. Michael Crowder, 'Whose dream was it anyway? Twenty-five years of African independence', *African Affairs,* 86 (1987), 7–24.

28. Perhaps the most thorough of which is Human Rights Watch (written by Alison Des Forges), *'Leave None to Tell the Story': Genocide in Rwanda* (New York, 1999).

29. Key exponents of a more realistic view are Norma Kriger, *Zimbabwe's Guerrilla War: Peasant Voices* (Cambridge, 1992); Colin Leys and John Saul, *Namibia's Liberation Struggle: The Two-Edged Sword* (London, 1995); Ineke van Kessel, *'Beyond Our Wildest Dreams': The United Democratic Front and the Transformation of South Africa* (Charlottesville, 2000).

30. Donald Crummey, 'Society, state and nationality in the recent historiography of Ethiopia', *Journal of African History,* 31 (1990), 103–19.

31. Cf. the attempt at renewal by Jean-François Bayart, 'Africa in the world: a history of extraversion', *African Affairs,* 99 (2000), 217–67.

32. E.g. Luise White, *The Comforts of Home: Prostitution in Colonial Nairobi* (Chicago, 1990).

33. E.g. Jocelyn Alexander, JoAnn McGregor and Terence Ranger, *Violence and Memory: One Hundred Years in the 'Dark Forests' of Matabeleland* (Oxford, 2000).

34. Megan Vaughan, *Curing Their Ills: Colonial Power and African Illness* (Cambridge, 1991); Nancy Rose Hunt, *A Colonial Lexicon: Of Birth Ritual, Medicalization, and Mobility in the Congo* (Durham, 1999).

35. Cf. Frederick Cooper, 'What is the concept of globalization good for? An African historian's perspective', *African Affairs,* 100 (2001), 189–214.

36. Deepak Lal, 'Asia and Western dominance: retrospect and prospect', International Institute of Asian Studies Annual Lecture, Leiden, 27 Oct. 2000, summarized in *IIAS Newsletter* 24 (Feb. 2001), 3. This is explored at full length in D. Lal, *Unintended Consequences: The Impact of Factor Endowments, Culture and Politics on Long-Run Economic Performance* (Cambridge, MA, 1998).

37. Rosalind O'Hanlon and David Washbrook, 'After Orientalism: culture, criticism and politics in the third world', *Comparative Studies in Society and History,* 34 (1992), 142.

38. Barraclough, *An Introduction to Contemporary History,* 12. Italics in the original.

39. Cf. David Anderson and Richard Rathbone (eds.), *Africa's Urban Past* (Oxford, 2000); there are also many rich suggestions in Iliffe, *Africans.*

40. This is not dissimilar to a suggestion made by Ali Mazrui, 'Identity politics and the nation-state under siege: towards a theory of reverse evolution', *Social Dynamics,* 25 (1999), 5–25.

41. Barraclough, *An Introduction to Contemporary History,* 8.

42. Henri Brunschwig, 'Histoire, passé et frustration en Afrique noire', *Annales,* 17 (1962), 875.

43. The main source on Africanist archives is the International Council on Archives, *Guide des sources de l'histoire de l'Afrique* (9 vols., Zug, 1970–83), the result of a UNESCO sponsored project that concerns almost entirely archives from pre-independence periods. There are regular descriptions of archives to be found in the journal *History in Africa.* E.g. 27 (2000) has articles on Ghanaian, Ugandan and Mozambican archives, on archives in Germany, on the papers of the White Sisters missionary order and on the documentary collection at South Africa's Fort Hare University.

44. Stephen Ellis, *The Mask of Anarchy: The Destruction of Liberia and the Religious Dimension of an African Civil War* (London, 1999), 322, based on information given to the author by the director-general of the National Documentation Center in Liberia.

45. Gregory Mann, 'Dust to dust: a user's guide to local archives in Mali', *History in Africa,* 26 (1999), 453–6.

46. Heike Behrend, *Alice Lakwena and the Holy Spirits: War in Northern Uganda 1986–87* (Oxford, 1999), 10–11.

47. E.g. Emmanuel Le Roy Ladurie, *Montaillou: Cathars and Catholics in a French Village, 1294–1324* (trans. Barbara Bray, London, 1978; first French edn. 1975); Carlo Ginzburg, *The Cheese and the Worms: The Cosmos of a Sixteenth-Century Miller* (trans. John and Anne Tedeschi, London, 1980; first Italian edn., 1976).

48. Charles van Onselen, *The Seed is Mine: The Life of Kas Maine, a South African Sharecropper, 1894–1985* (Oxford, 1996).

49. E.g. Kristin Mann, *Marrying Well: Marriage, Status and Social Change among the Educated Elite in Colonial Lagos* (Cambridge, 1985); Landeg White, *Magomero: Portrait of an African Village* (Cambridge, 1987).

50. The private papers of the Samkange family are described by Terence Ranger, *Are We Not Also Men? The Samkange Family and African Politics in Zimbabwe, 1920–64* (London, 1995), vii–x.

51. Among many publications of high quality, recent examples include John Thornton, *The Kongolese Saint Anthony: Dona Beatriz Kimpa Vita and the Anthonian Movement, 1684–1706.* (Cambridge, 1998); and Pier M. Larson, *History and Memory in the Age of Enslavement: Becoming Merina in Highland Madagascar, 1770–1882* (Oxford, 2000).

52. E.g. Leonard Brehun, *Liberia: The War of Horror* (Accra, 1991); Nkem Agetua, *Operation Liberty: The Story of Major General Joshua Nimyel Dogonyaro* (Lagos, 1992); Bayo Ogunleye, *Behind Rebel Line: Anatomy of Charles Taylor's Hostage Camps* (Enugu, 1995).

53. E.g. James Youboty, *Liberian Civil War: A Graphic Account* (Philadelphia, 1993).

54. André-Jean Tudesq, *Feuilles d'Afrique: étude de la presse de l'Afrique subsaharienne* (Talence, France, 1995), 327–30. The same author has written a series of books on various aspects of African mass media, including television.

55. A point noted by Clifford Geertz, who refers to on-line quotations 'disappearing like electronic wraiths when you look back for them'. 'Life Among the Anthros', *New York Review of Books*, 48 (8 Feb. 2001), 18, n. 5.

56. Robert Launay, 'Spirit media: the electronic media and Islam among the Dyula of north Côte d'Ivoire', *Africa*, 67 (1997), 441–53, is a study of the effects of video rather than a historical study using video as a primary source.

57. Northwestern University and the Library of Congress both have exceptional collections.

58. A historian who has written some well-known studies of the press in eighteenth-century France, Robert Darnton, is also a former journalist and has written penetratingly about modern American newspapers: *The Kiss of Lamourette: Reflections in Cultural History* (New York, 1990), 60–93.

59. James Sanders, *South Africa and the International Media, 1972–1979: A Struggle for Representation* (London, 2000), esp. ch. 1.

60. Rosalynde Ainslie, *The Press in Africa: Communications Past and Present* (London, 1966), 9–20.

61. Michael Schatzberg, for example, in a work in course of publication by Indiana University Press, has used newspapers from a range of African countries as sources for the analysis of prevailing ideas about political authority in what he calls 'middle Africa'. His published thoughts on the matter to date are in Michael Schatzberg, 'The household as model for legitimacy', *Africa,* 63 (1993), 445–61.

62. International Press Institute, *A Rural Press for Africa* (London, 1979), 4.

63. UNESCO, *Rapport mondial sur la culture, 2000* (Paris, 2000), 311. The same source has information on the availability of books, libraries, etc.

64. World Bank, *African Development Indicators* 2000 (Washington, 2000), 254.

65. A case-study is W. Joseph Campbell, *The Emergent Press in Benin and Côte d'Ivoire: From the Voice of the State to Advocate of Democracy* (Westport, 1998). The London-based organisation Article 19 has also published a series of good studies, as have African-based groups such as the Media Institute of Southern Africa.

66. Cf. Cornelis Nlandu-Tsasa, *La rumeur au Zaire de Mobutu: radio-trottoir à Kinshasa*, esp. 75–7.

67. Amadu Wurie Khan, 'Journalism and armed conflict in Africa: the civil war in Sierra Leone', *Review of African Political Economy*, 78 (1998), 594–5.

68. Claude Ake, 'What is the problem of ethnicity in Africa?', *Transformation*, 22 (1993).7.

69. Stephen Ellis, 'Reporting Africa', *Current History*, 99 (2000), 225–6.

70. Stephen Ellis, 'Tuning in to pavement radio', *African Affairs*, 88 (1989), 321–30.

71. Robert Darnton, 'Paris: the early Internet', *New York Review of Books*, 47, 11 (29 June 2000), 42.

72. Jean-Noel Kapferer, *Rumeurs: le plus vieux media du monde* (Paris, 1987), 19–22. An English translation was published in 1990.

73. Edward L. Bernays, *Propaganda* (New York, 1928), 9.

74. *Cameroon Tribune,* no. 3080, 21 September 1984, quoted in Ellis, 'Tuning in to pavement radio', 325.

75. Mary Myers, 'Community radio and development: issues and examples from francophone West Africa', in Richard Fardon and Graham Furniss (eds.), *African Broadcast Cultures: Radio in Transition* (Oxford, 2000), 97, n. 6. Matthew Schoffeleers, 'The AIDS pandemic, the prophet Billy Chisupe and the democratization process in Malawi', *Journal of Religion in Africa,* 39 (1999), 412–4, reports that many Malawians consider aid and AIDS to be closely connected.

76. On the attention paid, for example, by Nkrumah's government in Ghana, see M.N. Tetteh, *Anatomy of Rumour Mongering in Ghana* (Accra, 1976); on Zaire, Nlandu-Tsasa, *La rumeur au Zaire.*

77. Nicolas Martin-Granel, 'Rumeur sur Brazzaville: de la rue a l'écriture', *Canadian Journal of African Studies,* 33 (1999), 362–409; Jean-Claude Gakosso, *La nouvelle presse congolaise: du goulag a l'agora* (Paris, 1997), 59–65.

78. The same applies to many other parts of the world. See e.g. Anand A. Yang, 'A conversation of rumors: the language of popular *mentalités* in late nineteenth-century colonial India', *Journal of Social History*, 20 (1986–7), 485–505.

79. Tetteh, *Anatomy of Rumour Mongering*, 38–9.

80. Richard Rathbone, *Murder and Politics in Colonial Ghana* (New Haven, 1993).

81. Emmanuel Terray, 'Le pouvoir, le sang et la mort dans le royaume asante au dixneuvieme siecle', *Cahiers d'etudes africaines,* 136 (1994), 549–61.

82. Ellis, *The Mask of Anarchy,* esp. 245–66.

83. Kapferer, *Rumeurs,* 49.

84. Amid a large literature, works I have found particularly illuminating include Elizabeth Tonkin, *Narrating Our Pasts: The Social Construction of Oral History* (Cambridge, 1992) and Johannes Fabian, *Moments of Freedom: Anthropology and Popular Culture* (Charlottesville, 1998).

85. The literature starts with Jan Vansina, *Oral Tradition* (London, 1965; first French edn. 1961) and his later *Oral Tradition as History* (London, 1985); a neglected masterpiece is Alain Delivre, *L'histoire des rois d'Imerina: essai d'interpretation d'une histoire orale* (Paris, 1974).

86. Elizabeth Tonkin, 'Investigating oral tradition', *Journal of African History*, 27 (1986), 203–13.

87. Luise White, Speaking with Vampires: *Rumor and History in Colonial Africa* (Berkeley, 2000).

88. Luise White, 'The most telling: lies, secrets and history', *South African Historical Journal*, 42 (2000), 11–25.
89. For an example, Stephen Ellis, 'Rumour and power in Togo', Africa, 63 (1993), 462–76, set in context by Charles Piot, *Remotely Global: Village Modernity in West Africa* (Chicago 1999), 44–9.
90. Thomas Hobbes (C.B. Macpherson, ed.), *Leviathan* (1651; Pelican edn., London, 1968), 150.
91. Collingwood, *The Idea of History*, 25–8.
92. This has been the subject of an extensive theoretical debate, notably in a series of works by Hayden White suggesting that history-writing is similar to fiction in the sense of being a literary creation. For a summary and a response, see Roger Chartier, *Au bord de la falaise: l'histoire entre certitudes et inquiétude* (Paris, 1998), esp. 87–107.
93. Collingwood, *The Idea of History*, 240–2, 245–6.
94. Cf. Larry Diamond, 'Fiction as political thought', *African Affairs*, 88 (1989), 435–45.
95. Jeffrey S. Victor, 'Social construction of Satanic ritual abuse and the creation of false memories', in Joseph De Rivera and Theodore R. Sarbin (eds.), *Believed-In Imaginings: The Narrative Construction of Reality* (Washington DC, 1998), 194.
96. Tom Rosentiel, quoted in the *Washington Post*, 2 March 1999.
97. Mbembe, *On the Postcolony,* 1–23.
98. Bayart, 'Africa in the world'.
99. Sousa Jamba, 'The idea of Angola', *The Times Literary Supplement*, 8 June 2001, 12.
100. E.g. Fabian, *Moments of Freedom*, 87–101; Tamara Giles-Vernick, 'Doli: translating an African environmental history of loss in the Sangha River basin of equatorial Africa', *Journal of African History*, 41 (2000), 373.
101. Collingwood, *The Idea of History*, 24–5.
102. Achille Mbembe, 'A propos des écritures africaines de soi', *Politique africaine*, 77 (2000), 25–6.
103. Bernault, 'L'Afrique et la modernité'.
104. Frederick Cooper, 'What is the concept of globalization good for?'
105. Jean and John L. Comaroff, 'Occult economies and the violence of abstraction: notes from the South African postcolony', *American Ethnologist*, 26 (1999), 279.
106. Barraclough, *An Introduction to Contemporary History*, 15.

2. AFRICA'S WARS OF LIBERATION

1. Buijtenhuijs, R., 1971, 1978, 1987a.
2. Buijtenhuijs, R., 1993, 1998b.
3. Buijtenhuijs, R., 1996.
4. Vansina, J., 1994, pp. 40–59.
5. Johnson, S., 1921, was completed in 1897 but published only later.
6. Some US universities had previously had professional teachers of what would now be called African American studies and many black American intellectuals had drawn on African history in their work. Melville Herskovits is generally regarded as the first US academic Africanist to have had substantial influence

outside the established tradition of African American studies. Cf. Zeleza, P.T., 1997.

7. Deschamps, H., 1975; Vansina, J., *op. cit.*; Oliver, R., 1997.
8. Person Y., 1968–75. The first president of Guinea, Ahmed Sékou Touré, claimed descent from Samory Touré.
9. Jenkins, K., 1991.
10. Cf. Cohn, N., 1993.
11. Pomper, P., Elphick, R.H., and Vann, R.T., *World History: Ideologies, Structures, and Identities,* 1998, esp. the essay by William Green on pp. 53–65.
12. Brunschwig, H., 1962, pp. 874–5.
13. Davidson, B., 1970, pp. 266–8.
14. E.g. Gann, L., 1993.
15. Deschamps, H., *op. cit.*; Oliver, R., *op. cit*
16. At its inception in 1963, the Organisation of African Unity issued a call for the publication of a comprehensive history of Africa, an initiative which was to lead to the UNESCO African history series, authored largely by Africans, which eventually finished publication in 1993. See Vansina, J., 1993. Other institutions and even individuals have also attempted to write comprehensive histories of Africa, such as the eight-volume *Cambridge History of Africa,* begun in 1965 and completed in 1986. On the latter, Oliver, R., *op. cit.,* pp. 294–6.
17. Diop, C.A., 1960.
18. The pioneering work was Vansina, J., 1961.
19. Basil Davidson has published over 20 books on African history and politics and was also the presenter of a successful BBC-TV séries. For some short autobiographical elements, see Davidson, B., 1994, pp. 97–102.
20. Robinson, R., and Gallagher, J., 1962.
21. Ranger, 1968a.
22. Ranger, 1968b.
23. Quoted in *ibid.,* p. 437.
24. John Lonsdale, quoted in Cooper, F, 1994, p. 1520.
25. See e.g. Denoon, D, and Kuper, A., 1970.
26. Cf. Coquery-Vidrovitch, C. (1997), who believes that francophone scholarship on Africa has been rather poor in comparison with anglophone production.
27. Suret-Canale, J., 1982. I am not sure who first applied the term 'collaborators' to Africans who worked with colonial governments, but it seems to date from about 1960.
28. When a leading Oxford historian referred disdainfully to Africa's past in 1963 as the 'unrewarding gyrations of barbarous tribes', he was understandably treated to the scorn of all Africanists. See Fuglestad, F., 1992, esp. pp. 311–12.
29. South Africa had technically been an independent state since 1910, but its condition bore such an obvious similarity to colonial rule that the South African Communist Party considered apartheid to be 'colonialism of a special type'.
30. Ranger, T., 1968a, p. XXI
31. Crummey, D., 1986, and especially the essay by Ralph Austen on pp. 89–108.
32. Cf. Glassman, J., 1995.
33. Leys, C., 1996, esp. pp. 143–63.

34. E.g. Mbembe, A., 1991.
35. Cf. Toulabor, C., 1986; Mbembe, A., 1992.
36. Raison-Jourde, F., 1997.
37. Cf. Hansen, H.B., and Twaddle, M., 1991.
38. Crowder, M., 1987.
39. Leys, C., *op. cit.,* pp. 107–96.
40. E.g. Davidson, B., 1992. A similar view in French political science is expressed in Badié, B., 1992. An influential recent variant is Mamdani, M., 1996.
41. Geffray, C., 1990.
42. World Bank, 1989.
43. Buijtenhuijs, R., and Rijnierse, B., 1993, and Buijtenhuijs, R., and Thinot, C., 1995, provide useful surveys of much of this literature. This research was financed by the Netherlands Ministry of Development Cooperation.
44. Essack, K., 1994.
45. E.g. Bazenguissa-Ganga, R., 1999.
46. John Keegan, quoted in Mazower, M., 1999, p. XIV.
47. A recent summary is Berman, B., 1998.
48. Ake, C., 1996.
49. Leys C., and Saul, J., 1995.
50. E.g. Clapham, C., 1998; and Reno, W., 1998.
51. Kriger, N., 1992; Richards, P., 1995; Ellis, S., 1999; Human Rights Watch, 1999.
52. Cf. Ottaway, M., 1999.
53. There appears to be no full study of South Africa's African Renaissance. See e.g. *Indicator South Africa 1998.*
54. Notably Mbembe, A., 1992.
55. Ignazio Silone, quoted in Mazower, *op. cit.,* p. XI.
56. *Ibid.,* p. XII.
57. Mazower, M., *op. cit.,* p. XII.
58. Ellis, S., *op cit.*
59. Van Creveld, M., 1991.
60. On the looting of cities, see e.g. Bazenguissa-Ganga, R., *op. cit.*; Ellis, S., *op. cit.*
61. Keen, D., forthcoming.
62. I am grateful to Fredenk van Gelder of the Johann Wolfgang Goethe University, Frankfurt, for pointing this out to me using the example of Coetzee, J., 1980. I would add to his other examples, such as Kourouma, A., 1970; Achebe, C., 1966, and 1983.
63. Bayart, J.F., forthcoming.

3. TUNING IN TO PAVEMENT RADIO

1. The best academic treatment is David Bettison, 'Rumour under Conditions of Charismatic Leadership and Racial Political Tension', *African Social Research*, 6 (1968), 413–62. I am grateful to Richard Hodder-Williams for this reference. See also Toure Keita, 'Radio trottoir', *Index on Censorship*, (1986), No. 5, p. 27; Ekambo Duasange Ndundu, 'Radio trottoir: ses lois tendancielles', *Analyses Sociales*,

(laboratoire d'analyses sociales de Kinshasa), 3, No. 4 (July–Aug 1986), pp. 56–61. Articles in *Politique Africaine* have also touched on the subject.

2. Henri Lopès, *Le Pleurer-Rire* (Paris).
3. Personal communication by Tiébilé Dramé.
4. Leroy Vail and Landeg White, 'Forms of Resistance: songs and perceptions of power in colonial Mozambique', *American Historical Review*, 88, (1983), pp. 887–8.
5. Article 19, *Freedom of Information and Expression in Zaïre* (London, 1987), pp. 28–9.
6. *La lettre de l'Océan Indien*, 15 December 1984.
7. *Lakroa*, 23 December 1984.
8. M.E.F. Bloch, *Placing the Dead* (London and New York, 1971), pp. 31–2.
9. G. Berg, *Historical Traditions and the Foundations Monarchy in Imerina* (Univ. of California, Berkeley, Ph.D., 1975), p. 16.
10. Association of Recognized Professional Bodies, Accra, *News Beulltin* Vol. II, no. 2, 28 July 1982.
11. David Williams, *Malawi, the Politics of Despair* (New York 1978), pp. 252–3; G. Shepperson and T. Price, *Independent African* (Edinburgh U.P., 1958), pp. 9–10.
12. David Lan, *Guns and Rain* (London, James Currey 1985).
13. Quoted in Filio Bamose, 'Cameroun: de la rumeur publique', *Afrique-Asie* No. 332, p. 32.
14. Private communication.
15. International Press Institute, *A Rural Press for Africa* (London 1979), p. 4.
16. BBC World Service, press release, no date.
17. Graham Mytton, *Mass Communication in Africa* (London 1983), pp. 20–1.
18. *Africa Confidential*, Vol. 23 No. 12 (9 June 1982), p. 8.
19. For a general discussion of how government rhetoric is received, and often subverted by the use of humour, in popular discourse, see C. Dubuch, 'Langage du Pouvoir: pouvoir du langage', *Politique Africaine*, 20 (December 1985), pp. 44–53.
20. Amnesty International, *Annual Report 1988* (London, 1988). Cf. N. Mwambungu, Member of Parliament for Karonga North constituency in Malawi: 'A whisper which would lead to the breakdown of the Malawi government will be treated as treason', quoted in Williams, *Malawi*, p. 229.
21. François Callet (trans. G.S. Chapus and E. Ratsimba), *Histoire des Rois* (revised ed., Antananarivo, 1974–8), Vol. III, pp. 93–4.
22. Joseph Ki-Zerbo, 'Africa silent continent?' *Index on Censorship*, No. 2 (1986), pp. 16–18.
23. Jean-Pierre Challard, 'Signé Makaya!', *Africa International* (December 1985), pp. 33–6.
24. Peter Geschiere, *Village Communities and the State* (London, 1982), pp. 45–54.
25. Geschiere, *Village Communities*, pp. 45–54.
26. Bettison, 'Rumour under conditions of charismatic leadership'.
27. Roger Koumabila-Abougoué, '"N'gole", un fétiche anti-colonialiste de l'après-guerre (1945–1955)', *La Semaine Africaine*, 10–16 January 1985, pp. 15–16.
28. M. Anafu, 'The CPP and the chiefs', *West Africa*, 10 December 1984, pp. 2518–20.
29. Comi Toulabor, *Le Togo sous Eyadéma* (Paris, 1986)

4. RUMOUR AND POWER IN TOGO

1. I am grateful to Michael Schatzberg for drawing my attention to this reference.

5. VIOLENCE AND HISTORY

1. In addition to the available literature on the RUF, these last remarks are based on two periods of research, in 1998 and 2002, including interviews with former RUF leaders.
2. 'Libya/Liberian trained Special Forces Commando', document in author's possession.
3. A good overview is the collection by Clapham (1998).
4. This phrase has caught on: it produced more than 2,000 hits on an internet search engine.

6. THE POLITICAL ELITE OF IMERINA AND THE REVOLT OF THE *MENALAMBA*. THE CREATION OF A COLONIAL MYTH IN MADAGASCAR, 1895–1898

1. I am grateful to Madame Françoise Raison for her comments upon an earlier draft of this article.
2. *Rapport d'ensemble sur la pacification, l'organisation et la colonization de Madagascar* (Tananarive, 1899), p. 14.
3. The only full-length work on the *menalamba* is J. Rasoanasy, *Menalamba sy tanindrazana* (Tananarive, 1976). For a good discussion of the published evidence on the leadership of the *menalamba* see S. Ayache, 'Introduction à l'œuvre de Rainandriamampandry'. *Annales de l'Université de Madagascar, série lettres*, x (1969), 11–50.
4. The papers in question are those of the Laroche family, in Paris, and the Lyautey papers, soon to be transferred to a permanent archive in Paris. I am most grateful to Madame Laroche for permission to study her family papers in her own home, and to M.M.P. Toussaint and A. Le Révérend and Madame Bonazzi for permission to consult the Lyautey papers. See also note 73.
5. On the political factions see C. Le Myre de Vilers, 'Note sur la situation politique et morale', and 'Généalogie des principals familles Malgaches', 14 December 1888. Ministère des Affairs Etrangères (MAE), Paris, correspondance politique, Madagascar, ancience série, vol. 30, fols. 23–32 and 46–53; on the French party, see E.F. Knight, *Madagascar in War Time* (London, 1896), *passim*; for a brief biography of Rasanjy, *Notes, Reconnaissances et Explorations*, 111 (1898), 116–17.
6. R. Pascal, 'Les rapports de quinzaine d'Hippolyte Laroche', pt. v, *Bulletin de Madagascar*, CCXLVIII *bis* (February 1967), pp. 165–70, prints the treaty. See also A. Lebon, *La pacification de Madagascar* (Paris, 1928), *passim*, on French arguments over the government of Madagascar.
7. Dépôt des Archives d'Outre-Mer (DAOM), Aix-en-Provence, Madagascar 2 Z 326: memoranda by Ranchot, 14 and 29 Oct. 1895; and Madagascar 2 Z 342: Ranchot to minister des affaires étrangères, 15 November 1895.
8. DAOM, Mad. 2 Z 342: Ranchot to minister des affaires étrangères, 16 January 1896; Mad. 2 Z 365: General Voyron to minister de la guerre, 1 February 1896.

9. On the spread of the insurrection in northern Imerina, DAOM Mad. 6 (2) D 3: Ramampanenitra to Ramasoandromahamay (Rabozaka), 19 *Alakarabo* 1896; in southern Imerina, DAOM Mad. 2 Z 361, *passim*.
10. *Menalambo* means literally 'red shawls'. The most plausible explanation for the name is that the leaders wore red shawls as a traditional symbol of authority.
11. C. Savaron, *Mes souvenirs à Madagascar avant et après la conquête* (Tananarive, 1932), p. 287. The Laroche papers include the manuscript of the unpublished memoirs of Hippolyte Laroche, resident-general of Madagascar from January to October 1896. These include a chapter entitled 'La semaine sanglante', a record of the siege of Tananarive.
12. H. Laroche, 'Le pouvoir civil et le commandement', chapter XIII of his memoirs; A. Lebon, *La pacification, passim*.
13. H. Berthier, 'Le protectorat du ter Octobre 1895 au 18 Janvier 1896', *Bulletin de l'Acadèmie Malgache* (new series), xxiv (1941), 121.
14. 'Le service des renseignements militaires', chapter XII of Laroche's memoirs, typescript of 57 pages, Laroche papers. The original report of the conspiracy is in DAOM Mad. 2 Z 347: Voyron to Laroche, 18 June 1896.
15. Pascal, 'Les rapports de quinzaine', pt. IV, *Bull. De Madag.* CCXLVIII (January 1967), 73–86.
16. 'Compte-rendu de la reunion du 16 Juin 1896'. Laroche papers, rapports spéciaux.
17. Laroche papers: Gautier to Laroche, 1 June 1896; Bourde to Lebon, 10–11 July 1896, printed in Lebon, pp. 222–5; P. Bourde, 'Note sur les rapports du palais avec l'insurrection de l'Imerina', no date. Archives Nationales Section Outre-Mer (ANSOM), Paris, MAD 215 (445); DAOM Mad. 2 Z 347: Voyron to Laroche, 25 June 1896; Service historique de l'Armée (SHA), Vincennes, Madagascar ancient fonds carton 8: Voyron to ministre de la guerre, 11 June 1896.
18. ANSOM MAD 216 (447): Laroche to Lebon, 14 June 1896. For the opinions of the army see SHA, Mad AF 68, letters from Lt. de Cointet; also, Commandant Reibell, *Le Commandant Lamy, d'aprês sa correspondance et ses souvenirs de campagne* (Paris, 1903), 306–59.
19. ANSOM MAD 216 (453), *passim*, has a collection of relevant press-cuttings.
20. SHA, Mad. AF 44: Lebon to General Billot, 25 March 1896.
21. L. Brunet, *L'œuvre de la France à Madagascar* (Paris 1903), *passim*. Brunet was one of the deputies for Réunion.
22. H. Deschamps, *Histoire de Madagascar* (4th ed, Paris, 1972), p. 236, note 1.
23. H. Berthier, 'Le protectorat'; E-F. Gautier, *Trois Héros* (Paris, 1931), pp. 67–139; J. Carol (pasued.), *Chez les Hovas (Au pays rouge)*, (Paris, 1898). Cf. Ayache, 'Introduction à l'œuvre de Rainandriamampandry'.
24. 'Exécution du Ministre de l'Intérieur et du Prince Ratsimamanga', chapter XV of Laroche's memoirs. This text forms the basis for the following discussion of the trial.
25. *Ibid.*, p. 61 of typed draft.
26. According to Madame Laroche, her father-in-law's memoirs were written after 1904.
27. Archives of the United States' consulate at Tarnatave (US Consular), vol. x. Original in Washington. Microfilm copy in Archives Nationales (Arch. Nat.), Paris,

253 Mi 40: Welter to Rockhill, 19 October 1896; E. Grosclaude, *Un parisien à Madagascar* (2ⁿᵈ ed., Paris, 1898), 94–96; Grosclaude was probably also the author of the account in *Le Figaro*, 29 October 1896.

28. Cf. ANSOM MAD 215 (445): Gallieni to Lebon, 10 October 1896; H. Deschamps, *Histoire de Madagascar*, p. 235.

29. ANSOM MAD 216 (453): Laroche to Lebon, 20 July 1896.

30. Carol, *Chez les Hovas*, 272–4.

31. Gautier, *Trois Héros*, 67–139.

32. US Consular, vol. x (Arch. Nat. 253 Mi 40): Welter to Rockhill, 10 October and 3 December 1896; Lamy to Giraud, 3 December 1896, printed in Reibell, *Le Commandant Lamy*, p. 359; P. Solofo, *Hitako ny nitifirana an-dRainandriamampandry sy Ratsimamanga* (Tananarive, 1959), 14–15.

33. Brunet, *L'œuvre de la France*, 377 *et seq.*

34. Rainianjanoro, *Fampandrian-tony sy taniara maro samy hafa* (Tananarive, 1920), 11–12; Lyautey papers, ancient classement 455; Lyautey to chef de poste de Morafeno, 12 May 1897.

35. Rainianjanoro, *Fampandrian-tany*, 12–16; Rainianjanoro, 'Histoire de ce que Rainianjanoro 15 hrs. a fait dans la pacification du pays à Madagascar', 1 March 1899. Lyautey papers, a. cl. 445.

36. Lyautey papers, a. cl. 445: Rasanjy to Rainianjanoro, 22 May 1897; a cl. 31: Rémond to Lyautey, 8 October 1897.

37. Below, note 46.

38. Lyautey papers, a. cl. 455; Lyautey to Rémond, 28 May 1897.

39. Lyautey papers, a. cl. 453/1; Lyautey to Gallieni, 1 June 1897.

40. Ibid.

41. Lyautey to his brother, 24 May 1897, [*sic*], printed in L.H.G. Lyautey, *Lettres du Tonkin et de Madagascar* (2ⁿᵈ ed. Paris, 1921), 537–9. It is evident that the account was written many years later, and may have been deliberately misleading. Rémond is misspelt 'Raymond'; Lyautey was not at Antsatrana on 24 May 1897; nor is the date of the surrender correct.

42. Lyautey papers, a. cl. 452/2: Lyautey to Rémond, 11 June 1897.

43. Lyautey papers, a. cl. 455: Lyautey to Gallieni, 14 June 1897. Lyautey's italics.

44. Lyautey papers, a. cl. 446: Rabezavana to Rémond, 15 July 1897; ANSOM MAD 438 (1203): same to same, 16 July 1897, annexe no. 1 to Gallieni's political report of 26 August 1897.

45. The other letters are: 'Déposition de Rainibetsimisaraka', 26 July 1897, annexe no. 2 to Gallieni's report of 26 August 1897. ANSOM MAD 438 (1203): letters to and from Rabozaka annexed to H. Berthier, 'Le protectorat', in *Bull. De l'Acad. Malg.*; 'Déclaration de Rabozaka', no date, annexed to Gallieni's report of 27 March 1898, ANSOM MAD 374 (1015).

46. SHA, Mad. Nouveau fonds 15/28(2)/17: note on Rainianjanoro; *Journal Officiel de Madagascar et Dépendances*, CCXXXVI (16 April 1898), 1727–8.

47. *Rapport d'ensemble*, 14.

48. For example, 'Rapport du tournée du Gouverneur-Général dans le Betsilco', 13 September–6 October 1897. DAOM Mad. 2 D 95. The bulk of Gallieni's private papers remains with his family and is not available for consultation, but there is

much of interest in the archives départementales de l'Orne, Le Myre de Vilers papers, dossier 29: letters from Gallieni, 1896–1904.

49. 'Exécution du Ministre de l'Intérieur et du Prince Ratsimamanga', 63–4. Laroche papers; T.T. Matthews, *Thirty Years in Madagascar* (2nd ed., London, 1904), 319–20.

50. DAOM Mad. 6 (10) D 1.

51. Le Myre de Vilers papers, dossier 29: Gallieni to Le Myre de Vilers, 12 November 1898.

52. DAOM Mad. 2 Z 326: memorandum by Ranchot, 14 October 1895.

53. ANSON MAD 216 (447): Laroche to ministre des colonies, 25 February 1896. Enclosed is a French translation of the letter, dated 1 February 1896.

54. 'La lettre au gouverneur d'Ambohimanga', typescript of 6 pages, Laroche papers.

55. ANSOM MAD 216 (153): Laroche to Lebon, 20 July 1896.

56. 'Rapport de Monsieur le Commandant Gérard, Chef d'État-Major, sur la déposition de la Reine', March 1897, enclosed with Gallieni's report of 12 March 1897, ANSOM MAD 438 (1201).

57. ANSOM MAD 216 (447): Gautier to Laroche, 1 June 1896, annexe no. 1 to Laroche's report of 13 June 1896.

58. For intelligence reports warning of the approaching insurrection, see DAOM MAD. 2 Z 332 and 2 Z 364.

59. ANSOM MAD 216 (447): Laroche to ministre des colonies, 28 March 1896. A copy of the letter is enclosed: Ravaikafo (Rabezavana) to Ramahatra, 22 *Alohotsy* 1896.

60. C. Savaron, *Mes souvenirs*, 153 and 175. For a brief biography of Ramahatra, J. Chauvin, 'Le Prince Ramahatra', *Revue d'histoire des colonies,* XXVII, 11 (1939), 33–46.

61. DAOM Mad. 6 (2) D 3: Rainimafana to Ramasoandromahamay (Rabozaka), 16 *Adimizana* 1896.

62. On the circumstances surrounding the reception of the letter see SHA, Mad. NF 8/3/15: Ramahatra to secrétaire-général, 19 March 1896; H. Berthier, 'Le protectorat', 128; Berthier papers, Académie des Sciences d'Outre-Mer, Paris: Ramahatra to Rasanjy, 19 March 1896, and Ramahatra to Gallieni, 19 October 1896.

63. The evidence of the messenger who carried the letter to Ramahatra also throws doubt on the existence of any similar letter from Rabezavana to Rainandriamampandry. 'Déclaration du messager qui a porté la lettre au Prince Ramahatra...', March 1896, SHA, Mad. NF 8/3/15.

64. For example, SHA, Mad. NF 8/3/29: Captain Staup to Voyron, 7 April 1896.

65. DAOM Mad. 2 Z 361: Colonel Oudri to Voyron, 8 April 1896, and 'Rapport du Général Oudri', 8 May 1896. The translation from the Malagasy is mine.

66. Ambodirano was the scene of an unsuccessful rising in November 1895.

67. DAOM Mad. 2 Z 361: Oudri to Voyron, 8 April 1896.

68. SHA, Mad. AF 26: Oudri to ministre de la guerre, 25 August 1896.

69. Laroche papers: Besson to Laroche, 4 and 12 June 1896, quoted in part in R. Pascal, 'Les rapports de quinzaine', pt. 1, *Bull de Madag.* CCXLV (October 1966), 951, note 1.

70. ANSOM MAD 215 (445): Besson to Gallieni, 24 November 1896, annexe no. 6 to Gallieni's report of 13 December 1896.

71. Lyautey papers, a. cl. 35: Besson to Lyautey, 26 June 1903.

72. DAOM Mad. 2 Z 386, 'Journal de la résidence de Betafo', entries for 4 and 8 June 1896; Laroche papers: Besson to Laroche, 4 June 1896. See also the extracts from the *Norsk Missionstidende* translated into French in enclosures with Hanotaux to Lebon, 31 July 1896, ANSOM MAD 348 (931).

73. There are *menalamba* letters scattered in several archives in France and Madagascar, but the main collections are in DAOM Mad. 6 (2) d 3, and in the Archives de la République Malgache (ARM), Tananarive, series NN 91. Both consist mostly of letters captured from Rabozaka towards the end of 1897.

74. Laroche papers: Rafaralahimanavanana to Rainiketamanga and others, 19 *Asorotany* 1896 (French translation).

75. For example, DAOM Mad. 6 (2) D 3: Ranjiva to Ramahamay (Rabozaka), 12 *Alahasaty* 1896.

76. DAOM Mad. 2 Z 387. Alby to Laroche, 31 August 1896.

77. On Rainijirika, Laroche papers: note by resident-inspecteur Pradon, 5 September 1896. On Ramenamaso, Savaron, *Mes souvenirs*, 216–17.

78. For example, ARM NN 91: Ralaifanonitra to Ramasoandromahamay (Rabozaka), 22 *Adizaoza* 1896.

79. 'Proclamation d'un chef rebelle du Cercle d'Ambatomanga', no date, annexe no. 2 to Gallieni's report of 13 December 1896, ANSOM MAD 215 (445).

80. There is a play on words between '*Faranisay*' ('French') and '*Fara-tay*' (literally, 'the last excrement'). The *menalamba* often used this insulting pun.

81. It was a common belief among the rebels that the old prime minister, Rainilaiarivony, had been killed by the French. In fact he died of natural causes in exile in Algiers.

82. Cf. G.S. Chapus and E. Ratsimba, *Histoire des Rois* (4 vols., Paris, 1953–8), iv, 345. This is the French translation of Père Callet's *Tantaran' ny Andraina*. I am grateful to Françoise Raison for supplying this reference and also for drawing my attention to the influence of *The Pilgrim's Progress*.

83. W. Ellis, *The Martyr Church: a Narrative of the Introduction, Progress and Triumph of Christianity in Madagascar* (London, 1870), p. 107.

84. DAOM Mad. 6 (4) D 16, 'dossier Peill': proclamation by Rabezavana, 12 November 1896.

85. There is a fine discussion of the Merina concept of political authority in A. Delivré, *L'histoire des rois d'Imerina* (Paris, 1974), 139–74.

86. F. Raison, 'Les ramanenjana', *Asie du sud-est et le monde insulindien*, VII, ii–iii (1976) m 271–93. R. Delval, *Radama II, prince de la renaissance malgache* (Paris, 1972), 732–918, provides evidence that Radama II really did lead the insurgents of 1863, Madame Raison's view is the more convincing because the rebels of 1863, like those of 1896 and 1947, probably needed to believe that their movement was supported by a legitimate authority.

87. DAOM Mad. 2 Z 105, *kabary* of Queen Ranavalona II, June 1877 (French translation). 'Je sais que les fauteurs de troubles mettent mon nom en avant pour entraîner les gens à leur suite. Ils mentent; ce sont des ennemis de moi et du royaume eux et ceux qui les écountent; ils seront punis comme rebelles.'

88. J. Tronchon, *L'insurrection malgache de 1947* (Paris, 1974), 82–118.

89. DAOM Mad. 6 (2) D 3: Ramialanenina to Ramasoandromahamay (Rabozaka), 10 *Adimizana* 1896; ARM NN 91: Ralaifanenitra to Ramasoandromahamay (Rabozaka), 8 *Asorotany* 1896.

90. Lyautey papers, a. cl. 445: 'Patriote 16e honneur' to Rabezavana, 18 July 1896 (French translation). Added doubt is attached to the authorship of the letter by the penciled notes in the margin. By the signature an unknown hand (Lyautey?) has written 'Randriamampandry' [*sic*]. In the margin is written 'lettre de Randriamampandry—est-ce copie ou de mémoire?'.

91. Notably Gautier, *Trois Héros*, 132–3.

92. There is an incomplete list of such casualties in Laroche to Lebon, 10 July 1896, printed in Pascal, pt. IV, p. 89, note 1.

93. For some examples, see 'Notice concernant la région d'Andriamena', no date, DAOM Mad. 6 (9) D 27; archives of the London Missionary Society (LMS), London, Madagascar incoming letters 26/2/A: Sibree to Thompson, 22 April 1896; DAOM Mad. 6 (2) D 3: Rainimafana and others to Ramasoandromahamay (Rabozaka), 19 *Asambola* 1896.

94. Decree of Ranavalona III, 22 August 1896, DAOM Mad. 6 (10) D 1. On Rainandriamampandry's wealth, 'Exécution du Ministre de l'Intérieur et du Prince Ratimamanga', Laroche papers.

95. The comparison with the Dreyfus affair is an interesting one. The issues at stake between pro- and anti-military factions were similar in both cases. Laroche in chapter XV of his unpublished memoirs makes specific allusion to Dreyfus. It is ironic that one of the original charges against Dreyfus was that he had sold plans for the organization of the Madagascar expedition of 1894–5.

96. T.T. Matthews (trans.), 'Among the *Fahavalo*: perils and adventures of a prisoner for fourteen months in the rebel camp', *Antananarivo Annual*, VI (1897), 80–93.

97. Berthier papers: Penel to Laroche, 3–4 August 1896.

98. DAOM Mad. 6 (4) D 52: Besson to Gallieni, 10 February 1899.

99. Tronchon, *L'insurrection malgache*, p. 24.

100. The main protestant archives relating to the religious troubles are the LMS (London) and the Société des Missions Evangéliques (Paris). See also DAOM 6 (4) D 50–1. The Jesuit archives, which represent the catholic view, are surprisingly thin for this period.

101. Matthews, *Thirty Years*, 324.

102. Le Myre de Vilers papers, dossier 29: Gallieni to Le Myre de Vilers, *passim*.

103. Cf. G. Fenard, *Les indigènes fonctionnaires à Madagascar* (Paris, 1939), 239–40; H. Deschamps, *Les migrations intérieures à Madagascar* (Paris, 1959), 90; R. Archer, *Madagascar depuis 1972* (Paris, 1976), *passim*.

7. 'MBOKODO: SECURITY IN ANC CAMPS, 1961–1990'

1. Howard Barrell, review of Stephen Ellis and Tsepo Sechaba, *Comrades Against Apartheid: the ANC and the South African Communist Party in Exile* (James Currey, London and Indiana University Press, Bloomington, 1992) in *Journal of Southern African Studies,* 18 (1992), p. 857, n. 7.

2. Bandile Ketelo *et al.,* 'A Miscarriage of Democracy: the ANC Security Department in the 1984 Mutiny in *Umkhonto* in *Searchlight South Africa,* 5 (July 1990), pp. 35–65. The first known account of the mutiny had earlier appeared in *Africa Confidential,* Vol. 29, No. 24 (2 December 1988), then edited by the present author.

3. Real name Hermanus Gabriel Loots. Like most ANC members, Loots used a pseudonym or 'travelling name' while in exile. In the present text ANC members are referred to by the names by which they are best known, whether or not it is their original or real name.

4. 'Report: Commission of Inquiry into Recent Developments in the People's Republic of Angola' (Lusaka, 14 March 1984). Henceforth known as the Stuart Commission. Obtainable from ANC headquarters, Johannesburg. I am grateful to Carl Niehaus for supplying copies of this and other ANC reports.

5. 'Report of the Commission of Enquiry into Complaints by Former African National Congress Prisoners and Detainees' (August 1992). Henceforth known as the Skweyiya Commission.

6. 'Report of the Commission of Enquiry into Certain Allegations of Cruelty and Human Rights Abuse against ANC Prisoners and Detainees by ANC Members' (Johannesburg, 20 August 1993), pp. 53–4. Henceforth known as the Motsuenyane Commission.

7. See, for example, the interview with Chris Hani, member of the ANC's National Executive Committee and Secretary-General of the SACP, in *Work In Progress,* 92 (June 1992), pp. 18–20, in response to some of the allegations made by Ellis and Sechaba, *Comrades Against Apartheid.* On the debate inside the ANC over the constitution of the Skweyiya Commission, Paul Trewhela, 'The ANC Prison Camps: an Audit of Three Years, 1990–1993', *Searchlight South Africa,* 10 (April 1993), pp. 12–14.

8. Skweyiya Commission, p. 6.

9. See note 6 above.

10. 'Report on a Commission of Inquiry set up in November 1989 by the National Working Committee of the African National Congress to Investigate the Circumstances leading to the Death of Mzwakhe Ngwenya (also known as Thami Zulu or TZ)' (16 March 1990). Obtainable from ANC headquarters, Johannesburg.

11. Amnesty International, 'South Africa: Torture, Ill-Treatment and Executions in African National Congress Camps' (AFR 53/27/92, London, 2 December 1992). Obtainable from Amnesty International, London.

12. 'The Report of the Douglas Commission 1993' (January 1993). Obtainable from International Freedom Foundation, Johannesburg.

13. International Society for Human Rights, 'Human Rights and the African National Congress' (Frankfurt, 1993). Marc Gordon, an official of the International Freedom Foundation, was the ISHR's observer at the Motsuenyane Commission.

14. On the International Freedom Foundation, David Ivon, 'Touting for South Africa: International Freedom Foundation,' *Covert Action Information Bulletin,* 31 (1989), pp. 62–4.

15. Ronnie Kasrils, *Armed and Dangerous: My undercover struggle against apartheid* (Heinemann Educational, Oxford, 1993), p. 250.

16. Brian Sokutu, 'MK's toughest fight—keeping the troops happy', *Sunday Times* (Johannesburg), 12 September 1993.

17. Reported in. Trewhela, 'The ANC Prison Camps: an Audit of Three Years,' p. 17.

18. Stuart Commission, p. 24.

19. Mocsucnyant Commission, p. 25.

20. Kasrils, *Armed and Dangerous*, pp. 170–1.

21. Motsuenyane Commission, p. 26.

22. A biography of Sigxashe released by the SACP in December 1991 states that he joined the ANC in 1959 and the SACP in 1984. This last date appears to be a typographical error, as Sigxashe was certainly a Party member long before then.

23. Gerard Ludi and Blaar Grobelaar, *The Amazing Mr Fischer* (Nasionale Boekhandel, Johannesburg, 1966). Ludi was a police spy who infiltrated the SACP in the early 1960s.

24. 'Inside Quadro', *Searchlight South Africa*, 5 (July 1990), p. 31.

25. Jeremy Cronin, 'What Happened in Exile?', *Work in Progress*, 81 (March 1992), p. 35.

26. Kasrils, *Armed and Dangerous*, p. 253.

27. Ellis and Sechaba, *Comrades Against Apartheid*, p. 47, who mistakenly attribute the incident to the period before the Wankie campaign, rather than after.

28. Tom Lodge, *Black Politics in South Africa since 1945* (Longman, London, 1983), p. 300; Howard Barrell, *MK: the ANC's Armed Struggle* (Penguin, London, 1990), p. 20.

29. See Joe Slovo, 'J-B. Marks, Communist, Man of the People, Fighter for Freedom,' *The African Communist 95* (1983), pp. 88–9. This text, published in late 1983, seems to have had some influence on the attitude of ANC mutineers the following year.

30. Ellis and Sechaba, *Comrades Against Apartheid*, pp. 52–66.

31. Barrell, *MK: The ANC's Armed Struggle*, p. 19.

32. Stephen Davis, *Apartheid's Rebels* (Yale University Press, New Haven, 1987), p. 57.

33. Chief of Staff Siphiwe 'Gebuza' Nyande, quoted in Kaizer Nyatsumba, 'MK Registration Deadline', *The Star*, 15 September 1993, Jacklyn Cock, 'The Social Integration of the Demobilised Soldiers in Contemporary South Africa', *South African Defence Review*, 12 (1993), pp. 1–17

34. Stuart Commission, p. 24.

35. Affidavit of Joseph Tshepo Mamasela presented to the Harms Commission, 18 April 1990. Copy in the archives of the Independent Board of Inquiry, Johannesburg. Some background information on Mamasela, and corroboration of his testimony, is also contained in notes of interviews with former police captain Dirk Coetzee, contained in the same archive.

36. Ellis and Sechaba, *Comrades Against Apartheid*, pp. 116–8.

37. Ketelo *et al.*, 'Miscarriage of Democracy', pp. 38–42.

38. Ketelo *et al.*, 'Miscarriage of Democracy', p. 38.

39. Ketelo *et al.*, 'Miscarriage of Democracy', pp. 39–40.

40. Henry Pike, *A History of Communism in South Africa* (Christian Mission International of South Africa, 2nd edn., Germiston, 1988), p. 427.

41. Paul Trewhela, 'A Literature of Wolves', *Searchlight South Africa* 8 (January 1992), pp. 62–67.

42. Motsuenyane Commission, pp. 140–1.

43. Oyama Mabandla, '*Comrades Against Apartheid*: a Response by co-author Oyama Mabandla (Tsepo Sechaba) to a Review by Jeremy Cronin in *Work in Progress*, 811'.

Unpublished ms., October 1992. The journal *Work in Progress* declined to publish this rejoinder to Cronin in an acceptable form. Photocopies of this text are available on application to the author of the present article.

44. Mabandla, '*Comrades Against Apartheid*: a response by co-author Oyama Mabandla'. Cf. Kasrils, *Armed and Dangerous*, pp. 184–5.

45. Skweyiya Commission, pp. 24–5.

46. Skweyiya Commission, p. 36.

47. Ellis & Sechaba, *Comrades Against Apartheid*, p. 178.

48. Motsuenyane Commission, pp. 26–7.

49. Amnesty International, 'South Africa: Torture, Ill-Treatment and Executions in ANC Camps,' pp. 11–14.

50. '"The Enemy Hidden Under the Same Colour", statement by the Central Committee of the SACP on the activities of the "Gang of 8",' in *South African Communists Speak: Documents from the history of the South African Communist Party 1915–1980* (Inkululeko, London, 1981), pp. 400–17; Ellis & Sechaba, *Comrades Against Apartheid*, pp. 52–78.

51. Slovo, 'JB Marks', pp. 88–9.

52. Jobodwana Commission, esp. pp. 8–9.

53. Mabandla, '*Comrades Against Apartheid*: a response by co-author Oyama Mabandla'.

54. Author's interview with Jeremy Cronin, Johannesburg, March 1992.

55. See, for example, Kenneth Grundy, *The Militarization of South African Politics* (Oxford University Press, Oxford, 1988).

56. Among histories of the ANC, Francis Melt, *South Africa Belongs to Us* (James Currey, London, 1989) and Heidi Holland, *The Struggle: A History of the African National Congress* (George Braziller, New York, 1990), are highly partisan, P. Walshe, *The Rise of African Nationalism in South Africa: the African National Congress 1912–1952* (University of California Press, Berkeley and Los Angeles, 1971) is outdated.

57. Cf. William Cyrus Reed, 'International Politics and National Liberation: ZANU and the Politics of Contested Sovereignty in Zimbabwe', *African Studies Review*, 36, 2 (1993), pp. 31–59.

58. Trewhela, 'The ANC Prison Camps: an Audit of Three Years', pp. 12–14.

59. Skweyiya Commission, pp. 61–2.

60. Motsuenyane Commission, pp. 71 and 85.

61. African National Congress, 'African National Congress National Executive Committee's Response to the Motsuenyane Commission's Report', 29 August 1993.

62. Jacques Pauw and Shaun Johnson, 'MI Chief's Secret Parley', *The Star*, 27 August 1992.

63. Cf. Richard Carver, 'Zimbabwe: Drawing a Line Through the Past', *Journal of African Law,* 37, 1 (1993), pp. 69–81.

8. THE HISTORICAL SIGNIFICANCE OF SOUTH AFRICA'S THIRD FORCE

1. John Kane-Berman, *Political Violence in South Africa* (Johannesburg, South African Institute of Race Relations, 1993), pp. 15–27.

2. Morris Szeftel, 'Manoeuvres of War in South Africa', *Review of African Political Economy*, 51 (1991), pp. 63–76; Martin Murray, *The Revolution Deferred: the Painful Birth of Post-Apartheid South Africa* (London, Verso, 1994), esp. pp. 73–116.

3. Quoted in Rupert Taylor and Mark Shaw, 'The Dying Days of Apartheid', in Aletta Norval and David Howarth (eds), *South Africa in Transition: New Theoretical Perspectives* (London, Macmillan, forthcoming).

4. 'Interim Report on Criminal Political Violence by Elements within the South African Police, the KwaZulu Police and the Inkatha Freedom Party', by the Commission of Inquiry regarding the Prevention of Public Violence and Intimidation, 18 March 1994. Copy obtained from Human Rights Archive (HURISA), Sandton.

5. See, for example, Gavin Cawthra, *Policing South Africa: the South African Police and the Transition from Apartheid* (London, Zed Books, 1993); Herbert M. Howe, 'The South African Defence Force and Political Reform', *Journal of Modern African Studies*, 32, 1 (1994), pp. 29–51; Anthony Minnaar, Ian Liebenberg, Chari Schutte (eds), *The Hidden Hand: Covert Operations in South Africa* (Pretoria, Human Sciences Research Council, 1994); Annette Seegers, *The Military in the Making of Modern South Africa* (London, Tauris Academic Studies, 1996); Taylor and Shaw, 'The Dying Days of Apartheid'.

6. Allister Sparks, *Tomorrow is Another Country: the Inside Story of South Africa's Negotiated Revolution* (Struik Book Distributors, Sandton, 1994); Patti Waldmeir, *Anatomy of a Miracle: the End of Apartheid and the Birth of the New South Africa* (London, Viking, 1997).

7. Nelson Mandela, *Long Walk to Freedom* (London, Abacus, 1995), pp. 703, 705, 730.

8. See, for example, Timothy Sisk, *Democratization in South Africa: the Elusive Social Contract* (Princeton, Princeton University Press, 1995); Courtney Jung and Ian Shapiro, 'South Africa's Negotiated Transition: Democracy, Opposition and the New Constitutional Order', *Politics and Society*, 23, 3 (1995), pp. 269–308.

9. See, for example, Michael MacDonald, 'Power Politics in the New South Africa', *Journal of Southern African Studies*, 22, 2 (1996), pp. 221–233.

10. Thomas Hobbes, *Leviathan* (Harmondsworth, Pelican, edited by C.B. Macpherson, 1968), pp. 185–186.

11. State Archives, Pretoria: 'Strategie vir die bekamping van die revolusionere klimaat', appendix to minutes of State Security Council meeting 13/85 (SSC13/85): 26 August 1985.

12. Seegers, *The Military in the Making of Modern South Africa*, p. 185.

13. Brigadier C.A. Fraser, *Lessons Learnt from Past Revolutionary Wars*. This text received a restricted circulation in the SADF but was never published.

14. The ANC strategy, known as The Four Pillars of the Revolution, is perhaps most accessible in articles published in the ANC's official journal *Sechaba*. The best study is Howard Barrell, 'Conscripts to their Age: African National Congress Operational Strategy, 1976–1986' (University of Oxford, unpublished DPhil, 1991).

15. Quoted in *Pcircitus*, 25 September 1982. Article reprinted in Barry Streek, *South African Pressclips Supplement. South Africa's Intelligence Services, Part I* (Cape Town, mimeo, May 1991).

16. J.J. McCuen, *The Art of Counter-Revolutionary War: the Strategy of Counter-Insurgency* (London, Faber and Faber, 1966), p. 77.
17. Seegers, *The Military in the Making of Modern South Africa*, p. 125.
18. Joe Slovo, 'The Sabotage Campaign', *Dawn*, special anniversary issue [1986], p. 25.
19. Seegers, *The Military in the Making of Modern South Africa*, pp. 125–126.
20. Eschel Rhoodie, *P.W. Botha: the Last Betrayal* (Melville, SA Politics, 1989), is an essential, though partisan, source. For a more staid account, see Brian Pottinger, *The Imperial Presidency: P.W. Botha, the First Ten Years* (Johannesburg, Southern Book Publishers, 1988).
21. The official history of the SAP is Marius de W. Dippenaar, *The History of the South African Police, 1913–1988* (Silverton, Promedia, 1988). This may be read in conjunction with unofficial studies, such as Cawthra, *Policing South Africa*.
22. Ron Reid Daly, as told to Peter Stiff, *Selous Scouts: Top Secret War* (Alberton, Galago paperback edition, 1983), esp. pp. 175–181.
23. *Ibid*, p. 15.
24. Ken Flower, *Serving Secretly: Rhodesia into Zimbabwe, 1964–1981* (London, John Murray, 1987), p. 124.
25. Reid Daly, *Selous Scouts*, pp. 76, 478.
26. Colonel Eugene de Kock, interview with Phillip van Niekerk, Pretoria Central Prison, 3 March 1996. A brilliant film biography of De Kock is by Jacques Pauw. Entitled 'Prime Evil', it was first broadcast on South African Television on 21 October 1996.
27. Jim Hooper, *Beneath the Visiting Moon: Images of Combat in Southern Africa* (Lexington MA, Lexington Books, 1990), p. 110. A hostile view of Koevoet is Denis Herbstein and John Evenson, *The Devils are Among Us: the war for Namibia* (London, Zed Books, 1989), pp. 61–95.
28. Interview with Colonel Eugene de Kock by Phillip van Niekerk, Pretoria Central Prison, 3 March 1996. There is also abundant information in the records of De Kock's 1996 trial by the Pretoria Supreme Court.
29. Author's interviews with former members of CIO unit, Pretoria, May 1996. Also see Pauw, 'Prime Evil'. In 1996, the Pretoria Supreme Court convicted De Kock of 89 offences, including six murders.
30. Cawthra, *Policing South Africa*, p. 19.
31. *Ibid*, pp. 19, 27.
32. Patrick Laurence, *Death Squads: Apartheid's Secret Weapon* (London, Penguin Forum Series, 1990), pp. 63–69.
33. Works on the Broederbond include Ivor Wilkins and Hans Strydom, *The Super-Afrikaners: Inside the Afrikaner Broederbond* (Jonathan Ball, Johannesburg, 1978), and J.H.P. Serfontein, *Brotherhood of Power: an Expose of the Secret Afrikaner Broederbond* (London, Rex Collings, 1979).
34. C.A. Fraser, 'Revolutionary Warfare: Basic Principles of Counter-Insurgency', no place or date. Extracts from this work were translated into Afrikaans with a foreword by P.W. Botha and circulated to senior officials in 1986. See note 57, below. Extracts from the work of J.J. McCuen were similarly circulated among senior officials in abridged form.

35. Joseph Hanlon, *Beggar Your Neighbours: Apartheid Power in Southern Africa* (London, CIIR and James Currey, 1986).

36. Seegers, *The Military in the Making of Modern South Africa*, pp. 161–165.

37. Johan C.K. van der Merwe, 'Die Staatsveiligheidsraad: die Ontwikkeling van 'n Stelsel vir Veiligheidsbestuur in die Republiek van Suid-Afrika, 1972–1989' (unpublished PhD thesis, University of South Africa, 1990).

38. Deneys Coombe, 'The Trust Feed Killings', in Minnaar *et al.* (eds), *The Hidden Hand*, pp. 191–211.

39. Howard Barrell, 'The Turn to the Masses: the African National Congress's Strategic Review of 1978-79', *Journal of Southern African Studies,* 18, 1 (1992), pp. 46–92.

40. Confidential interview, 11 June 1997.

41. Minutes of SSC 4/84: 5 March 1984.

42. 'SA Defence Force Involvement in the Internal Security Situation in the Republic of South Africa', p. 24, unpublished document by South African National Defence Force, 1997.

43. Minutes of SSC 2/83: 7 February 1983.

44. Minutes of SSC 1/85: 21 January 1985.

45. Minutes of State Security Council (hereafter SSC) 5/85: 18 March 1985.

46. Minutes of SSC 6/85: 15 April 1985.

47. Confidential source.

48. Minutes of Extraordinary meeting of SSC, 18 July 1985.

49. *Ibid.*

50. Minutes of SSC 13/85: 26 August 1985.

51. The first such article in the file is Charles Nelson (of Thames Valley Police), 'Third Force: an International Police Association Scholarship Report', *Police Journal*, 53 (April 1980), pp. 138-146. SSC File 22/1/1/3/3, vol. I.

52. File 22/1/1/3/3, vol. 1, especially the report on behalf of the SADF by Brigadier B.A. Ferreira, 28 February 1986.

53. Minutes of SSC 7/86: 12 May 1986.

54. Author's interview with Colonel Eugene de Kock, Pretoria Central Prison, 4 May 1996.

55. Amnesty application by Major-Gen A.J.M. Joubert, May 1997.

56. Nicholas Haysom, *Mabangalala: the Rise of Right-wing Vigilantes in South Africa* (Occasional Paper No. 10, Centre for Applied Legal Studies, University of the Witwatersrand, Johannesburg, 1986). A book-length official report on the organisation of vigilantes is Major-General F.M.A. Steenkamp, 'Alternatiewe Strukture as Faktor in die Rewolusioriere Aanslag teen die RSA' (Pretoria, unpublished, South African Police HQ, February 1987).

57. C.A. Fraser, *Revolusionere Oorlogvoering: Grondbeginsels van Teeninsurgensie* (restricted circulation, 10 September 1986). This is an Afrikaans translation of extracts from Fraser's work referred to at note 34 above.

58. Fraser, *Lessons Learnt From Past Revolutionary Wars,* para. 33.

59. Sam Sole, 'The Hammer Unit and the Goniwe Murders', in Minnaar, Liebenberg and Schutte (eds), *The Hidden Hand*, pp. 277–286.

60. The documents in question were produced in evidence at the 1996 trial of Magnus Malan and others in Durban.
61. Confidential interview, 11 June 1997.
62. Seegers, *The Military in the Making of Modern South Africa*, p. 311.
63. Justice M.E. Kumleben, *Commission of Inquiry into the Alleged Smuggling of and Illegal Trade in Ivory and Rhinoceros Horn in South Africa* (Pretoria, State Printer, 1996).
64. Author's telephone interview with Major-Gen. A.J. van Deventer, Pretoria, 10 May 1996.
65. Adriaan Snyman, *Stem van 'n Profeet* (Mosselbaai, Hugenote Publikasies, 1993), p. 16.
66. Quoted in Waldmeir, *Anatomy of a Miracle*, p. 43.
67. For an acid portrait of Lieutenant-General Pieter van der Westhuizen, Chief of Staff (Intelligence) from 1978 to 1985, see Chester Crocker, *High Noon in Southern Africa: Making Peace in a Rough Neighbourhood* (Cape Town, Jonathan Ball, 1993), pp. 116–117.
68. Ina van der Linde, 'Die Manne Agter die Skerms Dink Na', *Vrye Weekblad*, 25 November 1993; author's interview with Major-General Chris Thirion, Pretoria, 7 May 1996.
69. Ros Reeve and Stephen Ellis, 'An Insider's Account of the South African Security Forces' Role in the Ivory Trade', *Journal of Contemporary African Studies*, 13, 2 (1995), p. 233.
70. Laurence, *Death Squads*, p. 68.
71. Quoted in Taylor and Shaw, 'The Dying Days of Apartheid'.
72. Mary Braid, 'Apartheid's Assassin Accuses P.W. Botha', *The Independent*, 18 September 1996.
73. This was part of the testimony of General Johan van der Merwe to the Truth and Reconciliation Commission. See 'Can PW Be Forced to Speak, or Pay?', *Weekly Mail and Guardian*, 25–31 October 1996.
74. Evidence of the corruption of the Brixton Murder and Robbery Squad was produced in court at the Pretoria trial of Charles Landman, former head of the unit, in 1996. Stefaans Brümmer, 'Tale of Top Cop's "Dicey Dealings"', *Weekly Mail and Guardian*, 6–12 December 1996.
75. De Wet Potgieter, 'Die Ferdi Bamard-Dossier', *Rapport*, 1 December 1996.
76. Mervyn Rees and Chris Day, *Muldergate* (Johannesburg, Macmillan South Africa, 1980).
77. Seegers, *The Military in the Making of Modern South Africa,* p. 286, note 16, remarks that the history of the Broederbond in the 1980s and 1990s is a subject in need of further study. See also 'Big Broeder Speaks', *NoseWeek,* 14 (March 1996), pp. 3–6. A rare study of the financial aspects of the total strategy, although it gives no attention to the role of the Broederbond, is Clive Scholtz, 'Drive Now and Pay Forever—the Apartheid Way', in R. Hengeveld and J. Rodenburg (eds), *Embargo: Apartheid's Oil Secrets Revealed* (Amsterdam, Amsterdam University Press, 1995), pp. 254–268.
78. Regter L.T.C. Harms, *Kommissie van Ondersoek na Sekere Moontlike Onreelmatighede. Hoofverslag* (Pretoria, Staatsdrukker, 1989). Vermaas, originally a lawyer to Department of Information chief Dr Eschel Rhoodie, was convicted by the Pretoria Supreme Court on 111 charges in December 1996.

79. Stephen Ellis, 'Africa and International Corruption. The Strange Case of South Africa and Seychelles', *African Affairs*, 95, 379 (1996), pp. 165–196.

80. De Wet Potgieter, *Contraband: South Africa and the International Trade in Ivory and Rhino Horn* (Cape Town, Queillerie, 1995), pp. 33–36, 178–182.

81. Sparks, *Tomorrow Is Another Country*, pp. 72–86.

82. Mandela, *Long Walk to Freedom*, pp. 609–668.

83. Author's interviews with Colonel Eugene de Kock and other members of Vlakplaas unit, Pretoria, May 1996.

84. Crocker, *High Noon in Southern Africa*, passim.

85. Wimpie de Klerk, *F. W. de Klerk, the Man in His Time* (Johannesburg, Jonathan Ball, 1991).

86. Author's confidential interview, Pretoria, 6 May 1996.

87. Sparks, *Tomorrow is Another Country*, pp. 72–73.

88. Confidential source.

89. Resolution of State Security Council meeting no. 13 of 1989, quoted in Sparks, *Tomorrow is Another Country*, p. 111. The original would have been in Afrikaans.

90. Robert d'A. Henderson, 'South African Intelligence Under De Klerk', *International Journal of Intelligence and Counterintelligence*, 8, 1 (1995), p. 60; author's interview with officer of SAPS, Johannesburg, 2 May 1996.

91. *Sechaba*, 24, 4 (1990), p. 18.

92. Anton du Plessis and Mike Hough (eds), *Selected Official South African Strategic Perceptions, 1989-1992* (Institute for Strategic Studies, University of Pretoria, *Ad hoc* publication no. 29, 1992), pp. 1–10.

93. Sparks, *Tomorrow is Another Country*, pp. 154–155.

94. Interview in *The Star*, 17 March 1990. A Broederbond document setting out a similar line of thinking is 'Basic Political Values for the Survival of the Afrikaner' [English translation], copy in Box 11.2, Institute voor Zuidelijk Afrika, Amsterdam. This document was first circulated for internal discussion in the Broederbond in 1986.

95. Hermann Giliomee and Lawrence Schlemmer, *From Apartheid to Nation-Building: Contemporary South African Debates* (Cape Town, Oxford University Press, 1989), p. 200.

96. Author's interview with Major-Gen. Tienie Groenewald, Pretoria, 19 May 1996.

97. Interview with Colonel Eugene de Kock by Phillip van Niekerk, Pretoria Central Prison, 18 February 1996.

98. Author's interview with Colonel Eugene de Kock, Pretoria Central Prison, 4 May 1996.

99. Author's interview with Peter Casselton, Pretoria, 19 May 1996.

100. On 32 Battalion, see Peta Thornycroft and Eddie Koch, '32 Battalion to Come Clean on Train Violence', *Weekly Mail and Guardian*, 29 November–5 December 1996; on Five Recce, see the testimony of Felix Ndimene, 'Confessions of an SADF Killer', *New Nation*, 26 July–1 August 1991, pp. 6–7. A chronology of the train violence is Independent Board of Inquiry, 'Blood on the Tracks: a Special Report on Train Attacks by the Independent Board of Inquiry', (Johannesburg, mimeo, undated).

101. Pauw, 'Prime Evil'.

102. Author's interview with General Johan van der Merwe, Pretoria, 21 May 1996.

103. 'Interim Report on Criminal Political Violence by Elements within the South African Police, the Kwazulu Police and the Inkatha Freedom Party', by the Commission of Inquiry regarding the Prevention of Public Violence and Intimidation, 18 March 1994. Available at HURISA, Sandton.

104. Kane-Berman, *Political Violence in South Africa*, p. 25.

105. On Operation Vula see Connie Braam, *Operatie Vula: Zuidafrikanen en Nederlanders in de Strijd Tegen Apartheid* (Amsterdam, Meulenhoff, 1992); also Robert d'A. Henderson, 'Operation Vula against Apartheid South Africa: a Case Study in Sub-State/Insurgent Intelligence Activities', awaiting publication.

106. Mark Shaw, 'South Africa's Other War: Understanding and Resolving Political Violence in Kwazulu-Natal (1985–?) and the PWV (1990–?)' (unpublished PhD thesis, University of the Witwatersrand, 1997), pp. 210–230.

107. Chris Hani, 'Just How Possible Is Peace?', *The African Communist,* 130 (1992), p. 8.

108. Anonymous, quoted in Waldmeir, *Anatomy of a Miracle,* p. 186.

109. *Ibid.,* p. 186.

110. Undated press clipping.

111. Author's interviews, Pretoria, May 1996.

112. Confidential source.

113. See articles by De Wet Potgieter in *Rapport,* 1 December 1996. Also see Pauw, 'Prime Evil'.

114. Sparks, *Tomorrow Is Another Country,* pp. 133–134.

115. Ronnie Kasrils, *Armed and Dangerous: My Undercover Struggle Against Apartheid* (Oxford, Heinemann, 1993), pp. 354–368.

116. Howe, 'The South African Defence Force and Political Reform', pp. 39–41.

117. Shaw, 'South Africa's Other War', pp. 210–230.

118. Jacques Pauw and Shaun Johnson, 'MI Chief's Secret Parley', *The Star*, 27 August 1992; Mark Shaw, 'Negotiating Defence for a New South Africa', in Jakkie Cilliers and Markus Reichardt (eds), *About Turn: the Transformation of the South African Military and Intelligence* (Halfway House, Institute for Defence Policy, n.d.), pp. 9–34.

119. Author's interview with General Constand Viljoen, Cape Town, 27 May 1996.

120. Phillip van Niekerk, 'De Vraag is Hoe Lang De Kock Zal Vastzitten', *De Volkskrant* [Amsterdam], 1 November 1996.

121. Ellis, 'Africa and International Corruption', pp. 170–178.

122. United Nations, 'Third Report of the International Commission of Inquiry (Rwanda)', 28 October 1996. Unpublished document.

123. South African Police Service, *Report on the Incidence of Serious Crime During 1995* (Pretoria, National Crime Information Management Centre, April 1996), p. 1.

124. Ineke van Kessel, '"Beyond Our Wildest Dreams": The United Democratic Front and the Transformation of South Africa' (unpublished PhD thesis, University of Leiden, 1995). This important work is to be published by the University of Virginia Press and the University of Natal Press.

125. Andre du Toit, *Understanding South African Political Violence: A New Problematic?* (Geneva, Discussion Paper no. 43, United Nations Research Institute for Social Development, 1993).

126. SAPS, *Report on the Incidence of Serious Crime During 1995,* pp. 31–32.

127. 'Ex-Policemen Crime Bosses, Says Mbeki', *The Mercury* [Durban], 15 July 1997.

128. Some interesting reflections on this are in Edward V. Badolato, 'International Crime Imperils South Africa's Security', *Counterterrorism and Security,* Fall/Winter 1995, pp. 25–30. The author is a former Deputy Assistant Secretary of the US Department of Energy.

129. Kumleben, *Commission of Inquiry into the Alleged Smuggling of and Illegal Trade in Ivory and Rhinoceros Horn;* Stephen Ellis, 'Of Elephants and Men: Politics and Nature Conservation in South Africa', *Journal of Southern African Studies,* 20, 1 (1994), pp. 53–70.

130. 'Surge in Gold Smuggling Robs Mines and Economy', *Business Day,* 9 May 1996.

131. On 'shadow states', see William Reno, *Corruption and State Politics in Sierra Leone* (Cambridge University Press, Cambridge, 1995). For a general view, Stephen Ellis, 'Africa After the Cold War: New Patterns of Government and Politics', *Development and Change,* 27, 1 (1996), pp. 1–28.

132. J. Michael Waller and Victor J. Yasmann, 'Russia's Great Criminal Revolution: the Role of the Security Services', *Journal of Contemporary Criminal Justice,* 11,4 (1995), pp. 277–297.

9. LIBERIA 1989–1994

1. Much of the information in this article was acquired during a field trip to Monrovia and Buchanan, Liberia, in July 1994. The article was drafted in August 1994 and takes no account of developments after that date. I am grateful to Fred van der Kraaij for his encouragement and for supplying literature from his own collection and to Binaifer Nowrojee and Jeanette Carter for their insights into Liberian politics, as well as to others who must remain anonymous.

2. Paul Richards, 'Rebellion in Liberia and Sierra Leone: a Crisis of Youth?', in O.W. Furley (ed.), Conflict in Africa (Tauris Academic Studies, London, 1995).

3. Leonard Brehun, *Liberia: the War of Horror* (Adwinsa Publications, Accra, 1991), p. 113.

4. For a short summary, see e.g. Yekutiel Gershoni, 'From ECOWAS to ECOMOG. The Liberian Crisis and the Struggle for Political Hegemony in West Africa', *Liberian Studies Journal,* XVIII, 1 (1993), pp. 21–43. Much of the following material was also widely reported in the international press in 1990. Leading sources include the Liberia Newsletter published by the Liberia Working Group in Bremen, Germany; the *Liberian Studies Journal,* which includes useful reprints of primary sources; and West Africa magazine. I am also grateful to Kofi Woods for making available back-numbers of Liberian newspapers.

5. Africa Watch, *Liberia: Flight from Terror: Testimony of Abuses in Nimba County* (New York, 1990). Reprinted in the *Liberian Studies Journal,* XV, 1 (1990), pp. 142–161.

6. Lawyers' Committee on Human Rights, *Liberia: a Promise Betrayed* (New York, 1986), p. 23.

7. Africa Watch, *Flight from Terror.*

8. Africa Watch, *Liberia: a Human Rights Disaster* (New York, 1990), p. 1. Reprinted in *Liberian Studies Journal,* XVI, 1 (1991), pp. 129–155.

9. Amnesty International, *Annual Report 1991* (London, 1991), entry on Liberia.

10. On Sanyang's role in the 1981 coup attempt, Arnold Hughes, 'The Attempted Gambian Coup d'État of 27 July 1981', in idem (ed), *The Gambia: Studies in Society and Politics* (African Studies Series No. 3, Centre of West African Studies, University of Birmingham 1991), pp. 92–106. This also documents the relationship between Liberian and Gambian radicals before 1980, notably on p. 96.

11. Author's interview, Monrovia, 24 July 1994; Barki Gbanaboma, '"Enfant terrible" Explains', *West Africa*, 4–10 May 1992, p. 756.

12. This fear was actually realised in an unexpected way: two coups, in Sierra Leone (1992) and Gambia (1994), have been successfully carried out by troops who had returned from peace-keeping service in Liberia.

13. E. John Inegbedion, 'ECOMOG in Comparative Perspective', in Timothy G. Shaw and Julius Emeka Okolo (eds.), *The Political Economy of Foreign Policy in ECOWAS* (Macmillan, London, 1994), pp. 218–244.

14. On this period, see Africa Watch, *Liberia: the Cycle of Abuse, Human Rights Violations since the November Ceasefire* (New York, 21 November 1991). Reprinted in Liberian Studies Journal, XVII, i (1992), pp. 128–164.

15. James Butty, 'What Does ULIMO Want?', *West Africa,* 7–13 September 1992, p. 1519.

16. Africa Watch, *Liberia: Waging War to Keep the Peace. The ECOMOG Intervention and Human Rights* (New York, June 1993). Reprinted in *Liberian Studies Journal*, XVIII, ii (1993), pp. 278–318.

17. William Reno, 'Foreign Firms and the Financing of Charles Taylor's NPFL', *Liberian Studies Journal*, XVIII, ii (1993), pp. 175–87, supplemented by author's interviews.

18. *The Harbel Area Massacres (at Carter Camp and Camp A). White Paper of the Interim Government of National Unity on the Matter* (Ministry of Foreign Affairs, Monrovia, 21 June (1993); 'Report of the Armed Forces of Liberia (AFL) on June 6, 1993, Carter Camp Massacre in Harbel', unpublished document, Ministry of Defence, Monrovia; 'The Carter Camp Massacre: Results of an Investigation by the Panel of Inquiry ... unpublished, United Nations, New York, 10 September 1993; 'AFL Reaction to the Wako Commission Report', submitted to the UN Secretary General by Lieut-Gen. J. Hezekiah Bowen, AFL Chief of Staff, unpublished.

19. 'Top AFL Man killed in LPC Area', *The Inquirer*, 25 May 1994.

20. The present author concluded on the basis of evidence available that the LPC was in fact a proxy force under the control of Krahn officers of the AFL. cf. Janet Fleischman, An Uncivil War', *Africa Report*, May–June 1993, pp. 56–9.

21. For census figures see Christopher Clapham, 'Liberia: Physical and Social Geography', *Africa South of the Sahara 1994* (Europa Publications, London, 1994), p. 492.

22. Some of the many excellent histories of Liberia include J. Gus Liebenow, *Liberia: the Quest for Democracy* (Indiana University Press, Bloomington, 1987); S. Byron Tarr and Elwood Dunn, *Liberia, a National Polity in Transition* (Scarecrow Press, Metuchen, New Jersey, and London, 1988); Amos Sawyer, *The Emergence of Autocracy in Liberia: Tragedy and Challenge* (Institute for Contemporary Studies, San Francisco, 1992).

23. Sawyer, *The Emergence of Autocracy*, p. 285.

24. Sawyer, *The Emergence of Autocracy*, p. 288.

25. Dunn and Tarr, *A National Polity*, pp. 125–6.

26. cf. H. Boima Fahnbulleh, 'Struggle for Democracy (2)', *West Africa*, 15–21 March 1993, pp. 418–420.

27. Amos Sawyer, *Effective Immediately: Dictatorship in Liberia 1980–1986: a Personal Perspective* (Liberia Working Group Paper No. 5, Liberia Working Group, Bremen, 1987), p. 5.

28. Sawyer, *Effective Immediately*, p. 5.

29. Sawyer, *Effective Immediately*, p. 8.

30. Sawyer, *Effective Immediately*, p. 8.

31. Sawyer, *Effective Immediately*, p. 4.

32. Dunn and Tarr, *A National Polity*, p. 97.

33. Above, note 6.

34. G.E. Saigbe Boley, *Liberia: the Rise and Fall of the First Republic* (Macmillan, London, 1983).

35. Tarr and Dunn, *A National Polity*, pp. 112–4.

36. Some interesting comments on Boley's career are to be found in S. Byron Tarr, 'Founding the Liberia Action Party', *Liberian Studies Journal*, XV, i (1990), pp. 13–47.

37. Sawyer, *Effective Immediately*, p. 6.

38. Sawyer, *Effective Immediately*, pp. 13–14.

39. Author's interview in Monrovia, 26 July 1994. Taylors's current companion, Agnes Reeves, is not his legal wife and is not to be confused with Quiwonkpa's kinswoman.

40. Augustine Konneh, 'Mandingo Integration in the Liberian Political Economy', *Liberian Studies Journal*, XVIII, i (1993), p. 55.

41. Lawyers' Committee for Human Rights, *Liberia: a Promise Betrayed*, esp. pp. 45–105.

42. Tarr and Dunn, *A National Polity*, pp. 112–4.

43. Brehun, *War of Horror*, p. 31. cf. 'Mandingoes: Who are They?', *Torchlight*, 28 July–3 August 1994.

44. S. Byron Tarr, 'The Ecomog Initiative' in, 'Liberia: a Liberian perspective', *Issue*, XXI, i-ii, 1993, pp. 78–9.

45. Press conference by Tom Woweiyu, Monrovia, 19 July 1994. Reproduced in *The News*, 22 July 1994.

46. 'Fahnbulleh on the Guns and the Actors', *New Democrat*, 21–27 July 1994. Text of a speech delivered at the University of Liberia on 1 July 1994 by H. Boirna Fahnbulleh.

47. Africa Watch, *A Human Rights Disaster*, p. 27.

48. Kwesi Yankah and Lazarus D Maayang, 'Charles Taylor: Dark Days in Ghana', *Uhuru* (Accra), 5 (1990), pp. 39–42. Much of this fascinating interview with a former cell-mate of Taylor in Accra was confirmed by my own interviews, including in March 1991 with a person who had been imprisoned with Taylor in Freetown.

49. Africa Watch, *Liberia: A Human. Rights Disaster*, pp. 5–11.

50. Tarr, 'The Ecomog Initiative', p. 78.

51. Reported in New Democrat, 23–29 June 1994.

52. Press conference by Tom Woweiyu, Monrovia, 19 July 1994. Reproduced in *The News*, 22 July 1994.

53. Professor NNK, 'The ULIMO Leadership Crisis: not a Krahn–Mandingo War', *Monrovia Daily News,* 29 June 1994.

54. This is based on the author's own observations in July 1994.

55. 'Split Mounts in the AFL', *New Democrat,* 28 July–3 August 1994.

56. 'NPFL on the Rampage', *The News,* 25 July 1994.

57. United Nations Security Council, *Third Progress Report of the Secretary General on the United Nations Observer Mission in Liberia* (S/1994/463, New York, 18 April 1994).

58. Cf. Stephen P. Reyna, *Wars without End: the Political Economy of a Precolonial African State* (University Press of New England, Hanover and London, 1990), for an interesting analysis of the mechanics of systems of this type.

59. Brehun, *War of Horror,* p. 89.

60. Interview with minister of the LNTG, 26 July 1994.

61. Interviews in Monrovia with refugees from Cape Mount County, 22 July 1994.

62. Interviews in Buchanan with refugees from Grand Bassa County, 29 July 1994; Human Rights Watch Africa, *Liberia: Human Rights Abuses by the Liberian Peace Council and the Need for International Oversight* (New York, 17 May 1994).

63. Reno, 'Foreign firms', p. 183.

64. Quoted in John H.T. Stewart, 'Taylor's Greater Liberia', *New Democrat,* 23–29 June 1994.

65. Author's interviews in Monrovia 26 July 1994, and Buchanan, 29 July 1994.

66. Sawyer, *Effective Immediately,* p. 5.

67. 'Libéria: trafics d'une guerre oubliée', *La Dépêche Internationale des Drogues,* 28 (Feb.,1994), pp. 6–7. I am grateful to Jean-François Bayart for this reference. Cf. the recollections of a former cell-mate of Charles Taylor, who recalls that '[Taylor] insisted that the major concern of African governments should be the prevention of domestic consumption of hard drugs. Once people are exporting such drugs from Africa, they should be allowed. He further stressed that we should think of cultivating coca and marijuana … as major exports. He was particularly peeved about the fact that African governments complain of lack of capital when they have the easy option of granting banking facilities to drug barons who have billions of dollars for laundering'. Yankah and Maayang, 'Charles Taylor: Dark Days in Ghana', p. 40.

68. Paul Gifford, *Christianity in Doe's Liberia* (Cambridge University Press, Cambridge, 1993).

69. A term favoured by Michel Foucault and used in regard to Africa notably by Jean-François Bayart, *L'État en Afrique: la politique du ventre* (Fayard, Paris, 1989), pp. 13–14.

70. Sawyer, *The Emergence of Autocracy,* pp. 43–60.

71. The following is based largely on Beryl L. Bellman, *The Language of Secrecy: Symbols and Metaphors in Poro Ritual* (Rutgers University Press, New Brunswick, 1984); and Kenneth Little, 'The Political Function of the Poro', part I, *Africa,* XXXV, iv (1965), pp. 349–365, and part II, *Africa,* XXXVI, i (1966), pp. 62–72. For a summary of the literature on the Poro society, Gunther Schröder, *Eine Verborgene Dimension Gesellschaftlicker Wirklichkeit* (Liberia Working Group Paper No. 6, Liberia Working Group, Bremen, 1988), pp. 3–12.

72. Schröder, *Eine Verborgene Dimension,* pp. 38–51.

73. Bellman, *The Language of Secrecy,* p. 8.

74. Quoted in Little, 'Poro', p. 355.

75. Liebenow, *Quest for Democracy*, p. 41.

76. Cf. Gunter Schröder and Dieter Seibel, *Ethnographic Survey of Southeastern Liberia: the Liberian Kran and the Sapo* (Liberian Studies Monograph Series No. 3, Liberian Studies Association in America, Newark, Delaware, 1974), pp. 82–88.

77. A distinguished exception to these remarks is Warren L. d'Azevedo, 'A Tribal Reaction to Nationalism', parts I–IV, in *Liberian Studies Journal* I, ii (1969), pp. 1–22; II, i (1969), pp. 43–63; II, ii (1970), pp. 99–115; III, i (1970–1), pp. 1–19.

78. Bellman, *The Language of Secrecy*, pp. 14, 17.

79. A documentary reference to this case is H. Boima Fahnbulleh, 'Struggle for Democracy (2)', *West Africa*, 15–21 March 1993, pp. 418–20. The fact that such an important case seems to have passed without mention in standard histories of the Tolbert period is itself testimony to the extent to which is aspect of Liberian political culture has been occulted in the past.

80. On the Gray Allison case, *West Africa*, 10–16 July 1989, p. 1150; 21–27 July 1989, p. 1397; 28 August–3 Sept. 1989, p. 1442. Other trials of ritual murder cases at the same period are reported in *West Africa*, 6–12 Feb. 1989, p. 206 and 24–30 July 1989, p. 1229.

81. Konneh, 'Mandingo Integration', p. 54.

82. Sawyer, *Effective Immediately*, p. 29.

83. Sawyer, *Effective Immediately*, p. 11.

84. Personal communication by Binaifer Nowrojee. On the symbolism of the Executive Mansion building, see John Momoh, 'Prized Edifice', *West Africa*, 25–31 March 1991, p. 439.

85. Tarr, 'The Ecomog Initiative', p. 77.

86. Konneh, 'Mandingo Integration', pp. 54–5.

87. cf. Brehun, *War of Horror*, pp. 27–8, 52–3, 90–1.

88. See *Neiu Democrat*, 23–29 June 1994.

89. Lawyers' Committee, *A Promise Betrayed*, pp. 50–62.

90. Quoted in Lawyers' Committee, *A Promise Betrayed*, p.58.

91. Some of these photos were published in *The Eye*, 28 April 1994. Other photographs from the same source, seen by the present author, were unpublished.

92. 'Catholics Frown on "Eating of Humans"', *The Inquirer*, 25 July 1994.

93. Schroder and Seibel, *Ethnographic Survey*, esp. pp. 34, 87.

94. Author's interviews with Liberian government minister, 26 July 1994. Cf. Brehun, *War of Horror*, pp. 1–2.

95. Cf. Gerrie ter Haar, *Spirit of Africa: the Healing Ministry of Archbishop Milingo of Zambia* (Hurst & Co., London, 1992), esp. pp. 97–164.

96. Liebenow, *Quest for Democracy*, p. 42.

97. Little, 'Poro', pt. I, pp. 350–1.

98. K.B. Wilson, 'Cults of Violence and Counter-Violence in Mozambique', *Journal of Southern African Studies*, XVIII, iii (1992), p. 554.

99. Bruce Berman and John Lonsdale, *Unhappy Valley: Conflict in Kenya and Africa* (James Currey, London, 1992), p. 215.

100. There exists a vast literature on this subject, but see especially Achille Mbembe, *Afriques Indociles. Christianisme, pouvoir et État en société postcoloniale* (Karthala, Paris, 1988).

101. See the interview with a child-fighter who, having been 'born again' in Christ, has 'taken an oath never to kill again. I'm now a complete born-again Christian and a child of God'. Charles Osagie-Usman, 'Mission of Revenge', *West Africa*, 7–13 February 1994, p. 205.

11. RELIGION AND POLITICS IN SUB-SAHARAN AFRICA

1. The popular works referred to in this article (such as those by Kaniaki and Mukendi, Pianim, and Okeke mentioned below) are taken from the authors' own private collections, having been bought in markets and shops in Africa. Even the excellent African Books Collective, the Oxford-based concern which distributes books outside Africa on behalf of some fifty leading African publishers, rarely handles the type of literature to which we refer.

2. For example, D.D. Kaniaki and Evangelist Mukendi, *Snatched from Satan's Claws: an amazing deliverance by Christ* (Nairobi, 1994) is published in both English and Kiswahili. This text will be discussed in more detail below. A related discussion on popular literature is Michael Schatzberg, 'Power, legitimacy and "democratisation" in Africa', *Africa*, 63, 4 (1993), 445–61.

3. For a spiritual journey in the form of modern literature, see e.g. Amos Tutuola, *My Life in the Bush of Ghosts* (London, 1954) and, more recently, Ben Okri, *The Famished Road* (London, 1991). A rare publication by a non-African with deep personal experience of the subject is Eric de Rosny, *Les Yeux de ma Chèvre* (Paris, 1981), which became a best-seller in Africa.

4. A pioneer in this field is Paul Gifford, whose work has inspired a growing interest among academics in the West. See Gifford, *The Religious Right in Southern Africa* (Harare, 1988); *Christianity and Politics in Doe's Liberia* (Cambridge, 1993); as well as two edited volumes, *New Dimensions in African Christianity* (Nairobi, 1992), and *The Christian Churches and the Democratisation of Africa* (Leiden, 1995). A number of African scholars have also written on this subject, particularly in Ghana and Nigeria, but have attracted less international attention. See e.g. Matthews Ojo, 'The growth of campus Christianity and charismatic movements in western Nigeria' Ph.D., University of London (1986); Ojo, 'Deeper life Christian Ministry: a case study of the charismatic movements in western Nigeria', *Journal of Religion in Africa*, 18 (1988), 141–62; and 'The contextual significance of the charismatic movements in independent Nigeria', *Africa*, 58 (1987), 175–92; Kingsley Larbi, 'The development of Ghanaian Pentecostalism: a study of the appropriations of the Christian gospel in twentieth century Ghana setting with special reference to the Christ Apostolic Church, the Church of Pentecost and the International Central Gospel Church', Ph.D., University of Edinburgh (1995).

5. See e.g. Abdou Touré and Yacouba Konaté, *Sacrifices dans la ville: le citadin chez le divin en Côte d'Ivoire* (Abidjan, 1990).

6. On recent transformations of Muslim societies, see Louis Brenner (ed.), *Muslim Identity and Social Change in Sub-Saharan Africa* (London, 1993), and Mervyn Hiskett, *The Course of Islam in Africa* (Edinburgh, 1995).

7. David Martin, *Tongues of Fire: the explosion of protestantism in Latin America* (Oxford, 1990), and David Westerlund (ed.), *Questioning the Secular State: the worldwide resurgence of religion in politics* (London, 1996).

8. For a comprehensive survey, see Robert H. Bates, V.Y. Mudimbe and Jean O'Barr (eds.), *Africa and the Disciplines* (Chicago and London, 1993).

9. E.g. Jeff Haynes, *Religion in Third World Politics* (Boulder, 1994); Leonardo A. Villalon, *Islamic Society and State Power in Senegal: disciples and citizens in Fatick* (Cambridge, 1995). A wide-ranging, although now rather dated, survey is Terence Ranger, 'Religious movements and politics in Sub-Saharan Africa', *African Studies Review*, 29, 2 (1986), 1–69.

10. E.g. T. O. Ranger and I. N. Kimambo (eds.), *The Historical Study of African Religion* (London, 1972); Françoise Raison-Jourde, *Bible et pouvoir à Madagascar au XIXe siècle* (Paris, 1991).

11. Jean-François Bayart, *L'État en Afrique: la politique du ventre* (Paris, 1989). Other relevant works from the same school include Jean-François Bayart, Achille Mbembe and Comi Toulabor, *Religion et modernité politique en Afrique noire* (Paris, 1993), and François Constantin and Christian Coulon (eds.), *Religion et transition démocratique en Afrique* (Paris, 1997).

12. World Bank, *Sub-Saharan Africa: from crisis to sustainable growth* (Washington DC, 1989), p. 60.

13. Two bibliographical surveys which include useful references to the literature on governance are Rob Buijtenhuijs and Elly Rijnierse, *Democratisation in Sub-Saharan Africa 1989–1992,* Research Reports no. 51, Afrik-studiecentrum (Leiden, 1993); Rob Buijtenhuijs and Céline Thiriot, *Democratization in Sub-Saharan Africa, 1989–1992* (Leiden, Bordeaux, 1995).

14. Sally Falk Moore, *Anthropology and Africa: changing perspectives on a changing scene* (Charlottesville and London, 1994), pp. 15–28.

15. An early example of this trend is John Peel, *Aladura, a Religious Movement Among the Yoruba* (London, 1968).

16. Influential examples are Jean Comaroff, *Body of Power, Spirit of Resistance: the culture and history of a South African people* (Chicago and London, 1985), and David Lan, *Guns and Rain: guerrillas and spirit mediums in Zimbabwe* (London, 1985).

17. E.g. Maurice Bloch, *From Blessing to Violence: history and ideology in the circumcision ritual of the Merina of Madagascar* (Cambridge, 1986); Richard Werbner, *Ritual Passage, Sacred Journey: the process and organisation of a religious movement* (Manchester, 1989); Jean and John Comaroff (eds.), *Modernity and its Malcontents: ritual and power in postcolonial Africa* (Chicago and London, 1993); Pascal Boyer (ed.), *Cognitive Aspects of Religious Symbolism* (Cambridge, 1993); Boyer, *The Naturalness of Religious Ideas: a cognitive theory of religion* (Berkeley, CA, 1994).

18. Cf. Jean and John Comaroff, *Of Revelation and Revolution: christianity, colonialism and consciousness in South Africa* (Chicago and London, 1991).

19. This definition of religion originates with Sir Edward Burnett Tylor (1832–1917).

20. Both quotations are from Robin Horton, *Patterns of Thought in Africa and the West: essays on magic, religion and science* (Cambridge, 1997), p. 306.

21. For a discussion of the role of religion in African philosophy, see e.g. Kwame Anthony Appiah, *In My Father's House: Africa in the philosophy of culture* (New York, 1992), pp. 107–36. That not all Africans are religious is made clear by Éloi Messi

Metogo, *Dieu peut-il mourir en Afrique? Essai sur l'indifférence religieuse et l'incroyance en Afrique noire* (Paris, 1997).

22. Reflections on the rise of new religious movements include Bennetta W. Jules-Rosette (ed.), *The New Religions of Africa* (Norwood, NJ, 1997); Rosalind Hackett (ed.), *New Religious Movements in Nigeria* (Lewiston, NY, 1987); Hackett, 'Revitalisations in African traditional religion', in Jacob Olupona (ed.), *African Traditional Religions in Contemporary Society* (New York, 1991), pp. 135–48; Hackett, 'African new religious movements', in Ursula King (ed.), *Turning Points in Religious Studies: essays in honour of Geoffrey Parrinder* (Edinburgh, 1990), pp. 192–200; Paul Gifford, 'Some recent developments in African Christianity', *African Affairs*, 93, 373 (1994), 513–34.

23. For a critique of the notion of fundamentalism, see Gerrie ter Haar, *Halfway to Paradise: African Christians in Europe* (Cardiff, 1998), ch. 9. We will follow some scholars of Islam in labelling modern exponents of political Islam as Islamists.

24. On the Moonie presence in Zaire and Angola, see 'Angola: oily enclave', *Africa Confidential*, 37, 1 (5 January 1996), 7.

25. Isak Niehaus, 'Witch-hunting and political legitimacy: continuity and change in Green Valley, Lebowa, 1930–91', *Africa*, 63, 4 (1993), 498–530.

26. D.D. Kaniaki and Evangelist Mukendi, *Snatched from Satan's Claws*, p. 38.

27. Ibid., p. 39.

28. Ibid., p. 41.

29. Ibid., p. 41.

30. Ibid., p. 42.

31. E.g. Wyatt MacGaffey, *Modern Kongo Prophets: religion in a plural society* (Bloomington, IN 1983), pp. 126–7.

32. Cf. Victoria Eto, *Exposition on Water Spirits* (Nigeria, 1988); Kathleen O'Brien Wicker, 'Mami water in African religion and spirituality', in Jacob K. Olupona and Charles H. Long (eds.), *African Spirituality* (forthcoming).

33. Ernest Pianim, *Ghana in Prophecy* (Kumasi, 1995). This view seems to be related to the recent migration of Ghanaians to Europe.

34. S.N.I. Okeke, *Satanic Minister: the ministries of Lucifer* (Lagos, 1991), p. 4.

35. *Africa Research Bulletin*, 33, 10 (1996), 12442a.

36. Yann Droz, 'Si Dieu veut ... ou suppôts de Satan? Incertitudes, millénarisme et sorcellerie chez les migrants kikuyu', *Cahiers des Études Africaines*, 37, 145 (1997), 85–117.

37. Martin, *Tongues of Fire*.

38. Hackett, 'Revitalisations in African traditional religion'.

39. Kenneth Little, 'The political function of the Poro', *Africa*, 35, 4 (1965), 349–65, and 36, 1 (1966), 62–72.

40. Donal B. Cruise O'Brien, *Saints and Politicians: essays in the organisation of a Senegalese peasant society* (Cambridge, 1975).

41. Lan, *Guns and Rain*.

42. Hugo Hinfelaar, *Bemba-Speaking Women of Zambia in a Century of Religious Change (1892–1992)* (Leiden, 1994).

43. Jacques Baulin, *La politique intérieure d'Houphouët-Boigny* (Paris, 1982), pp. 116–18.

44. Samba Diarra, *Les faux complots d'Houphouët-Boigny* (Paris, 1997), pp. 223–43.

45. Beatwell Chisala, *The Downfall of President Kaunda* (Lusaka, 1994), pp. 45–51.

46. Personal communication by Tiébilé Dramé, former minister of the Malian government.

47. Maurice Chabi, *Banqueroute, mode d'emploi: un marabout dans les griffes de la maffia béninoise* (Porto Novo, no date).

48. Personal communication by Solofo Randrianja, historian at the University of Tamatave.

49. Jean-François Bayart, 'L'Afrique invisible', *Politique internationale*, 70 (1995), 287–99. Claude Wauthier, 'L'étrange influence des franc-maçons en Afrique francophone', *Le Monde Diplomatique*, 522 (Sept. 1997), 6–7, mentions the competition between Rosicrucianism and Freemasonry for the allegiance of francophone heads of state.

50. This was widely reported in the Dutch press when the Mozambican government negotiated an arrangement with a TM foundation in the Netherlands.

51. On *radio trottoir* in general, Stephen Ellis, 'Tuning in to Pavement Radio', *African Affairs*, 88, 352 (1989), 321–30. For a specific case, Sabakinu Kivilu, 'Le radio-trottoir dans l'exercice du pouvoir politique au Zaïre', in B. Jewsiewicki and H. Moniot (eds.), *Dialoguer avec le léopard?* (Paris, 1988), pp. 179–193.

52. Robert B. Charlick, *Niger: personal rule and survival in the Sahel* (Boulder, 1991), pp. 69–70.

53. Camilla Strandsbjerg, 'Religion and the interpretation of political power: aspects of political thinking in Benin', paper presented at the conference on Religion and Politics in Africa and the Islamic World, University of Copenhagen, 1–3 Oct. 1997.

54. Gerrie ter Haar, *Spirit of Africa: the healing ministry of Archbishop Milingo of Zambia* (London, 1992), pp. 199–200.

55. Metena M'Nteba, 'Les conférences nationales africaines et la figure politique de l'évêque-président', *Zaïre-Afrique*, 276 (1993), 361–72.

56. Allen F. Roberts, 'L'authenticité, l'aliénation et l'homicide: une étude sur le processus social dans les zones rurales au Zaïre', in Jewsiewicki and Moniot, *Dialoguer avec le léopard?*, pp. 327–51.

57. Comi Toulabor, *Le Togo sous Eyadéma* (Paris, 1986), esp. pp. 105–31.

58. A good example is Simon Kimbangu, concerning whom see Marie-Louise Martin, *Kimbangu: an African prophet and his church* (Oxford, 1975). Karen E. Fields, *Revival and Rebellion in Colonial Central Africa* (Princeton, 1985) studies the reaction of colonial administrations to a range of spiritual movements.

59. Examples include the role of the Unification Church in Korea, the rise of the Religious Right in the United States and the establishment of an Islamic government in Iran.

60. This was the date of application of the first Structural Adjustment Programme, concerning Senegal.

61. For a statement of these norms, expressed by a leading theorist who was writing at precisely the time such institutions were being introduced in Africa, see Max Weber (ed. Max Rheinstein), *Max Weber on Law in Economy and Society* (Cambridge, MA, 1954).

62. W.J.F. Jenner, *The Tyranny of History: the roots of China's crisis* (London, 1992), pp. 198–200.

63. Jean-François Bayart, 'L'historicité de l'état importé', in J.F. Bayart (ed.), *La greffe de l'État* (Paris, 1996), pp. 11–39.

64. Alan Bullock and Oliver Stallybrass (eds.), *The Fontana Dictionary of Modern Thought* (London, 1977), p. 490.

65. Nietzsche, *The Will to Power*, quoted in *The Penguin Dictionary of Political Quotations* (Harmondsworth, 1986), p. 122.

66. Ineke van Kessel, '"From Confusion to Lusaka": the youth revolt in Sekhukhuneland', *Journal of Southern African Studies*, 19, 4 (1993), 593–614.

67. Peter Geschiere, *Sorcellerie et politique au Cameroun: la viande des autres* (Paris, 1995), pp. 125–63, describes how villagers may perceive national political problems as a form of witchcraft. For a discussion of the idea of spirit possession on a national scale, Gerrie ter Haar and Stephen Ellis, 'Spirit possession and healing in modern Zambia: an analysis of letters to Archbishop Milingo', *African Affairs*, 87, 347 (1988), 185–206. Paul Richards, *Fighting for the Rain Forest: war, youth and resources in Sierra Leone* (London and Portsmouth, NH, 1996), pp. xxiv–xxv, sees fear of cannibalism as a form of similar moral panic on a national scale.

68. A good example appears to be the Ugandan prophetess Alice Lakwena. Tim Allen, 'Understanding Alice: Uganda's Holy Spirit Movement in context', *Africa*, 61, 3 (1991), 370–99.

69. Jean-Pierre Diamani, 'L'humour politique au *Phare* du Zaïre', *Politique africaine*, 58 (1995), 151–7.

70. P.F. Bradford, D.J. Williams, Y. Pwol, C.H. Cheal and T.B. Dankwa, *The Christian Attitude: witchcraft and charms, drinking, cults, marxist socialism, sickness* (Achimota, Ghana, 1980), pp. 54–9, is a popular work which explicitly labels Rosicrucianism as a devilish cult.

71. Emmanuel Milingo, *Face to Face with the Devil* (Victoria, Australia 1991).

72. Emmanuel Milingo, *Plunging into Darkness* (Victoria, Australia 1993).

73. Geschiere, *Sorcellerie et politique*, pp. 125–40.

74. Ibid., pp. 20–1, and pp. 279–86. A further useful survey of the literature on witchcraft is Simeon Mesaki, 'The evolution and essence of witchcraft in pre-colonial African societies', *Transafrican Journal of History*, 24 (1995), 162–77. The originator of much of the vocabulary in use is Edward Evans-Pritchard, *Witchcraft, Oracles and Magic among the Azande* (1st edn 1937; reprint Oxford, 1977), pp. 8–12.

75. Cf. Arthur F. Kulah, *Theological Education in Liberia: problems and opportunities* (Lithonia, GA, 1994), esp. pp. 45–61.

76. ter Haar, *Spirit of Africa*.

77. K.B. Wilson, 'Cults of violence and counter-violence in Mozambique', *Journal of Southern African Studies*, 18, 3 (1992), 527–82. A general survey of traditional religion and warfare is Stephen L. Weigert, *Traditional Religion and Guerrilla Warfare in Modern Africa* (New York, 1996).

78. Malyn Newitt, *A History of Mozambique* (London, 1995), p. 576.

79. Bruce Berman and John Lonsdale, *Unhappy Valley: conflict in Kenya and Africa* (London, 1992), p. 215.

80. Gifford, *The Religious Right*.

81. H.A.S. Johnston, *The Fulani Empire of Sokoto* (London, 1967), pp. 26–102.

82. On exoticism in African studies, see Christian Coulon, 'L'exotisme peut-il être banal? L'expérience de *Politique africaine*', *Politique africaine*, 65 (1997), 77–95.

12. THE OCCULT DOES NOT EXIST

1. Until the 1970s, concepts such as 'magic' and 'primitive religion' were generally seen by scholars as unproblematic and of universal application within an evolutionary framework. In a classic work on British history, for example, Keith Thomas (1973: 52) specifically compares early modern England to Africa. For a discussion on the applicability of the term 'witchcraft' today, see the introductory chapter in ter Haar (2007).

2. In the social sciences, the most influential proponent of the idea that religion is something that binds people is Durkheim (1912).

13. WITCH-HUNTING IN CENTRAL MADAGASCAR 1828–1861

1. Alan Macfarlane, *Witchcraft in Tudor and Stuart England* (London, 1970); Keith Thomas, *Religion and the Decline of Magic: Studies in Popular Beliefs in Sixteenth- and Seventeenth-Century England* (London, 1971).

2. For example, Geoffrey Parrinder, *Witchcraft: European and African* (1958; London, 1963), esp. 128–9.

3. For example, Max Marwick (ed.), *Witchcraft and Sorcery* (London, 1970).

4. Mary Douglas (ed.), *Witchcraft Confessions and Accusations* (London, 1970), p. xx.

5. For example, Stuart Clark, *Thinking with Demons: The Idea of Witchcraft in Early Modern Europe* (Oxford, 1997); Stuart Clark (ed.), *Languages of Witchcraft: Narrative, Ideology and Meaning in Early Modern Culture* (Basingstoke, 2001).

6. The quotation is from Blair Rutherford, 'To Find an African Witch: Anthropology, Modernity and Witch-Finding in North-West Zimbabwe', *Critique of Anthropology*, xix (1999), 91. The most influential studies of the type criticized by Rutherford are Jean and John Comaroff (eds.), *Modernity and its Malcontents: Ritual and Power in Postcolonial Africa* (Chicago, 1993) and Peter Geschiere, *The Modernity of Witchcraft: Politics and the Occult in Postcolonial Africa* (Charlottesville, 1997), who gives a brief summary of the literature on Africa on pp. 215–23.

7. A definition in the tradition of the anthropologist E. B. Tylor.

8. Clifford Geertz, 'Religion as a Cultural System', in Michael Banton (ed.), *Anthropological Approaches to the Study of Religion* (London, 1966), 42.

9. Maia Green, 'Witchcraft Suppression Practices and Movements: Public Politics and the Logic of Purification', *Comparative Studies in Society and History*, xxxix (1997), 319.

10. South Africa–Netherlands Research Programme on Alternatives in Development, *Crossing Witchcraft Barriers in South Africa* (Utrecht and Turfloop, SA, n.d.), 2–3. This is the preliminary report of a project directed by S. T. Kgatla and G. ter Haar.

11. Malcolm Crick, *Explorations in Language and Meaning: Towards a Semantic Anthropology* (London, 1976), 112. This forms part of a discussion of 'witchcraft' on pp. 109–27.

12. Barry Hallen and J. O. Sodipo, *Knowledge, Belief and Witchcraft: Analytic Experiments in African Philosophy* (London, 1986), ch. 3.

13. Steven Feierman, 'African Histories and the Dissolution of World History', in R.H. Bates, V.Y. Mudimbe and Jean O'Barr (eds.), *Africa and the Disciplines: The Contributions of Research in Africa to the Social Sciences and Humanities* (Chicago, 1993), 178–9.

14. E.E. Evans-Pritchard, *Witchcraft, Oracles and Magic among the Azande* (Oxford, 1937), 9–10.

15. Marwick (ed.), *Witchcraft and Sorcery*, 11–14. A recent study of Sri Lanka speaks of 'sorcery', where Africanists would be more likely to refer to 'witchcraft': Bruce Kapferer, *The Feast of the Sorcerer: Practices of Consciousness and Power* (Chicago and London, 1997),

16. Mary Douglas, 'Sorcery Accusations Unleashed: The Lele Revisited, 1987', *Africa*, lxix (1999); Isak Niehaus, with Eliazaar Mohlala and Kally Shokane, *Witchcraft, Power and Politics: Exploring the Occult in the South African Lowveld* (London, 2001), 31–6.

17. Quoted in Rodney Needham, 'Polythetic Classification: Convergence and Consequences', *Man*, new ser., x (1975), 365.

18. William Ellis, *History of Madagascar*, 2 vols. (London, 1838), i, 461, has a fine drawing.

19. For a brief survey of historical references, see Raymond Decary, *Les Ordalies et sacrifices rituels chez les anciens malgaches* (Paris, 1959), 11–30.

20. J. Richardson, *A New Malagasy–English Dictionary* (1885; Farnborough, 1967), 444.

21. Pierre Verin, *Madagascar* (Paris, 1990), ch. 2.

22. See the journal of the Dutch ship *Barneveld*, 1719, in *Collection d'ouvrages anciens concernant Madagascar*, ed. Alfred and Guillaume Grandidier *et al.*, 9 vols. (Paris, 1903-20), v, 23.

23. The name Imerina originally designated a purely geographical area, and it may be that it was not applied to a political formation before the late eighteenth century: Pier Larson, 'Desperately Seeking the Merina (Central Madagascar): Reading Ethnonyms and their Semantic Fields in African Identity Histories', *Jl Southern African Studies*, xxii (1996).

24. Alain Delivre, *L'Histoire des rois d'Imerina: interpretation d'une tradition orale* (Paris, 1974), 188–90.

25. The best study of nineteenth-century Imerina, the most important polity in the island at that time, is Françoise Raison-Jourde, *Bible et pouvoir a Madagascar au XIX siecle* (Paris, 1991).

26. Ellis, *History of Madagascar*, i, ch. 17; J.J. Freeman and D. Johns, *A Narrative of the Persecution of the Christians in Madagascar* (London, 1840).

27. Recorded in the journal of Father M. Finaz, for the years 1855–7, Archives historiques de l'archevêché, Andohalo, Antananarivo, sér. 'Diaries', no. 20, 33–4. This archive includes Finaz's original diary, plus a manuscript copy by Father A. Boudou. Extensive extracts from Finaz's journal are published in C. de la Vaissiere, *Histoire de Madagascar, ses habitants et ses missionnaires*, 2 vols. (Paris, 1884).

28. Gwyn Campbell, 'The State and Pre-Colonial Demographic History: The Case of Nineteenth-Century Madagascar', *Jl African Hist.*, xxxii (1991), 419.

29. Ellis, *History of Madagascar*, i, 487.

30. C. Caillon-Filet, 'Jean Laborde et l'Océan Indien' (Univ. of Aix-en-Provence *thèse de 3ème cycle*, 1978), 287–94; C. Buet, *Six mois à Madagascar* (Paris, 1894), 262; G.S. Chapus and G. Mondain, 'Le Tanguin', *Bulletin de l'Académie malgache*, new ser., xxvii (1946), 176; book 3 of Rainandriamampandry's unpublished history 'Tantarany Madagascar', Archives de la République malgache (ARM), Antananarivo: Royal Archives, sér. SSI2, fo. 97.

31. Campbell, 'State and Pre-Colonial Demographic History', 437–9.

32. Ellis, *History of Madagascar*, i, 460. This is also mentioned in the leading nineteenth-century Malagasy source, *Histoire des rois d'Imerina*, ed. Francois Callet, trans. G.S. Chapus and E. Ratsimba, 5 vols. (Antananarivo, 1953–78), iii, 225–6, which indeed gives the recipe for the slaves' restorative. Subsequent references will use the title of the Malagasy original by which this work is best known, *Tantaran' ny Andriana* (1878–81). Volume and page numbers refer to the French translation.

33. The main collection is *Collection d'ouvrages anciens concernant Madagascar,* ed. Grandidier et al.

34. See esp. Étienne de Flacourt, *Histoire de la grande isle Madagascar*, ed. Claude Allibert (1658; Paris, 1995).

35. Raison-Jourde, however, notes that Flacourt, writing in the mid seventeenth century, could find many points of similarity between Malagasy society and his own, whereas the rise of a different type of state in Europe after his time made such understanding progressively more difficult: Raison-Jourde, *Bible et pouvoir à Madagascar*, 51, 52 (n. 1).

36. The best-known of which is *Tantaran' ny Andriana*. A guide is Delivré, *L'Histoire des rois d'Imerina*.

37. Flacourt, *Histoire de la grande isle Madagascar*, 153.

38. A French translation is Lucile Rabearimanana, 'Mystique et sorcellerie dans le manuscrit de l'ombiasy', *Omaly sy Anio,* i–ii (1975). A number of detailed descriptions and quotations from invocations used in the administration of the poison are contained in nineteenth-century publications; an example in English is Ellis, *History of Madagascar*, i, ch. 17.

39. Ravelonahina, quoted in Louis Chevalier, *Madagascar: populations et ressources* (Paris, 1952), 66. I am grateful to Solofo Randrianja for this reference.

40. Before the nineteenth century, literacy in Arabic script was limited to a tiny number of people who used it as an esoteric skill: see Ludvig Munthe, *La Tradition arabico-malgache vue à travers le manuscrit A-6 d'Oslo et d'autres manuscrits disponibles* (Antananarivo, 1982). Literacy in the Latin alphabet, coupled with a growing tendency to use writing for mundane purposes, spread from the early nineteenth century: Françoise Raison-Jourde, 'L'Échange inégale de la langue: la pénétration des techniques linguistiques dans une civilisation de l'oral (Imerina, debut du XIXe siècle)', *Annales E.S.C.,* xxxii (1977).

41. Mentioned, for example, by Flacourt, in his *Histoire de la grande isle Madagascar,* 184. On *hasina*, see Delivré, *L'Histoire des rois d'Imerina,* 140–71.

42. See Paul Ottino, *L'Étrangère intime: essai d'anthropologie de la civilisation de L'ancien Madagascar*, 2 vols. (Paris, 1986), i, 9–10.

43. Raison-Jourde, *Bible et pouvoir à Madagascar*, 84.

44. Françoise Raison-Jourde (ed.), *Les Souverains de Madagascar: l'histoire royale et ses résurgences contemporaines* (Paris, 1983), esp. 18–35.

45. Sovereigns were more often men than women. But, for most of the nineteenth century Imerina was ruled by queens, increasingly manipulated, after the coup of 1828, by a government dominated by military men.

46. Two excellent eyewitness descriptions of the same Sakalava king, Andriamaheininarivo—probably the most powerful ruler in Madagascar at that time—are by merchants of the Dutch East India Company. See the description by O.L. Hemmy (1741) in *Collection d'ouvrages anciens concernant Madagascar*, ed. Grandidier *et al.*, vi, 52–196, and the journal (*dagregister*) of the *Schuylenburg* (1752), the most accessible copy of which is in the Rijksarchief, The Hague, VOC 10814.

47. On the meaning of ethnicity in modern Africa, see Bruce J. Berman, 'Ethnicity, Patronage and the African State: The Politics of Uncivil Nationalism', *African Affairs*, xcvii (1998).

48. Hendrik Frappe, 'Korte Beschrijving van 't Eiland Madagascar of St Laurens aan de Westsijde', in National Library of South Africa, Cape Town, MS D 3, fo. 16.

49. James Sibree, *Madagascar before the Conquest* (London, 1896), 152–3. A description of Merina political culture in Andrianampoinimerina's time is in Raison-Jourde, *Bible et pouvoir à Madagascar*, chs. 1–2.

50. Cf. William Ellis, *Three Visits to Madagascar* (London, 1858), 78.

51. Maurice Bloch, *From Blessing to Violence: History and Ideology in the Circumcision Ritual of the Merina of Madagascar* (Cambridge, 1986), esp. chs. 7–8.

52. Pointed out by Ottino, and quoted in Allibert's edition of Flacourt, *Histoire de la grande isle Madagascar*, 498 (n. 6). See also Pierre Colin, *Aspects de l'âme malgache* (Paris, 1959), 25–8.

53. Frappe, 'Korte Beschrijving van 't Eiland Madagascar', fo. 19.

54. Raombana, *Histoires*, ed. Simon Ayache, 2 vols. (Fianarantsoa and Antananarivo, 1980–94), i, 155–83.

55. Gerald M. Berg, 'Writing Ideology: Ranavalona, the Ancestral Bureaucrat', *History in Africa*, xxii (1995), 73.

56. Charles Renel, *Les amulettes malgaches, ody et sampy*, special issue of *Bulletin de l'Académie malgache*, new ser., ii (1915), 63–70, 134.

57. *Ibid.*, 241–2.

58. Ellis, *History of Madagascar*, i, 397.

59. *Tantaran' ny Andriana*, iii, 102–4.

60. Raombana, *Histoires*, ed. Ayache, i, 233. The grammatical errors are reproduced here as in the original.

61. *Ibid.*, 149.

62. The trader Lebel, quoted in Pier M. Larson, *History and Memory in the Age of Enslavement: Becoming Merina in Highland Madagascar*, 1770–1822 (Portsmouth, Oxford and Cape Town, 2000), 97.

63. As reported by a French agent in Fort-Dauphin to the governor of Bourbon: Archives départementales, Ile de la Réunion, France, sér. 1 M 48c: de Roland to de Freycinet, 20 June 1822. On the same phenomenon on West Africa, see Rosalind Shaw, 'The Production of Witchcraft / Witchcraft as Production: Memory,

Modernity, and the Slave Trade in Sierra Leone', *Amer. Ethnologist*, xxiv (1997), 861–5.

64. Raison-Jourde, *Bible et pouvoir à Madagascar*, 106.

65. *Ibid.,* 189–91.

66. *Tantaran' ny Andriana*, iii, 206, 213–14, which also names some of these officers.

67. See Ellis, *History of Madagascar*, ii, 411–12, and Raombana, *Histoires,* ed. Ayache, ii, 253–63, for British and Malagasy accounts of some similar anecdotes.

68. Quoted in Decary, *Les ordalies et sacrifices rituels*, 15.

69. Raombana, *Histoires*, ed. Ayache, ii, 267.

70. *Boky Firaketana ny Fiteny sy ny Zavatra Malagasy* [Treasury of Malagasy Expressions and Things] (publication in instalments, Antananarivo, 1937–), entry on 'Andriamihaja'.

71. Larson, *History and Memory in the Age of Enslavement*, 223–4.

72. Raombana, *Histoires,* ed. Ayache, i, 47.

73. Georges Condominas, *Fokon'olona et collectivités rurales en Imerina* (Paris, 1960), 119–30, refers to the orders of Merina society as 'castes', although most anthropologists avoid the term.

74. Archives of the London Missionary Society (LMS), School of Oriental and African Studies, London: Incoming letters, box 2, folder 4, jacket D: Jones to Arundel, Antananarivo, 10 Sept. 1828.

75. This procedure is described in *Tantaran' ny Andriana,* iii, 217–26; for the 1829 episode, see ibid., v, 104–5.

76. *Boky Firaketana ny Fiteny sy ny Zavatra Malagasy*, 'Andriamihaja'.

77. Freeman and Johns, *Narrative of the Persecution of the Christians in Madagascar,* 17.

78. *Ibid.; Tantaran' ny Andriana*, v, 122–5; *Boky Firaketana ny Fiteny sy ny Zavatra Malagasy,* 'Andriamihaja'.

79. C. de la Vaissiere, *Vingt ans à Madagascar* (Paris, 1885), 123. The source is Jean Laborde.

80. Recorded in the journal of Finaz, for the years 1855–7 (see n. 27 above). The story of Rainiharo's family is in the copy by Boudou, 246. It is almost certain that Laborde was Finaz's source.

81. Rainandriamampandry, 'Tantarany Madagascar', ARM, Royal Archives, sér. SS12, fo. 97.

82. Bloch, *From Blessing to Violence*, 118.

83. Public Record Office, London, Foreign Office Papers, ser. 48, file 1: Johns to col. sec. Mauritius, 30 Oct. 1837, quoted in G.S. Chapus, 'Nouveaux documents sur l'époque de Radama 1er et Ranavalona 1ère', typescript copies of archives from London and Mauritius, Académie malgache, Antananarivo, AM 325, 289–92.

84. Raombana, 'Annales', 932–55, 1058–68 of original text (to be published, ed. Simon Ayache).

85. Manuscript by Raalbert, quoted in Chevalier, *Madagascar,* 66 (n. 2).

86. Listed in W.E. Cousins, *Fomba Malagasy* [Malagasy Customs], ed. H. Randzavola (1876; Antananarivo, 1955), 84–98.

87. See n. 32 above.

88. *Tantaran' ny Andriana*, iii, 102.

89. Ida Pfeiffer, *Voyage à Madagascar (avril-septembre 1857)* (1862; Paris, 1981), 150–1.

90. Finaz, original diary (see n. 27 above), 44.

91. For example, ARM, Royal Archives, sér. Ill CC 146: Rainimanga to Ranavalona I, 5 Adijady 1857.

92. This was based on my own rapid search in 1999, and is also confirmed by Françoise Raison-Jourde.

93. Campbell, 'State and Pre-Colonial Demographic History', 438, thinks otherwise, but I can see no evidence for this.

94. Finaz, original diary (see n. 27 above), 38–9.

95. *Ibid.*, 45.

96. *Ibid.*, entry for May 1857.

97. Karen Fields, 'Political Contingencies of Witchcraft in Colonial Central Africa: Culture and the State in Marxist Theory', *Canadian Jl African Studies, xvi* (1982), 586.

98. J.S. La Fontaine, *Speak of the Devil: Tales of Satanic Abuse in Contemporary England* (Cambridge, 1998), 14.

99. *Ibid.*, 180.

100. J. Arch Getty and Oleg V. Naumov, *The Road to Terror: Stalin and the Self-Destruction of the Bolshevikss 1932–1939* (New Haven, 1999), 7.

101. La Fontaine, *Speak of the Devil.*

102. Raison-Jourde, *Bible et pouvoir a Madagascar*, 106.

103. *Ibid.,* 289.

104. Christina Larner, *Witchcraft and Religion: The Politics of Popular Belief* (Oxford, 1984), 89–90, 124, 128.

105. Campbell, 'State and Pre-Colonial Demographic History'.

106. Peter Pels, 'The Magic of Africa: Reflections on a Western Commonplace', *African Studies Rev.,* xli (1998), 195.

107. LMS Journals 1/7: Griffiths, Jones, Canham entry for 16 Sept. 1823.

108. Raison-Jourde, *Bible et pouvoir à Madagascar*, 133–8.

109. Quoted in Bloch, *From Blessing to Violence*, 19.

110. Decary, *Les Ordalies et sacrifices rituels,* 24–7.

111. Quoted in Campbell, 'State and Pre-Colonial Demographic History', 437.

112. James Sibree, *The Great African Island* (London, 1880), 282.

113. Finaz, quoted in de la Vaissière, *Histoire de Madagascar*, i, 256.

114. Diaire d'Ambohidratrimo, entry for 14 June 1880, Archives historiques de l'archevêché, Andohalo, Antananarivo, sér. 'Diaires', no. 98.

115. H.H. Cousins, 'Tanghin, or the Poison Ordeal of Madagascar', *Antananarivo Annual*, v (1896), 387.

116. Maianjaona Rakotomalala, Sophie Blanchy and Françoise Raison-Jourde, *Madagascar: les ancêtres au quotidien* (Paris, 2001), 14–16.

117. Edmund Leach, quoted in Elizabeth Tonkin, 'Masks and Power', *Man*, new ser., xiv (1979), 247.

14. THE NEW FRONTIERS OF CRIME IN SOUTH AFRICA

1. 'South Africa: Drugs—Mandela's new struggle', *The Geopolitical Drug Dispatch,* No. 54 (April 1996), pp. 1–3.

2. Some observers regard the Sharpeville massacre of 1960 as the true beginning of the war. The South African Communist Party and the African National Congress, both of which had been banned by law, formed an armed wing, Umkhonto we Sizwe, which issued a formal declaration of war on 16 December 1961. On 27 April 1994, South Africa's first general election resulted in the election of a government with a majority from the ANC.

3. 'Surge in gold smuggling robs mines and economy', *Business Day,* 9 May 1996.

4. On 'shadow states', see Reno, 1995; for a general view, see Ellis, 1996b.

15. AFRICA AND INTERNATIONAL CORRUPTION

1. For some definitions, see Arnold J. Heidenheimer, Michael Johnston and Victor Levine (eds.), *Political Corruption: a Handbook* (Transaction Publishers, New Brunswick, 1989), pp. 3–68.

2. Robert Williams, *Political Corruption in Africa* (Gower, Aldershot, 1987). A useful periodical source is the journal *Corruption and Reform,* including a special number on Africa, 7, 3 (1992–3). On corruption and development, George Moody-Stuart, *A Good Business Guide to Bribery: Grand corruption in Third World development* (Transparency International, Berlin, 1994).

3. Jean-François Médard, 'L'État patrimonial en Afrique noire', in *États d'Afrique noire: formation, mécanismes et crise* (Kathala, Paris, 1987), pp. 323–53.

4. Richard Joseph, *Democracy and Prebendal Politics in Nigeria: The rise and fall of the Second Republic* (Cambridge University Press, Cambridge, 1987).

5. Stanislav Andreski, 'Kleptocracy as a System of Government in Africa', in Arnold J. Heidenheimer (ed.), *Political Corruption: readings in comparative analysis* (Holt, Rinehart and Winston, New York, 1970), pp. 346–57.

6. World Bank, *Sub-Saharan Africa: from crisis to sustainable growth* (Washington DC, 1989), p. 60.

7. Useful overviews of the literature on democratization in Africa, including some studies of governance, are Rob Buijtenhuijs and Elly Rijnierse, *Democratization in Sub-Saharan Africa, 1989–1992: an overview of the literature* (Research report 51, Afnka-studiecentrum, Leiden, 1993), and Rob Buijtenhuijs and Ciline Thiriot, *Democratization in Sub-Saharan Africa, 1992–1995: an overview of the literature* (Afrika-studiecentrum, Leiden, and Centre d'étude d'Afrique noire, Bordeaux, 1995).

8. A non-governmental organization established in Germany in 1993, Transparency International, studies international aspects of corruption in the third world. German Foundation for International Development, Accountability and Transparency in International Economic Development: the launching of transparency international (Zentralstelle für Wirtschafts- und Sozialentwicklung, Berlin, 1993). There is an abundant literature on illicit international business practices, money-laundering etc., in which Africa receives little attention since, in world terms, the African role in international business is small. See for example, Ingo Walter, *Secret Money* (Unwin, London, 2nd edn., 1989).

9. Jean Houbert, 'The Indian Ocean Creole Islands: Geo-Politics and Decolonization', *Journal of Modern African Studies*, 30, 3 (1992), pp. 465–84.

10. Jonathan Bloch & Patrick Fitzgerald, *British Intelligence and Covert Action* (Brandon, Dingle, Co. Kerry, 1983), pp. 196–9. Cf. Mancham's own account in James Mancham, *Paradise Raped* (Methuen, London, 1983).

11. Philippe Leymarie, *L'océan Indien: le nouveau coeur du monde* (Karthala, Paris, 1981).

12. Andri Oraison, 'Les avatars du BIOT (British Indian Ocean Territory). Le processus de l'implantation militaire américaine à Diego Garcia', *Annuaire des pays de l'océan Indien*, vol. VI (Editions du CNRS, Paris, and Presses universitaires d'Aix-Maraeilles, Aix-en- Provence, 1979), pp. 177–209.

13. Christopher Lee, *Seychelles: Political castaways* (Elm Tree Books, London, 1976), pp. 1–3.

14. Among several books on security in the Indian Ocean produced in the 1970s, see e.g. W.A.C. Adie, *Oil, Politics and Seapower: the Indian Ocean vortex* (Crane, Russak, New York, 1975). On the later period, Leymarie, *L'ocean Indien*.

15. Philip M. Allen, *Security and Nationalism in the Indian Ocean* (Westview Press, Boulder and London, 1987), p. 123.

16. 'An Indian Ocean Face-Off', *Newsweek*, 17 September 1984.

17. Affidavit dated 11 October 1986 submitted by G. Mario Ricci to the High Court of Justice of England and Wales, Queen's Bench Division, case of Giovanni Mario Ricci versus Paul Chow, 1986 R. No. 183: copy in the possession of the author. Also, François d'Aubert, *L'argent sale: enquête sur un krach retentissant* (Plon, Paris, 1993), pp. 155–65.

18. Gianfranco Turano, 'Promette il Paradiso', *Il Mondo,* 30 March–8 April 1991, pp. 75–9.

19. See Ricci's introduction to Claude Pavard, *Seychelles, from one island to another* (Editions Dellroisse, no place or date). Also *Indian Ocean Newsletter,* 7 March 1992.

20. Interview with Mario Ricci in *L'Espresso,* 27 January 1985.

21. Barrie Penrose and Simon Freeman, 'The Plotters in Room 412', *Sunday Times* (London), 24 October 1982.

22. Interview with President René in *The Indian Ocean Newsletter*, 6 and 13 September 1986.

23. *Seychelles Freedom Herald* No. 7, September 1985, p. 3.

24. Interview with President René in *The Indian Ocean Newsletter*, 6 and 13 September 1986.

25. Michael Gillard, 'Banking Ripples from Seychelles', *The Observer*, 18 July 1982.

26. Martin Bailey, 'Unchivalrous World of the Bogus Knights', *The Observer*, 15 March 1987.

27, *Indian Ocean Newsletter*, 19 July 1992.

28. Giuseppe Meroni, 'La Victoria degli Italiani', *Capital*, August 1986, pp. 72–5.

29. 'GMR Group in South Africa', company brochure, no date. Also, 'G.M.R. Group alle Seychelles: Programma di Vendita di Azioni e di Obbligazioni Convertibili,' company brochure, May 1981.

30. Obituary notice: 'Eschel Rhoodie', by Rex Gibson, *The Independent,* 28 July 1993. See also Mancham, *Paradise Raped.*

31. Mervyn Rees and Chris Day, *Muldergate* (Macmillan South Africa, Johannesburg, 1980).

32. Joseph Hanlon, *Beggar Your Neighbours: apartheid power in Southern Africa* (James Currey, London, 1986), pp. 7–16.

33. Shipping Research Bureau (R. Hengeveld & J. Rodenburg, eds.), *Embargo: apartheid's oil secrets revealed* (Amsterdam University Press, Amsterdam, 1995).

34. Mike Hoare, *The Seychelles Affair* (Corgi edition, London, 1987), pp. 1–108.

35. Joseph Lelyveld, 'New Role for Pretoria Army Intelligence Unit?', *International Herald Tribune*, 11 May 1982.

36. Hoare, *The Seychelles Affair*, p. 77.

37. White Paper on Aggression of November 25th 1981 against the Republic of Seychelles (Department of Information, Victoria, Seychelles, 1982).

38. Two memoirs of the incident are Hoare, *The Seychelles Affair*, and Jerry Puren (with Brian Pottinger), *Mercenary Commander* (Galago, Alberton, South Africa, 1986).

39. *The Independent*, 29 July 1992.

40. Author's interview with former Foreign Minister Maxime Ferrari, Paris, 22 April 1993.

41. Lelyveld, 'New Role for Pretoria Army Intelligence Unit?'

42. Arthur Gavshon, 'Seychelles Policies are Shifting to the West', *The Star*, 3 October 1983. This was confirmed by the author's own interviews with Seychellois officials.

43. 'Crackdown Seen as Part of Pik's New Diplomatic Drive', *Star*, 25 January 1984. Tony Stirling, 'Foiled Plot as "Double Agent" Claim, *The Citizen*, 9 December 1983.

44. Jacques Pauw, *In the Heart of the Whore* (Southern Book Publishers, Halfway House, South Africa, 1991), pp. 59–60.

45. Phillip van Niekerk, 'How We Bombed London', *The Observer,* 19 February 1995.

46. 'GMR Group in South Africa,' company brochure, no date.

47. Kitt Katzin, 'Ricci Exposé: the Inside Story', *Sunday Star,* 7 February 1988.

48. Kitt Katzin, 'Nat Superspy's Shadowy Boss,' *Sunday Star,* 19 April 1987.

49. Sarah Sussens, 'Superspy Williamson Turns to Sanctions.' *Sunday Tribune,* 30 November 1986.

50. *The Observer*, 26 April 1987.

51. Byline Africa News Feature Service, 11/S04/87.

52. Richard Dowden and Stephen Ellis, 'The Anatomy of a Conspiracy', *The Independent*, October 1987.

53. Phillip van Niekerk, 'How Apartheid Conned the West', *The Observer*, 16 July 1995. See also Longreach registration records: Company file 86 02070/07, Registrar of Companies, Pretoria.

54. Author's interview with Major Michael Irwin, Longreach Managing Director, London, July 1987.

55. Kitt Katzin, 'Superspy and the Jackal', *Sunday Star*, 28 February 1988; *idem*, 'Williamson Admits Tie to Mystery Mercenary,' *Sunday Star*, 6 March 1988.

56. Louise Flanagan, 'PW Knew of SADF Plan to Topple Sebe', *Weekly Mail*, 26 March to 1 April 1993. On the background, Jeff Peires, 'The Implosion of Transkei and Ciskei', *African Affairs*, 364, 91 (1992), pp. 365–87.

57. BBC Summary of World Broadcasts, 3 April 1991.

58. Sam Sole, 'Former PW Man in Rwanda Arms Link', *Sunday Tribune*, 3 July 1994.

59. *Indian Ocean Newsletter*, 16 July 1994.

60. File number 86/02890/07, GMR Group South Africa (pty) Ltd., Registrar of Companies, Pretoria.

61. Human Rights Watch Arms Project, *Rwanda/Zaire: Rearming with impunity* (Vol. 7, no. 4, Washington and New York, May 1995). Stefaans Brümmer, 'SA's Arms-Dealing Underworld', *Weekly Mail & Guardian*, 2–8 June 1995.

62. A subject recently investigated by a judicial commission of inquiry in South Africa, the Cameron Commission.

63. Stephen Ellis, 'Of Elephants and Men: Politics and nature conservation in South Africa', *Journal of Southern African Studies*, 20, 1 (1994), pp. 53–70.

64. Environmental Investigation Agency, *Under Fire: Elephants in the front line* (London, 1992), p. 35.

65. Van Niekerk, 'How Apartheid Conned the West'.

66. Kitt Katzin, 'The R 100-m Puzzle: Who is Backing Chieftain Airlines?', *Sunday Star*, undated clipping. On Chieftain Airlines, see Kommissie van Ondersoek ita Sekere Moonthke Oreëlmatighede, Hoqfverslag, Sy Edele Regter L.T.C. Harms (Staatsdrukker, Pretoria, 1989). Henceforth called the Harms Commission.

67. Samantha Weinberg, *Last of the Pirates: the search for Bob Denard* (Jonathan Cape, London, 1994), pp. 108–9. For background, see W. Andrew Terrill, 'The Comoro Islands in South African Regional Strategy', *Africa Today*, 33, 2–3 (1986), pp. 59–70.

68. Annette Seegers, 'South Africa's National Security Management System, 1972–90', *Journal of Modern African Studies*, 29, 2 (1991), pp. 253–73.

69. Ros Reeve and Stephen Ellis, 'An Insider's Account of the South African Security Forces' Role in the Ivory Trade', *Journal of Contemporary African Studies*, 13, 2 (1995), esp. pp. 231–3.

70. Rees and Day, *Muldergate*.

71. Harms Commission.

72. 'A Cute Little Bankhaus in Bisho', *Noseweek*, 9 (Sept, 1994), pp. 4–6. On Palazzolo, Ralph Blumenthal, *Last Days of the Sicilians* (Times Books, New York, 1988), esp. p. 316.

73. On the use of SADF front companies for political purposes in the homelands, Peires, 'The Implosion of Transkei and Ciskei'.

74. Shipping Research Bureau, *Embargo*, pp. 77–84.

75. 'Dr Rhoodie 'Talks about "South Africa's Biggest Secret"', *Noseweek*, July 1993, p. 5.

76. Reeve and Ellis, 'An Insider's Account of the South African Security Forces' Role in the Ivory Trade', p. 232.

77. Gianfrancesco Turano, 'Quells Banca d'Altura', *Il Morula*, 30 March–8 April 1991; d'Aubert, *L'argent sale*, p. 162.

78. Martin Short, *Inside the Brotherhood* (Grafton Books, London, 1990), pp. 160–2, 537–63.

79. Alexander Stille, *Excellent Cadavers: the Mafia and the death of the First Italian Republic* (Jonathan Cape, London, 1995), esp. pp. 11–12.

80. Jan van der Putten, 'Italiaans Staatsoliebedrijf Kampioen Smeergeldbetaler,' *De Volksrant*, 18 February 1993.

81. Jean-François Médard, 'Les relations Nord-Sud: l'Afrique, les démocracies occidentales, et la corruption', *Revue Internationale des sciences sociales* (UNESCO, Paris, Sept, 1996), forthcoming.

82. Charles Raw, *The Money-Changers* (Harvill, London, 1992), p. 4.

83. Commissione Parlamentare d'Inchiesta sulla Loggia Massonica P2, *Allegaa Alla Relazione*, serie II (Vol. II, Rome, 1984), pp. 586–92.

84. Jonathan Kwitny's stories on Pazienza in *The Wall Street Journal*, 8 August 1985, and 9 August 1985. See also Larry Gurwin, *The Calvi Affair* (Pan, London, 1983), p. 191.

85. Raw, *The Money-Changers*, pp. 322–6.

86. Kwitny, *The Wall Street Journal*. See also the interview with Pazienza in *Oggi*, 5 June 1985; *Seychelles Freedom Herald*, August 1985. Supplemented by author's telephone interviews with Pazienza.

87. Kwitny, *The Wall Street Journal*.

88. On Fiorini, see d'Aubert, *L'argent sale*, pp. 97–167.

89. Gurwin, *The Cahn Affair*, pp. 60–1, 131.

90. A good short description of SASEA is in two articles by Larry Gurwin & M. Bakker, 'Waarom Hangt er zo'n Vieze Lucht rond Sasea?', *FEM: Financial Economisch Magazine*, 11–19 May 1990; and 'Italiaans Ovemarae-Duo Botst met Beurzen', *FEM*, 20–28 May 1990.

91. D'Aubert, *L'argent sale*, p. 132.

92. D'Aubert, *L'argent sale*, pp. 123–51.

93. Florio Fiorini, Ricordàn … da Lontano (Videopool, Milano, 1993), pp. 119–23.

94. D'Aubert, *L'argent sale*, pp. 152–5.

95. *Seychelles Freedom Herald*, August 1985.

96. *The Observer*, 26 April 1987.

97. Author's confidential interview, November 1988.

98. Larry Gurwin, personal communication.

99. 'Flying in the Face of Sanctions', *Africa Analysis*, October 1987. List of LAS shareholders in the author's possession.

100. D'Aubert, *L'argent sale*, pp. 151, 154.

101. On Parretti, Edward Jay Epstein, 'The Mystery of the Instant Mogul', *Spy*, June 1990, pp. 85–93.

102. Assemblée Nationale, *Rapport de la commission d'enquête sur le Crédit Lyonnais* (2 vols., Rapport no. 1480, Paris, 1994), I, pp. 71–86.

103. Assemblée Nationale, *Rapport de la commission d'enquête sur le Crédit Lyonnais*.

104. D'Aubert, *L'argent sale*.

105. Assemble Nationale, *Rapport de la commission d'enquête sur le Crédit Lyonnais*, I, p. 82.

106. D'Aubert, *L'argent sale*, pp. 416–8.

107. *The Geopolitical Drug Dispatch*, No 48 (October 1995), p. 8.

108. Assemblée Nationale, *Rapport de la Commission d'enquête sur le Crédit Lyonnais*, I, 23, 71–86.

109. Joseph Persico, *Casey: from the OSS to the CIA* (Viking, New York, 1990), p. 575.

110. 'Contra Links Go Unnoticed,' *Southscan*, 15 October 1987; Bob Woodward, *Veil: The secret wars of the CIA, 1981–1987* (Pocket Books, New York, 1987), p. 300; Steven Emerson, *Secret Warriors: inside the covert military operations of the Reagan era* (G.P. Putnam's Sons, New York, 1987), p. 222.

111. Author's confidential interview, Chicago, November 1988. See also correspondence between Peter Teeley and David Macdonald and Mario Ricci obtained from US Justice Department under the Foreign Agents' Registration Act.

112. David R. Macdonald to President René, 8 March 1985, obtained from US Justice Department.

113. Correspondence between Peter Teeley and David Macdonald and Mario Ricci obtained from US Justice Department. Supplemented by author's confidential interview, Chicago, November 1988.

114. On the WACL, Scott Anderson and Jon Lee Anderson, *Inside the League* (Dodd, Mead & Co., New York, 1986).

115. Kenneth Timmerman, *The Death Lobby: how the West armed Iraq* (Bantam, London, 1992), pp. 227–30.

116. Amnesty International, *Seychelles: Political Imprisonment and Allegations Regarding the 'Disappearance' or Extrajudicial Execution of Suspected Opponents of the Government* (AFR 50/02/85, London, 1985).

117. Notably in his newsletter, *Seychelles Freedom Herald*.

118. Author's phone interview with Ambassador David Fischer, February 1993. Also author's interview with Maxime Ferrari, Paris, 22 April 1993.

119. 'Mombasa Promises to Drive out the Mafia', *The Times* (London), 16 March 1987; 'Minister Warns Hotels on Mafia', *Sunday Times* (Kenya), 29 March 1987. I am grateful to Martin Short for providing further background information on this case.

120. *Indian Ocean Newsletter*, 7 March 1992.

121. *Indian Ocean Newsletter*, 14 January 1995.

122. *Indian Ocean Newsletter*, 7 March 1992; d'Aubert, *L'argent sale*, pp. 148–51.

123. *Indian Ocean Newsletter*, 18 November 1995.

124. Quoted in 'Revealed: Paradise for Crooks', *Sunday Times* (London), 14 January 1996.

125. Stille, *Excellent Cadavers*, pp. 9–10.

126. Ellis, 'Of Elephants and Men'.

127. 'Weapons for Sale', *The Economist*, 29 July 1995, and material published in the South African press concerning Executive Outcomes Lid.

128. Stille, *Excellent Cadavers*; Alfred W. McCoy, *The Politics of Heroin: CIA complicity in the global drug trade* (Lawrence Hill, New York, 1991).

129. Roy Pateman, 'Intelligence Agencies in Africa—a Preliminary Assessment', *Journal of Modern African Studies*, 30, 4 (1992), pp. 569–85. On South Africa, Robert d'A. Henderson, 'South African Intelligence under de Klerk', *International Journal of Intelligence and Counter Intelligence*, 8, 1 (1995), pp. 51–89.

130. Stephen Smith and Antoine Glaser, *Ces Messieurs Afrique* (Calmann Livy, Paris, 1992).

131. United States Department of State, Bureau for International Narcotics and Law Enforcement Affairs, *International Narcotics Control Strategy Report* (Washington DC, March 1995).

132. D'Aubert, *L'argent sale*, p. 545.

133. The Centre d'études des recherches internationales, Paris, represented by Jean-François Bayart and Béatrice Hibou, and the Afnka-studiecentrum, Leiden, represented by myself, are currently carrying out a project on the Criminalization of the State in Africa.

134. Peter Truell and Larry Gurwin, *False Profits: the inside story of BCCI, the world's most corrupt financial empire* (Houghton Mifflin, New York, 1992).

16. THIS PRESENT DARKNESS

1. *Opgelicht,* TROS-TV, Nederland 1, 9 May, 3 October 2006.
2. Ibid.
3. *The Times* [London], 21 July 2005, p. 40.
4. BBC News, 'Spain Holds Lottery Scam Suspects', 17 April 2008.
5. IPOL, *Nationaal Dreigingsbeeld 2012: Georganiseerde criminaliteit* (Dienst IPOL, Zoetermeer, 2012), p. 139.
6. Quoted in Henry Louis Gates, 'Powell and The Black Elite', *The New Yorker,* 25 September 1995.
7. There is no generally accepted definition of organised crime: Nikos Passas, 'Introduction', pp. xiii–xix, *Organized Crime* (Dartmouth Publishing Co., Aldershot, 1995). See Chapter Eleven for further discussion.
8. National Archives of Nigeria [NAN], Ibadan, Oyo Prof. 1, 4113: 'Crime and its Treatment'; report to the Governor by Alexander Paterson, February 1944.
9. http: / /archiveswiki.historians. org/index.php /National_Archives_of_ Nigeria [accessed 26 July 2015].
10. http://www.archives.gov/dc-metro/college-park/
11. http://www.nationalarchives.gov.uk/
12. Ogechi Ekeanyanwu, 'Zungeru, Town of Amalgamation, in Shambles', *Premium Times,* 16 March 2013, http://www.premiumtimesng.com/arts- entertainment/125291- zungeru-town-of-amalgamation-in-shambles.html [accessed 1 May 2015].
13. Helen Callaway and Dorothy O. Helly, 'Crusader for Empire: Flora Shaw/ Lady Lugard', in Nupur Chaudhuri and Margaret Strobel (eds), *Western Women and Imperialism: Complicity and Resistance* (Indiana University Press, Bloomington and Indianapolis, 1992), pp. 79–97.
14. Written as Ibo in older texts.
15. 'Introduction', in A.H.M. Kirk-Greene (ed.), *Lugard and the Amalgamation of Nigeria: A Documentary Record* (Frank Cass, London, 1968), p. 27. A recording of Lugard's amalgamation speech may be heard at https:// www.youtube.com/ watch?v=C5Xom7T6-yU [accessed 13 May 2015].
16. Quoted in Henry L. Bretton, *Power and Stability in Nigeria:The Politics of Decolonization* (Frederick A. Praeger, NewYork, 1962), p. 127.
17. Quoted in James Booth, *Writers and Politics in Nigeria* (Hodder & Stoughton, London, 1981), p. 23.
18. Attributed to Sir Ahmadu Bello.
19. I.F. Nicolson, *The Administration of Nigeria 1900–1960: Men, Methods and Myths* (Clarendon Press, Oxford, 1969), p. 8.
20. Sir F.D. Lugard, 'Report on the Amalgamation of Northern and Southern Nigeria', in A.H.M. Kirk-Greene (ed.), *Lugard and the Amalgamation of Nigeria*, p. 67.
21. Ibid.
22. Ibid.
23. G.H. Findlay, report on the reorganisation of the Colony, 1927, cited by L.C. Gwam in his catalogue to the colonial archives at the National Archives of Nigeria, Ibadan.
24. John Iliffe, *Honour in African History* (Cambridge University Press, 2005), p. 121.
25. Lugard, 'Report on the Amalgamation of Northern and Southern Nigeria', p. 68.

26. Ibid., p. 67.

27. Ibid., pp. 68–9.

28. Margery Perham, *Native Administration in Nigeria* (1937; 2nd impression, Oxford University Press, 1962), pp. 73–4.

29. Ibid., p. 43.

30. Robin Horton 'Stateless Societies in the History of West Africa', in J.F. Ade Ajayi and Michael Crowder (eds), *History of West Africa* (2 vols, Harlow 1985), I, p. 87.

31. Lugard, 'Report on the Amalgamation of Northern and Southern Nigeria', p. 72.

32. Sir Bernard Bourdillon, *Memorandum on the Future Political Development of Nigeria* ('confidential', Government Printer, Lagos, 1939), p. 4. Copy in the National Archives of Nigeria, Ibadan, at MN/B4A.

33. Frederick Lugard, *The Dual Mandate in British Tropical Africa* (1922; 5th edn, Frank Cass, London 1965).

34. Michael Crowder, 'Indirect Rule: French and British Style', *Africa,* 34, 3 (1964), pp. 197–205.

35. Hubert Deschamps, 'Et maintenant, Lord Lugard?', *Africa,* 33, 4 (1963), pp. 293-306.

36. William Malcolm Hailey, *An African Survey* (Oxford University Press, London, 1938), p. 272.

37. Ibid., p. 273.

38. Remi Brague (trans. Lydia G. Cochrane), *The Law of God: The Philosophical History of an Idea* (University of Chicago Press, Chicago and London, 2007).

39. Obafemi Awolowo, *Awo: The Autobiography of Chief Obafemi Awolowo* (Cambridge University Press, 1960), p. 12.

40. Simeon O. Eboh, 'Law and Order in the Society: The Nigerian Experience', *The Nigerian Journal of Theology,* 18 (2004), p. 23.

41. Ibid., p. 24.

42. Biko Agozino, 'Crime, Criminology and Post-Colonial Theory: Criminological Reflections on West Africa', in James Sheptycki and Ali Wardak (eds), *Transnational and Comparative Criminology* (Glasshouse Press, London), p. 125.

43. Lugard to Lady Lugard, 13 Nov. 1912, quoted in Kirk-Greene, 'Introduction', p. 13.

44. Stephen Ellis and Gerrie ter Haar, *Worlds of Power: Religious Thought and Political Practice in Africa* (Hurst & Co., London, 2004), p. 14.

45. Marcel Gauchet (trans. Oscar Burge), *The Disenchantment of the World: A Political History of Religion* (Princeton University Press, Princeton, NJ, 1999).

46. Awolowo, *Awo*, pp. 8–9.

47. Frank Hives and Gascoine Lumley, *Ju-Ju and Justice in Nigeria* (1930; Penguin edn., Harmondsworth, 1940), p. 111.

48. Obafemi Awolowo, *The Path to Nigerian Freedom* (Faber & Faber, London, 1947), p. 97.

49. Ibid.

50. Perham, *Native Administration in Nigeria*, p. 71.

51. Ibid, p. 76.

52. Iliffe, *Honour in African History*, p. 214.

53. A.A. Lawal, *Corruption in Nigeria: A Colonial Legacy* (University of Lagos, text of an inaugural lecture on 7 June 2006).

54. David Pratten, *The Man-Leopard Murders: History and Society in Colonial Nigeria* (Edinburgh University Press, Edinburgh, 2007), p. 88.

55. Ogbu U. Kalu, 'Missionaries, Colonial Government and Secret Societies in South-Eastern Igboland, 1920–1950', *Journal of the Historical Society of Nigeria*, 9, 1 (1977), pp. 75–90.

56. National Archives of Nigeria, Ibadan [NAI], M.L.G. (W) 17887, 'Reformed Ogboni Fraternity': Otu Edu to Chief Commissioner, Western Province, et al., 1 April 1950.

57. Pratten, *The Man-Leopard Murders*, p. 88.

58. Ibid., p. 86.

59. Record of the second meeting of the colonial Local Government Advisory Panel, 22 Oct. 1948, in Martin Lynn (ed.), *British Documents on the End of Empire. Series B, Country Volumes, Volume 7* (vol. I, the Stationery Office, London, 2001), pp. 162–4.

60. David Pratten, *The Man-Leopard Murders*, p. 97.

17. WEST AFRICA'S INTERNATIONAL DRUG TRADE

1. UNODC, *Cocaine Trafficking in West Africa: The threat to stability and development* (UNODC, Vienna, 2007), <http://www.uNODC.org/documents/data-and-analysis/west_ africa_cocaine_report_2007-12_en.pdf> (31 January 2008).

2. For example: NRC Handelsblad (Rotterdam), 4 August 2008; *Financial Times*, 4 November 2008.

3. UNODC, *Cocaine Trafficking in West Africa*, p. 8.

4. *Ibid.*, p. 3.

5. David Blair, 'Special report: West Africa welcomes Latin America's drug barons', *Daily Telegraph*, <www.telegraph.co.uk/new/worldnews/africaandindianocean/senegal/3456011/S> (9 December 2008).

6. Gleaned during a visit to Monrovia, 11–14 January 2009.

7. Interview, law-enforcement officer, Accra, 31 August 2008.

8. Interviews, US government officials, Washington DC, 6 June 2008.

9. US National Archives and Records Administration [NARA II], Maryland, RG 84, general records of foreign service posts: records of the consulate-general, Lagos, 1940–63, box 2, 'Smuggling of narcotics'.

10. Antonio L. Mazzitelli, 'Transnational organized crime in West Africa: the additional challenge', *International Affairs* 83, 6 (2007), pp. 1075–6.

11. UNODC, *Cocaine Trafficking in West Africa*, pp. 11–16.

12. Jean-François Bayart, Stephen Ellis, and Beatrice Hibou, *The Criminalization of the State in Africa* (James Currey, Oxford, 1999), especially Bayart's Chapter 2.

13. Emmanuel Kwaku Akyeampong, 'Diaspora and drug trafficking in West Africa: a case study of Ghana', *African Affairs* 104, 416 (2005), pp. 429–47.

14. National Archives, Ibadan, Oyo Prof 1/1321: correspondence concerning coca cultivation.

15. National Archives, Ibadan, Ekiti Div 1/1, 1085, Indian hemp: circular from Acting Permanent Secretary, Ministry of Local Government, Western Region, 7 December 1954.

16. NARA II, RG 84, records of the consulate-general, Lagos, 1940–63, box 2, 'Smuggling of narcotics': Erwin P. Keeler to Department of State, 3 February 1954.

17. *Ibid.*: Erwin P. Keeler to Department of State, 4 December 1952.
18. *Ibid.*: memorandum for Mr Ross, 21 August 1952, attached to Robert W. Ross to Department of State, 28 August 1952.
19. *Ibid.*: Erwin P. Keeler to Department of State, 4 December 1952.
20. Cf. Alfred W. McCoy, *The Politics of Heroin: CIA complicity in the global drug trade* (Lawrence Hill Books, New York, 1991).
21. Press release number 295, Federal Ministry of Information, Lagos, 22 March 1971, contained in press cuttings file in Nigerian Institute of International Affairs, Lagos.
22. 'The cost of war against smuggling', *New Nigerian*, 31 August 1979.
23. 'Avoid Indian Hemp', leaflet c. 1974, in 'Nigeria: drugs, 1979–', press cuttings file in Nigerian Institute of International Affairs, Lagos.
24. Umoh James Umoh and Alhaji Nurudeen Adio-Saka, 'The problem of smuggling among pilgrims', *Daily Times*, 13 July 1972. In 1972, 44,061 Nigerians officially went on the hajj, the second-largest national contingent after Yemenis.
25. Penny Green, *Drugs, Trafficking and Criminal Policy: The scapegoat strategy* (Waterside Press, Winchester, 1998), p. 46.
26. *Sunday Times* (Lagos), 10 March 1974; 'The redeemer is not near', *Daily Sketch* (Lagos), 28 July 1974.
27. National Archives of the United Kingdom, Kew: FCO 65/1530: Reuters report, 23 August 1974.
28. 'Organized crime: Nigeria' (paper presented at UNODC workshop on West African organized crime, Dakar, 2–3 April 2004).
29. Mark Shaw, *Crime as Business, Business as Crime: West African criminal networks in southern Africa* (South African Institute of International Affairs, Johannesburg, 2003), p. 11.
30. Statement by US Embassy, Lagos, published in *Daily Times* (Lagos), 10 December 1984, p. 3.
31. Rasheed Williams, 'Nigeria, a leading heroin market', *National Concord* (Lagos), 8 April 1985.
32. Statement by US Embassy, Lagos, published in *Daily Times,* 10 December 1984, p. 3.
33. *Ibid.*
34. Quoted in the *Daily Times,* 26 November 1984.
35. Quoted in '… and its Nigerian connection', *Guardian* (Lagos), 30 December 1984.
36. According to the newsletter *Drug Force,* the official publication of the Nigerian Drug Law Enforcement Agency, quoted in *Daily Champion* (Lagos), 9 May 1993.
37. '2,000 Nigerians in foreign jails for drug offences', *New Nigerian,* 13 May 1988.
38. The *Guardian* (Lagos) carried a series of reports on this matter in May and June 1983. See also Axel Klein, 'Trapped in the traffick: growing problems of drug consumption in Lagos', *Journal of Modern African Studies* 32, 4 (1994), pp. 657–77.
39. Address by Alain Labrousse, director of Observatoire Géopolitique des Drogues, Bordeaux, 28 April 1994; interviews, US law-enforcement officer, Bangkok, 16 May 2005, and former Liberian presidential aide, Amsterdam, 4 November 2004.
40. Mark Shaw, 'The political economy of crime and conflict in sub-Saharan Africa', *South African Journal of International Affairs* 8, 2 (2001), p. 66.

41. A reference to the notorious Four One Nine advance fee fraud. See Daniel Jordan Smith, *A Culture of Corruption: Everyday deception and popular discontent in Nigeria* (Princeton University Press, Princeton, NJ, 2007), especially Chapter 1.

42. Speech on 19 January 2006, reported in *Punch* (Lagos), 20 January 2006.

43. Peter Lewis, 'From prebendalism to predation: the political economy of decline in Nigeria', *Journal of Modern African Studies* 34, 1 (1996), p. 97. The reference to 'Zairianisation' is on p. 80.

44. Stanislav Andreski, *The African Predicament: A study in the pathology of modernisation* (Michael Joseph, London, 1968). A definition of 'kleptocracy' is on p. 109.

45. See the unofficial version of the Oputa Panel report released on 1 January 2005 by the National Democratic Movement (Washington, DC), Vol. 4, p. 104, <http://www.dawodu.com/ oputa1.htm> (24 November 2008). Further information is in Richard Akinnola (ed.), *The Murder of Dele Giwa: Cover-up—revelations* (Human Rights Publications, Lagos, 2001).

46. *The BCCI Affair: A report to the Committee on Foreign Relations, United States Senate by Senator John Kerry and Senator Hank Brown* (US Government Printing Office, Washington DC, 1993), pp. 99–104. The quotation is on p. 49.

47. Peter Truell and Larry Gurwin, *False Profits: The inside story of BCCI, the world's most corrupt financial empire* (Houghton Mifflin, Boston and New York, 1992), p. 162.

48. United States Information Service (USIS) press release, 2 March 1998, quoted in *Punch,* 5 March 1998.

49. Kofi Bentsum Quantson, *Travelling and Seeing: Johnny just come* (NAPASVIL Ventures, Accra, 2002), p. 67.

50. '2,000 Nigerians in foreign jails for drug offences', *New Nigerian,* 13 May 1988.

51. Jonas Okwara, 'Three Nigerians held weekly in US on drug charges', *Guardian,* 15 July 1990.

52. Jackson Akpasubi, 'US says "no" to Nigeria', *Sunday Concord,* 30 June 1991. Eric Fottorino, *La Piste blanche: L'Afrique sous l'emprise de la drogue* (Balland, Paris, 1991), p. 19, gives the same figure of 15,433 for Nigerians arrested for drug offences between 1979 and 1989.

53. Fottorino, *La Piste blanche,* p. 19.

54. Segun Babatope, 'Drug trafficking: a nation under siege', *National Concord,* 3 February 1992.

55. Nnamdi Obasi, 'Drug trafficking', *Weekend Concord,* 1 June 1991.

56. Green, *Drugs, Trafficking*, p. 48.

57. 'Adegoke's ill-fated deal with skypower', *National Concord,* 30 April 1989.

58. Editorial, *Nigerian Tribune,* 24 March 2006.

59. 'NDLEA stinks—Bamaiyi', *Daily Times,* 18 February 1994.

60. Fottorino, *La Piste blanche,* pp. 57, 60.

61. Stephen Ellis, 'Les prolongements du conflit israélo-arabe: le cas du Sierra Leone', *Politique africaine* 30 (1988), pp. 69–75.

62. Robert I. Friedman, *Red Mafiya: How the Russian mob has invaded America* (Little, Brown, Boston, MA, 2000), pp. 57–8.

63. Akyeampong, 'Diaspora and drug trafficking in West Africa', p. 441.

64. Author's interviews with former aide to President Charles Taylor, 2002–4.

65. Kwesi Yankah and Lazarus D. Maayang, 'Charles Taylor: dark days in Ghana', *Uhuru* (Accra), 3 (1990), p. 40.

66. The International Consortium of Investigative Journalists, *Making a Killing: The business of war* (Public Integrity Books, Washington, DC, 2003), especially chapters 7 and 10.

67. Nya Kwiawon Taryor (ed.), *Justice, Justice: A cry of my people* (Strugglers' Community Press, Chicago, IL, 1985), p. 54; phone interview, former aide to Charles Taylor, 4 November 2004.

68. Interview, Ghanaian police officer, Accra, 31 August 2008.

69. *Jane's Intelligence Review*, 1 July 2005. Antony Altbeker, *A Country at War with Itself: South Africa's crisis of crime* (Jonathan Ball, Johannesburg and Cape Town, 2007), pp. 124–5, argues that South Africans often exaggerate the impact of foreign organized crime in their own country. However, his concern in this passage is to refute any suggestion that South African crime is foreign rather than homegrown.

70. USIS press release, 2 March 1998, quoted in *Punch,* 5 March 1998.

71. Fottorino, *La Piste blanche,* pp. 60–1; see also allegations in *Liberian Diaspora* 3, 12 (1993), p. 4 (to be viewed with caution, as this was a propaganda sheet for Charles Taylor).

72. 'Drug: NDLEA sends officers' names to presidency', *Guardian*, 9 November 1998.

73. See interview with General Bamaiyi in *Sunday Champion,* 20 June 1999.

74. John K. Cooley, *Unholy Wars: Afghanistan, America and international terrorism* (third edition, Pluto Press, London and Sterling, VA, 2002), p. 143.

75. Laolu Akande, 'Nigeria high on US fraud, drugs list', *Guardian,* 18 August 1999.

76. UNODC, *Transnational Organized Crime in the West African Region* (New York, NY, 2005), p. 21.

77. Sisca Agboh, 'NDLEA impounds N1b worth of cocaine', *Post Express* (Lagos), 31 August 2002.

78. Laolu Akande, 'Nigerian boy, 12, swallows 87 condom wraps of heroin', *Guardian,* 13 April 2002.

79. UNODC, *Transnational Organized Crime in the West African Region,* p. 48.

80. 'Italy police arrest mafia suspect', BBC News, 14 November 2003, <http://news.bbc.co.uk/2/hi/europe/3270935.stm> (24 November 2008).

81. Statement to the Senate Foreign Relations Committee Subcommittee on African Affairs, 20 July 1995, obtained from the US Information Resource Center, US Embassy, The Hague.

82. Henry Mintzberg, *Structure in Fives: Designing effective organizations* (1983; second edition, Prentice Hall, Englewood Cliffs, NJ, 1993), p. 254. The term 'adhocracy' was coined by Alvin Toffler in his bestseller *Future Shock* (Bantam Books, New York, NY, 1972).

83. Interview, Lagos, 24 October 2007.

84. '237 Nigerian drug convicts in arrive [sic] today', *Guardian,* 29 March 2003.

85. 'African community at Pratunum, Bangkok' (paper presented by Royal Thai Police, African Criminal Networks conference, Bangkok, 16–19 May 2005).

86. 'Dongri nightlife', *Time Out Mumbai* 2, 24 (July–August 2006), <http://www.timeoutmumbai.net/mumbailocal/mumbailocal_details.asp?code= 11&source= 1 > (24 November 2008).

87. 'Nigerian drug barons invade South Africa', *Guardian,* 11 April 1998.
88. The name has been suppressed for legal reasons. Information obtained from official source, Lagos, 24 October 2007.
89. Reuben Abati, 'The hanging of Amara Tochi in Singapore', *Guardian,* 28 January 2006.
90. Nigerian Drug Law Enforcement Agency (NDLEA), 'An analysis of the drug trafficking issues and trends at the Murtala Muhammed International airport, Ikeja, Lagos (MMIA)' (unpublished paper, 7 pp., September 2007).
91. *Ibid.*
92. *Ibid.*
93. Franco Prina, 'Trade and exploitation of minors and young Nigerian women for prostitution in Italy', 2003, Chapter 1, <http://www.unicri.it/wwd/trafficking/nigeria/docs/rr_prina_eng.pdf> (24 November 2008).
94. Cf. Kate Meagher, 'Social capital, social liabilities, and political capital: social networks and informal manufacturing in Nigeria', *African Affairs* 105, 421 (2006), pp. 553–82.
95. Stephen Ellis, 'The Okija shrine: death and life in Nigerian politics', *Journal of African History* 49, 3 (2008), pp. 445–66.
96. Joe Igbokwe, *Igbos: 25 years after Biafra* (Advent Communications, no place given, 1995), p. 40.
97. Joe Brown Akubueze v The Federal Republic of Nigeria, 4 March 2003. Available via Toma Micro Publishers Ltd., <http://www.tomalegalretrieve.org/phplaw/site/index.php> (23 July 2008).
98. Flemming Quist, 'Drug trafficking in West Africa 2000–2004 in an international perspective' (UNODC workshop on West African organized crime, Dakar, 2–3 April 2004).
99. *Ibid.*
100. *Ibid.*
101. *Ibid.*
102. Johan van den Dongen and Bart Olmer, 'Vloedgolf van drugs', *De Telegraaf* (Amsterdam), 26 October 2006.
103. Interview, Dutch judicial officer, Amsterdam, 13 December 2006; cf. Bart Middelburg and Paul Vugts (eds), *De Endstra-Tapes: De integrale gesprekken van Willem Endstra met de Recherche* (Nieuw Amsterdam publishers, Amsterdam, 2006), p. 324, a record of police interviews with a leading figure of the Dutch underworld, the late Willem Endstra.
104. ISN Security Watch, 27 February 2008, <www.isn.etnz.ch> (28 February 2008).
105. Mazzitelli, 'Transnational organized crime in West Africa', p. 1075.
106. UNODC, 'Cocaine trafficking in western Africa, situation report', October 2007, pp. 3–5, <http://www.google.com/search?hl=en&q=UNODC±Situation±Report%E2%80%99%2C±   October±2007&btnG=Search> (24 November 2008).
107. *Ibid.,* p. 5.
108. *This Day,* 10, 13, 15 June 2006.
109. Interview, Lagos, 24 October 2007.
110. UNODC, 'Cocaine trafficking in Western Africa, situation report', October 2007, p. 6.

111. Presentation by DEA agent, Washington DC, 6 June 2008.

112. 'Bissau drugs probe death threats', BBC News, 30 July 2008, <http://news.bbc. co.uk/ go/pr/fr/-/2/hi/africa/7532466.stm> (31 July 2008).

113. International Crisis Group, Guinée-Bissau: Besoin d'Ètat (Africa report No.142, Dakar/Brussels, July 2008).

114. Mazzitelli, 'Transnational organized crime in West Africa', p. 1076, note 23. UNODC, 'Drug Trafficking as a Security Threat in West Africa' (November 2008), p. 13, gives the origin as Guinea-Bissau, <http://www.unodc.org/unodc/en/frontpage/drug-trafficking-as-a-security- threat-in-west-africa.html> (4 February 2009).

115. Interviews, Accra, 31 August 2008; 'West Africa/drugs', Africa Confidential 49, 6 (14 March 2008).

116. Alistair Thomson, 'Drug trade threatens to corrode Ghana's image', International Herald Tribune, 23 December 2008.

117. Africa Confidential 49, 6 (14 March 2008), 'West Africa/drugs'.

118. Interviews, Lagos and Abuja, October 2007; '"Blood oil" dripping from Nigeria', BBC News, 27 July 2008, <http://news.bbc.co.uk/2/hi/africa/7519302.stm> (25 November 2008).

119. 'Mali cocaine haul after firefight', BBC News, 4 January 2008, <http://news. bbc.co.uk/ 2/hi/africa/7171219.stm> (17 January 2008). UNODC, 'Drug Trafficking as a Security Threat', p. 32, reports the discovery of a similar amount of hashish. It is not clear if this is a coincidence or a reporting error.

120. Heba Saleh, 'Islamist militants rise again in Algeria', Financial Times, 1 September 2008; cf. International Crisis Group, Islamist Terrorism in the Sahel: Fact or fiction? (Africa report No. 92, Dakar/Brussels, 2005), pp. 18–19.

121. Presentation by DEA officers, Washington DC, 6 June 2008.

122. UNODC, Cocaine Trafficking in West Africa, p. 20.

123. Francisco E. Thoumi, 'The rise of two drug tigers: the development of the illegal drugs industry and drug policy failure in Afghanistan and Colombia', in F. Bovenkerk and M. Levi (eds), The Organized Crime Community: Essays in honor of Alan A. Block (Studies of Organized Crime No. 6, Springer Science and Business Media, New York, NY, 2007), p. 126.

124. Ibid.

125. Ibid.

126. Ibid., p. 127.

127. UNODC, Cocaine Trafficking in West Africa, p. 1.

128. 'UN fears over West Africa drugs', BBC News, 27 November 2007, <http:// news.bbc. co.uk/2/hi/africa/7114593.stm> (25 November 2008).

129. UNODC, Crime and Development in Africa (Vienna, 2005), p. 67, <http://www. unodc.org/unodc/en/data-and-analysis/Studies-on-Drugs-and-Crime.html> (26 November 2008).

130. Ibid.

131. Cf. Manuel Castells, End of Millennium (second edition, Blackwell, Oxford, 2000), Vol. 3 of the Information Age trilogy, pp. 82–118.

132. William Reno, Corruption and State Politics in Sierra Leone (Cambridge University Press, Cambridge, 1995), p. 3. Interestingly, the expression 'shadow state' was used

long before, by Jean Suret-Canale, 'La Guinee dans le systeme colonial', *Presence Africaine* 29 (1959–60), p. 97.

133. Reno, *Corruption and State Politics,* p. 2

134. Cf. Tekena Tamuno and Robin Horton, 'The changing position of secret societies and cults in modern Nigeria', *African Notes* 5, 2 (1969), pp. 36–62.

135. Castells, *End of Millennium,* p. 98; see also Bayart *et al., The Criminalization of the State in Africa,* chapters 1 and 2.

136. 'Chinese gangs in Africa for long haul', *Jane's Intelligence Digest,* 8 July 2008.

20. SOUTH AFRICA AND THE DECOLONIZATION OF THE MIND

1. BBC News, 'South Africa appeal on xenophobia', 11 May 2009: http://news.bbc. co.uk/2/hi/africa/8044186.stm [accessed 11 May 2009].

2. Shireen Hassim, Tawana Kupe and Eric Worby (eds.), *Go Home or Die Here: Violence, xenophobia and the reinvention of difference in South Africa* (Wits University Press, Johannesburg, 2008), p.16.

3. Brigadier C.A. Fraser, 'Lessons learnt from past revolutionary wars', p. 5, unpublished text circulated among senior officers of the South African Defence Force. Copy in the author's possession.

4. Official South African police statistics reported at http://www.saps.gov.za/ statistics/reports/crimestats/2008/crime_stats_2008.htm [accessed 26 March 2009].

5. The pre-1994 statistics are notoriously unreliable. Mark Shaw, *Crime and Policing in Post-Apartheid South Africa: Transforming under Fire* (C. Hurst & Co., London, 2002), pp.15–17.

6. Antony Altbeker, *A Country at War with Itself: South Africa's crisis of crime* (Jonathan Ball Publishers, Johannesburg and Cape Town, 2007).

7. His own memoir is *Barend Strydom Die Wit Wolf: 'n belydenis* (Vaandel Uitgevers, Mosselbaai, 1997).

8. *Truth and Reconciliation Commission of South Africa Report* (5 vols., Cape Town, 1998), 3, p. 511.

9. See note 4.

10. Altbeker, *A Country at War.*

11. Among a spate of recent work occasioned by the bicentenary of abolition, see e.g. Adam Hochschild, *Burying the Chains: The British struggle to abolish slavery* (Macmillan, London, 2005).

12. E.g. William Ellis, *History of Madagascar,* 2 vols. (Fisher, Son, & Co., London and Paris), I, p. 82.

13. Tom Porteous, *Britain in Africa* (Zed Books and University of KwaZulu-Natal Press, London, New York and Pietermaritzburg, 2008), p. 42.

14. The text of the speech is available at http://www.bartleby.com/124/pres53.html [accessed 23 February 2008].

15. Christopher Andrew and Vasili Mitrokhin, *The Mitrokhin Archive II: The KGB and the world* (Allen Lane, London, 2005), ch.23, esp. pp. 480–1.

16. Frank Myers, 'Harold Macmillan's "winds of change" speech: a case study in the rhetoric of policy change', *Rhetoric and Public Affairs,* 3, 4 (2000), pp. 555–75.

Although the speech has gone down in history as the 'winds of change', Macmillan in fact referred only to 'wind' in the singular.

17. A phrase apparently invented by Karl Popper, *The Poverty of Historicism* (1957; Routledge, London and New York, 2002), pp. 38–9.

18. John Lonsdale, 'States and social processes in Africa: a historiographical survey', *African Studies Review,* 24, 2–3 (1981), p.139.

19. Zbigniew Brzezinski, *Out of Control: Global turmoil on the eve of the twenty-first century* (Charles Scribner's Sons, New York, 1993), p.17.

20. Manuel Castells, *End of Millennium* (1998; Second edn., Blackwell, Malden MA etc., 2000), p. 63.

21. John Iliffe, *Africans: The history of a continent* (2nd edn., Cambridge University Press, 2007), p. 2.

22. Breyten Breytenbach, 'Mandela's smile: Notes on South Africa's failed revolution', *Harper's Magazine* (December 2008): http://www.thetruthseeker.co.uk/article. asp?ID=9848 [accessed 28 May 2009].

23. Cf. Kenneth Pomeranz, *The Great Divergence: China, Europe, and the making of the modern world economy* (Princeton University Press, Princeton and Oxford, 2000).

24. Dipesh Chakrabarty, *Provincializing Europe: Postcolonial thought and historical difference* (Princeton University Press, Princeton and Oxford, 2000), p. 5.

25. Crawford Young, 'The end of the post-colonial state in Africa? Reflections on changing African political dynamics', *African Affairs,* 103, 410 (2004), pp. 23–49.

26. I. William Zartman (ed), *Collapsed States: The disintegration and restoration of legitimate authority* (Lynne Rienner, Boulder, CO, 1995).

27. She used this phrase at her first press conference after her appointment, on 24 January 1997: http://www.pbs.org/newshour/bb/white_house/january97/albright_1-24.html [accessed 27 December 2008].

28. Cf. Ngugi wa Thiong'o, *Decolonising the Mind: The politics of language in African literature* (James Currey, London, 1986). It is striking how often key insights into Africa's societies and politics have come from novelists sometimes decades before they have been identified by social scientists.

29. Martin Luther King, 'Beyond Vietnam: a time to break silence', published at http://www.hartford-hwp.com/archives/45a/058.html [accessed 18 June 2009].

AFTERWORD

1. J.F. Bayart, *État et religion en Afrique* (Paris: Karthala, 2018). See also, J.F. Bayart, *Violence et Religion en Afrique* (Paris, Karthala, 2018), which bears the inscription, '*À Stephen Ellis, qui a compris mieux et plus vite que d'autres l'importance du fait religieux en Afrique*'.

2. On the impact of these optical effects on the interpretation of the alleged 'religious renewal', see Eric Morier-Genoud, 'Renouveau religieux et politique au Mozambique: entre permanence, rupture et historicité', *Politique africaine,* 134, June 2014, pp. 155–177.

3. Terence Ranger, 'Scotland Yard in the bush: medicine, murders, child witches and the construction of the occult. A literature review', *Africa,* 77 (2), 2007, pp. 272–283; Gerrie ter Haar and Stephen Ellis, 'The occult does not exist: a response

to Terence Ranger', *Africa*, 79 (3), 2009, pp. 399–412; Peter Geschiere, *The modernity of witchcraft: politics and the occult in postcolonial Africa*, translated by Peter Geschiere and Janet Roitman (Charlottesville, VA and London: University Press of Virginia, 1997) and *Witchcraft, Intimacy and Trust. Africa in Comparison* (Chicago, IL: The University of Chicago Press, 2013). On fears surrounding contemporary witchcraft, see Andrea Ceriana Mayneri, *Sorcellerie et prophétisme en Centrafrique. L'imaginaire de la dépossession en pays banda* (Paris: Karthala, 2014) and Adam Ashworth, *Madumo. A Man Bewitched* (Chicago, IL: The University of Chicago Press, 2000).

4. Eric Hobsbawm and Terence Ranger (eds.), *The Invention of Tradition* (Cambridge: Cambridge University Press, 1983).

5. Wolfram Eberhard, *Conquerors and Rulers: Social Forces in Medieval China* (Leiden: E.J. Brill, 1965), pp. 1–17 (p. 14).

6. Peter Geschiere, *Village Communities and the State. Changing Relations among the Maka of Southeastern Cameroon since the Colonial Conquest* (London: Kegan Paul International, 1982), pp. 241–242.

7. Henry J. Drewal, 'Mami Wata shrines: exotica and the construction of self' in Mary J. Arnoldi, Christraud M. Geary and Kris L. Hardin (eds.), *African Material Culture* (Bloomington, IN: Indiana University Press, 1996), chapter 13; Bogumil Jewsiewicki, *Mami Wata. La peinture urbaine au Congo* (Paris: Gallimard, 2003).

8. Patrick Haenni, *L'Islam de marché. L'autre révolution conservatrice* (Paris: Le Seuil, 2005).

9. Gwenaël Njoto-Feillard, *L'Islam et la réinvention du capitalisme en Indonésie* (Paris: Karthala, 2012).

10. Paul Veyne, 'L'interprétation et l'interprète. A propos des choses de la religion', *Enquête*, 3, 1996, p. 7; available online: http://enquete.revues.org/sommaire332.html.

11. Alf Lüdtke (ed.), *The history of everyday life: reconstructing historical experiences and ways of life,* translated by William Templer (Princeton, N.J.; Chichester: Princeton University Press, 1995) and *Des ouvriers dans l'Allemagne du XXe siècle. Le quotidien des dictatures* (Paris: L'Harmattan, 2000).

12. Veyne, 'L'interprétation et l'interprète'. Here, Veyne is very close to Weber's concept of *Veralltäglichung* or 'becoming like every day'. Jean-Pierre Grossein, in his fundamental work of translation and exegesis, translated this into French as '*quotidiannisation*', rejecting the usual but erroneous translation ('routinisation'), taken from Talcott Parsons. See Jean-Pierre Grossein, 'Peut-on lire en français *L'Éthique protestante et l'esprit du capitalisme?*', *European Journal of Sociology*, 40 (1), May 1999, pp. 125–147 and 'A propos d'une nouvelle traduction de *L'Éthique protestante et l'esprit du capitalisme*', *Revue française de sociologie*, 43 (4), 2002, pp. 653–671.

13. Terence Ranger, *Are We Not Also Men? The Samkange Family and African Politics in Zimbabwe, 1920–64* (London: James Currey, 1995).

14. Max Weber, *L'Éthique protestante et l'esprit du capitalisme, suivi d'autres essais*, translated by Jean-Pierre Grossein (Paris: Gallimard, 2003), pp. 133–134. The standard English translation of this work is Max Weber, *The Protestant Ethic and the Spirit of Capitalism*, translated by Talcott Parsons (London; New York: Routledge, 2001,

first published in 1930); cf. also the later version edited and translated by Stephen Kalberg (Chicago, IL and London: Fitzroy Dearborn, 2001). The very normative translation of Weber's concepts by Talcott Parsons has been criticised. It seems to me that Weber's words are best rendered in Guenther Roth and Claus Wittich's translation of *Economy and Society. An Outline of Interpretive Sociology*, Berkeley, University of California Press, 1978.

15. Max Weber, *The Sociology of Religion*, translated by Ephraim Fischoff (London: Methuen and Co., 1965), and *Economy and society: an outline of interpretive sociology*

16. Xavier Audrain, *Des 'punks de Dieu' aux 'taalibe-citoyens'. Jeunesse, citoyenneté et mobilisation religieuse au Sénégal. Le mouvement mouride de Cheikh Modou Kara (1980– 2007)*, PhD thesis, Paris, Université de Paris-1 Panthéon Sorbonne, 2013. See also Jean-François Havard, 'Le "phénomène" Cheikh Bethio Thioune et le djihad migratoire des étudiants sénégalais "Thiantakones"' in Fariba Adelkhah and Jean-François Bayart (eds.), *Voyages du développement. Emigration, commerce, exil* (Paris: Karthala, 2007), p. 321, and Jean-François Bayart, 'La cité bureaucratique en Afrique subsaharienne' in Béatrice Hibou (ed.), *La Bureaucratisation néolibérale* (Paris: La Découverte, 2013), pp. 291–313.

17. Paolo Prodi, *Christianisme et monde moderne. Cinquante ans de recherche* (Paris: Gallimard, Seuil, 2006), p. 185, p. 203, pp. 210ff., pp. 250ff., p. 293; Richard W. Southern, *Western Society and the Church in the Middle Ages*, revised edition (London: Penguin, 1990); Michel de Certeau, *Le Lieu de l'autre. Histoire religieuse et mystique* (Paris: Gallimard, Le Seuil, 2005), pp. 24ff.; Antonio Padoa-Schioffa (ed.), *Justice et législation* (Paris: PUF, 2000); Fariba Adelkhah, *Being Modern in Iran* (New York: Columbia University Press, 2000); and Jean-François Bayart, *L'Islam républicain. Ankara, Téhéran, Dakar* (Paris: Albin Michel, 2010), chapter 4.

18. Weber, *L'Éthique protestante*, p. 124 and pp. 277ff.

19. Ruth Marshall, *Political Spiritualities. The Pentecostal Revolution in Nigeria* (Chicago, IL: The University of Chicago Press, 2009).

20. James F. Searing, *'God Alone is King': Islam and Emancipation in Senegal. The Wolof Kingdoms of Kajoor and Bawol, 1859–1914* (Portsmouth: Heinemann, 2002).

21. Mohamed Tozy, 'Des oulémas frondeurs à la bureaucratie du "croire". Les péripéties d'une restructuration annoncée du champ religieux au Maroc' in Hibou (ed.), *La Bureaucratisation néolibérale*, pp. 129–154, and 'Du service de Dieu au service du Prince. Entre bavardage médiatique et vœu de silence' in Ariane Zambiras and Jean-François Bayart (eds.), *La Cité culturelle. Rendre à Dieu ce qui revient à César* (Paris: Karthala, 2015), pp. 119–154.

22. Michel de Certeau, *The Writing of History*, translated by Tom Conley (New York and Chichester: Columbia University Press, 1988), pp. 118ff. Apart from Michel de Certeau's studies of mysticism in the 16th and 17th centuries, see Avihu Zakai, *Exile and Kingdom. History and Apocalypse in the Puritan Migration to America* (Cambridge: Cambridge University Press, 1992).

23. Carlo Ginzburg, *The night battles: witchcraft and agrarian cults in the sixteenth and seventeenth centuries*, translated by John and Anne Tedeschi (London: Routledge & Kegan Paul, 1983) and Jeanne Favret-Saada, *Les Mots, la mort, les sorts: la sorcellerie dans le Bocage* (Paris: Gallimard, 1977). [The Bocage is a rural area in western France—Trans.]

24. François de Polignac, *Cults, territory, and the origins of the Greek city-state*, translated by Janet Lloyd (Chicago, IL: University of Chicago Press, 1995); Jean-François Bayart (ed.), *Religion et modernité politique en Afrique noire. Dieu pour tous et chacun pour soi* (Paris: Karthala, 1993); Zambiras and Bayart (eds.), *La Cité cultuelle*.

25. Jean-François Bayart, *Global Subjects: a political critique of globalization*, translated by Andrew Brown (Cambridge: Polity Press, 2007).

26. Prodi, *Christianisme et monde moderne*, p. 253. See also Joseph R. Strayer, *On the Medieval Origins of the Modern State* (Princeton, NJ: Princeton University Press, 1970), and Southern, *Western Society and the Church*, who writes: 'The habit of separating ecclesiastical history from secular history has tended to make everything ecclesiastical appear more rarefied than it really is. It is only when we study church history as an aspect of secular history that we can begin to understand the limitations and opportunities of the medieval church [...]' (p. 360).

27. See Paul Veyne, *L'Inventaire des différences* (Paris: Le Seuil, 1976), p. 35, and my commentary: Jean-François Bayart, 'Comparer en France: petit essai d'autobiographie disciplinaire', Politix, 21 (83), October 2008, pp. 201–228, available online: https://www.tandfonline.com/doi/abs/10.1080/03085148200000009?journalCode=reso20

28. I am here borrowing the formula used by Giovanni Levi. See also Paul Veyne: 'In history the questions, which are sociological, are of more importance than the answers, which are matters of fact' (*L'Inventaire des différences*, p. 61).

29. John D. Y. Peel, *Religious Encounter and the Making of the Yoruba* (Bloomington, IN: Indiana University Press, 2000); Anne Hugon, *Un Protestantisme africain au XIXe siècle. L'implantation du méthodisme en Gold Coast (Ghana). 1835–1874* (Paris: Karthala, 2007); John K. Thornton, *The Kingdom of Kongo. Civil War and Transition, 1641–1718* (Madison, WI: University of Wisconsin Press, 1983) and *The Kongolese Saint Anthony. Dona Beatriz Kimpa Vita and the Antonian Movement, 1684–1706* (Cambridge: Cambridge University Press, 1998).

30. Ghislaine Gydon, *On Trans-Saharan Trails. Islamic Law, Trade Networks, and Cross-Cultural Exchange in Nineteenth-Century Western Africa* (Cambridge: Cambridge University Press, 2009); Daniel J. Schroeter, *Merchants of Essaouira. Urban Society and Imperialism in South-Western Morocco, 1844–1886* (Cambridge: Cambridge University Press, 1988).

31. See Zekeria Ould Ahmed Salem, *Prêcher dans le désert. Islam politique et changement social en Mauritanie* (Paris: Karthala, 2013).

32. Prodi, *Christianisme et monde moderne*, p. 32.

33. Prodi, *Christianisme et monde modern*; Southern, *Western Society and the Church*. Terence Ranger was one of the first to insist on the importance of lay movements in sub-Saharan Africa: 'Religious movements and politics in Sub-Saharan Africa', *African Studies Review*, 29 (2), June 1986, p. 37.

34. Achille Mbembe, *Afriques indociles. Christianisme, pouvoir et État en société postcoloniale* (Paris: Karthala, 1988).

35. De Certeau, *Le Lieu de l'autre*, pp. 23ff.

36. Terence Ranger, 'Religious development and African Christian identity' in K.H. Petersen (ed.), *Religion, Development and African Identity* (Uppsala: Scandinavian Institute of African Studies, 1987), pp. 29–57, and 'Religious movements and politics', pp. 37ff.

37. Zambiras and Bayart (eds.), *La Cité cultuelle*.

38. See Bayart, *L'Islam républicain*.

39. De Certeau, *Le Lieu de l'autre*, pp. 28–29.

40. See Jean-François Bayart, 'Postface: la cité cultuelle à l'âge de la globalisation' in Zambiras and Bayart (eds.), *La Cité cultuelle*, pp. 155–187.

41. Bayart, *Global Subjects*.

42. For a contemporary example, see Julien Bonhomme, *Les Voleurs de sexe. Anthropologie d'une rumeur africaine* (Paris: Seuil, 2009).

43. See Gilles Holder (ed.), *L'Islam, nouvel espace public en Afrique* (Paris: Karthala, 2009). See also Christian Coulon, *Les Musulmans et le pouvoir en Afrique noire. Religion et contre-culture* (Paris: Karthala, 1983).

44. Luis Martínez, *The Algerian Civil War 1990–1998*, translated by Jonathan Derrick (London and Paris: Hurst in association with the Fondation Nationale des Sciences Politiques. Centre d'Ètudes et de Recherches Internationales, 2000).

45. Philip S. Gorski, *The Disciplinary Revolution. Calvinism and the Rise of the State in Early Modern Europe* (Chicago, IL: University of Chicago Press, 2003).

46. See Kenneth J. Orosz, *Religious Conflict and the Evolution of Language Policy in German and French Cameroon, 1885–1939* (New York: Peter Lang, 2008) for the particularly interesting case of Cameroon, due to the change of colonial powers in the wake of the First World War, and Didier Péclard, *Les Incertitudes de la nation en Angola. Aux racines sociales de l'Unita* (Paris: Karthala, 2015).

47. Southern, *Western Society and the Church*; Prodi, *Christianisme et monde moderne*; Gorski, *The Disciplinary Revolution*.

48. Béatrice Hibou (ed.), *La Privatisation des États* (Paris: Karthala, 1999); Jean-François Bayart, Stephen Ellis and Béatrice Hibou, *The Criminalisation of the State in Africa* (Oxford: James Currey, 1998).

49. I am here drawing on Guy Hermet's notion as developed in connection with religious organizations in authoritarian situations, in *Revue française de science politique*, 23 (3), June 1973.

50. John Iliffe, *A History of the African AIDS Epidemic* (Athens, OH: Ohio University Press, 2006), chapter 10.

51. Wyatt MacGaffey, *Modern Kongo Prophets. Religion in a Plural Society* (Bloomington, IN: Indiana University Press, 1983); Susan Asch, *L'Église du Prophète Kimbangu. De ses origines à son rôle actuel au Zaïre* (Paris: Karthala, 1983).

52. Weber, *Sociology of Religion* and *Economy and Society*.

53. Jean-François Bayart, *The State in Africa: the politics of the belly* and Jean-François Bayart (ed.), special issue on 'L'argent de Dieu. Eglises africaines et contraintes économiques', *Politique africaine* 35, September 1989.

54. See Comi M. Toulabor, 'Mgr Dosseh, archevêque de Lomé', *Politique africaine*, 35, October 1989, pp. 68–76.

55. Marshall, *Political Spiritualities*.

56. Morier-Genoud, 'Renouveau religieux et politique au Mozambique', pp. 171–172.

57. Olivier Carré and Gérard Michaud, *Les Frères musulmans. Egypte, Syrie (1928–1982)* (Paris: Gallimard, Julliard, 1983); Mohamed Tozy, *Monarchie et islam politique au Maroc*, revised and enlarged edition (Paris: Presses de Sciences Po, 1999); Youssef

Belal, *Le Cheikh et le calife. Sociologie religieuse de l'islam politique au Maroc* (Lyon: ENS éditions, 2011).

58. Gerrie ter Haar, *Spirit of Africa: the healing ministry of Archbishop Milingo of Zambia* (London: Hurst, 1992). On the other hand, the Supreme Pontiff was not averse to Mgr Milingo's therapeutic activities, and allowed him to practise his ministry of healing in Rome.

59. *Le Monde*, 6 November 2014.

60. Jean-François Bayart, 'Another look at the Arab Springs', *Sociétés politiques comparées*, 35, 2013, pp. 1-34, available online: http://www.fasopo.org/reasopo/n35/art_n35_eng.pdf. For a shorter, updated version, see Jean-François Bayart, 'Retour sur les Printemps arabes', *Politique africaine*, 133, March 2014, pp. 153-175.

61. Guy Hermet, *Aux frontières de la démocratie* (Paris: Presses universitaires de France, 1983), p. 207.

62. Audrain, *Des 'punks de Dieu'*; Marshall, *Political Spiritualities*. Michel de Certeau noted that, in modern Europe, 'through the mystics' confrontations with the power that connects heaven to the earth, there is sketched out, from England to Spain, a spiritual form of what will become the "citizen", separating from power a transcendental or ethical principle of society' (*The Mystic Fable*, vol. 2, *The Sixteenth and Seventeenth Centuries*, translated by Michael B. Smith (Chicago, IL: University of Chicago Press, 2015), p. 16).

63. See Holder (ed.), *L'Islam*.

64. See Ramon Sarró's fine study, *The Politics of Religious Change on the Upper Guinea Coast. Iconoclasm done and undone* (Edinburgh: Edinburgh University Press, 2009).

65. Jeanne-Françoise Vincent, *Traditions et transition. Entretiens avec des femmes beti du Sud-Cameroun* (Paris: ORSTOM, Berger-Levrault, 1976).

66. Richard Elphick and Rodney Davenport (eds.), *Christianity in South Africa. A Political, Social, and Cultural History* (Berkeley, CA: University of California Press, 1997).

67. Marshall, *Political Spiritualities*.

68. This is the expression used with regard to Iran by Fariba Adelkhah in *La Révolution sous le voile. Femmes islamiques d'Iran* (Paris: Karthala, 1991). Since the publication of this work, several studies have investigated the place of women in Islam, and in particular these forms of 'Islamic feminism'. See Adeline Masquelier, *Women and Islamic Revival in a West African Town* (Bloomington: Indiana University Press, 2009).

69. Nadine Picaudou, *L'Islam entre religion et idéologie. Essai sur la modernité musulmane* (Paris: Gallimard, 2010).

70. Bayart, *L'Islam républicain*, chapter 5.

71. Philippe Chanson, Yvan Droz, Yonatan N. Gez and Edio Soares (eds.), *Mobilité religieuse. Retours croisés des Afriques aux Amériques* (Paris: Karthala, 2014).

72. Prodi, *Christianisme et monde moderne*.

73. Jean-François Havard, 'Le "phénomène" Cheikh Bethio Thioune et le djihad migratoire des étudiants sénégalais "Thiantakones"', in Adelkhah and Bayart (eds.), *Voyages du développement*.

74. Jean-François Bayart, 'A nouvelles pratiques religieuses, nouveaux instruments d'analyse? L'écriture abiographique des plans de foi' in Chanson, Droz, Gez and Soares (eds.), *Mobilité religieuse*, pp. 39–52.

75. Fabien Eboussi Boulaga, *Christianisme sans fétiche. Révélation et domination* (Paris: Présence africaine, 1981). See also Pius Ngandu Nkashama, *Eglises nouvelles et mouvements religieux. L'exemple zaïrois* (Paris: L'Harmattan, 1990).

76. Murray Last, 'Muslims and Christians in Nigeria: an economy of political panic', *The Round Table*, 96 (392), October 2007, pp. 605–616; Peel, *Religious Encounter*; Marshall, *Political Spiritualities*.

77. Prodi, *Christianisme et monde moderne*, pp. 12ff, p. 18, p. 32, p. 63, p. 87, pp. 93ff.

78. Iliffe, *A History of the African AIDS Epidemic*.

79. Gorski, *The Disciplinary Revolution*; Prodi, *Christianisme et monde moderne*, pp. 107ff, pp. 138ff, pp. 291ff, pp. 377–378.

80. De Certeau, *Le Lieu de l'autre*, p. 24.

81. Bayart, *The State in Africa* and 'Africa in the world: a history of extraversion', *African Affairs*, 99 (395), April 2000, pp. 217–267—this article was originally written in French and admirably translated by Stephen Ellis.

82. Bayart (ed.), 'L'argent de Dieu'.

83. Mbembe, *Afrique indocile*.

84. See Henri Bergson, *Time and Free Will. An Essay on the Immediate Data of Consciousness*, translated by F.L. Pogson (London: George Allen and Unwin, 1910). Michel de Certeau talks of how time can be 'flaky'.

85. De Certeau, *Le Lieu de l'autre*, p. 22.

86. Veyne, *L'Inventaire des différences*.

87. See Prodi, *Christianisme et monde moderne*, especially pp. 366–368 and pp. 382ff.; Southern, *Western Society and the Church*, chapter 7.

88. Prodi, *Christianisme et monde moderne*, pp. 190ff.

89. Jean-François Bayart, Achille Mbembe and Comi Toulabor, *Le Politique par le bas en Afrique noire*, new and revised edition (Paris: Karthala, 2008), pp. 9–16.

90. Weber, *L'Éthique protestante et l'esprit du capitalisme*, especially pp. LX-LXI for Grossein's commentary, and *Sociology of Religion*.

91. Walter Benjamin, 'Theses on the Philosophy of History' in *Illuminations*, translated by Harry Zohn, edited by Hannah Arendt, pp. 196–209 (p. 200 and p. 205).

92. Sanjay Subrahmanyam, 'Du Tage au Gange au XVIe siècle: une conjoncture millénariste à l'échelle eurasiatique', *Annales HSS*, 56 (1), January–February 2001, pp. 51–84.

93. Catherine Maire, 'Les jansénistes et le millénarisme. Du refus à la conversion', *Annales HSS*, 63 (1), January-February 2008, pp. 7–36 and *De la cause de Dieu à la cause de la Nation. Le jansénisme au XVIIIe siècle* (Paris: Gallimard, 1998).

STEPHEN ELLIS BIBLIOGRAPHY

JOS DAMEN

(African Studies Centre Leiden)

A digital version of this bibliography can be downloaded from Leiden University Repository, https://hdl.handle.net/1887/67223

BOOKS

The Rising of the Red Shawls. A Revolt in Madagascar 1895-1899. Cambridge, Cambridge University Press, 1985. ISBN 0-521-26287-9

French edition: *L'Insurrection des menalamba. Une révolte à Madagascar.* Pref. de Faranirina V. Rajaonah; trad. de l'anglais par Ginette Randriambeloma. Paris, Editions Karthala, 1998. ISBN 2-86537-796-2

Un complot colonial à Madagascar. L 'affaire Rainandriamampandry. Pref. de Jean-François Bayart. Paris, Karthala & Antananarivo, Editions Ambozontany, 1990. ISBN 2-86537-160-3

(with Tsepo Sechaba), *Comrades Against Apartheid. The South African Communist Party and the ANC in Exile, 1960-1990.* London, James Currey & Bloomington, Indiana University Press, 1992. ISBN 0-85255-353-6.

(with Yves Faure, eds.), *Entreprises et entrepreneurs africains.* Paris, Editions Karthala & Paris, Orstom, 1995. ISBN 2-86537-530-7.

(ed.), *Africa Now. People, Policies and Institutions.* London, James Currey, 1996. ISBN 085255-232-7.

Dutch edition: *Afrika nu. Mensen, beleid en instellingen.* Den Haag, Ministerie van Buitenlandse zaken, 1995. ISBN 90-5328-100-2

French edition: *Afrique maintenant.* Paris, Editions Karthala, 1995. ISBN 2865376028

(with Jean-François Bayart & Beatrice Hibou), *La criminalisation de l'État en Afrique.* Bruxelles, Editions Complexe, 1997. ISBN 2-87027-674-5

627

English edition: (with Jean-François Bayart & Beatrice Hibou), *The Criminalization of the State in Africa*. Oxford, James Currey (etc.) & Bloomington, Indiana University Press, 1999. ISBN 0-85255-813-9

The Mask of Anarchy. The Destruction of Liberia and the Religious Dimension of an African Civil War. London, C. Hurst & New York, New York University Press, 1999. ISBN 1-85065-417-4.

The Mask of Anarchy. The Destruction of Liberia and the Religious Dimension of an African CivilWar. 2ⁿᵈ ed., revised and updated with new preface. London, Hurst & New York, New York University Press, 2007. ISBN 978-0-8147-2211-4.

(with Gerrie ter Haar), *Worlds of Power. Religious Thought and Political Practice in Africa*. London, Hurst & New York, Oxford University Press, 2004. ISBN 1-85065734-3. [Special edition: Johannesburg, Wits University Press, 2004. ISBN 019522017X]

Spanish edition: (with Gerrie ter Haar, translation by Francisco Ramos Mena), *Mundos de Poder. Pensiamento religioso y practica politica en Africa*. Barcelona, Edicions Bellaterra, 2005. ISBN 8472902838.

(with Solofo Randrianja), *Madagascar. A Short History*. London, Hurst & Chicago, Chicago University Press, 2009. ISBN 978-1-85065-947-1.

(with Ineke van Kessel, eds.), *Movers and Shakers. Social Movements in Africa* Leiden, Brill, 2009. ISBN 978-90-04-18013-0; Online version: http://hdl.handle.net/1887/18530

Season of Rains. Africa in the World. Forew. by Archbishop Desmond Tutu. Auckland Park, Jacana & London, Hurst & Co., 2011. ISBN 978-1-8490-4180-5

Dutch translation: *Het regenseizoen.Afrika in de wereld*. Amsterdam, Prometheus & Bert Bakker, 2011, ISBN 978-90-351-3631-1

External Mission. The ANC in Exile, 1960–1990. Johannesburg, Jonathan Ball & London, Hurst & Co, 2012 & New York, Oxford University Press, 2013. ISBN 978-1-8490-4262-8.

This Present Darkness.A History of Nigerian Organized Crime. London, Hurst & Co. & New York, Oxford University Press, 2016. ISBN 978-0-19-049431-5 [SA edition: Pretoria, Jacana, 2016. ISBN 978-1-4314-2374-3]

ARTICLES & BOOK CHAPTERS

'Un texte du XVIIieme siecle sur Madagascar'. *Omaly sy Anio*, 9 (1), 1979, pp.151-166.

'The political elite of Imerina and the revolt of the menalamba. The creation of a colonial myth in Madagascar, 1895-1898'. *The Journal of African History*, Vol. 21, No. 2 (1980), pp. 219-234.

'Les traditionalistes menalamba et leur conception de la royaute: Études sur la nature de la monarchie en Imerina', in Françoise Raison-Jourde (ed), *Les Souverains de Madagascar* (Paris, Karthala, 1983), pp.373-390.

(with Gerrie ter Haar), 'Spirit possession and healing in modern Zambia: An analysis of letters to Milingo', *African Affairs,* 87 (347) (1988), pp.185-206.

'Les prolongements du conflit israelo-arabe: le cas du Sierra Leone', *Politique Africaine,* 30 (1988), pp.69-75.

'Tuning in to pavement radio', *African Affairs* 88 (352) (1989), pp.321-330.

'The ANC in Exile', *African Affairs,* 90 (1991), pp.439-447.

'The South African Communist Party and the Collapse of the Soviet Union', *The Journal of Communist Studies,* 8, ii (1992), pp. 145-159. Reprinted in A. Hughes (ed.), *Marxism's Retreat from Africa* (London, Frank Cass, 1992), pp.145-159.

'Defense d'y voir: la politisation de la protection de la nature', *Politique africaine,* 48, (December 1992), pp. 7-21.

'De Klerk–Mandela: l'inevitable entente,' *Politique internationale* 59 (1993), 307-320.

'Democracy in Africa: Achievements and prospects', in D. Rimmer (ed.), *Action in Africa* (Royal African Society/James Currey, London, 1993), pp.133-143. Also published in Van den Berg & Bosma (below, 1994).

'Rumour and Power in Togo', *Africa,* 63, 4 (1993), 362-376.

'Democracy and human rights', in R. van den Berg & U.T. Bosma (eds), *Historical Dimension of Development, Change and Conflict in the South* (Poverty and Development No. 9, Directorate General for International Cooperation, the Hague, 1994), pp. 115-126.

'Government and rituals in old Madagascar', in *Afrika: Een sprekend verleden* (Univ. of Utrecht, 1994), pp.103-109.

'Of elephants and men: Politics and nature conservation in South Africa, *Journal of Southern African Studies,* 20, i (1994), pp.53-69.

'*Mbokodo.* Security in ANC camps, 1961-1990', *African Affairs,* 93 (1994), 371, pp.279-298.

'De crisis van de staat in Afrika', *Internationale Spectator,* 48, x (October 1994), pp.498-503.

'Nigeria: een onmogelijke dictatuur', *Internationale Spectator,* 49, i (January 1995), pp.19-23.

(with Ros Reeve), 'An insider's account of the South African security forces' role in the ivory trade', *Journal of Contemporary African Studies,* 13, ii (1995), pp.227-244.

'Liberia 1989-1994: a study of ethnic and spiritual violence', *African Affairs,* vol.94 (July 1995), 375, pp.165-197.

'Wer zahmt die Macht der Masken?', *der Uberblick* (Hamburg), 2 (1995), pp.5-15.

Democracy in Sub-Saharan Africa. Where does it come from? Can it be supported? (ECDPM, Working Paper No.6, Maastricht, 1995).

'Africa after the Cold War: new patterns of government and politics', *Development and Change,* 27, i, (1996), pp.1-28.

'Africa and international corruption: The strange case of South Africa and Seychelles', *African Affairs,* 95 (1996), 379, pp. 165-196.

'The strange life of African states', *Africa Insight,* 26, 1 (1996), pp. 2-3.

(with Janet MacGaffey), 'Research on Sub-Saharan Africa's unrecorded international trade: Some methodological and conceptual problems, *African Studies Review,* 39, 2 (1996), 19-41.

French (rev.) version, 'Le commerce international informel en Afrique sub-saharienne. Quelques problèmes méthodologiques et conceptuels'. In: *Cahiers d'Études Africaines* 145, vol.XXXVIII-1 (1997), pp.11-37.

'Les nouvelles forces de sécurité sud-africaines', *Herodote,* 82-3 (1996), pp. 177-184.

'Analysing Africa's wars', *Anthropology in Action,* vol.3, no.3 (1996), pp.18-21.

'Nieuwe machtspatronen in Afrika', *Internationale Spectator,* 51, 4 (1997), pp.201-204.

'Criminal and political violence in South Africa', in Bas de Gaay Fortman and Marijke Veldhuis (eds.), *Internal Conflicts, Security and Development* (RAWOO, publication no.14, Den Haag, 1997), pp.52-56.

'Réalités et incertitudes intérieures en République Sud-Africaine', in J-P. Doumenge et J-F. Lionnet (eds), *Regards sur l'Afrique (1996-7)* (Centres des Hautes Études sur l'Afrique et l'Asie Modernes, Paris, 1997), pp.55-57.

'Liberia—the Heart of a West African Struggle', *News from Nordiska Afrikainstitutet,* 1 (Jan.1998), pp.2-4.

'Commentary', in M. Kuitenbrouwer and N. van der Werff (eds), *Incomplete Transitions in Southern Africa* (Utrecht, 1998), pp.42-46.

'The Grey Economy', in J. Middleton (ed), *Encyclopaedia of Africa* (4 vols., Charles Scribner's Sons, New York, 1998).

'Verschwindet der moderne Staat aus Afrika?', *der Uberblick,* 1 (1998), pp.37-41.

'The Historical Significance of South Africa's Third Force', *Journal of Southern African Studies,* 24, 2 (1998), pp.261-299.

(with Gerrie ter Haar), 'Religion and Politics in sub-Saharan Africa', *Journal of Modern African Studies,* 36, 2 (1998), pp.175-201.

'Liberia's Warlord Insurgency', in C. Clapham (ed.), *African Guerrillas* (James Currey, Oxford, 1998), pp.155-171.

'War in southern Africa: Some implications for the environment', in Charl Schutte, Ian Liebenberg and Anthony Minnaar (eds), *The Hidden Hand: covert operations in South Africa* (2nd edn., Human Sciences Research Council, Pretoria, 1998), pp.439-456.

'Regional dimensions of proliferation of light weapons in West Africa', in Sarah Meek (ed.), *Controlling Small Arms Proliferation and Reversing Cultures of Violence in Africa and the Indian Ocean* (ISS Monograph series, 30, Johannesburg, 1998), pp.16-18.

(with Solofo Randrianja), 'The First Malagasy', *IIAS Newsletter,* 17 (Dec. 1998), p.21.

'Mafias, milices, le crime et l'État en Afrique', *Panoramiques: l'enfer des mafias* (ed. Michel Serceau), (Paris, Editions Corlet, 1999), pp.128-131.

'Africa and international corruption: the strange case of South Africa and Seychelles', reprinted in John Mukum Mbaku (ed.), *Corruption and the Crisis of Institutional Reforms in Africa* (Edwin Mellen Press, New York, 1998), pp.193-236.

(with J-F. Bayart & B. Hibou), 'L'Afrique du Sud à la veille d'une consultation décisive', *Politique africaine,* 73 (1999), 137-145.

'Staatsinrichting in Afrika: import of eigen kweek?', *Internationale Spectator* 53, 5 (1999), pp.294-298.

'A Golden Age of Archives', *NVAS nieuwsbrief,* 2, 3 (1999), pp.4-5.

'Vérité sans reconciliation en Afrique du Sud', *Critique Internationale,* 5 (Oct.1999), pp.125-137.

'Elections in Africa in historical context', in J. Abbink and G. Hesseling (eds), *Election Observation and Democratization in Africa* (Macmillan and St Martin's Press, Basingstoke and New York, 1999), pp.37-48.

'Reporting Africa', *Current History,* vol.99, no.627 (May 2000), pp.221-226.

(with D. Killingray), 'Introduction', centenary issue of *African Affairs,* vol.99, no.395 (April 2000), pp.177-182.

Review essay: 'Truth and Reconciliation Commission of South Africa report', *Transformation,* 42 (2000), pp.57-72.

'Crime, Politics and States in Southern Africa', *The World Today,* 56, 10 (October 2000), pp.17-19.

'Armes mystiques: Quelques éléments de réflexion à partir de la guerre du Liberia', *Politique africaine,* 79 (October 2000), pp.66-82.

'Africa's wars of liberation: some historiographical reflections', in P. Konings, W. van Binsbergen and G. Hesseling (eds.), *Trajectoires de libération en Afrique contemporaine* (Karthala, Paris, 2000), pp.69-91.

'Gedachten over Afrika', *Internationale Spectator,* LV, 4 (April 2001), pp.180-184.

'Sierra Leone', in Nina Tellegen (ed.), *Afrika-expertbijeenkomst: Ghana, Mali, Mozambique, Sierra Leone, Congo, Rwanda* (Min. Van Buitenlandse Zaken en Afrika-Studiecentrum, Den Haag en Leiden, 2001), pp.63-67.

'Fit to Print? Comparing Standards of News', *Harvard International Review,* XXIII, (Spring 2001), pp.56-59.

'Les guerres en Afrique de l'Ouest: le poids de l'histoire', *Afrique contemporaine,* 198, (2001), 51-56.

'Mystical weapons: some evidence from the Liberian war', *Journal of Religion in Africa,* XXXI, 2 (2001), 222-236.

'War in West Africa', *The Fletcher Forum of World Affairs,* 25, 2 (2001), 33-39.

'Writing histories of contemporary Africa', *Journal of African History,* 43, 1 (2002), pp.1-27.

(with David Killingray) 'Africa after 11 September 2001', *African Affairs,* 101, 402, pp.5-8.

(with Gerrie ter Haar), 'Religion and Politics in Africa', *Afrika Zamani,* 5/6 (1997-8), 221-246.

(with Amanda Dissel), 'Ambitions réformatrices et inertie du social dans les prisons sud-africaines', *Critique Internationale,* 16 juillet 2002, pp.137-152.

'Witch-hunting in central Madagascar, 1828-61', *Past and Present* 175 (2002), pp.90-123.

'Briefing: West Africa and its oil', *African Affairs,* 102, 406 (2003), pp.135-138.

'Colonial conquest in central Madagascar. Who resisted what?', in J. Abbink, M. de Bruijn and K. van Walraven (eds.), *Rethinking Resistance: Revolt and violence in African History* (Brill, Leiden, 2003), pp.69-86.

Translated as *A proposito de resisir: Repensar la insurgencia en Africa* (Oozebap, Barcelona, 2003), pp.111-136.

'The old roots of Africa's new wars', *Internationale Politikund Gesellschaft,* 2, pp.29-43.

Republished (English version) in *Militaire Spectator,* 173, 1 (2004), pp.25-33.

'L'évolution politique de l'Afrique: les formes se renouvellent, les modèles restent à inventer', *Marches tropicaux et méditerranéens,* 3000 (9 May 2003), pp.970-974.

'History and Violence: a response to Thandika Mkandawire', *Journal of Modern African Studies*, 41, 3 (2003), 457-475.

'Briefing: the Pan-Sahel initiative', *African Affairs* 103, no 412 (2013), pp.459-464.

'International elements of West Africa's wars: the role of regional and non-African actors', in Karim Hussein & Donata Gnisci (eds), *Conflict and Development Policy in the Mano River region and Côte d'Ivoire* (OECD, Paris, 2003), pp.23-26.

'Africa's Wars: the historical context', *New Economy* (Institute for Public Policy Research—IPPR) (Sept. 2004), pp.144-147.

'Interpreting violence: Reflections on West African Wars', in Neil L. Whitehead (ed), *Violence* (School of American Research Press/James Currey, Santa Fe and Oxford), pp.107-124.

'La violence dans l'histoire de l'Afrique', in *La Mémoire du Congo: le temps colonial,* (Eds. Noeck/Musée royale de l'Afrique central, Tervuren, 2005), pp.37-42.

(with Gerrie ter Haar), 'Afrika: Spiritualitat und politische Praxis', *Der Uberblick,* 41, 1, 2005, pp.45-48.

'Liberia', in Andreas Mehler, Henning Melber and Klaas van Walraven (eds), *Africa Yearbook 2004: Politics, Economy and Society South of the Sahara* (Brill, Leiden), pp.101-109.

'How to Rebuild Africa', *Foreign Affairs,* 84, 5 (2005), pp.135-148.

'A Visit to the National Archives of Liberia', *African Research and Documentation,* 99 (2005), p. 49.

'The roots of African corruption', *Current History,* 105, 691 (May 2006), pp.203-208.

'Coming changes to Africa's system of government', *African Analyst,* 1 (2006), pp.31-42.

(with Gerrie ter Haar), 'The Role of Religion in Development: Towards a New Relationship between the European Union and Africa', *European Journal of Development Research,* vol.18, no.3 (2006), pp.351-367.

'Liberia', in Andreas Mehler, Henning Melber and Klaas van Walraven (eds), *Africa Yearbook 2005: Politics, Economy and Society South of the Sahara* (Brill, Leiden, pp.105-112.

'Witching-times: A theme in the histories of Africa and Europe', in Gerrie ter Haar (ed), *Imagining Evil: Witchcraft beliefs and accusations in contemporary Africa* (Africa World Press, Trenton, NJ, 2007), pp.31-52.

Preface in Armando Marques Guedes and Maria Jose Lopes (eds), *State and Traditional Law in Angola and Mozambique* (Amedina, Lisbon, 2007), pp.7-9.

'The Sahara and the "War on Terror"', *Anthropology Today*, 23, 3 (June 2007), pp.21-22.

'How to Rebuild Africa', in Princeton N. Lyman and Patricia Dorff (eds), *Beyond Humanitarianism* (Council on Foreign Relations, New York, 2007), pp.151-164 [reprint of 2005 article in *Foreign Affairs*].

(with Gerrie ter Haar), 'Religion and politics: Taking African epistemologies seriously', *Journal of Modern African Studies*, 45, 3 (2007), pp.385-401.

'Tom and Toakafo: The Betsimisaraka kingdom and state formation in Madagascar, c.1715-1750', *Journal of African History*, 48, 3 (2007), pp.439-455.

'AHR Conversation: Religious Identities and Violence' [roundtable], *American Historical Review*, 112, 5 (December 2007), pp.1432-1481.

'Liberia', in Andreas Mehler, Henning Melber and Klaas van Walraven (eds), *Africa Yearbook: Politics, Economy and Society South of the Sahara in 2006* (Brill, Leiden, pp.115-122.

'Reflections on libraries and archives', *African Research & Documentation*, 105 (2007), pp.5-8.

(with Gerrie ter Haar), 'Africa's religious resurgence and the politics of good and evil', *Current History*, 107, 708 (April 2008), pp.180-185.

'Beside the State: an epilogue', in Alice Bellagamba and Georg Klute (eds), *Beside the State: Emergent powers in contemporary Africa* (Rudiger Koppe Verlag, Koln), pp.197-204.

'Liberia', in Andreas Mehler, Henning Melber and Klaas van Walraven (eds), *Africa Yearbook: Politics, Economy and Society South of the Sahara in 2007* (Brill, Leiden, 2008), pp.117-124.

'The Okija shrine: Death and life in Nigerian politics', *Journal of African History*, 49, 3, (2008), pp.445-466.

'West Africa's International Drug Trade', *African Affairs*, 108, no.431 (2009), pp.171-196.

'The history of sovereigns in Madagascar: new light from old sources', in Didier Nativel and Faranirina V. Rajaonah (eds), *Madagascar revisitée: en voyage avec Françoise Raison-Jourde* (Karthala, Paris, 2009), pp.405-431.

(with Gerrie ter Haar), 'The Occult does not Exist: a Response to Terence Ranger', *Africa*, 69, 3 (2009), pp.399-412.

'Nigeria's Campus Cults: an Anti-Social Movement', in Stephen Ellis and Ineke van Kessel (eds.), *Movers and Shakers: Social Movements in Africa* (African Dynamics series, Brill, Leiden, 2009), pp.221-236. Online: http://hdl.handle.net/1887/18530

(with Ineke van Kessel), 'Introduction', in Stephen Ellis and Ineke van Kessel (eds.), *Movers and Shakers: Social Movements in Africa* (African Dynamics series, Brill, Leiden, 2009), pp.1-16. Online: http://hdl.handle. net/1887/18530

'Tráfico de drogas en Africa Occidental', in Colectivo Maloka (ed), *La Economía de las drogas ilícitas: Escenarios de conflictos y derechos humanos* (Generatliat de Catalunya, 2009), pp.33-41.

South Africa and the Decolonization of the Mind. Inaugural lecture, Desmond Tutu chair in the Faculty of Social Sciences, VU University, Amsterdam, 2009. No ISBN Online version: http://hdl.handle.net/1871/15351

'The Mutual Assimilation of Elites: The Development of Secret Societies in Twentieth Century Liberian Politics', in J. Knorr and W. Trajano Filho (eds), *The Powerful Presence of the Past: Integration and Conflict along the Upper Guinea Coast* (African Studies series, Brill, Leiden, 2010), pp. 185-204

'Development and invisible worlds', in B. Bompani & M. Frahm-Arp (eds), *Development and Politics from Below: Exploring Religious Space in the African State* (Palgrave-MacMillan, London, 2010), pp.23-39.

'Fifty years of independence', in Pirogue Collective, *Imagine Africa* (Island Position, New York/Goree, 2011), pp.167-176.

(with Aurelia Segatti), 'The Role of Skilled Labor', in Aurelia Segatti and Loren B. Landau (eds), *Contemporary Migration to South Africa* (World Bank, Washington, 2011), pp.67-80.

'The Genesis of the ANC's Armed Struggle in South Africa, 1948-1961', *Journal of Southern African Studies,* 37, 4 (2011), pp.657-676.

'Written history of Liberia for the film *Pray the Devil Back to Hell* ', (Fork Films NYC) 1 October 2011

(with Gerrie ter Haar), 'Religion and politics in Africa', in Elias Bongmba (ed), *The Wiley-Blackwell Companion to African Religions* (Blackwell, Oxford, 2012), pp.457- 465.

'Nigerian Organized Crime', in F. Allum and S. Gilmour (eds), *Routledge Handbook of Transnational Organized Crime* (Routledge, London and New York, 2012), pp.127-142.

(with Brooke Stearns Lawson): *'A Slow Burning Fuse'. Narcotics in the Mano River Union Region of West Africa.* Washington, USAID, 2012.

(with Will Reno, Brooke Stearns Lawson and Ben Farley) *Narcotics and development assistance in Ghana.* USAID Field Assessment Washington, USAID, Dec. 2012

'Nigeria: corrupt, chaotisch, maar nog steeds Afrika's slapende reus', *Internationale Spectator,* 66, 5 (May 2012), pp.250-252.

'China and Africa's Development: The Testing Ground of a World Power', *IIAS Newsletter,* 60, (Summer 2012), p.30.

'Politics and Crime: Reviewing the ANC's Exile History', *South African Historical Journal*, 64, 3 (2012), pp.622-636.

(with Sakhela Buhlungu), 'The trade union movement and the Tripartite Alliance: A tangled history', in Sakhela Buhlungu and Malehoko Tshoaedi (eds), *Cosatu's Contested Legacy: South African Trade Unions in the Second Decade of Democracy* (HSRC Press, Cape Town, 2012, pp.259-282, and ASC series vol. 28, Brill, Leiden, 2013).

'The African National Congress in Exile', *Current Intelligence*, 31 January 2013 (with Gerrie ter Haar).

'Religion and politics', in Nic Cheeseman et al (eds), *Routledge Handbook of African Politics* (Routledge, London and New York, 2013), pp.121-132.

(with Gerrie ter Haar), 'Spirits in politics: some theoretical reflections', in A. Steinforth and B. Meier (eds), *Spirits in Politics: Uncertainties of Power and Healing in African Societies* (Campus verlag, Frankfurt and New York, 2013), pp.37-48.

'Conclusion', Martin Shipway (ed), *The Rise and Fall of Modern Empires*, vol IV (Ashgate, London, 2013), pp.69-87.

Translation: 'West Africa's International Drug Trade', in Takehiko Ochiai (ed), *Africa and Drugs* (Koyo Shobo, Japan, 2014).

'Face to Face with England's Libel Laws', *Socio*, 3 (2014), pp.49-61.

'The African National Congress and the international community—1960 to 1990', in Kwandiwe Kondlo, Christopher Saunders and Siphamandla Zondi (eds), *Treading the Waters of History. Perspectives on the ANC* (Africa Institute of South Africa, Pretoria, 2014), ISBN: 978-0-7983-04521-3, pp. 38-51.

'De dreiging van Boko Haram', *Internationale Spectator*, 68, 11 (Nov 2014), pp.17- 21.

'Rethinking the Past', in Toyin Falola, ed, *Mandela: Tributes to a Global Icon* (Carolina Academic Press, Durham, NC, 2014), pp.311-312.

'South Africa: Introduction', in Bert Klandermans and Cornelis van Stralen (eds), *Movements in Times of Democratic Transition* (Temple University Press, Philadelphia PA, 2015), pp.209-215.

'Response to Hugh Macmillan', *Africa*, 85, 1 (2015), pp 156-158.

(with Mark Shaw) 'Does organised crime exist in Africa?', *African Affairs*, vol. 114, nr. 457 (2015), pp. 508-528.

'Nelson Mandela, the South African Communist Party and the origins of Umkhonto we Sizwe', *Cold War History*, vol. 16. nr. 1, February 2016, pp. 1-18.

(with Gerrie ter Haar) 'The History of Witchcraft Accusations and Persecutions in Africa', in Wolfgang Behringer, Sonke Lorenz and

Dieter R. Bauer (eds), *Spate Hexenprozesse: Der Umgang der Aufklarung mit dem Irrationalen,* Gutersloh: Verlag fur Regionalgeschichte, 2016, pp. 332-345 (Hexenforschung Band 14).

(with Gerrie ter Haar) 'Religion and politics: taking African epistemologies seriously', in Nicholas Cheeseman (ed.), *African Politics: Major Works* (4 volume set), vol. 3: *Identity Politics, Conflict and Accommodation: Class, Religion and Ethnicity,* London: Routledge, 2016, pp. 93-108 (originally published in *JMAS,* 2007).

BOOK REVIEWS

Review of Bonar A. *Gow, Madagascar and the Protestant Impact. In the Journal of African History*, 21, 4 (1980), pp.561-562.

Review of Raymond K. Kent, *Madagascar in History: Essays from the 1970s. In the Journal of African History*, 21, 4 (1980), pp.561-562.

Review of *Omaly Sy Anio (Hier et Aujourd'hui)* (University of Madagascar). In the *Journal of African History,* 22, 3 (1981), pp.431-432.

Review of Antoine Bouillon, *Madagascar: le colonisé et son 'âme'. Essai sur le discourspsychologique colonial.* In the *Journal of African History*, 24, 1 (1983), pp.134-135.

Review of Liliana Mosca, *Il Madagascar nella vita di Raombana primo storico malgascio (1809–1855).* In the *Journal of African History*, 24, 3 (1983), pp.393-394.

Review of Bernard Schlemmer, *Le Menabe: histoire d'une colonisation. In the Journal of African History*, 26, 2 (1985), pp.264-265.

Review of Maurice Bloch, *From Blessing to Violence. History and Ideology in the circumcision ritual of the Merina of Madagascar. In the Journal of African History,* 28, 3 (1987), pp.465-466.

Review of John Mack, *Madagascar, island of the ancestors.* In the *Journal of African History*, 28, 3 (1987), pp 465-466.

Review of Jaccques Tronchon, *L'Insurrection malgache de 1947.* In the *Journal of African History*, 29, 1 (1988), pp. 133-134.

Review of S. Johns and R. Hunt Davis, *Mandela, Tambo and the African National Congress. The Struggle against Apartheid 1948–1990.* In the *Journal of Southern African Studies*, 17, 4 (1991), pp.773-774.

Review of Y.-G. Paillard, *Les incertitudes du colonialisme. Jean Carol à Madagascar.* In *Journal of African History* 33, ii (1992), pp.349-350.

Review of F. Raison-Jourde, *Bible et Pouvoir à Madagascar au XIXe siecle.* In *Journal of African History,* 33, iii (1992), pp.510-12. Translated in *Omaly sy Anio,* 29-32 (1989-90), p.469-471.

Review of G. Feeley-Harnik, *The Green Estate. Restoring Independence in Madagascar*. In *Africa*, 61, ii (1993).

Review of H. Bradt, with M. Brown, *Madagascar*. In *Bulletin of the School of Oriental and African Studies*, LVII, 3 (1994), p.653.

Review of Ronnie Kasrils, *Armed and Dangerous*, in *Africa*, 62, iv (1994), pp.593-595.

Review of Malyn Newitt, *A History of Mozambique*, in *Journal of Imperial and Commonwealth History*, 23, 3 (1995), pp.528-529.

Review of Mervyn Brown, *A History of Madagascar*, in *IIAS Newsletter*, 7 (1996), p.32.

Review of Shipping Research Bureau, *Embargo: Apartheid's Oil Secrets Revealed*, in *Amandla*, May 1996, pp.20-21.

Review of Colin Leys, *The Rise and Fall of Development Theory*, in *Development Policy Review*, Vol. 14, no. 3 (1996), pp.304-305.

Review of Edmond Keller and Donald Rothchild (eds), *Africa and the New International Order*, in *Development Policy Review*, 15, 2 (1997), pp.213-214.

Review of Robin Renwick, *Unconventional Diplomacy in Southern Africa*, and Jakkie Cilliers and Markus Reichardt (eds), *About Turn, the transformation of the South African military and intelligence*, in *Survival*, 39, 4 (1997), pp.191-192.

Review of Richard Werbner and Terence Ranger (eds), *Postcolonial Identities in Africa*, in *Development Policy Review*, 16, 3 (1998), pp.317-318.

Review of Pieter Boele van Hensbroek, *African Political Philosophy, 1860-1995*, in *Internationale Spectator*, 11 November 1998, pp.599-600.

Review of Michel Prou, *Malagasy, un pas de plus, vol. III*. In *Journal of African History*, 40, (1999), p.345.

Review of Jean-Roland Randriamaro, *Padesm et luttes politiques a Madagascar*. In *Journal of African History*, 40, 1 (1999), pp.149-150.

Review of *Les drogues en Afrique sub-saharienne* by Observatoire globale de drogues, *Politique africaine*, 75 (1999), pp.184-185.

Review of Claude Allibert (ed.), *Histoire de la Grande Isle Madagascar*, in *Journal of African History*, 40, 2 (1999), p.348.

Review of Mark Israel, *South African Political Exile in the United Kingdom*, for *Journal of Modern African Studies*, 37, 4 (1999), pp.738-739.

Review of Mark Huband, *The Liberian Civil War*, in *Africa*, 69, 4 (1999) pp.636-637.

Review of Abdel-Fatau Musah and J. Kayode Fayemi (eds.), *Mercenaries: an African security dilemma*, in *Journal of Modern African Studies*, 38, 3 (2000), pp.541-542.

Review of Mats Berdal and David M. Malone (eds), *Greed and Grievance: Economnic Agendas in Civil Wars*, in *Canadian Journal of African Studies*, 35, 1 (2001), pp.174-175.

Review of R. Fardon and G. Furniss (eds), *African Broadcast Cultures: radio in transition*, for *Bulletin of the School of Oriental and African Studies*, 64, 2 (2001), pp. 303-304.

Review of Pier M. Larson, *History and Memory in the Age of Enslavement: Becoming Merina in Highland Madagascar, 1770-1822,* for *Journal of Commonwealth and Imperial History*, 29, 3 (2001), pp.119-121. Also reviewed for H-Net, internet book review service: http://www2.h-net.msu.edu/reviews/

Review of Achille Mbembe, *On the Postcolony,* for *African Affairs,* 100, no 401 (2001), pp.670-671.

Review of Karen Middleton (ed.), *Ancestors, Power and History in Madagascar*, for the *Journal of Religion in Africa*, 32, 3 (2002), p.398.

Review of Deryck Scarr, *Seychelles since 1770: History of a Slave and Post-Slavery Society*, in *Journal of Imperial and Commonwealth History*, 30, 1 (2002), pp. 165-166.

Review of April and Donald Gordon (eds), *Understanding Contemporary Africa,* for *Round Table,* 367 (2002), p.678.

Review of M. Rakotomalala et al, *Usages sociaux des religions sur les Hautes Terres malgaches*, in *Politique africaine*, 86 (2002), pp.205-206.

Review of S. Randrianja, *Société et luttes anticoloniales à Madagascar*, in *Politique africaine*, 86 (2002), pp.206-207.

Review of Jennifer Cole, *Forget Colonialism? Sacrifice and the Art of Memory in Madagascar*, for *The Journal of African History*, 44, 1 (2003), pp.190-191.

Review of Isaac Phiri, *Proclaiming Political Pluralism: Churches and Political Transitions in Africa*, for *Commonwealth and Comparative Politics*, 41, 1 (2003), pp.135-136.

Review of Terry Bell and Dumisa Ntsebeza, *Unfinished Business: South Africa, apartheid and truth*, in *Journal of Modern African Studies*, 42, 3 (2004), p.469-470.

Review of James Barber, *Mandela's World: the International Dimension of South Africa's Political Revolution 1990–99*, for *Africa*, 75, 2 (2005), pp.249-250.

Review of Jason Burke, *Al-Qaeda: The True Story of Radical Islam*, in *The Round Table*, 378, (2005), pp.145-165.

Review of Paul Nugent, *Africa Since Independence: A Comparative History*, in *African Research and Documentation*, 97, 2005, pp.49-51.

Review of Jonathan Fox and Shmuel Sandler, *Bringing Religion into International Relations,* in *The Round Table*, 94, 382, (2005), pp.661-662.

Review of Tatah Mentan, *Dilemmas of Weak States: Africa and Transnational Terrorism in the Twenty-First Century*, in *The Round Table*, 94, 380 (2005), p. 398.

Review of Tibamanga Mwene Mushanga, *Criminology in Africa*, for *Journal of Modern African Studies*, 43, 4 (2005), pp.674-675.

Review of Niels Kastfelt (ed), *Religion and African Civil Wars*, in *The Round Table*, 94, 382 (2005), pp.660-661.

Review of Robert Dick-Read, *Phantom Voyagers*, in *African Affairs*, 104, 417 (2005), pp.706-710.

Review of Finn Fuglestad, *The Ambiguities of History*, in *African Affairs*, 105, 418 (2006), pp.151-153.

Review of Adam Ashforth, *Witchcraft, Violence, and Democracy in South Africa*, in *American Anthropologist*, 108, 2 (2006), p.401.

Review of Gwyn Campbell, *An Economic History of Imperial Madagascar, 1750– 1895: The Rise and Fall of an Island Empire*, in *Journal of Southern African Studies*, 32, 4 (2006), pp.840-841.

Review of Didier Nativel, *Maisons royales, demeures des grands a Madagascar. L'inscription de la réussite sociale dans l'espace urbain de Tananarive au XIXe siècle*, for *Africa*, 76, 4 (2006), pp.601-602.

Review of Mary H. Moran, *Liberia: The violence of democracy* for *African Studies Review*, 49, 3 (2006), pp.161-162.

Review of Stewart & Strathern, *Witchcraft, Sorcery, Rumour and Gossip*, in *The Round Table*, 95, 385 (2006), pp.477-479.

Review of Amos Sawyer, *Beyond Plunder: Toward Democratic Governance in Liberia*, for the *Canadian Journal of African Studies*, 41,2, (2007), pp. 362-364.

Review of Guy Arnold, *Africa: A Modern History*, for *Journal of African History*, 48, (2007), pp.317-318.

Review of Martin Thomas (ed), *European Decolonization*, for *The Round Table*, 97, 394 (2008), pp.165-166.

Review of Preben Kaarsholm (ed), *Violence, Political Culture and Development in Africa*, for *Africa Today*, 54, 4 (2008), pp.99-100.

Review of Raymond K. Kent, *The Many Faces of an Anti-Colonial Revolt: Madagascar's Long Journey into 1947*, for *The Journal of African History*, 49, 1, pp.158-159.

Review of Steven Robins, *From Revolution to Rights in South Africa: Social Movements, NGOs and Popular Politics after Apartheid*, for *The Round Table*, 98, 404 (October 2009), pp.630-631.

Review of Toyin Falola and Matthew M. Heaton, *A History of Nigeria*, for *The Round Table*, 98, 404 (October 2009), pp.627-628.

Review of Anthony Butler, *Contemporary South Africa*, for *The Round Table*, 99, 408 (June 2010), p.341.

Review of Pier M. Larson, *Ocean of Letters: Language and Creolization in an Indian Ocean Diaspora*, for *Social History*, 36, 1 (February 2011), pp.25-27.

Review of P.C. Swanepoel, *Really Inside Boss*, in *Journal of Southern African Studies*, 37, 1 (2011), pp.193-194.

Review of Ruth Marshall, *Political Spiritualities*, in *Politique Africaine* 124 (December 2011), pp.203-205.

Review of Adekeye Adebajo, *The Curse of Berlin: Africa after the Cold War*, in *African Affairs*, 111, 442 (2012), pp.152-153.

Review of Sabine Marschall, *Landscape of Memory: Commemorative Monuments, Memorials and Public Statuary in post-Apartheid South Africa*, for *Time & Society*, 21 (2012), p.137.

Review of Didier Galibert, *Les gens du pouvoir à Madagascar*, in *Politique Africaine*, 125 (March 2012), p.236.

Review of M. Gould, *The Biafran War: The Stuggle for Modern Nigeria*. In: *Journal of the Royal United Services Institute*, 157, 2 (2012), pp. 78-79.

Review of Nelson Tshabalala, *Smoke of Forgiveness*, for *NVAS Newsletter*, October 2013.

Review of Robert I. Rotberg, *Africa Emerges*, for *International Affairs* 90, 2 March, pp.482-483.

Review of Howard W. French, *China's Second Continent*, *Wall Street Journal*, 7 June 2014, pp.C5-C6: http://online.wsj.com/articles/book-review-chinas-second-continent- by-howard-w-french-1402089810

BLOGS

Indicting a head of state is a political act, [on Omar al-Bashir], *African Arguments*, 10 July 2008 http://africanarguments.org/2008/07/10/indicting-a-head-of-state-is-a-political-act/

Madagascar, Roots of Turmoil, 23 March 2009. Blog *Open Democracy* http://www.opendemocracy.net/article/madagascar-roots-of-turmoil

West Africa's international drugs trade, CSIS notes, 6 November 2009 http://csis.org/blog/west-africa%E2%80%99s-international-drug-trade

The Sahara's new cargo: drugs and radicalism, 14 April 2010. Blog *Open Democracy* http://www.opendemocracy.net/stephen-ellis/saharas-new-cargo-drugs-and-radicalism

What Future for Africa? *African Arguments*, 20 June 2011 http://africanarguments.org/2011/06/20/what-future-for-africa-by-stephen-ellis/

Drugs in West Africa, *Jurist*, 9 March 2012 http://iurist.org/hotline/2012/03/stephen-ellis-africa-crime.php

Introduction to ANC webdossier *(The ANC at 100)*, for ASC Library, August 2012 http://www.ascleiden.nl/content/webdossiers/african-national-congress-100

Review of Neil Carrier and Gernot Klantschnig, *African Arguments*, 22 October 2012 http://africanarguments.org/category/politics-now/africa-and-the-war-on-drugs/

The Mali Effect, *Open Democracy* Blog 7 March 2013, http://www.opendemocracy.net/stephen-ellis/mali-effect

New light on Nelson Mandela's autobiography. *Politicsweb, 13* January 2014. http://www.politicsweb.co.za/opinion/new-light-on-nelson-mandelas-autobiography

The ANC and SACP: In Search of a New Legend, *Politicsweb,* 24 March 2014 http://www.politicsweb.co.za/politicsweb/view/politicsweb/en/page71619?oid=576632&sn=Detail&pid=71619

Democratic Elections in Nigeria, *Thesigers,* 28 January 2015 http://thesigers.com/analysis/2015/1/28/democratic-elections-in-nigeria

PRESS ARTICLES

'De lange arm van het Wereld Natuur Fonds', *de Volkskrant,* 24 August 1991

'Leger van Suid Afrika is nauw betrokken bij ivoorstroperij', *de Volkskrant,* 2 March 1992

'Wereldnatuurfonds diende belangen van Zuid-Afrika', *de Volkskrant,* 6 March 1992

'De SACP staliniseerde de ANC in ballingschap,' Second Amandla Lecture, *Amandla,* June-July 1992

'Chris Hani: tot praten bekeerde communist', *NRC Handelsblad,* 23 April 1993

'De verstrengeling van politiek en geweld in Zuid-Afrika,' *de Volkskrant,* 17 March 1993

'France: African Policy', *Oxford Analytica* daily brief, 21 December 1993

'Zuid Afrika op weg naar democratie', *Zuid-Afrika,* 71, i (1994), p.12

'Radio trottoir als speerpunt van democratie', *Wordt vervolgd,* April 1994

'Looters' Paradise?', *Focus on Africa,* V, iv (1994), p.14

'A Time to Heal', *Woord en Daad,* 349 (1995)

'Wer zahmt die Macht der Masken?', *Frankfurter Rundschau,* 4 August 1995

'Verval van Afrika is zorg voor Europa', *NRC Handelsblad,* 12 January 1996

'Westerse wereld moet leren leven met opkomst van nieuwe mafia-staten', *NRC Handelsblad,* 9 April 1996, p.7

'Liberia: In den letzten sechs Jahren dreizehn Friedensabkommen', *Das Parlament,* 16-17 (April 1996), p.4

Guest-column: *NRC Handelsblad,* 20 July 1996

'The Business of Crime', *Weekly Mail & Guardian* (South Africa), 25 April 1997

'Do We Really Know Africa?', *Weekly Mail & Guardian* (South Africa), 9 May 1997

'Futile Drug Ban Fuels Criminal Syndicates' *Weekly Mail & Guardian* (South Africa), 25-31 July 1997, p.4

'Profiteering from War' *Weekly Mail & Guardian* (South Africa), 25-31 July 1997, p.29

'Zuid Afrikaanse Huurlingen Waken over Afrika', *Zuidelijk Afrika,* 1, 2 (1997), pp.25-27

'Heldenverering voor de nieuwe Afrikaanse leiders is misplaatst', *NRC Handelsblad,* 10 July 1997, p.7

'Taylor dans ses habits de presidentiable', *L'autre Afrique,* 8 (9-15 July 1997), pp.38-39

'De staat als boef', *Zuidelijk Afrika,* 2, 1 (1998), pp.20-21

'Nigeria's president tegen wil en dank verdient steun', *Trouw,* 30 July 1998, p.11

'Hart van Afrika heeft nieuwe grenzen nodig', *Algemeen Dagblad,* 15 August 1998, p.8

'Afrika verandert fundamenteel door oorlogen', *NRC Handelsblad,* 20 January 1999, p.9

'Westen is in Afrika blind voor de waarheid', *NRC Handelsblad,* 19 May 1999, p.13

'Geen echte vrede in Sierra Leone', *Trouw,* 16 July 1999, p.15

'Relatie rijke landen en Afrika in impasse', *NRC Handelsblad,* 14 September 1999

'Afrika en Europa zijn onlosmakelijk verbonden', *NRC Handelsblad,* 7 April 2000, p.7

'De cultus van cultuur', in 'Boekenodyssee', supplement to *Internationale Samenwerking,* September 2000, pp.5-7

'The Mask Slips' (by Bram Posthumus), *Index on Censorship,* 5 (2000), pp.23-25

'Hulp aan derde wereld eist nieuwe visie', *NRC Handelsblad,* 31 October 2000, p.8

'La contagion de la guerre libérienne', *La Libre Belgique,* 11-12 January 2003, p.11

(with Gerrie ter Haar), 'Why religion has become the new politics', *Financial Times,* 18 January 2005

(with Gerrie ter Haar), 'Religion and development', *Harvard International Review,* 2 May, http://hir.harvard.edu/religion-and-development/ (Comment in *The Broker,* 6 February 2008), pp.9-19

(with Gerrie ter Haar), 'Verbunden mit der Welt der Geister', *Welt-Sichten,* August 2008, pp.30-33

(with Gerrie ter Haar), 'Religion ist Macht', *Afrikapost,* December 2008, pp.24-25

'The Financial crisis and Africa', *Habari,* 24 (2009), pp.10-11

'When the ANC refuses to listen', *Weekly Mail & Guardian,* 6 November 2009, p.28. http://www.mg.co.za/article/2009-11-06-when-the-anc-refuses-to-listen#comments

'West Africa's international drug trade: a maritime risk?', article for *Risk Intelligence*

'Democratie in Afrika', *De Helling,* 23, 2 (2010), 31-33

(with Gerrie ter Haar), 'Africa's invisible world', *The Geographer,* Winter 2010-11, pp.12-13

Signatory to open letter, 'Ivory Coast: the war against civilians', *Foreign Policy,* 31 January 2011

'Na Gbagbo komt het gezonde verstand', *NRC Next,* 11 April 2011

Liberia and Norway, in *Africa Confidential* 53, 14 (2012)

Reader's letter [on Mali], *London Review of Books,* 35, 5 (7 March 2013), p.4

Reader's letter [on *Mandela & Communism*], *New York Review of Books,* LX, 13, 15 August 2013 http://www.nybooks.com/articles/2013/08/15/mandela-and-communism/

Reader's letter [on *C.I.A. and Mandela's Arrest*], *New York Times,* 11 December 2013 http://www.nytimes.com/2013/12/10/opinion/cia-and-mandelas-arrest.html

'ANC suppresses real history to boost its claim to legitimacy', *Mail and Guardian,* 3 January 2014

'ANC sticks to its stories', *Mail and Guardian,* 24 January 2014

Reader's letter in *Business Day,* 28 January 2014

Reader's letter [on South Africa], *London Review of Books,* 36, 3 (6 February 2014), p.4

Reader's letter in *Business Day,* 14 February 2014

Reader's letter in *Business Day,* 18 February 2014

Reader's letter, 'The Real Roots of the Armed Struggle', *Business Day*, 24 February 2014

Reader's letter, 'SACP's Central Role', *Business Day*, 5 March 2014

Reader's letter, 'SACP not conventional', *Business Day*, 11 March 2014

De Groene Amsterdammer, 13 March 2014, pp. 36-37

Reader's letter, 'Jordan in denial again', *Business Day*, 24 March 2014

Reader's letter, 'Mao supported ANC', *Business Day*, 8 September 2014

Reader's letter, 'Harvey's view is right', *Business Day*, 25 November 2014

Reader's letter, 'Clandestine SACP', *Business Day*, 3 December 2014

INTERVIEWS

(This section is incomplete, esp. before 1991)

Interview with Wim Bossema, *De Volkskrant*, 10 August 1991

Interview with *Mare*, 6 September 1991

Interview with *NRC Handelsblad*, 11 September 1991

Interview with Frans Crols, *Trends magazine*, 26 September 1991

Interview in *IMWOO bulletin*, 4th quarter 1991

Interview in *The Star, Johannesburg*, 8 April 1992

Interview in *Die Suid-Afrikaan*, No 38 April-May 1992

Interview in *Amandla*, May 1992

Interview in *Algemeen Dagblad*, 13 June 1992

Interview with *De Telegraaf*, 11 June 1992

Interview in *Elsevier*, 15 August 1992

Interview in *Het Nieuwsblad*, 19 August 1992

Interview with *HP/De Tijd* on South Africa, 30 March 1993

Interview with *Tam Tam* (Benin), 4 March 1994

Interview with Fred Bridgland, *Sunday Telegraph*, 3 April 1994

Interview with *Mare*, 14 April 1994

Interview with *Brabant Pers*, 25 April 1994

Interview with *Reflector*, September 1994

Interview with *Internationale Samenwerking*, November 1995

Interview with *Onze Wereld*, December 1995

Interview in *Reformatorish Dagblad*, 7 March 1996, p.15

Interview in *Trouw*, 6 April 1996

Interview with *de Volkskrant* on Liberia, 10 April 1996

Interview with *de Standaard* on Liberia, 11 April 1996

Interview with *Reformatorisch Dagblad* on Liberia, 18 April 1996

Interview with *Algemeen Dagblad* on the OAU, 12 July 1996

Interview with *Reformatorisch Dagblad* on Burundi, 27 July 1996

Interview with *Nederlands Dagblad* on Burundi, 1 August 1996
Interview in *Internationale Samenwerking,* February 1997, pp.30-4
Interview in *De Standaard* (Belgium), 17 July 1997
Interview in *Reformatorisch Dagblad,* 28 June 1997
Interview in *Boston Globe,* 25 August 1997
Interview in *Trends,* 21 August 1997, p.3
Interview in *de Volkskrant,* Fred de Vries, 14 January 1998
Interview in *Hervormd Nederland,* 54, 10 (7 March 1998), pp.8-11
Interview in *Reformatorisch Dagblad,* 27 March 1998, p.6
Interview on *Nigeria in Reformatorisch Dagblad,* 13 June 1998, p.13
Interview on Sierra Leone, *Internationale Samenwerking,* July-August 1998, pp.28-29
Interview on mercenaries in *Croissance,* Paris, 15 January 1999
Interview on Sierra Leone in *De Standaard, Belgium,* 13 January 1999, p.9
Interview in *Information* (Denmark), 19 April 1999
Interview on Uganda in *Trouw,* 19 June 1999, p.6
Interview in *Vrij Nederland,* 33, 21 August 1999, pp.19-21
Interview in *De Standaard,* 24 January 2000, p.4
Interview in *VPRO Gids,* 29 January 2000, pp.4-5
Interview in *Information* (Denmark), 23 February 2000, p.6
Interview in *Mare,* 25, 30 March 2000, p.7
Interview in *Skript,* 22, 3 (2000), pp.5-16
Interview in *Trouw,* 16 January 2001
Interview in *Information* (Denmark), 17 January 2000
Interview in *Trouw,* 17 February 2001
Interview in *Trouw,* 16 August 2001
Interview in *Trouw,* 17 February 2002
Interview in *La Liberté* (Fribourg), 6 July, p. 10
Interview in *Suddeutsche Zeitung,* 'Der ansteckende Krieg', 30 July 2002
Interview on Religion in Africa, http://www.religioscope.com/dossiers/geo/africa.htm
Interview in *Information* (Copenhagen), 20 September 2002, p.5
Interview in *Trouw,* 'Ivorianen slachtoffer van etnische politiek', 5 October 2002, p.7
Interview in *Financieel-Economische Tijd* (Antwerp), 21 November 2002, p.5
Interview with Damien Conare, *Courrier de la Planète,* 16 March 2006
Interview with *New York Times* on Liberia, 2 April 2006
Interview with Sibylla Claus, *Trouw,* on Liberia, 4 April 2006
Interview with Dick Wittenberg, *NRC Handelsblad,* 8-9 April 2006
Interview with Hans Buddingh, *NRC Handelsblad,* on Liberia, 21 April 2006

Interview with *de Volkskrant,* on Liberia, 24 April 2006

Interview in *Courrier de la Planète,* 79 (January-March 2006), pp. 56-7

Interview in *El Watan* [Algeria], 13 June 2007

Interview in *De Morgen* [Antwerp], 26 January 2008

Interview in *Lloyd's List,* 4 July 2008

Interview in *de Volkskrant,* 5 July 2008

Interview in *IRIN News,* 19 February 2009

Interview in *De Standaard,* Brussels, on Gabon, 3 September 2009

Interview in *The Observer,* London, on the drug trade, 29 November 2009

Interview in *La Croix,* Paris, 20-21 February 2010

Interview in *Dagblad De Pers,* 1 March 2010

Interview in *Wordt Vervolgd,* 43, 6 June 2010, p. 12

Interview with *Helsingin Sanomat* (Helsinki), 29 June 2010

Interview with *AFP* on Madagascar, 29 August 2010

Interview with *de Volkskrant,* 23 July 2011

Online interview at 'New book in African Studies', http://newbooksinafiricanstudies.com/2011/07/26/stephen-ellis-season-of-rains-africa-in-the-world-hurst-2011/

Interview in *Internationale Samenwerking,* 8 October 2011, pp. 36-7.

Interview in *Libération,* 11 November 2011

Interview, *Reuters,* 8 Jan. 2012, http://www.reuters.com/article/2012/01/08/us-safrica-anc-centenary-idUSTRE80709A 20120108

'Analysis: Nigeria: will it fall apart or can it hold?' Quoted: Stephen Ellis, *Reuters,* 15 Jan. 2012. http://www.reuters.com/article/2012/01/15/us-nigeria-fractures-idUSTRE80E0FJ20120115

Interview, Radio Nederland Wereldomroep, 'Les "y-en-a-marre" touareg'. 18 October 2012

'Mr Marlboro: the jihadist back from the "dead" to launch Algerian gas field raid'. Peter Beaumont in *The Guardian,* 17 January 2013. Quoted: Stephen Ellis. http://www.guardian.co.uk/world/2013/jan/17/mokhtar-belmokhtar-algeria-hostage-crisis

Other media quoting Ellis on this story: *Daily Mail, IB Times, Business Insider, Yahoo News, BBC News* http://www.bbc.co.uk/news/world-africa-21061480 and *Het Parool* 18 January 2013

Interview in *Sanlian Lifeweek,* China, 22 January 2013

Interview with Classic FM South Africa (on *ANC in Exile*), 14 January 2014

Film interview, *Camp 72,* documentary on Liberia, 25 February 2014

Interview with *BNR radio* on Nigeria, 9 May 2014

Interview with *Radio 1 OVT* on the history of Nigeria, 11 May 2014

Interview with *National Public Radio* (on Liberia), 22 May 2014

Interview with *de Volkskrant* (on Liberia), 22 August 2014

Interview with *France Culture* (on ebola), 11 September 2014

Interview with *BNR radio* (on Nigeria), 12 September 2014

Interview with *Belgian radio* (on ebola), 17 September 2014

Interview with *Jeune Afrique* on Liberia, 17 September 2014

Interview with *Radio1 OVT* on: 'Ebola, Liberia & Amerika', 21 September 2014

Interview with *Radio Vatican* on Liberia, 24 September 2014

Interview *Met het Oog op Morgen*, Saturday 19 October

Interview with *BNR*, Monday 21 October 2014

Interview with *Deutsche Welle*, 10 December 2014

Interview with *Deutsche Welle* on terror in Africa, 16 December 2014

Interview with *BBC French Service* on Boko Haram, 16 January 2015

Interview with *de Volkskrant* (on removal of statues in South Africa), 8 April 2015

COPYRIGHT PERMISSIONS AND PUBLISHER'S ACKNOWLEDGEMENT

The Publishers, Dr Tim Kelsall and Professor Gerrie ter Haar gratefully acknowledge the following for kindly granting permission to reproduce the following copyright material in this volume. In addition, Tim Kelsall would like to give heartfelt thanks to Gerrie ter Haar for her permission to publish co-authored articles, and for her close support and encouragement in producing the entire volume.

Cambridge University Press for

Ch 1, 'Writing Histories of Contemporary Africa', *Journal of African History*, 2002, 43, 1-26.

Ch 4, 'Rumour and Power in Togo', *Africa*, 1993, 63, 4, 462-476.

Ch 5, 'Violence and History', 'Violence and history: a response to Thandika Mkandawire', *Journal of Modern African Studies*, 41, 2003 (3), 457-75.

Ch 6, 'The Political Elite of Imerina', 'The political elite of Imerina and the revolt of the menalamba. The creation of a colonial myth in Madagascar, 1895-1898'. *The Journal of African History*, vol. 21, no. 2, 1980, 219-234.

Ch 10, 'Religion and Politics: Taking African Epistemologies Seriously' (with Gerrie ter Haar), 'Religion and politics: Taking African epistemologies seriously', *Journal of Modern African Studies*, 2007, 45, 3, 385-401.

Ch 11, Religion and Politics in Sub-Saharan Africa', (with Gerrie ter Haar), 'Religion and Politics in sub-Saharan Africa', *Journal of Modern African Studies*, 1998, 36, 2, 175-201.

Ch 12, 'The Occult Does Not Exist', (with Gerrie ter Haar), 'The Occult does not Exist: a Response to Terence Ranger', *Africa,* 2009, 69, 3, 399-412.

The Royal African Society and Oxford University Press for

Ch 3, 'Tuning in to Pavement Radio', *African Affairs*, 1989, 88 (352), pp. 321-30.

Ch 7, 'Mbokodo: Security in ANC Camps', 'Mbokodo: security in ANC camps, 1961–1990', *African Affairs*, 1994, 93 (371), 279-98.

Ch 9, 'Liberia 1989–1994: A Study of Ethnic and Spiritual Violence', *African Affairs*, 1995, 94 (375), 165-98.

Ch 15, 'Africa and International Corruption', 'Africa and international corruption: the strange case of South Africa and the Seychelles', *African Affairs*, 1996, 95 (165-196).

Ch 17, 'West Africa's International Drug Trade', *African Affairs*, 2009, 108 (431), 171-96.

Past and Present and Oxford University Press for

Ch 13, 'Witch-Hunting in Central Madagascar 1828–1861', *Past and Present* (175), 90-123.

Karthala Publishers for

Ch 2, 'Africa's wars of liberation: some historiographical reflections', which was first published as 'Les guerres de liberation de l'Afrique: quelques reflexions historiographiques', in *Trajectoires de liberation en Afrique contemporaine* (P. Konings, W. van Binsbergen et G. Hesseling, eds) © Karthala, 22/24 boulevard Arago, 75013 Paris, France.

Boydell and Brewer for

Ch 14, 'The new frontiers of crime in South Africa' was first published as Stephen Ellis, 'The new frontiers of crime in South Africa' in Jean-Francois Bayart, Stephen Ellis and Beatrice Hibou (eds), *The*

Criminalization of the State in Africa, © James Currey Publishers (an imprint of Boydell & Brewer), 1999, pp. 49-68.

The Council on Foreign Relations, Inc., for

Ch 18, 'How to rebuild Africa', reprinted by permission of FOREIGN AFFAIRS, (Sept/Oct 2005), © (2005) by the Council on Foreign Relations, Inc. www.ForeignAffairs.com.

The University of California Press for

Ch 19, 'The roots of African corruption', which was first published as 'The Roots of African Corruption', *Current History*, 1 May 2006; 105 (691): 203–208, © the University of California Press.

Taylor & Francis for

Ch 8, 'The Historical Significance of South Africa's Third Force', *Journal of Southern African Studies*, 1998, 24, 2, pp. 261-299, © the Editorial Board of the *Journal of Southern African Studies*, reprinted by permission of Taylor & Francis Ltd, http://www.tandfonline.com on behalf of The Editorial Board of the *Journal of Southern African Studies*.

VU University, Amsterdam for

Ch 20, 'South Africa and the Decolonization of the Mind', Inaugural lecture, Desmond Tutu chair in the Faculty of Social Sciences, VU University, Amsterdam, 2009. No ISBN Online version: http://hdl.handle.net/1871/15351.